124148

D1320883

A–Z of
EMPLOYMENT
LAW

A–Z of

EMPLOYMENT

LAW

FOURTH EDITION

A Complete Reference Source for Managers

PETER CHANDLER

KOGAN
PAGE

First published in Great Britain in 1995
Second edition 1997
Third edition 2000
Fourth edition 2003

Kogan Page Limited
120 Pentonville Road
London N1 9JN
United Kingdom
www.kogan-page.co.uk

© Peter Chandler, 1995, 1997, 2000, 2003

British Library Cataloguing in Publication Data

A CIP record for this book is available from the British Library.

ISBN 0 7494 3889 4

Typeset by Saxon Graphics Ltd, Derby
Printed and bound in Great Britain by Creative Print and Design Wales, Ebbw Vale

Contents

Table of Statutes, Regulations and Orders   *viii*
Table of Cases   *xiv*
Preface   *xix*

Absenteeism   1
Access to employment   4
Adoption leave and pay   12
Advertisements (discriminatory)   15
Advisory, Conciliation & Arbitration Service   21
Age of majority   24
Attachment of earnings   25
Bad workmanship, penalties for   29
Bank and public holidays   30
Birth certificates   33
Canteens and rest rooms for employees   34
Central Arbitration Committee   37
Children, employment of   41
Closed shop   47
Codes of practice   48
Collective agreements   52
Commission for Racial Equality   57
Compromise agreements   59
Conciliation officers   65
Constructive dismissal   69
Continuous employment, meaning of   76
Contract of employment   85
Convicted persons, employment of   92
Cooperation, employee's duty of   103
Data protection   106
Deductions from pay   114
Disabled persons   121
Disciplinary rules and procedure   133
Disclosure of information   149
Dismissal   168
Dismissal and 'TUPE' transfers   198
Dismissal because of a statutory restriction   200
Dismissal for asserting a statutory right   201
Dismissal for incompetence   204
Dismissal for lack of qualifications   206
Dismissal for misconduct   208

Dismissal for refusing Sunday work   214
Dismissal for 'some other substantial reason'   217
Dismissal for taking industrial action   219
Dismissal in health and safety cases   224
Dismissal of a pension scheme trustee   227
Dismissal of an employee or workforce representative   228
Dismissal on grounds of disability   231
Dismissal on grounds of ill-health   232
Dismissal on grounds of redundancy   241
Dismissal on grounds of trade union membership or non-membership   243
Disobedience   245
EEA nationals, employment of   248
Employment agencies   250
Employment Appeal Tribunal   258
Employment tribunals and procedure   260
Equal Opportunities Commission   279
Equal pay and conditions   280
European Works Councils   285
Fidelity and trust, employee's duty of   297
Fixed-term employees   303
Flexible working   310
Foreign nationals, employment of   314
Frustration of contract   327
Grievances and procedure   330
Guarantee payments   334
Holidays, annual   338
Independent trade union   351
Induction training   353
Insolvency of employer   356
Inventions, patents and copyright   359
Itemised pay statement   362
Job title   366
Jury service   368
Lay-offs and short-time working   372
Lock-outs   375
Maternity rights   377
Medical reports, access to   405
National minimum wage   410
Notice of termination of employment   420
Overtime employment   425
Parental leave   431
Part-time workers   438
Paternity leave   444
Pension schemes   447

Picketing	450
Posted workers	452
Pregnant employees and nursing mothers	458
Public interest disclosures	461
Racial discrimination	467
Redundancy	474
References	489
Rest breaks and rest periods	492
School leaving date	502
Sex discrimination	502
Shop assistants	521
Sickness and statutory sick pay	523
Strikes and other industrial action	541
Sunday work	553
Suspension from work on maternity grounds	564
Suspension from work on medical grounds	573
Suspension with/without pay	576
Time off for dependants	578
Time off for study or training	581
Time off work: employee representatives	587
Time off work: pension scheme trustees	589
Time off work: pregnant employees	590
Time off work: public duties	593
Time off work: redundancy	596
Time off work: safety representatives	598
Time off work: trade union members	602
Time off work: trade union officials	603
Trade disputes and arbitration	607
Trade union members	608
Trade union membership and activities	614
Trade union recognition	617
Training of employees	629
Transfer of undertakings	634
Victimisation	649
Wages, payment of	661
Women and young persons, employment of	662
Working hours	667
Written reasons for dismissal	678
Written statement of employment particulars	679
Wrongful dismissal	685
Appendix: Continuous employment	687
Index	*695*

Table of Statutes, Regulations and Orders

Part I Statutes
Access to Medical Reports Act 1988   239, 405 *et seq*
Adoption Act 1976   12
Adoption (Scotland) Act 1978   12
Air Force Act 1955   96
Army Act 1955   96
Asylum & Immigration Act 1996   8, 49, 248, 314, 468
Attachment of Earnings Act 1971   25

Banking & Financial Dealings Act 1971   31
Betting, Gaming & Lotteries Act 1963   215, 429, 553, 562, 663
Births & Deaths Registration Act 1953   33

Children Act 1989   101
Children & Young Persons Act 1933   42, 43, 94, 95–96
Children & Young Persons Act 1963   42
Children & Young Persons (Scotland) Act 1937   43, 95
Chiropractors Act 1994   97
Chronically Sick and Disabled Persons Act 1970   130
Companies Act 1985   129, 150
Copyright, Designs & Patents Act 1988   361
Criminal Law Act 1977   95
Criminal Procedure (Scotland) Act 1975   94, 96

Data Protection Act 1984   108, 112
Data Protection Act 1998   103, 106 *et seq*, 491
Deregulation & Contracting Out Act 1994   250, 522, 554, 562
Disabled Persons (Employment) Acts 1944 & 1958   121, 127
Disability Discrimination Act 1995   5, 8, 15, 16, 59, 60, 86, 121 *et seq*, 173, 188,
    231, 449, 649, 657
Disability Rights Commission Act 1999   49, 121

Education Act 1996   502
Education (Scotland) Act 1980   502, 594
Education (Work Experience) Act 1973   42, 46
Employer's Liability (Compulsory Insurance) Act 1969   629
Employment Act 1989   492
Employment Act 2002   (*Numerous throughout*)
Employment Agencies Act 1973   250, 256
Employment of Children Act 1973   42, 44

Employment of Women, Young Persons & Children Act 1920   42, 45
Employment Protection Act 1975   21, 258
Employment Protection (Consolidation) Act 1978   68, 242
Employment Relations Act 1999 *(Numerous throughout)*
Employment Rights Act 1996 *(Numerous throughout)*
Employment Rights (Dispute Resolution) Act 1998   22, 52, 62, 121, 185, 189, 260, 474
Employment Tribunals Act 1996   68, 259, 261, 271
Equal Pay Act 1970   89, 262, 267, 279, 281 *et seq*, 504

Family Law Reform Act 1969   24
Fire Precautions Act 1971   355, 632
Further & Higher Education (Scotland) Act 1992   594

Gaming Act 1968   101

Health & Safety at Work etc Act 1974   46, 49, 86, 87, 135, 164, 267, 353, 428, 459, 522, 564, 630

Insolvency Act 1986   356

Juries Act 1974   368 *et seq*

Licensing Act 1964   663
Licensing (Scotland) Act 1976   663
Local Government Act 1972   593
Local Government (Scotland) Act 1973   593
Local Government etc. (Scotland) Act 1994   593
Lotteries & Amusements Act 1976   101

National Health Service Act 1977   693
National Health Service & Community Care Act 1990   594
National Health Service (Scotland) Act 1978   594
National Lottery etc Act 1993   101
National Minimum Wage Act 1998   59, 60, 86, 149, 167, 177, 202, 418, 649
Naval Discipline Act 1957   96

Osteopaths Act 1993   97

Patents Act 1977   359
Payment of Wages Act 1960   662
Pension Schemes Act 1993   176, 186, 358, 447 *et seq*
Pensions Act 1995   284, 449, 589
Police Act 1996   593
Police Act 1997   92, 99

Prisons Act 1952   594
Prisons (Scotland) Act 1989   594
Professions Supplementary to Medicine Act 1960   98
Protection from Harassment Act 1997   516
Public Health Act 1936   665
Public Interest Disclosure Act 1998   148, 151, 176, 264, 461 *et seq*
Public Order Act 1986   516

Race Relations Act 1976   5, 7, 15, 19, 49, 57, 60, 86, 124, 173, 188, 254, 262, 467
    et seq, 649
Race Relations (Remedies) Act 1994   473
Redundancy Payments Act 1965   474
Registration of Births, Deaths & Marriages (Scotland) Acts 1854 to 1938   33
Rehabilitation of Offenders Act 1974   10, 92, 99, 102, 173
Reserve Forces (Safeguard of Employment) Act 1985   691
Road Transport Act 1968   675

School Boards (Scotland) Act 1988   594
Sex Discrimination Act 1975   7, 15, 16, 49, 59, 60, 86, 124, 173, 188, 254, 262,
    279, 283, 385, 503 *et seq*, 522, 526, 649
Sex Discrimination Act 1986   53, 284
Shops Act 1950   521, 554
Social Security Contributions & Benefits Act 1992   78, 377, 524, 538, 690
Sunday Trading Act 1994   214, 429, 523, 553
Superannuation Act 1972   689

Tax Credits Act 2002   177, 202, 261, 649, 658
Teaching & Higher Education Act 1998   582
Town & Country Planning Act 1990   130
Trade Union & Labour Relations (Consolidation) Act 1992 *(Numerous
    throughout)*
Trade Union Reform & Employment Rights Act 1993   53

Wages Act 1986   429, 661

Part II Statutory Instruments (Regulations & Orders)

Air Navigation Order 1985 (SI 1985/1643)   568, 666

Children (Performances) Regulations 1968 (SI 1968/1728)   42, 46
Children (Protection at Work) Regulations 1998 (SI 1998/276)   42, 43
Collective Redundancies & Transfer of Undertakings (Protection of
    Employment) (Amendment) Regulations 1999 (SI 1999/1925)   153, 157,
    482, 587

Conduct of Employment Agencies and Employment Businesses Regulations 1976 (SI 1976/715) 252
Control of Asbestos at Work Regulations 2002 (SI 2002/2675) 36, 354, 501
Control of Lead at Work Regulations 2002 (SI 2002/2677) 36, 135, 165, 354, 454, 460, 501, 564, 567, 573, 665
Control of Substances Hazardous to Health Regulations 2002 (SI 2002/2677) 36, 165, 354, 454, 501, 573

Deregulation (Deduction from Pay of Union Subscriptions) Order 1998 (SI 1998/1529) 119
Disability Discrimination (Meaning of Disability) Regulations 1996 (SI 1966/1455) 128
Disability Discrimination (Questions & Replies) Order 1996 (SI 1996/2793) 125, 231

Education (School Leaving Date) Order 1997 (SI 1997/1970) 502
Electricity at Work Regulations 1989 (SI 1989/635) 165
Employment Appeal Tribunal Rules 1993 (SI 1993/2854) 258
Employment Protection (Continuity of Employment) Regulations 1996 (SI 1996/3147) 82, 83
Employment Protection (Part-time Employees) Regulations 1995 (SI 1995/31) 77
Employment Protection (Recoupment of Jobseeker's Allowance & Income Support) Regulations 1996 (SI 1996/2349) 189, 276
Employment Tribunals (Constitution & Rules of Procedure) Regulations 2001 (SI 2001/1171) 266, 282
Employment Tribunals Extension of Jurisdiction (England & Wales) Order 1994 (SI 1994/1623) 68, 424, 577
Employment Tribunals Extension of jurisdiction (Scotland) Order 1994 (SI 1994/1624) 68, 424, 577
Equal Opportunities (Employment Legislation) (Territorial Limits) Regulations 1999 (SI 1999/3163) 453
Equal Pay (Amendment) Regulations 1983 (SI 1983/1794) 281

Fair Employment & Treatment (Northern Ireland) Order 1998 (SI 1998/3162) 10, 15, 173
Fire Precautions (Workplace) Regulations 1997 (SI 1997/1840) 632
Fixed-term Employees (Prevention of Less Favourable Treatment) Regulations 2002 (SI 2002/2034) 32, 57, 150, 180, 229, 307 *et seq*, 454, 529, 649, 659
Flexible Working (Procedural Requirements) Regulations 2002 (SI 2002/3207) 304
Flexible Working (Eligibility, Complaints & Remedies) Regulations 2002 (SI 2002/3236) 304
Food Safety (General Food Hygiene) Regulations 1995 (SI 1995/1763) 134, 633

Health & Safety (Consultations with Employees) Regulations 1996 (SI 1996/1513)   149, 165, 166, 225, 600
Health & Safety (Display Screen Equipment) Regulations 1992 (SI 1992/2792)   165, 354
Health & Safety (First Aid) Regulations 1981 (SI 1981/917)   632
Health & Safety (Young Persons) Regulations 1997 (SI 1997/135)   354

Ionising Radiations Regulations 1999 (SI 1999/3232)   36, 460, 501, 564, 567, 573, 666

Management of Health & Safety at Work Regulations 1999 (SI 1999/3242)   45, 149, 165, 166, 354, 399, 459, 564, 567, 598, 630
Manual Handling Operations Regulations 1992 (SI 1992/2793)   165
Maternity & Parental Leave, etc Regulations 1999 (SI 1999/3312)   174, 371, 431, 458, 580
Maternity & Parental Leave (Amendment) Regulations 2002 (SI 2002/2789)   377 *et seq*, 658
Merchant Shipping (Medical Examination) Regulations 1983 (SI 1983/808)   666

National Minimum Wage Regulations 1999 (SI 1999/584)   410 *et seq*

Part-time Workers (Prevention of Less Favourable Treatment) Regulations 2000 (SI 2001/1551)   32, 86, 150, 202, 438 *et seq*, 454, 649, 659
Part-time Workers (Prevention of Less Favourable Treatment) Regulations 2000 (Amendment) Regulations 2002 (SI 2002/2035)   439
Passenger & Goods Vehicles (Recording Equipment) Regulations 1979 (SI 1979/1746)   676
Paternity & Adoption Leave Regulations 2002 (SI 2002/2788)   12, 14, 444 *et seq*
Personal Protective Equipment at Work Regulations 1992 (SI 1992/2966)   165
Police Act (Enhanced Criminal Record Certificates Protection of Vulnerable Adults) Regulations 2002 (SI 2002/446)   101
Provision & Use of Work Equipment Regulations 1998 (SI 1998/2306)   165
Public Interest Disclosure (Prescribed Persons) Order 1999 (SI 1999/1549)   472

Race Relations (Questions & Replies) Order 1977 (SI 1977/842)   472
Rehabilitation of Offenders Act 1974 (Exceptions) Order 1975 (SI 1975/1023)   94, 97
Right to Time Off for Study or Training Regulations 1999 (SI 1999/986)   582, 652

Safety Representatives & Safety Committees Regulations 1977 (SI 1977/500)
149, 166, 224, 599

Sex Discrimination (Gender Reassignment) Regulations 1999 (SI 1999/1102)
5, 503, 526

Sex Discrimination & Equal Pay (Remedies) Regulations 1993 (SI 1993/2798)
503, 517

Sex Discrimination (Questions & Replies) Order 1975 (SI 1975/2048)　518

Statutory Maternity Pay (Compensation of Employers) Amendment
Regulations 1999 (SI 1999/363)

Statutory Maternity Pay (General) Regulations 1986 (SI 1986/1960)　393,
402

Statutory Sick Pay & Statutory Maternity Pay (Decisions) Regulations 1999
(SI 1999/776)　539

Statutory Sick Pay (General) Regulations 1982 (SI 1982/894)　238, 524, 525,
531

Transfer of Undertakings (Protection of Employment) Regulations 1981 (SI
1981/1794)　55, 84, 161, 176, 191, 198, 229, 264, 587, 634 *et seq*

Transnational Information & Consultation of Employees Regulations 1999
(SI 1999/3323)　40, 150, 260, 285 *et seq*

Work in Compressed Air Regulations 1996 (SI 1996/1656)　36

Working Tax Credit (Payment by Employers) Regulations 2002 (SI 2002/2172)
178, 363

Working Time (Amendment) Regulations 2002 (SI 2002/3128)　425, 522,
665, 672

Working Time Regulations 1998 (SI 1998/1833)　32, 56, 60, 86, 87, 104, 175,
186, 191, 202, 229, 256, 338, 425, 492, 649, 662, 667

Workplace (Health, Safety & Welfare) Regulations 1992 (SI 1992/3004)　34,
36, 165, 501

Table of Cases

Adams v Charles Zub Associates Limited [1978] IRLR 551   72
Allen v Flood [1898] AC 1   4
Allen v Robles [1969] 1 WLR 1193   73
Asda Stores v Thompson & Others [2002] IRLR 245   213
Ayse Süzen v Zehnacker Gebäudereinguing GmbH Krankenhausservice and Lefarth GmbH [1997] IRLR 255   645

Barber & others v RJB Mining (UK) Limited [1999] IRLR 308   87, 668
Batisha v Say & Longleat Enterprises [1976] 19 Man. Law 23   18
Bentley Engineering Co Ltd v Crown & Miller [1976] ICR 225   78
Bernadone v Pall Mall Services Group & Others [2000] IRLR 487   637
Betts v Brintel Helicopters Limited and KLM Era Helicopters [1997] IRLR 361   646
Blackburn & Others v Gridquest Ltd [2002] IRLR 604   344
Bracebridge Engineering Limited v Darby [1990] IRLR 3   514
British Aircraft Corporation v Austin [1978] IRLR 332   72
British Home Stores Limited v Burchell [1978] IRLR 379   298
British Sugar plc v Kirker [1998] IRLR 624, EAT   231
Burrett v West Birmingham Health Authority [1994] IRLR 7   510

Castledine v Rothwell Engineering Ltd [1973] IRLR 99   492, 679
Caterleisure Ltd v TGWU, unreported, 14 October 1991, EAT   644
Christel Schmidt v Spar-und Leihkasse der früheren Amter Bordesholm, Kiel under Cronshagen [1995] ICR 237; [1994] IRLR 302, ECJ   645
Church v West Lancashire NHS Trust [1998] ICR 423   480
Clark v Novacold [1999] IRLR 318   125
Collinson v British Broadcasting Corporation [1998] IRLR, EAT 238   81
Cooperative Wholesale Society Limited v Squirrell [1974] IRLR 45   210
Coral Leisure Group Limited v Barnett [1981] IRLR 204   91
Corner v Buckingham County Council [1978] ICR 836   595
Coverfoam (Darwen) Ltd v Bell [1981] IRLR 195   237
Credit Suisse First Boston (Europe) Limited v Padiachy [1998] IRLR 504, QBD   636
Credit Suisse First Boston (Europe) Limited v Lister [1998] IRLR 700, CA   636

Dalgleish & Others v Lothian & Borders Police Board [1991] IRLR 422   299
Davies & Alderton v Head Wrighton Teesdale Ltd [1979] IRLR 170   605
Dekker v Stichting Vormingscentrum Voor Jong Volwassenen (VJV-Centrum Plus) [1991] IRLR 27   506
Dines v Initial Health Care Services Ltd [1994] IRLR 336, CA   644
Dr Sophie Redmond Stichting v Bartol & Others [1992] IRLR 366   643

Dutton & Clark Ltd v Daly [1985] IRLR 363   72
Dutton v Hawker Siddeley Aviation Limited [1978] IRLR 390   597

ECM (Vehicle Delivery Service) Limited v Cox [1999] IRLR 416   646
E C Cook v Thomas Linnell & Sons Limited [1977] IRLR 132   204
East Lindsey District Council v Daubney [1977] IRLR 181   236
Elliott Turbomachinery Ltd v Bates [1981] ICR 218   480
Ellis v Brighton Cooperative Society [1976] IRLR 419   217
Emmerson v Commissioners of Inland Revenue [1977] IRLR 458   595
Etam plc v Rowan [1989] IRLR 150   17, 508

Faccenda Chicken Limited v Fowler & Others [1986] IRLR 69   299
Ford v Milthorn Toleman Ltd [1980] IRLR 31   70
Ford v Warwickshire County Council [1983] ICR 273   78
Foreningen af Arbejdsledere i Danmark v Daddy's Dance Hall A/S [1988] IRLR 41,
   EAT   636, 644
Francisco Hernández Vidal v Gomez Perez [1999] IRLR 132   646
Fuller v Mastercare Service & Distribution (EAT/0707/00)   510
Futty v Brekkes (D & D) [1974] IRLR 130   73

Garricks (Caterers) Limited v Nolan [1980] IRLR 259   239
General & Municipal Workers Union v Certification Officer [1977] ICR 183   352
General Bill Posting v Atkinson [1909] AC 118   301
Gimber v Spurrett (1967) 2 ITR 308   480
Graham Oxley Tool Steels Ltd v Firth [1980] IRLR 135   72

Habermann-Bettermann v Arbeiterwohlfahrt, Bezirksverband Ndb/Obf e V (No. c-
   421/92)   507
Hare v Murphy Brothers [1974] ICR 603 CA   90
Harman v Flexible Lamps Limited [1980] IRLR 418   238
Harper v National Coal Board [1980] IRLR 260   236
Harrington v Kent [1980] IRLR 353   90
Harris (Ipswich) Limited v Harrison [1978] IRLR 382   210, 298
Harrison v George Wimpey & Company Limited [1972] 7 ITR 438   328
Harrison Bowden Ltd v Bowden [1994] ICR 186, EAT   644
Hay v George Hanson (Building Contractors) Ltd [1996] IRLR 427   638
Hayes v Malleable Working Men's Club & Institute [1985] ICR 703   511
Herbert Morris Ltd v Saxelby [1916] 1 AC 688   301
Hill v Chappell (EAT/1250/01)   347
Hitchcock v St Ann's Hosiery Company Ltd [1971] ITR 98, QBD   481
Hivac Ltd v Park Royal Scientific Instruments Ltd [1946] 1 All ER 350, CA   302
Houston v Zeal (CH) Limited [1972] ITR 331   210
Hurley v Mustoe [1981] IRLR 208   504, 657
Hussain v Elone plc [1999] IRLR 420   212
Hussein v Saints Complete House Furnishers [1979] IRLR 337   20, 470

Industrial Rubber Products v Gillon [1977] IRLR 389   70
Ingram v Foxon [1984] ICR 685   81
Isle of Wight Tourist Board v Coombes [1976] IRLR 413   73

JMA Spijkers v Gebroers Benedik Abbatoir CV [1986] 2 CMLR 296, ECJ   643, 644
John Laing & Son Ltd v Best [1968] ITR 3   481

K Sherrier v Ford Motor Company [1976] IRLR 141   212
Katsikas v Konstantinidis [1993] IRLR 179, ECJ   638
Kenny v South Manchester College [1993] IRLR 265   127, 643
Kigass Aero Components v Brown [2002] IRLR 312, EAT   343
King v Webb's Poultry Products (Bradford) Ltd [1975] IRLR 135   73

Ladbroke Racing Limited v Arnott [1979] IRLR 192   139
Landorganisationen i Danmark v Ny Molle Kro [1989] ICR 330, ECJ   643
Laws Stores Limited v Oliphant [1978] IRLR 251   139
Lawton v BOC Transhield Ltd [1987] IRLR 404   489
Leverton v Clwyd County Council [1989] IRLR ICR   281
Levez v Jennings (Harlow Pools) Ltd, unreported EAT/812/94   124
Lewis v Motorworld Garages Ltd [1985] IRLR 465   74
Lewis Shops Group v Wiggins [19731 IRLR 205   139
Lightfoot v D & J Sporting Ltd [1996] IRLR 64   91
Litster v Forth Dry Dock and Engineering Co Ltd [1989] ICR 341, HL   638
LMC Drains Ltd & Metro-Rod Services Ltd v Waugh [1991] 3 CMLR 172   644
Louies v Coventry Hood & Seating Co [1990] IRLR 324, EAT   213
Lunt v Merseyside TEC Ltd [1999] ICR 17   60

Macarthys Limited v Smith [1980] IRLR 211   282
Mahlburg v Land Mecklenburg-Vorpommern [2000] IRLR 276   507
Marleasing SA v La Comercial Internacional de Alimentacion [1990] ECR 4153, ECJ   644
Marshall v Southampton and South-West Hampshire Area Health Authority (No. 2) (Case No. C271/91)   6
Martin v Lancashire County Council [2000] IRLR 487 CA   637
Martin v Yorkshire Imperial Metals [1978] IRLR 440   211
McLellan v Cody and Cody, unreported, 7 October 1986, EAT   643
McNeill v Charles Crimin (Electrical Contractors) Ltd [1984] IRLR 179   70
Merseyside & North Wales Electricity Board v Taylor [1975] IRLR 80, QBD   236
Meyer Dunmore International Limited v Rogers [1978] IRLR 167   212
MPB Structure Ltd v Munro [2002] IRLR 601   344
Moore v Dupont Furniture Products Ltd [1980] IRLR 158, CA   66
Morris v Walsh Western UK Ltd [1997] IRLR 562   81
Murphy v Sheffield Hallam University (1998),(unreported)ET 2800489/98   123
Murray & Another v Foyle Meats Ltd [1999] ICR 827   480

Napier v National Business Agency Ltd [1951] 2 All ER 264   78, 91
Nash v Mash/Roe Group Ltd [1999] IRLR 168   169
Nasse v Science Research Council and Vyas v Leyland Cars [1979] IRLR 465   491
Newland v Simons & Willer (Hairdressers) Limited [1981] ICR 521   78
Nordenfelt v Maxim Nordenfelt Guns & Ammunition Co Ltd [1894] AC 535   301
Nottinghamshire County Council v Bowly [1978] IRLR 252   211

O'Neill v Symm & Co Ltd [1998] IRLR 233   124

P v S and Cornwall County Council (Case No C-13/94)   503
P Bork International A/S v Foreningen af Arbejdsledere i Danmark [1989] IRLR
   41, ECJ   638
Pepper & Hope v Daish [1980] IRLR 13 EAT   70
Polkey v Dayton Services Limited [1987] IRLR 503   104, 136, 237
Post Office v Jones [1977] IRLR 422   236
Prestwick Circuits Limited v McAndrew [1990] IRLR 191   71
Price v Civil Service Commission [1977] IRLR 291   512
Printers & Finishers Ltd v Holloway [1965] RPC 239   299
Pritchard-Rhodes Ltd. v Boon and Milton [1979] IRLR 19   479
Property Guards Limited v Taylor & Kershaw [1982] IRLR 175   94

R v Secretary of State for Employment, ex parte Equal Opportunities Commission
   [1994] ICR 317   76
Rask v ISS Kantineservice A/S [1993] IRLR 133   636, 643
Ratcliffe v Dorset County Council [1979] IRLR 191   595
Rex Stewart Jeffries Parker Ginsberg Ltd v Parker [1988] IRLR 483   301
Ridout v TC Group [1998] IRLR 628   122
Roadburg v Lothian Regional Council [1976] IRLR 283   18
Robinson v Crompton Parkinson [1978] IRLR 61   70
Rock-It Cargo Ltd v Green [1997] IRLR 58   61
Ross v Delrosa Caterers Ltd [1981] ICR 393   81
Rowan v Machinery Installations (South Wales) Limited [1981] ICR 386   81
Rutherford v Harvest Town Circle & Bently v DTI (No. 2) [2002] IRLR 768   169
Rygaard v Stro Molle Akustik [1996] IRLR 151   645

Safebid Ltd v Ramiro, unreported, 3 May 1990, EAT   643
Salveson v Simmons [1994] IRLR 52   92
Sanchez Hidalgo & Others v Asociación de Servicios Aser & Sociedad Cooperativa
   Minerva [1999] IRLR 136   646
Sandhu v London Borough of Hillingdon [1978] IRLR 209   200
Saunders v Richmond Upon Thames Borough Council [1977] IRLR 363   506
Savoia v Chiltern Herb Farms Ltd [1982] IRLR 166 CA   75
Schmidt v Austicks Bookshops Ltd [1977] IRLR 360   510
Scott Packing and Warehousing Company Limited v Patterson [1978] IRLR 167
   218

Scottish Special Housing Association v Cooke [1979] IRLR 264   211
Sharman v Hindu Temple (1991), unreported, EAT 253/90   91
Sheffield v Oxford Controls Co Ltd [1979] IRLR 133 (EAT)   74
Shields v Coombes (Holdings) Ltd [1978] ITR 473   280
Singh v Rowntree Mackintosh Ltd [1979] IRLR 199   470
Skyrail Oceanic Limited t/a Cosmos Tours v Coleman[1978] IRLR 226   218
Smith v Safeway plc [1996] IRLR 456   511
Smiths Industries Aerospace & Defence Systems Limited v Brookes [1986] IRLR 434   238
Snowball v Gardner Merchant Limited [1987] IRLR 397   514
Spencer v Paragon Wallpapers Ltd [1976] IRLR 373   237
Spring v Guardian Royal Exchange [1993] IRLR 122   489
Stephenson Jordan & Harrison Ltd v MacDonald & Evans [1952] 1 TLR 101, CA 234   299
Strathclyde Regional Council v Porcelli [1986] IRLR 134 CS   513
Sutcliffe & Eaton v Pinney [1977] IRLR 349   201
Sutton & Gates (Luton) Limited v Boxall [1978] IRLR 486   206
Sweeney v J & S Henderson (Concessions) Ltd [1999] IRLR 306, EAT   78

Taylor v Alidair Limited [1978] IRLR 82   204, 210
Thompson v Walon Car Delivery and BRS Automotive Ltd [1997] IRLR 343   643
Tiptools Limited v T W Curtis [1973] IRLR 276   205
Treganowan v Robert Knee & Company Limited [1975] IRLR 247   218
Trust House Forte Ltd v D J Murphy [1977] IRLR 187   298
Trust Houses Forte Leisure Ltd v J Aquilar [1976] IRLR 251   210

United Bank Limited v Akhtar [1989] IRLR 507   71

Vilella v MFI Furniture Centres Limited [1999] IRLR 468   238

W J Thompson v Eaton Limited [1976] IRLR 308   220
W E Cox Toner (International) Ltd v Crook [1981] IRLR 443 (EAT)   73
Wallace v South Eastern Education & Library Board [1980] IRLR 193   506
Webb v EMO Air Cargo (UK) Ltd [1993] IRLR 27   506
Wendelboe v L J Music Aps [1985] ECR 457, ECJ   638
Western Excavating (ECC) Ltd v Sharp [1978] 2 WLR 344, CA   69
Wetherall (Bond St W1) Ltd v Lynn [1978] ICR 203   70
Wileman v Minilee Engineering Ltd [1988] IRLR 144   514
Wilson v St Helen's Borough Council/BFL v Baxendale & Meade [1998] IRLR 706 636
Woods v W M Car Services (Peterborough) Ltd [1982] IRLR 413, CA   69
Wylie v Dee & Co [1978] IRLR 103   17, 508
Wynes v Southrepps Hall Broiler Farm [1968] ITR 407   475

Zarcynska v Levy [1978] IRLR 532   471

Preface

These past two years have witnessed a not wholly unexpected flood of new legislation enhancing the rights of employees (and workers) and imposing yet more duties and responsibilities on employers. This fourth edition of the handbook has been appropriately updated and provides practical guidance on the new legislation and on selected and pertinent decisions by the tribunals and courts.

Enhanced maternity rights mean that pregnant employees whose babies are due on or after 6 April 2003 may now take up to 52 weeks' maternity leave (with substantial improvements in the amount of statutory maternity pay payable during their maternity pay periods). Similar rights are also available to the parents of adopted children. Fathers, for their part, may take one or two weeks' paid (or unpaid) paternity leave; while the parents of a child under the age of six (or under the age of 18, if disabled) may apply for more flexible working arrangements. Another development is the right of women to question their employers (using a new form designed for that purpose) if they suspect that they are being paid less than comparable male employees working in the same establishment. Following full implementation of Council Directive 94/33/EC 'on the protection of young people at work', and concomitant amendments to the Working Time Regulations 1998, young persons under the age of 18 (who have lawfully left school) may not be required to work for more than 40 hours a week or for more than eight hours on any day. Their ability to work at night has also been severely curtailed. The recent abolition of the so-called '13-week rule' means that all workers (regardless of their contractual status) will begin to accrue an entitlement to paid annual holidays from day one of their contracts. Once the new 'dispute resolution' provisions of the Employment Act 2002 (summarised in this fourth edition) come into force, all employers (whatever the size of the businesses or undertakings) will be duty-bound to adopt minimum statutory procedures (DDPs and GPs) for dealing with workplace dismissals and grievances.

My thanks as always to my publishers and to my family for their unswerving support throughout this project. Dedicated to the memory of Frances, a dear friend and sister.

A

ABSENTEEISM

Key points

- Employers should have no need to remind employees that they are expected to turn up for work on time and to remain at their desks or workstations until the end of their working day or shift. People who are routinely late for work, or who take extended lunch breaks, or who are in the habit of slipping away early, or who take an unauthorised day off every now and again to attend the funeral of yet another distant relative, are putting their jobs at risk. They are in breach of their contracts of employment and should not be surprised if their employer decides that 'enough is enough'.

The reasonable employer

- The *reasonable* employer will first seek out the malingerer, invite him (or her) into his office 'for a chat', listen to his explanations and (if those explanations are unacceptable or incredible) warn him that he will be dismissed if he does not mend his ways. Fortunately, most malingerers are quickly identified and uprooted – long before they have earned the right to pursue a complaint of unfair dismissal before an employment tribunal.

- As a matter of good industrial relations practice, an employer should never presume that an absentee employee is malingering. Common sense alone dictates that he (or she) take reasonable steps to find out why the employee has not turned in for work on time, why he has not yet returned from his lunch-break, why he slipped away early, or why he took a day off work without permission. It could be that the employee has suddenly been taken ill or has been injured and unable to contact his employer. He may have suffered a bereavement or have been distracted by a serious domestic crisis. If he is yet again late for work, he could have been delayed by traffic, or whatever.

- The reasonable employer will ask the right questions, consider the facts as he knows them, review the employee's punctuality and attendance record, reflect on his (or her) general attitude and demeanour, and take his decision accordingly. This latter approach is particularly important in the case of a long-serving and otherwise well-respected employee whose recent and uncharacteristically poor attendance record may be symptomatic of emergent domestic, emotional or financial worries which may not have been fully explored or investigated. Although his conduct may be no less disruptive than that of the professional malingerer, his peremptory dismissal would undoubtedly be viewed as unfair by an employment tribunal.

- An employee who is disciplined or dismissed because of his (or her) unacceptable attendance record should be afforded an opportunity to appeal against that decision if he considers that he has been unfairly treated.

- Although employees are well aware that persistent late attendance and unauthorised absenteeism will inevitably invite disciplinary action, section 3 of the Employment Rights Act 1996 nonetheless requires employers to include a note in the written statement issued to each employee 'specifying any disciplinary rules applicable to the employee or referring to a document that is reasonably accessible to the employee and that specifies such rules'.

  Note: For the time being at least, this requirement does not apply to a small firm or business in which the total number of persons employed (including persons employed in other branches of the same business or by any associated employer) is less than twenty (*ibid.* section 3(3)). However, from September 2003, when section 36 of the Employment Act 2002 is expected to come into force, that exemption disappears. What this means is that all employers will henceforth be required to adopt minimum rules and procedures for dealing with disciplinary issues within the workplace. For further particulars, see *Disciplinary rules & procedures* (elsewhere in this handbook).

- High levels of absenteeism can be very costly and damaging, especially to the small business. When drawing up his disciplinary rules or explaining his situation to the job applicant or new recruit, an employer should stress the importance of good timekeeping and should point out the consequences if an employee ignores prior warnings and routinely takes time off work without good reason or prior authorisation. Most employers insist that people who are likely to be late or who will not be attending for work on any day should contact them as soon as possible, certainly within one hour of their normal starting time on that day. See also **Dismissal on grounds of ill-health** and **Sickness and statutory sick pay** elsewhere in this handbook.

- ACAS Code of Practice 1 (*Disciplinary & Grievance Procedures*) urges that, except for gross misconduct, no employee should be dismissed for a first breach of discipline. But, a great deal will depend on the circumstances, including the size and administrative resources of the employer's undertaking. As was suggested earlier, few professional malingerers will survive with an employer long enough to qualify to pursue a complaint of unfair dismissal before an employment tribunal. So far as the longer-serving employee is concerned, it will be for the tribunal to decide whether, in the circumstances, the employer had acted reasonably in taking the decision to dismiss. Copies of ACAS Code of Practice 1 (Ref. COP1) are available from ACAS Reader Limited on 0870 242 9090.

Deductions from pay

- An employer does, of course, have every right to withhold the wage or salary otherwise due to an employee in respect of a period of unauthorised absence from work. But to withhold an excessive amount (for example, by deducting a half hour's pay to punish an employee who is five minutes late for work) is tantamount to imposing a fine. This is illegal, unless:

  (a) the employee had given his (or her) *prior written consent* to the making of that additional deduction; or

  (b) the employer's right to make that deduction had been expressly incorporated in the employee's contract of employment or had previously been notified to the employee in writing.

- An employee cannot be required to give retroactive consent to the making of a deduction from his (or her) pay packet. In other words, an employer's policy in relation to late attendance and unauthorised absenteeism must be made known to every employee before he can presume to put that policy into effect (see section 13 of the Employment Rights Act 1996). See also **Deductions from pay, Dismissal for misconduct, Dismissal on grounds of ill health** and **Wages, payment of** elsewhere in this handbook.

Time off work

- The reader will be aware that certain categories of employee have the statutory right to be permitted a reasonable amount of paid (or unpaid) time off work to enable them to carry out their functions or duties (as trade union officials, trade union members, officials of specified public bodies, employee and workforce representatives, safety representatives, pension scheme trustees, and so on). The pregnant employee likewise has a right to paid time off work for ante-natal care; and the redundant employee, paid time off to look for work or to arrange for re-training. Employees also have the right to be permitted a reasonable amount of unpaid time off work to attend to the needs of dependants; while the parents (or adoptive parents) of children under the age of five may take up to 13 weeks' unpaid parental leave. For further particulars, please turn to the sections titled **Parental leave** and **Time off work** (of which there are several) elsewhere in this handbook.

Absences following maternity leave

- A new mother, who is prevented by illness or injury from returning to work after a period of ordinary or additional maternity leave, does not forfeit her right to return to work so long as she informs her employer that she is ill and produces a doctor's sick note (or a self-certificate for illness) in keeping with the usual sickness absence procedures laid down in her contract of employment. For further particulars, please turn to the section titled **Maternity rights** elsewhere in this handbook.

ACCESS TO EMPLOYMENT

Key points

- Under the common law, an employer cannot be compelled either to employ a particular job applicant or to reinstate or re-engage someone who has been dismissed. As Lord Davey remarked in *Allen v Flood* [1898] AC 1: 'An employer may refuse to employ [a workman] for the most mistaken, capricious, malicious or morally reprehensible motives that can be conceived, but the workman has no right of action against him.' And again: 'A man has no right to be employed by any particular employer, and has no right to any particular employment if it depends on the will of another.'

- Although an employer retains his (or her) common law right to pick and choose the people he employs, there may be a price to pay for exercising that right. In short, an employer can be ordered to pay compensation to a job applicant if a tribunal or court is satisfied that the employer acted unlawfully in refusing (or deliberately omitting) to employ the person concerned on grounds of:

(a) sex, marital status, pregnancy or gender reassignment;

(b) colour, race, nationality, or national or ethnic origins;

(c) disability;

(d) trade union membership or non-membership;

(e) religion or political opinion (Northern Ireland only); or

(f) a 'spent' conviction.

Recent developments: In December 2001, the Government published a consultation document (entitled *Towards Equality and Diversity*) outlining its proposals for implementing EU Directives 2000/43/EC and 2000/78/EC, the first of which prohibitions discrimination on grounds of race and ethnic origin; and the second, discrimination on grounds of sexual orientation, religion or belief, disability, or age. The consultation period ended on 29 March 2002. Legislation on sexual orientation and religion (including technical amendments to the Race Relations Act 1976) will be implemented in the second half of 2003. Legislation ending the exemption for small employers in the Disability Discrimination Act 1995 (as well as other amendments to that Act) will be brought into force in October 2004. However, legislation prohibiting discrimination on grounds of age is unlikely to be introduced before December 2006. Copies of the Consultation Document may be accessed and downloaded from website www.dti.gov.uk.

Sex discrimination

- Discrimination on grounds of sex, marital status or 'gender reassignment' (see next paragraph) is prohibited by the Sex Discrimination Act 1975. An employer's refusal or deliberate failure to offer employment on such grounds will very likely prompt a complaint to an employment tribunal. If such a complaint is upheld, the employer will be ordered to pay compensation to the complainant of an unspecified amount that includes damages for loss of prospective earnings and injury to feelings (plus interest on the sum awarded).

- Discrimination against transsexuals (more precisely, against persons who intend to undergo, are undergoing or have undergone gender reassignment) was outlawed on 1 May 1999 by the Sex Discrimination (Gender Reassignment) Regulations 1999.

Note: Following the decision of the European Court of Justice in *Marshall v Southampton and South-West Hampshire Area Health Authority (No. 2)* (Case No. C271/91) and the coming into force on 22 November 1993 of the Sex Discrimination & Equal Pay (Remedies) Regulations 1993 employers should by now be aware that there is no longer a ceiling or upper limit on the amount of compensation that may be awarded to a job applicant unlawfully denied access to employment on grounds of sex, marital status or (now) gender reassignment.

- An employer may be able to justify his refusal to employ a particular job applicant on the grounds that being a woman or a man (or being married) is a *genuine occupational qualification* for the job in question *(ibid.* section 7). The genuine occupational qualification defence is also permissible in certain circumstances involving gender reassignees. For further particulars, please turn to the section titled **Sex discrimination** elsewhere in this handbook.

- If an employment tribunal (at the suit of the Equal Opportunities Commission [EOC]) finds that an employer had yielded to third party pressure to discriminate against a job applicant on grounds of sex, marital status or gender reassignment, and that the third party concerned is likely to do so again, the EOC may apply to the county court for an injunction restraining that person from committing any further unlawful acts *(ibid.* sections 40 and 72).

- A complaint of unlawful discrimination under the 1975 Act must be presented to an employment tribunal not later than three months after the date on which the act complained of was done *(ibid.* section 76(1)).

Pregnancy

- It is not at all clear whether a refusal to employ a woman because she is pregnant (or for a connected reason) is in the same legal category as a refusal to employ a woman simply because she *is* a woman. Although *prima facie* tantamount to unlawful discrimination on grounds of sex, there may well be circumstances in which an employer's refusal to engage a pregnant job applicant could be justified before an employment tribunal.

- For example, an employer will be disinclined (understandably) to recruit a heavily-pregnant woman as a marketing manager (however well-qualified or better-qualified she may be than other candidates for the post) if one of her first duties is to exercise her undoubted skills to launch a major new product range at a time when she will be off work preparing for childbirth or having her baby – and likely to be absent from work on maternity leave for up to 52 weeks. Arguably, the employer's refusal to employ would have little to do with the woman's being pregnant. Indeed, an employer would be equally disinclined to appoint a man to the same post knowing that, within a matter of weeks, he would be going into hospital for several months, at a time when the survival of the employer's business might very well hinge on the new appointee being at work at the very time he is likely to be away. But comparing a healthily-pregnant woman with a sick man is risky, especially in the current climate. Should such a case go before an employment tribunal, the employer would need to advance a very strong case indeed.

Note: Section 51 of the Sex Discrimination Act 1975 allows that it is not unlawful for an employer to refuse to employ a woman if doing so would be in breach of health and safety legislation restricting or prohibiting the employment of women in certain hazardous occupations. However, in *Mahlburg v Land Mecklenburg-Vorpommern [2000] IRLR 276(*, the European Court of Justice (ECJ) held that it is not permissible to refuse to employ a new or expectant mother in work otherwise prohibited to her on health and safety grounds if the employment is intended to be *permanent* and she is the best candidate for the job. In a not dissimilar case, that of *Webb v EMO Air Cargo (UK) Ltd (No. 2)* [1994] ICR 770 ECJ, a woman initially recruited as a replacement for a key employee during her absence on maternity leave (with a promise of permanent employment when the person she was replacing returned to work) was dismissed when it was discovered that she too was pregnant and would be taking maternity leave at the same time as the colleague she was meant to replace. An employment tribunal, the EAT and the Court of Appeal all agreed that the woman had been dismissed not because she was pregnant but because she would not have been available to carry out her primary task of doing the work of the other employee during the latter's absence on maternity leave. Her dismissal, they said, was therefore fair. The House of Lords were not so sure. Mrs Webb had been employed for an indefinite period, even though initially employed to take over the work of a woman who would be absent for several weeks on maternity leave. Their Lordships referred the matter to the European Court of Justice (ECJ) which, on 14 July 1994, held that the woman's dismissal amounted to unlawful sex discrimination in breach of the 1976 European Union directive on equal treatment for men and women in the workplace. The ECJ also put a great deal of emphasis on the fact that Mrs Webb had been employed for an indefinite period. Had Mrs Webb been recruited specifically to replace the other employee, and had she been informed from the very outset that she would be dismissed once the permanent encumbent had returned to work, the outcome might well have been different.

Colour, race, nationality or ethnic or national origins

- Section 4 of the Race Relations Act 1976 cautions that it is *prima facie* unlawful to refuse or 'deliberately omit' to offer employment to a person because of his or her race, colour, nationality or ethnic or national origins, unless being of a particular racial group is a *genuine occupational qualification* for the job in question (*ibid.* section 5). If a tribunal upholds a complaint of unlawful racial discrimination, it will order the employer to pay compensation including damages for injured feelings and loss of potential earnings. With the coming into force on 3 July 1994 of the Race Relations (Remedies) Act 1994, there is no longer an upper limit on the amount of compensation that an employer may be ordered to pay in such circumstances. For further particulars, please turn to the section titled **Racial discrimination** elsewhere in this handbook.

Note: The reader will be aware that section 8 of the Asylum & Immigration Act 1996 prohibits the employment in the UK of any person aged 16 or over who is either an illegal immigrant or who does not have the legal and still valid right to seek and obtain employment during his (or her) stay in the UK. The penalty for a breach of this requirement is a fine of up to £5,000. See **Foreign nationals, employment of** elsewhere in this handbook.

- The Commission for Racial Equality (CRE) may, for its part, institute proceedings before an employment tribunal against any person or organisation that has either induced or attempted to put pressure on an employer to discriminate against job applicants on racial grounds. If the tribunal confirms that such pressure had been brought to bear and that the guilty party is likely to do so again, the CRE may apply to a designated county court (or to a sheriff court) for an order restraining the person or organisation concerned from committing any further unlawful acts (*ibid.* sections 31 and 63).

- A complaint of unlawful discrimination under the 1976 Act must be presented within three months of the date on which the act complained of was done (*ibid.* section 69(1)).

Disability discrimination

- Under section 4 of the Disability Discrimination Act 1995, it is unlawful for an employer (in a business or organisation that employs 15 or more people) to refuse to interview or employ an otherwise well-qualified job applicant simply because that applicant is disabled. Nor can an employer justify that refusal by claiming that the premises (ie, the building or location in which the applicant would be required to work) are not suitable for use by disabled persons in general or for the particular job applicant in the light of his (or her) disability.

- It is also unlawful for an employer to instruct some other person or body (eg, the personnel department or an employment agency) not to interview or recruit disabled job applicants or (in the case of an agency) submit such candidates for employment.

- A disabled job applicant may complain to an employment tribunal if denied an interview or an offer of employment because of his (or her) disability. If the tribunal finds the complaint to be well-founded, it will make a declaration to that effect and will order the respondent employer (agency or organisation) to pay compensation to the complainant – including compensation for injury to feelings (*ibid.* section 8). For further particulars, please turn to the section titled **Disabled persons** elsewhere in this handbook.

Trade union membership or non-membership

- Section 137 of the Trade Union & Labour Relations (Consolidation) Act 1992 warns that 'it is unlawful to refuse a person employment because he (or she) –

(a) is, or is not, a member of a trade union, or

(b) is unwilling to accept a requirement –

    (i)   to take steps to become or cease to be, or to remain or not to become, a member of a trade union, or

    (ii)   to make payments or suffer deductions for not being a member of a trade union'.

What this means in effect is that an employer must disregard a job applicant's membership or non-membership of a trade union when determining his or her suitability for employment. Nor is it lawful for an employer to require a job applicant to agree to pay money (to a charity, or whatever) or to have money deducted from his or her pay packet as an alternative to the payment of trade union dues. Any term in a contract of employment or collective agreement (express or implied) that purports to override an employee's statutory rights in this respect is null and void.

- A job applicant denied an interview or refused employment on grounds of his (or her) trade union membership or non-membership may complain to an employment tribunal. If such a complaint is upheld, the tribunal will order the employer to pay the complainant up to £53,500 in compensation. A complaint may also be presented if there is reason to suspect that the employer refused to entertain or process a job application because of the applicant's trade union membership or non-membership – without regard to the latter's capabilities or qualifications for the job in question.

- In some trades and industries, employers would only accept job applications from members of a particular trade union whose names had been put forward by that trade union. Such an arrangement or practice (if it still persists) is unacceptable if its effect is to exclude applications from persons who are not members of a particular trade union or of any trade union. Indeed, any employer party to such an arrangement or practice will nowadays be deemed *without more* to have unlawfully refused to employ a particular job applicant because he or she was not a member of a trade union *(ibid.* section 137(4)).

- If, on a complaint under section 137 of the 1992 Act, it is alleged that a trade union or other person threatened the employer with a strike or some other form of industrial action if he recruited a nonunion employee, the job applicant or the employer may request the employment tribunal to direct that the person who exercised that pressure be joined (or, in Scotland, sisted) as a party to the tribunal proceedings. If the complaint is upheld, the trade union official or member concerned will be ordered to pay the whole or part of any award of compensation payable to that job applicant *(ibid.* section 142). See **Trade union membership and activities** and **Closed shop** elsewhere in this handbook.

Religion or political opinion

- Under the Fair Employment & Treatment (Northern Ireland) Order 1998, an employer is liable to heavy penalties if he (or she) refuses to employ a job applicant because of that person's religious belief or political opinion. In practice, this means that Protestants and Catholics must be afforded equal access to job opportunities and must not be denied employment or refused an interview because of their religious or political affiliations. It is as well to note that discrimination on grounds of religion is to be outlawed throughout the UK when legislation implementing Employment Directive 2000/78/EC comes into force in the second half of 2003.

'Spent' convictions

- Section 4(2) of the Rehabilitation of Offenders Act 1974 states that a person may not lawfully be excluded from any office, profession, occupation or employment because of a 'spent' conviction. Indeed, 'where a question seeking information with respect to a person's previous convictions, offences, conduct or circumstances is put to him (or her)…the question shall be treated as not relating to spent convictions or to any circumstances ancillary to spent convictions, and the answer thereto may be framed accordingly'.

- In short, any job applicant with a 'spent' conviction has the legal right to lie about that conviction when asked by a prospective employer if he or she has ever been in prison or been convicted of an indictable offence. The exceptions to this rule are explained elsewhere in this handbook in the section titled **Convicted persons, employment of**.

- Although it is *prima facie* unlawful to refuse to employ a person on discovery that he (or she) has a 'spent' conviction, the 1974 Act does not offer a remedy for a person discriminated against in this way. At best, the applicant can apply to the court for a declaration of 'unlawfulness'. But that falls far short of any award of compensation for loss of potential earnings and injured feelings.

  Note: To dismiss an otherwise competent employee on discovery that he (or she) had concealed details of a spent conviction (and for that reason alone) will almost certainly lead to a finding of unfair dismissal and an award of compensation (unless the employee in question was in an *excepted* occupation).

Activities of employment agencies and businesses

- Any employment agency that discriminates against (or denies its services to) job applicants on grounds of race, colour, ethnic origins, nationality, sex, marital status, gender reassignment, disability, or trade union membership or non-membership (whether of its own initiative or on the instructions of a client employer) could be ordered to pay the whole or part of any compensation awarded to a disgruntled job applicant.

- In the appropriate circumstances, the person (or persons) running the agency could be served with a prohibition order by an employment tribunal (at the suit of the Secretary of State) effectively prohibiting any such person from carrying on (or being in any way concerned with the carrying on) of an employment agency or business for a period of up to 10 years. A failure to comply with the terms of a prohibition order is a serious offence for which the penalty, on summary conviction, is a fine of up to £5,000 (per sections 3 to 3D, Employment Agencies Act 1973). See also **Employment agencies** elsewhere in this handbook.

ADOPTION LEAVE AND PAY

Key points

- From 6 April 2003, an employee who has been newly-matched with a child for adoption, or whose partner has been newly-matched with a child for adoption, or who is one of a couple who have been newly matched with a child for adoption (in each case, by an approved adoption agency), and who has been continuously employed by his or her employer for 26 weeks or more leading into the week in which notification of being matched occurred, has the right to take up to 26 weeks' ordinary adoption leave, followed immediately by up to 26 weeks' additional adoption leave. An employee with average earnings of £75 or more per week will qualify to be paid statutory adoption pay (SAP) during his or her ordinary adoption leave period. The relevant legislation is to be found in the Paternity & Adoption Leave Regulations 2002 which came into force on 8 December 2002.

  Note: By definition, the right to adoption leave is not available to a step-father or mother who adopts his or her partner's children.

- It is as well to point out that the right to take up to 52 weeks' adoption leave is available to those eligible employees only who were informed on or after 6 April 2003 that they had been matched with a child for adoption – unless the notification occurred before 6 April 2003, but the child was not actually placed with them (or their partners) until 6 April 2003 or later. Furthermore, the right to adoption leave is available to one member only of a couple (whether married or otherwise) who have had a child placed with them for adoption – in which event, it is up to the adoptive parent or parents to decide which of them takes the adoption leave. However, the other partner may be entitled to take one or two weeks' paid paternity leave during the eight weeks following adoption and up to 13 weeks' unpaid parental leave, as to which please turn to the sections on **Parental leave** and **Paternity leave** elsewhere in this handbook.

Disrupted placement in the course of adoption leave

- An employee who has already begun a period of adoption leave, in anticipation of being placed with a child, may remain on adoption leave for up to eight weeks (or, where appropriate, for a further eight weeks) if, for one reason or another, the expected placement does not occur or if the child dies or is returned to the adoption agency under section 30(3) of the Adoption Act 1976 or section 30 of the Adoption (Scotland) Act 1978.

Statutory Adoption Pay

- An employee who qualifies for adoption leave, and who earns an average of £77 or more per week (during the period of eight weeks ending with the last payday before the end of the week in which notice of being matched for adoption was given) will normally qualify for up to 26 weeks' Statutory Adoption Pay (SAP) during his or her ordinary adoption pay period. The adoption pay period is the period that begins on the Sunday immediately following the day on which an employee begins his or her ordinary adoption leave.

- There are two rates of SAP, the higher rate and the lower rate. The higher rate is an amount equivalent to nine-tenths of the employee's average weekly earnings and is payable for each of the first six weeks of the adoption pay period. The lower rate, payable for the remaining (up to) 20 weeks, is £100 a week or 90 per cent of the employee's average weekly earnings, whichever is the lower of those amounts. An employer who has lawfully paid SAP to an employee may reclaim 92 per cent of the amount paid by deducting the amount in question from payments of employees' and employers' NI contributions made to the Collector of Taxes at the end of each tax month. Employers who are eligible for small employers' relief may recover 100 per cent of the amount of SAP paid, plus an additional amount (currently 4.5 per cent) in compensation for the employer's portion of NI contributions paid on SAP.

Notification procedure

- To exercise his (or her) right to adoption leave, an employee must (within seven days of the date on which he was notified of having been matched with a child for adoption) inform his employer (in writing, if requested to do so) of his intention to take ordinary adoption leave, specifying:

  (a) the date on which the child is expected to be placed with him for adoption; and

  (b) the date on which he has elected to take adoption leave (which may begin either on the date on which the child is placed with him for adoption or no more than 14 days before the expected placement date).

  Where his employer requests it, the employee must also produce documentary evidence (letters, certificates, etc) issued by the adoption agency confirming the name and address of the agency, the name and date of birth of the child, the date on which the agency informed him that he had been matched with that child; and the date on which the agency expects to place the child with him.

- Employees who have correctly notified their employers of the date on which they intend to start their adoption leave may change their minds, so long as they inform their employers at least 28 days beforehand of the revised start date.

- An employer, who has been correctly notified of the date on which an employee intends to start his or her adoption leave, must write to the employee in question, within the next 28 days, setting out the date in which the employee would be expected to return to work on completion of his or her full entitlement to adoption leave.

Statutory rights during and after adoption leave

- While absent from work on adoption leave, an employee has rights similar to those available to employees on maternity leave (as to which, see **Maternity rights** elsewhere in this handbook). In short, an employee absent from work on adoption leave has the right:

  - if made redundant during his or her ordinary or additional adoption leave period, to be offered suitable alternative employment under a new contract of employment to begin on the day immediately following the day on which his or her previous contract of employment came to an end;

  - to the continuation of certain contractual rights and duties while absent from work on adoption leave (save for the right to be paid his or her normal wages or salary while absent on adoption leave);

  - to return to work after adoption leave in his or her original (or in a substantially equivalent) job;

  - to ask for more flexible working arrangements on his or her return to work (as to which, see **Flexible Working** elsewhere in this handbook); and

  - not to be dismissed, selected for redundancy, victimised, or subjected to any other detriment for exercising or asserting his or her rights under the Paternity & Adoption Leave Regulations 2002.

- Employees on adoption leave, who wish to return to work earlier than the date on which they are otherwise due to return, must notify their employers of the proposed earlier date of return at least 28 days beforehand. Should they fail to do so, their employers are within their rights to delay their return until those 28 days have elapsed or until the date on which they are otherwise due to return, whichever occurs sooner.

Claims and remedies

- Eligible employees who are denied their entitlement to adoption leave, or who are dismissed, selected for redundancy, victimised, or subjected to any other detriment for asserting their rights under the Paternity & Adoption Leave Regulations 2002, may complain to an employment tribunal and will be awarded appropriate compensation if their complaints are upheld.

  See also **Flexible working, Maternity rights, Parental leave**, and **Paternity leave** elsewhere in this handbook.

ADVERTISEMENTS (DISCRIMINATORY)

Key points

- A job advertisement that indicates (or could be construed as indicating) an intention to discriminate against would-be job applicants on grounds of sex, marital status, gender reassignment, colour, race, nationality or national or ethnic origins, or on grounds of disability, is unlawful by virtue of section 38 of the Sex Discrimination Act 1975, section 29 of the Race Relations Act 1976, and section 11 of the Disability Discrimination Act 1995.

  Note: It is not yet unlawful in the UK for an employer to discriminate against a job applicant (or existing worker) on grounds of age, political conviction, or religion – except in Northern Ireland where discrimination on grounds of religion or political opinion is outlawed by the Fair Employment & Treatment (Northern Ireland) Order 1998. However, the UK Government has three years within which to introduce legislation implementing the EU's Employment Directive 2000/78/EC, which prohibitions discrimination on grounds of sexual orientation, religion, or age. Legislation prohibiting discrimination on grounds of sexual orientation or religion is expected to come into force in the second half of 2003. However, exercising its right to do so, the Government has yet to decide whether to exercise its right to delay the introduction of Regulations prohibiting discrimination on grounds of age until December 2006.

- Proceedings in such cases will ordinarily be brought by the Equal Opportunities Commission, the Commission for Racial Equality or the Disability Rights Commission (either of their own initiative or in response to a complaint from a member of the public).

Disability Discrimination Act 1995

- If a job advertisement suggests an intention to discriminate against disabled persons, a disabled job applicant who responds to that advertisement and is either denied an interview or is refused (or not offered) the employment because of his disability, may complain to an employment tribunal and will be awarded compensation if his complaint is upheld. Furthermore, the publisher of the offending advertisement, as well as the person who inserted it, is liable to be fined – unless the publisher can show in his defence that he published the advertisement in reliance on a statement by the advertiser that it would not be unlawful to do so, and that it was reasonable for him to rely on that statement.

Note: The Disability Rights Commission (DRC), which has powers similar to those available to the Equal Opportunities Commission (EOC) and the Commission for Racial Equality (CRE) may caution any person (employer, employment agency, or publisher) who publishes a discriminatory advertisement that he (or she) is liable to be served with a non-discrimination notice unless he can satisfy the Commission that no discrimination was intended or occurred.

Sex Discrimination Act 1975

- Section 38 (3) of the 1975 Act cautions that the use of a job title with a gender-specific connotation (such as 'waiter', 'salesgirl', 'postman' or 'stewardess') will be taken to indicate an intention to discriminate unless the advertisement in which that title appears clearly invites applications from persons of either sex. Incidentally, there is no law that requires an employer to use terms such as 'manageress' or 'chair' or other convoluted (or 'politically correct') versions of such traditional job titles. But giving undue prominence to a job title such as 'Air Stewardess' or publishing an advertisement for the more politically-acceptable 'Flight Attendant' in a woman's magazine (but in no other publication) could be construed as overtly discriminatory – notwithstanding a disclaimer to the effect that the vacancy is open to persons of either sex.

- However, there are exceptions to this rule. An employer may decline to employ a man, woman or gender reassignee in a particular job if the sex of the successful applicant is a *genuine occupational qualification* (or, in the case of a gender reassignee, a *supplementary genuine occupational qualifi-*

cation) for that job. Furthermore, there are some industrial processes and occupations in which the employment of women is prohibited by health and safety regulations – as to the latter, please turn to the sections titled **Sex discrimination** and **Women and young persons, employment of,** elsewhere in this handbook.

- To summarise: a job may be restricted to persons of a particular sex:

  (a) if it is likely to involve physical contact with women/men in circumstances where those women or men might reasonably object to its being carried out by a man/woman;

      Note: Employers should be careful not to interpret sub-paragraph (a) or, for that matter, (b) too literally. In *Etam plc v Rowan* [1989] IRLR 150, an employer was held to have discriminated against a man on grounds of sex when she refused to employ him to sell women's lingerie. In a not dissimilar case, that *of Wylie v Dee Co.* [1978] IRLR 103, a woman was refused a job as sales assistant with a firm of gentlemen's outfitters because her duties would involve taking a man's inside leg measurements. The tribunal held that there was more to working in a menswear store than measuring a man for a pair of trousers. Should a customer object to being attended to by a woman in this way, there was nothing to prevent her seeking help from one of her male colleagues.

  (b) if the holder of the job is likely to do her work in circumstances where men might reasonably object to the presence of a woman because they are in a state of undress or are using sanitary facilities (and *vice versa*);

  (c) if, in the case of a person who intends to undergo, is undergoing or has undergone gender reassignment, the job in question would involve the holder being liable to be called upon to perform intimate physical searches (pursuant to statutory powers);

  (d) if, because of the nature or location of the employer's establishment, it would be impracticable for the holder of the job to live other than in dormitories (or similar) occupied, or normally occupied, by persons of the opposite sex – if the accommodation in question is not equipped with separate sleeping arrangements, washrooms or toilets – but only for so long as it remains unreasonable to expect the employer to provide separate facilities for women (or men);

  (e) if, in a situation similar to that described in (d) above, other employees sharing such accommodation and facilities might reasonably object (in the interests of preserving decency and privacy) to the presence of a person who intends to undergo, or is undergoing, gender reassignment – always provided that it would be unreasonable to expect the employer either to equip those premises with suitable accommodation or to make alternative arrangements;

(f) if, on health and safety grounds, the job cannot lawfully be offered to a woman of whatever age, or to a woman of reproductive capacity, or to one who is either pregnant or breastfeeding or has recently given birth (eg, in work involving exposure to ionising radiations or to lead or lead compounds)(but see the *Note* on page 507);

(g) if the job needs to be filled by a man because it is likely to involve work   outside the United Kingdom in countries (eg, certain Middle Eastern countries) whose laws and customs are such that the work could not (or could not effectively) be carried out by a woman;

(h) if the job is one of two intended to be filled by a married couple (eg, caretaker and cook) sharing accommodation provided by the employer on the employer's premises.

There are similar exceptions in relation to jobs in hospitals, prisons, and other establishments for persons requiring special care, supervision or attention; childcare jobs; and jobs that provide individuals with personal services promoting their welfare or education.

• Being a man or a woman is also a genuine occupational qualification if the job in question calls for a man (or a woman) for reasons of physiology (eg, fashion model, club hostess) or authenticity (eg, in dramatic performances and other forms of entertainment). However, a job applicant's supposed physical strength or stamina may *not* be used as a basis for refusing to entertain applications from women (for instance, for work as a builder's labourer). If there is to be a test of strength or stamina, all job applicants (male as well as female) should be invited to submit to that same test.

Case Law: Cases decided in this area include that of *Roadburg v Lothian Regional Council* [1976] IRLR 283 when it was held that an existing imbalance of the sexes in a team of voluntary services officers was not a reason sufficient to justify a refusal to recruit a woman to that team; and that of *Batisha v Say & Longleat Enterprises* [1976] 19 man. Law 23, when it was held that unlawful discrimination occurred when a woman was denied employment as a cave guide.

If an employer instructs one of his subordinates (eg, a personnel manager or factory foreman) to commit an unlawful discriminatory act, he (or she) is guilty of an offence and liable to be proceeded against by the Equal Opportunities Commission.

Race Relations Act 1976

- An employer is at liberty to discriminate against job applicants on racial grounds if he (or she) can prove that being of a particular racial, national or ethnic group is a *genuine occupational qualification* for the vacancy in question. Such an exception is permissible:

  (a) if the job requires participation in a dramatic performance or other entertainment in a capacity for which a person of a particular racial group is required for reasons of authenticity;

     Note: In this context, the expression *racial group* means a group of persons defined by reference to colour, race, nationality or ethnic or national origins, and references to a person's racial group refer to any racial group in which he or she falls (section 3(1), 1976 Act).

  (b) if the job involves participation as an artist's or photographic model in the production of a work of art, visual image or sequence of visual images for which a person of a particular racial group is required for reasons of authenticity;

  (c) if the job involves employment in a place (such as a Chinese restaurant) where food or drink is (whether for payment or not) provided to and consumed by members of the public or a section of the public in a particular setting for which, in that job, a person of a particular racial group is required for reasons of authenticity;

  (d) if the intended occupant of the job will be required to provide persons of the same racial group with personal services promoting their welfare, and those services can most effectively be provided by a person of that racial group.

- A job advertisement will be deemed unlawful if it imposes restrictions or requirements that (albeit unintentionally) effectively discriminate against persons on grounds of colour, race, nationality, or ethnic or national origins. An example of this would be an advertisement that requires candidates to possess qualifications gained entirely (or available only) in the United Kingdom. Another would be an advertisement lodged in a newspaper or journal whose circulation is known to be restricted to persons from a particular racial group.

Case Law: In Hussein v Saints Complete House Furnishers [1979] IRLR 337, a small firm of household furnishers in Liverpool declined to recruit job applicants from postal districts 7 and 8 because persons previously recruited from those areas tended to bring with them, or attract, unemployed friends of their own age who were in the habit of loitering about the front of the shop. The Tribunal found that, although the employer had not intended to discriminate against the complainant, his exclusion of candidates from postal districts 7 and 8 effectively denied job opportunities to some 50 per cent of the black community in Merseyside. The firm's recruitment policy was indirectly discriminatory and, therefore, unlawful.

Enforcement

- Job advertisements that are perceived to be discriminatory on grounds of sex, race or disability will be dealt with by the Equal Opportunities Commission (EOC), or the Commission for Racial Equality (CRE) or the Disability Rights Commission (DRC). Any one of those bodies may serve notice on the offending employer or newspaper proprietor that he (or she) will be issued with a *Non-Discrimination Notice* unless able to satisfy the Commission (within the period specified in the notice) that no discrimination was intended or occurred.

- A Non-Discrimination Notice enjoins the employer who inserted (and/or newspaper proprietor who published) the offending advertisement to end his (or her) unlawful discriminatory practices and to furnish evidence of compliance. The employer who repeats the offence within a period of five years is likely to be taken to court and served with an injunction that is enforceable by committal for contempt.

- Although a member of the public cannot bring legal proceedings against an employer (or newspaper proprietor) in respect of a discriminatory advertisement, a job applicant denied an interview or an offer of employment on grounds of sex, race or disability (perhaps as a consequence of that same job advertisement) may present a complaint of unlawful discrimination to an employment tribunal – as to which, see **Racial discrimination** and **Sex discrimination** elsewhere in this handbook. See also **Access to employment** and **Disabled persons**.

| **ADVISORY, CONCILIATION & ARBITRATION SERVICE** |

Key points

- The Advisory, Conciliation & Arbitration Service (referred to below as 'ACAS' or 'the Service') is an independent statutory body, first established on 1 January 1976 under section 1 of the (since repealed) Employment Protection Act 1975 and continued by section 247 of the Trade Union & Labour Relations (Consolidation) Act 1992.

    Note: ACAS performs its functions (and those of its officers and servants) on behalf of the Crown, 'but not so as to make it subject to directions of any kind from any Minister of the Crown as to the manner in which it is to exercise its functions under any enactment' (*ibid.* section 247(3)).

Constitution of ACAS

- ACAS is directed by a Council which consists of a Chairman and nine ordinary members appointed by the Secretary of State for Employment. Following consultations with the bodies concerned, three of the ordinary members are appointed from organisations representing employers and three from organisations representing workers. If he thinks fit, the Secretary of State may appoint a further two ordinary members (one representing employers; the other, workers). He may also appoint up to three Deputy Chairmen, either from the existing ordinary members or in addition to those members. The Council's Chairman, Deputy Chairmen and ordinary members may be either full-time or part-time and hold office for a maximum of five years. However, previous membership does not affect a person's eligibility for reappointment. With the consent of the Secretary of State as to their numbers, manner of appointment and terms and conditions of service, the Council may appoint a Secretary and such other officers and staff as it may determine (*ibid.* section 251).

Conciliation officers

- 'ACAS shall designate some of its officers to perform the functions of conciliation officers under any enactment (whenever passed) relating to matters that are or could be the subject of proceedings before an employment tribunal' and 'references in any such enactment to a conciliation officer are to an officer designated under this section' (*ibid.* section 211). For further details, please turn to the section in this handbook titled **Conciliation officers**.

Issue of codes of practice

- ACAS may issue codes of practice containing such practical guidance as it thinks fit for the purpose of promoting the improvement of industrial relations (*ibid.* section 199). For further particulars, please turn to the section titled **Codes of practice**.

Functions of ACAS

- Under section 209 of the 1992 Act (as amended by the Employment Rights (Dispute Resolution) Act 1998), the general duty of ACAS is to promote the improvement of industrial relations. No longer does it have a particular duty to concentrate on the settlement of trade disputes. Its role in dispute prevention is likely to assume equal, if not greater, importance.

Advice

- ACAS may, either of its own initiative or at the request of employers, employers' associations, workers and trade unions, give such advice as it thinks appropriate on matters concerned with or affecting (or likely to affect) industrial relations. The Service may also publish general advice on industrial relations matters (*ibid.* section 213).

Conciliation

- ACAS may, either at the request of one or other of the parties (and with the consent of both) or of its own initiative, help (or offer to help) settle a trade dispute by conciliation – either by one of its own officers or by some other person nominated by the Service. Before intervening, ACAS will first encourage the parties to use their own agreed procedures (if any) for negotiation or the settlement of disputes (*ibid.* section 210). See also **Trade disputes and arbitration** elsewhere in this handbook.

Arbitration

- If a trade dispute is unlikely to be settled by conciliation *and* existing disputes procedures have been used and failed, ACAS may, at the request of one or more of the parties to the dispute (but only with the consent of *all* of the parties), refer that dispute to arbitration – either by the Central Arbitration Committee (CAC) or by one or more arbitrators appointed by the Service for that purpose. If two or more arbitrators (or arbiters) are appointed, ACAS will appoint one of them to act as chairman. If a trade dispute is settled by arbitration, ACAS may (with the consent of all the parties) publish details of the award (*ibid.* section 212). See also the sections titled **Central Arbitration Committee** and **Trade disputes and arbitration** elsewhere in this handbook.

ACAS arbitration scheme

- Under the so-called 'ACAS Arbitration Scheme', independent arbitrators (appointed by ACAS) are empowered to adjudicate on disputes between employers and employees about the fairness or otherwise of an employee's dismissal. The aim of the Scheme is to promote the settlement of unfair dismissal disputes in a confidential, informal, relatively fast and cost-efficient way. Unlike the handling of such complaints before the employment tribunals, the new arbitration scheme avoids the use of formal pleadings, witnesses and documentary procedures. The usual rules of evidence do not apply nor is strict law or legal precedent a determining factor. Instead, in reaching their decisions, the arbitrators will take into account the general principles of fairness and good conduct laid down in ACAS Code of Practice 1 on *Disciplinary & Grievance Procedures* and in related ACAS publications, notably its *Discipline at Work* Handbook. Arbitral decisions (or awards) will be final, with very limited opportunities for the parties to appeal or otherwise challenge the outcome.

Note: Information and guidance on the ACAS Arbitration Scheme can be obtained, free of charge, from ACAS Reader Limited on **0870 242 9090** or may be accessed and downloaded from website www.acas.org.uk/arbitration.htm.

Inquiry

- Where appropriate, ACAS may inquire into any question relating to industrial relations generally or to industrial relations in any particular industry, undertaking or part of an undertaking. The Service may publish a report of its findings following any such inquiry if it considers that publication is desirable for the improvement of industrial relations, either generally or in relation to the specific question inquired into. But it will not publish its report without first sending a draft to the parties concerned and taking account of their views.

Fees

- Under section 251A of the 1992 Act, ACAS may charge a fee for its services – but only in a case where it considers it appropriate to do so. Furthermore, it may charge a fee whether or not an employer or trade union (or individual) has asked for or invited its services. For some services, the Secretary of State may direct ACAS to charge a fee – either at the full economic cost of the service in question or at a specified proportion or percentage of that cost. However, ACAS may not charge a fee for its services unless it first forewarns a 'client' employer, trade union or individual that a fee will (or may) be levied. If the 'client' is not forewarned, there is no liability to pay.

Future developments

- In the *Explanatory Notes* to the Employment Act 2002, the Government acknowledges that an ACAS-brokered settlement of a dispute between an employer and one or more of his employees is often reached at the very last moment before the case comes before an employment tribunal. Delayed settlements, says the *Notes*, are costly in terms of the time, money and other resources, not only to the parties in dispute but also to ACAS and the Employment Tribunals Service. Regulations to be made under section 24 of the 2002 Act (on a date yet to be specified) will amend section 7 of the Employment Tribunals Act 1996 to allow for the postponement of the fixing of a time and place for a hearing in order for the proceedings to be settled through conciliation. The regulations will set out the length of the conciliation period and will provide for its extension where the conciliator considers that settlement within a short additional timeframe is very likely. Section 24 of the 2002 Act further provides that ACAS's duty to conciliate cases will revert to a power to conciliate after the compulsory conciliation period has ended. The effect will be that, once the conciliation period is over, the conciliation officer will be able to judge whether to continue to conciliate the case or to pass it back to the Employmrent Tribunals Service so that a time and place can be fixed for a hearing.

See also **Conciliation officers** and **Employment tribunals and procedure** elsewhere in this handbook.

AGE OF MAJORITY

Key points

- The 'age of majority' was reduced from 21 to 18 years by the Family Law Reform Act 1969. Any person under the age of 18 is treated in law as a 'minor'.

- An 18-year-old can be bound by the terms of a contract of employment, whether or not that contract acts to his or her benefit. However, a person under the age of 18 (classified as a 'minor') can only be so bound if the contract (taken as a whole) is considered to be to his or her benefit.

- For further particulars, please refer to the sections titled **Children, employment of** and **Women and young persons, employment of** elsewhere in this handbook. See also **Birth certificates**.

ATTACHMENT OF EARNINGS

Key points

- From time to time, the courts will serve so-called 'attachment of earnings' orders on employers requiring them to make periodical deductions from an employee's weekly or monthly pay cheque and to forward the money to the collecting officer of the court (section 6(1), Attachment of Earnings Act 1971). Similar legislation applies in Scotland and Northern Ireland.

- An attachment of earnings order may be made:

    (a) by the High Court, to secure payments under a High Court maintenance order;

    (b) by a county court, to secure payments under a High Court or a county court maintenance order or the payment of a judgement debt; or payments under an administration order;

    (c) by a magistrates' court, to secure payments under a magistrates' court maintenance order or the payment of any sum adjudged to be paid by a conviction or the payment of any sum required to be paid by a legal aid contribution order (*ibid.* section 1).

    Note, however, that an attachment of earnings order cannot be made against payments of statutory maternity pay (SMP).

Contents of order

- Unless made to secure maintenance payments, an attachment of earnings order will specify the whole amount payable under the relevant adjudication (or so much of that amount as remains unpaid), including any relevant costs.

- An attachment of earnings order will also specify the *normal deduction rate*, that is to say, the rate (expressed as a sum of money per week, month or other period) at which the court thinks it reasonable for the employee's earnings to be applied to meeting his (or her) liability under the relevant adjudication (ie, the conviction, judgement, order or other adjudication from which the employee's liability arises).

- An order will also specify a *protected earnings rate*, ie, the rate below which, having regard to the employee's resources and needs, the court thinks it reasonable that the earnings actually paid to him should not be reduced (*ibid.* section 6(5)). Thus, if the employee in question is a piece-worker, whose earnings vary from week to week, the court may order that his take-home pay should not be less than a specified amount. If, for example, the prescribed attachment is £25 a week, and the employee earns an average £130 per week (net of income tax and national insurance contributions, etc), the court may decide that his take-home pay should never be less than £100 a week (his *protected earnings rate*). If, in any week, his net earnings are less than £125, the employer may only deduct the difference between his net earnings and that protected earnings rate. The shortfall would be carried forward and recovered in ensuing weeks until the full amount is paid to the collecting officer of the court.

Compliance by employer

- If served with an attachment of earnings order, the employer must comply with its terms within seven days (*ibid.* section 7(1)).

- If the employee in question is no longer employed by the employer, or subsequently resigns or is dismissed, the employer must notify the court of that fact within 10 days of the date on which the order was served or (as appropriate) within 10 days of the date on which the employee left his employ (*ibid.* section 7(2)).

Example

- John Smith is a salesman with average earnings, after deduction of tax and national insurance contributions, of £400 a week. A county court has served an attachment of earnings order on John's employer directing him to deduct £65 per week from John's pay packet in respect of payments under a maintenance order. The court has decided on a protected earnings limit of £325, which means that his take-home pay must not be less than that amount. As John's income varies from week to week, there will be occasions when his employer must deduct less than £65 so as not to reduce his take-home pay below £325. However, any deficit (or arrears) must be carried forward from week to week. The picture over the first few weeks may be demonstrated by the following table:

Week No.	Net or 'attachable' earnings	Deductions under the order	Take-home pay	Arrears carried forward
1	£415	£65	£350	Nil
2	£410	£65	£340	Nil
3	£387	£62	£325	£3
4	£375	£50	£325	£18
5	£380	£55	£325	£28
6	£440	£93	£347	Nil

Every time the employer deducts money from John's wages, in compliance with an attachment of earnings order, he may also deduct £1.00 towards his own clerical and administrative costs which additional deduction (if made) must be listed on the itemised pay statement given to John with his weekly payslip.

Employer's administrative costs

- Each time an employer deducts money from an employee's wages or salary, in compliance with the terms of an attachment order, he is entitled to deducted a further £1.00 towards his clerical and administrative costs (*ibid.* section 7(4)(a)). This figure is reviewed regularly.

Notification to employee

- Likewise, on each occasion that an employer deducts money from an employee's earnings, in compliance with the terms of an attachment of earnings order, he must provide the employee with a written statement of the total amount of the deduction (*ibid.* section 7(4)).

Power of court to obtain information

- Before making an attachment of earnings order, a court may order the relevant employer to provide a signed statement giving specified particulars of the relevant employee's earnings and anticipated earnings (*ibid.* section 14).

Offences

- If an employer fails to comply with an attachment of earnings order, or fails to notify the court that the employee in question is no longer in his employ or has left his employ, or refuses or neglects to provide a statement of the employee's earnings and projected earnings, he is guilty of an offence and liable to a fine of up to £200. Furthermore, if he makes any statement to the court that he knows to be false in a material particular, he may be sent to prison for up to 14 days (*ibid.* section 23).

B

BAD WORKMANSHIP, PENALTIES FOR

Key points

- It is unusual nowadays for an employer to dock an employee's wages or salary because of accidental damage to property or goods. In any event, an employer's right to do so is strictly regulated by Part II (*Protection of Wages*) of the Employment Rights Act 1996. Save for deductions in respect of income tax (PAYE) and National Insurance contributions (and other exceptions), an employer does not have the legal right to deduct money from an employee's wages or salary (or demand any payment) without that employee's express consent. If an employer wishes to deduct monies (or demand a payment from an employee) for bad workmanship:

  - his (or her) right to do so and the reason for making that deduction must be clearly laid down in the employee's contract of employment (a copy of which must have previously been supplied to the employee *before* the incident that prompted the making of that deduction);

  - alternatively, the employee must have previously given his (or her) consent in writing to the making of such a deduction for the purposes for which it is to be made – which consent may not be given or have effect retrospectively.

Even if an employee has given his (or her) written consent to the making of a deduction from his pay (or to accepting a demand for payment) in respect of damaged goods, the amount deducted (or payment demanded) should reflect the actual loss or damage suffered. However, there is nothing to prevent an employer disciplining or, indeed, dismissing an employee who wilfully or persistently causes damage to the employer's property or goods. Any monies outstanding on termination of employment in respect of damaged goods may be recovered in full from the wages or salary (and other contractual payments, including accrued holiday pay) due to the employee at that time.

- If an employer does not comply with these requirements, an employee has three months in which to complain to an employment tribunal. If the complaint is upheld, the employer will be ordered to reimburse the full disputed amount. Bearing in mind that an employee has no need to resign in order to assert his (or her) statutory rights before an employment tribunal, the law warns that an employer will be liable to pay heavy compensation if an employee is dismissed or selected for redundancy for questioning or challenging any alleged infringement of his rights under the 1996 Act or for pursuing the matter before an employment tribunal (*ibid*. section 104). This rule applies whether or not the employee is entitled to the disputed right and regardless of the outcome of the proceedings. See also **Deductions from pay** and **Dismissal for asserting a statutory right** elsewhere in this handbook.

BANK AND PUBLIC HOLIDAYS

Key points

- The following days are bank and public holidays in England and Wales:

  New Year's Day (1 January)
  Good Friday
  Easter Monday
  the first Monday in May
  the last Monday in May
  the last Monday in August
  Christmas Day (25 December)
  Boxing Day (26 December)

  27 December (if either of Christmas Day or Boxing Day falls on a Sunday) or any days substituted for those days (or added to those days) by government or Crown proclamation (eg, New Year's Eve, 1999).

- In Scotland, bank and public holidays fall on:

  New Year's Day (1 January) (or 2 January, if New Year's Day falls on a Sunday)
  2 January (or 3 January, if 2 January falls on a Sunday)
  Good Friday
  Easter Monday
  the first Monday in May

the last Monday in May
the first Monday in August
Christmas Day (or 26 December, if Christmas Day falls on a Sunday)
26 December (if it is not a Sunday).

- And in Northern Ireland:

New Year's Day (1 January)
St Patrick's Day (17 March) (or 18 March, if 17 March is a Sunday)
Good Friday
Easter Monday
the first Monday in May
the last Monday in May
12 July
the last Monday in August
Christmas Day (25 December)
Boxing Day (26 December)
27 December (if either of Christmas Day or Boxing Day falls on a Sunday).

- Strictly speaking, Christmas Day and Good Friday are common law *public* holidays in England, Wales and Northern Ireland; whereas the remainder are *bank* holidays as defined by the Banking & Financial Dealings Act 1971. For our purposes, the distinction is somewhat academic. Bank and public holidays are routinely referred to, collectively, as public holidays.

Rights of employees

- Although employees have no statutory right to public holidays (paid or otherwise), it has long since been customary for employees to be given paid time off work on those days (or on days substituted for those days). If employees are required (or volunteer) to work normally on a public holiday, they will ordinarily expect to be paid at premium rates (eg, time-and-a-half or double time) for such work and/or to be granted equivalent paid time off work in lieu (to be taken within a specified period after the day in question). However, it should again be emphasised that premium payments for work on a bank or public holiday is not a statutory requirement.

Contracts of employment and collective agreements

- Much will depend on what is written into the individual contract of employment or in the terms of a (local or industry-wide) collective agreement. To ensure that employees are made aware of their rights (if any) in relation to holidays (including bank and public holidays), section 1 of the Employment Rights Act 1996 requires employers to give each employee a written statement containing specified particulars of the terms and conditions of his (or her) employment, including particulars of his or her 'entitlement to holidays, *including* public holidays, and holiday pay (the particulars given being sufficient to enable the employee's entitlement, including any entitlement to accrued holiday pay on the termination of employment, to be precisely calculated)'.

Details to be given in the 'principal statement'

- It is as well to point out here that it is no longer lawful for a written statement (or contract of employment) to refer an employee to the provisions of a collective agreement or to a staff handbook (or similar document) for information about his (or her) entitlement (if any) to public holidays and holiday pay. That information must be given in the *principal statement*. If the statement makes no mention of public holidays, an employee may ask an employment tribunal to intervene and to decide what information should have been included in the statement. If the employer responds by dismissing the employee, the dismissal will be held to have been unfair and the employer will be ordered to pay compensation. See also **Dismissal for asserting a statutory right** and **Written particulars of terms of employment** elsewhere in this handbook.

Working Time Regulations 1998

- Given that there is no statutory right to paid bank or public holidays, employers may (subject to any contrary provision in their workers' contracts) offset *paid* bank and public holidays against their obligation under regulation 13 of the Working Time Regulations 1998 to provide four weeks' paid annual holidays to each of those workers. But, if those same workers have long enjoyed an express or implied contractual right to bank and public holidays, in addition to their paid annual holidays, it would be a breach of contract for the employer unilaterally to override that right in order to modify the impact of regulation 13. Furthermore, employing part-time, casual, or seasonal workers on terms and conditions less favourable to them than those enjoyed by comparable full-time employees within the same establishment will undoubtedly fall foul of the Part-time Workers (Prevention of Less Favourable Treatment) Regulations 2000, let alone (in the case of temporary or fixed-term employees) the Fixed-term Employees, etc Regulations 2002. For further information, please turn to the section on **Holidays, annual** elsewhere in this handbook. See also **Part-time workers** and **Fixed-term employees**.

BIRTH CERTIFICATES

Key points

- Nowadays, there are comparatively few restrictions on the working hours and periods of employment of young persons between the ages of 16 and 18. However, there *are* strict limits on the employment of persons under the age of 16. In law, the latter are regarded as children.

- Once a person has reached the age of 18 (ie, the age of majority), he or she is capable of being bound by the terms of a contract of employment. For a person under that age, such a contract cannot be enforced unless, taken as a whole, it acts to that person's benefit. For further particulars, see **Age of majority** elsewhere in this handbook.

- If doubtful about the true age of a job applicant or young person already in his employ, an employer should either insist on the production of a birth certificate (or equivalent document, such as a passport) or obtain a certified copy of the relevant entry in the register provided under the Births and Deaths Registration Act 1953 (or, in Scotland, the Registrations of Births, Deaths & Marriages (Scotland) Acts 1854 to 1938). Employers have the legal right to obtain such a certificate on payment of a small fee. The prescribed *Form of Requisition for Certificate of Birth* will be supplied without charge by any local registrar or superintendent registrar of births, deaths and marriages.

  Legal restrictions on the employment of children and young persons are discussed elsewhere in this handbook under **Children, employment of** and **Women and young persons, employment of**.

C

CANTEENS AND REST ROOMS FOR EMPLOYEES

Key points

- Whether or not employers are legally-bound to provide their workers with dedicated canteens or rests room will depend in large part on the type of activity or process in which an employer is engaged. Regulation 25(5) of the Workplace (Health, Safety & Welfare) Regulations 1992 – that apply to *every* workplace – states that 'suitable and sufficient facilities shall be provided for persons at work to eat meals where meals are regularly eaten in the workplace'.

- By way of explanation, the accompanying Approved Code of Practice points out that 'seats in work areas can be counted as eating facilities provided they are in a sufficiently clean place and there is a suitable surface on which to place food. Eating facilities', it continues, 'should include a facility for preparing or obtaining a hot drink, such as an electric kettle, a vending machine or a canteen'. Furthermore, 'workers who work during hours or at places where hot food cannot be obtained in, or reasonably near to, the workplace should be provided with the means for heating their own food'.

  Note: Copies of the code of practice referred to above (titled: *Workplace Health, Safety and Welfare: Approved Code of Practice and Guidance Notes* (L24) (ISBN 0 11 886333 9) can be purchased from HSE Books (Telephone: 01787 881165; Fax: 01787 313995).

- Although there are circumstances in which employers must provide a separate canteen or mess room where their workers can take their meals (see *Factory workers* below), there is no legislation that requires them to provide a full catering service.

  Note: The expression *workplace* means 'any premises or part of premises which are not domestic premises and are made available to any person as a place of work, and includes any place within the premises to which such person has access while at work and any room, lobby, corridor, staircase, road or other place used as a means of access to and egress from the workplace or where facilities are provided for use in conjunction with the workplace other than a public road' (*ibid.* regulation 2(1)).

All workers

- All workers who take their meals on their employers' premises are entitled to do so in relative comfort and in hygienic surroundings, seated on chairs or benches, with a sufficient number of tables or desk tops on which to place their food. Where a separate canteen, mess room or eating area is provided, it too must be furnished with a sufficient number of tables and chairs (with backrests) and must comply with current food safety and hygiene regulations. Furthermore, the employer must nominate a person (or persons) whose job it is to keep the room or area clean and tidy.

Office workers

- Regulation 25 does not give office workers the right to a separate eating area or canteen. Most office workers have a desk and chair and very little face-to-face contact with the public. Under the 1992 Regulations, a chair counts as a 'suitable eating facility' provided it is in a sufficiently clean place (such as an office) and there is a suitable surface (such as a desk top) on which an employee can place his or her food. Even so, the employer must provide a facility (such as an electric kettle or vending machine) for preparing or obtaining a hot drink. And, if his (or her) employees work at times or in places where hot food cannot be readily obtained, he must also provide a small cooker, hotplate or microwave oven in (or on) which his employees can heat their own food.

Shop assistants

- Shop assistants spend most of their time on their feet. Whether or not they have their main meals on the premises, their employer must set aside a rest room or screened-off area where they can relax or 'put their feet up' during their morning and afternoon tea breaks or when business is slow. The rest room (or area) must be furnished with a sufficient number of chairs (with backrests) and tables, and be equipped with an electric kettle or a hot drinks vending machine. If there is no nearby café, snack bar or pub where they can readily buy hot food, their employer must also provide a hot plate (or a small cooker) on or in which they can heat their own food.

Factory workers

- Workers in factories, workshops, warehouses and the like are entitled to separate eating facilities (away from their work areas) if their food is likely to be contaminated by dust, water, fumes or hazardous substances, or if they work in premises or are engaged in processes where eating, drinking (or smoking) is prohibited by regulations made under (or saved by) the Health & Safety at Work etc Act 1974. Their employer must provide an electric kettle or hot drinks vending machine and, if any employees work at night or in a place where it is difficult or inconvenient to purchase a hot meal, a hot plate, cooker or microwave oven in (or on) which they can heat their own food.

- Eating, drinking, smoking, etc are currently prohibited in workplaces regulated by:

  - the Work in Compressed Air Regulations 1996;
  - the Control of Asbestos at Work Regulations 2002;
  - the Workplace (Health, Safety & Welfare) Regulations 1992;
  - the Control of Lead at Work Regulations 2002;
  - the Control of Substances Hazardous to Health Regulations 2002; and
  - the Ionising Radiations Regulations 1999.

Pregnant employees and nursing mothers

- Nowadays, every workplace must be equipped with suitable rest facilities for use by employees who are pregnant or breastfeeding including a place where they can lie down when the need arises. The facilities should be situated close to (or as near as reasonably possible to) female toilets and washrooms (regulation 25(4), Workplace (Health, Safety & Welfare) Regulations 1992. Common sense will dictate what is suitable (or practicable) for one workplace and what is unsuitable in relation to another. In a large factory, office block, hotel or department store, an employer would be expected to set aside a small well-ventilated room furnished with one or more beds or reclining chairs and equipped with a toilet and washbasin. In a small establishment (where space is at a premium), a curtained-off area with a comfortable reclining chair (and some guarantee of privacy) would probably suffice.

  Note: A free HSE leaflet titled *Occupational health aspects of pregnancy* (MA6, 1989) is available on request from the Health & Safety Executive's 'Freeleaflet" line (Tel: 01787 881165 or Fax: 01787 313995).

Passive smoking

- Regulation 25(3) of the 1992 Regulations (see above) also imposes a duty on employers to take such steps as are necessary to ensure that their employees can retire to a room or area where they can take a rest break, drink or eat their sandwiches (or whatever) in relative comfort –

without experiencing discomfort from tobacco smoke. If there are no separate facilities for smokers and nonsmokers, the rest room must be designated a 'No Smoking' area. Although employers may be prepared to set aside a room or special area for the use of smokers, they are not legally-bound to do so. Indeed, in a small office or shop, where there is no separate rest room, and in which staff are expected or accustomed to taking their meals and rest breaks at their desks (or in a curtained-off area at 'the back of the shop'), the employer will have little choice but to introduce a 'No Smoking' rule throughout his premises.

Note: The issues associated with passive smoking in the workplace are reviewed in a free HSE leaflet titled *Passive smoking at work* (INDG 63), available from HSE Books, PO Box 1999, Sudbury, Suffolk, CO10 6FS; Tel: 01787 881165; or Fax: 01787 313995. In a consultative document titled *Proposals for an Approved Code of Practice on passive smoking at work* (published on 29 October 1999), the Health & Safety Commission propose, *inter alia,* that the risk assessment compulsorily carried out by all employers in accordance with the Management of Health & Safety at Work Regulations 1999 should include an assessment of the risks from passive smoking at work to the health of people who already suffer from asthma or chronic bronchitis. From this assessment, employers should determine what their options are for controlling exposure to environmental smoke, such as: banning smoking in the workplace (either completely or partially); physically segregating non-smokers from tobacco smoke; providing adequate ventilation; or adopting a system of work that reduces the time an employee is exposed to environmental tobacco smoke.

Offences and penalties

- Non-compliance with health and safety legislation is a criminal offence which could lead to prosecution and a fine of up to £20,000. In some circumstances, the offending employer is liable to a fine of an unlimited amount and/or imprisonment for a period of up to two years.

See also **Rest breaks and rest periods** elsewhere in this handbook.

CENTRAL ARBITRATION COMMITTEE

Key points

- The Central Arbitration Committee (or CAC) is the senior standing arbitration tribunal in Great Britain. A successor to both the Industrial Court (set up in 1919) and the Industrial Arbitration Board (1971), the CAC's constitution and independent status are presently described in sections 259 to 265 of the Trade Union & Labour Relations (Consolidation) Act 1992.

- The CAC comprises a Chairman and one or more deputy chairmen appointed by the Secretary of State (after consultation with ACAS and other persons) and several members experienced in industrial relations also appointed by the Secretary of State. Those other members (apart from the Chairman) must include some persons whose experience is as representatives of employers and some whose experience is as representatives of workers. Members will normally hold office for a maximum of five years. Cases brought before the CAC are normally heard by the Chairman (or one of the deputy chairmen) and two members (one from each side of industry) (*ibid.* sections 259 and 260, as amended by section 22 of the Employment Relations Act 1999).

Trade disputes

- Any matter constituting a trade dispute may be referred to the CAC for arbitration, so long as both parties to the dispute agree. However, all requests for voluntary arbitration must first be channelled through ACAS (the Advisory, Conciliation & Arbitration Service). Voluntary arbitration hearings are held in private unless the parties wish otherwise. The CAC's decision is not normally announced at the hearing (which is usually completed in a day) but is relayed in writing to the parties at a later date. See **Trade disputes and arbitration** elsewhere in this handbook.

    Note: Although the parties to a trade dispute are under no legal obligation to honour an award made by the CAC, such awards are invariably accepted.

- Section 183 of the 1992 Act allows that a trade union may complain to the CAC either that an employer has failed to disclose to representatives of the union information that he is required by section 181 to disclose for the purposes of collective bargaining or that he has failed to confirm such information in writing in accordance with that section. The complaint must be in writing and in such form as the CAC may require. If an employer fails to comply with the CAC's decision in such cases, the CAC will make an award on the claim that has effect as part of the contracts of employment of the employees concerned. For further particulars, please turn to the section titled **Disclosure of information**.

Disclosure of information for the purposes of collective bargaining

- A recognised independent trade union may complain to the CAC that an employer has failed to comply with his (or her) duty under section 181 of that Act to disclose information without which the union would be to a material extent impeded in carrying on collective bargaining with that employer (*ibid.* section 183). For further details, please turn to the section titled **Disclosure of information** elsewhere in this hand-book.

Recognition agreements and collective bargaining

- Should an employer have rejected a trade union's request for recogni-tion for collective bargaining purposes, in respect of a group or groups of workers (or if negotiations for a voluntary recognition agreement have broken down), the union in question may apply to the CAC for compulsory recognition. No such request will be valid unless, on the day on which it was made, the employer employed at least 21 workers (including workers employed by any associated employer) or had employed an average of at least 21 workers in the 13 weeks ending with that day (per sections 70A, 70B, 263A and Schedule A1 of the Trade Union & Labour Relations (Consolidation) Act 1992).

- When asked to assist or intervene over an employer's rejection of a trade union's request for recognition, the CAC will not only have to decide the appropriate bargaining unit but must also satisfy itself that 10 per cent of the workers constituting that bargaining unit are members of the union. Furthermore, it must be persuaded that a major-ity of the workers in that bargaining unit would be likely to favour recognition. If the majority of workers in the bargaining unit are members of the union, the CAC will ordinarily issue a declaration of recognition without further ado. But if, notwithstanding majority membership, the CAC is not convinced that there is sufficient support for recognition, it will arrange for a secret ballot to be conducted by a qualified independent person within 20 working days of the latter's appointment. For further particulars, please turn to the section on **trade union recognition** elsewhere in this handbook.

- If a majority of the workers voting in the secret ballot (and at least 40 per cent of the workers constituting the bargaining unit) vote in favour of recognition, the CAC will issue a declaration to the effect that the union is recognised as entitled to conduct collective bargaining with the employer on behalf of the bargaining unit.

- The CAC may again be called upon to intervene if, within 30 working days after its declaration of recognition, the parties have been unable to agree a method by which they will conduct collective bargaining. If, within the next 20 working days, and in spite of the CAC's further intervention, there is still no procedural agreement, it will be for the CAC to determine the method by which the parties are to conduct their collective bargaining. The CAC's method will have effect as if it were contained in a legally enforceable contract made between the employer and the relevant trade union. The same applies even if the parties subsequently agree in writing to vary or replace the method specified by the CAC. See **Trade union recognition** elsewhere in this handbook.

Derecognition

- Schedule A1 to the 1992 Act also lays down procedures for derecognition and for the intervention of the CAC if the original bargaining unit ceases to exist or is no longer an appropriate bargaining unit.

European Works Councils

- Under the Transnational Information & Consultation of Employees Regulations 2000, which came into force on 15 December 1999, the central management of a multi-national company may apply to the CAC for a declaration as to the validity of a request by 100 or more of the company's employees (or by representatives of those employees) for the initiation of negotiations for the establishment of a European Works Council (EWC) (or an information and consultation procedure). Disputes about other specified matters (mainly procedural) arising prior to the establishment of an EWC may also be referred to the CAC. A failure to comply with a CAC declaration is punishable as if it were a contempt of court. For further particulars, please turn to the section titled **European Works Councils** elsewhere in this handbook.

CAC proceedings

Trade disputes

- Before a CAC hearing takes place, the parties concerned will be asked to exchange evidence in the form of written statements. In disclosure of information cases (that are not routed through ACAS), the Chairman (or one of the deputy chairmen) will normally arrange an informal, joint meeting of the parties to clarify the issues and to give the parties an opportunity to resolve their difficulties (either themselves or with the help of ACAS) before a full hearing is arranged.

Recognition disputes

- For the purpose of discharging its functions under Schedule A1 of the Trade Union & Labour Relations (Consolidation) Act 1992 ('Collective Bargaining: Recognition'), the chairman of the CAC will establish a three-person panel consisting of the chairman himself or herself (or a deputy chairman), a member of the Committee whose experience is as a representative of employers, and a member of the Committee whose experience is as a representative of workers. The panel may, at the discretion of its chairman, sit in private. If there is no unanimous decision, the question before the panel will be decided according to the majority opinion. If the majority of the panel do not have the same opinion, it will be up to the panel's chairman to decide the question (acting with the full powers of an umpire or, in Scotland, an oversman) (*ibid.* section 263A).

Guidance notes

- Guidance on the procedure at CAC hearings and on the preparation of written statements is given in a booklet titled *Notes for Guidance*, available from the following address:

The Secretary
Central Arbitration Committee
Brandon House
180 Borough High Street
London
SE1 1LW
Telephone: 020 7210 3737/3738

The booklet referred to above will undoubtedly be revised in light of the expansion of the CAC's functions under the Employment Relations Act 1999.

Further information about the CAC's activities is to be found in the Committee's Annual Reports, copies of which will also be supplied on request.

CHILDREN, EMPLOYMENT OF

Key points

- A child is a person who is not over 'compulsory school age'. In England and Wales a child who turns 16 during a school year cannot lawfully leave school until the last Friday in June. A child who turns 16 after that last Friday in June, but *before* the beginning of the next school year, may likewise lawfully leave school on that last Friday in June. In Scotland, a child who turns 16 during the period from 1 March to 30 September, inclusive, may leave school on 31 May of that same year. Children whose 16th birthdays occur outside that period must remain at school until the first day of the Christmas holidays.

- These provisions are currently to be found in section 8 of the Education Act 1996, supported by the Education (School Leaving Date) Order 1997, and (for Scotland) in section 31 of the Education (Scotland) Act 1980.

- Given the many restrictions on the employment of school-age children, employers (or would-be employers) who have doubts about the true age of young-ish employees and job applicants would be wise to contact their local education authorities for further particulars. Alternatively, they should insist on the production of a birth certificate or (as is their right and on payment of a small fee) apply to the registrar or superintendent registrar of births, deaths and marriages for a certi-fied copy of that birth certificate; as to which, see **Birth certificates** else-where in this handbook.

Legal restrictions on the employment of children

- Statues and Regulations prohibiting or restricting the employment of children in prescribed circumstances include:

  (a) Employment of Women, Young Persons & Children Act 1920 (as amended);

  (b) Children & Young Persons Act 1933 (as amended);

  (c) Children & Young Persons (Scotland) Act 1937 (as amended);

  (d) Children & Young Persons Act 1963 (as amended);

  (e) Children (Performances) Regulations 1968;

  (f) Employment of Children Act 1973;

  (g) Education (Work Experience) Act 1973 (as amended); and

  (h) The Children (Protection at Work) Regulations 1998, implementing EC Council Directive 94/33/EC on the protection of young people at work.

  Prohibitions on the employment of young persons (which expression includes children) in certain hazardous occupations are discussed else-where in this handbook in the section titled **Women & young persons, employment of**.

Children & Young Persons Acts 1933 & 1937

- The Children & Young Persons Acts 1933 & 1937 (as amended by the Children (Protection at Work) Regulations 1997 *(qv)* state that no child shall be employed:

  1. so long as he (or she) is under the age of fourteen years; or

  2. to do any work other than light work (see below); or

  3. before the close of school hours on any day on which he (or she) is required to attend school; or

  4. before seven o'clock in the morning or after seven o'clock in the evening on any day; or

  5. for more than two hours on any day on which he (or she) is required to attend school; or

  6. for more than two hours on any Sunday; or

  7. for more than eight hours or, if he (or she) is under the age of 15, for more than five hours on any day (other than a Sunday) on which he is not required to attend school; or

  8. for more than 35 hours or, if under the age of 15, for more than 25 hours in any week in which he (or she) is not required to attend school; or

  9. for more than four hours in any day without a rest break of one hour; or

  10. at any time in a year unless, at that time, he (or she) has had, or could still have, during school holidays, at least two consecutive weeks without employment.

  The expression 'light work' means work of a kind that is unlikely to affect the safety, health or development of a school age child or to interfere with the child's education or regular and punctual attendance at school.

- Within seven days of employing a school age child, employers must apply to the local education authority (on a form supplied by the authority) for an Employment Certificate. The application form will seek a brief explanation of the type of employment in question and will ask for information about daily working hours, intervals for meals and rest, and so on. A copy of the Certificate approving the employment in question will be sent, as a matter of routine, to the child's Head Teacher. The consent of the child's parents or guardian will also be required (see also *Information to parents* below). Before applying for an Employment Certificate, employers should make it their business to obtain a copy of the local authority's byelaws on the employment of children (although these will often be provided automatically when the application form is sent or delivered to the employer).

- Local authority byelaws may distinguish between children of different ages and sexes and between different localities, trades, occupations, and circumstances. They may prohibit absolutely the employment of children in specified occupations, and may (notwithstanding the general prohibition on the employment of children under the age of 14) contain provisions authorising the employment by the parents or guardians of children under 14 in light agricultural or horticultural work. Such byelaws may also authorise the employment of children aged 13 years in certain categories of light work and may allow children under 14 to work for up to an hour before the start of school on any day in which they are required to attend school.

  Note: Under the Employment of Children Act 1973, the power of local authorities (or, in Scotland, education authorities) to make byelaws regulating the employment of children is replaced by a power of the Secretary of State for Employment to make cognate regulations. To date, the Secretary of State has not exercised that power.

Other prohibited occupations

- Many local authorities prohibit the employment of children in the following occupations:
  - in the kitchen of any hotel, cook shop, fried fish shop, restaurant, snack bar or cafeteria;
  - as a marker or attendant in any billiards or pools saloon, licensed gaming house or registered club;
  - in, or in connection with, the sale of alcohol, except where alcohol is sold exclusively in sealed containers;
  - in collecting or sorting rags, scrap metal or refuse;
  - as a fairground attendant or assistant;
  - in any slaughterhouse;
  - in, or in connection with, any racecourse or race-track, or other place where any like sport is carried on;
  - in any heavy agricultural work;
  - in, or in connection with, the sale of paraffin, turpentine, white spirit, methylated spirit or petroleum spirit;

- touting or selling from door to door; or

- as a window cleaner.

As was indicated earlier, copies of local authority byelaws (including applications for a permit to employ a child) are available on request from the relevant local authority for the district in which the would-be employer conducts his or her business.

Industrial undertakings

- Section 1(1) of the Employment of Women, Young Persons & Children Act 1920 prohibits the employment of any child in an 'industrial undertaking', which includes particularly:

  - mines and quarries;

  - industries in which articles are manufactured, altered, cleaned, repaired, ornamented, finished, adapted for sale, broken up or demolished, or in which materials are transformed;

  - construction, reconstruction, maintenance, repair, alteration or demolition of any building, railway, harbour, dock, pier, canal, inland waterway, road, tunnel, bridge, viaduct, sewer, drain, well, gaswork, waterwork or other work of construction, including the preparation for or laying the foundations of any such work or structure;

  - transport of passengers or goods by road, rail or inland waterway, including the handling of goods at docks, quays, wharves and warehouses, but excluding transport by hand.

The 1920 Act cautions that the relevant local authority (in Scotland, the education authority) must be consulted if the employer is in any doubt about the lines or divisions between industry, commerce and agriculture.

Information to parents

- Before employing a child, a would-be employer must not only obtain the consent of one or other of the child's parents or guardians, but must also provide that parent or guardian with relevant and comprehensible information about any health and safety risks associated with the job in question. That information must include particulars about the preventive and protective measures the employer proposes to adopt (or has already put in place) to eliminate or minimise those risks (regulation 10(2), Management of Health & Safety at Work Regulations 1999).

Work experience

- Under the Education (Work Experience) Act 1973, the restrictions otherwise imposed on the employment of school age children (in relation to working hours and periods of employment) do not apply during their last academic year at school (the GCSE year) if the employment in question is part of a local authority-approved work experience programme. The 1973 Act does not, however, permit the employment of such children in work otherwise prohibited by statute or local authority byelaws.

Public performances

- Under the Children (Performances) Regulations 1968, a school age child may take part in a public performance (stage work, television broadcasts, etc) in prescribed circumstances, subject to the issue of a licence by the relevant local authority or a Justice of the Peace. Would-be employers or agents in such circumstances should enquire of the local authority for the area in which the child attends school.

Offences and penalties

- If a child is employed in contravention of any of the statutes or byelaws discussed above, the employer (or, as appropriate, the parent or guardian) will be guilty of an offence and liable, on summary conviction, to a fine of up to £200, rising to £500 if convicted on a second or subsequent occasion. The penalty for an offence under health and safety legislation restricting or prohibiting the employment of children in certain occupations is a fine of up to £2,000 or a fine of an unlimited amount if a conviction is obtained on indictment. If the offence constitutes a failure on the part of an employer to discharge a duty to which he is subject under sections 2 to 6 of the Health & Safety at Work, etc Act 1974, the fine on summary conviction could be as much as £20,000.

  See also **Women & young persons, employment of** elsewhere in this handbook.

CLOSED SHOP

Key points

Meaning of 'closed shop'

- In simple terms, a closed shop (or union membership agreement) is an understanding or agreement between an employer and one or more trade unions whereby the employer agrees not to employ (or to continue to employ) any person who is not a member of one or other of the trade unions party to that agreement.

Protection of job applicants and existing employees

- Nowadays, the closed shop is a legal irrelevancy. It can no longer be used as an excuse for denying a person a job or for dismissing (or disciplining) a person who refuses to be or remain a member of a trade union (even if the union in question is recognised by the employer as having bargaining rights in respect of a particular class or group of employees). Furthermore, an employer cannot lawfully demand a payment from a non-union employee (or presume to make a deduction from that employee's wages or salary) as an alternative to the payment of trade union dues. In short, an individual has the absolute right to decide whether or not he or she wishes to join (or remain a member of) a trade union. Any employer who undermines that right (or bows to trade union pressure to dismiss or victimise an employee who refuses to 'fall into line'), will be liable to pay very heavy compensation indeed. For further particulars, please turn to the sections titled **Dismissal** and **Dismissal on grounds of trade union membership** elsewhere in this handbook.

- It is also unlawful for an employer to refuse to interview or employ a job applicant who is not a member of a trade union (or of a particular trade union) or who has made it clear that he (or she) has no intention of joining a particular trade union or any trade union. A job applicant may complain to an employment tribunal if he (or she) suspects that he has been denied a job (or a job interview) for one or other of those reasons. The complaint must be presented within three months of the alleged unlawful act. If the complaint is upheld, the tribunal will order the employer to pay up to £53,500 by way of compensation (section 137 and 140, Trade Union & Labour Relations (Consolidation) Act 1992).

- A person will be taken to have been refused employment because of his (or her) non-membership of a trade union (or because of his refusal to join a trade union) if an employer offers him a job on terms that no reasonable employer who wished to fill the post would offer.

  See also **Access to employment** and **Victimisation** elsewhere in this handbook.

CODES OF PRACTICE

Key points

- An 'approved' code of practice is a document (approved, in most instances, by Parliament) that contains practical guidance on the law. In the context of employment law, a code of practice interprets the duties and responsibilities of employers and the rights of employees under this or that statute and/or its associated regulations and orders.

Legal status of a code of practice

- A failure on the part of any person (employer, trade union official, or employee) to observe any provision of an approved Code of Practice does not of itself render him (or her) liable to proceedings before a court or tribunal. But in such proceedings, that failure is admissible in evidence and, if any provision of the code appears to the court or tribunal to be relevant to any question arising in the proceedings, it shall be taken into account in deciding that question.

- In other words, the codes of practice referred to in this section have much the same status as has the Highway Code in respect of breaches of road traffic legislation. A motorist will not be prosecuted for a breach of the Highway Code. But, if he is prosecuted for an alleged offence under the Road Traffic Acts, his failure to observe any relevant provisions of the Highway Code will be admissible in evidence in proceedings before the magistrates' court.

Who issues codes of practice?

- In the employment arena, codes of practice may be issued by:
  - the Advisory, Conciliation & Arbitration Service (ACAS) – to promote the improvement of industrial relations (per sections 199 to 202, Trade Union & Labour Relations (Consolidation) Act 1992);

–   the Secretary of State for Trade & Industry – 'for the purpose (a) of promoting the improvement of industrial relations, or (b) of promoting what appear to him to be desirable practices in relation to the conduct by trade unions of ballots and elections' (*ibid.* sections 203 to 206);

–   the Disability Rights Commission – on how to avoid discrimination or with a view to promoting the equalisation of opportunities for disabled persons and persons who have a disability, or encouraging good practice regarding the treatment of such persons (per section 53A, Disability Rights Commission Act 1999);

–   the Equal Opportunities Commission (EOC) – (a) for the elimination of discrimination in the field of employment; and/or (b) the promotion of equality of opportunity in that field between men and women (per section 56A, Sex Discrimination Act 1975);

–   the Commission for Racial Equality – 'for either or both of the following purposes: (a) the elimination of discrimination in the field of employment; (b) the promotion of equality of opportunity in that field between persons of different racial groups' (per section 47, Race Relations Act 1976); and

–   the Health & Safety Commission (HSC) – 'for the purposes of providing practical guidance with respect to the provisions of sections 2 to 7 of the Health & Safety at Work etc Act 1974 or of health and safety regulations or of any of the existing statutory provisions' (*ibid.* section 16).

A code of practice requires prior consultation with interested parties, the consent of the Secretary of State and approval (in all but one instance) by resolution of both Houses of Parliament.

•   Under the Asylum & Immigration Act 1996 (as amended by section 22 of the Immigration & Asylum Act 1999):

–   the Secretary of State *must* issue a code of practice as to the measures which an employer is to be expected to take, or not to take, in order to avoid unlawful discrimination on grounds of race when establishing (as every employer is duty-bound to do) whether a job applicant 'subject to immigration control' has the legal right either to enter (or remain) in the UK or to take up employment while in the UK.

In preparing a draft of the code, the Home Secretary must consult the Commission for Racial Equality (CRE) or (in Northern Ireland) the

Equality Commission for Northern Ireland, and such organisations and bodies as he (or she) considers appropriate. The draft will then be laid before both Houses of Parliament, after which the Secretary of State may bring the code into operation by an order made by statutory instrument (*ibid.* sections 8 and 8A).

Advisory, Conciliation & Arbitration Service (ACAS)

- When proposing to issue a code of practice (or a revised code), ACAS must first prepare and publish a draft of the code. It must then consider any representations made to it about the draft and may modify the draft accordingly. It must then transmit the draft to the Secretary of State for Employment who, if he approves of it, will lay it before both Houses of Parliament for approval by resolution.

- To date, ACAS has issued three approved codes of practice. These are:

  COP 1: *Disciplinary & Grievance Procedures* (2000)

  COP 2: *Discosure of information to trade unions for collective bargaining purposes* (1998)

  COP 3: *Time off for trade union duties & activities* (1998)

  copies of which are available from: ACAS Reader Limited, PO Box 16, Earl Shilton, Leicester LE9 8ZZ (Telephone: 0870 242 9090).

Department of Trade & Industry

- If the Secretary of State for Trade & Industry proposes to issue a code of practice (or a revised code), he must first consult with ACAS, then publish a draft of the code and, after considering any representations by interested bodies (that may prompt him to modify the draft), lay it before both Houses of Parliament for their approval by resolution. Once approved, the code comes into effect on 'such day as the Secretary of State may by order appoint'.

- To date, three approved codes have been published. These are:

  Code of Practice: Picketing (1992);

  Code of Practice: Industrial action ballots and notice to employers (2000)

  Code of Practice: Access to workers during recognition and derecognition ballots (2000)

These are available from: DTI Publications Order Line, Admail 528, London SW1W 8YT (Telephone: 0870 1502 500) (email: publications@dti.gsi.gov.uk).

For further particulars, please turn to **Picketing, strikes and other industrial action** and **Trade union recognition** elsewhere in this handbook.

Equal Opportunities Commission (EOC), Commission for Racial Equality (CRE) and Disability Rights Commission (DRC)

- When proposing to issue a code of practice, the EOC, the CRE and the DRC must follow a procedure similar to that prescribed for ACAS. However, the Sex Discrimination, Race Relations and Disability Discrimination Acts specifically caution those bodies to first consult with organisations or associations representative of employers or of workers, and with 'such other organisations or bodies as appear to the Commission to be appropriate'. There are currently five codes of practice in force. These are:

  Code of Practice on sex discrimination, equal opportunties policies, procedures and practices in employment (1985)

  Code of Practice on equal pay (1997) (available, together with the code above, from: Marketing & Communications Department, Equal Opportunities Commission, Overseas House, Quay Street, Manchester M3 3HN)

  Code of Practice for the elimination of racial discrimination and the promotion of equal opportunity in employment (available from: Commission for Racial Equality, Elliot House, 10–12 Arlington Street, London SW1E 5EH (Telephone: 020 7828 7022))

  Code of Practice for the elimination of discrimination in the field of employment against disabled persons or persons who have had a disability (1996)

  Code of practice on the duties of trade organisations to their disabled members and applicants (1999)

Health & Safety Commission

- As might have been expected, the Health & Safety Commission has produced a considerable number of codes of practice on health and safety issues. Of immediate relevance are:

Code of Practice: Safety Representatives and Safety Committees (1978)

Code of Practice: Time off for the training of safety representatives (1978)

copies of which are available from HSE Books, PO Box 1999, Sudbury, Suffolk CO10 6FS (Tel: 01787 881165, Fax: 01787 313995, and email: www.hsebooks,gov.uk).

See also the sections titled **Commission for Racial Equality, Disabled persons, Equal Opportunities Commission, Equal pay and conditions, Racial discrimination, Sex discrimination,** and **Time off work: safety representatives.**

COLLECTIVE AGREEMENTS

Key points

- A collective agreement (as defined by section 178 of the Trade Union & Labour Relations (Consolidation) Act 1992) is an agreement or arrangement between one or more employers (or employers' associations) and one or more trade unions dealing with one or other of the following matters:

    - 'terms and conditions of employment, or the physical conditions in which any workers are required to work;

    - engagement or non-engagement, or termination or suspension of employment or the duties of employment, of one or more workers;

    - allocation of work or the duties of employment between workers or groups of workers;

    - matters of discipline;

    - a worker's membership or non-membership of a trade union;

    - facilities for officials of trade unions; and

    - machinery for negotiation or consultation, and other procedures, relating to any of the above matters, including the recognition by employers or employers' associations of the right of a trade union to represent workers in such negotiation or consultation or in the carrying out of such procedures.'

Note: Any term in a collective agreement which purports to discriminate against women (or men) is void and unenforceable (*per* section 6, Sex Discrimination Act 1986, as amended by the Trade Union Reform & Employment Rights Act 1993).

Is a collective agreement legally binding?

- A collective agreement will be conclusively presumed not to be legally enforceable unless it is in writing; and contains a provision that (however expressed) states that the parties intend it to be legally enforceable.

- A collective agreement will be enforceable in a court of law if, but only if, it satisfies both of those conditions. The same applies if there is a provision in a collective agreement that specifies that one or more parts of that agreement (but not the whole agreement) are intended by the parties to be legally enforceable (*ibid.* section 179).

- As a collective agreement often deals with matters such as rates of pay, entitlement to holidays, disciplinary rules and procedures, etc, those provisions will usually be incorporated in the contracts of employment of the employees covered by the agreement and will (if need be) be enforced by the tribunals and courts. Indeed, the written particulars of employment required to be issued to employees when they first start work must specify any collective agreement that directly affects their terms and conditions of employment. If the employer was not himself a party to that agreement, the written statement must identify the persons by whom the agreement was made (section 1(4)(j), Employment Rights Act 1996). For further details, see **Written particulars of terms of employment** elsewhere in this handbook.

'No strike' clauses

- If there are any terms in a collective agreement that purport to prohibit or restrict the right of workers to take part in a strike or other form of industrial action (or have the effect of prohibiting or restricting that right), those terms will not form part of an employee's contract of employment unless the collective agreement itself:

  (a) is in writing;

  (b) contains a provision expressly stating that those terms shall (or may be) incorporated in such a contract;

  (c) is reasonably accessible at his place of work to the worker to whom it applies and is available for him to consult during working hours;

(d) is one where each trade union that is a party to the agreement is an independent trade union; and

provided also that the contract between the worker and the person for whom he works expressly or impliedly incorporates those terms (section 180, Trade Union & Labour Relations (Consolidation) Act 1992).

Note: An independent trade union is a trade union that (a) is not under the domination or control of an employer or group of employers (or of one or more employers' associations) and (b) is not liable to interference by an employer or any such group or association (arising out of the provision of financial support or material support or by any other means whatsoever) tending towards such control; and references to *independence* shall be construed accordingly (*ibid.* section 5).

Dismissal procedures agreement

- A 'dismissal procedures agreement' (as defined in section 235 of the Employment Rights Act 1996) is an agreement (in writing) between an employer and a trade union, the effect (or intended effect) of (or of one or more which is to substitute for the statutory right of an employee to complain of unfair dismissal to an employment tribunal. A dismissal procedures agreement may be a separate agreement or it may form part of a collective agreement. Either way, it will not be legally binding unless specifically 'designated' as such by order of the Secretary of State for Employment. Nor will the Secretary of State make an order designating such an agreement as having effect in substitution for the unfair dismissal provisions of the 1996 Act unless it satisfies all of following conditions prescribed by section 110 of that Act:

  1. Every trade union party to the agreement must be an independent trade union.

  2. The procedures laid down in the agreement for determining the fairness or otherwise of a dismissal (or intended dismissal) must be accessible without discrimination to all employees falling within any description to which the agreement relates.

  3. The remedies provided by the agreement in respect of unfair dismissal must, on the whole, be as beneficial as (but not necessarily identical to) those available to the employment tribunals under Chapter II of Part X of the 1996 Act.

  4. The agreement must include provision either for arbitration in every case or for:

(a) arbitration where (by reason of an equality of votes or for any other reason) a decision under the agreement cannot otherwise be reached; and

(b) a right to submit to arbitration any question of law arising out of such a decision.

5. The provisions of the agreement must be such that it can be determined with reasonable certainty whether a particular employee is one to whom the agreement applies or not *(ibid.* section 110(3)).

But, if the agreement states that it does *not* apply to particular descriptions of dismissals (eg, the right of an employee under section 99 of the 1996 Act not to be dismissed (or selected for redundancy) on grounds of pregnancy or childbirth (or for a connected reason), the agreement will *not* operate in relation to a dismissal of any such description *(ibid.* section 110(2), as substituted by section 12 of the Employment Rights (Dispute Resolution) Act 1998).

- An award made under a designated dismissal procedures agreement may be enforced (in England and Wales) by leave of the county court, in the same manner as a county court judgment to the same effect is enforced. In Scotland, such an award may be recorded for execution in the Books of Council and Session, and will be enforceable accordingly *(ibid.* section 110(6), inserted by section 13(3) of the Employment Rights (Dispute Resolution) Act 1998).

- Section 110(4) of the 1996 Act points out that one or other of the parties to a designated dismissal procedures agreement may apply to the Secretary of State for Employment for an order revoking an order made under section 110(3). The Secretary of State will revoke the order if all parties are agreed or if satisfied that the agreement no longer satisfies *all* of conditions 1 to 5 above.

Collective agreements and TUPE transfers

- If there is a collective agreement in force when a business or undertaking is sold or otherwise disposed of, the organisation that purchases or acquires that business inherits that agreement (and all of the seller's obligations under that agreement) in the same way as it inherits the contracts of employment of the persons employed in that business and covered by the provisions of that agreement (regulation 6, Transfer of Undertakings (Protection of Employment) Regulations 1981).

- Furthermore, if the person selling or transferring his (or her) business recognises an independent trade union as having bargaining rights in respect of some or all of his employees, the new owner must likewise recognise that same trade union in respect of those same employees – although there is nothing to prevent him varying or rescinding that agreement at a later date. However, this rule does not apply *unless* the business (or part of the business sold) maintains an identity distinct from the remainder of the purchaser's business. If the new owner simply absorbs the business, or merges it with his existing business, the recognition agreement no longer applies (*ibid.* regulation 9). See also **Continuous employment** elsewhere in this handbook.

Collective agreements: detriment and dismissal

- Section 17 of the Employment Relations Act 1996 empowers the Secretary of State to make regulations about cases where a worker is either dismissed or subjected to detriment by his (or her) employer for refusing to enter into a contract which includes terms which differ from the terms of a collective agreement which applies to that worker. At the time of writing, section 17 had not as yet been brought into force.

Working Time Regulations 1998

- Regulation 23 of the Working Time Regulations 1998 (as amended) allows that a collective agreement may (in relation to particular workers or groups of workers) modify or exclude those provisions in the regulations which relate to daily and weekly rest periods and in-work rest breaks – but only for adult workers (that is to say, workers aged 18 and over) – so long as the agreement clearly allows those workers to take equivalent periods of compensatory rest (*ibid.* regulations 23 and 24).

- Save for young workers under the age of 18, the night work limits imposed by the 1998 Regulations may also be excluded or modified (for all workers, including adolescents) by a collective agreement – so long as an adult worker's average weekly hours (including hours worked at night) do not exceed 48 during the agreed reference period, which latter may be extended (for objective or technical reasons associated with the organisation of work) from 17 to 52 weeks. However, any term in a collective (or workforce) agreement that presumes to override a worker's right not to work more than an average 48 hours a week is void and unenforceable.

- Finally, a worker's entitlement to a minimum four weeks' paid annual holidays is also sacrosanct – although a collective agreement may determine when the holiday year begins and ends, the procedures to be followed by workers before taking their holidays, and the method to be used to calculate a worker's residual entitlement to holiday on the termination of his (or her) employment. It may also contain a provision allowing a worker who has resigned or been dismissed to compensate his (or her) employer for holidays taken in excess of his statutory entitlement – whether by a payment, by undertaking additional work, or otherwise (*ibid.* regulation 14(4)).

Other legislation

- Information about the role and validity of collective (or workforce) agreements in the context of the rights of fixed-term employees under the Fixed-term Employees (Prevention of Less Favourable Treatment) Regulations 2002, is to be found elsewhere in this handbook in the section titled **Fixed-term employees**.

  See also **Holidays, annual, Rest breaks and rest periods, Trade union recognition**, and **Working hours**.

COMMISSION FOR RACIAL EQUALITY

Key points

- The Commission for Racial Equality (CRE) which replaced the former Race Relations Board and the Community Relations Commission, was established by section 43 of the Race Relations Act 1976. The CRE has at least eight (but not more than 15) Commissioners, including a chairman and one or more deputy chairmen, all appointed on a full-time or part-time basis by the Secretary of State for Employment.

- The duties of the CRE are to work towards the elimination of racial discrimination and to promote equality of opportunity and good relations between different racial groups. It monitors observance of the 1976 Act and is empowered to conduct investigations, serve non-discrimination notices, and to apply to the court for an injunction or order against persistent offenders. The CRE may also issue codes of practice containing practical guidance on methods for the elimination of discrimination in the field of employment.

Power of the CRE to obtain information

- The CRE may order an employer to furnish written information about his employment policies and practices or serve notice on him to appear before the Commission at a specified time and place (bringing with him any and all documents relating to the matters specified in the notice). If an employer refuses or fails to cooperate, the CRE may apply to a county court (or, in Scotland, the sheriff court) for an order directing him to comply. If an employer wilfully alters, suppresses, conceals or destroys any document that he has been ordered to produce, or knowingly or recklessly makes any statement that is false in a material particular, he is guilty of an offence and liable on summary conviction to a fine of up to £5,000.

Non-Discrimination Notices

- If, in the course of a formal investigation, the CRE are satisfied that an employer is committing (or has committed) an unlawful discriminatory act, they may serve on him a 'Non-Discrimination Notice' ordering him to comply with the law and cautioning him that, if there is any repetition during the next five years, the matter will be placed in the hands of the county (or sheriff) court.

- The CRE will not normally serve a Non-Discrimination Notice on an employer without first warning him of the possibility (and the legal implications) and giving him 28 days within which to put his side of the story (orally or in writing). An employer has six weeks within which to appeal to an employment tribunal (or, where appropriate, to a designated county or a sheriff court) against any requirement of a Non-Discrimination Notice on the ground either that it is unreasonable (because it is based on an incorrect finding of fact) or for any other reason. In the event, the court will either confirm or quash the requirement or substitute a new requirement.

Help for persons suffering racial discrimination

- An employee (or job applicant) who has already registered a complaint of unlawful racial discrimination with an employment tribunal (or who is contemplating doing so) may apply to the CRE for help and advice. The CRE will usually agree to help if the case is unduly complex or raises a question of principle, or if there are any other special considerations. Their help may include procuring (or attempting to procure) an out-of-court settlement (eg, by a direct approach to the employer in question); arranging for the giving of advice by a solicitor or counsel; or, in the final analysis, seeing to it that the employee is adequately represented at the tribunal hearing. See also **Racial discrimination**.

See also **Codes of practice.**

COMPROMISE AGREEMENTS

Key points

- Any provision in a contract of employment (or in any other form of agreement) which purports to override an employee's statutory right to bring proceedings before an employment tribunal is void and unenforceable (section 203, Employment Rights Act 1996). There are analogous provisions in the Sex Discrimination Act 1975, the Race Relations Act 1976, the Trade Union & Labour Relations (Consolidation) Act 1992; the Disability Discrimination Act 1995, the Working Time Regulations 1998; and the National Minimum Wage Act 1998.

- However, there are exceptions to this rule. There are three forms of 'out of court' settlement, each of which is legally binding on the signatories, effectively preventing an employee (that is to say, the would-be complainant) bringing or continuing with proceedings before an employment tribunal. The first of these is the so-called COT 3 agreement; the second, the 'compromise agreement'; and the third, an arbiteral agreement under the so-called ACAS arbitration scheme.

Compromise agreements

- The compromise agreement is a form of agreement that does *not* require the intervention of ACAS. It is an agreement between an employer and an employee that, if properly concluded, is also legally binding on the parties. By entering into a compromise agreement with his (or her) employer, an employee who believes that he has been unfairly or unlawfully dismissed or that his employer has infringed one or other of his statutory rights in employment, agrees to waive his right to pursue his complaint before an employment tribunal in return for an agreed amount of compensation or some other consideration.

- It is important to note that the point of a compromise agreement is to settle an *existing* dispute (or two or more existing disputes, eg, an allegation of unfair dismissal allied to a dispute about the non-payment of statutory redundancy pay) which are or may be the subject of proceedings before an employment tribunal. A compromise agreement cannot be used as a 'catch-all' vehicle for the settlement of disputes which may arise in the future (per the Employment Appeal Tribunal in *Lunt v Merseyside TEC Ltd* [1999] ICR 17).

Procedural requirements

- Before entering into a compromise agreement, an employee *must* receive advice from a *relevant independent adviser* (see below) as to the terms and effect of the proposed agreement and, in particular, as to its effect on his (or her) ability to pursue his rights before an employment tribunal. Furthermore, the agreement itself must satisfy certain other conditions. It must be in writing and must relate to specific proceedings by a named employee. It must also name the person who gave the independent advice and must include a statement to the effect that the agreement satisfies the conditions regulating compromise agreements (or contracts), laid down in whichever of the following statutes or regulations applies:

  - Sex Discrimination Act 1975 (section 77(4A));

    Note: Section 77(4A) extends to compromise agreements settling complaints under the Equal Pay Act 1970.

  - Race Relations Act 1976 (section 72(4A));

  - Trade Union & Labour Relations (Consolidation) Act 1992 (section 288(2B));

  - Disability Discrimination Act 1995 (section 9(3));

  - Employment Rights Act 1996 (section 203(3));

  - Working Time Regulations 1998 (regulation 35);

  - National Minimum Wage Act 1998 (section 49).

A compromise agreement will be invalid and unenforceable if the relevant independent adviser was also acting in the matter for the employer (or an associated employer) or was himself (or herself) a party to the dispute; or if, at the time he (or she) gave that advice, he was not covered by either of a valid contract of insurance or an indemnity provided for members of a profession or professional body covering the risk of a claim by the employee in respect of any loss arising in consequence of that advice.

Meaning of 'relevant independent adviser'

- The term 'relevant independent adviser' means a person who:
  - is a qualified lawyer, that is to say, as respects England and Wales, a barrister, a solicitor who holds a practising certificate, or an autho-rised advocate or litigator; and, as respects Scotland, an advocate (whether in practice as such or employed to give legal advice), or a solicitor who holds a practising certificate;
  - is an officer, official, employee or member of an independent trade union who has been certified in writing by the trade union as competent to give advice and as authorised to do so on behalf of the trade union;
  - works at an advice centre (eg, the Citizens' Advice Bureau), whether as an employee or a volunteer, and has been certified in writing as competent to give advice and authorised to do so on behalf of the centre; or
  - is a person of a description specified by order of the Secretary of State.

Non-payment by the employer

- Payments due to an employee under a valid compromise agreement arising out of a complaint of unfair dismissal may be enforced by an employment tribunal (under its 'breach of employment contracts' juris-diction), so long as the issue is referred to a tribunal within three months of the employer's refusal or failure to pay (*per Rock-It Cargo Limited v Green* [1997] IRLR 58).

- Should an employer become insolvent, or otherwise renege on a compromise agreement settling a dispute over the non-payment of a redundancy or severance payment, the employee in question may apply to the Secretary of State (in practice, the Department for Education & Employment) for payment of the amount due out of the National Insurance Fund – always provided that the employee had first taken all reasonable steps (including a complaint to an employment tribunal, or proceedings to enforce a decision or award of an employ-ment tribunal) to recover that amount. The amount payable by the Secretary of State in these circumstances is restricted to whichever is the lesser of the *statutory* redundancy payment payable to the employee and the amount specified in the relevant compromise agree-ment. The Secretary of State will seek to recover the amount paid to the employee from the employer himself or (if the latter is insolvent) from the employer's trustee in bankruptcy, liquidator, administrator, receiver or manager (per Chapter VI, Employment Rights Act 1996, as amended by section 11 of the Employment Rights (Dispute Resolution) Act 1998). For further particulars, please turn to the section titled **Insolvency of employer** elsewhere in this handbook.

Example of a 'compromise agreement'

- The following is a suggested example of a compromise agreement. However, employers would be well-advised to develop their own forms of compromise agreement following consultations with a solicitor or with their own legal departments. For information about COT 3 agreements, see the next section, titled **Conciliation officers**.

SAMPLE COMPROMISE AGREEMENT

Note: Any person or organisation who/which borrows or adapts this sample compromise agreement solely for the purpose for which it is intended does so on the strict understanding that he/she/it thereby indemnifies the author and the publishers of this book against any liability arising out of its use, misuse or adaptation. Reproduction of this simple agreement for another purpose and without the prior written permission of the publishers is strictly prohibited.

Agreement (*delete where inapplicable*) under section 77(4)(aa) of the Sex Discrimination Act 1975 and/or, as appropriate, section 72(4)(aa) of the Race Relations Act 1976, section 288(2A) of the Trade Union & Labour Relations (Consolidation) Act 1992, section 9(2)(b) of the Disability Discrimination Act 1995, or section 203(2)(f) of the Employment Rights Act 1996, regulation 35 of the Working Time Regulations 1998, or section 49 of the National Minimum Wage Act 1998.

This Agreement is made the _____ day of _____ 200__ **between**:

_____

(hereinafter referred to as 'the employer') and

_____

(hereinafter referred to as 'the employee')

and is made in resolution of a dispute concerning an alleged breach by the employer of one or more of the employee's statutory rights under (*delete where inapplicable*) the Sex Discrimination Act 1975/the Race

Relations Act 1976/the Trade Union & Labour Relations (Consolidation) Act 1992/the Disability Discrimination Act 1995/the Employment Rights Act 1996/the Working Time Regulations Act 1998/the National Minimum Wage Act 1998, which matters are outlined in Appendix I hereto.

It is agreed that:

1. The employee has received advice from a relevant independent adviser as to the terms and effect of this Agreement and, in particular, its effect on the employee's ability to pursue his/her rights before an employment tribunal.

2. The employee hereby waives his/her right to bring or continue with proceedings before an employment tribunal arising out of the matters outlined in Appendix I hereto.

3. (delete if inapplicable) The employee's employment terminated/willterminate on _____ (*date*).

4. On the date hereof, the employer will pay to the employee the sum of £ _____ by way of compensation for the loss of his/her employment and/or for the alleged breach or breaches of those of his/her statutory employment rights as are outlined in Appendix I hereto – which compensation is calculated in the manner and for the purposes described in Appendix III hereto, in consideration of which the employee will indemnity the employer in respect of any tax liability which may arise in respect of the whole or any part of that payment.

5. (*delete if inapplicable*) The employer will.......... (*for example: reinstate, re-engage, transfer, promote, provide training etc*)......... the employee in accordance with the terms and conditions outlined in Appendix II hereto.

6. The payments and/or other consideration made or accorded to the employee under paragraphs 4 and/or 5 hereof are in full and final settlement of any claim or claims by the employee arising out of the matters outlined in Appendix I hereto.

7. By his signature hereto the employee agrees to refrain from instituting or continuing proceedings before an employment tribunal or court in respect of the matters outlined in Appendix I hereto.

8. This Agreement or any of the terms it contains will not be communicated to any third party other than as required by law or in the circumstances described in paragraph 6 hereto without the express written consent of both parties.

    By his/her signature hereto the relevant independent adviser (hereinafter referred to as 'the advisee') warrants and declares that:

9. His/her name and address is as follows:

    _____

    _____

10. (*delete where inapplicable*)

    He/she is a qualified lawyer.

    He/she is an officer/official/employee/member of an independent trade union who has been certified in writing by the trade union as competent to give advice and as authorised to do so on behalf of the trade union.

    He/she works at an advice centre and has been certified in writing by the centre as competent to give advice and as authorised to do so on behalf of the centre.

11. At the time he/she advised the employee as to the terms and effect of this Agreement, he/she was covered by (*delete where inapplicable*) a contract of insurance/an indemnity provided for members of a profession or professional body, against the risk of a claim by the employee in respect of any loss arising in consequence of that advice.

12. In all respects, this Agreement satisfies the conditions relating to compromise agreements under the relevant provisions of (*delete where inapplicable*) the Sex Discrimination Act 1975, the Race Relations Act 1976, the Trade Union & Labour Relations (Consolidation) Act 1992, the Disability Discrimination Act 1995, the Employment Rights Act 1996, the Working Time Regulations 1998, the National Minimum Wage Act 1998, the Part-time Workers (Prevention of Less Favourable Treatment) Regulations 2000, or the Fixed-term Employees (Prevention of Less Favourable Treatment) Regulations 2002.

Signed: _____
(*the employee*)

Signed: _____
(*the adviser*)

Signed: _____
(*the employer*)

Note: The parties to this Agreement should also sign or initial each of Appendices I, II and III to this Agreement – suggested examples of which are not included here.

CONCILIATION OFFICERS

Key points

- The role of the Advisory, Conciliation & Arbitration Service (ACAS) is to provide an independent and impartial service to prevent and resolve disputes between employers and employees. Conciliation officers appointed by ACAS have a statutory duty to promote settlements of complaints arising out of a breach (or alleged breach) of an employee's rights under contemporary employment and industrial relations legislation which are or could be the subject of proceedings before the employment tribunals (*per* Part IV, Chapter IV of the Trade Union & Labour Relations (Consolidation) Act 1992 and sections 18 and 19 of the Employment Tribunals Act 1996).

- If there is a dispute between an employer and an employee concerning an alleged infringement of one or other of the employee's statutory rights (including his or her right not to be unfairly dismissed), either party to that dispute may request a conciliation officer to make his (or her) services available to them. It is a conciliation officer's duty to endeavour to promote a settlement – before the employee decides to take the matter further by presenting a complaint to an employment tribunal (section 18(2), Employment Tribunals Act 1996). If an employee has already complained to an employment tribunal, a copy of his (or her) 'originating application' (Form IT1) plus a copy of his employer's (or former employer's) response (Form IT3) to that application, will be sent automatically to the appropriate regional office of ACAS. A conciliation officer will then contact both parties offering to help settle the 'dispute' between them. However, he cannot proceed further unless *both* parties accept that offer of help. But see *Future developments* at the end of this section.

- It is not the function of conciliation officers to comment on the merits or otherwise of an employee's complaint (or to attempt to persuade an employee to withdraw that complaint). Their role is to help the parties establish the facts and clarify their views, without allowing their own views to intrude. In short, a conciliation officer is neither an arbitrator nor an investigator. Nor is anything said to a conciliation officer in the course of discussions admissible as evidence in proceedings before an employment tribunal.

COT 3 agreements

- If a conciliation officer succeeds in promoting an 'out-of-court' settlement, details of the settlement will be recorded on form COT 3 (signed by both parties). Once this is done, the employee cannot then change his (or her) mind and press ahead with the original complaint (see *Moore v Dupont Furniture Products Limited* [1980] IRLR 158 (CA)). Each party keeps a copy of form COT 3. A third copy is sent to the Central Office of the Employment Tribunals which will register the complaint as having been settled by conciliation. Another (relatively new) form of binding agreement reached without the intervention of a conciliation officer – is the so-called 'compromise agreement' (discussed in the previous section).

General

- If an employer fails to honour the terms of a COT 3 settlement, the employee may apply to the county court for an order enforcing compliance.

- If an out-of-court settlement is reached without the intervention of a conciliation officer (and there has been no 'compromise agreement'), the employee is free to change his (or her) mind and can insist on having his complaint heard by an employment tribunal – regardless of how the settlement was framed.

- Nothing communicated to a conciliation officer during his (or her) attempts to promote a settlement is admissible in evidence before an employment tribunal – unless the party concerned gives his express consent.

Complaints of unfair dismissal

- If an employee has presented a complaint of unfair dismissal to an employment tribunal, the conciliation officer's first duty is to explore

the possibility of reinstatement or re-engagement. If this is impracticable or unacceptable (usually because the relationship between the
parties has soured), he (or she) will invite the parties to consider the
question of compensation. Although conciliation officers are free to
explain the formulae used by employment tribunals to calculate
awards of compensation for unfair dismissal, it is *not* their function to
recommend an appropriate amount.

Note: A conciliation officer will intervene on a complaint of unfair dismissal if satisfied
either that a dismissal (including an alleged 'constructive' dismissal) has actually
occurred or that the employee has either been dismissed or has resigned but is still
serving out his (or her) notice period.

Dismissal for asserting a statutory right

- A conciliation officer may also intervene when an employee claims that
  he (or she) was dismissed for having challenged his employer's
  infringement of one or other of his statutory employment rights or for
  having referred the alleged infringement to an employment tribunal
  (section 104, Employment Rights Act 1996). For further particulars, see
  Dismissal for asserting a statutory right elsewhere in this handbook.
  See also **Victimisation**.

Alleged infringement of other employment rights

- A conciliation officer will also intervene, or offer his (or her) services,
  before or after a complaint has been presented to an employment tribunal, in complaints (or likely complaints) arising out of an alleged
  (suspected or potential) infringement by an employer of an employee
  or worker's statutory rights under contemporary employment legislation:

Breach of employment contract disputes

- The employment tribunals also have jurisdiction *(see Note* below) to
  hear most breach of employment contract disputes that arise (or remain
  unresolved) on the termination of an employee's period of employment. At the request of both parties (if a complaint has already been
  presented) or of either party (if there has not yet been a formal
  complaint), a conciliation officer is duty-bound to try to settle such a
  dispute before it proceeds to a full tribunal hearing. A conciliation
  officer will not take the initiative in such cases unless he (or she)
  believes that he has a reasonable prospect of success.

Note: The Employment Tribunals Extension of Jurisdiction (England & Wales) Order 1994 and the Employment Tribunals Extension of Jurisdiction (Scotland) Order 1994 were made by the Lord Chancellor and the Lord Advocate, respectively, under the then section 131 of the Employment Protection (Consolidation) Act 1978 (now section 3 of the Employment Tribunals Act 1996). The orders, which came into force on 12 July 1994, enable the employment tribunals to hear all breach of employment contract disputes that arise (or remain unresolved) at the end of an employee's period of employment – except for claims relating to personal injury, intellectual property, tied accommodation, obligations of confidence, and covenant e, which latter remain outside the tribunals' jurisdiction.

Future developments

- As is pointed out in the *Explanatory Notes* accompanying the Employment Act 2002, the duty of ACAS (through its conciliation officers) is to continue to seek a conciliated settlement between an employer and an employee for so long as the two parties to the dispute want to carry on. This can sometimes lead to an ACAS-brokered agreement being reached at the very last moment – before an employee's complaint comes before an employment tribunal – 'the result', say the *Notes*, of the parties being unwilling to focus on the importance of agreement until the reality of the tribunal hearing is upon them. But delayed settlements 'cost time and resource to the parties involved, to ACAS, and to the tribunal services. The objective, therefore, is to introduce a system that encourages earlier conciliated settlement where this is possible, without preventing last minute settlements if there is good reason for them'.

- To that end, section 24 of the 2002 Act establishes a fixed period of conciliation for claims to an employment tribunal. Once section 24 is brought into force (possibly in the second half of 2003), section 7 of the Employment Tribunals Act 1996 will be amended by regulations to enable the postponment of the fixing of a time and place for a tribunal hearing in order for the proceedings to be settled through conciliation. Regulations will set out the length of the conciliation period and will provide for its extension only in cases where the conciliation officer considers that settlement within a short additional time frame is very likely. Once the conciliation period is over, it will be for a conciliation officer (and he or she alone) to judge whether to continue to conciliate the case or to pass it back to the Employment Tribunal Service so that a time and place can be fixed for a hearing. Copies of the 2002 Act (ISBN 0 10 542202 9) and its accompanying *Explanatory Notes* (ISBN 0 10 56202 8), may be purchased from the Stationery Office (0845 7 023474) or by email from book.orders@tso.co.uk.

See also **Compromise agreements, Disabled persons, Employment tribunals and procedure, Equal pay and conditions, Racial discrimination, Sex discrimination, Trade union membership and activities,** and **Victimisation,** elsewhere in this handbook.

CONSTRUCTIVE DISMISSAL

Key points

- In law, a constructive dismissal occurs when '(an) employee terminates (his or her) contract of employment, with or without notice, in circumstances such that he is entitled to terminate it without notice by reason of the employer's conduct' (section 95(l)(c), Employment Rights Act 1996).

- The authoritative test of constructive dismissal was given by Lord Denning in *Western Excavating (ECC) Ltd v Sharp* [1978] 2 WLR 344, CA. 'An employee,' he said, 'is entitled to treat himself as constructively dismissed if the employer is guilty of conduct which is a significant breach going to the root of the contract of employment; or which shows that the employer no longer intends to be bound by one or more of the essential terms of the contract.'

- In giving his judgement in the *Western Excavating* case, Lord Justice Lawton acknowledged that people without legal training may be unfamiliar with the principles of law that operate to bring a contract of employment to an end by reason of an employer's conduct. On the other hand, he said, 'sensible persons have no difficulty in recognising such conduct when they hear about it. Persistent and unwanted amorous advances by an employer to a female member of his staff would, for example, clearly be such conduct; and,' he continued, 'for a chairman of an employment tribunal in such a case to discuss with his lay members whether there had been a repudiation or a breach of a fundamental term by the employer would be, for most lay members, a waste of legal learning.'

- In *Woods v W M Car Services (Peterborough) Ltd* [1982] IRLR 413, CA, Mr Justice Browne-Wilkinson stated that there is an implied term in every contract of employment that an employer will not, without reasonable and proper cause, conduct himself in a manner calculated or likely to destroy or seriously damage the relationship of confidence and trust between employer and employee. Any employer, he said, who persistently attempts to vary an employee's terms and conditions of employment with a view to getting rid of him, is in clear breach of that implied duty. Such a breach, he concluded, is a fundamental breach amounting to a repudiation, since it necessarily goes to the root of the employment contract.

- A false allegation of dishonesty, unreasonably made, or other conduct by an employer showing a lack of trust and confidence in an employee, may also amount to a repudiation of the contract of employment sufficient to entitle the employee to terminate his employment and present a complaint of unfair constructive dismissal (*vide Robinson v Crompton Parkinson* [1978] IRLR 61).

Other examples

- Other examples of conduct recognised by the tribunals and courts as being tantamount to a repudiation of contract (in the particular circumstances of each case) include:

    - reducing (or attempting to reduce) an employee's rate of pay or changing the way in which his pay is calculated (*Industrial Rubber Products v Gillon* [1977] IRLR 389);

    - demoting an employee, changing his job content, duties, responsibilities, working hours (or shift) without first consulting him and/or obtaining his agreement (*Ford v Milthorn Toleman Ltd* [1980] IRLR 31);

    - undermining the authority vested in a manager or supervisor by criticising or abusing him (or her) in the presence of junior staff (*Wetherall (Bond St W1) Ltd v Lynn* [1978] ICR 203);

    - refusing to give an agreed pay rise (*Pepper & Hope v Daish* [1980] IRLR 13 EAT);

    - transferring (or attempting to transfer) an employee to another job, premises or location in the absence of any express (or, less often, an implied) contractual right to do so (*McNeill v Charles Crimin (Electrical Contractors) Ltd* [1984] IRLR 179);

    - persistent sexual (or racial) harassment (*Western Excavating, qv*); and

    - failure to provide a safe or secure place of work or appropriate safety equipment (see *Safety at work* below).

- It should be stressed that a contract of employment is an agreement made between two parties. It is not open to one of those parties (invariably the employer) to presume to change any term of that contract without seeking and obtaining the agreement of the other party (the employee). To do otherwise is a breach of contract. It will be for the tribunals and courts to decide whether the breach is so significant as to entitle the employee to consider his (or her) contract of employment to be at an end.

Mobility clauses

- Many cases alleging unfair constructive dismissal hinge on the existence or otherwise of an express or implied 'mobility clause' in an employee's contract of employment. In *United Bank Limited v Akhtar* [1989] IRLR 507, a junior bank employee with a sick wife and two small children was given just six days in which to settle his affairs and move from Leeds to another branch of the bank in Birmingham. Although there was a clearly-stated mobility clause in Mr Akhtar's contract of employment, giving his employers the right to transfer him from one branch of the bank to another, Mr Akhtar found it impossible to comply with the bank's request. After pleading with his employers to give him more time, Mr Akhtar resigned. Upholding his complaint of unfair constructive dismissal, the Employment Appeal Tribunal remarked that 'in our view, [a mobility clause in a contract] includes, as a necessary implication, first, the requirement to give reasonable notice and, secondly, the requirement so to exercise the discretion to give relocation or other allowances, in such a way as not to make performance of the employee's duties impossible'.

- In *Prestwick Circuits Limited v McAndrew* [1990] IRLR 191, which turned on an employer's implied right to order a transfer from one place of employment to another, the Court of Session stated that any such implied right 'must be subject to the implied qualification that reasonable notice must be given in all the circumstances of the case'.

- Few forward-thinking employers nowadays would exercise their contractual right to transfer an employee from one location to another without first talking to him (or her), reviewing his domestic situation, offering relocation counselling, sending the employee and his family on an expenses-paid trip to the new location (to look at housing, schools, etc), offering a measure of financial assistance and agreeing a reasonable period to enable the employee to put his affairs in order.

Safety at work

- Every employer has a common law, statutory (and implied contractual) duty to protect his employees from risks to their health and safety at work. In *British Aircraft Corporation v Austin* [1978] IRLR 332, the tribunal held that an employee was entitled to resign and claim constructive dismissal when her employer failed, in spite of repeated reminders, to provide her with safety spectacles made up to her own prescription. In *Graham Oxley Tool Steels Ltd v Firth* [1980] IRLR 135, there was a similar outcome when an employee resigned because she could no longer work in a temperature of 49°F. The tribunal held that the employers were in breach of contract by failing to provide the employee with a 'suitable working environment'.

- In another case, that of *Dutton & Clark Ltd v Daly* [1985] IRLR 363, a cashier resigned when the building society in which she worked was robbed twice in the space of two months. An employment tribunal upheld her complaint that her employers had failed in their duty to provide her with a safe system of work – even though the employers had clearly spent a great deal of money fitting their premises with security cameras, alarm buttons, thick steel plates and reinforced glass screens. The EAT allowed the employers' appeal and remitted the case to a differently-constituted tribunal. The scope of the duty of an employer to provide a safe system of work can be expressed, said the EAT, as the taking of *reasonable* steps or the taking of such steps as are *reasonably practicable* to prevent exposure to unnecessary risk. The tribunal should have examined the employer's security arrangements from the point of view of any reasonable employer. In the High Court, said Sir Ralph Kilner Brown, Mrs Daly would never have persuaded a judge that her employers had broken a fundamental term of her contract of employment.

  Note: Sections 44, 100 and 108 of the Employment Rights Act 1996 state that (in the absence of a safety representative, a representative of employee safety, a safety committee, or competent person designated to keep a 'watching brief' on health and safety issues, an employee who is victimised or subjected to any detriment, or dismissed (or forced to resign), for expressing a reasonable concern about his (or her) employer's approach to such issues, may bring proceedings before an employment tribunal regardless of his age or length of service at the material time.

Premature resignation

- Case law suggests that an employee should not act too hastily in interpreting an apparent breach of contract as an intention on the part of his employer to repudiate the contract. Thus, in *Adams v Charles Zub Associates Limited* [1978] IRLR 551, the EAT held that an employee had been wrong to resign when his employer had twice failed to pay him his salary on time. Although his employer had been technically in breach of contract, the employee was well aware that the delays in payment were entirely due to circumstances beyond the employer's control. There was no intention not to be bound by the relevant term in the employee's contract of employment.

- In *Futty v Brekkes (D & D)* [1974] IRLR 130, a fish filleter resigned and claimed constructive dismissal when his foreman told him, 'If you do not like the job, f— off.' The tribunal dismissed his complaint, pointing out that the language used by the foreman was not uncommon in the fish trade and that he would have used more precise language had he truly intended to dismiss the man. The complainant, said the tribunal, had acted too hastily.

- However, in a not dissimilar case, a manager was told (during an argument with a director and in the presence of several of his subordinates) to 'piss off and f— off'. The director continued to abuse the manager all the way to the car park where he relieved him of the keys to his company car, telling him again to 'piss off'. An employment tribunal held that the manager had been constructively dismissed (*King v Webb's Poultry Products (Bradford)* Ltd [1975] IRLR 135). Likewise, in *Isle of Wight Tourist Board v Coombes* [1976] IRLR 413, the EAT held that a company director had shattered the relationship of trust and confidence between himself and his personal secretary when he informed her (in the presence of a third party) that she was 'an intolerable bitch on a Monday morning'. The secretary, who was unaccustomed to such abuse and resigned on the spot, was held to have been unfairly and constructively dismissed.

Acceptance of repudiation

- If an employer has demonstrated that he no longer intends to be bound by an essential term of an employment contract, the employee has two options. He (or she) may either accept the repudiation by promptly resigning (with or without notice) or protest about the repudiation and carry on working in the hope that he can persuade his employer to change his stance. In *W E Cox Toner (International) Ltd v Crook* [1981] IRLR 443 (EAT), Browne-Wilkinson J stated that an employee in that position 'is not bound to elect (one or other of those options) within a reasonable or any other time. Mere delay by itself (unaccompanied by any express or implied affirmation of the contract) does not constitute affirmation of the contract. But, if it is prolonged, it may be evidence of an implied affirmation' (*vide Allen v Robles* [1969] 1 WLR 1193). He went on to say that, 'provided the employee makes clear his objection to what is being done, he is not to be taken to have affirmed the contract by continuing to work and draw pay for a limited period of time, even if his purpose is merely to enable him to find another job'.

- A similar view was taken by the Court of Appeal in *Lewis v Motorworld Garages Ltd* [1985] IRLR 465, when they overturned the decisions of an employment tribunal and the EAT. An employee, said the Court, may be subjected to a barrage of humiliation and unjustified criticism of his work spread over many months. He could have resigned on a number of occasions and would have had every justification in bringing a complaint of unfair constructive dismissal. The fact that he decides to carry on working, in the faint hope that matters might improve, does not mean that he cannot rely on those earlier breaches of contract when he finally says to his employers: 'Enough is enough!'

Use of grievance procedure

- As soon as an employer has made it clear (by his words or actions) that he no longer intends to be bound by one or other of the essential terms of a contract of employment, the employee is entitled to consider his employment to be at an end, and to resign then and there. However, under the 'statutory grievance procedures' provisions of the Employment Act 2002, employment tribunals will not entertain certain complaints until 28 days after the parties to a dispute have completed Step 1 of the grievance procedure. Indeed, the tribunals are empowered to vary compensatory awards for failures to use the statutory grievance procedure by between 10 and 50 per cent; as to which see **Grievances and procedure** elsewhere in this handbook.

Resign or be sacked!

- An employer who threatens to dismiss an employee unless he (or she) resigns is in breach of the employment contract and can expect to face a complaint of unfair constructive dismissal. But, if an employee agrees to resign in return for a satisfactory financial inducement (even though there may be a threat of dismissal lurking in the background), his contract of employment will be treated as having been terminated by mutual consent. In disputed cases the question an employment tribunal will ask is: 'Was it the threat of dismissal which "persuaded" the employee to resign, or was it the inducement (money or whatever) offered by the employer and willingly accepted by the employee?' (*vide Sheffield v Oxford Controls Co Ltd* [1979] IRLR 133 (EAT)).

- Employers who offer financial inducements to employees to encourage them to resign would be well-advised to put any resultant agreement in writing (signed by both parties) to avoid any subsequent (and, possibly, opportunistic) complaints of unfair constructive dismissal. See also **Conciliation officers** and **Compromise agreements** elsewhere in this handbook.

Can a constructive dismissal be fair?

- In *Savoia v Chiltern Herb Farms Ltd* [1982] IRLR 166 CA, Lord Justice Waller remarked that, 'although it may be more difficult for an employer to say that a constructive dismissal was fair, nevertheless there may well be circumstances where it is perfectly possible to do so'.

- In the *Savoia* case, the employers were unhappy with the way in which a supervisor carried out his duties. Their solution was to promote him to foreman (with a pay rise) and transfer him to another department. The employee objected on medical grounds, claiming that he had a conjunctivitis problem that would be aggravated by the heat and smoke given off by the ovens in the new department. However, when challenged, he refused to provide a doctor's certificate and would not submit to an independent medical examination by a doctor nominated by the company. In the event, he resigned and presented a complaint of unfair constructive dismissal. The Court of Appeal agreed with the employment tribunal which heard his complaint (and with the EAT which rejected his appeal) that the complainant had indeed been constructively dismissed – given that he was under no contractual obligation, express or otherwise, to accept a promotion. However, his refusal to cooperate with his employers, coupled with their sound operational reasons for wanting to transfer him to another department, rendered his dismissal 'fair'.

Qualifying period and upper age limit

- To qualify to present a complaint of unfair dismissal (constructive or otherwise), an employee must ordinarily have been under *normal retiring age* and have been employed for a continuous period of one year or more ending with *the effective date of termination* of his (or her) employment. For the meanings of the italicised expressions, please turn to the section titled **Dismissal** (notably pages 169 and 194 to 196).

Inadmissible reasons for dismissal

- The qualifying conditions referred to in the previous paragraph, do not, however, apply when an employee claims that he (or she) has been dismissed (or selected for redundancy) for carrying out (or attempting to carry out) his duties as an employee representative, workforce representative, pension scheme trustee, safety representative (or representative of employee safety) or because of his trade union membership (or non-membership) or activities. Nor do they apply to a dismissal (or selection for redundancy) on grounds of race, sex, marital status, gender reassignment or disability (or for connected reasons), or for asserting a statutory right, or for reasons related to pregnancy, childbirth or maternity, or (in the case of a *protected or opted-out* shop worker or betting worker) a dismissal for refusing Sunday work. People in those categories (discussed elsewhere in this handbook) may register a complaint of unfair dismissal regardless of their age or length of continuous service at the material time. For a more comprehensive list of inadmissible (or automatically unfair) reason for dismissal, please turn to page 173 of this handbook.

  See also the sections titled **Contract of employment, Disabled persons, Dismissal, Dismissal in health and safety cases, Dismissal of an employee or workforce representative, Dismissal of a pension scheme trustee, Dismissal for asserting a statutory right, Dismissal for refusing Sunday work, Maternity rights, Racial discrimination, Sex discrimination, Trade union membership and activities,** and **Victimisation.**

CONTINUOUS EMPLOYMENT, MEANING OF

Key points

- To qualify for most statutory rights in employment, an employee must be in *continuous* employment and must have been *continuously employed* for a specified period. That period is expressed in months or years – a month meaning a calendar month; and a year, a year of 12 calendar months. The rules are laid down in Part XIV, Chapter I (sections 210 to 219) of the Employment Rights Act 1996 – reproduced as the Appendix to this handbook.

- Following the decision of the House of Lords in *R v Secretary of State for Employment, ex parte Equal Opportunities Commission* [1994] ICR 317, and the subsequent introduction of the Employment Protection (Part-Time Employees) Regulations 1995, part-time employees are nowadays entitled to the same statutory employment rights as their full-time colleagues, and are subject to the same qualifying conditions for access to those rights. See also the section titled **Part-time workers** elsewhere in this handbook.

The continuity of a period of employment

- Any employee who is in continuous employment will ultimately have been employed for a period sufficient to qualify for most (if not all) of the statutory rights outlined both in the Employment Rights Act 1996 and in related legislation (such as the Trade Union & Labour Relations (Consolidation) Act 1992). For example, an employee who has been continuously employed for one month up to the day preceding a *workless day* will qualify to be paid a guarantee payment in respect of that and (within prescribed limits) any subsequent workless days. A pregnant employee, who has been continuously employed for one year or more at the beginning of the 11th week before the expected week of childbirth, will qualify for up to 29 weeks additional maternity leave. An employee with one or more years' service at the effective date of termination of his (or her) employment has the right to pursue a complaint of unfair dismissal. An employee with two or more years' continuous service from the age of 18, has the right to be paid (or to claim) a redundancy payment; and so on.

- In computing an employee's period of continuous employment, any question whether the employee's employment is of a kind counting towards a period of continuous employment or whether periods (consecutive or otherwise) are to be treated as forming a single period of continuous employment, is determined week by week.

- But, where it is necessary to compute the length of an employee's period of employment in order to determine whether he (or she) qualifies for a statutory right which is dependent on a period of continuous employment, different rules apply, as is explained later in this section under the headings: *When does a period of continuous employment begin?* and *And when does it end?*

Weeks that count

- Every week during the whole or part of which an employee's relations with his (or her) employer are governed by a contract of employment counts in computing that employee's period of employment (*ibid.*

section 212(1)). It follows that the continuity of an employee's period of employment with the one employer is not broken if the employee is re-employed by that same employer (whether in the same or a different job) during the week immediately following the week in which his previous employment ended – even if the employee has worked (albeit briefly) for another employer in the days preceding his re-employment (*per Sweeney v J & S Henderson (Concessions) Ltd* [1999] IRLR 306 (EAT)).

- Under normal circumstances a week which does not count in the computation of a period of employment breaks the continuity of that period of employment. If, for example, the employee in the previous paragraph had not been re-engaged by his former employer for a further week, the continuity of his period of employment with that employer would have been broken. However, as is explained later in this section, there *are* circumstances in which an interval of more than one week between two consecutive periods of employment with the same employer will nonetheless be treated as part of an employee's total period of continuous employment with that employer.

Note: The continuity of a period of employment will be broken if an otherwise legal contract is performed illegally (eg, by a fraud on the Inland Revenue) (*Napier v National Business Agency Limited* [1951]2 All ER 264) unless the employee was unaware, for example, that his (or her) employer had been acting unlawfully (*Newland v Simons & Willer (Hairdressers) Limited* [1981] ICR 521). For further particulars, please turn to the section titled **Contract of employment** elsewhere in this handbook.

Weeks that do not count but do not break continuity

- Any week, during the whole or part of which an employee takes part in a strike, must be discounted when computing the employee's total period of continuous employment. However, the loss of that week does not destroy the continuity of that period of employment. See also *Industrial disputes* below.

- Weeks during the whole or part of which an employee works (or worked) outside Great Britain ordinarily count as part of that employee's total period of continuous employment, except in the case of a week (or part week) in which the employee was not an employed earner for the purposes of the Social Security Contributions & Benefits Act 1992 in respect of whom a secondary Class 1 National insurance contribution was payable under that Act (whether or not the contribution was in fact paid). In the latter situation, the week or weeks in question do not break the continuity of a period of employment but do not count as part of the employee's total period of continuous employment.

When does a period of continuous employment begin?

- To determine whether an employee has been continuously employed for a period sufficient to qualify for one or other of his (or her) statutory rights under the Employment Rights Act 1996, his period of continuous employment *begins* with the day on which he first started work with his employer and *ends* with the day by reference to which the length of his period of continuous employment falls to be ascertained (but see *Industrial disputes* below).

- This rule applies to all statutory employment rights which are dependent on a period of continuous employment, except in relation to an employee's right to a statutory redundancy payment. In the latter instance, any employee who started work with his (or her) employer *before* his 18th birthday is deemed to have started work on that 18th birthday (*ibid.* section 211(2)).

And when does it end?

- A period of continuous employment will end on the *effective date of termination* of the employee's contract of employment. For the meaning of *effective date of termination*, please turn to the section titled **Dismissal** elsewhere in this handbook. However, continuity will be preserved if an unfairly dismissed employee is reinstated or re-engaged by his former employer (or by an associated or successor employer) at the direction of an employment tribunal. See *Reinstatement or re-engagement* below. See also *Circumstances that do not break continuity*.

Presumption of continuity

- Section 210(5) of the 1996 Act cautions that 'a person's employment during any period shall, unless the contrary is shown, be presumed to have been continuous'. This means that, when confronted with a tribunal situation, an employer must be prepared to produce evidence to support his (or her) assertion that the applicant employee (the complainant) had not been continuously employed for a period sufficient to qualify him (or her) to pursue a complaint of unfair dismissal before an employment tribunal or to lay claim to a particular statutory right (such as a redundancy payment or any other statutory right that he claims has been denied him).

- To pursue a complaint before an employment tribunal concerning an alleged breach of one or other of his (or her) statutory rights, an employee must complete Form IT1 (*Originating Application to an*

Employment Tribunal) and send it to his (or her) nearest regional (ROET) or other office (OET) of the employment tribunals explaining the nature of his (or her) complaint. Within a week or two, a copy of that form will be forwarded to the employer (as well as to ACAS) together with Form IT3, inviting him (or her) to respond to the employee's complaint. It is at this point that the employer must be prepared to refute the employee's contention that he had (or has) been continuously employed for a period sufficient to qualify him for the right he now claims has been denied him. If the employer neglects to do so (either at this stage or at the subsequent tribunal hearing), the tribunal will proceed on the assumption that the disputed period of employment was continuous.

Circumstances that do not break continuity

- There are circumstances in which continuity of employment is not broken even though an employee's contract of employment has come to an end:

  - If an employee has been dismissed (or has resigned) on grounds of ill-health, his (or her) intervening period of absence will be treated as part of his total period of employment *if*, but only if, he is reinstated or re-engaged by the same employer within 26 weeks of the date on which his employment under his previous contract came to an end (the 'effective date of termination') (*ibid.* section 212(3)(a)).

  - If, on the other hand, an employee is dismissed on account of a temporary cessation of work, or in circumstances such that, by custom or arrangement, he (or she) is regarded as continuing in the employment of his employer (eg, seasonal workers), continuity of employment will be preserved if, at some later date, he is re-employed or reinstated by the same (or an associated) employer (*ibid.* section 212(3)(b) and (c)). Thus, if a factory is destroyed by fire and the workforce is necessarily dismissed pending rebuilding, the intervening period of interruption of employment will ordinarily count as a period of employment, notwithstanding that some or all of the workforce may have accepted work elsewhere while waiting to return to their original jobs (see *Bentley Engineering Co Ltd v Crown & Miller* [1976] ICR 225 when employment was interrupted in similar circumstances for 21 months and two years, respectively, without loss of continuity). See also the decision of the House of Lords in *Ford v Warwickshire County Council* [1983] ICR 273.

- In contentious cases, it will be (as always) a matter for the tribunals and courts to determine whether a break in employment preserves the continuity of a period of employment. In *Ingram v Foxon* [1984] ICR 685, it was held that an agreement between an employer and a returning employee – that the interval between the latter's dismissal and subsequent re-employment would form part of the employee's total period of continuous employment – could be categorised as an 'arrangement or custom' sufficient to bind the employer to that agreement. That decision was disputed by the EAT in *Morris v Walsh Western UK Limited* [1997] IRLR 562 and rejected by the EAT in *Collinson v British Broadcasting Corporation* [1998] IRLR 238 (EAT). In short, the concept of 'continuity of employment' is a statutory concept, and not one that can be vitiated by a compromise agreement or any other form of agreement between an employer and an employee. See also *Reinstatement or re-engagement* below.

Special provisions for redundancy payments

- The continuity of a period of employment is broken – but only for redundancy qualification and payment purposes – if an employee who has been paid a statutory redundancy payment is subsequently re-engaged by his (or her) former employer in circumstances which do not otherwise destroy continuity. This means that, although continuity is preserved for all other purposes – qualifying periods for unfair dismissal, additional maternity leave, notice, etc – the re-engaged employee will not again qualify for a redundancy payment until such time as he again satisfies the prescribed qualifying conditions for such a payment (in terms of length of service and age) (*ibid.* section 214).

  Note: In *Rowan v Machinery Installations (South Wales) Limited* [1981] ICR 386, and again in *Ross v Delrosa Caterers Limited* [1981] ICR 393, it was held that section 214 of the 1996 Act applies to a statutory redundancy payment (as defined in section 162 of the 1996 Act). It does not apply to a severance or other form of 'redundancy payment' which an employer is not legally required to make.

- The same rule applies when an employee, who has previously been paid a statutory redundancy payment, is reinstated or re-employed by his employer (or by a successor or associated employer):

  (a) following the intervention of an ACAS conciliation officer (and the conclusion of a COT 3 agreement); or

  (b) as the result of a relevant compromise agreement; or

  (c) as the result of an 'arbitral agreement' delivered by an independent arbitrator under the ACAS Arbitration Scheme; or

  (d) in compliance with a tribunal order for reinstatement or re-engagement (see below).

However, continuity will be preserved *for all purposes* (including entitlement to a statutory redundancy payment) if the terms on which the employee is reinstated or re-engaged include a provision that the employee repay the amount of any statutory redundancy payment previously paid to him (or her) – so long as the employee complies with that provision (*ibid.* section 219 as modified by the Employment Protection (Continuity of Employment) Regulations 1996).

Industrial disputes

- The continuity of a period of employment is *not* destroyed when an employee takes part in a strike (or is absent from work because of a lock-out). However, the number (or aggregate number) of days lost through strike action (or a lock-out) must be discounted when computing an employee's total period of continuous employment for the purpose of establishing his or her right (or otherwise) to one or other of the statutory employment rights listed in the 1996 Act. The date on which the employee's period of employment actually began must then be treated as postponed by the number of days in question (*ibid.* sections 211(3) and 216).

- For example, unless dismissed for an inadmissible or unlawful reason, an employee will not qualify to present a complaint of unfair dismissal to an employment tribunal if he (or she) had not been continuously employed for one calendar year or more at the effective date of termination of his contract of employment. When calculating an employee's period of continuous employment for this purpose (perhaps in response to a Form IT3), the respondent employer will first need to establish the number of days (if any) during which the employee took part in a strike or was absent from work because of a 'lock-out' – counting the number of days (in each case) between the last working day between the day on which each strike or lock-out began and the day on which the employee returned to work. If these add up to, say, five days, the employer must then treat the date on which the employee first started work as postponed by that same number of days. If the employee in question started work on 3 May 1999, he will be treated for these purposes as having started work on 8 May 1999. If his employment ended on 5 May 2000, he will not have completed the necessary one calendar year's service and will have forfeited his right to challenge the fairness of his dismissal before an employment tribunal.

Reinstatement or re-engagement

- If an employer (or a successor or associated employer) complies with a tribunal or court order to reinstate or re-engage an unfairly dismissed employee, the period of the employee's absence from work (ie, from the time his (or her) employment ended to the date on which he was reinstated or re-engaged) will count as part of his total period of continuous employment (*ibid.* section 219 and regulation 3 of the Employment Protection (Continuity of Employment) Regulations 1996 (*qv*)).

- In a situation involving an unfair redundancy dismissal, the continuity of employment, otherwise broken for redundancy qualification and payments purposes, will be re-established for those and all other purposes if the terms on which the employee is to be reinstated or re-engaged include a provision that the employee repay the amount of any statutory redundancy payment paid to him (or her) by his employer at the time of his dismissal, so long as the employee complies with that provision (*ibid.* sections 214 and 219, and regulation 4 of the Employment Protection (Continuity of Employment) Regulations 1996 (*qv*)). See also *Special provisions for redundancy payments* earlier in this section.

Continuity and a change of employer

- A change of employer does not break the continuity of a period of employment if the employer's business is acquired by, or transferred to, another owner or employer; or if the employer dies and his personal representatives or trustees continue to run the business; or if there is a change in the partners, personal representatives or trustees; or if the employee transfers from one employer to another when, at the time of the transfer, the two employers are associated employers (*ibid.* section 218).

- Two employers will be treated as associated 'if one is a company of which the other (directly or indirectly) has control, or if both are companies of which a third person (directly or indirectly) has control; and *associated employer* shall be construed accordingly' (section 231, Employment Rights Act 1996). A successor employer in relation to an employee, means a person who, in consequence of a change occurring (whether by virtue of a sale or other disposition or by operation of law) in the ownership of the undertaking, or of part of the undertaking, for the purposes of which the employee was employed, has become owner of the undertaking or part (*ibid.* section 235(1)).

Transfer of undertakings

- Under the provisions of the Transfer of Undertakings (Protection of Employment) Regulations 1981, as amended, an employee's contractual rights are safeguarded when the company (organisation or business) for which he (or she) works is sold or transferred as a going concern to another employer. This means that the new owner inherits the contracts of employment of the persons employed by the former owner immediately before the transfer or sale took place. He (or she) cannot pick or choose which employees to take over. They all go with the business – unless an employee makes it known, either to his existing employer or to the new owner, that he objects to becoming employed by the new owner. If this happens, there is no dismissal in law and the employee has no grounds for pursuing a complaint of unfair dismissal against either his former employer or the new owner of the business (*ibid.* regulations 5(4A) and (4B)).

- If the original employer dismisses one or more of his (or her) employees simply because he has sold (or is in the process of selling or transferring) his business (or in order to strike a better deal with the prospective purchaser), that employee will be treated in law as having been unfairly dismissed – unless the employer can show that the dismissal was for 'an economic, technical or organisational [ETO] reason entailing changes in the workforce'. The same applies if the new owner or employer sets about dismissing one or other of the employees he has inherited, unless he too can justify the dismissals in ETO terms. However, an employee dismissed in these circumstances will not qualify to pursue a complaint of unfair dismissal unless he (or she) had been continuously employed for one year or more at the effective date of termination of his contract of employment (*ibid.* regulations 5 and 8).

- It follows that the transfer or sale of an undertaking (company/partnership, business firm, or franchise) does not break the continuity of employment of the persons employed in that undertaking before the transfer or sale occurred. Indeed, section 4 of the 1996 Act imposes a duty on the new employer to issue a written statement to each of those employees giving his or her name (ie, the name of the employing organisation) and the date on which the employee's period of continuous employment began ('taking into account any employment with a previous employer which counts towards that period'). That written statement must be issued 'at the earliest opportunity and, in any event, not later than one month after the change' to which it refers.

See also **Contract of employment, Transfer of undertakings** and **Written particulars of terms of employment** elsewhere in this handbook.

CONTRACT OF EMPLOYMENT

Key points

- A person enters into a contract of employment (or contract of service) with an employer when he (or she) agrees to undertake specified duties (and assume specified responsibilities) in return for an agreed wage or salary. The two essential features of a contract of employment are control and mutuality of obligation. There is 'control' when an employer tells the employee *what* to do, *when* to do it and how it is to be done (or, in the case of a highly-qualified and skilled employee, the *manner* in which it is to be done). But the most important ingredient is 'mutuality of obligation'.

- As a rule of thumb, there is 'mutuality of obligation'

    (a) when an employer undertakes to provide a person with work on specified days of the week, for a specified number of hours, and for a specified or indefinite period; and

    (b) the person in question accepts the employer's offer of employment and undertakes to carry out that work with due diligence and efficiency for an agreed wage or salary, under agreed terms and conditions, and to obey the employer's lawful instructions.

Workers who are hired on a casual or 'as and when required' basis, who can come and go as they please, and who are free (without penalty) to accept or reject any offer of occasional work that comes their way, are not 'employees' in the strict legal sense of the word. Such workers are said to be hired or engaged under contracts *suorum generum* (that is to say, of their own kind). However, once any such casual arrangement is regularised; once an employer puts such an arrangement on a permanent footing (whether for an indefinite period, or for a specified number of days, weeks or months), and the worker agrees to work for the employer for that period (and on mutually agreed terms and conditions), the worker becomes an 'employee' in the strict legal sense of the word.

Note: Workers who are not employees nonetheless enjoy the rights and protection afforded to all workers (including employees) by legislation such as the Working Time Regulations 1998, the National Minimum Wage Act 1998, the Part-time Workers (Prevention of Less Favourable Treatment) Regulations 2000, the Health & Safety at Work etc Act 1974, the Sex Discrimination Act 1975, the Race Relations Act 1976, and the Disability Discrimination Act 1995.

- This over-simplified definition of a contract of employment (which has no statutory definition) also highlights the difference between an *employee* and a *self-employed person*. A self-employed person is engaged under a contract for services. He (or she) owes no loyalty to the person who hires him other than to complete one or more specific tasks within specified time limits in return for an agreed fee. He is his own master, normally provides and uses his own tools and equipment, submits invoices for services rendered, prepares annual accounts for scrutiny by the Inland Revenue, and pays his own taxes and national insurance contributions. He is in business to make a profit and is personally responsible for any losses. He must register for VAT if his annual turnover exceeds a specified amount.

- A contract of employment comes into being and is enforceable as such as soon as employment commences. The written statement of initial employment particulars required to be issued by an employer to every new employee is not, as is often supposed, a contract of employment. It merely provides evidence of the contractual terms, particularly if the information it contains is limited to that prescribed by sections 1 to 7 of the Employment Rights Act 1996. Other evidence of the contractual terms can be adduced, for example, from a collective agreement, the employee's job description, staff and works handbooks, policy documents, safety rules, custom and practice within the employing organisation or industry, and so on. There are also implied terms.

- When an employee remarks (or complains to an employment tribunal) that he (or she) has not yet received his 'contract of employment' he is, in reality, talking about the written statement referred to in the previous paragraph. The employer who neglects to provide an employee with a written statement explaining the terms and conditions of the latter's employment is not thereby denying that employee his contractual rights (as some employers appear to believe). Nor does an employer have anything to gain by withholding the written statement until two months after the date on which the employee was recruited. The sooner an employee knows what is expected of him (and what his contractual rights and obligations are), the better.

Working time as a term of contract?

- Under regulation 4(1) of the Working Time Regulations 1998, an adult worker (whether employee or otherwise) has the statutory right not to work more than an average 48 hours in any week (calculated over a reference period of 17 consecutive weeks). In *Barber & others v RJB Mining UK Limited* [1999] IRLR 308, the High Court declared that, notwithstanding an employer's duty under regulation 4(2) to take all reasonable steps to comply with regulation 4(1), paragraphs (1) and (2) did not need to be read together. Regulation 4(1) stood alone, and clearly imposed a contractual obligation on an employer to ensure that no person in his employ works more than an average 48 hours a week. That, said Mr Justice Gage, was a mandatory requirement which had to be applied to all contracts of employment. See also *Complaints arising out of a breach of contract* below.

Duties of employer

- Although a contract of employment or written statement will rarely say so in as many words, an employer owes a common law and implied contractual duty to his (or her) employees to take reasonable care for their safety. He must provide a safe place of work, safe working methods, safe plant and equipment, suitable training and instruction, competent supervision, and so on. An employee who is injured as a direct result of his (or her) employer's negligence, may sue for damages in the ordinary courts. If the employer is in breach of his statutory duty to ensure, so far as is reasonably practicable, the health, safety and welfare at work of the employee in question, he runs the risk also of being prosecuted under the Health & Safety at Work etc Act 1974.

- An employee has an implied contractual right to be treated with dignity and respect. He (or she) need not submit to foul language or abuse, or to false accusations or, indeed, to any conduct that destroys the very basis of the employment contract. If he is victimised, harassed, disciplined, subjected to any other detriment, dismissed (or selected for redundancy) on grounds of sex, marital status, gender reassignment, colour, race, nationality, disability, trade union membership (or non-membership), or for asserting one or other of his statutory rights in employment (including his right to health and safety protection), he can complain to an employment tribunal. A woman (or man) is entitled to the same pay and conditions enjoyed by men (or women) in the same employment if she (or he) is employed on like work or on work rated as equivalent, or on work of equal value.

- Any term in a contract of employment that purports to override or negate an employee's common law or statutory employment rights is null and void.

Duties of employee

- For his (or her) part, the employee must serve his employer honestly and faithfully. He must respect his employer's property and trade secrets, and must carry out his duties to the best of his abilities. If he ignores his employer's lawful instructions, or is uncooperative, disruptive or negligent in doing the job he is employed to do, he is in breach of contract and runs the risk of being dismissed. However, the common law right of an employer to dismiss an employee is vitiated to an extent by the statutory right of most employees not to be unfairly dismissed (a subject that is discussed at length elsewhere in this handbook).

Restrictive covenants

- The insertion, and validity of, restrictive covenants in contracts of employment are discussed elsewhere in this handbook in the section titled **Fidelity and trust, employee's duty of**.

Strikes and other industrial action

- A strike, 'go slow' and (in some circumstances) a 'work to rule' is a breach by the employee of his (or her) implied duty to cooperate with his employer. Under the common law, an employee who withdraws his labour or services in this way is deemed to have repudiated his contract and has effectively dismissed himself. In practice, it is open to the employer either to accept the repudiation and bring the contract of employment to an end or to affirm the contract and allow the employee to return to work after the industrial action is over.

- However, under statute law (notably the Trade Union & Labour Relations (Consolidation) Act 1992, as amended), the selective dismissal of one or more (but not all of the striking workers) or the selective reinstatement or re-engagement of one or more striking workers (following the dismissal of all of them), can be challenged before an employment tribunal – if, but only if, the strike was official (ie, endorsed by the trade union in question following a vote in favour of such action). Any person taking part in an unofficial strike or other unofficial industrial action thereby forfeits his right to complain of unfair dismissal and can be dismissed with impunity (*ibid.* sections 237, 238 and 238A). For further particulars, please turn to the sections titled **Dismissal for**

taking industrial action, Lock-outs and **Strikes and other industrial action** elsewhere in this handbook.

Equality clause

- Section 1 of the Equal Pay Act 1970 (as amended) cautions that 'if the terms of a contract under which a woman is employed at an establishment in Great Britain do not include (directly or by reference to a collective agreement or otherwise) an *equality clause*, they shall be deemed to include one'. This means that, if a woman is employed on like work with a man (or on work rated as equivalent, or on work of equal value) any term in her contract that is, or becomes, less favourable to her than a term of a similar kind in the man's contract shall be treated in law as so modified as not to be less favourable. For further particulars, please turn to the sections titled **Equal pay and conditions** and **Pension schemes** elsewhere in this handbook.

Collective agreements

- To the extent that a collective agreement between an employer (or an employers' association) and one or more trade unions includes provisions relating to remuneration, working hours, holidays, sickness benefits, and so on, that agreement will be deemed to form part of the individual employee's contract of employment – always provided that his (or her) rights under that agreement are included (or, in one or two instances, referred to) in the written statement of terms of employment issued in accordance with sections 1 to 7 of the 1996 Act (as to which, see **Written particulars of terms of employment** elsewhere in this handbook).

Termination of contract

- There are a number of ways in which the contract of employment may be brought to an end. An employee may end his (or her) employment simply by giving the notice prescribed by his contract (or the minimum notice prescribed by section 86 of the 1996 Act, whichever is the greater). He is under no obligation to state his reasons for resigning and may leave once the period of notice has expired. If, on the other hand, he simply walks off the job without giving notice, he is in breach of contract and may, in theory at least, be sued for damages. In practice, few employers would consider the exercise worthwhile. If, on the other hand, an employee terminates his employment without notice, in circumstances in which he is entitled to do so by virtue of his employer's conduct, he has been effectively dismissed and may (subject to the usual qualifying conditions) pursue a complaint of unfair 'constructive' dismissal before an employment tribunal (as to which, see **Constructive dismissal** elsewhere in this handbook).

- Under the common law doctrine of frustration, a contract of employment may also be brought to an end by the death, imprisonment or prolonged illness of either party to that contract. However, in the light of the provisions of the 1996 Act, an employer would be ill-advised to invoke the doctrine of frustration when challenged to explain the 'dismissal' of a sick or injured employee absent from work for a prolonged period. On the other hand, frustration may be invoked if an employee has been sentenced to a lengthy term of imprisonment (even if he or she has lodged an appeal) (*per Hare v Murphy Brothers* [1974] ICR 603 (CA) *and Harrington v Kent* [1980] IRLR 353). See **Frustration of contract** elsewhere in this handbook.

- A contract of employment may also be terminated by the employer – either because the contract itself (being a 'limited-term contract') has expired (and is not renewed under the same contract), or for a reason related to the capability, qualifications or conduct of the employee, or if the termination in question is tantamount to a constructive dismissal. Section 98(2) of the 1996 Act allows that an employee can also be lawfully dismissed because his (or her) continued employment would be illegal, or on grounds of redundancy, or for 'some other substantial reason' of a kind such as to justify the dismissal of an employee holding the position which that employee held. Whether or not an employer acted reasonably and fairly in taking the decision to dismiss (for whatever reason) is a matter for an employment tribunal to decide. See also **Constructive dismissal**, **Dismissal**, and **Fixed-term employees** elsewhere in this handbook.

Complaints arising out of a breach of contract

- Since 12 July 1994, the jurisdiction of the employment tribunals has included all breach of employment contract cases on termination of employment – except for personal injury claims, cases (outside the tribunals' normal field of expertise) relating to intellectual property, tied accommodation, obligations of confidence, and covenants in restraint of trade. It is important to stress that the jurisdiction of the employment tribunals in these circumstances is limited to cases that *arise or are outstanding on the termination of an employee's contract of employment*, and not otherwise. A claim for damages arising out of an alleged breach of contract by an employer must be presented within three months of the effective date of termination of the employee's contract of employment. Counter-claims must be submitted by an employer not later than six weeks from the date on which the employer receives a copy of the employee's originating application (Form IT1) from the Secretary to the Tribunals.

- There is an upper limit of £25,000 on the amount a tribunal may award in breach of employment contract cases. A claimant seeking higher damages should do so in the civil courts (which retain concurrent jurisdiction).

Illegal contracts

- Any employee who enters into an illegal contract of employment may find to his (or her) cost that the contract in question will be held to be void and unenforceable by the tribunals and courts. Such an employee would be denied his common law right to sue for wrongful dismissal, and would be unable to enforce his statutory employment rights including his right to claim a redundancy payment or to present a complaint of unfair dismissal (which latter rights are dependent on the existence of a valid contract of employment and a period of continuous service under that contract).

- What then is an illegal contract? Such a contract may include an undertaking by an employer not to deduct PAYE tax or National Insurance contributions from the employee's earnings (*Napier v National Business Agency Limited* [1951] 2 All ER 264). However, in *Lightfoot v D & J Sporting Limited* [1996] IRLR 64, it was pointed out that there *is* a distinction between tax evasion (which is unlawful) and tax avoidance (which is perfectly legitimate). A contract is not rendered illegal by an employee's lawful efforts to minimise his tax liabilities.

- A contract under which an employee is hired specifically to carry out illegal or immoral acts (eg, to procure prostitutes for the entertainment of his employer's business clients) will also be unenforceable (*Coral Leisure Group Limited v Barnett* [1981] IRLR 204), as would a contract under which an employer recruits an illegal immigrant, in contravention of the Asylum & Immigration Act 1996, or in circumstances in which the employee does not possess a valid work permit (*Sharman v Hindu Temple* (1991) unreported, EAT 253/90) – although the outcome in each case will depend on its particular circumstances.

- In the *Coral* case referred to in the previous paragraph, a public relations executive occasionally procured prostitutes at his employer's behest for the entertainment of his employer's business clients. The tribunal held that, although the employee had acted unlawfully in carrying out his legitimate duties, he had not been hired for that specific purpose. His contract remained valid and enforceable and he retained the right to present a complaint of unfair dismissal. Were this not the case, an HGV driver or sales representative (in less dramatic circumstances) would run the risk of invalidating his (or her) contract of employment every time he ignored a red traffic light or exceeded the speed limit in the course of carrying out his normal duties.

- A contract of employment entered into legally at the outset may become illegal with the passage of time. This may arise if, for example, an employer decides at some later date not to deduct tax or national insurance contributions from an employee's wages. A similar situation arose in *Salveson v Simmons* [1994] IRLR 52, when a farm manager illegally arranged to have part of his salary paid tax-free into a business that he owned. When the farm changed hands, the new owner refused to continue this arrangement. The farm manager resigned and presented a complaint of unfair constructive dismissal. The tribunal held the tax evasion to which he had been a party had rendered his contract void, in spite of his claim that he did not know that the arrangement had been illegal. Ignorance of the law is no excuse.

See also the sections titled **Collective agreements, Conciliation officers, Cooperation, employee's duty of, Disobedience, Equal pay and conditions, Fidelity and trust, employee's duty of, Notice of termination of employment**, and **Written statement of employment particulars**.

CONVICTED PERSONS, EMPLOYMENT OF

Key points

- The Rehabilitation of Offenders Act 1974 effectively entitles a person with a previous criminal record to withhold information about any *spent* convictions when he (or she) applies for a job. Although there are exceptions to this general rule (see below), the rationale behind the 1974 Act is to encourage the rehabilitation of people whose criminal records would otherwise deny them an opportunity to seek, obtain or retain gainful employment.

Note: Under Part V of the Police Act 1997 (discussed later in this section), employers seeking reassurance about the suitability of job applicants for certain types of work (eg, work involving the care and supervision of persons under the age of 18) will be afforded an opportunity to seek and obtain information about convictions which have not become *spent* or, in exceptional circumstances, to receive details about all of an employee's (or would-be employee's) convictions (*spent* and otherwise).

- A conviction becomes *spent* if the person in question is not again convicted of an indictable offence within a specified period of years beginning with the date on which he (or she) was convicted and sentenced. As is illustrated by **Tables A** and **B** below, the length of the rehabilitation period is determined by the nature of the offence, the length of sentence imposed by the court, and the age of the offender at the material time.

  Note: An 'indictable offence' is an offence triable by a judge and jury in the Crown Court.

Effect of a 'spent' conviction

- Once a conviction has become *spent*, the person convicted is treated in law (subject to exceptions) as if the offence and the conviction had never occurred. Although there is nothing to prevent a prospective employer asking a job applicant whether he (or she) has ever been convicted of an indictable offence inside or outside Great Britain, or served time in prison, or been in trouble with the police, the candidate is equally entitled to answer 'No' in relation to any convictions that are spent. He cannot lawfully be refused employment for failing to reveal details of those convictions; nor can he be dismissed or otherwise prejudiced if, at a later date, his employer discovers that he concealed details of a spent conviction at the employment interview. Section 4(2) of the Act states that 'where a question seeking information with respect to a person's previous convictions, offences, conduct or circumstances is put to him the question shall be treated as not relating to spent convictions or to any circumstances ancillary to spent convictions, and the answer thereto may be framed accordingly'.

- It follows that any employee dismissed for having (or concealing) a spent conviction would be justified in presenting a complaint of unfair dismissal to an employment tribunal – given that the reason for his (or her) dismissal is unlikely to amount to 'some other substantial reason of a kind such as to justify the dismissal of an employee holding the position which that employee held' (but see *Excepted occupations* below). But, to qualify to bring a complaint of unfair dismissal, such an employee would need to have been continuously employed for at least one year and have been under *normal retiring age* at the *effective date of termination* of his contract of employment. Without those qualifying conditions, his only other recourse would be to pursue an action for damages in the ordinary courts.

Note: In *Property Guards Limited v Taylor & Kershaw* [1982] IRLR 175, the EAT held that the dismissal of a security guard, for failing to disclose a 'spent' conviction, was unfair – the more so as the job of security guard (although requiring a person of good character) is not one of the excepted occupations listed in the Rehabilitation of Offenders Act 1974 (Exceptions) Order 1975 (see *Excepted occupations* below).

Sentences excluded from rehabilitation

- Certain sentences are excluded from rehabilitation even if the person convicted is released from prison (for whatever reason) before serving-out his full sentence. These are:

  - a sentence of imprisonment for life;

  - a sentence of imprisonment, youth custody, detention in a young offender institution, or corrective training for a term exceeding 30 months;

  - a sentence of preventive detention;

  - a sentence of detention during Her Majesty's pleasure, or for life, or under section 205(2) or (3) of the Criminal Procedure (Scotland) Act 1975, or for a term exceeding 30 months, passed under section 53 of the Children & Young Persons Act 1933 (young offenders convicted of grave crimes) or under section 206 of the 1975 Act (detention of children convicted on indictment) or a corresponding court martial punishment; and a sentence of custody for life.

  Any other conviction and sentence is subject to rehabilitation under the 1974 Act.

Rehabilitation periods for particular sentences

- The rehabilitation periods for particular sentences are as specified in Tables A and B below. It is important to stress that the length of the rehabilitation period is determined by the length or type of sentence imposed – not, in the case of a sentence of imprisonment, on the length of time served in prison. In other words, the fact that a offender may have served only part of his (or her) sentence (eg, early release for good behaviour) does not alter the length of the rehabilitation period. This rule does not, however, apply to imprisonment with an order under section 47(1) of the Criminal Law Act 1977. In such a case, the person convicted will be treated as having served the sentence as soon as he completes service of so much of the sentence as was by that order required to be served in prison (*ibid.* section 1(2A), inserted by section 47 of the Criminal Law Act 1977).

Table A

REHABILITATION PERIODS FOR PARTICULAR OFFENCES SUBJECT TO REDUCTION BY HALF FOR PERSONS UNDER 18

A sentence of imprisonment or youth custody or detention in a young offender institution or corrective training for a term exceeding six months but not exceeding 30 months.	10 years
A sentence of cashiering, discharge with ignoring or dismissal with disgrace from Her Majesty's service.	10 years
A sentence of imprisonment or youth custody or detention in a young offender institution for a term not exceeding six months.	7 years
Any sentence of detention in respect of a conviction in service disciplinary proceedings.	5 years
A sentence of dismissal from Her Majesty's service.	7 years
A fine or any other sentence subject to rehabilitation under the Rehabilitation of Offenders Act 1974 (not being a sentence to which Table B below applies) (See also *Note* below).	5 years

Note: Suspended sentences are treated as if they had not been suspended. The rehabilitation period for an absolute discharge is six months; and, for probation, conditional discharge or binding over, one year. For fit persons orders, supervision orders and care orders under section 57 of the Children & Young Persons Act 1933, or section 61 of the Children & Young Persons (Scotland) Act 1937, the rehabilitation period is also one year. In the case of remand home orders, approved school orders, residential training orders, attendance centre orders and community supervision orders, the rehabilitation period runs on for one year after the relevant order expires. For hospital orders under the Mental Health Acts, the rehabilitation period is the period of five years from the date of conviction or a period beginning with the date on which the hospital order ceases or ceased to have effect, whichever is the longer.

Table B

REHABILITATION PERIODS FOR CERTAIN SENTENCES CONFINED TO YOUNG OFFENDERS

A sentence of Borstal training.	7 years
A custodial order under Schedule 5A to the Army Act 1955 or the Air Force Act 1955, or under Schedule 4A to the Naval Discipline Act 1957, where the maximum period of detention specified in the order is more than six months.	7 years
A custodial order under section 71AA of the Army Act 1955 or the Air Force Act 1955, or under section 43AA of the Naval Discipline Act 1957, where the maximum period of detention specified in the order is more than six months.	7 years
A sentence of detention for a term exceeding six months but not exceeding 30 months passed under sections 53 of Children & Young Persons Act 1933 (young offenders convicted of grave crimes) or under section 206 of the Criminal Procedure (Scotland) Act 1975 (detention of children convicted in indictment).	5 years
A sentence of detention for a term not exceeding six months passed under either of the Children & Young Persons Act 1933 or the Criminal Procedure (Scotland) Act 1975.	3 years
An order for detention in a detention centre made under section 4 of the Criminal Justice Act 1982, or section 4 of the Criminal Justice Act 1961.	3 years
A custodial order made under any of the Schedules to the Army Act 1955, the Air Force Act 1955 and the Naval Discipline Act 1957, where the maximum period of detention specified in the order is six months or less.	3 years
A custodial order under section 71AA of either of the Army Act 1955 or the Air Force Act 1955, or under section 43AA of the Naval Discipline Act 1957, where the maximum period of detention specified in the order is six months or less.	3 years

Sentences imposed by courts outside Great Britain

- A sentence imposed by a court outside Great Britain is treated as a sentence which most nearly corresponds to one of the descriptions mentioned in Tables A or B above, or in the paragraphs preceding those Tables.

Unauthorised discovery or disclosure of 'spent' convictions

- In practice, it is unlikely that an employer will learn of a spent conviction through official channels. Indeed, if he attempts to obtain such information from police or court records (or from records maintained by a local authority or other official agencies), he will meet with a sharp rebuff. If he obtains any information concerning a spent conviction by fraud, dishonesty or bribe, he is guilty of an offence and is liable, on summary conviction, to a fine of up to £5,000 and/or to imprisonment for a term not exceeding six months. See also *References* below.

- It is an offence also for any person having custody of or access to official records to reveal information about a person's convictions to a third party. The penalty on conviction is a fine of up to £2,500.

Excepted occupations

- Under the Rehabilitation of Offenders Act 1974 (Exceptions) Order 1975, as amended, and by the Osteopaths Act 1993 and the Chiropractors Act 1994, convicted persons seeking employment in the occupations listed below do not enjoy the protection of the 1974 Act. Thus, any person with a spent conviction applying for employment as a:
    - medical practitioner;
    - barrister, advocate (in Scotland) or solicitor;
    - chartered accountant, certified accountant;
    - dentist, dental hygienist, dental auxiliary;
    - veterinary surgeon;
    - nurse, midwife;
    - ophthalmic optician, dispensing optician;
    - pharmaceutical chemist;
    - registered teacher (in Scotland);

- or any profession to which the Professions Supplementary to Medicine Act 1960 applies;
- registered osteopath; or
- registered chiropractor,

must reveal details of any and all convictions, including *spent* convictions. Such information must also be disclosed in relation to:

- judicial appointments;
- employment in the police force, or in the prison service, or as a traffic warden, or in certain occupations involving the provision of social services or health services; and
- work concerned with the provision to persons aged under 18 of accommodation, care, leisure and recreational facilities, schooling, social services, supervision or training.

Other regulated occupations include that of firearms dealer; a director, controller or manager of an insurance company; a dealer in securities; a manager or trustee under a unit trust scheme; a person applying to the police or to a court of summary jurisdiction for a licence to keep explosives; and a person seeking a Gaming Board licence.

- Answers to questions relating to any offence involving fraud or dishonesty, which are put to a person by a building society (or by or on behalf of the Building Societies Commission), in order to assess the suitability of that person to be a director or other officer of a building society, must likewise reveal details of all such convictions (spent or otherwise).

References

- An employer *may* disclose details of a spent conviction in a reference given to a prospective employer, always provided that the disclosure is made without malice or as the result of information improperly obtained. Otherwise, he could be sued for damages for libel and will not be entitled to rely upon the defence of 'justification'. If he chooses not to reveal that information and is subsequently sued by the second employer for the tort of deceit, the 1974 Act provides him with a statutory defence. Section 4(2)(b) states that any person questioned by another person about an employee's (or would-be employee's) previous convictions 'shall not be subjected to any liability or otherwise prejudiced in law by reason of any failure to acknowledge or disclose a spent conviction or any circumstances ancillary to a spent conviction'.

On balance, an employer would be well-advised to keep such information to himself. See also **Data protection** and **References** elsewhere in this handbook.

Personnel records

- Personnel records containing details of employees' convictions should likewise be kept well away from prying eyes, bearing in mind also that any convictions that were not spent at the time those records were prepared could well become spent with the passage of time.

Police Act 1997

- Provisions in the Police Act 1997 enable employers who are suspicious (or remain unconvinced) that people applying for *excepted occupations* and other sensitive jobs (including work with children and young persons under 18) are telling the whole truth when claiming that they have no criminal convictions (spent or otherwise).

  The scheme is administered by the Criminal Records Bureau (CRB) (an executive agency of the Home Office)(see *Further information* below). The Bureau may issue:

  (a) a criminal conviction certificate (CCC);

  (b) a criminal record certificate (CRC); or

  (c) an enhanced criminal record certificate (ECRC)

  to any individual (or, where appropriate, to any registered body corporate or unincorporate) who or which applies for such a certificate (using a form prescribed for that purpose) and who pays the prescribed disclosure fee (£12). The registration fee for bodies corporate or unicorporate is £300 (and for each countersignatory: £5).

Criminal conviction certificate

- An employer seeking to fill a particular vacancy (eg, as a nightwatchman or as a security guard) may require a job applicant to produce a criminal conviction certificate (CCC) in support of his (or her) application. The latter will give prescribed details of the applicant's every criminal conviction (other than a conviction which has since become *spent* within the meaning of the Rehabilitation of Offenders Act 1974). If there is no record of any unspent convictions, the CCC will state that fact (*ibid.* section 112).

- An applicant who has been issued with a CCC will not normally be issued with another CCC for a prescribed period. In this context, the term 'prescribed' means prescribed by regulations made by the Secretary of State.

Criminal record certificate

- A criminal record certificate (or CRC) is a certificate which gives the details of *every* conviction (including every *spent* conviction) and every police caution in respect of an offence admitted to by the applicant at the time the caution was given. A CRC may be required by a would-be employer in support of a person's application for employment in (or appointment to) one of the *excepted occupations* listed earlier in this section. As with a CCC, a CRC may also state that the applicant has had no criminal convictions or cautions (*ibid.* section 113).

- Every application for a CRC using the prescribed form must be counter-signed by a *registered person* and be accompanied by the prescribed fee. A copy of the CRC, once issued, will be sent directly to that registered person. The term 'registered person' means either a body corporate or unincorporate (eg, a private or public limited company, or a partnership), or a person appointed to an office by virtue of an Act of Parliament, or an individual who employs others in the course of a business. The names of all persons or bodies registered for these purposes will be listed in a register maintained by the Secretary of State.

- A body or individual applying for registration must satisfy the Secretary of State that he (or she) is likely to ask *exempted questions* or, in the case of a body corporate, is likely to countersign applications for CRCs at the request of bodies or individuals asking such questions. Exempted questions are questions relating to an *excepted occupation* (see above) in response to which a job applicant *is* obliged to disclose details of every criminal conviction, spent or otherwise.

  Note: An application for a CRC by (or on behalf of) a Minister of the Crown must be accompanied by a statement by that Minister that the certificate is required for the purposes of an exempted question asked in the course of considering the applicant's suitability for an appointment by or under the Crown.

Enhanced criminal record certificate (ECRC)

- An enhanced criminal record certificate (ECRC) will be available to individuals applying for positions which involve regular caring for, training, supervising or being in sole charge of young persons under 18. It will also be available to people applying for certain statutory licensing purposes (see below) and for those being considered for judicial appointments. As is the case with the criminal records certificate (CRC), the ECRC will contain information on 'spent' and 'unspent' convictions and police cautions. It will also include information from local police files including elevant non-conviction information. It could also be made available to those caring for vulnerable adults (*per* the Police Act (Enhanced Criminal Record Certificates) (Protection of Vulnerable Adults) Regulations 2002 and the eponymous Scotland Regulations 2002 (*ibid.* sections 115 and 116).

- The procedure for applying for an ECRC is the same as that for a CRC except that an application for an ECRC must be accompanied by a statement by the registered person who countersigns it that the certificate is required for the purposes of an exempted question asked:

(a) in the course of considering the applicant's suitability for a position (whether paid or unpaid) which involves regularly caring for, training, supervising or being in sole charge of persons under 18; or for a position with the same or similar duties and responsibilities which is of a kind specified in regulations made by the Secretary of State; or

(b) for a purpose relating to:

- gaming certificates, certificates of consent or licences as prescribed by the Gaming Act 1968;

- registration or certification under the Lotteries & Amusements Act 1976 (societies, schemes and lottery managers);

- a licence under the National Lottery, etc Act 1993 (running or promoting lotteries);

- registration under the Children Act 1989 or under article 118 of the Children (Northern Ireland) Order 1995 (child minding and day care);

- the placing of children with foster parents in accordance with any provision of, or made by, the Children Act 1989 or the Children (Northern Ireland) Order 1995 (welfare of privately fostered children);

- the approval of any person as a foster carer by virtue of the relevant provisions of the Social Work (Scotland) Act 1968, the exercise by a local authority of their functions under the Foster Children (Scotland) Act 1984, or the placing of children with foster parents by virtue of section 70 of the Children (Scotland) Act 1995 (disposal of referral by children's hearing).

Evidence of identity

- A person applying for a CCC, CRC or ECRC will be expected to produce evidence of his (or her) identity. If there is any doubt as to the true identity of an applicant, he may be required to have his fingerprints taken. Regulations dealing with the taking of fingerprints may make provision requiring their destruction in specified circumstances and by specified persons (*ibid.* section 118).

Offences: unauthorised disclosure

- Any member, officer or employee of a body registered for the purposes described above who discloses information contained in a CRC or ECRC is guilty of an offence under the 1997 Act unless he (or she) discloses it in the course of his duties to other members, officers or employees of that registered body who have a direct interest in the information contained in the certificate. The penalty on summary conviction for unlawful disclosure is imprisonment for a term not exceeding six months and/or a fine of up to £1,000 (*ibid.* section 124).

- However, no offence is committed if the information contained in a CRC or ECRC is disclosed:

  (a) with the written consent of the applicant for the certificate; or

  (b) to a government department; or

  (c) to a person appointed to an office by virtue of any enactment; or

  (d) in accordance with an obligation to provide information under or by virtue of any enactment; or

  (e) for the purpose of answering an exempted question in relation to an application for employment in (or appointment to) an *excepted occupation* within the meaning of the Rehabilitation of Offenders Act 1974 (as discussed earlier in this section); or

  (f) for some other purpose specified in regulations made by the Secretary of State (*ibid.*).

Further information

- For further information on the work of the CRB (registration, applications forms, codes of practice, publications, frequently asked questions, etc) the reader is commended to websites www.crb.gov.uk and www.disclosure.gov.uk. Employers may write to the CRB at PO Box 110, Liverpool, L3 6ZZ or telephone the CRB's Information Line on 0870 90 90 811.

Data protection implications

- Under the Data Protection Act 1998, sensitive information, including information about an employee's criminal convictions, may not be stored in a paper-based or computerised filing system without the employee's express permission – unless there is some justification for the keeping of that information and appropriate measures are taken to prevent unauthorised access to it. For further particulars, please turn to the section titled **Data protection** elsewhere in this handbook.

COOPERATION, EMPLOYEE'S DUTY OF

Key points

- Implicit in every contract of employment is the employee's duty to cooperate with his (or her) employer. This means obeying his employer's lawful and reasonable instructions, and doing his job efficiently and to the best of his capabilities.

- The shop assistant who is dilatory in attending to the needs of customers, or the secretary who takes two hours to type a one-page memorandum, could each be said to be lacking in cooperation even though both might argue that they are doing what they have been paid to do, if not as fast as their employer might wish.

- The receptionist at the front desk who is always grubby and untidy, or who deals with clients and visitors in a peremptory fashion, is not only damaging his (or her) employer's good name and commercial objectives, but is also in breach of contract and is liable to be dismissed.

- Whether or not such conduct justifies summary dismissal would depend on the seriousness of the offence, its immediate consequences, the size of the employer's organisation and the damage it has caused. The manager who swears at a valued client could justifiably be dismissed 'on the spot', although a preliminary investigation of the facts and circumstances is always advisable in such cases (especially if his (or her) conduct is wholly out of character). An employee, on the other hand, who is somewhat curt with a client, should be taken to one side and cautioned that a repetition could result in dismissal.

Note: As was pointed out by the House of Lords in *Polkey v Dayton Services Limited* [1987] IRLR 503, it is an unwise employer indeed who ignores his (or her) own disciplinary procedures when dismissing an allegedly uncooperative employee (or, for that matter, any employee). A failure to consult or warn an employee about the consequences of his (or her) actions (or to dismiss that employee on the spot without benefit of even a cursory investigation of the circumstances) will usually be held to have been unfair.

- The implied duty of cooperation often finds expression in the disciplinary or house rules made known to employees when they first start work with their employer. In the absence of such rules, an employment tribunal might well challenge an employer's 'reasonableness' in dismissing an employee who is unaware of the standard of conduct expected of him (or her) (see **Disciplinary rules and procedures** elsewhere in this handbook).

Overtime working

- An employee who refuses to work overtime on an isolated occasion would be less at risk than the employee who refuses to work overtime on any occasion (but see *Note* below). Again, a great deal will depend on the circumstances at the relevant time (including the size and administrative resources of the employer's undertaking). For example, a refusal to work overtime in a small organisation employing just a handful of staff could do serious damage to the employer's business; in which event, a dismissal for a first refusal might well be justified. In a larger establishment, such as a factory employing several hundred people, a first refusal might lead to a verbal or written warning.

Note: The reader will be aware that, under the Working Time Regulations 1998, adult workers have the right to refuse to work more than an average 48 hours a week (including overtime hours) and young workers more than 40 hours a week. An employer who flouts the 1998 Regulations is liable to prosecution and a heavy fine. Furthermore, any worker who is subjected to a 'detriment', or dismissed or selected for redundancy, for refusing to work more than an average 48-hour week, may complain to an employment tribunal and will be entitled to compensation. For further particulars, please turn to the section titled **Working hours** elsewhere in this handbook.

- If an employee is expected to work overtime, when and as asked to do so, that requirement should be spelled out in no uncertain terms at the job interview and reinforced in the written statement of terms and conditions of employment issued to employees in accordance with sections 1 to 7 of the Employment Rights Act 1996.

Mobility clauses

- The employee who refuses to transfer from one location to another (eg, from a factory in Manchester to a sister factory in Bristol) could not be said to be lacking in cooperation if there is no express (or implied) mobility clause in his (or her) contract of employment. Indeed, an employer's insistence on such a transfer could very well prompt the employee to resign and pursue a complaint of unfair constructive dismissal (see **Constructive dismissal** elsewhere in this handbook). In some organisations (banks, hotels, building societies) it is standard practice for up-and-coming junior managers and graduate trainees to 'move about' – both to gain experience in their particular business or industry and to enhance their career prospects. Although there will undoubtedly be circumstances in which employment tribunals will identify an implied mobility clause in an employee's contract of employment, employers would be well-advised to stress this requirement both at the initial employment interview and as an express term in the written statement (or job description) issued to an employee when he or she first starts work. See also **Fidelity, employee's duty of** elsewhere in this handbook.

D

DATA PROTECTION

Key points

- Under the Data Protection Act 1998, employers who store and process personal data about their employees – whether in a computerised, paper-based or other relevant filing system – must ensure that the data in question serves a legitimate purpose; that it is kept under 'lock and key'; and that it is not deliberately or unwittingly disclosed to unauthorised third parties. Employees, for their part, have the right to be informed of the nature and scope of the data held on their personal files, the source of that data (*Who provided it?*), and the names or job titles of the people to whom that data has been or may be disclosed. They have the right also (on payment of a fee of up to £10) to inspect and take copies of most (if not all) of the documents concerning personal data about them that is held in their employers' filing systems. Although the term 'employee' is used throughout this section, it is as well to point out that the 'data protection' and 'subject access' provisions of the 1998 Act apply equally to casual, seasonal and temporary workers who may or may not be 'employees' in the strict legal sense of the word.

- Employees may challenge the relevance or accuracy of any personal data about them that is held on their employers' files and may apply to the High Court or county court for an order directing their employers to rectify, block, erase or destroy that data and any other personal data which contains an expression of opinion which appears to the court to be based on inaccurate data. But see *Transitional provisions* below.

  Note: 'Processing', in relation to information or data, whether done manually or by computer, means obtaining, recording, or holding the information or data; or carrying out any operation or set of operations on that information or data, including organising, adapting, altering, retrieving, disclosing, erasing or destroying it.

- The term 'relevant filing system' encompasses any non-automated or manual filing system that is structured either by reference to individuals or by reference to criteria relating to individuals, and that is assembled in such a way that specific information relating to a particular individual is readily accessible. Arguably, the contents of the typical personnel file are neither 'structured'; nor 'readily accessible'. Indeed, some commentators have expressed the view that, because they are unstructured, such files fall outside the scope of the 1998 Act. Others have argued, equally cogently, that they do not. Wiser counsel urges employers to err on the side of caution by applying the 1998 Act's 'data protection principles' (see below) to all personal data which relates to individual employees.

- Although the processing of personal data on a computer in a coded format may be appropriate from the point of view of security, it does not relieve employers of their statutory duty to disclose that data when an employee asks to see it. Coded data must, of course, be translated into plain English (and a hard copy produced) before it is made available to the employee.

Meaning of 'personal data'

- 'Personal data' means data or information relating to a living person (whether employee or worker, job applicant or former employee) who can be readily identified from that data (or from any other data held by, or likely to come into the possession, of that individual's employer (or former employer), including any expression of opinion about that individual and any indication of the employer's intentions in respect of that individual. But see *Information that need not be disclosed* below.

Sensitive personal data

- The 1998 Act lays down rules concerning the processing of so-called 'sensitive personal data' – that is to say, data that consists of information relating to a person's racial or ethnic origins, or to his (or her) religious beliefs, political opinions, trade union membership, physical or mental health, sexual life, or criminal convictions.

- An employer may not process sensitive personal data about an employee (or reveal such data to a third party) without the employee's express consent, preferably in writing, unless the data in question is needed for legal reasons or in compliance with an employer's statutory duties. Indeed, the 1998 Act allows that the 'processing' of data about an employee's racial or ethnic origins may be justified if the employer's aim is to monitor the effectiveness of his equal opportunities policy.

- Job application forms that require a would-be employee to reveal sensitive data should explain why that information is needed. For example, in certain trades and industries involving exposure to specified hazardous substances, health and safety legislation effectively requires women of 'reproductive capacity' to disclose whether they are pregnant or are breastfeeding or have recently given birth. Such information will need to be kept on file for obvious reasons (at least for so long as it remains relevant). Job applicants who have a liability to epileptic seizures, or who are insulin-treated diabetics, or who have a alcohol or continuing drug dependency, or who have suffered from a psychotic illness within the previous three years, may not be employed to drive large vehicles; and so on. The Rehabilitation of Offenders Act 1974 also requires job applicants (and, in some cases, existing employees) who are applying for appointment or transfer to particular occupations to disclose details of any and all criminal convictions (including 'spent' convictions).

The eight 'data protection principles'

- The 1998 Act lists eight data protection principles that differ slightly in subject-matter and content from the seven principles laid down in the now-repealed 1984 Act. Under the 1998 Act, personal data about an individual (whether 'processed' by automated or non-automated means):

    1. must be processed fairly and lawfully;

    2. must be obtained for one or more specified lawful purposes;

    3. must be adequate, relevant and not excessive in relation to the purposes for which it is processed;

    4. must be accurate and, where necessary, kept up to date;

    5. must not be kept longer than is necessary;

    6. must be processed in accordance with the rights of employees (or former employees);

    7. must be safeguarded (by appropriate technical or organisational measures) against unauthorised or unlawful processing, and against accidental loss, damage or destruction; and

    8. must not be transferred to a country or territory outside the European Economic Area unless that country or territory ensures an adequate level of protection for the rights and freedoms of data subjects (this principle is new in the 1998 Act).

In brief, an employer should only process personal data if the information held on an employee's file (computerised or otherwise) is necessary or justifiable:

- for the purposes of entering into a contract of employment (employee's name, address, age, sex, address, marital status, number of dependants, schooling, academic qualifications, employment history, etc); or

- in the context of an employee's (or employer's) statutory or contractual rights, duties or obligations (eg, doctor's sick notes, attendance records, performance appraisals, disciplinary records and warnings, health assessments, information about accidents, injuries or diseases); or

- for PAYE tax, National Insurance, or occupational pension scheme purposes.

- Personal data about an employee or worker should only be kept on file for so long as is strictly necessary. It follows, that personnel files should be 'laundered' at regular intervals to remove extraneous, invalid, irrelevant or out of date information (particularly important in the case of former employees). If an employee asks for inaccurate, false or irrelevant material to be removed from his (or her) personal file, the employer should comply, unless of course he disagrees with the employee's assessment of that information; in which event, the matter may be referred to the High Court or a county court for determination, although the latter option will not be available in relation to data held in manual or paper-based filing systems in existence before 24 October 1998 (see *Transitional provisions* below)

- Finally, and most importantly, an employer must ensure that appropriate security measures are in place to prevent personal data held on computer or in paper-based filing systems falling into the wrong hands. As indicated earlier, sensitive personal data should not be kept on file without the express permission of the individual(s) concerned unless there is an overriding legal or practical requirement for the retention of such data.

Access to personal data

- Under the 'subject access' provisions of the 1998 Act, employees have the right (at reasonable intervals and without undue delay, and on payment of a fee of up to £10) to be informed about any personal data concerning them that is held by their employers either electronically (that is to say, in a computerised format) or in their manual or paper-based filing systems. They have the right also to examine that data and to ask for the correction, updating or erasure of any data that they consider to be inaccurate or irrelevant. What constitutes *reasonable* access will depend on the particular circumstances. But two or three times a year would not be unreasonable.

Note: If revealing the source of contentious information on an employee's file means disclosing the identity of the person who provided that information in the first place, the employer must first obtain the permission of that person before doing so. If that permission is withheld, the employer must edit the information in such a way as to omit that person's name or other identifying particulars.

- Finally, an employee should not expect to be given access to personal data at a moment's notice. He may have to wait up to 40 days (the maximum under the Act), before that information is supplied. An employer who refuses to supply such data (or needlessly delays issuing that data) is guilty of an offence and liable on summary conviction to a fine of up to £5,000.

Evaluating an employee's capabilities

- Information held on computer or on an employee's personnel file, which expresses an opinion about that employee's capabilities, character, attitudes, conduct, performance, etc must be disclosed to that employee on request.

- Furthermore, an employee may challenge his (or her) employer's *sole* reliance on the computerised processing of his personal data to evaluate his work performance, capabilities, reliability, conduct, etc – the more so if decisions stemming from that automated evaluation are likely to have a significant impact on the employee's prospects for advancement or career development within the employing organisation. In short, the employee has the right to demand an intelligible explanation of the logic involved in such decision-taking and may write to his employer requiring him to ensure that no such decision is to be taken based solely on a computerised evaluation of his personal data.

Information that need not be disclosed

- The definition of *personal data* in the 1998 Act includes any indication of an employer's intentions with respect to an individual employee – which, at first sight, would appear to suggest that an employee is entitled to know whether he (or she) has been earmarked for a pay rise, promotion, redundancy, disciplinary action or dismissal. However, that is not the case. Schedule 7 to the Act (*Miscellaneous Exemptions*) makes it clear that employees have no statutory right to demand to see (or to be provided with copies of) documents whose contents comprise information processed for the purpose of management forecasting or planning

– the more so if the premature disclosure of such information is likely to prejudice the conduct of the employer's business (*ibid.* Schedule 7, paragraph 6).

- Nor need an employer disclose the contents of a reference relating to an existing or former employee that he (or she) has sent in confidence to a prospective new employer. Nor need he reveal the contents of a reference sent to some other body or institution which is considering an employee for further education or training, or that relates to the appointment (or prospective appointment) of an employee to any public office; or that is given in respect of any service the employee hopes or intends to provide to another person or organisation (*ibid.* Schedule 7, paragraph 1).

- Although not obliged to disclose the contents of references sent to other employers, that same prohibition does not apply to references supplied by one or other of an employee's former employers. However, section 7 of the 1998 Act cautions that an employer should be wary of disclosing the contents of a reference supplied in confidence by a former employer unless it is possible to do so by deleting the name and job title of the person who wrote the reference as well as those of any other person named or referred to in the reference. Furthermore, in deciding whether it is reasonable to supply a copy of a reference without the consent of the person who wrote it (or that of any other person named or identified in it), the employer must pay due regard to any duty of confidentiality owed to the individuals in question; the steps that have been, or should have been, taken to obtain their consent; whether they are capable of giving their consent; and whether they have expressly refused to give their consent.

Transitional provisions

- The 1998 Act allows of two transitional periods. The first transitional period ended on 23 October 2001; the second ends on 23 October 2007. During the first transitional period, personal data held in automated or computerised filing systems was exempt from some but not all of the 1998 Act's provisions. The processing of data stored on computer must now comply fully with the 1988 Act. However, as is explained in the next paragraph, most employers have until 23 October 2007 to comply fully with Act's provisions relating to manual or paper-based filing systems.

- During the second transitional period, manual (or paper-based) files in existence before 24 October 1998, need not comply with the first data protection principle (save for the right of an employee to access personal data held on those files), nor with the second, third, fourth and fifth data protection principles until the end of the second transitional period (that is to say, until 24 October 2007). Nor do employees have the right, during that second transitional period, to apply to the county court (or High Court) for an order requiring their employers to rectify, block, erase or destroy inaccurate data held on those files. In short, employers processing personal data held in manual files (set up before 24 October 1998) have some five years in all in which to 'put their houses in order' – by auditing and sanitising those files and putting the necessary compliance procedures in place.

- What is not yet clear (and this has been the subject of some speculation) is whether personal data added to manual or paper-based files on or after 24 October 1998 'enjoys' the benefit of the same seven (now four) year transitional period or whether such data should now comply fully with the 1998 Act. In her *Introduction to the Data Protection Act 1998*, the Data Protection (now Information) Commissioner states that personal data about existing employees added to files that came into being before 24 October 1998 is 'unlikely' to alter the character of those files unless that additional material 'produces a different effect on the overall processing operation'. Further information about compliance with the 1998 Act (notably on this latter point) on this point may be obtained by telephoning the data protection Information Line on 01625 545745. See also *Further information* at the end of this section.

Notification

- Under the since-repealed Data Protection Act 1984, UK employers who kept personal data about their employees in a computerised filing system or by other electronic means (eg, in a mainframe, desk-top, laptop computer, or on a floppy disc or CD), or who used the services of a computer bureau to store or process any such data, had no need to register that fact with the then Data Protection Commissioner if the data in question was held solely for the purposes of calculating and paying wages, salaries and pension monies. Even though registration was not required in the latter situation, the data stored on computer could not then (and cannot now) legally be used for any other purpose. Nor may it be disclosed to any other person except for the purpose of obtaining actuarial advice on pension issues or for use in medical research into the health and accident records of persons employed in particular occupations.

- With the coming into force on 1 March 2000 of the 1998 Act, and the concomitant repeal of its predecessor, the former system of registration has been replaced by a new notification regime. Under that regime, employers who store and process personal data about their employees (whether on computer or in paper-based filing systems) need not notify the Information Commissioner of that fact (although they may choose to do so voluntarily) if the processing is done purely for staff administration purposes – eg, for recruitment and selection or payroll purposes or in connection with an employee's employment and career history, qualifications, experience, promotion, transfer or training, performance, health and attendance, conduct and capabilities, or related personnel issues. Nor is notification required if employers do not use computers for processing personal data about their employees. However, notification is required if personal data about an individual is processed on computer for pensions administration purposes. Further advice may be obtained from the Notification Helpline on 01625 545745 (Fax: 01625 545748 or email: data@notification.demon.co.uk).

Employment Practices Data Protection Code

- In March and September 2002, respectively, the Information Commissioner published the first and second parts of a planned four-part *Employment Practices Data Protection Code*. Part 1 (*Recruitment and Selection*) and Part 2 (*Records Management*) may be downloaded from website www.dataprotection.gov.uk/dpr/dpdoc.nsf. Part 3 of the code (*Monitoring at Work*), in draft form, was published on 8 July 2002, and may also be downloaded from the same website. At the time of writing, a consultation draft of Part 4 of the code (*Medical Information*) had not yet been produced. It is as well to point out that the new code will not come into force until its four constituent parts have been formally agreed and published.

Further information

- It is important to stress that the above is little more than a summary of the principal provisions of the 1998 Act and should not be relied upon by any reader as his (or her) primary source of information on the 1998 Act – the more so as the Act itself is not only lengthy and complex, but contains a great many 'ifs' and 'buts' which have not been explored in any detail in these pages. Copies of the *The Data Protection Act 1998 – Legal Guidance* can be downloaded from website www.dataprotection.gov.uk. or may be obtained (along with related publications, guidance notes and codes of practice) from:

Publications
Information Commissioner's Office
Wycliffe House
Water Lane
Wilmslow
Cheshire
SK9 5AF

Telephone: (01625) 545700

See also the sections titled **Convicted persons, employment of, Disclosure of information, Medical reports, access to, Public interest disclosures,** and **References**, elsewhere in this handbook.

DEDUCTIONS FROM PAY

Key points

- As a general rule (there are exceptions) a worker's wages or salary are inviolate. This means that, in the absence of any statutory duty to make certain deductions from a worker's pay (eg, in respect of PAYE (income tax) and National Insurance contributions) or a relevant provision in the worker's contract of employment, an employer must not presume to deduct any other sum of money (for whatever purpose) without the written permission of the worker concerned or without the authority of a court order.

Protection of wages

- Legislation regulating deductions from pay (and demands for payment) is to be found in Part II of the Employment Rights Act 1996, section 13 of which states (*inter alia*) that an employer must not deduct any sum from the wages or salary of any worker unless:

  (a) his (or her) right to make that deduction is clearly laid down *in writing* in the worker's contract, or in the written statement of employment particulars necessarily issued to every worker (*qua* employee) in accordance with sections 1 to 7 of the Employment Rights Act 1996, or in some associated document, signed and dated, a copy of which must have been supplied to the worker in advance of any deduction; or

  (b) the worker had previously given his consent in writing to the making of that deduction.

- Furthermore, any term in a worker's contract relating to deductions from pay will apply only to incidents or events occurring *after* the date on which that term was agreed to by the worker and inserted in his (or her) contract. Likewise, any subsequent written consent given by a worker (concerning deductions from his pay) will apply only to events or incidents occurring *after* the date on which that consent was given. What this means is that an employer cannot lawfully require a worker to give retrospective consent to a deduction from his pay in respect of an incident (such as a cash shortage or damage to goods) that occurred before that consent was obtained (*ibid.* section 13).

Demands for payment

- The same principles apply when an employer demands a payment from an employee. An employer cannot insist on an employee paying him a sum of money (for whatever reason) unless his right to do so, and the circumstances in which he can exercise that right, are clearly laid down in the employee's contract of employment (a copy of which must have been made available to the employee *before* the incident that prompted the employer's subsequent demand for the sum of money in question). Alternatively, the employee must have consented in writing to pay a sum of money on demand. Again, the employee must not only have given his (or her) written consent *before* the incident that prompted the demand for payment but must also have specified in that consent the particular circumstances that would entitle the employer to demand such a payment (*ibid.* section 15).

Exceptions

- The rule restricting the right of an employer to deduct money from an employee's pay or to make a demand for payment does not apply:

  (a) to the recovery or reimbursement of overpaid wages or salary, or any overpayment in respect of business expenses incurred by the employee in carrying out his employment;

  (b) to third party requests for deductions (eg, under an SAYE scheme) in accordance with any relevant provision in the employee's contract of employment or that the employee had previously authorised in writing;

  (c) to attachment of earnings (or garnishee) orders made by a court (see Attachment of Earnings, elsewhere in this handbook);

  (d) to deductions (or payments) made (or required) by the employer on account of the worker's having taken part in a strike or other industrial action; and

(e) to deductions or demands for payment in response to a court or tribunal order requiring the payment of the amount in question by the worker to the employer (*ibid.* section 14).

- Although Part II of the Employment Rights Act allows that inadvertent overpayments of wages or salary may be recouped from an employee's pay packet without the prior written authority of that employee, doing so could give rise to problems under the common law unless the employee in such a situation is forewarned that any overpayments will be recouped and is afforded an opportunity to discuss alternative means of repaying the amount overpaid. Employers should make it clear to their employees (by whatever means) that overpayments of wages or salary, advances on pay, loans (and the like), will be recouped – either by a single deduction on the next available payday or (if this is likely to cause hardship) by a series of deductions over an agreed sequence of paydays. In other words, the employee in such a situation should be given an opportunity to talk the matter over with his (or her) employer before the latter acts to recover the amount overpaid.

Meaning of wages or salary

- The expression *wages* (or *salary or pay*) in this context includes any and all bonuses, commissions, fees, holiday pay, sick pay (including statutory sick pay) and other contractual emoluments paid (or payable) to an employee. It also includes statutory maternity pay, guarantee payments, and amounts ordered to be paid by an employment tribunal in respect of a breach of a worker's statutory rights (or in pursuance of an order for reinstatement or re-engagement).

- However, it does *not* include any payment to a worker by way of an advance or loan; any reimbursement of expenses incurred by the employee in connection with his (or her) work; any payment by way of a pension, allowance or gratuity in connection with a worker's retirement or as compensation for loss of office; any redundancy payment; or any payment to a worker otherwise than in his capacity as a worker. Also excluded are payments or benefits in kind except a 'payment' in the form of a voucher, stamp or similar document that has a fixed value expressed in monetary terms and is capable of being exchanged for money, goods or services (or for any combination of two or more of those things) (*ibid.* section 27).

Recovery of cash shortages from retail workers

- Persons in retail employment (shop assistants, tellers, cashiers, bar staff, waiters and waitresses, etc) may be required under the terms of their contracts (or have already agreed in writing) to reimburse their employer for any cash shortages or stock deficiencies for which they are responsible. If there is no such term in an employee's contract (or no prior written agreement), the employer cannot lawfully deduct a sum of money from that employee's pay packet (or lawfully demand a payment from that employee) in respect of such a shortage or deficiency (*ibid.* sections 17 to 21).

- Even if an employer does have the contractual right (or an employee's prior written authority) to deduct a sum of money from an employee's wages or salary in respect of a cash shortage or stock deficiency, the amount deducted must not exceed one-tenth of the *gross* pay due to the employee on that pay day. This means, in practice, that the employer may have to recover the full amount owed by instalments (*ibid.* section 18).

- Demands for payment from an employee in respect of a cash shortage or stock deficiency must be preceded by a letter or memorandum notifying the employee of the total amount payable in respect of that cash shortage or stock deficiency and of the payday (or series of paydays) on which payment (or payment by instalments) is to be made. Second and subsequent demands for payment must also be made in writing and must be made on the pay day on which payment is required. Any demand for payment on a day other than a payday will be null and void. As with deductions from pay, the amount paid by an employee on any one pay day must not exceed one-tenth of the *gross* pay due to the employee on that pay day (*ibid.* section 18).

- The one-tenth upper limit in respect of deductions or payments applies whatever the amount owed by the employee. If he or she is found to have been responsible for more than one cash shortage or stock deficiency, the aggregate of any deductions or payments must still not exceed one-tenth of the employee's gross wages or salary on any one pay day (*ibid.*).

- If, as is sometimes the case, a worker's gross pay in respect of a particular period is determined by reference to any cash shortages or stock deficiencies occurring during that period:

(a) his (or her) true gross pay for that period will be held to be the gross amount he would have received had there been no cash shortages or stock deficiencies during that period; and

(b) the difference between those two amounts will be held to be a deduction from the employee's pay on account of those cash shortages or stock deficiencies.

In other words, it is not open to an employer to exercise his contractual right to reduce an employee's gross pay because of a cash shortage and then to deduct or demand a further 10 per cent from the employee's reduced gross pay to recover the amount in question. The total of those two amounts must not exceed 10 per cent of the employee's true gross pay as defined in (a) above (*ibid.*).

Example: A cashier is ordinarily paid £200 per week. However, there is a term in his contract of employment that states that his gross pay for any week will reduce by £10 if he is responsible for a cash shortage or stock deficiency during that week. If there is a cash shortage of, say, £150 (for which the cashier is responsible), the maximum amount that may be deducted from his pay packet for the week in question is £20 (ie, 10 per cent of £200). As £10 has already been deducted, the maximum additional amount that may be deducted is also £10.

- Finally, an employer cannot legally deduct money from a worker's pay packet (or demand a payment from a worker) in respect of a cash shortage or stock deficiency if the pay day on which that deduction or payment takes place (or on which the first of a series of such payments or deductions takes place) falls after the end of the period of 12 months beginning the date when the employer found out about the shortage or deficiency (or, if earlier, the date on which he ought reasonably to have done so). In other words, an employer has 12 months within which to recover (or to begin to recover) the amount of any cash shortage or stock deficiency. If he ought to have established the existence of that shortage or deficiency much earlier than he says he did, an employment tribunal might well order him to repay any deduction made or any payment received 'out of time' (*ibid.* sections 18(2) and (3) and 20(2) and (3)).

Monies still owing on the termination of employment

- Should a person in retail employment resign or be dismissed before he (or she) has repaid the full amount of any monies owed to the employer in respect of cash shortages or stock deficiencies, the employer may (in accordance with previous arrangements, *but not otherwise*) either deduct all or part of the amount outstanding from any final payment of wages or salary due to the employee or demand repayment of that outstanding amount. In the event of a refusal to pay, the employer may have to sue for recovery in the ordinary courts (*ibid.* section 22).

Complaints to an employment tribunal

- A worker who considers that his employer has made an unauthorised deduction from his (or her) pay (or has demanded and received an unauthorised payment), may lodge a complaint with the Secretary to the Employment Tribunals. If a tribunal upholds his complaint, it will make a declaration to that effect and will order the employer to reimburse the full disputed amount. In certain cases, the tribunal will direct that any amount owed by an employee to his employer in respect of a cash shortage or stock deficiency is to be reduced by the amount of any unauthorised deduction or payment – in spite of the fact that the employer has already been ordered to reimburse that same amount to the employee (*ibid.* section 23).

- Complaints to an employment tribunal under the 'Protection of Wages' provisions of the 1996 Act must be lodged with the Secretary to the Employment Tribunals within three months of the date on which the relevant unauthorised deduction or payment was made. It is as well to point out that (as with most other statutory rights in employment) an employee does *not* have to resign his (or her) job in order to enforce those rights. Indeed, if an employee is dismissed (or selected for redundancy) for asserting a statutory right (whether before an employment tribunal or otherwise), his dismissal will be automatically unfair – regardless of his age or length of service at the material time even if it later transpires that the employee was not entitled to the right he believes was infringed (*ibid.* section 104).

Trade union dues

- An employer must not deduct trade union dues (ie, membership subscriptions) from a worker's pay (in accordance with check-off arrangements previously agreed with a trade union) unless he has received written authorisation from each of the workers concerned (*per* section 68, Trade Union & Labour Relations (Consolidation) Act 1992, as amended by the Deregulation (Deduction from Pay of Union Subscriptions) Order 1998).

Note: Itemised pay statements necessarily issued to employees must identify deductions in respect of trade union dues (as to which, please turn to the section titled **Itemised pay statement** elsewhere in this handbook).

- If a worker writes to his (or her) employer asking him to stop deducting union dues from his wages or salary, the employer must act on that request on the worker's next pay day or (if the request was not received in time) as soon as 'reasonably practicable' after that pay day (*ibid.*).

- Under section 68A of the 1992 Act, a worker may complain to an employment tribunal that his employer has deducted union dues from his pay in contravention of these requirements. The complaint must be presented within the period of three months beginning with the date on which the unauthorised deduction was made or (if there have been a number of such deductions) the date on which the last of those deductions was made. If the complaint is upheld, the tribunal will make a declaration to that effect and will order the employer to make restitution.

Political fund contributions

- Although content to have his membership subscription (or union dues) deducted from his pay packet under a 'check-off' arrangement, a worker may be less than happy about contributing to the union's political fund. To ensure that no such contributions are deducted from his (or her) pay, the worker must first write to his trade union in the following terms (*ibid.* section 84):

To: *(Name of trade union)*

POLITICAL FUND (EXEMPTION NOTICE)

I give notice that I object to contributing to the Political Fund of the Union, and am in consequence exempt, in manner provided by Chapter VI of Part I of the Trade Union & Labour Relations (Consolidation) Act 1992, from contributing to that fund.

Signature of Member:

Address:...Date: ....

The next step is to write to his employer confirming that he has written to his trade union in the terms outlined above and certifying that he is exempt from any obligation to contribute to his trade union's political fund. The employer must respond on the first payday on which it is reasonably practicable for him to do so by ensuring that no amount representing any such contribution is deducted from the worker's pay (*ibid.* section 86).

- A worker, who has instructed his (or her) employer to cease deducting political fund contributions from his pay, may complain to an employment tribunal if his employer has ignored his instructions or has responded by refusing to deduct any union dues from the worker's pay (while continuing to operate a 'check-off' arrangement for other members of the same trade union). If the complaint is upheld, the tribunal will make a declaration to that effect and will order the employer to repay the amount wrongly deducted from the worker's pay. Non-compliance with the terms of such an order (within the next four weeks) will prompt a further complaint to a tribunal and an order directing the employer to pay the worker the equivalent of two weeks' pay (*ibid.* section 87, as substituted by section 6 of the Employment Rights (Dispute Resolution) Act 1998).

See also **Bad workmanship** and **Dismissal for asserting a statutory right**, elsewhere in this handbook.

DISABLED PERSONS

Key points

- With the repeal of the largely ineffective provisions of the Disabled Persons (Employment) Acts 1944 and 1958, legislation relating to the employment of (and discrimination against) disabled persons is now to be found in the Disability Discrimination Act 1995, which came into force on 2 December 1996. Employers no longer need employ a quota or percentage of registered disabled persons; nor need they reserve 'designated employments' to be filled only by such persons.

  Note: Under the Disability Rights Commission Act 1999, the Disability Rights Commission (DRC) has powers akin to those enjoyed by the EOC and CRE (including the right to issue non-discrimination notices, to prepare and issue codes of practice, and to advise and represent complainants in court and tribunal proceedings.

- For the time being at least, the 1995 Act does not apply to firms or businesses that have fewer than 15 people on the payroll (*ibid.* section 7(1), as amended). However, that exemption is to be removed once the

Government has implemented EU Council Directive 2000/78/EC of 27 November 2000 'establishing a general framework for equal treatment in employment and occupation'. The exemption is to be removed on 1 October 2004, once the draft Disability Discrimination Act 1995 (Amendment) Regulations 2003 come into force. A copy of those draft regulations (published for consultation purposes only) may be accessed and downloaded from website www.dti.gov.uk/er/equality/disabili-tyregs.pdf.

Discrimination in recruitment

- It is unlawful for an employer to discriminate against a disabled person (who is a job applicant):

  (a) in the arrangements which he makes for the purpose of determining to whom he should offer employment;

  (b) in the terms on which he offers that person employment; or

  (c) by refusing to offer, or deliberately not offering, him employment (*ibid*. section 4(1)).

  In short, it is unlawful for an employer to discriminate against a disabled person by taking steps to ensure that no disabled person is interviewed or short-listed for any job vacancy within his organisation (regardless of the applicant's qualifications or experience or evident suitability for the job in question), or (if he is prepared to employ disabled persons) by offering employment on terms less favourable than those offered to able-bodied candidates appointed to the same job.

- This is not to say that it is unlawful *per se* for an employer to refuse to employ disabled persons. If a particular vacancy can only be filled by an able-bodied person, or is unsuitable for people with particular disabilities (perhaps because of the risks to health and safety associated with doing that job), or because the means of access or work equipment is incapable of being modified, the employer is not obliged to employ a disabled person to fill that job. If the rejected job applicant is unhappy with the employer's decision and decides to complain to an employment tribunal, it will be for the employer to show that the applicant's disability militated against his or her being offered employment in that job or that the workplace and associated equipment was incapable of being modified to accommodate the applicant.

Note: In *Ridout v TC Group* [1998] IRLR 628, a rejected job applicant suffering from photosensitive epilepsy claimed that she had been unlawfully discriminated against on the grounds of disability because her would-be employer had failed to make 'reasonable adjustments' (contrary to the 1995 Act) by interviewing her under fluorescent lights. The EAT held that a reasonable employer could not be expected to be aware of the problem unless she had taken the trouble to forewarn him of her sensitivity to such lights. In a not dissimilar case, that of *Murphy v Sheffield Hallam University* (1998) unreported, ET 2800489/98, an employer's failure to provide a sign language interpreter when interviewing a profoundly deaf job applicant was held to be unlawful, the more so as the applicant had made it clear, when completing his job application, that an interpreter would be needed. The employer was ordered to pay £2,500 in compensation.

- Any advertisement for a job vacancy (whether published in the local or national press, or distributed internally, or posted in an employment agency or newsagent's window), that suggests that the employer who placed it will discriminate against disabled job applicants, or that demands patently unnecessary qualifications, or that uses words or phrases such as 'dynamic', 'energetic', 'alert', 'articulate', 'must have a pleasing appearance or personality' (and so on), may be introduced as evidence before an employment tribunal in support of a disabled job applicant's claim that he was unlawfully discriminated against by the employer who placed that advertisement (even if the advertisement in question appeared after the applicant approached the employer for employment) (*ibid.* section 11).

- Furthermore, the newspaper proprietor or agency that knowingly publishes or publicises patently discriminatory advertisements is guilty of an offence under the 1995 Act unless he (or she) can show that he acted in reliance on a statement made by the employer that the advertisement was not unlawful under the 1995 Act and it was reasonable for him to rely on that statement. The penalty on summary conviction is a fine of up to £5,000. An employment agency or business convicted in these circumstances also risks forfeiting its operating licence (*ibid.* section 57).

Discrimination in employment

- It is also unlawful for employers to discriminate against disabled persons in their employ by paying them lower wages or salaries (or associated payments) solely because they are disabled, or by offering other less favourable terms and conditions of employment. To refuse to promote or transfer a disabled employee, or to deny him (or her) opportunities for training for further advancement or to improve his skills, is likewise unlawful. An employee, who believes he has been discriminated against in this way, has every right to challenge his employer's actions before an employment tribunal, and is under no obligation to terminate his employment in order to do so. If his employer responds by victimising or disciplining the employee for having the effrontery to question his authority, that too is unlawful and will inevitably lead to a further hearing before a tribunal (*ibid.* sections 4(2) and 55). For further particulars, please turn to the section titled **Victimisation** at the end of this handbook.

Dismissing the disabled employee

- It would be a foolhardy employer indeed who would dismiss a disabled employee (or select him or her for redundancy ahead of other more suitable candidates) because that employee is disabled, and for no other reason. If the purported reason had to do with the employee's conduct, capabilities, attendance record, lack of qualifications, or 'some other substantial reason' of a kind such as to justify the dismissal, it will be for the employer to satisfy an employment tribunal that he had acted reasonably and fairly in all the circumstances. In other words, an employer's decision to dismiss a disabled employee (or to select him for redundancy) is likely to be more closely scrutinised for evidence of unlawful discrimination than would be his decision to dismiss an able-bodied employee.

- In *Levez v Jennings (Harlow Pools) Ltd*, unreported, EAT/812/94, the EAT held that the admittedly less favourable treatment of a disabled employee who has been dismissed because of his disability can be legally justified. The defence of 'justification' is available to employers under the 1995 Act (but not under either the Sex Discrimination Act 1975 or the Race Relations Act 1976). If an employer finds it impossible or impracticable to make reasonable adjustments to accommodate an employee's disability, he may be left with no choice but to dismiss. In deciding whether such a dismissal is fair or unfair, said the EAT, an employment tribunal will need to balance the interests of the employer against those of the employee.

- In *O'Neill v Symm & Co Ltd* [1998] IRLR 233, the EAT held that an employer could not be held to have contravened the 1995 Act, when he dismissed a disabled employee with a poor attendance record, if he was unaware that she had been diagnosed as suffering from chronic fatigue syndrome (ME), no more than an employer could be held to have dismissed a woman for a reason connected with pregnancy if she had neglected to inform him that she was pregnant. Application forms inviting (understandably reluctant) job applicants to indicate whether they are disabled (or whether they are pregnant, breastfeeding or have recently given birth – a statutory requirement in some instances) should be accompanied by a statement explaining why that information is needed; although employers should be mindful of their duties (and the rights of employees) under the Data Protection Act 1998.

Complaints to an employment tribunal

- A complaint of unlawful discrimination under section 8 of the 1995 Act must normally be presented to an employment tribunal within three months of the alleged unlawful act – although a complaint presented out of time may be considered, if the tribunal considers that it is just and equitable to do so (*ibid.* Schedule 3, Part I).

   Note: In *Clark v Novacold* [1999] IRLR 318 (the first case to be heard by the Court of Appeal under the 1995 Act), it was held that a disabled person has no need to compare the treatment meted out to him (or her) with that meted out to an able-bodied person in similar circumstances. It is sufficient that his disability was the reason for his treatment. In short, a wheelchair-bound employee with a poor timekeeping record should not be treated less favourably than an employee who is never late for work. If the nature of his disability is the reason for his poor timekeeping, he has been treated less favourably in law. In such a case, it will be for the employer to satisfy a tribunal or court that his treatment of that employee had been justified.

Questions and replies

- Any disabled employee (or job applicant), who believes that he (or she) has been unlawfully discriminated against in contravention of the Disability Discrimination Act 1995 (whether by his employer, a prospective employer, or whomever), may question the person concerned about the reasons for his or her apparently unlawful actions. If dissatisfied with that person's written explanation (if, indeed, an explanation is offered), the person aggrieved may admit that explanation (or failure to explain) as evidence in any ensuing proceedings before an employment tribunal (*ibid.* section 67).

- The procedure is explained in the Disability Discrimination (Questions & Replies) Order 1996. The form prescribed for this purpose is Form DL56, copies of which (with accompanying explanatory notes) are available free of charge from the Disability Rights Commission (tel: 0870 600 5522) or may be downloaded from website www.drc.gov.uk/drc/informationandlegislation/page312.asp

Decision of tribunal and compensation

- If an employment tribunal upholds a complaint of unlawful discrimination, it will make a declaration to that effect and will order the employer to pay compensation to the employee (which may include compensation for injury to feelings). The amount of the compensation will be calculated by applying the principles applicable to the calculation of damages in claims in tort or (in Scotland) in reparation for breach of statutory duty (*ibid.* section 8(3) and (4)).

- The tribunal may also recommend that the employer take appropriate steps to remedy the situation that prompted the employee to pursue a complaint of unlawful discrimination. This means that the tribunal may recommend adjustments to the workplace, adaptation of, or modifications to, plant and equipment (including the means of access and egress), reallocating certain duties, and so on (see next paragraph). If the employer fails or refuses to comply with any such recommendation, the tribunal may increase the amount of compensation payable to the complainant (*ibid.* section 8).

Employer's duty to make adjustments

- If an employer's job specifications, terms and conditions of employment (including working hours and start and finishing times) or his recruitment, promotion, training or transfer policies place disabled job applicants and employees at a substantial disadvantage relative to their more able-bodied colleagues, the employer is duty-bound to review those arrangements with a view to eliminating their discriminatory impact and accommodating the needs of those applicants and employees (*ibid.* section 6).

- The same applies to any physical features of the employer's premises that could militate against the employment of disabled persons in those premises or prevent them carrying out their work efficiently. If the way furniture and equipment is arranged or designed inhibits access to a work bench or desk or makes it difficult for a disabled employee to carry out his (or her) duties, the employer will need to consider what adjustments are necessary to accommodate a disabled person. If some of the work a disabled person is employed to do is beyond his or her capabilities, the employer should consider the practicability of allocating those duties to another employee. He might also transfer the employee to another vacancy; alter his working hours; assign him to a different place of work; allow him to be absent during working hours for rehabilitation, assessment or treatment; and provide appropriate training. Instruction manuals and testing or assessment procedures may need to be modified. It may also be necessary to provide a reader or interpreter.

- Clearly, it would not be viable for all employers to invest large sums of money altering their premises to accommodate the needs of disabled persons – bearing in mind that those alterations may not prove to be cost-effective and may not be wholly successful in removing the discriminatory impact on disabled employees. Whether or not an employer faced with a complaint of unlawful discrimination had done all that could reasonably be expected of him to accommodate the needs of disabled persons, in the light of his financial and other resources, will be a matter for a tribunal to decide (*ibid.* section 6(3) and (4)).

Note: In *Kenny v Hampshire Constabulary* [1999] IRLR 76 (EAT), the Employment Appeal Tribunal held that an employer's duty under the 1995 Act to make 'reasonable adjustments' to accommodate a disabled employee did not extend to providing a carer (or nominating another employee) to assist the employee when visiting the toilet. Nor would they extend, said the EAT, in the case of a wheelchair-bound employee, to providing transport to and from the employee's place of work.

Meaning of 'disability' and 'disabled person'

- A person has a disability for the purposes of the 1995 Act if he (or she) has a physical or mental impairment that has a substantial and long-term effect on his ability to carry out normal day-to-day activities (*ibid.* section 1).

   Note: Any person registered as disabled under the Disabled Persons (Employment) Acts 1944 and 1958 is deemed 'disabled' for the purposes of the 1995 Act and for an initial period of three years from 2 December 1996; after which, he or she will be deemed to have had a disability and hence to have been a disabled person during that period. The certificate of registration issued to a person under regulations made under section 6 of the Act of 1944 will be conclusive evidence of that disability (1995 Act, Schedule 1, para 7).

- The expression 'mental impairment' includes an impairment resulting from or consisting of mental illness only if the illness is a clinically well-recognised illness. The effect of an impairment (physical or mental) is a long-term effect if it has lasted (or is likely to last) at least 12 months or it is likely to last for the rest of the life of the person affected. If an impairment ceases to have a substantial adverse affect on a person's ability to carry out normal day-to-day activities, it is to be treated as continuing to have that effect if that effect is likely to recur (*ibid.* Schedule 1, paras 1 and 2).

- An impairment is to be taken to affect the ability of the person concerned to carry out normal day-to-day activities only if it affects one of the following:

   (a) mobility;

   (b) manual dexterity;

   (c) physical coordination;

(d) continence;

(e) ability to lift, carry or otherwise move everyday objects;

(f) speech, hearing or eyesight;

(g) memory or ability to concentrate, learn or understand;

(h) perception of the risk of physical danger.

A person who has a progressive condition (such as cancer, multiple sclerosis, or muscular dystrophy or infection by the human immuno-deficiency virus) will be taken to have an impairment that has a substantial adverse effect on his ability to carry out normal day-to-day activities if the condition is likely to result in his having such an impairment (*ibid.* Schedule 1).

Severe disfigurement, tattoos etc

- A severe disfigurement is to be treated as a disability for the purposes of the 1995 Act unless it consists of either a tattoo (which has not been removed) or a piercing of the body for decorative or other non-medical purposes, including any object attached through the piercing for such purposes (*ibid.* Schedule 1, para 3 as modified by the Disability Discrimination (Meaning of Disability) Regulations 1996, referred to in the following paragraphs as 'the 1996 Regulations'.

Addictions

- A job applicant or employee who is addicted to alcohol, nicotine or any other substances is not thereby a disabled person within the meaning of the 1995 Act – unless the addiction (in the case of an addiction to drugs) was originally the result of administration of medically prescribed drugs or other medical treatment (regulation 3 of the 1996 Regulations).

Other conditions not to be treated as impairments

- Seasonal allergic rhinitis (otherwise known as hayfever) does not amount to a disability for the purposes of the 1995 Act unless the condition aggravates the effect of another condition. Nor are the following personality disorders to be treated as disabilities for those purposes:

(a) a tendency to set fires;

(b) a tendency to steal;

(c) a tendency to physical or sexual abuse of other persons;

(d) exhibitionism; and

(e) voyeurism.

Code of practice and guidance

- The following (priced) publications are available from the Stationery Office (Tel: 0870 600 5522) or by email from books.orders@tso.co.uk. Free text versions may also be downloaded from website www.drc.gov.uk/drc/informationandlegislation/page312.asp

  A Code of Practice for the Elimination of Discrimination in the Field of Employment Against Disabled Persons or Persons Who Have Had a Disability

  Disability Discrimination Act 1995 Code of Practice: Rights of Access, Goods, Facilities, Services & Premises

  Guidance on Matters to be Taken into Account in Determining Questions Relating to the Definition of Disability

  See also *Useful publications* below.

Occupational pension schemes

- Under section 16 of the 1995 Act, every occupational pension scheme will be taken to include 'a non-discrimination rule' relating to the terms on which persons become members of the scheme and members of the scheme are treated. The rule requires the trustees or managers of the scheme to refrain from any act or omission which, if done by an employer, would amount to unlawful discrimination under the 1995 Act.

Statements in director's reports

- Under paragraph 9 of Schedule 7 to the Companies Act 1985, every company employing an average of more than 250 people per week (including part-timers, but excluding persons working wholly or mainly outside the UK) must include in the directors' report attached to its annual accounts a statement outlining the company's policy in relation to the employment, training, career development and promotion of registered disabled persons.

Chronically sick and disabled persons

- Section 8A of the Chronically Sick and Disabled Persons Act 1970 (inserted by the Chronically Sick and Disabled Persons (Amendment) Act 1976) imposes a duty on the owners and developers of proposed new offices, shops, railway premises, factories, and other commercial and industrial premises, to consider the needs of disabled persons when designing the means of access to (and within) those premises, including the means of access to parking facilities, toilets, cloakrooms and washing facilities.

- Although the owners or developers of premises intended for use as offices, shops, factories, workshops, etc cannot be prosecuted for failing to comply with their duties under the 1970 Act, there is nothing to prevent a disabled person denied ready access to such premises (or injured as a direct consequence of the owner or developer's breach of his statutory duty under the 1970 Act) from pursuing a civil action for damages. In any event, when granting planning permission for new offices, shops, factories, etc (or for the conversion of existing buildings), local authorities are duty-bound to draw the attention of the person to whom planning permission has been granted to the relevant provisions of the 1970 Act and to the Code of Practice for Access for the Disabled to Buildings (per section 76, Town & Country Planning Act 1990).

- See also **Dismissal for asserting a statutory right** and **Victimisation** elsewhere in this handbook.

Useful publications

- The following leaflets are available free from the Disability Rights Commission on 0870 600 5522. Most of these may also be downloaded from website www.drc.gov.uk/drc/informationandlegislation/page312.asp, All are available in alternative formats (eg, Braille and audio cassette).

  A Brief Guide to the Disability Discrimination Act (DL 40)

  The Disability Discrimination Act 1995: The Questions Procedure (DL56)

  The Disability Discrimination Act 1995: Some Useful Suggestions (DL200)

  The Disability Discrimination Act 1995: What Employers Need to Know (DL170)

  Definition of Disability (DL 60)

Employment (DL 70)
Access to Goods, Facilities and Services (DL 80)
Letting or Selling Land or Property (DL 90)
Definition of Disability (DX1)
Education (DL 100)
Public Transport Vehicles (DL 110)

A complete list of free and priced DRC publications is available from the same website.

**Copies of the Statutes, Regulations and Orders referred to
throughout this handbook are obtainable from**

STATIONERY OFFICE PUBLICATIONS CENTRE

(Mail, fax and telephone orders only)

PO Box 276, London SW8 5DT

Telephone orders:	0870 600 5522
Fax orders:	0870 600 5533
General enquiries:	0870 600 5522
e-mail orders:	books.orders@tso.co.uk

and from
Stationery Office Bookshops

123 Kingsway
London WC2B 6PQ
Telephone: 020 7242 6393
Fax: 020 7242 6394

9–21 Princess Street
Manchester M60 8AS
Telephone: 0161 834 7201
Fax: 0161 833 0634

68/69 Bull Street
Birmingham B4 6AD
Telephone: 0121 236 9696
Fax: 0121 236 9699

16 Arthur Street
Belfast BT1 4GD
Telephone: 028 9023 8451
Fax: 028 9023 0782

33 Wine Street
Bristol BS1 2BQ
Telephone: 0117 926 4306
Fax: 0117 929 4515

71 Lothian Road
Edinburgh EH3 9AZ
Telephone: 0870 606 5566
Fax: 0870 606 5588

18–19 High Street
Cardiff CF1 2BZ
Telephone: 029 2039 5548
Fax: 029 2033 8437

DISCIPLINARY RULES AND PROCEDURE

Key points

The written statement of employment particulars necessarily issued to each and every employee, in compliance with sections 1 to 7 of the Employment Rights Act 1996, must include a note:

- specifying any *disciplinary rules* applicable to that employee or referring him (or her) to some other document that specifies those rules (always provided that the employee has reasonable opportunities of reading that other document during his working hours, or it is made reasonably accessible to him in some other way);

- specifying the name or job title of the person to whom that employee can apply if he or she is dissatisfied with any disciplinary action taken (or penalty imposed) for any alleged breach of those rules; and

- specifying the *procedure* (including the time limits) for presenting and pursuing any such application.

If (as is often the case in larger organisations) an employee has the right of appeal to progressively higher levels of management, the procedure for doing so must be explained, either in the written statement itself or in the alternative document referred to in (a) above.

Exemption for small employers

- Until late 2003, when the present law is to be changed, employers with fewer than 20 people 'on the payroll' (including persons employed in other branches of the same business, as well as those employed by associated employers), need *not* include a note in the written statements issued to their employees specifying their disciplinary rules and procedures. Nor need the statement refer those employees to some other document containing that information (*ibid.* section 3). However, once sections 29 to 34 of the Employment Act 2002 come into force, that exemption is to be removed. After then, all employers, large as well as small, will be duty-bound to develop minimum statutory disciplinary and dismissal procedures (DDPs) (as well as statutory grievance procedures). Indeed, it will be an implied term of every contract of employment that the statutory DDP is to apply in circumstances specified in regulations to be made by the Secretary of State for Trade & Industry. Under those regulations, employment tribunals will be empowered to vary compensatory awards by up to 50 per cent where either the employer or the applicant employee has failed to use those minimum statutory procedures.

- The statutory DDP will comprise a three-step standard procedure for dealing with disciplinary issues in the workplace. For small employers, there will be a modified two-step procedure. Both will involve meetings between one or more members of management and an employee.

Disciplinary rules

- In the interests of health, safety and efficiency, let alone good order and satisfactory working relations, an employer should see to it that his employees know and understand what is expected of them and what penalties will be imposed if they break the rules. Some forms of behaviour will be self-evidently unacceptable; others, not. For instance, the average employee should not need to be reminded that anti-social behaviour (such as fighting, physical or verbal assault, sexual harassment, racial abuse, drunkenness, lewdness, theft, fraud, or the use of non-prescribed drugs) is just as unacceptable in a working environment as insubordination, persistent absenteeism, malingering, sluggishness, a breach of confidentiality, damage to company property, and any intentional or reckless disregard for health and safety rules.

- But some forms of conduct will not be so self-evidently wrong or dangerous. For instance, it would be *prima facie* unreasonable and unfair to dismiss a young or inexperienced catering worker for a first breach of the Food Safety (General Food Hygiene) Regulations 1995 if he or she had never been told of the existence (let alone the requirements) of those regulations. The same applies to the factory worker unfamiliar with health and safety legislation or with the risks associated with certain hazardous substances.

- ACAS Code of Practice 1 on *Disciplinary & Grievance Procedures* reminds employers that, when drawing up their rules, their aim should be to specify clearly and concisely those necessary for the efficient and safe performance of work, and those whose purpose it is to maintain satisfactory relations within the workforce and between employees and management. 'Rules,' says the Code, 'should be set out clearly and concisely in and be readily available to all workers, for example, in handbooks or company Intranet sites. Managers should make every effort to ensure that all workers know and understand the rules, including those whose first language is not English or who have a disability or impairment (eg, the inability to read). This may be best achieved by giving every employee a copy of the rules and by explaining them orally. In the case of new employees, this should form part of an induction programme. It is also important that managers at all levels and worker representatives are fully conversant with the disciplinary rules and that the rules are regularly checked and updated where necessary. Copies of the Code are available from ACAS Reader Ltd, PO Box 16, Earl Shilton, Leicester LE9 8ZZ (Tel: 0870 242 9090) or from website: www.acas.org.uk.

Note: Although the ACAS Code of Practice encourages employers to draw up rules necessary for the 'efficient and *safe* performance of work', section 3(2) of the 1996 Act states that the requirement to specify disciplinary rules and procedure does *not* apply to rules, disciplinary decisions or procedure relating to health or safety at work. However, it should be pointed out that section 2(2)(c) of the Health & Safety at Work etc Act 1974 imposes a duty on every employer to provide 'such information, instruction, training and supervision as is necessary to ensure, so far as is reasonably practicable, the health and safety at work of his employees'. Similar reinforcing provisions are to be found in regulations made under, or saved by, the 1974 Act.

- Many disciplinary rules will be common to all employing organisations. Others will be specific to the trade or industry in which the employee is engaged. For example, the licensee in a public house or hotel (anxious not to forfeit his or her liquor licence) would make it clear to his staff that they will be summarily dismissed if they sell or supply alcohol to persons who are, or appear to be, under the age of 18. The factory manager will be inclined to deal equally severely with employees found eating, drinking or smoking in prohibited areas (eg, in premises regulated by the Control of Lead at Work Regulations 2002). And so on.

- Most disciplinary rules will impose greater or lesser penalties for the following:

  (a) Persistent late attendance/poor timekeeping.

  (b) Theft or fraud.

  (c) Unauthorised possession of (or wilful damage to) company property.

  (d) Disclosure or misuse of confidential information concerning the company's business dealings, processes, methods of operation, activities or plans.

  (e) Drunkenness or the use of non-prescribed drugs while on duty.

  (f) Gross insubordination.

  (g) Fighting, physical assault, or abusive or threatening behaviour directed at customers, clients or fellow employees.

(h) Intentional or reckless disregard for safety and hygiene rules.

(i) Sexual harassment, racial abuse, abuse of the disabled, and other forms of socially-unacceptable conduct.

(j) Abuse of the employer's sick pay scheme.

The list is not intended to be exhaustive, but it does encompass problems common to (or likely to be encountered at one time or another within) most employing organisations.

- Once he has drawn up his rules, the employer should make it known to his employees that certain types of misconduct will warrant summary dismissal for a first offence and that other, less serious, offences will usually lead to dismissal (or a lesser penalty) if the offender fails to respond to formal verbal and written warnings. For instance, unauthorised absenteeism in a large organisation will ordinarily prompt a word of caution from the employee's supervisor, followed by a formal verbal warning and one or two written warnings if the offence is repeated. In the small organisation with just a handful of staff (eg, an office, shop, workshop or cafeteria), a single instance of unexplained (or inexcusable) absenteeism could be very damaging to the employer's business and might well prompt a warning that a repetition will result in immediate dismissal. The important thing is that employees should be aware of the distinction between serious and minor offences and the penalties that apply to each.

Note: As was pointed out by the House of Lords in *Polkey v Dayton Services Ltd* [1987] IRLR 503, employers should think twice before abandoning their disciplinary rules and procedures when prompted to dismiss an employee for misconduct or any related reason. A failure to follow those procedures (even in a situation in which an employer is convinced that following them would make no difference to the final outcome) will usually lead to a finding of unfair dismissal. However, once sections 29 to 34 of the Employment Act 2002 come into force (late 2003?), with the concomitant introduction of statutory dismissal and disciplinary procedures (DDPs), the tribunals will be empowered to disregard procedural mistakes, beyond the statutory minimum procedures, in unfair dismissal cases, if following full procedures would have made no difference to the outcome.

Disciplinary procedure

- No employee should be dismissed (with or without notice) until he (or she) has been given a chance to explain his conduct. The expression 'summary dismissal' should not be taken to mean a right to order an employee off the employer's premises without benefit of an interview or an investigation of the facts. If an employee's alleged misconduct is so gross as to warrant immediate dismissal, he should first be given a chance to explain his actions. If this cannot be done immediately, the employee should be suspended on full pay for a brief period (perhaps a day or two) until all the evidence has been collected, sifted and evaluated. If the misconduct is confirmed, then, and only then, should the employee be dismissed. These and related considerations are covered by paragraphs 5 to 33 of the Code of Practice referred to above.

- Paragraph 9 of the code states that disciplinary procedures should:

  (a) be in writing;

  (b) specify to whom they apply;

  (c) be non-discriminatory;

  (d) provide for matters to be dealt without undue delay;

  (e) provide for proceedings, witness statements and records to be kept confidential;

  (f) indicate the disciplinary actions that may be taken;

  (g) specify the levels of management that have the authority to take the various forms of disciplinary action;

  (h) provide for workers to be informed of the complaints against them and, where possible, all relevant evidence before any hearing;

  (i) provide workers with an opportunity to state their case before decisions are reached;

  (j) provide workers with the right to be accompanied (see *Note* below);

  (k) ensure that, except for gross misconduct, no worker is dismissed for a first breach of discipline;

  (l) ensure that disciplinary action is not taken until the case has been carefully investigated; and

  (m) ensure that individuals are given an explanation for any penalty imposed;

  (n) provide a right of appeal – normally to a more senior manager – and specify the procedure to be followed.

Note: Any worker who is required or invited by his (or her) employer to attend a disciplinary or grievance hearing, has the statutory right to be accompanied at that hearing by a co-worker, a shop steward or a full-time trade union official (*per* section 10, Employment Relations Act 1999). The chosen companion (if a fellow worker) is entitled to paid time off work to attend the hearing, may address the hearing itself or confer with the worker during the hearing, but will not be permitted to answer questions on behalf of the worker. An employer who denies a worker his (or her) statutory right to be accompanied at a disciplinary or grievance hearing will be ordered to pay the worker up to two weeks' pay by way of compensation. A worker who is disciplined, victimised, dismissed or selected for redundancy by his employer for having exercised that statutory right may likewise complain to an employment tribunal (regardless of his age or length of service at the material time) and will be awarded substantial compensation if his complaint is upheld. In cases of alleged unfair dismissal or selection redundancy on those same grounds, the worker in question may also apply to the tribunal for interim relief (see Index for further particulars).

- Section 13 of the Employment Relations Act 1999 defines 'disciplinary hearing' as meaning a hearing which could result in the administration of a formal warning to a worker or the taking of some other action in respect of the worker by his (or her) employer, or the confirmation of a warning issued or some other action taken. A 'grievance hearing', on the other hand, is a hearing which concerns the performance of a duty by an employer in relation to a worker.

Verbal and written warnings

- As was indicated earlier, a manager or supervisor will ordinarily intervene with a friendly word of caution (in private) when an employee commits a minor infringement of his employer's 'house rules'. This approach will usually resolve most minor 'misunderstandings' quickly. But, if stronger action (other than summary dismissal) is called for, the following procedure (as laid down in paragraphs 11 to 16 of the Code of Practice (*qv*)) should be observed.

  (a) The employee should first be given a formal verbal warning; or, if the issue is more serious, a first written warning setting out the nature of the offence and the likely consequences if the employee is again guilty of misconduct within a specified period. The employee should be advised that this is the first formal stage of the disciplinary procedure and that a record of that warning will be kept on his or her personal file.

  (b) If there is a repetition of the same (or the commission of a similar) offence, the next step will be a first or final written warning (as appropriate) that should again specify the offence (or series of offences) and include a statement that a recurrence will lead to suspension or dismissal, or some other penalty, as the case may be.

  (c) The final step will either be a final written warning or dismissal or, if allowed for by an express or implied term in the employee's contract of employment, demotion, a cut in pay, transfer to another location or department, or suspension without pay. However, disciplinary suspension without pay should not normally be for a prolonged period.

At each of stages (a), (b) and (c), the employee should be interviewed by his (or her) immediate supervisor in the presence of a more senior manager. The employee should be reminded of his statutory right to be accompanied and represented by a colleague of his own choosing or by his trade union representative, either to act as a silent witness or ready and willing to speak up on his behalf. The employee should be reminded of his alleged misconduct and asked to explain his conduct before a decision is taken. He should also be informed of his right of appeal to a higher level of management and the procedure for exercising that right if he considers that the penalty imposed at each of stages (a), (b) or (c) is unfair or unduly harsh.

Records

- An employer should keep a note or copies of all formal verbal and written warnings served on an employee. These should be treated as confidential and kept under lock and key. Except in agreed special circumstances, they should be destroyed if there are no further instances of misconduct within a period of, say, six or 12 months after those warnings were served; as to which, see **Data protection** elsewhere in this handbook

Fairness of disciplinary rules and procedures

- To be effective, an employer's disciplinary rules and procedure must be accepted as reasonable by those who are covered by them and by those who administer them. In other words, the tribunals and courts can and will challenge the fairness of an employer's disciplinary rules and their attendant penalties if relatively minor offences are characterised as major breaches of discipline and if the rules are interpreted inflexibly.

- In *Laws Stores Limited v Oliphant* [1978] IRLR 251, a supermarket cashier was summarily dismissed for neglecting to ring up a single jar of coffee on her cash register. Although there was no suggestion that the employee had been dishonest, the company nonetheless adhered to its own strict rule that a failure to observe the correct till procedure would result in instant dismissal. The Employment Appeal Tribunal (EAT) held that it was unreasonable for the company to impose the extreme sanction of dismissal for a single unexplained departure from the laid-down procedure.

- There was a similar outcome in the case of *Ladbroke Racing Limited v Arnott* [1979] IRLR 192. There, a cashier in a betting shop was dismissed for placing a bet on behalf of a pensioner. The employee's contract of employment clearly stated that staff were forbidden to place bets at any time in any of the company's betting shops, and warned that the penalty for a breach of that rule was summary dismissal. The EAT commented that rules that clearly warn of the inevitability of dismissal for certain offences must, nonetheless, be applied sensibly and fairly.

Status of a code of practice

- The ACAS code of practice referred to in this section lays down guidelines for employers in the preparation, dissemination and application of disciplinary rules and procedures. Although a failure on the part of any person to observe any provision of a code of practice does not of itself render him liable to legal proceedings, that breach is nonetheless admissible in evidence in proceedings before an employment tribunal. But, as Sir Hugh Griffiths remarked in *Lewis Shops Group v Wiggins* [1973] IRLR 205: 'Even in a case in which the code of practice is directly in point, it does not follow that a dismissal must, as a matter of law, be deemed unfair, because an employer does not follow the procedures recommended in the code. The code,' said Sir Hugh, 'is, of course, always one important factor to be taken into account in the case, but its significance will vary according to the particular circumstances of each individual case.' Once Part III of the Employment Act 2002 comes into force (late 2003?), the code of practice is likely to be amended to remind employers of the need to follow minimum statutory dismissal and disciplinary procedures (DPPs) before taking a decision to dismiss an employee.

Employment Act 2002

- Once section 29 and Schedule 2 of the Employment Act 2002 come into force (probably in the second half of 2003), all employers (regardless of the number of people they employ) will be required to adopt statutory dismissal and disciplinary procedures (DPPs) which may or may not fall short of their existing rules and procedures. Furthermore, the DPP is to be imported as an implied term in every contract of employment. There is to be a standard DPP and a modified DPP. As indicated in Tables 1 and 2 below, the standard DPP comprises a three-step procedure; and the modified version, a two-steps procedure. Regulations to be made under Part III of the 2002 Act will outline the circumstances in which either of these procedures is to be applied. However, section 31 of the 2002 Act allows that a failure to follow those minimum procedures will result in tribunal awards of compensation for unfair dismissal being increased or reduced by between 10 and 50 per cent. The award will be increased by between 10 and 50 per cent if the failure is attributable to inaction on the part of a respondent employer, or reduced by between 10 and 50 per cent if attributable to a refusal or failure by the complainant employee to comply with requirements of either procedure or to exercise his or her right of appeal under that procedure.

Table 1

DISMISSAL AND DISCIPLINARY PROCEDURE
Standard procedure

Schedule 2, Part 1, Chapter 2, Employment Act 2002
Crown copyright ©. Reproduced with acknowledgements

"Step 1: Statement of grounds of action and invitation to meeting

(1) The employer must set out in writng the employee's alleged conduct or characteristics, or other circumstances, which lead him to contemplate dismissing or taking disciplinary action against the employee.

(2) The employer must send the statement or a copy of it to the employee and invite the employee to attend a meeting to discuss the matter.

Step 2: Meeting

(1) The meeting must take place before action is taken, except in the case where the disciplinary action consists of suspension.

(2) The meeting must not take place unless the employer has informed the employee what the basis was for including the statement under paragraph 1(a) the ground or grounds given in it, and the employee has had a reasonable opportunity to consider his response to that information.

(3) The employee must take all reasonable steps to attend the meeting.

(4) After the meeting, the employer must inform the employee of his decision and notify him of the right of appeal against the decision if he is not satisfied with it.

Step 3: Appeal

(1) If the employee does wish to appeal, he must inform the employer.

(2) If the employee informs the employer of his wish to appeal, the employer must invite him to attend a further meeting.

(3) The employee must take all reasonable steps to attend the meeting.

(4) The appeal meeting need not take place before the dismissal or disciplinary action takes place.

(5) After the appeal meeting, the employer must inform the employee of his final decision".

Table 2

DISMISSAL AND DISCIPLINARY PROCEDURE
Modified procedure

Schedule 2, Part 1, Chapter 2, Employment Act 2002
Crown copyright ©. Reproduced with acknowledgements

"Step 1: Statement of grounds for action

4.   The employer must –

(a) set out in writing:

(i)   the employee's alleged misconduct which has led to the dismissal,

(ii) what the basis was for thinking, at the time of the dismissal that the employee was guilty of the alleged misconduct, and

(iii) the employee's right to appeal against dismissal, and

(b) send the statement or a copy of it to the employee.

Step 2: Appeal

5.   (1) If the employee does wish to appeal, he must inform the employer.

(2) If the employee informs the employer of his wish to appeal, the employer must invite him to attend a meeting.

(3) The employee must take all reasonable steps to attend the meeting.

(4) After the appeal meeting, the employer must inform the employee of his final decision".

See also the sections titled **Cooperation, employee's duty of, Dismissal for misconduct, Fidelity and trust, employee's duty of,** and **Suspension with/without pay** elsewhere in this handbook.

- The following is a suggested example of an organisation's 'Disciplinary Rules and Procedure', which readers are free to adopt (or adapt) for their own purposes. In doing so, they should bear in mind that once sections 29 to 34 and Schedule 2 to Employment Act 2002 come into force (very likely in the second half of 2003), those procedures may need be modified to ensure compliance with the minimum three or two-step statutory dismissal and disciplinary procedures (DPPs) discussed in the preceding paragraphs.

SAMPLE DISCIPLINARY RULES AND PROCEDURE
XYZ Company Limited

PART 1: DISCIPLINARY POLICY

The success of our business depends in large part on the qualities and capabilities of the people we employ; on their capacity for hard-work; and on their ability to work as a team. People who are disruptive or uncooperative, who indulge in anti-social behaviour or who are always challenging the authority of their supervisors and managers, not only undermine morale and good working relations, but sap the strength of the business. In some situations, they put their own health and safety at risk, as well as that of our customers and their fellow-employees. If such people do not respond to help, counselling, training or warnings, the Company may have no choice but to dismiss them.

However, we accept that every employee has the right to be treated fairly and consistently. If you fail to meet the requirements of your job – in terms of your conduct, attitude or performance – your supervisor or head of department will explain your shortcomings to you in private, will listen to what you have to say, and will ensure that you receive as much training, advice and encouragement as is necessary to help you improve. This approach will normally resolve most difficulties and misunderstandings. However, there will be times when a more formal approach is needed. Unless your conduct is so serious or damaging as to warrant summary dismissal (see below), the following procedure will apply.

Right to be accompanied at disciplinary hearings

Please note that you have a contractual (and legal) right to be accompanied and represented at all formal stages of the disciplinary procedure by a companion of your own choosing (who may be a working colleague, a shop steward or a full-time union official, but not otherwise). Your chosen companion will be allowed paid time off work to attend the hearing with you, and will have the right to address the disciplinary hearing and to confer with you during the hearing. However, he (or she) does not have the right to answer questions on your behalf. You have the company's assurance that you will not be disciplined, dismissed, selected for redundancy, or subjected to any other detriment for exercising your right to be accompanied and represented in this way.

Formal Verbal Warning

If you have been guilty of misconduct, or appear unable or unwilling to do your job properly (in spite of counselling, training and advice), you will be asked to attend an interview with your immediate supervisor or head of department. If your explanations are unacceptable, you will be formally cautioned that unless matters improve within a stated period, you will receive a formal written warning and could be dismissed.

A note of that formal verbal warning will be placed on your personal file – to be destroyed six months later if your supervisor or head of department has no further occasion to speak to you about your conduct within that period.

Formal Written Warning

If a formal verbal warning has not achieved the desired result, you will be called to attend a second meeting with your immediate supervisor or head of department (in the presence of the General Manager) and will be invited to bring along with you a colleague (or your shop steward) to speak on your behalf.

If your explanations are unacceptable, the General Manager will issue you with a formal written warning. The warning will state why it has been given; will name dates, times and places; will mention what additional counselling, training and assistance you can expect to receive (when and by whom); and will caution you that, if your conduct, attitude or performance does not improve within a stated number of weeks or months, you will be dismissed.

A copy of that formal written warning will be placed on your personal file. The warning will be destroyed after 12 months, if the Company has no further reason to discipline you during the intervening period.

Dismissal

If the formal written warning has not achieved the desired improvement, you will again be interviewed by the General Manager in the presence of your own supervisor or manager. You will be given a final opportunity to explain your misconduct or continued deterioration in work performance and may again call on a fellow employee or your shop steward to accompany you at the interview and to make representations on your behalf. If your explanations are unacceptable, you will be dismissed. You will be told when your employment is to end and will be sent or handed a letter (within the next three working days) explaining the reasons for your dismissal. The letter will also tell you what to do if you wish to appeal against your dismissal.

If you are dissatisfied with the Company's decision to dismiss you, you have seven working days within which to lodge an appeal. You should write to the Managing Director explaining why you believe you have been unfairly treated. The Managing Director will consider what you have to say, study the facts and the available evidence, speak to each of the parties concerned, and will make arrangements to interview you personally.

Appeals Procedure

The Managing Director's decision will be conveyed to you in writing within 14 working days of the receipt of your letter of appeal. His decision in the matter will be final. If he upholds the company's decision to dismiss you, he will notify you in writing and will inform you of your right (if any) to present a complaint of unfair dismissal to an employment tribunal. If he decides that dismissal is too harsh a punishment, he may offer you the option of a period of suspension without pay, a demotion, a transfer to another department or job, a reduction in pay, or a combination of one or more of those options (subject, in each case, to your written agreement in the presence of a witness). If he decides that you have been unfairly treated, he will order your reinstatement on full pay and (where appropriate) the destruction of all records relating to the incident or series of incidents that prompted your dismissal.

PART II: REASONS FOR DISMISSAL

The Company will not dismiss any employee without good reason. All allegations of misconduct, insubordination or poor work performance will be investigated. Unless you are guilty of gross industrial misconduct (that may lead to your immediate dismissal following a brief period of suspension on full pay while the matter is investigated), you will be given a second chance to set matters to rights. If you have a satisfactory explanation for your undisciplined conduct or your apparent inability to cope with the demands of your job, you will be given a fair hearing. If further 'on-the-job' training is seen to be necessary, it will be provided. If you believe that you have been treated unreasonably, you can appeal to the Managing Director. The penalty of dismissal will only be used as a last resort.

The Employment Rights Act 1996 lists a number of legitimate or 'permitted' reasons for dismissal. These are:

1. Incompetence – that is to say, an employee's proven inability to cope with the demands of his or her job, caused or aggravated by a lack of the necessary qualifications, skills or experience.

2. Repeated or long-term absences from work because of ill-health or injury.

   Note: It is clearly inappropriate to speak in terms of disciplining an employee whose frequent or prolonged absences from work are due to genuine illness or injury. In such cases, the Company will adopt a sympathetic approach and will reach a decision based on available medical evidence, the employee's age and length of service, discussions with the employee himself (or herself) and the nature and importance of the work he does.

3. Misconduct – including theft, fraud, damage to company property, disclosing confidential information to third parties (eg about the company's trade secrets, business dealings, pricing policies, etc), rudeness to clients, poor attendance and timekeeping, fighting, physical assault, sexual harassment, racial abuse (or other forms of bullying, on whatever grounds) and intentional or reckless disregard for basic rules of health, safety and hygiene, and other forms of socially-unacceptable behaviour.

4. Any legal disqualification – such as the expiry and non-renewal of a work permit, forfeiture of driving licence (if employed as a driver), etc.

5. Redundancy.

6. Some other substantial reason – such as an unreasonable refusal to accept changes in working hours, shift patterns or working methods, or the introduction of new machines, processes or technology, etc introduced in the interests of greater business efficiency and profitability.

Summary (or Instant) Dismissal

Should you be accused of gross misconduct, which amounts to a serious breach of your contract of employment, you will be dismissed summarily (that is to say, 'on the spot'), without benefit of the notice to which you would otherwise be entitled to terminate your employment with the Company. Any allegation of gross misconduct will be investigated speedily and thoroughly. If those investigations cannot be carried out immediately, you will be suspended from work on full pay until all the facts are available. You will then be interviewed by the General Manager in the presence of your immediate supervisor or manager and will be given an opportunity to state your case. If you wish, you may be accompanied by a colleague of your own choosing, by your shop steward or by a full-time trade union official.

If the evidence confirms that you have been guilty of gross misconduct, you will be informed that you have been dismissed and will be asked to leave the premises immediately. Written reasons for your dismissal will be sent to you within the next five working days.

Examples of conduct that will result in instant dismissal include:

- Theft, fraud, or unlawful possession of Company property.
- Wilful damage to Company property.
- Disclosure to an unauthorised third party of confidential information relating to the Company's activities, trade secrets, marketing strategy, pricing policy, etc. *(Note:* This does not apply to 'protected disclosures' under the Public Interest Disclosure Act 1998.)
- Drunkenness (or consumption of alcohol) while on duty.
- The use or distribution of non-prescribed drugs.
- Gross insubordination.
- Physical or sexual assault.
- Gross indecency or lewd behaviour.
- Abusive or offensive behaviour towards clients, customers or visitors.
- Intentional or reckless disregard for safety and hygiene rules.

In cases of unauthorised possession of company property, theft or fraud, or the use, sale or distribution of unauthorised drugs on the Company's premises, the Company reserves the right to refer such matters to the police.

Appeal Against Summary Dismissal

If you are summarily dismissed, you nonetheless have the right to appeal (in writing) to the Managing Director. If your appeal is upheld or a lesser penalty is imposed, you will either be reinstated in your old job or will be invited to accept a transfer to a different job or location within the Company at the same or a lower rate of pay. Subject to your written agreement, the lesser penalty of suspension without pay (for a *maximum* period of five working days) may be imposed in certain circumstances as the more desirable alternative to dismissal. The decision of the Managing Director will be final and will be relayed to you in writing within 10 working days of the day in which your appeal was received.

DISCLOSURE OF INFORMATION

Key points

- An employer has a legal duty to disclose specified information about his (or her) business activities and plans to:

  (a) *trade union representatives* for the purposes of collective bargaining;

  (b) *the appropriate representatives* (and to the Department of Trade & Industry), when contemplating redundancies;

  (c) *the appropriate representatives* when proposing the sale or transfer of the business (or part of the business) or when contemplating the purchase of another business;

  (d) *safety representatives* (appointed under the Safety Representatives, etc Regulations 1977), and to *competent persons* (designated as such by their employer under the Management of Health & Safety at Work Regulations 1999 and related legislation) to enable them to carry out their duties effectively; and

  (e) *employees* directly or to *representatives of employee safety* (*elected* by the employees, in circumstances in which there are no trade union-appointed safety representatives) on issues affecting (or likely to affect) their health and safety at work (*per* the Health & Safety (Consultations with Employees) Regulations 1996).

- Under the National Minimum Wage Act 1998, an employer has 14 days within which to produce the 'relevant records' (ie, wage and payroll records) to:

(f) a *worker* who has properly exercised his (or her) right under section 10 of that Act to inspect, examine and copy those records – in circumstances in which the worker has reasonable grounds for believing that he has been paid less than the national minimum wage.

- Under the Part-time Workers (Prevention of Less Favourable Treatment) Regulations 2000,

    (g) part-time workers may write to their employers seeking a written explanation for any alleged infringement of their rights under those Regulations. That written explanation must be produced within the next 21 days.

- Under the Fixed-term Employees (Prevention of Less Favourable Treatment) Regulations 2002, an employee engaged under a fixed-term or task-related contract may demand a written explanation from the employer,

    (h) if he (or she) believes that he is being treated less favourably than a comparable permanent employee working in the same establishment.

- Under the Transnational Information and Consultation of Employees Regulations 1999, a multinational employer must relay certain information to:

    (i) employees and their representatives in anticipation of (and following) the establishment of European Works Council (discussed at length, elsewhere in this handbook, in the section titled **European Works Councils**).

- Finally, under Schedule 7, para. 9 to the Companies Act 1985, the annual directors' report of every company employing 250 or more people must contain a statement describing such policy as the company had applied during the relevant financial year:

    For giving full and fair consideration to job applications from disabled persons ('having regard to their particular aptitudes and abilities'); for continuing the employment of, and arranging appropriate training for, those of their employees who have become disabled persons during their employment with the company; and otherwise for the training, career development and promotion of the disabled persons employed by the company.

Public Interest Disclosure Act 1998

- Under the Public Interest Disclosure Act 1998 (commonly referred to as 'the Whistleblower's Act'), workers (including employees), who make so-called 'protected disclosures' about wrongdoing within the organisations for which they work, have the right not to be dismissed or subjected to any detriment for making such a disclosure. A successful complaint to an employment tribunal is likely to result in the employer being ordered to pay the worker a substantial amount of compensation. The Act, which came into force on 2 July 1998, is discussed more in the section titled **Public interest disclosures** elsewhere in this handbook.

Collective bargaining

- Any employer who recognises an independent trade union as having bargaining rights on behalf of a particular group or class of employee, must disclose to representatives of that trade union information without which they would find it difficult to formulate their wage and associated demands – information that an employer would ordinarily be expected to disclose in the interests of good industrial relations practice. This requirement is laid down in section 181 of the Trade Union & Labour Relations (Consolidation) Act 1992 ('the 1992 Act').

Meaning of 'independent trade union'

- Section 5 of the 1992 Act (*qv*) *defines independent trade union as* meaning a trade union that:

   (a) is not under the domination or control of a particular employer or group of employers (or of one or more employers' associations); and

   (b) is not liable to interference by an employer or by any such group or association of employers (arising out of the provision of financial or material support or by any other means whatsoever) tending towards such control.

Information that should be disclosed

- Guidance on the type of information that an employer might reasonably be expected to disclose is given in ACAS Code of Practice 2 (*Disclosure of Information to Trade Unions for Collective Bargaining Purposes*) (Code CPO2), available from ACAS Reader Limited, PO Box 16, Earl Shilton, Leicester LE9 8ZZ (tel: 0870 242 9090).

Although the Code of Practice is couched in general terms, it cautions negotiators on both sides to take account of several factors when discussing which information should be disclosed. These include: the subject matter of negotiations and the issues raised by those negotiations; the level at which negotiations take place (department, plant, division or company-wide); the size of the company; and the type of business or activity in which the company is engaged.

The following points should be noted:

(a) An employer may, if he or she chooses, insist that trade union representatives submit their requests for information in writing (*ibid.* section 181(3)).

(b) Trade union representatives, for their part, may likewise insist that the information they ask for be disclosed or confirmed in writing (*ibid.* section 181(5)).

(c) An employer is *not* obliged to disclose information that, if made public, could do 'substantial injury' to his or her business or undertaking (for reasons other than its effect on collective bargaining). Nor need an employer disclose information that:

  – would be against the interests of national security;

  – has been communicated to him or her in confidence or that has otherwise been obtained in consequence of the confidence reposed in him or her by another person;

  – relates to a specific individual (without that person's consent);

  – is *sub judice* or was obtained by the employer for the purpose of bringing, prosecuting or defending any legal proceedings (*ibid.* section 182(1)).

Finally, an employer cannot be required to produce, or allow inspection of, any original document (other than a document prepared for the purpose of conveying or confirming information requested by trade union representatives). Nor can an employer be required to compile or assemble information if the time, effort and expense involved is out of all reasonable proportion to the value of that information in the conduct of collective bargaining (*ibid.* section 182(2)).

Failure to disclose information

• If an employer refuses or fails to disclose information to a recognised independent trade union for collective bargaining purposes, the representatives of that trade union may present a written complaint to the Central Arbitration Committee (CAC). If the Committee believes that the complaint can best be resolved by conciliation, it will first refer the matter to the Advisory, Conciliation & Arbitration Service (ACAS), which body will seek to promote a settlement. If ACAS is unsuccessful, the CAC will proceed to hear and determine the complaint, and will make a declaration stating whether it finds the complaint well-founded and giving the reasons for its findings. The CAC's declaration will specify what information the employer must disclose and within what time limits. If, in spite of the CAC's findings, the employer remains obstinate, the complaint will be referred back to the CAC which, after due deliberation, will make an award of terms and conditions to the employees represented by that trade union as specified in the original claim. If need be, the award will be enforced by an employment tribunal or, if preferred, by a civil court (*ibid.* sections 183 to 185).

- In other words, an employer who persistently refuses to disclose information, that the CAC considers to be essential to the collective bargaining process, may well have to accept wage increases and/or other improvements in the terms and conditions of his or her employees that might not otherwise have been conceded. In short, the CAC's award of terms and conditions would form part of the contracts of employment of those employees and would be enforceable as such.

Collective redundancies

- An employer proposing to make 20 or more employees redundant, within a period of 90 days or less, is duty-bound to discuss his or her proposals with the appropriate employee representatives. The employer must also inform the Secretary of State for Trade & Industry (in practice, the Department of Trade & Industry (DTI)).

- These requirements (explained in more detail below) are to be found in sections 188 to 198 of the Trade Union & Labour Relations (Consolidation) Act 1992, as amended by the Collective Redundancies & Transfer of Undertakings (Protection of Employment) (Amendment) Regulations 1995, and by the eponymous 1999 Regulations, which latter came into force on 28 July 1999 (but only in respect of redundancy dismissals taking effect on or after 1 November 1999).

Meaning of 'appropriate representatives'

- For these purposes, the term *appropriate representative* means either of a trade union appointed (or elected) representative or (in a non-union situation) an employee representative elected or appointed by fellow employees to represent their interests in discussions with their employer.

- Before the 1999 Regulations (*qv*) came into force, it was up to the employer to decide whether to consult with trade union-elected (or appointed) representatives or with employee-elected representatives. Under the new rules, that choice is removed. If the *affected employees* (that is to say, the employees likely to be affected by the proposed redundancy dismissals or by measures taken in connection with those dismissals) are of a description in respect of which the employer recognises an independent trade union, then the employer must consult about those dismissals with representatives of that trade union.

- Where there is no trade union representation, the employer may either discuss his or her redundancy proposals with existing employee representatives (ie, employees previously appointed or elected by the affected employees to represent their interests in a variety of situations) or invite the affected employees to elect one or more of their number specifically to represent their interests in respect of the proposed redundancies.

Election of employee representatives

- If there *is* to be an election of employee representatives, the employer must see to it that votes are cast and counted before the redundancy consultation process is scheduled to begin. The employer has the right to decide on the number of representatives to be elected (so long as that number is sufficient to represent the interests of all the affected employees) and must make such arrangements as are reasonably necessary to ensure that the election is conducted fairly. To that end, the employer must see to it that those entitled to vote in the election can do so in secret. Before the election takes place, the employer must:

   (a) decide on the term of office of the persons who are to be elected as employee representatives (ensuring that it is sufficient to enable completion of the consultation process);

   (b) make it known that every affected employee has the right to submit his (or her) name as a candidate for election; and

   (c) ensure that all affected employees have the opportunity to vote on the day on which votes are to be cast and that each employee has the right to vote for as many candidates as there are representatives to be elected.

Finally, the employer must ensure that the votes given at the election are accurately counted (*ibid.* section 188A).

Note: An employee has the statutory right not to be disciplined, victimised or subject to any other detriment by his (or her) employer for taking part in an election of employee representatives. Nor may he be dismissed (or selected for redundancy) on such grounds (per sections 47(1A), 103(2) and 105(3), Employment Rights Act 1996, as inserted by regulations 12 and 13 of the 1999 Regulations referred to earlier in this section). For further particulars, please turn to the sections titled **Dismissal** and **Victimisation** elsewhere in this handbook.

- If the affected employees decline their employer's invitation to elect one or more of their number as employee representatives, or fail to conduct the election within a reasonable time, the employer must write to each affected employee giving the information he or she would otherwise have had to disclose to those representatives (as to which, see *Information to be disclosed to representatives* below) (*ibid.* section 188(7B)).

When must consultations begin?

The timing of consultations is important. Section 188(2) of the 1992 Act cautions that consultations must begin at the very earliest opportunity – before the first of the redundancy dismissals takes effect. Specifically:

(a) where 100 or more employees are to be dismissed as redundant *at one establishment* within a period of 90 days or less, consultations with the appropriate representatives must begin at least 90 days before the first of those dismissals is to take place;

(b) where 20 to 99 employees are to be dismissed as redundant *at one establishment* within a period of 90 days or less, consultations must begin at least 30 days before the first of those dismissals is to take place.

Note: Use of the expression 'at one establishment' means that the redundancy consultation period may vary from factory to factory or from office to office within the same organisation. If, for example, a bank plans to make several hundred of its staff redundant throughout Great Britain over a given period, the length of the consultation period will vary from branch to branch – depending on the number of people to be made redundant at each of those branches.

- Although consultations must begin at least 30 or 90 days before the first of any dismissals takes place, there is nothing to prevent an employer issuing advance redundancy notices to the employees in question – bearing in mind that some long-serving employees may be entitled to notice (contractual or statutory) longer than the minimum consultation period.

Information to be disclosed to representatives

- For consultation purposes, an employer must write to each of the appropriate representatives explaining or describing:

  - why the redundancies are necessary;

  - the numbers and job titles or descriptions (but not necessarily the names) of the employees whom he proposes to make redundant;

  - the total number of employees of every such description (or job title) employed at the establishment in question;

  - how the employees to be made redundant were (or are to be) selected;

  - the proposed method of carrying out the dismissals, with due regard to any agreed procedure, including the period over which the dismissals are to take effect; and

  - how redundancy payments are to be calculated (if other than in accordance with statutory requirements).

  The letter or document containing that information must either be handed or sent by post to the appropriate representatives (to an address each has notified), or (in the case of trade union-elected or appointed representatives) sent by post to the union's head office (*ibid.* section 188(4) and (5)).

  Note: Where affected employees have declined their employer's invitation to elect one or more of their number to enter into consultations with their employer, the latter must write to each of those employees giving the information listed above (*ibid.* section 188(7B)).

The consultation process

- An employer's consultations with the *appropriate representatives* must include discussions about ways and means of avoiding the dismissals altogether, about reducing the numbers of employees to be dismissed, and about mitigating the consequences of the dismissals. Finally, they *must* be undertaken by the employer with a view to reaching agreement (*ibid.* section 188(6)).

Complaints

- An employee representative or (in the case of a failure relating to trade union representatives) the relevant trade union may present a complaint to an employment tribunal that an employer has failed to comply with his (or her) duty to consult about his redundancy proposals (including a refusal to discuss ways and means of avoiding dismissals or reducing their number, etc), or that the employer has failed to disclose written information needed for the purposes of consultation. Any such complaint must be presented to the tribunal either before any redundancy dismissals take place or within the period of three months beginning with the date of the first dismissal (*ibid.* section 189).

- An affected employee may complain to an employment tribunal that his (or her) employer had failed to comply with the rules relating to the election of employee representatives, or had refused to allow such elections to take place, or (in the absence of appropriate representatives) had failed to provide the written information that should have been provided in respect of the proposed redundancy dismissals. The burden of proof in such cases rests squarely on the shoulders of the employer (*ibid*).

- An employer may argue in his (or her) defence that there were special circumstances which made it impracticable for him to comply with his duty to consult appropriate representatives about his redundancy proposals, or to allow fair elections to take place, or to disclose the prescribed information in writing, or that he took all 'reasonably practicable' steps to comply with those requirements. However, it will *not* be a defence for him to contend that he was unable to disclose information about impending redundancies because that information had been withheld from him by the controlling employer (eg, a holding company, head office, or an employer located overseas) (*ibid.* section 188(7)).

Protective award

- An employment tribunal that upholds a complaint concerning an employer's failure to comply with his duties under sections 188 or 188A of the 1992 Act, will make a declaration to that effect and may order the employer to pay a protective award to each of the affected employees. A protective award is equivalent in effect to an employee's normal earnings, paid for a 'protected period' not exceeding 90 days (*ibid.* section 189, as amended by the Collective Redundancies & Transfer of Undertakings (Protection of Employment) (Amendment) Regulations 1999.

  Note: The rate of remuneration payable to an employee under a protective award is a week's pay for each week of the protected period and *pro rata* for odd days within that period – calculated in accordance with Chapter II, Part XIV of the Employment Rights Act 1996.

Non-redundancy dismissals and trial period

- If an employee resigns or is fairly dismissed (for a reason other than redundancy) during the protected period referred to in the previous paragraph, the employer's obligation to pay the remainder of the protective award ceases (*ibid.* section 191(1)).

- Likewise, if an employer offers to renew the contract of employment of an otherwise redundant employee or to re-engage him or her in suitable alternative employment during the protected period, and the employee unreasonably refuses that offer, the employer need not pay the remainder of the protective award always provided that the provisions of the renewed or new contract do not differ from the corresponding provisions of the previous contract (*ibid.* section 191(2)).

- If the new or renewed contract referred to in the previous paragraph is tantamount to a different job (perhaps with different duties and responsibilities), albeit on the same terms and conditions as the employee's previous job, the employee has a right to 'try out' that new job for a trial period of four weeks or for such longer period (as may be needed to retrain the employee) as is specified in a *written* agreement between the parties. If the employee not unreasonably decides (during or at the end of the trial period) that the job is unsuitable, the contract may be terminated *without more* and payments (if any) under the protective award reinstated. The same applies if it is the employer who decides that the employee is not suited to the new or alternative job and terminates the employee's contract of employment (with or without notice) (*ibid.* section 191(4) to (7)).

Complaint by redundant employee

- If an employer does not comply with an order to pay remuneration to an employee under a protective award (or ceases paying the award for whatever reason), it is up to that employee (not his (or her) employee representative or trade union representative) to refer the matter for adjudication by an employment tribunal. The employee must present his complaint on Form ET1 or by letter within three months of the date on which the employer's refusal or failure occurred. If the complaint is upheld, the employer will be ordered *without more* either to pay the amount due to the employee or face proceedings for contempt of court (*ibid.* section 192).

Collective agreements on redundancies

- If there is a collective agreement in force between an employer and one or more independent trade unions which establishes:

    - arrangements for providing alternative employment for employees to whom the agreement relates if they are dismissed as redundant; or

    - arrangements for the handling of redundancies; and

    - those arrangements are, on the whole, at least as favourable to those employees as the provisions of sections 188 to 197 of the 1992 Act,

    the parties to that agreement may apply to the Secretary of State (in practice, the Department for Education & Employment) for an order adapting, modifying or excluding any of those provisions both in their application to any or all of those employees and in their application to any other employees of the employer in question (*ibid.* section 198).

- However, the Secretary of State will not make such an order unless the agreement itself contains satisfactory procedures for the settlement of disputes concerning the application (or implementation) of the agreement – eg, arbitration or adjudication by an independent referee – or the agreement indicates that any employee covered by the agreement may present a complaint to an employment tribunal that one or other of the parties to the agreement has not complied with its provisions (*ibid.* section 198(3)).

Duty to notify the Secretary of State for Trade & Industry

- An employer who is contemplating 100 or more redundancies *at one establishment* within a period of 90 days or less must forewarn the Department of Trade & Industry (DTI) (in practice, the nearest DTI Redundancy Payment Office: see below) at least 90 days before the first of those dismissals takes effect. If he (or she) plans to make 20 or more employees redundant at one establishment within a period of 90 days or less, he must do so at least 30 days before the first of those dismissals takes effect (*ibid.* section 193). The prescribed form for this purpose is HR1. A copy of that form (once completed) must also be delivered or sent to the appropriate employee representative(s) or, in the case of a trade union representative, sent by post to the union's head or main office (*ibid.* section 193(6)). If the DTI asks for further information about the proposed redundancies, the employer must supply that information.

- Redundancy Payments Offices are situated at the following addresses:

PO Box 15 Exchange House 60 Exchange Road Watford WD1 7SP Tel: 01923 210 700	Covering all London boroughs, Essex, Hertfordshire, Kent, Surrey and Sussex
Ladywell House Ladywell Road Edinburgh EH12 7UR Tel: 0131 316 5600	Covering Scotland, plus Cleveland, Cumbria Durham, Northumberland, Tyne & Wear
7th Floor Hagley House 83–85 Hagley Road Birmingham B16 8NF Tel: 0121 456 4411	Covering Wales and all other counties of England

---

FREE TELEPHONE HELPLINE

The Department of Trade & Industry has provided a free redundancy
helpline for employees, employers and trade unions in Great Britain.
The number to call is 0500 848 489

Penalty for failure to notify Secretary of State

- An employer who refuses or neglects to notify the DTI about his (or her) redundancy proposals is guilty of an offence and liable on summary conviction to a fine of up to £5,000. If an offence committed by a body corporate is proved to have been committed with the consent or connivance of, or to be attributable to neglect on the part of, any director, manager, company secretary, personnel manager, etc (or by any similar officer of the body corporate), he (or she), as well as the body corporate, is also guilty of the offence and liable to be proceeded against and punished accordingly (*ibid.* section 194).

- For further particulars, please turn to the section titled **Redundancy** elsewhere in this handbook. See also **Dismissal on grounds of** redundancy, **Dismissal of an employee representative, Time off work: employee representatives, Time off work: trade union officials,** and **Victimisation,** elsewhere in this handbook.

Transfer or sale of an employer's business

- Any employer who has begun negotiations either to sell his (or her) business (or part of that business), as a going concern, or to expand his business by buying another business, is duty-bound to inform and consult the *appropriate representatives* of those of his employees (the *affected employees*) who may be affected either by the transfer itself or by measures to be taken in connection with that transfer. The discussions and consultations with the appropriate representatives must begin long enough before the relevant transfer so as to enable the exchange of information and meaningful discussions to take place (regulation 10, Transfer of Undertakings (Protection of Employment) Regulations 1981, as amended).

- In this context, the term 'appropriate representatives' means the representatives of an independent trade union recognised by an employer for collective bargaining purposes. If there is no trade union representation, the employer must conduct the information and consultation process with employee-elected or -appointed representatives (that is to say, persons previously appointed or elected by the affected employees to represent their interests in consultations with their employer) or with representatives specifically elected by affected employees to discuss the implications of the relevant transfer with their employer (*ibid*).

Note: If there are no employee-elected representatives, the employer must invite the affected employees to elect one or more of their number to represent their interests in relation to the relevant transfer (*ibid.* regulation 10A(1)). If the employees decline that invitation, or fail to conduct elections within a reasonable time, the employer must write to each of those employees giving the information summarised below in the paragraph titled *Duty to inform and consult*. An employer's role and duties in relation to the election of employee representatives are as described on page 154 above under the paragraph titled *Election* of *employee representatives*.

Additional note: An employee has the statutory right not to be disciplined, victimised or subject to any other detriment by his (or her) employer for having taken part in an election of employee representatives. Nor may such an employee be dismissed (or selected for redundancy) on such grounds (*per* sections 47(1A), 103(2) and 105(3), Employment Rights Act 1996, as inserted by regulations 12 and 13 of the 1999 Regulations referred to earlier in this section). For further particulars, please turn to the sections titled **Dismissal** and **Victimisation** elsewhere in this handbook.

- These requirements are to be found in regulations 10 and 10A of the Transfer of Undertakings (Protection of Employment) Regulations 1981, as amended by the Collective Redundancies & Transfer of

Undertakings (Protection of Employment) (Amendment) Regulations 1995, the Collective Redundancies & Transfer of Undertakings (Protection of Employment) (Amendment) Regulations 1999, and the Transfer of Undertakings (Protection of Employment) Regulations 1999. The 1981 Regulations (as amended) safeguard the contractual and statutory rights of employees when their employer's business (or part of that business) is sold as a going concern or transferred to another employer. It is as well to note that the 1981 Regulations apply only to transfers where there is a change of employer, eg where a part or whole of a business is sold, or where two businesses or companies combine to form a new business. In other words, the Regulations do not apply to a share take-over that does not involve a change of employer. But sale of a franchise operation is now covered.

Note: When an employer purchases a business as a going concern, he (or she) not only acquires a new business but also inherits the contracts of employment of the persons employed in that business at the time the sale or transfer was effected. If the employer dismisses one or more of those employees solely because of the purchase (or for a connected reason), the dismissal will be held to be unfair and he will be ordered to pay compensation. The same general rule applies if an employer selling (or negotiating the sale of) his business dismisses one or more of his employees in order to hasten proceedings or as a condition of sale. However, the 1981 Regulations allow of an exception if the dismissal of an employee before or after the sale or transfer of a business was for an economic, technical or organisational (ETO) reason entailing changes in the workforce. Even so, the respondent employer will need to persuade an employment tribunal that he had acted reasonably in the circumstances and that the dismissal was fair (*ibid.* regulation 8). For further particulars, please see **Dismissal and a change of employer** elsewhere in this handbook.

Duty to inform and consult

- As was indicated earlier, the representatives of an independent trade union recognised by one or other, or both, of the employers involved in the sale or transfer of a business, or (in the absence of such representation) representatives appointed or elected by their fellow affected employees, must be informed about the proposed sale, purchase or transfer by their respective employers and must be consulted about the likely effect on them of that sale, purchase or transfer. Specifically, each employer must inform those representatives:

    (a) either that the business is to be sold as a going concern or that he (or she) intends to expand the business by acquiring another business;

    (b) when the proposed sale or purchase is (or is likely) to take place;

    (c) why he is selling his business or buying another business, as the case may be;

    (d) what the legal, economic and social implications will be for employees affected by the sale or purchase;

(e) about any measures he envisages he will take (in connection with the transfer) in relation to his employees or, if he envisages that no measures will be so taken, that fact; and

(f) if he is the employer selling or transferring his business, what he knows about the purchaser's plans in relation to those of his own employees who will remain with the business after the sale or transfer has been effected or, if their situation is unlikely to change, that fact – which information must be made known to him by the intending purchaser in sufficient time to enable him to comply with this requirement.

- Consultations with trade union or employee representatives about the proposed sale or purchase of a business (a relevant transfer) must be conducted with a view to seeking agreement about the likely impact on employees affected by that sale or purchase. In the course of consultations, the employer must consider and reply to any suggestions or counter-proposals put forward by those representatives (and, if he (or she) is minded to reject them, must state his reasons for doing so) (*ibid.* regulation 10(5) and (6)).

- The 1981 Regulations acknowledge that negotiations for the sale or acquisition of a business may be jeopardised by too early an announcement of either party's intentions. If there are 'special circumstances' that render it not reasonably practicable to inform and consult employee or trade union representatives, the parties to the negotiations must nonetheless take all such steps towards complying with their duty to inform and consult as are reasonably practicable in the circumstances. Whether or not the delay was justified will be a matter for an employment tribunal to decide (*ibid.* regulation 10(7)).

- The information that is to be given to employee representatives must either be delivered to them or be sent by post to an address already notified or, if representatives of a recognised independent trade union are involved in the consultation process, to the head or main office of the union in question (*ibid.* regulation 10(4)). The consultation process itself must, of course, be conducted 'face to face'.

Employer's failure to inform or consult

- An employee representative or (in the case of a failure relating to one or more trade union representatives) the relevant trade union may present a complaint to an employment tribunal that an employer has failed to comply with his (or her) duty to consult him, her or them about his plans to sell or transfer his business or to acquire another business, or that he has failed to disclose written information needed for the purposes of such consultations. Any such complaint must be presented to the tribunal within three months of the date on which the relevant transfer took place or, in the case of an employer's failure to pay the compensation ordered to be paid by the tribunal, within three months of the date on which the tribunal's order was made (*ibid*. regulations 10 and 11(8)). The burden of proof in such cases rests squarely on the shoulders of the employer (*ibid*).

- An affected employee may likewise complain to an employment tribunal that his (or her) employer had failed to comply with the rules relating to the election of employee representatives, or had refused to allow such elections to take place, or (in the absence of appropriate representatives) had failed either to provide him with the written information that he should have provided in respect of that transfer and/or had failed to consult him about the proposed transfer (*ibid*. regulation 11).

- If the tribunal finds any such complaint to be well-founded, it will make a declaration to that effect and may order the employer to pay the complainant a sum not exceeding 13 weeks' pay by way of compensation. A further complaint may be presented if an employer fails or refuses to comply fully with the tribunal's order. If such a complaint is upheld, the respondent employer will once again be ordered either to comply with the original order or face proceedings before the county court (*ibid*. regulation 11).

  See also **Continuous employment, Dismissal and a change of employer**, and **Dismissal for asserting a statutory right** elsewhere in this handbook.

Health and safety at work

- Every employer has a general duty under section 2(2)(c) of the Health & Safety at Work etc Act 1974 to provide his (or her) employees with as much information, instruction, training and supervision as is necessary to ensure, so far as is reasonably practicable, their health, safety and welfare at work. Noncompliance with that duty is a criminal offence that could result in prosecution and a fine (if convicted) of up to £20,000 or, if the employer is convicted on indictment, a fine of an unlimited amount.

- This means, in practice, that employees must know and understand the risks inherent in the type of work they are employed to do; what safeguards have been put in place to avoid exposure to those risks; what additional precautions they must take for the avoidance of injury; and what instruction and training (or further training) they will receive when new processes, technology, systems of work or hazardous substances are introduced to the workplace, or when they are transferred to different work or given a change of responsibilities.

- An employer's general duty to inform, instruct, supervise and train has been reinforced in recent years by specific duties laid down in regulations made under the 1974 Act, of which the following are the most far-reaching:

  - the Electricity at Work Regulations 1989;

  - the Health & Safety (Display Screen Equipment) Regulations 1992;

  - the Manual Handling Operations Regulations 1992;

  - the Personal Protective Equipment at Work Regulations 1992 ;

  - the Workplace (Health, Safety & Welfare) Regulations 1992;

  - the Health & Safety (Consultation with Employees) Regulations 1996;

  - the Control of Lead at Work Regulations 2002.

  - the Provision & Use of Work Equipment Regulations 1998;

  - the Control of Substances Hazardous to Health Regulations 2002; and

  - the Management of Health & Safety at Work Regulations 1999.

  Copies of these regulations (discussed more fully in the current edition of our companion volume titled *An A-Z of Health & Safety Law*) are available from The Stationery Office (see page 132).

Employer's safety policy

- It is the duty of every employer of five or more persons to prepare and, as often as necessary, revise a written statement of his general policy with respect to the health and safety at work of his employees. The statement must include details of the organisation and arrangements put in hand by the employer to ensure that his (or her) policy is carried out. This includes naming the persons concerned (or their job titles) and spelling out their responsibilities, as well as developing and updating a body of safety rules and procedures. The policy statement must be brought to the notice of (and preferably explained to) each and every employee. A failure to provide or update a safety policy is an offence which could result in prosecution and the risk of heavy penalties under the Health & Safety at Work etc Act 1974 (*ibid.* sections 2(3) and 33).

Safety representatives and 'competent persons'

- Regulation 7 of the Safety Representatives & Safety Committees Regulations 1977 entitles a trade union-appointed safety representative to inspect and take copies of any document relevant to the workplace (or to the employees whom the safety representative represents) that his (or her) employer is required to keep by virtue of any health and safety legislation, including regulations made under, or saved by, the Health & Safety at Work etc Act 1974 – unless the document in question consists of, or relates to, the health record of an identifiable individual. An employer who denies a safety representative access to any relevant health and safety document is guilty of an offence and liable to prosecution under the 1974 Act (with the attendant heavy penalties if convicted).

- The Health & Safety (Consultation with Employees) Regulations 1996 apply to premises in which there is no recognised independent trade union representing the interests of employees and in which (accordingly) there are no trade union-appointed safety representatives under the 1977 Regulations (see the previous paragraph). In such a situation, the employer is duty-bound to consult with the employees directly on health and safety issues or with so-called *representatives of employee safety* elected by those employees to act on their behalf. Furthermore, he (or she) must make available whatever *information* is necessary to enable the employees or their elected representatives to participate fully and effectively in the consultation process.

- Regulation 7 of the Management of Health & Safety at Work Regulations 1999 imposes a duty on every employer to designate one or more employees to be 'competent persons' to assist him (or her) to do what needs to be done to comply with his duties under relevant health and safety legislation. Furthermore, he must ensure (*inter alia*) that the person or persons appointed by him to assist him with health and safety measures receive adequate *information* and support.

- Any employer who seeks to prevent a safety representative, or a *representative of employee safety*, or a designated 'competent person' carrying out his (or her) legitimate functions (for example, by withholding vital information about new processes, machines, equipment, or hazardous substances) is guilty of an offence under the 1974 Act and is liable to prosecution and a heavy fine. An employer who compounds that refusal by victimising or dismissing such an employee (or selecting that employee for redundancy), for carrying out (or attempting to carry out) those functions, may be called upon to respond to a complaint to an employment tribunal and could well be ordered to pay substantial compensation to those employees – which matters are dealt with in the sections titled **Dismissal in health and safety cases** and **Victimisation** elsewhere in this handbook.

See also **Time off work: safety representatives**.

National Minimum Wage Act 1998

- Any worker who has reason to believe that he (or she) has been paid less than the national minimum wage during a particular pay reference period may write to his employer asking him (or her) to produce the relevant extract from his payroll records. The employer has 14 days within which to produce that extract (either at the worker's place of work or, if the records are held elsewhere, at that other place), and must give the worker reasonable notice of the time and place at which the documents will be produced. The worker has the right both to inspect and examine the documents and to make copies. He has the right also to be accompanied at that time by another person of his own choosing.

- An employer who fails to respond to any such request within the prescribed 14-day period, or who either refuses to produce the necessary documents or withholds some of them, or who fails to allow the worker to inspect and take copies of those records, will be ordered by an employment tribunal to pay the worker a sum equal to 80 times the hourly amount of the then current national minimum wage. A complaint brought by a worker in these circumstances must be presented within three months of the employer's refusal or failure to cooperate (*ibid.* section 11).

- The 1998 Act is 'policed' by Inland Revenue enforcement officers. Apart from the remedies available to individual workers, employers who stubbornly refuse to pay the national minimum wage to their workers will be served with enforcement notices by Inland Revenue officers which, if not complied with, will result in their being ordered by an employment tribunal to pay to the Secretary of State a financial penalty equivalent to twice the hourly amount of the national minimum wage in respect of each and every worker to whom the failure to comply relates for each day during which the failure to comply has continued.

For further particulars, please turn to the section titled **National minimum wage** elsewhere in this handbook.

Employee's duty of fidelity

- It is as well to point out that, implicit in every contract of employment, is the duty of fidelity and trust owed by an employee to his (or her) employer. An employee must not disclose his employer's trade secrets to any unauthorised person or organisation or reveal confidential information about his employer's business dealings (eg, pricing policy, marketing strategy, customer lists, etc) that could be used to advantage by a competitor or other interested party. An employment tribunal would uphold the prerogative of an employer to dismiss any employee who abuses the confidence placed in him. Provided the employer has acted reasonably, and has taken the time and trouble to ascertain the true state of affairs, such a dismissal would be considered fair.

- However, as was indicated earlier in this section, an employee is not obliged to conceal the commission of a crime or other unlawful act perpetrated or contemplated by his (or her) employer. Indeed, he has an obligation to pass on such information to the proper authorities. See also **Fidelity and trust, employee's duty of** and **Public interest disclosures** elsewhere in this handbook.

DISMISSAL

Key points

- Section 94 of the Employment Rights Act 1996 states that every employee shall have the right not to be unfairly dismissed. But, as sections 108 and 109 point out, an employee does *not* qualify for the right to present a complaint of unfair dismissal to an employment tribunal unless he or she:

  - had been continuously employed for a minimum period of one year at the *effective date of termination* of his (or her) contract of employment, and

  - was, at that time, either under the age of 65 or under the *normal retiring age* for an employee (male or female) holding the position which that employee held (as to which, see *Normal retiring age* below).

Exceptions to the rule

- There are, of course, exceptions to the age and service rule mentioned above. Any employee who has been dismissed for an unlawful or inadmissible reason (or for asserting a statutory right) has the right to complain to an employment tribunal, regardless of his (or her) age or length of service at the material time – which issues are discussed later in this section.

  Note: An employee dismissed for having been suspended from work on medical grounds need only have completed one month's service in order to qualify to pursue a complaint of unfair dismissal (*ibid.* section 64(2)). For further particulars, see **Suspension from work on medical grounds** elsewhere in this handbook.

Effective date of termination

- For the meaning of the expression *effective date of termination* (which occurs frequently in the following pages), see pages 194 to 196.

Normal retiring age

- Under the 1996 Act, men and women in the same employment occupying the same or similar jobs must be permitted to retire at the same age. If an employment tribunal hearing a complaint of unfair dismissal is unable to ascertain from the complainant's contract of employment (or from custom and practice, or from the available evidence) what is or was the *normal retiring age* for an employee holding the position that the complainant held, it will deem that normal retiring age to be 65 (*ibid.* section 109(l)). If, for example, a female employee is forced to retire at age 60, when her male colleagues (or predecessors) doing the same or similar work were/are not required to retire until age 65, her dismissal (or selection for redundancy) for that reason alone will ordinarily be held to have been unfair.

  Note: In *Nash v Mash/Roe Group Ltd* [1999] IRLR 168, and more recently in *Rutherford v Harvest Town Circle & Bentley v DTI* (unreported), the employment tribunals acknowledged that UK employment legislation that prevents employees aged 65 or over from pursuing claims for unfair dismissal or redundancy payments could be in breach of EU law. Although neither decision is likely to have an impact, unless ratified by the higher courts or the European Court of Justice, the UK Government is now committed to implementing Council Directive 2000/78/EC of 27 November 2000, which prohibits direct or indirect discrimination (inter alia) on grounds of age. Although Member States have until 2 December 2003 to introduce legislation prohibiting discrimination based on religion or belief or sexual orientation, Article 18 allows that Member States may, if necessary, have an additional three years (that is to say, until 2 December 2006) to implement the Directive's provisions relating to age and disability discrimination. The UK Government has indicated that it will be taking advantage of that option.

Restrictions on contracting out

- Any term in a contract of employment or other agreement is void if it purports to exclude or limit the operation of any provision of the Employment Rights Act 1996, or to preclude any person from bringing proceedings under that Act (*ibid.* section 203). But the prohibition on contracting-out rule does *not* apply to so-called COT 3 agreements, 'compromise agreements', 'arbitral agreements' (see *ACAS arbitration agreements* below) or (designated) 'dismissal procedures agreements'.

COT 3 agreements

- An employee is precluded from presenting a complaint of unfair dismissal to an employment tribunal if – with the assistance of a conciliation officer from ACAS – both he (or she) and the employer agree to settle their differences 'out of court'. The agreement (known as a COT 3 agreement, after the form on which it is formally recorded) must be in writing and must be signed by both the employee and the employer. Each party keeps a copy of the signed agreement, the original of which is sent to the Secretary to the Tribunals. The complaint will then be registered in the form of a decision as having been settled by conciliation. An employee who has reached a COT 3 settlement of his (or her) complaint cannot then change his mind. For further particulars, please turn to the section on **Conciliation officers**.

'Compromise' agreements

- Another type of agreement is the so-called 'compromise' agreement, introduced by the Trade Union Reform & Employment Rights Act 1993. If the agreement satisfies each of the conditions spelled out in section 203(3) of the 1996 Act *(qv)* or in related statutes, the employee who signs that agreement thereby renounces his (or her) right to present a complaint of unfair dismissal to an employment tribunal (or a complaint concerning an alleged infringement of any of his other statutory employment rights) (as to which, see **Compromise agreements**, elsewhere in this handbook).

Dismissal procedure agreements

- A 'dismissal procedure agreement' is an agreement between an employer and a trade union, the effect (or intended effect) of which is to substitute for the statutory right of an employee to present a complaint of unfair dismissal to an employment tribunal. A dismissal procedure agreement may be a separate agreement or it may form part of a collective agreement. Either way, it will not be legally binding unless specifically 'designated' as such by order of the Secretary of State for Education & Employment (*ibid.* sections 65 and 66). For further particulars, please turn to the section on **Collective agreements** elsewhere in this handbook.

ACAS arbitration scheme

- Since 21 May 2001, when the 'ACAS Arbitration Scheme' came into operation, disagreements about the fairness or otherwise of an employee's dismissal may now be referred to one of a number of independent arbitrators appointed by the Advisory, Conciliation & Arbitration Service (ACAS). The aim of the Scheme is to promote the settlement of unfair dismissal disputes in a confidential, informal, relatively fast and cost-efficient way. Unlike the handling of such complaints before the employment tribunals, the new arbitration scheme avoids the use of formal pleadings, and formal witness and documentary procedures. The usual rules of evidence do not apply nor will strict law or legal precedent be a determining factor. Instead, in reaching his or her decision, the ACAS-appointed arbitrator will take into account the general principles of fairness and good conduct laid down in ACAS Code of Practice 1 on *Disciplinary & Grievance Procedures* (discussed elsewhere in this section) and in related ACAS publications, notably its *Discipline at Work* handbook. Arbitral decisions (or awards) will be final, with very limited opportunities for the parties to appeal or otherwise challenge the result.

Readers seeking further information and guidance on the ACAS Arbitration Scheme should access website www.acas.org.uk/arbitration.htm or telephone ACAS Reader Limited on 0870 242 9090.

Excluded classes of employment

- The right to present a complaint of unfair dismissal to an employment tribunal does *not* apply to:

  - employment as master or as a member of the crew of a fishing vessel where the employee is remunerated only by a share in the profits or gross earnings of the vessel (*ibid.* section 199(2)); or

  - employment under a contract of employment in police service or to persons engaged in such employment (*ibid.* section 200).

Meaning of dismissal

- There is a dismissal in the legal (as well as the accepted) sense when an employee's contract of employment is terminated by his or her employer, with or without notice and for whatever reason. This is the usual form of dismissal. An employer simply informs the employee, either orally or in writing, that his or her employment is at an end – either immediately (which is a summary dismissal) or at the end of a specified period (which is a dismissal with notice).

- There are, however, two other forms of termination of employment, each of which constitutes a dismissal in law. Thus, an employee will be treated as having been dismissed by his (or her) employer:

  (a) if he is employed under a limited-term contract and that contract terminates by virtue of the limiting event without being renewed under the same contract (*ibid.* section 95(1)(b), as to which, see **Fixed-term employees,** elsewhere in this handbook; or

  (b) if the employee resigns, with or without notice, in circumstances such that he (or she) is entitled to resign without notice by reason of his employer's conduct – as to which, see **Constructive dismissal** elsewhere in this handbook (*ibid.* section 95(1)(c)).

Legitimate reasons for dismissal

- Section 98 of the 1996 Act (*qv*) lists seven 'legitimate' or permitted reasons for dismissal. These are dismissal on grounds of:

  (a) incompetence;

  (b) ill-health (including mental disability);

  (c) lack of qualifications;

  (d) misconduct;

  (e) redundancy;

  (f) illegality of continued employment; or

  (g) some other substantial reason of a kind such as to justify the dismissal of an employee holding the position which that employee held.

  Although these may be legitimate reasons for dismissal, the question of 'fairness' will be a matter for an employment tribunal to decide (see page 181). Each of reasons (a) to (g) is discussed elsewhere in this handbook under the subject heads listed at the end of this section.

Note: If an employee serving out his (or her) notice of dismissal decides to hand in his resignation, to take effect before the date on which his employer's notice is due to expire, he will nonetheless be treated in law as having been dismissed by his employer for the reason (or reasons) given by the employer when he dismissed the employee in the first place (*ibid*. section 55(3)). in other words, the employee's resignation in such circumstances does not undermine his right to present a complaint of unfair dismissal, if minded to do so.

Unlawful and inadmissible reasons for dismissal

- An employee who has been dismissed for an allegedly 'inadmissible' or unlawful reason may complain to an employment tribunal regardless of his (or her) age or length of service at the material time (*ibid*. section 109(2)). In other words, the usual qualifying conditions for bringing a complaint of unfair dismissal do not apply in such cases.

- It is *prima facie* unlawful (or inadmissible) and, therefore, unfair to dismiss an employee or select him (or her) for redundancy:

Discrimination cases

(a) on grounds of sex, marital status or gender reassignment (section 6, Sex Discrimination Act 1975);

(b) on racial grounds, that is to say, on grounds of colour, race, nationality or national or ethnic origins (section 4, Race Relations Act 1976);

(c) on grounds of disability or for a connected reason (Disability Discrimination Act 1995); or

(d) (in Northern Ireland only) on grounds of religion or political opinion (Fair Employment & Treatment (Northern Ireland) Order 1998);

'Spent' conviction cases

(e) because the employee had failed to reveal details of a *spent* conviction, unless employed in an excepted occupation or profession and therefore obliged to reveal details of all convictions, spent or otherwise (section 4(3)(b), Rehabilitation of Offenders Act 1974).

Note: Section 4(3)(b) of the Rehabilitation of Offenders Act 1974 reads as follows: 'A conviction which has become spent, or any circumstances ancillary thereto, or any failure to disclose a spent conviction or any such circumstances, shall not be a proper ground for dismissing or excluding a person from any office, profession, occupation or employment.' For further information, please refer to the section in this handbook titled **Convicted persons**.

Pregnancy, maternity and 'family reasons' cases

(f) If the reason (or, if more than one, the principal reason) for the dismissal or selection for redundancy was a reason connected with pregnancy, childbirth, maternity leave, adoption leave, parental leave, paternity leave, a request for flexible working arrangements, or time off for dependants; or a reason relating to action which an employee took, agreed to take, or refused to take, in respect of a collective or workforce agreement dealing with parental leave (Section 99, Employment Rights Act 1996, and regulation 20 of the Maternity & Parental Leave etc regulations 1999 (as amended);

(g) if the reason (or, if more than one, the principal reason) for the dismissal was that the employee was redundant (when others occupying similar positions had not been made redundant) and it is shown that the reason (or, if more than one, the principal reason) for his or her selection for redundancy was a reason of a kind specified in (f) above (*ibid.*);

(h) if a woman had been made redundant during her ordinary or additional maternity leave period but her employer (or his successor or an associated employer) had refused or failed to offer her suitable alternative employment under a new contract to take effect immediately on the ending of her employment under her original contract (*ibid.*);

Health and safety cases

(i) if the reason (or, if more than one, the principal reason) for the dismissal or selection for redundancy was that the employee had carried out (or proposed to carry out) activities in connection with preventing or reducing risks to health and safety at work having been *designated* or *appointed* by his or her employer to carry out just such activities (*ibid.* sections 100 and 105(3));

(j) if the reason (or, if more than one, the principal reason) for the dismissal or selection for redundancy was that the employee being an appointed safety representative, or a member of a safety committee (if acknowledged as such by the employer) had performed, or proposed to perform, his or her legitimate functions in one or other of those capacities (*ibid.*);

(k) if the reason (or, if more than one, the principal reason) for the dismissal or selection for redundancy was that the employee at a place where there was no safety representative or safety committee (or there *was* such a representative or committee but it was not reasonably practicable for the employee to raise the matter by those means) – brought to his (or her) employer's attention, by reasonable means, circumstances connected with his work that he reasonably believed were harmful or potentially harmful to health or safety (*ibid.*);

(l) if the reason (or, if more than one, the principal reason) for the dismissal or selection for redundancy was that, in circumstances of danger, that he (or she) reasonably believed to be serious and imminent and that he could not reasonably have been expected to avert, left (or proposed to leave), or (while the danger persisted) refused to return to, his place of work or any dangerous part of his place of work (*ibid.*);

(m) if the reason (or, if more than one, the principal reason) for the dismissal or selection for redundancy was that, in circumstances of danger, the employee took, or proposed to take, appropriate steps to protect himself (or herself) or other persons from the danger (*ibid.*);

Note: However, in such a case, the dismissal will not be held to have been unfair 'if the employer shows that it was, or would have been, so negligent for the employee to take the steps that he took, or proposed to take, that a reasonable employer might have dismissed him for taking, or proposing to take, them' (sections 103 and 105). Whether the steps that the employee took, or proposed to take, were 'appropriate' will be judged by reference to all the advice available to him at the time (*ibid.* section 100(2)).

Sunday working cases

(n) if the reason (or, if more than one, the principal reason) for the dismissal or selection for redundancy of a *protected or opted-out* shop worker or betting worker was that he (or she) had refused, or proposed to refuse, to do shop work or betting work on a Sunday or on a particular Sunday (sections 101 and 105(4), Employment Rights Act 1996);

Working time cases

(o) if the reason (or principal reason) for the dismissal or selection for redundancy was that the worker (qua employee):

– had refused (or proposed to refuse) to comply with a requirement which the employer had imposed (or had proposed to impose) in contravention of the Working Time Regulations 1998;

– had refused (or proposed to refuse) to forgo a right conferred on him (or her) by those Regulations;

> – had failed to sign a workforce agreement for the purposes of those Regulations, or to enter into, or agree to vary or extend, any other agreement with his (or her) employer which is provided for in those Regulations; or

> – being a representative of members of the workforce for the purposes of Schedule 1 to those Regulations, or a candidate for election as such a representative, had performed (or had proposed to perform) any functions or activities as such a representative or candidate;

(*per* sections 101A and 105(4A) of the Employment Rights Act 1996, as inserted by regulation 32 of the Working Time Regulations 1998);

Pension scheme trustee cases

(p) if the reason (or, if more than one, the principal reason) for the dismissal or selection for redundancy was that the employee, in his (or her) capacity as a trustee of a relevant occupational pension scheme, performed (or proposed to perform) any functions as such a trustee (*ibid.* sections 102(1) and 105(2));

Note: 'Relevant occupational pension scheme' means an occupational pension scheme (as defined in section 1 of the Pension Schemes Act 1993) established under a trust.

Employee representative cases

(q) if the reason (or, if more than one, the principal reason) for the dismissal or selection for redundancy was that the employee – in his (or her) capacity as an elected employee representative (or candidate for election as such a representative), for the purposes of Chapter II of Part IV of the Trade Union & Labour Relations (Consolidation) Act 1992 (*collective redundancies*) or regulations 10 and 11 of the Transfer of Undertakings (Protection of Employment) Regulations 1981 – had performed (or proposed to perform) any functions or activities as such an employee representative (or candidate) (*ibid.* sections 103 and 105(6));

Protected disclosure cases

(r) if the reason (or principal reason) for the dismissal or selection for redundancy was that the employee had made a protected disclosure (per sections 103A and 105(6A), Employment Rights Act 1996, as inserted by sections 5 and 6 of the Public Interest Disclosure Act 1998);

Assertion of statutory right cases

(s) if the reason (or, if more than one, the principal reason) for the dismissal or selection for redundancy was that the employee had brought proceedings against his (or her) employer to enforce one or other of his statutory rights, or supposed statutory rights, under the Employment Rights Act 1996 or the Trade Union & Labour Relations (Consolidation) Act 1992 (sections 104 and 105(7), Employment Rights Act 1996);

(t) if the reason (or, if more than one, the principal reason) for the dismissal or selection for redundancy was that the employee had, in good faith, alleged that his (or her) employer had infringed one or other of the statutory rights referred to in sub-paragraph (h) above (*ibid.*);

National minimum wage cases

(u) if the reason (or principal reason) for the dismissal or selection for redundancy was that action had been taken (or proposed), by or on behalf of the employee, with a view to enforcing (or otherwise securing) the employee's statutory right to be paid the national minimum wage (per sections 104A and 105(7A), Employment Rights Act 1996, as inserted by section 25(1) of the National Minimum Wage Act 1998);

(v) if the reason (or principal reason) for the dismissal or selection for redundancy was that the employer had been prosecuted for an offence under section 31 of the National Minimum Wage Act 1998 as a result of action taken by (or on behalf of) the employee for the purpose of securing (or enforcing) the employee's right to be paid the national minimum wage (*ibid.*);

(w) if the reason (or principal reason) for the dismissal or selection for redundancy was that the employee qualified (or would or might have qualified) for the national minimum wage or for a particular rate of the national minimum wage (*ibid.*);

Tax Credits Act 2002 cases

(x) if the reason (or, if more than one, the principal reason) for the dismissal or selection for redundancy was:

– that action had been taken (or proposed) by or on behalf of an employee with a view to enforcing or otherwise securing a right conferred on the employee by regulations made under sections 25 of the Tax Credits Act 2002; or

–   that a penalty had been imposed on the employer (or proceedings for a penalty had been brought against the employer) under that Act, as a result of action taken by or on behalf of the employee for the purpose of enforcing, or otherwise securing the benefit of, such a right; or

–   that the employee was entitled (or would or may have been entitled) to a child tax credit and/or a working tax credit (*ibid.* sections 104B & 105(7B));

Note: Under the Working Tax Credit (Payment by Employers) Regulations 2002, which came into force on 1 March 2003, employers are duty bound to pay child tax credits and/or working tax credits to specified employees through the payroll. The Tax Credits Office (TCO) will instruct employers to make such payments for an initial period of up to 26 weeks. An employer may recover the amount paid to qualified employees by deducting it from returns of PAYE tax, National Insurance contributions and student loan deductions sent monthly or quarterly to the Inland Revenue. It is inadmissible and automatically unfair to dismiss an employee, select him (or her) for redundancy, or otherwise penalise him for being entitled to a tax credit or for taking steps to enforce his right to be paid those tax credits though the payroll.

Trade union membership cases

(y) if the reason (or, if more than one, the principal reason) for the dismissal or selection for redundancy was that the employee:

–   was, or proposed to become, a member of an independent trade union; or

–   had taken part, or proposed to take part, in the activities of an independent trade union at an appropriate time; or

–   was not a member of any trade union, or of a particular trade union, or of one of a number of particular trade unions, or had refused, or proposed to refuse, to become or remain a member; or

–   in consequence of a refusal to be or remain a member of a particular trade union or of any trade union, had refused (or proposed to refuse) to pay a sum of money or to have money deducted from his or her wages or salary in lieu of trade union membership – whether or not any such requirement was laid down in the employee's contract of employment or elsewhere in writing (sections 152 and 153, Trade Union & Labour Relations (Consolidation) Act 1992).

Unofficial strike and other industrial action cases

(z) Ordinarily, an employee forfeits his (or her) right to complain of unfair dismissal of unfair selection for redundancy if, at the material time, he was taking part in an unofficial strike or some other form of unofficial industrial action. However, that exclusion does not apply if it is shown that the reason (or principal reason) for the employee's dismissal or selection for redundancy was one of those specified in sections 99(1) to (3), 100, 101A(d), 103, 103A, or 104 of the Employment Rights Act 1996 (ie, dismissal in maternity, health and safety, employee representative and protected disclosure cases, or in 'time off for dependants' cases (per section 237, Trade Union & Labour Relations (Consolidation) Act 1992, as amended by Schedule 4, paragraphs 1 to 3 to the Employment Relations Act 1999));

Official (or 'protected') industrial action cases

(aa) if the reason (or, if more than one, the principal reason) for the employee's dismissal or selection for redundancy was that he (or she) had taken official industrial action and the dismissal or selection took place

– *within* the first eight weeks of that period of official industrial action; or

– *after* those first eight weeks (the employee having returned to work within that eight-week period); or

– *after* those first eight weeks if the employee was still taking official industrial action at the time but the employer had failed to take reasonable procedural steps with a view to resolving the dispute to which the official industrial action related (*per* section 238A, Trade Union & Labour Relations Consolidation Act 1992 and section 105(7C) of the Employment Rights Act 1996).

Part-time workers cases

(ab) If the reason (or, if more than one, the principal reason) for which the worker (*qua* employee) was dismissed or selected for redundancy was one specified in paragraph (3) of regulation 5 of the Part-time Workers (Prevention of Less Favourable Treatment) Regulations 2000 (read with paragraph (4) of that regulation) – as to which, please turn to the section titled **Part-time workers** elsewhere in this handbook.

Fixed-term employees cases

(ac) if the reason or, if more than one, the principal reason for the employee's dismissal or selection for redundancy was one of those specified in para (3) of regulation 6 of the Fixed-term Employees (Prevention of Less Favourable Treatment) Regulations 2002 – as to which, please turn to the section titled **Fixed-term employees** elsewhere in this handbook.

- To reiterate: A complaint of unfair dismissal for one or other of inadmissible or unlawful reasons listed in paragraphs (a) to (ac) above may be presented to an employment tribunal regardless of the employee's age or length of service at the effective date of termination of his or her contract of employment. Complaints to an employment tribunal under paragraph (e) above should be capable of being pursued on the basis that a *spent* conviction does not *per se* rank as a legitimate or 'permitted' reason for dismissal; nor would it ordinarily constitute *some other substantial reason* of a kind such as to justify the dismissal (or selection for redundancy) of a person holding the position which that person held.

Complaint of unfair dismissal

- A complaint of unfair dismissal must be presented in writing to the nearest regional or local office of the employment tribunals (preferably using Form IT1) before the end of the period of three months beginning with the effective date of termination of the employee's contract of employment, or within such further period as the tribunal considers reasonable in a case where it is satisfied that it was not reasonably practicable for the employee to have presented his or her complaint sooner (*ibid.* section 111).

Note: An employee given notice of dismissal may present a complaint of unfair dismissal while serving out the notice period (that is to say, while still employed) (*ibid.* section 111(3) an (4)). Clearly, this is not an option available to persons who have been summarily dismissed, but would certainly appeal to an employee who has resigned with notice, because of his (or their) employer's conduct, in circumstances which he believes are tantamount to unfair 'constructive' dismissal.

- When an employee's complaint of unfair dismissal is brought before an employment tribunal, it is the responsibility of the employer to explain:

- why the employee was dismissed or, if there was more than one reason, what the principal reason for the dismissal was; and

- that the reason was a legitimate or permitted reason.

The issue of fairness

- If satisfied on both those counts, the tribunal must then decide whether the dismissal was fair. The answer to that question will depend on whether, in the circumstances (including the size and administrative resources of the employer's undertaking), the employer had acted reasonably in treating his stated reason for dismissing the employee as a sufficient reason for dismissal – and that question, says the 1996 Act, will be determined in accordance with equity and the substantial merits of the case (*ibid.* section 98(4)).

- In other words, an employer responding to a complaint of unfair dismissal must not only satisfy the tribunal that he had a legitimate reason for dismissing the complainant, but that he had acted reasonably in doing so. If, for instance he dismissed an employee for incompetence, he will need to satisfy the tribunal not only that he had reasonable grounds for believing that the employee *was* incompetent but also that he had done all that could reasonably be expected of him to improve the employee's capabilities and skills before taking the decision to dismiss. For example, an otherwise satisfactory employee transferred to a different department in a job requiring new or different skills could not reasonably be expected to achieve the desired level of competence without a degree of instruction and advice, supported by on-the-job training or supervision. If the evidence before a tribunal shows that the employer failed the employee on one or more of those counts, or denied the employee an opportunity to improve his level of competence, the tribunal might well decide that the dismissal was unfair. See **Dismissal for incompetence** elsewhere in this handbook.

- Much the same approach will be adopted by the tribunals in cases of dismissal for alleged misconduct. Was the employee fully aware of the standard of conduct expected of him? Was he given an opportunity to explain? Was his misconduct so serious as to warrant dismissal for a first and possibly uncharacteristic breach of the rules? Did the employer follow his own laid-down procedures for dealing with issues of misconduct? And so on. If dismissed for redundancy, why was the employee selected ahead of other employees more junior or less competent and experienced than himself? If dismissed because of ill-health, was any effort made to establish his chances of making a complete recovery and returning to work in the short term? These and related issues (or reasons for dismissal) are discussed elsewhere in this handbook under the subject heads listed at the end of this section.

- The procedure at an employment tribunal hearing is summarised elsewhere in this handbook in the section titled **Employment tribunals and procedure**. There is also a useful booklet titled *Hearings at Employment Tribunals* (Ref ITL4), published by the Department of Trade & Industry, which can be obtained by contacting the DTI Publications Order Line on 0870 1502 500 (email: www.publications,dti.gsi.gov.uk). Another booklet, *What to do if taken to an employment tribunal (Ref ITL3)*, is available from the same source.

Reinstatement or re-engagement?

- On a finding of unfair dismissal, a tribunal has two options. It may make an order directing the employer to reinstate or re-engage the dismissed employee (having first ascertained that the employee wishes to be reinstated or re-engaged) or it will order the employer to pay compensation.

- Although an employment tribunal is duty-bound to enquire whether an employee wishes to be reinstated or re-engaged, it is under no legal obligation to make an order for reinstatement or re-engagement (regardless of the employee's wishes). Indeed, over the years, there have not been a great many tribunal orders for reinstatement or re-engagement; nor is it usual for unfairly dismissed employees to ask to be reinstated or re-engaged.

- If a tribunal has it in mind to make an order for reinstatement or re-engagement, it must not only take account of the employee's wishes in the matter but must also consider the practicability of doing so – in the light both of the employer's circumstances (which may have changed since the employee was dismissed) and the extent, if any, to which the employee caused (or contributed to) his own dismissal. A tribunal will not be swayed by evidence that the employer has already recruited a replacement employee – unless it is demonstrably clear that the job previously held by the dismissed employee had to be filled quickly or that the employer could not afford to wait any longer, having already waited a reasonable time without having heard any word from the employee that he (or she) wished to be reinstated or re-engaged (*ibid.* sections 112 to 117).

- An order for reinstatement effectively requires the employer to rein-state the employee in all respects as if he (or she) had never been dismissed. The order will specify any amount payable to the employee in respect of any benefit that he might reasonably be expected to have had but for his dismissal (including arrears of pay, for the period between the date of his dismissal and the date of his reinstatement) and the rights and privileges, including seniority and pension rights, that must also be restored to the employee. The order will also specify the date by which it must be complied with (*ibid.* section 114).

- An order for re-engagement on the other hand (usually made when there has been a change in the employer's circumstances or when an employee has been found to have caused or contributed to some extent to his own dismissal) will direct the employer to re-engage the employee in comparable employment – either with the same or with an associated employer. The order will specify the job, the wages or salary to be paid (including arrears of pay), the rights and privileges (if any) to be restored to the employee, and the date by which the order must be complied with. In the absence of any evidence that the employee had caused or contributed to any extent to his own dismissal, the terms of an order for re-engagement must, so far as is reasonably practicable, be as favourable to the employee as an order for reinstatement (*ibid.* section 115).

- When determining the amount of any arrears of pay owing to the employee, in connection with an order for reinstatement or re-engage-ment, the tribunal will take into account any moneys received by the employee between the date on which he was dismissed and the date of his reinstatement or re-engagement, including:

  - money in lieu of notice and any *ex gratia* payments paid by his former employer; and

  - any wages or salary received in respect of any intervening period of employment with another employer;

  and such other benefits as the tribunal thinks appropriate in the circumstances (*ibid.* section 115(3)).

A refusal to reinstate or re-engage

- An employer who refuses to comply with a tribunal order for reinstate-ment or re-engagement, will be ordered by the tribunal to pay the affected employee each of a *basic,* a *compensatory* and an *additional* award of compensation for unfair dismissal (each of which is discussed in more detail later in this section). The basic award is calculated in much the same way as the statutory redundancy payment and is (presently) subject to an upper limit of £7,800. The compensatory award has an upper limit of £53,500 (although there are exceptions, discussed later in this section); and the additional award is an amount not less than 26 nor more than 52 weeks' pay. An employer will not be ordered to pay the additional award if he (or she) can satisfy the tribunal that it was not practicable to reinstate or re-engage the employee in compliance with the original order (*ibid.* section 117(3) and (4)).

Note: The upper limit of £53,500 on the compensatory award may be exceeded to the extent necessary to enable the aggregate of the compensatory and additional awards fully to reflect the loss (including arrears of pay) sustained by the employee in consequence of the employer's refusal to reinstate or re-engage (*ibid.* section 124(4)).

Partial compliance with an order to reinstate or re-engage

- An employer who reinstates or re-engages a dismissed employee, in compliance with a tribunal order, but fails to comply fully with the terms of that order, will be ordered by the tribunal to compensate the employee for any loss he (or she) has sustained as a consequence of that failure. There is an upper limit of £52,600 on the amount of compensation that may be awarded in such circumstances (*ibid.* sections 117(1) and (2)).

Note: The upper limit of £52,600 on the amount of the compensation that may be awarded in the circumstances described above may be exceeded to the extent necessary to enable the award fully to reflect the amount payable by the employer in respect of any benefit which the employee might reasonably be expected to have had but for his dismissal (including arrears of pay) for the period between the date on which the dismissal took place and the date of reinstatement or re-engagement (*ibid.* section 1240)).

Compensation for unfair dismissal

Note: The upper limits on the awards of compensation for unfair dismissal discussed in the following pages were previously reviewed each year by the Secretary of State. However, with the coming into force of section 34 of the Employment Relations Act 1999, those upper limits are presently reviewed every September and are linked to September on September changes in the retail prices index. If the index for September is higher or lower than the index for the previous September, the upper limits on the awards will be increased or decreased (from 1 February of the following year) by the same percentage as the amount of the increase or decrease in the index (rounded up or down to the nearest £10 or £100, as appropriate).

- Although an employment tribunal may *order* an employer to reinstate or re-engage a dismissed employee, it cannot force him (or her) to do so – however reprehensible the employer's motives in dismissing the employee in the first place. But, there is a price to pay. As was indicated earlier, a refusal to reinstate or re-engage will result in the employer having to pay an *additional* award of compensation that is to say, an amount over and above (including arrears of pay) sustained by the aggregate of the *basic and compensatory* awards for unfair dismissal discussed below.

- If no order for reinstatement or re-engagement is made and the evidence shows that the employer had *written* to the employee at the time of his (or her) dismissal informing or reminding him of his right (under his contract or otherwise) to appeal against his dismissal, but the employee declined to exercise that right, the tribunal may *reduce* the amount of the additional award by an amount not exceeding the equivalent of two weeks' pay. If, on the other hand, the evidence shows that the employer had denied the employee his right of appeal (or had prevented him from exercising that right), the tribunal may *increase* the amount of the compensatory award by an amount of a maximum two weeks' pay (*ibid.* section 127A, as inserted by section 13, Employment Rights (Dispute Resolution) Act 1998).

Three heads of compensation

- Thus, there are three heads of compensation for unfair dismissal:
  - the *basic* award;
  - the *compensatory* award; and
  - the *additional* award;

  each of which we now consider in more detail.

The basic award

- The basic award of compensation for unfair dismissal is calculated in much the same way as a statutory redundancy payment (except that service before the age of 18 is not discounted) – its purpose being to compensate an employee for the loss of his (or her) 'property rights' in his job. Service in excess of 20 years is discounted, as are earnings in excess of £260 per week – the latter amount being the amount for the year beginning on 1 February 2003. Accordingly, the current maximum basic award of compensation is £7,800 payable to an employee with 20 years' service after the age of 41 and with an average or actual income equal to or in excess of £260 at the effective date of termination of his contract of employment (viz, $20 \times 1.5 \times £260$).

Note: Under Section 119(3) & (4) of the Employment Rights Act 1996, 'the amount of the basic award shall be calculated by reference to the period, ending with the effective date of termination, during which the employee has been... employed, by starting at the end of that perfect and reckoning backwards the number of years of employment falling within that period, and allowing:

(a)   one-and-a-half week's pay for each such year of employment in which the employee was not below the age of forty-one;

(b)   one week's pay for each such year of employment not falling within paragraph (a) in which the employee was not below the age of twenty-two; and

(c)   half a week's pay for each such year of employment not falling within either of paragraph (a) and (b).

(d)   Where, in reckoning the number of years of employment in accordance with subsection (3), twenty years of employment have been reckoned, no account shall be taken of any year of employment earlier than those twenty years.'

The amount of the basic award of compensation payable to an employee aged 64 at the time of his (or her) dismissal will be reduced by one-twelfth for each whole month beyond that age on the date of his dismissal (*ibid.* section 119(4) and (5)). It follows that an employee aged 64 years and six months at the time of his (or her) dismissal will be awarded a basic award of compensation for unfair dismissal equal to half the amount he would otherwise have been awarded had he been dismissed before his 64th birthday.

- The basic award of compensation will be a minimum £3,500 if a tribunal finds that the reason or principal reason for the dismissal (or selection for redundancy) was that the employee in question had carried out (or proposed to carry out) his (or her) functions either as

  –   a safety representative;

  –   a representative of employee safety;

  –   a member of a safety committee;

  –   a person designated by his employer to carry out activities in connection with preventing or reducing risks to health and safety at work;

  –   a workforce representative (or a candidate for election as such a representative) (for the purposes of the Working Time Regulations 1998);

  –   a trustee of a relevant occupational pension scheme (as defined in section 1 of the Pension Schemes Act 1993) established under a trust; or

  –   an employee representative (or a candidate for election as such a representative) for the purposes of Chapter II of Part IV of the Trade

Union & Labour Relations (Consolidation Act 1992 (collective redundancies) or for the purposes of regulations 10 and 11 of the Transfer of Undertakings (Protection of Employment) Regulations 1981 (section 120, Employment Rights Act 1996).

The same minimum basic award of £3,500 will be made if the tribunal finds that an employee was dismissed (or selected for redundancy) for refusing to be or remain a member of an independent trade union or for taking part at 'an appropriate time' in the activities of any such trade union *(per* section 156, Trade Union & Labour Relations (Consolidation) Act 1992).

Note: The expression 'an appropriate time' means (a) a time outside the employee's working hours, or (b) a time within his working hours at which, in accordance with arrangements agreed with (or consent given by) his employer, it is permissible for him to take part in the activities of a trade union. For this purpose, 'working hours' means any time when, in accordance with his contract of employment, the employee is required to be at work (section 152, Trade Union & Labour Relations (Consolidation) Act 1992).

- An employment tribunal will reduce the amount of a basic award of compensation for unfair dismissal by the amount of any statutory redundancy payment paid to the employee at the time of his or her dismissal (always provided that the employee was genuinely redundant at the material time). It may also reduce (or further reduce) that award by such amount as it considers just and equitable in the light of the employee's conduct in the period preceding the date of the dismissal (or the date on which notice of dismissal was given). A still further reduction may be imposed if there is evidence that the employee unreasonably refused his former employer's offer (if any) to reinstate him in his employment (in all respects, as if he had not been dismissed in the first place).

- An employee found to have been unfairly dismissed on grounds of redundancy, but who does not otherwise qualify for a statutory redundancy payment will nonetheless be awarded a basic award of compensation of a minimum two weeks' pay – which amount will be subject to the reductions referred to in the preceding paragraphs (*ibid.* section 121).

The compensatory award

- The *compensatory* award (payable in addition to the basic award and in circumstances in which either no order for reinstatement or re-engagement is made, or the employer has failed to comply with the terms of any such order) 'will be such amount' (not exceeding £53,500) as the tribunal considers just and equitable in all the circumstances, having regard to the loss sustained by the complainant in consequence of his (or her) dismissal or his employer's failure to comply with an order for reinstatement or re-engagement. However, that upper limit may be exceeded if an employment tribunal deems it necessary to do so to enable the award fully to reflect the loss (including arrears of pay) sustained by an employee as a consequence of his employer's actions (*ibid.* sections 123 and 124). For further particulars, please see earlier in this section under *Reinstatement or re-engagement?*

- Furthermore, that £53,500 upper limit does not apply to compensation awarded, or a compensatory award made, to an employee who is regarded as having been unfairly dismissed (or unfairly selected for redundancy):

   (a) in a health and safety case (see **Dismissal in health and safety cases** elsewhere in this handbook); or

   (b) for having made a 'protected disclosure' (under the Public Interest Disclosure Act 1998) (see **Public interest disclosures**)

   (*ibid.* section 124(1A), inserted by section 37(1), Employment Relations Act 1999).

   Note: As there is no upper limit on the amount of compensation that may be awarded to an employee held to have been unlawfully dismissed (or discriminated against) on grounds of sex, marital status, pregnancy, childbirth, race or disability, an employee seeking compensation for unlawful dismissal on such grounds may consider it more advantageous to pursue his or her claim for compensation under the Sex Discrimination Act 1975, the Race Relations Act 1976 or the Disability Discrimination Act 1995. For further particulars, please refer to the sections titled **Racial discrimination** and **Sex discrimination** elsewhere in this handbook. See also **Disabled persons**.

- Factors that will determine the precise amount of the compensatory award include the employee's immediate and projected loss of earnings and associated benefits, any loss of pension rights, the likelihood of his (or her) finding another job given his age, qualifications, skills, the unemployment situation in the area in which he lives, any damage to his reputation, any expenses incurred by him as a direct consequence of his dismissal; and so on. In assessing the award, the tribunal will also take into account the extent of the employee's efforts to mitigate his loss and the extent also to which he caused or contributed to his dismissal by his own actions.

- If an employment tribunal has *not* ordered the reinstatement or re-engagement of an unfairly dismissed employee and it is shown in evidence that the employer had *written* to the employee at the time of his (or her) dismissal informing or reminding him of his right (under his contract or otherwise) to appeal against his dismissal, but the employee declined to do so, the tribunal may *reduce* the amount of the compensatory award otherwise payable to that employee by an amount not exceeding the equivalent of two weeks, pay. If, on the other hand, the employer had denied the employee his right of appeal (or had prevented him from exercising that right), the tribunal may *increase* the amount of the compensatory award by an amount of a maximum two weeks' pay (*ibid.* section 127A, as inserted by section 13, Employment Rights (Dispute Resolution) Act 1998).

Additional award of compensation

- As was discussed earlier in this section, an employer who refuses or fails to comply with a tribunal order to reinstate or re-engage a dismissed employee will be ordered to pay that employee an *additional* award of compensation (that is to say, an amount in addition to the amount of any basic or compensatory award) unless he (or she) can satisfy the tribunal that it was not practicable to comply with that order. The additional award will be an amount not less than 26 nor more than 52 weeks' pay (*ibid.* section 117(3), as amended by section 33, Employment Relations Act 1999).

- Given the current upper limit of £260 (2003/04) on the amount of a week's pay, the maximum *additional* award of compensation is £13,520 (ie, 52 × £260); and the minimum, £6,760 (ie, 26 × £260) (*ibid.*).

Social Security Benefits

- Under the Employment Protection (Recoupment of Jobseeker's Allowance & Income Support) Regulations 1996 (as amended) the Secretary of State is empowered to recover from any award of compensation made to a dismissed employee an amount equal to the amount of any jobseeker's allowance or income support (or related benefits) received by the employee between the date of his (or her) dismissal and the date of the tribunal hearing (or reinstatement/re-engagement, as the case may be).

- What this means in practice is that the Department for Work & Pensions will serve a *recoupment notice* on the employer (not the employee) requiring him to deduct a specified sum of money from the compensation payable to the dismissed employee and to return that money to the Department. The Regulations state that an employer must not pay any award of compensation to a dismissed employee until he has received a recoupment notice (which may constitute a 'Nil' return). When making an award of compensation for unfair dismissal or ordering reinstatement or re-engagement, an employment tribunal will ordinarily remind the employer of that requirement.

Pressure to dismiss

- When determining the fairness or otherwise of a dismissal, an employment tribunal will *not* be influenced by any claim by the employer that a trade union or other person had induced him to dismiss the employee by calling, organising, procuring or financing a strike or other industrial action, or by threatening to do so; and that the pressure was exercised because the employee was not a member of any trade union or of a particular trade union or of one of a number of particular trade unions. In other words, it will be no defence for an employer to argue that he dismissed the employee to avoid the threat of industrial action, and that he really had no choice but to give in to that pressure (section 160, Trade Union & Labour Relations (Consolidation) Act 1992).

- However, if such pressure had been brought to bear, the employer or the employee (the complainant) may request a tribunal to direct that the person who exercised that pressure (shop steward, works convenor, or whoever) be joined or, in Scotland, sisted as a party to the subsequent tribunal hearing. Such a request *will* be granted if made before the tribunal hearing begins, but may be refused after that time. However, it will not be granted under any circumstances if made after the tribunal has made an award of compensation for unfair dismissal or an order for reinstatement or re-engagement. If the tribunal upholds the complaint of unfair dismissal and the employer's contention that he was pressurised into dismissing the employee, it may order the person responsible for exercising that pressure to pay the whole or part of any award of compensation made to the employee (*ibid.* section 160(2) and (3)).

Interim relief

- An employee who presents a complaint to an employment tribunal that he (or she) has been unfairly dismissed and that the reason (or, if more than one, the principal reason) for his dismissal was one of those listed in (a) to (e) below, may apply to the tribunal for *interim relief* (briefly, a direction to his employer or former employer ordering him to reinstate or re-engage him pending the determination of his complaint of unfair dismissal at the subsequent full tribunal hearing) (section 128(1), Employment Rights Act 1996).

- The reasons (or principal reasons) for an employee's dismissal which would entitle him (or her) to apply for a tribunal order for interim relief are as follows:

  (a) that he was (or had proposed to become) a member of an independent trade union or that he had taken part (or proposed to take part), at an appropriate time, in the activities of such a union, or that he was not a member of a trade union, or of one of a number of particular trade unions, or that he had refused, or proposed to refuse, to become or remain a member (sections 152 and 161, Trade Union & Labour Relations (Consolidation) Act 1992);

  (b) that he had carried out (or had proposed to carry out) his functions as a *safety representative* or as a *representative of employee safety,* or as a *member of a safety committee,* or his activities as a person designated by his employer to carry out activities in connection with preventing or reducing risks to health and safety at work (section 100(1)(a) and (b), Employment Rights Act 1996);

  (c) that, being a *workforce representative* for the purposes of Schedule 1 to the Working Time Regulations 1998 (or being a candidate for election as such a representative), he (or she) had performed (or proposed to perform) any functions or activities as such a representative (or candidate) (*ibid.* section 101A(d));

  (d) that he had carried out (or proposed to carry out) his functions as a *trustee of a relevant occupational pension scheme (ibid.* section 102(1));

  (e) that he had carried out (or proposed to carry out) his functions or activities as an *employee representative* elected by his peers to represent their interests in consultations relative to proposed collective redundancies or in circumstances covered by the Transfer of Undertakings (Protection of Employment) Regulations 1981 (*ibid.* section 103); or that he had made a protected disclosure (as to which, please turn to the section titled **Public interest disclosures** elsewhere in this handbook) (*ibid.* section 103A).

Collective bargaining: trade union recognition

- Under the 'collective bargaining and trade union recognition' provisions of the Trade Union & Labour Relations (Consolidation) Act 1992, an employee may likewise apply for an order for interim relief if he has presented a complaint to an employment tribunal that he (or she) has been unfairly dismissed and that the reason (or, if more than one, the principal reason) for his dismissal was that he:

(a) had acted with a view to obtaining or preventing recognition of a union (or unions) by his employer; or

(b) had indicated that he supported or did not support such recognition; or

(c) had acted with a view to securing or preventing the ending of bargaining arrangements under a recognition agreement; or

(d) had indicated that he supported or did not support the ending of those bargaining arrangements; or

(e) had influenced or sought to influence the way in which votes were to be cast by other workers in a ballot for union recognition; or

(f) had influenced or sought to influence other workers to vote or to abstain from voting in such a ballot; or

(g) had voted in such a ballot; or

(h) had proposed to do, or failed to do, or proposed to decline to do any of the things referred to in paragraphs (a) to (g) above.

(*ibid.* paragraph 161(2) and Schedule A1).

For further particulars, please turn to the section on **Trade union recognition** elsewhere in this handbook.

Procedure for obtaining interim relief

• An application for *interim relief* in the circumstances described *must* be submitted to an employment tribunal within seven days of the effective date of termination of the employee's contract of employment.

  Note: If the essence of the employee's complaint is that he (or she) had been dismissed (or is under notice of dismissal) for exercising his right to be or remain a member of an independent trade union (or to take part at an appropriate time in the activities of such a union), the application must be accompanied by a certificate signed by an authorised official of the union in question stating that there appear to be reasonable grounds for supposing that the employee has been dismissed because of his trade union membership or activities.

• An employment tribunal is duty-bound to hear an application for interim relief as quickly as possible, but only after having sent the employer a copy of the employee's application (plus, where appropriate, a copy of the certificate signed by the employee's trade union), together with at least seven days' advance written notice of the date, time and place fixed for the hearing.

Outcome of employee's application for interim relief

- If, on hearing the employee's application for interim relief, the tribunal agrees that there is a likelihood that his (or her) complaint of unfair dismissal will be upheld at a full tribunal hearing (which may not take place until several weeks or months later), it will order the employer to reinstate or re-engage the employee until the date set for the full hearing. If the employer fails to attend the interim hearing or has made it clear that he has no intention of reinstating or re-engaging the employee, the tribunal will make an order for the continuation of the employee's contract of employment. This means, in effect, that the employer must continue to pay the employee his (or her) normal wages or salary (less any reduction in respect of payments already made) until the employee's complaint of unfair dismissal is finally heard and decided.

- A failure to comply with an order for reinstatement or re-engagement (following a successful application for interim relief) will prompt the tribunal to order the continuation of the employee's contract of employment. It will also order the employer to pay the employee such compensation as it considers 'just and equitable' in all the circumstances having regard to the infringement of the employee's right to be reinstated or re-engaged and any loss he (or she) may have suffered in consequence of the employer's non-compliance. A failure to comply with the terms of a *continuation order* will likewise attract an award of compensation that, if need be, will be enforced by the ordinary courts.

- The meaning of the expression *effective date of termination*, is explained in **Table 1** below.

Table 1

Meaning of
'EFFECTIVE DATE OF TERMINATION'

Notes

The expression *effective date of termination* occurs frequently in the Employment Rights Act 1996 in relation to dismissal and redundancy. It has two meanings, depending on its intended purpose.

A complaint of unfair dismissal must ordinarily be presented to an employment tribunal within the period of three months beginning with the *effective date of termination* of the employee's contract of employment (as defined in boxes **1**, **2** and **3** below).

But, to qualify to present a complaint of unfair dismissal or to lay claim to a statutory redundancy payment, an employee must have been continuously employed for one year (or, in the case of any entitlement to a statutory redundancy payment, two years) ending with the effective date of termination (as defined in boxes **4** and **5** following).

EFFECTIVE DATES OF TERMINATION AND TIME LIMITS FOR COMPLAINTS

1. If a contract of employment is terminated by notice (whether given by the employer or the employee), the *effective date of termination* of that contract (for the purpose described in **1A** opposite) is the date on which that notice expires (*ibid.* section 97(l)(a)).	**1A.** Any employee minded to present a complaint of unfair dismissal to an employment tribunal must do so within the period of three months beginning with the *effective date of termination* (as defined in **1** opposite). *Note:* This rule applies even if the employee was given less than the statutory minimum notice pre- scribed by section 86 of the 1996 Act or less notice than that laid down in his contract of employment.
2. If an employee's contract of employment is terminated without notice (as happens when an employee is either summarily dismissed or resigns without notice), the *effective date of termination of* that employee's contract is the date on which the dismissal or departure actually took place (*ibid.* section 97(l)(b)).	**2A.** An employee who is dismissed without notice (or who resigns without notice) has three months from the *effective date of termination* (as defined in **2** opposite) within which to present his (or her) complaint of unfair dismissal (or unfair 'constructive dismissal') to an employment tribunal.
3. If a 'limited-term' contract expires without being renewed under the same contract, the *effective date of termination* of that contract is the date on which that limited term expired (*ibid.* section 97(l)(c)).	**3A.** The employee's complaint of unfair dismissal in such a case must be presented to an employment tribunal within three months of the *effective date of termination* as defined in **3** opposite.

QUALIFYING PERIOD OF CONTINUOUS EMPLOYMENT

4. Where a contract of employment is terminated by the employer and the notice required by section 86 to be given by the employer would, if duly given on the *material date*, expire on a date later than the *effective date of termination* (as defined in boxes **1, 2** and **3** above) then, for the purposes of sections 108(1), 119(1) and 227(3) of the 1996 Act, the later date shall be treated as the *effective date of termination* for the purposes of determining the employee's total period of continuous employment.

Note: The expression *material date* used above means the date on which notice of dismissal was given by the employer or, if the employee was summarily dismissed (ie, without benefit of notice), the date on which that dismissal occurred (*ibid.* section 97(3)).

4A. The definition of the term *effective date of termination* in **4** opposite is used:

(a) to determine whether a dismissed employee had been continuously employed for the minimum period required to qualify him (or her) either to present a complaint of unfair dismissal or to demand a written statement of reasons for dismissal;

(b) to establish a redundant employee's total period of continuous service, for the purposes of determining his entitlement (if any) to a statutory redundancy payment.

5. Where the contract of employment is terminated by the employee and:

(a) the *material date* does not fall during a period of notice given by the employer to terminate the contract; and

(b) had the contract been terminated not by the employee but by notice given on the *material date by* the employer, that notice would have been required by section 86 to expire on a date later than the *effective date of termination* (as defined by subsection (1)), then, for the purposes of section 118(1), 119(1) and 227(3) of the 1996 Act, the later date shall be treated as the effective date of termination in relation to the dismissal (*ibid.* section 97(4)).

5A. This definition applies when an employee resigns, with or without notice, in circumstances such that he (or she) is entitled to resign without notice by reason of his employer's conduct (that is to say, in circumstances in which an employee plans to pursue a complaint of unfair 'constructive' dismissal). In such a situation, the *effective date of termination* (as defined in **5** opposite) will determine whether the employee had been continuously employed for the prescribed minimum period of one year or more to qualify him to pursue that complaint.

Note: The expression *material date* (see opposite) means the date when the employee handed in his notice of resignation *or*, if he resigned without notice, the date-of his simultaneous resignation and departure (*ibid.* section 97(5)).

- Dismissal and the reasons for dismissal are discussed in more detail in the following sections:

Constructive dismissal
Dismissal and TUPE transfers
Dismissal because of a statutory restriction
Dismissal for asserting a statutory right
Dismissal for incompetence
Dismissal for lack of qualifications
Dismissal for misconduct
Dismissal for refusing Sunday work
Dismissal for 'some other substantial reason'
Dismissal for taking industrial action
Dismissal in health and safety cases
Dismissal of a pension scheme trustee
Dismissal of an employee or workforce representative
Dismissal on grounds of disability
Dismissal on grounds of ill-health
Dismissal on grounds of redundancy
Dismissal on grounds of trade union membership
Wrongful dismissal

See also the sections titled:

Collective agreements
Contract of employment
Convicted persons, employment of
Disabled persons
Frustration of contract
Maternity rights
National minimum wage
Parental leave
Fixed-term employees
Public interest disclosures
Racial discrimination
Redundancy
Sex discrimination
Sunday work

DISMISSAL AND 'TUPE' TRANSFERS
(Transfer of an undertaking)

Key points

- The rights of employees are safeguarded when an employer sells, transfers or otherwise disposes of his (or her) undertaking or part of his undertaking (trade, business or company) as a 'going concern' to another employer.

- Regulation 8 of the Transfer of Undertakings (Protection Of Employment) Regulations 1981 (the 'TUPE Regulations'), as amended by the Collective Redundancies & Transfer of Undertakings (Protection of Employment) (Amendment) Regulations 1999, states that where, either before or after the sale or transfer of a business, a person employed by either of the transferor (the seller) or the transferee (the buyer) is dismissed, that employee will be treated in law as having been unfairly dismissed, if the sale or transfer (or a reason connected with it) was the reason or principal reason for the dismissal. But see *ETO reasons* for dismissal below.

- However (and somewhat curiously), the right to present a complaint of unfair dismissal, in the circumstances described in the previous paragraph, is available only to those employees who have been continuously employed for one year or more (and who were under normal retiring age) at the effective date of termination of their contracts of employment. For the meaning of the expressions *effective date of dismissal and normal retiring age*, please turn to the section titled **Dismissal** (notably the **Tables** at the end of that section).

  Note: The 1981 Regulations came into force on 1 May 1982, implementing European Community Directive 77/187/EEC on 'acquired lights'. The regulations apply to a transfer from one person to another of an undertaking (or part of an undertaking), (including any non-commercial undertaking, situated immediately before the transfer in the United Kingdom – whether the transfer is effected by sale or by some other disposition or operation of law. Such a transfer may be effected by a series of two or more transactions and may take place whether or not any property is transferred to the transferee by the transferor. In other words, the Regulations also apply to transfers of franchises or sub-contracts. However, share takeovers, that do not result in a change of employer, are *not* covered by the Regulations.

- When a trade, business or undertaking changes hands, the contracts of employment of the persons employed in that business at the time of the relevant transfer do not come to an end (as was formerly the case under the common law). Nowadays, those contracts automatically transfer to the new owner (the transferee) together with the transferor's rights, duties, obligations and liabilities under or in connection with those contracts. The transferee cannot pick or choose which employees to take on (*ibid.* regulation 5).

- An otherwise transferred employee cannot, of course, be forced to move. If he (or she) objects to becoming employed by the transferee, he must inform the transferor or transferee of that fact. However, by doing so, the employee effectively terminates his contract of employment with the transferor. The Regulations make it clear that that does not amount to a dismissal in law, which means that the employee automatically forfeits his right (if any) to pursue a complaint of unfair dismissal – unless he has terminated his contract (with or without notice) in circumstances which entitle him to do so because of a substantial and detrimental change in his working conditions (ie, a constructive dismissal). Incidentally, the transferor is under no obligation to retain the services of an employee who objects to becoming employed by the transferee (although he may be happy to do so) even if just part of the transferor's business has been (or is about to be) sold or transferred as a going concern (*ibid.* regulation 5(4A) and (4B)).

ETO reasons

- Regulation 8(2) of the 1981 Regulations does, however, acknowledge that an employer (whether transferor or transferee) may have sound economic, technical or organisational (ETO) reasons for wanting to trim his (or her) workforce before or after the acquisition or the sale of the transferor's business. An ETO reason will be an acceptable reason for the dismissal of an employee if, but only if, it entails a change in the workforce. If that condition is satisfied (and it will be for an employment tribunal to decide whether it is or not), the dismissal will be treated in law as having been 'for a substantial reason of a kind such as to justify the dismissal of an employee holding the position which that employee held'. On a complaint of unfair dismissal, the employer in question would, nonetheless, need to persuade the tribunal that he had acted reasonably in treating that reason as a sufficient reason for dismissing that employee.

Complaints to an employment tribunal

- A complaint of unfair dismissal in the circumstances described above must be 'presented' to the nearest regional office (or office) of the employment tribunals within three months of the effective date of termination of the employee's contract of employment – as to which, please turn to the section titled **Dismissal** elsewhere in this handbook, which section also contains information about awards of compensation for unfair dismissal, etc.

- For further information about the impact and effect of the 1981 Regulations, please turn to **Collective agreements**, **Continuous employment**, and **Transfer of undertakings** elsewhere in this handbook. See also **Redundancy**.

DISMISSAL BECAUSE OF A STATUTORY RESTRICTION

(The illegality of continued employment)

Key points

- An employer who cannot *lawfully* continue to employ a person in a particular job, may be left with no alternative but to dismiss that employee; in which event, the dismissal will ordinarily be held to have been fair (section 98(2)(d), Employment Rights Act 1996).

- Thus, a van driver or sales representative risks losing his (or her) job if the magistrates' court has deprived him of his driving licence. The foreign national will have to leave the country if he (or she) is an illegal immigrant, or if his work permit has expired or has not been renewed. An under-age barman (or barmaid) can expect to be sacked for lying about his age; and so on.

- However, in spite of restrictions imposed by statute law, the test of 'reasonableness' will still apply. Thus, an employment tribunal might well want to know whether the van driver could not have been offered something else to do pending the restoration of his licence; or whether sufficient enquiries had been made concerning the possibility of renewing or extending the foreign national's work permit. An employer is not obliged to create a new job simply to accommodate an employee who has been foolish enough to forfeit his driving licence; nor need he take the Home Secretary to court for refusing to renew an overseas worker's work permit.

- But factors, such as an employee's status and length of service, will be relevant (in appropriate cases) in determining whether the dismissal of such an employee was fair or unfair. In *Sandhu v London Borough of*

Hillingdon [1978] IRLR 209 the Employment Appeal Tribunal pointed out that it is not automatically fair to dismiss an employee because his continued employment would be unlawful. In that case, a probationary teacher was dismissed when the Education Department ruled that he was unsuitable as a teacher. Although Schools Regulations forbade the employment of such a teacher, the borough council should first have satisfied themselves that the teacher had been treated fairly during his probationary period. In *Sutcliffe & Eaton v Pinney* [1977] IRLR 349, a trainee Hearing Aid Dispenser was dismissed when he failed to pass a Hearing Aid Council examination. The tribunal held that the man's employer could have secured an extension of the training period without running the risk of prosecution.

Complaint to an employment tribunal

- Any employee dismissed in the circumstances described in this section may pursue a complaint of unfair dismissal if he (or she) had been employed for a continuous period of one or more years and was under normal retiring age at the effective date of termination of his contract of employment. The complaint must be presented within three months of that effective date of termination. If a complaint is presented out of time, the tribunal will not accept it unless satisfied that it was not reasonably practicable for the complainant to have acted sooner (*ibid.* sections 108, 109 and 111). If the employee's complaint is upheld, the employer will be ordered either to reinstate or re-engage the employee and/or to pay compensation, as to which please turn to the section titled **Dismissal** elsewhere in this handbook.

Note: Most statutory restrictions on the employment of women and young persons in industrial undertakings (and elsewhere) were repealed by the Employment Act 1989. Those that remain are for the most part concerned with the protection of woman at work in circumstances connected with pregnancy and childbirth, exposure to lead and ionising radiations, and so on. See also Suspension from on maternity grounds and **Women and young persons, employment of** elsewhere in this handbook.

DISMISSAL FOR ASSERTING A STATUTORY RIGHT

Key points

- Sections 104 and 105 of the Employment Rights Act 1996 protect employees who are dismissed (or selected for redundancy) for complaining that their employer has infringed one or other of their statutory rights in employment. The dismissal of an employee in such circumstances will be treated as automatically unfair if the reason for it (or, if more than one, the principal reason) was that the employee:

(a) had brought proceedings against his (or her) employer to enforce a right of his that is a *relevant statutory right*; or

(b) alleged that the employer had infringed a right of his (or hers) that is a *relevant statutory right*.

Furthermore, an employee dismissed in such circumstances may present a complaint of unfair dismissal to an employment tribunal regardless of his (or her) age or length of service at the material time (*ibid.* sections 108 and 109).

• It is as well to point out that such a dismissal will be treated as unfair even if the employee was not entitled to the disputed right, and regardless of whether the employer had actually infringed that right or not. If the employee made his claim 'in good faith', he (or she) should not have been dismissed for doing so. Indeed, the same protection applies even if the employee was uncertain or confused about the precise right he claims had been infringed – so long as he had made it reasonably clear to his employer what that right was.

Meaning of 'relevant statutory right'

The following statutory rights are *relevant* for these purposes, namely:

(a) any rights conferred by the Employment Rights Act 1996, (discussed throughout this handbook) for which the remedy for their infringement is by way of a complaint or reference to an employment tribunal;

  Note: Those rights include the right to be paid the appropriate national minimum wage rate and the right of the employee (where appropriate) to be paid tax credits through the payroll (*ibid.* sections 104A and 104B, as inserted, respectively, by the National Minimum Wage Act 1998 and the Tax Credits Act 2002).

(b) the right of an employee to a minimum period of notice (as conferred by section 86 of the Employment Rights Act 1996);

(c) rights conferred by the Working Time Regulations 1998 (the limit in working hours, and the right to daily and weekly rest breaks and rest periods, in-work rest breaks, and paid annual holidays);

(d) rights conferred by the Part-time Workers (Prevention of Less Favourable Treatment) Regulations 2000;

(e) rights conferred by the Fixed-term Employees (Prevention of Less Favourable Treatment) Regulations 2002;

(f) the following rights (conferred by the Trade Union & Labour Relations (Consolidation) Act 1992), namely:

- the right of an employee to stop the deduction of union dues from his or her pay (*ibid.* section 68);

- the right of an exempt employee to demand that no amount representing a contribution to a trade union political fund be deducted from his or her pay (*ibid.* section 86);

- the right of an employee not to have action short of dismissal taken against him (or her) as an individual on grounds related to his trade union membership or activities or because of his refusal to be or remain a member of a particular trade union or of any trade union (*ibid.* section 146);

- the right of an official of a recognised independent trade union to be permitted paid time off work to carry out his or her duties as such an official (*ibid.* sections 168 and 169);

- the right of an employee who is a member of a recognised independent trade union to be permitted a reasonable amount of time off work in order to take part in appropriate activities of that trade union (*ibid.* section 170).

Time limit for proceedings

- As was indicated earlier in this section, an employee who has been dismissed (or selected for redundancy) for asserting a statutory right may present a complaint of unfair dismissal regardless of his (or her) age or length of service at the material time. The complaint must be presented to an employment tribunal within three months of the effective date of termination of the employee's contract of employment. A tribunal will not hear a complaint presented out of time unless satisfied that it was not reasonably practicable for the complainant to have done so within the three-month limit (*ibid.* section 111(2)). If the employee's complaint is upheld, the employer will be ordered either to reinstate or re-engage the employee and/or to pay compensation. For further details, please turn to the section titled **Dismissal** elsewhere in this handbook.

See also the sections titled **Deductions from pay**, **Dismissal for refusing Sunday work**, **Notice of termination of employment**, **Time off work** (various), **Trade union membership and activities**, **Victimisation** and **Wages, payment of** elsewhere in this handbook.

DISMISSAL FOR INCOMPETENCE

Key points

- If an employee is dismissed on grounds of incompetence, the question whether his (or her) dismissal was fair or unfair will depend on whether, in the circumstances (including the size and administrative resources of his business or undertaking), the employer had acted 'reasonably' in treating incompetence as a sufficient reason for dismissing that employee; and that question shall be determined in accordance with equity and the substantial merits of the case (section 98, Employment Rights Act 1996).

- Incompetence (or lack of capability) is a legitimate reason for dismissing an employee. In the Court of Appeal decision in *Taylor v Alidair Limited* [1978] IRLR 82, Lord Denning commented: 'Whenever a man is dismissed for incapacity or incompetence, it is sufficient that the employer honestly believes on reasonable grounds that the man is incapable or incompetent. It is not necessary for the employer to prove that he is in fact incapable or incompetent.' And, in *E C Cook v Thomas Linnell & Sons Limited* [1977] IRLR 132, the Employment Appeal Tribunal added that it is enough to establish incompetence as a reason for dismissal if a responsible employer came to that conclusion after a reasonable time and there is evidence to back that conclusion.

- The tribunals and courts have applied a number of yardsticks over the years in determining the question whether an employer had acted reasonably or unreasonably when treating incompetence as a sufficient reason for dismissing an employee. These are explained in the following paragraphs.

Length of service

- How long had the employee worked for his (or her) employer? If an employee has given several years' satisfactory service in the same or a similar job with the same employer, an employment tribunal is likely to be suspicious of the employer's contention that the employee was incompetent. The tribunal will want to see evidence of any deterioration in performance sufficient to justify dismissing that employee. If, on the other hand, the employee was a relative newcomer (or a long-serving employee transferred to a new department), the fault may very well rest with the employer's recruitment, selection and training techniques. In which case, the tribunal may well ask to see evidence of a programmed attempt to train the employee and to improve his or her performance to the required standard.

Warning of shortcomings

• Was the employee warned of his (or her) shortcomings? Were there any circumstances that may have prompted a temporary shortfall in performance? In other words, was the employee warned or given a chance to explain? Did discussions take place? Did the employer expect too much of the employee? Were there any circumstances that may have been overlooked? Did the employee have a debilitating or distracting domestic problem (eg, a sick child or spouse)? Were there factors beyond the employee's control that had a major and unforeseen effect on his or her performance, such as persistent staff shortages, a breakdown in communications, the loss of a major account, non-delivery of raw materials etc?

Provision of training and advice

• What steps were taken to improve performance? Was training provided as an ongoing feature? If not, it is hardly reasonable to appoint, promote or transfer a man (or a woman), to deny him training, counselling and advice, and then dismiss him as incompetent. Nor is it reasonable to leave an employee to his own devices for weeks or months at a time on the assumption (too often misplaced) that he will have the sense to seek help and advice when he needs it.

Suitable alternative employment

• Was the employee made aware of the consequences of his (or her) continued failure to improve his performance in his job? In *Tiptools Limited v T W Curtis* [1973] IRLR 276, the then National Industrial Relations Court took the view that a failure to warn an employee of the likelihood of dismissal could render the subsequent dismissal unfair, particularly if it is felt that a warning would have prompted an improvement in performance. Furthermore, if an employee has been appointed, promoted or transferred beyond the level of his abilities, his employer is under an obligation to consider the possibility of a transfer to more suitable work (if such work is available).

Incompetent or just lazy?

• An employer must take care to distinguish between incompetence due to an inherent inability to function and the case of an employee whose poor work record is due to his (or her) own carelessness, negligence or idleness. The latter situations are more appropriately dealt with as cases of misconduct rather than of capability – when different criteria will be applied by the tribunals (see *Sutton & Gates (Luton) Limited v Boxall* [1978] IRLR 486).

Additional notes

- An employee who is genuinely incapable of doing his (or her) job well should not be treated in quite the same way as the employee who is guilty of misconduct. Lack of capability (or incompetence) can be demonstrated in a number of ways, such as lack of skill and aptitude, poor qualities of leadership, lack of initiative, and so on. A long-serving employee, who is genuinely unable to adapt to modern techniques or technology, should not simply be discarded. He has an investment in his job and deserves as much consideration as the law and natural justice can provide. If an employer is careless in his recruitment and selection techniques, or fails to provide the necessary training and guidance needed to improve the qualities and abilities of his workforce, the employee can hardly be criticised for the shortcomings of his superiors. The test of *reasonableness* is likely to be more stringently applied in this area than in any other.

Complaints

- An employee dismissed on grounds of alleged incompetence does not qualify to pursue a complaint of unfair dismissal unless he (or she) was under normal retiring age and had been continuously employed for one year or more at the effective date of termination of his contract of employment. For further information, please turn to the section titled **Dismissal**, elsewhere in this handbook. See also **Cooperation, employee's duty of** and **Fidelity and trust, employee's duty of**.

DISMISSAL FOR LACK OF QUALIFICATIONS

Key points

- 'Lack of qualifications' is one of the permitted (or legitimate) reasons for dismissal listed in section 98(2) of the Employment Rights Act 1996. The expression *qualifications* means any degree, diploma or other academic, technical or professional qualification relevant to the position that a dismissed employee held (*ibid.* section 98(3)(b)).

- Although an employee can legitimately be dismissed for not having the qualifications needed to do his (or her) job, that is not necessarily an end to the matter. What an employment tribunal must decide is whether the dismissal was fair. Given the particular circumstances (including the size and administrative resources of his undertaking) did the employer act reasonably or unreasonably in treating the employee's lack of qualifications as a sufficient reason for dismissing him? That question, says section 98(4) of the 1996 Act, shall be determined 'in accordance with equity and the substantial merits of the case'.

- To dismiss an employee because he (or she) does not have the qualifications needed to do the job he is paid to do is tantamount to an admission by an employer that his recruitment and selection procedures are fundamentally flawed. If the evidence shows that an employee deliberately concealed his lack of qualifications at the employment interview, or lied about them, or produced phoney or falsified certificates, an employment tribunal is unlikely to challenge the fairness of the employer's decision to dismiss him. But, an employment tribunal might well adopt a different stance if the evidence suggests that the employee was recruited on the basis of glowing and essentially accurate references provided by previous employers, or that his employer failed to ask the right questions at the employment interview, or that he acted on the assumption that a clearly experienced job applicant also had the necessary technical or professional qualifications.

The test of 'reasonableness'

- The question that an employment tribunal might well ask in doubtful cases (and there are very few reported decisions turning on a complainant's lack of qualifications) is whether the qualifications in dispute are relevant to the job that the employee was employed to do. Although every case will turn on its merits, it may well be held to have been unfair to dismiss an otherwise respected and competent employee with many years service on discovery that he (or she) does not have the qualifications specified in the job description. Although the employee may have been economical with the truth when first interviewed for the vacancy, his performance in that job over the intervening years will undoubtedly be a factor in deciding whether or not his employer had acted reasonably in treating his lack of qualifications as a sufficient reason for dismissing him.

Note: *Qualifications* in this context are not to be confused with skill. To dismiss an employee who is unable to perform his (or her) job satisfactorily has more to do with his level of competence than with his lack of formal qualifications, although the two may be linked. See **Dismissal for incompetence** elsewhere in this handbook.

Complaint of unfair dismissal

- An employee who has been dismissed for a reason related to his (or her) qualifications may present a complaint of unfair dismissal if continuously employed for one year or more and under normal retiring age at the effective date of termination of his contract of employment. Such a complaint must be presented within three months, although a tribunal will occasionally accept a complaint presented 'out of time' if satisfied that it was not reasonably practicable for the complainant to have presented it sooner (*ibid.* sections 108, 109 and 111). If the employee's complaint is heard and upheld, the employer will be ordered either to reinstate or re-engage the dismissed employer and/or to pay compensation; as to which, please turn to the section titled **Dismissal** elsewhere in this handbook.

DISMISSAL FOR MISCONDUCT

Key points

- When an employee first starts work with an employer, he (or she) is entitled to receive a written statement containing specified particulars of the terms and conditions of his employment. The written statement (often inaccurately described as the 'contract of employment') must include particulars of any disciplinary rules the employee will be expected to observe during the course of his employment. Alternatively, the statement must refer the employee to some other document (such as a staff handbook) that is 'conveniently accessible' to him and that explains those rules or standards of conduct (section 1(3), Employment Rights Act 1996). See **Written particulars of terms of employment** elsewhere in this handbook.

- The duty to include a note specifying disciplinary rules does not apply to rules or procedures relating to health or safety at work, although there is nothing to prevent an employer outlining such rules (*ibid.* section 3(2)).

- The written statement or handbook (or whatever) must also give the name or job title of the person within the organisation to whom the employee can apply if he (or she) is dissatisfied with any disciplinary decision relating to him, and the procedure for registering his dissatisfaction. In other words, an employee who believes that he has been undeservedly reprimanded or warned for alleged misconduct should know what to do and who to see in order to have the issue aired and resolved. Furthermore, if the employer's disciplinary procedure allows for appeals to progressively higher levels of management (a facility usually only available in the larger organisation), that procedure must also be explained in writing and made known to the employee (*ibid.*). Note, however, that until section 36 of the Employment Act 2002 comes into force (in the second half of 2003), these requirements do not apply to organisations with fewer than 20 people on the payroll (including persons employed by any associated employer and those employed in other branches of the same business) (*ibid.* section 3(3)).

Code of practice

- Practical guidance on how to draw up disciplinary rules and procedures, and how to operate them effectively, is given in Code of Practice 1 (*Disciplinary and Grievance Procedures*) issued by the Advisory, Conciliation and Arbitration Service (ACAS), and should be studied with care. The Code stresses that employers must make every effort to ensure that employees know and understand the standards of conduct expected of them. This, says the Code, is best achieved by giving every employee a copy of the rules and by explaining them orally. In the case of new employees, this should form part of an induction training programme.

- A failure to follow the guidelines laid down in the Code of Practice will not of itself make a dismissal unfair. Although a departure from those guidelines is admissible in evidence in any proceedings, in the final analysis it will be for an employment tribunal to decide whether in the circumstances (including the size and administrative resources of his undertaking), an employer had acted reasonably or unreasonably in treating misconduct as a sufficient reason for dismissal (see **Disciplinary rules and procedure** elsewhere in this handbook).

Gross misconduct

- Paragraph 7 of the Code of Practice urges that employees be made aware of the likely consequences of breaking rules and, in particular, they should be given a clear indication of the type of conduct that may warrant summary dismissal.

- Unless guilty of gross misconduct, an employee should not normally be dismissed for a first breach of discipline. However, the expression *gross misconduct* is not defined. Indeed, no such definition is possible. If, for example, a shop assistant is occasionally rude or short-tempered with customers, he (or she) can expect to be taken aside by his employer and warned, in no uncertain terms, that, unless his conduct improves, he will be dismissed. A great deal will depend on the circumstances. Just how long an employer can be expected to tolerate such conduct will depend on the circumstances and the likely damage to his business. In an extreme case, a restaurateur might be well within his rights to dismiss a waitress on the very first occasion that she is rude to a customer, without affording her yet another opportunity to further damage his reputation (see *Houston v Zeal (CH) Limited* [1972] ITR 331). In such cases, it is not the role of the tribunal to decide whether or not an employee was guilty of misconduct at the time of his (or her) dismissal, but whether the employer had acted reasonably in the circumstances, having regard to equity and the substantial merits of the case (see *Trust Houses Forte Leisure Ltd v J Aquilar* [1976] IRLR 251).

- For the avoidance of doubt, an employer should always take the time and trouble to explain to his (or her) employees that certain forms of misconduct will not be tolerated. Conduct that could cause serious damage to an employer's reputation, or that exposes members of the public to risk to their health and safety (eg the night porter in a hotel, drunk or asleep at his post), will almost invariably justify summary dismissal. On the other hand, no employee should be dismissed until all the circumstances have been thoroughly investigated and the employee has been provided with an opportunity to explain his (or her) side of the story. In *Cooperative Wholesale Society Limited v Squirrell* [1974] IRLR 45, it was held that an uncharacteristic act of gross misconduct, by a long-serving employee with a previously unblemished record, should not render such an employee liable to dismissal.

Dishonesty and theft

- 'If a man is dismissed for stealing, as long as the employer honestly believes it on reasonable grounds, that is enough to justify dismissal. It is not necessary for the employer to prove that he was in fact stealing' (per the Court of Appeal in *Taylor v Alidair Limited* [1978] IRLR 82). Again, it is not the role of an employment tribunal to establish an employee's guilt or innocence. Nor does it necessarily follow that, because an employee is later acquitted of an offence alleged to have been committed in the course of his employment, his dismissal for that offence was unfair (*Harris (Ipswich) Limited v Harrison* [1978] IRLR 382).

- However, a charge of theft, proffered by the police against an employee does not, of itself, constitute grounds for dismissal. On a complaint of unfair dismissal, the employer must show that he (or she) had reasonable grounds for believing that the employee had committed the offence based on his own reasonable investigation of the circumstances (*Scottish Special Housing Association v Cooke* [1979] IRLR 264).

Criminal offences outside employment

- Generally speaking, an employer may not act on a misdemeanour, however serious, that took place outside normal working hours. To justify dismissal in such circumstances, the employer must convince an employment tribunal that the employee's conduct had done harm to his (or her) business or had affected the employee's ability to work effectively. Paragraph 15(c) of Code of Practice I (*qv*) cautions that criminal offences outside employment 'should not be treated as automatic reasons for dismissal, regardless of whether the offence has any relevance to the duties of the individual as an employee. The main considerations,' says the code, 'should be whether the offence is one that makes the individual unsuitable for his (or her) type of work or unacceptable to other employees. Employees should not be dismissed solely because a charge against them is pending or because they are absent through having been remanded in custody.'

- Thus, in *Nottinghamshire County Council v Bowly* 1978 RLR 252, an employee was dismissed without warning after having been convicted of gross indecency with another man in a public lavatory. The Employment Appeal Tribunal held that, although the employee's sexual misconduct outside normal working hours had not been particularly extreme, his employer had not acted unreasonably in deciding that his conviction no longer made him suitable to continue in his employment as a teacher.

Breach of safety rules

- An employer, who has taken the trouble to explain to employees the importance of observing safety procedures and standards, may be justified in treating a single isolated breach of the safety rules as conduct justifying summary dismissal without further warning. Thus, in *Martin v Yorkshire Imperial Metals* [1978] IRLR 440, a machine operator was dismissed 'on the spot' when it was discovered that he had deliberately deactivated a dual safety control on his machine. In evidence, it was demonstrated that the employee was well aware of the likely consequences of his actions, even though his employer's disciplinary rules did not specify dismissal as the automatic penalty for a breach of the safety rules.

- Any wilful misconduct on the part of an employee, that is likely to endanger the safety and security of fellow-employees, let alone that of clients, customers, etc would almost certainly justify that dismissal of that employee without further warning. Although there appears to be no case law on the subject, an employer could not be expected to tolerate a repetition of an incident that could have led to a major disaster or loss of life (eg, a night porter in a hotel drunk or asleep at his post).

Fighting and physical assault

- Fighting or physical assault is invariably categorised as gross misconduct justifying the summary dismissal of one or other (or, in some cases, both) of the protagonists. However, the duty of an employer to investigate the circumstances, and to invite those concerned to explain their conduct, is well illustrated by the case of *K Sherrier v Ford Motor Company* [1976] IRLR 141. There, two employees were discovered fighting. One was dismissed; the other merely reprimanded. The employee who had been dismissed complained to an employment tribunal that he had been unfairly treated relative to his colleague who had not been dismissed. However, his dismissal was held to have been fair when it was revealed in evidence that he had worked for the company for just two years and had already received six prior warnings for misconduct. His companion, on the other hand, had worked for the employers for several years and had a previous good record. In a similar case, that of *Meyer Dunmore International Limited v Rogers* [1978] IRLR 167, the Employment Appeal Tribunal held that summary dismissal for fighting is fair if there is a clear rule, that is well understood, that fighting is a serious matter and an inquiry is properly and fairly conducted.

Misconduct and witness statements

- Witness statements often have an important role to play in misconduct cases, especially in cases involving fighting and physical assault. While other employees (bystanders) might well be prepared to give written statements to their employer explaining what they saw or did not see, they might be less than eager (understandably, in some cases) to repeat their allegations before, or have the existence and content of those statements made known to the latter at a disciplinary hearing.

- In *Hussain v Elone plc* [1999] IRLR 420, an employee dismissed for head-butting another employee appealed to the Court of Appeal against the decision of an employment tribunal that his dismissal had been fair, a decision upheld on appeal by the EAT. He argued (through counsel) that it was contrary to natural justice for his employer to have repeated those allegations at a disciplinary hearing without either acknowledging the existence of, or affording him access to, witness statements obtained from four of his working colleagues.

- In rejecting Mr Hussain's appeal, the Court of Appeal held that, so long as an employer has carried out a fair and reasonable investigation of alleged misconduct before dismissing an employee, 'there is no universal requirement of natural justice or general principle of law that an employee must be shown in all cases copies of witness statements obtained by an employer about the employee's conduct. It is a matter of what is fair and reasonable in each case.' Mr Hussain had been informed of the allegations made against him and had been given every opportunity to respond to them. The person whom he had been accused of assaulting was also present at the hearing to give his version of events. Mr Hussain had been treated fairly and reasonably because he was told of the accusations against him and was given a full opportunity to respond to them.

- The outcome might well have been different, said Lord Justice Mummery, if the essence of the case against Mr Hussain was contained in statements which had not been disclosed to him, and where he had not otherwise been informed at the disciplinary hearing, or orally or in other manner, of the nature of the case against him. In *Louies v Coventry Hood & Seating Co Ltd* [1990] IRLR 324, EAT, cited by counsel for Mr Hussain, the substance of the case against the appellant was contained in statements which the employee had asked to see and which had not been shown to him, without good reason, and on which the employer had placed substantial reliance in reaching the decision to dismiss him. That, said Lord Mummery, is not the case here.

- In a more recent case, that of *Asda Stores Ltd v Thompson & Others* [2002] IRLR 245, the EAT held that an employment tribunal had been wrong to order the disclosure 'in their totality' of witness statements provided by other employees confirming allegations of gross misconduct and criminal activities by two of their colleagues – the more so as those statements had been provided under a guarantee of confidentiality. In short, said the EAT, the tribunal had failed properly to exercise its long-established discretionary power to direct disclosure of documents in an anonymised or edited form in order to conceal the identity of the witnesses and to maintain the employer's promise of confidentiality. If statements have not only to be anonymised but also edited to achieve this objective, that is what the tribunal should direct. In investigating complaints in cases such as this, where hard drugs are allegedly involved, it is entirely proper for an employer to give a promise of confidentiality – a promise that a tribunal should respect. Nothing should be disclosed, said the EAT, that in any way identifies the makers of any of the statements, unless they specifically agree to be identified. If this means that some statements have to be excluded in their entirety because it is not possible to conceal the identities of the people who made them, that is what will have to occur and the question of the fairness of the dismissal will have to be judged in due course by the employment tribunal on that basis.

Dismissal of trade union officials

- Paragraph 26 of Code of Practice 1 (*qv*) points out that 'disciplinary action against a trade union official can lead to a serious dispute if it is seen as an attack on the union's functions. Although normal disciplinary standards should apply to their conduct as to other employees, no disciplinary action beyond oral warning should be taken until the circumstances of the case have been discussed with a senior trade union representative or full-time official.' See also **Cooperation, employee's duty of Fidelity, employee's duty of** and **Written particulars of terms of employment**.

Complaint to an employment tribunal

- In the circumstances described above, an employee would not ordinarily qualify to pursue a complaint of unfair dismissal before an employment tribunal *unless* under normal retiring age and continuously employed for one year or more at the effective date of termination of his (or her) contract of employment. The complaint must be presented within three months of the effective date of termination of the employee's contract of employment. If his complaint is upheld, the employer will be ordered either to reinstate or re-engage the employee and/or pay an award of compensation; as to which, please turn to the section titled **Dismissal**, elsewhere in this handbook.

DISMISSAL FOR REFUSING SUNDAY WORK

Key points

- The Sunday Trading Act 1994 (which came into force on 26 August 1994) gave *shop workers* in England and Wales the right to opt-out of Sunday work, and the right also not to be dismissed, selected for redundancy, or victimised, for exercising that right. Shop workers employed before 26 August 1994 were also given the right to opt-out of any contractual obligation to work on Sundays. On 3 January 1995, that same right was extended to *betting workers* under analogous provisions inserted in the Betting, Gaming & Lotteries Act 1963. Since then, the relevant provisions of the 1994 and 1963 Acts have been repealed and have re-emerged in the (consolidating) Employment Rights Act 1996 (sections 36 to 43, 45, 101, 197(2), 232 and 233).

- For obvious reasons, the right to refuse to work on Sundays does *not* apply to *opted-in* shop and betting workers; that is to say, workers who have entered into an agreement with their employers to do shop work or betting work on Sundays; nor does it apply to shop or betting workers who have been employed specifically to work on Sundays only. For further particulars, see **Sunday work** elsewhere in this handbook.

Meaning of 'shop worker'

- A *shop worker* is an employee who, under his (or her) contract of employment, is required to do shop work or may be required to do such work. *Shop work* means work in or about a shop in England or Wales on a day on which the shop is open for the serving of customers. The expression *shop* includes any premises where any retail trade or business is carried on – including the business of a barber or hairdresser, the business of hiring goods otherwise than for use in the course of a trade or business, and retail sales by auction. But it does *not* include restaurants, cafeterias, coffee shops, tea rooms, public houses, bars, or the public dining rooms in hotels where meals, refreshments or intoxicating liquor are sold for consumption on the premises. Nor does it apply to any 'take-away' establishment in which meals or refreshment are prepared to order for immediate consumption off the premises (*ibid.* section 232).

- A *protected* shop worker is one who was employed as a shop worker before 26 August 1994, and is still so employed. The term *protected* also applies to shop workers recruited on or after that date on contracts of employment that do not and cannot require them to work in their employer's shop on Sundays.

- An *opted-out* shop worker is a shop worker employed on or after 26 August 1994 who has exercised his (or her) legal right to opt-out of a term in his contract of employment requiring him to work on Sundays.

- An *opted-in* shop worker is one who has renounced his (or her) *protected or opted-out* status and has entered into an agreement with his employer to work on Sundays or on nominated Sundays. An opted-in shop worker who reneges on that agreement can be fairly dismissed for doing so.

Meaning of 'betting worker'

- A betting worker is an employee who, under his (or her) contract of employment, is either required to do betting work or may be required to do so. *Betting work* means work for a bookmaker at a track in England or Wales on a day on which the bookmaker acts as such at that track, being work that consists of, or includes, dealing with betting transactions. The expression also encompasses work in a licensed betting office in England or Wales on a day on which that office is open for use for the effecting of *betting transactions*. The latter expression includes the collection or payment of winnings on a bet and any transaction in which one or more of the parties is acting as a bookmaker (*ibid.* section 233).

Complaint to an employment tribunal

- A *protected* or *opted-out* shop worker or betting worker, who has been dismissed or selected for redundancy for refusing to work on Sundays (or on a particular Sunday), can complain to an employment tribunal, regardless of his (or her) age or length of service at the time the dismissal occurred (*ibid.* section 108(3)). If the complaint is upheld, the employer will be ordered either to reinstate or re-engage the shop work and/or pay compensation. An employer who unreasonably refuses to comply with an order for reinstatement or re-engagement in these circumstances will very likely be ordered to pay an additional award of compensation. For further particulars, see **Dismissal** elsewhere in this handbook.

  Note: An *opted-in* shop worker or betting worker who has been dismissed or selected for redundancy for refusing or failing to work on Sundays (or on a particular Sunday) can also register a complaint of unfair dismissal if he (or she) believes that, in the particular circumstances, he had been unreasonably or unfairly treated by his employer. However, to pursue such a complaint, he would need to have worked for his employer for a continuous period of one year (and be under normal retiring age) at the effective date of termination of his contract of employment.

- A complaint of unfair dismissal in the circumstances described above must be presented within three months of the effective date of termination of the shop or betting worker's contract of employment. A tribunal will not normally hear a complaint that has been presented 'out of time' unless satisfied that it was not reasonably practicable for the complainant to have acted sooner. For the meaning of the expression *effective date of termination*, please turn to the section titled **Dismissal** earlier in this handbook. See also **Dismissal for asserting a statutory right**.

DISMISSAL FOR 'SOME OTHER SUBSTANTIAL REASON'

Key points

- Section 98 of the Employment Rights Act 1996 allows that there will be occasions when it may be fair to dismiss an employee for reasons other than those relating to his (or her) capability, qualifications, conduct, redundancy, or the illegality of continued employment.

- However, whether a dismissal for 'some other substantial reason' was fair or unfair will depend on whether, in the circumstances (including the size and administrative resources of his business), the employer had acted reasonably or unreasonably in treating that reason as a legitimate reason for dismissing the employee in question (*ibid.* section 98(l)(b)).

Business reorganisation

- For example, an employer may need to restructure or reorganise his (or her) business in the interests of efficiency, profitability or survival. This could involve a change in working methods and related manpower arrangements. At such a time, the employer would ordinarily discuss his problems and his proposals with employees or their representatives. However, at the end of the day, the decision must be his. The employment tribunals will not deny an employer's prerogative to manage his business as best he can. If an employer's proposals meet with resistance in some quarters, or if one or more employees are totally uncompromising in their attitudes, he may be left with no other alternative but to dismiss those employees. In *Ellis v Brighton Cooperative Society* [1976] IRLR 419, a foreman who refused to accept new working methods involving longer working hours and more onerous duties was held to have been fairly dismissed notwithstanding that he was not contractually bound to go along with those changes.

Pressure from dissatisfied clients

- In *Scott Packing and Warehousing Company limited v Patterson* [1978] IRLR 167, an employee was dismissed when a major client threatened to withhold further contracts unless that employee was taken off an existing contract. The client suspected the employee of pilfering. The Employment Appeal Tribunal held that pressure of this type amounted to 'some other substantial reason' to dismiss, but questioned the employer's 'reasonableness' in not considering the possibility of finding another job for the employee elsewhere within his organisation.

Clashes of personality

- An employee who causes tension and disharmony amongst fellow employees could also be a candidate for dismissal. Thus, in *Treganowan v Robert Knee & Company Limited* [1975] IRLR 247, an employee who boasted of her sexual exploits, and caused disharmony amongst her fellow employees, was adjudged to have been fairly dismissed for 'some other substantial reason'.

Confidential information

- In *Skyrail Oceanic Limited t/a Cosmos Tours v Coleman* [1978] IRLR 226, an employee was dismissed when it became known that she was to marry an employee of a rival travel operator. Both employers had met to discuss the possibility of confidential information being divulged. The decision was taken to dismiss the wife on the premise that the husband was the breadwinner. The Employment Appeal Tribunal held that her employer had been justifiably concerned about the possible risks to his business interests and that her dismissal was for 'some other substantial reason'. However, he had acted unreasonably in not forewarning the employee of the likelihood of dismissal.

Dismissing a replacement employee

- Section 106 of the 1996 Act deals with the situation confronting an employer who recruits a 'temporary' employee specifically to take on the work of one of his permanent employees who is either absent from work on maternity leave or who has been suspended from work on maternity or medical grounds (as provided by *ibid.* sections 64 and 66).

- In such circumstances, the dismissal of the replacement employee will be treated as having been 'for a substantial reason of a kind such as to justify the dismissal of an employee holding the position which that employee held', if:

– when engaging or recruiting the temporary employee, the employer made it clear to him (or her) *in writing* that he would be dismissed as soon as the employee he was replacing returned to work after maternity leave or resumed his (or her) normal duties at the end of the period of suspension.

Should the matter go before an employment tribunal (on a complaint by the 'temporary' or replacement employee that he or she had been unfairly dismissed), the employer will nonetheless need to satisfy the tribunal that he had acted reasonably and fairly in dismissing that employee when the permanent employee returned to work (*ibid.* sections 106(4) and 98(4)).

Complaint to an employment tribunal

- An employee does not ordinarily qualify to pursue a complaint of unfair dismissal *unless* he (or she) has been continuously employed for one year or more at the effective date of termination of his (or her) contract of employment. He or she must also have been under normal retiring age at that time. If the employee's complaint is upheld, the employer will be ordered either to reinstate or re-engage the employee and/or to pay an award of compensation; as to which, please turn to the section titled **Dismissal** elsewhere in this handbook.

DISMISSAL FOR TAKING INDUSTRIAL ACTION
(*Strikes and other industrial action*)

Key points

- Under the common law, any employee who withdraws his (or her) labour, by participating in a strike or other form of industrial action, has repudiated his contract of employment and has effectively dismissed himself – although, in practice, the employer would be expected to accept the repudiation by informing the employee that his employment has ended.

- In the ordinary course of events, an employment tribunal does not have the jurisdiction to decide whether the 'dismissal' of a striking worker was fair or unfair. Section 237 of the Trade Union & Labour Relations (Consolidation) Act 1992 states unequivocally that 'an employee has no right to complain of unfair dismissal if at the time of the dismissal he was taking part in an unofficial strike or other unofficial industrial action'. However, as is explained below, section 237 of the 1992 Act does extend a measure of protection to workers who have been dismissed during a lock-out conducted or instituted by their employer *or* while taking part in an *official* strike or other *official* industrial action.

Note: The expression *other industrial action* is not defined by the 1992 Act. However, in *W J Thompson v Eaton Limited* [1976] IRLR 308, the Employment Appeal Tribunal held that workers were engaged in *other industrial action* when they surrounded a new machine installed by their employer with a view to resisting their employer's (*sic*) 'unlawful coercive action' in attempting to enforce the installation of machines to which the employees objected.

Meaning of 'unofficial' industrial action

- A strike or other form of industrial action is *unofficial* in relation to an employee unless (a) he (or she) is a member of a trade union and the action is authorised or endorsed by that union or (b) he (or she) is not a member of a trade union but there are among those taking part in the industrial action members of a trade union by which the action has been authorised or endorsed. What this means in effect is that industrial action will not be regarded as unofficial if none of those taking part in it are members of a trade union.

- It should be noted that unofficial industrial action will *not* be treated as having been authorised or endorsed by a trade union if the executive, president or general secretary of that union repudiates that action as soon as is reasonably practicable after it has been brought to their attention. For the repudiation to be effective, the executive, general secretary or president of the union must:

    (a) write to the committee members or officials who called the industrial action in the first place, informing them that the union has repudiated their actions; and

    (b) do its best to give individual written notice of the fact and date of repudiation, without delay:

        (i)   to every member whom the union has reason to believe is taking part, or might take part, in the industrial action in question; and

        (ii) to the employer of every such member.

- The notice given to the members under (i) above must contain the following statement:

> 'Your union has repudiated the call (or calls) for industrial action to which this notice relates, and will give no support to unofficial industrial action taken in response to it (or them). If you are dismissed while taking unofficial industrial action, you will have no right to complain of unfair dismissal.'

If the general secretary, president or executive of the union repudiates unofficial industrial action in this way and the repudiation is genuine (see below), the strike or other industrial action will not be treated in law as unofficial before the end of the next working day after the day on which the repudiation takes place (*ibid.* section 237(4)). In other words, the striking workers have a limited time within which to return to work before running the risk of being dismissed and forfeiting their right to complain of unfair dismissal.

Example: A dozen or more production workers in a factory in the Midlands are called out on unofficial strike by their shop steward in a dispute about overtime payments. They normally work a five day week, Monday to Friday, inclusive. The strike starts on Thursday. In the meantime, the General Secretary of the union has been alerted and immediately writes to the shop steward and to each of the union's members who are involved in the strike telling them in effect (in the terms outlined above) to call off their action and get back to work. He also writes in similar terms to the workers' employer. If the striking workers receive the General Secretary's letter on the following Monday morning, they will have a little over a day-and-a-half to make up their minds about calling off the strike. Indeed, if they are not back at work at their normal starting time on Wednesday morning, their employer can dismiss them with impunity and they will forfeit their right to complain of unfair dismissal.

Repudiation or not?

- A trade union's purported repudiation of unofficial industrial action will not be treated in law as genuine if, at any time after that repudiation, the executive or president or general secretary of the union behaves in a manner that is inconsistent with that repudiation. Nor will there have been a genuine repudiation if, in response to a request made within the next six months by a person who has not been notified in writing of the repudiation (or by a party to a commercial contract whose performance has been interfered with as a result of the unofficial action), the executive or president or general secretary of the union does not forthwith confirm in writing that the industrial action had been repudiated (*ibid.* sections 20(2) and 21).

Note: Any act done by a trade union to induce a person to take part, or continue to take part, in industrial action is not protected (ie, is actionable in tort) unless the industrial action has the support of a ballot, has been called by a specified person, and takes place before the ballot ceases to be effective (ie, within the period of four weeks beginning with the date of the ballot (*ibid*. sections 226 and 233). In short, any form of industrial action that does not satisfy those requirements is *unofficial* and, therefore, unprotected. For further details, see **Strikes and other industrial action** elsewhere in this handbook.

Complaints by employees dismissed during official industrial action

- An employment tribunal *does* have jurisdiction to hear a complaint of unfair dismissal brought by an employee dismissed for taking part in *official* industrial action if the employee in question can show that one or more of his (or her) striking colleagues had not been dismissed, or that his employer had offered to re-employ one or more of the latter within three months of his own dismissal, but had not offered to re-employ him (*ibid*. section 238(2)).

- Save for an amendment introduced recently by the Employment Relations Act 1999 (see *Exceptions to the selective dismissal and re-employment rule* below), this means, in effect, that the only way an employer can avoid a complaint of unfair dismissal in such circumstances is to dismiss every striking employee and to resist the temptation to re-employ any one of their number for a period of three months beginning with the date on which the last striking worker was dismissed.

- An employer may defend his (or her) selective re-engagement of some, but not all, workers involved in a strike or lock-out by demonstrating to an employment tribunal that his actions were entirely 'reasonable' in the circumstances. For instance, his business may have suffered as a result of a prolonged strike or lock-out, to the point where he had no choice but to employ a much-reduced workforce (*ibid*. section 239(1), read with section 98(4) of the Employment Rights Act 1996). Notwithstanding this argument, the employer may, nonetheless, be called upon to justify his re-selection procedure – the more so if he has rejected so-called 'troublemakers' in favour of those less prone to take industrial action.

Exceptions to the selective dismissal and re-employment rule

- However, there is to be an exception to the rule relating to the selective dismissal or re-employment of employees who took part in official industrial action.

- Sections 238(2B) and 238A of the Trade Union & Labour Relations (Consolidation Act 1992 (as inserted by section 16 and Schedule 5 to the

Employment Relations Act 1999) caution employers that, notwithstanding section 238(2) of the 1992 Act, dismissing an employee for taking part in an *official* strike (or other form of *official* industrial action) will be treated as unfair (regardless of the employee's age or length of service at the material time) if:

(a) the dismissal occurred within the period of eight weeks beginning with the day on which the employee started to take official industrial action; or

(b) the dismissal occurred more than eight weeks after the day on which the employee first took official industrial action, in circumstances in which the employee had returned to work within those first eight weeks; or

(c) the dismissal occurred more than eight weeks after the employee first went on strike (or took some other form of official industrial action), in circumstances in which the employee had not returned to work and his employer had failed to take all reasonable steps to resolve the dispute to which the official industrial action related.

Note: Whether or not the employer in (c) above had taken reasonable procedural steps to resolve the industrial dispute will depend in large part on the extent to which either party had complied with (or had been willing to comply with) any previously agreed 'dispute resolution procedure' (eg, as laid down in a collective agreement), or on the willingness of either of the parties to commence or resume negotiations with a view to bringing the industrial action to an end, or whether an offer of conciliation by ACAS had been made and rejected (and by whom), or whether either or both of the parties had unreasonably refused a request that mediation services be used in relation to procedures to be adopted with a view to ending the dispute.

Complaint to employment tribunal

- An employment tribunal will not consider a complaint of unfair dismissal, in the circumstances described in this section, unless it is 'presented' within six months of the effective date of termination of the employee's contract of employment, or within such further period as the tribunal considers reasonable, if the tribunal is satisfied that it was not reasonably practicable for the complaint to be presented before the end of that period (*ibid.* section 239). Furthermore, unless dismissed in the circumstances described above ('*Exceptions to the selective dismissal and re-employment rule*'), the complainant must have been employed for a continuous period of one year or more and must have been under normal retiring age at the effective date of termination of his (or her) contract of employment (sections 108 and 109, Employment Rights Act 1996). If the employee's complaint is upheld, the employer will be ordered either to reinstate or re-engage the employee and/or pay an award of compensation to that employee; as to which, please turn to the section titled **Dismissal** elsewhere in this handbook.

Continuity of employment

- Days on which an employee is on strike against his (or her) employer (or is absent from work because of a lock-out by his employer) do not destroy the continuity of employment of a period of employment, but must nonetheless be discounted when computing that employee's total period of continuous employment (*ibid.* section 212). In practice, this means that the day on which the employee first started work with his employer is treated as postponed by the number (or aggregate number) of days during which he took part in strike action or was locked-out (including, in each case, the day on which he went on strike, or was locked-out, but excluding the day on which he returned to work).

- For further particulars, see **Continuous employment**, elsewhere in this handbook. See also **Lock-outs, Strikes and other industrial action, Trade union members,** and **Trade union membership and activities**.

DISMISSAL IN HEALTH AND SAFETY CASES

Key points

- It is inadmissible and automatically unfair for an employer to recruit or 'designate' an employee either as a safety officer or 'competent person' and then to dismiss or select that same employee for redundancy for carrying out (or proposing to carry out) his (or her) legitimate duties or functions (section 100, Employment Rights Act 1996).

  Note: Regulation 7 of the Management of Health & Safety at Work Regulations 1999 requires an employer to 'appoint one or more competent persons to assist him in undertaking the measures he needs to take to comply with the requirements and prohibitions imposed upon him by or under the relevant statutory provisions' (that is to say, under the Health & Safety at Work etc Act 1974 and statutes and regulations made under or saved by that Act).

- The same rule applies if an employee is dismissed or selected for redundancy:

  (a) for performing (or proposing to perform) his functions as an appointed *safety representative* or as a *member of a safety committee* (under the Safety Representatives & Safety Committees Regulations 1977);

(b) for performing (or proposing to perform) his functions as a *representative of employee safety*, having been elected as such by his or her fellow-employees (under the provisions of the Health & Safety (Consultation with Employees) Regulations 1996).

- Any employee designated, appointed or elected to represent the interests of fellow-employees on issues affecting (or likely to affect) their health and safety at work, has the legal right to carry out his (or her) functions without being victimised or threatened with dismissal for doing so. If such a person is dismissed for that reason, he may pursue a complaint of unfair dismissal regardless of his (or her) age or length of service at the time his employment ended.

- It is *also* automatically unfair to dismiss an employee or select him (or her) for redundancy:

  (a) for bringing to the employer's attention, by reasonable means, circumstances connected with his work that he reasonably believed to be harmful or potentially harmful to health or safety (in a situation in which there either is no safety representative or safety committee or representative of employee safety, or it was not reasonably practicable to contact or involve such persons);

  (b) for leaving (or proposing to leave) his place of work in circumstances of danger (that he reasonably believed to be serious and imminent and that he could not reasonably have been expected to avert) or for refusing to return to that place of work or to the dangerous part of that place of work while the danger persisted;

  (c) for taking (or proposing to take) *appropriate* steps to protect himself or other persons from a danger that he reasonably believed to be serious and imminent.

Whether the steps that an employee took (or proposed to take) under (c) above were *appropriate* is to be judged by all the circumstances including, in particular, his (or her) knowledge and the facilities and advice available to him at the material time (*ibid.* section 100(2)).

However, section 100(3) provides that a dismissal under (c) above will *not* be treated as having been unfair if the employer can satisfy an employment tribunal that it was (or would have been) so negligent of the employee to do what he (or she) did (or proposed to do) that *any* reasonable employer would have reacted by dismissing him.

Interim relief

- Any safety officer, safety representative, 'competent' person, 'designated' person, or member of a safety committee bringing a complaint of unfair dismissal to an employment tribunal, in the circumstances described above, may apply to the tribunal for *interim relief* (briefly, a direction to the employer or former employer ordering him (or her) to reinstate or re-engage the employee pending the determination of the latter's complaint at the subsequent full tribunal hearing).

- An application for interim relief *must* be submitted to an employment tribunal within seven days of the effective date of termination of the employee's contract of employment.

- An employment tribunal must hear an application for interim relief as quickly as possible, but not before sending the employer a copy of the employee's application and giving the employer at least seven days' advance written notice of the date, time and place for the hearing.

- If, on hearing the employee's application for interim relief, the tribunal agrees that there is a likelihood that the complaint will be upheld at a full tribunal hearing (which may not take place until several weeks or months later), it will order the employer to reinstate or re-engage the employee until the date set for the full hearing. If the employer fails to attend the interim hearing or has made it clear that he has no intention of reinstating or re-engaging the employee, the tribunal will make an order for the continuation of the employee's contract of employment. This means, in effect, that the employer must continue to pay the employee his or her normal wages or salary (less any reduction in respect of payments already made) until the employee's complaint is finally heard and decided. A failure to comply with the terms of a 'continuation order' will likewise attract an award of compensation which, if need be, will be enforced by the ordinary courts.

- If the employee's complaint of unfair dismissal is subsequently upheld at the full tribunal hearing, the employer will be ordered either to reinstate or re-engage the employee and/or pay an award of compensation to that employee. For further particulars, please turn to the section titled **Dismissal** elsewhere in this handbook.

  See also **Employment tribunals and procedure, Dismissal for asserting a statutory right, Time off work: safety representatives**, and **Victimisation** elsewhere in this handbook.

DISMISSAL OF A PENSION SCHEME TRUSTEE

Key points

- An employee who is a trustee of a relevant occupational pension scheme relating to his (or her) employment has the legal right to perform his duties as such a trustee without fear of being dismissed. Furthermore, he is entitled to a reasonable amount of paid time off work (during normal working hours) to enable him to carry out those duties and, if need be, to undergo training relevant to the performance of those duties (sections 58, 59 and 102, Employment Rights Act 1996).

    Note: The expression 'relevant occupational pension scheme' means an occupational pension scheme established under a trust by the employee's employer, as defined in section 1 of the Pension Schemes Act 1993.

Complaint to an employment tribunal

- If an employer dismisses an employee (or selects him (or her) for redundancy) for performing (or proposing to perform) his duties as a pension fund trustee, the dismissal will be regarded as unfair. The trustee may present a complaint of unfair dismissal to an employment tribunal, regardless of his age or length of service at the material time, and will be awarded compensation (including a minimum basic award of £3,500 – which latter is reviewed annually) if his complaint is upheld. The complaint must, however, be presented to the tribunal within three months of the effective date of termination of the employee's contract of employment.

Application for interim relief

- A pension fund trustee who has registered a complaint of unfair dismissal with the Secretary to the Tribunals, in the circumstances described above, may apply to an employment tribunal for *interim relief* (briefly, a direction to his (or her) employer, or former employer, ordering him either to reinstate the employee in his old job or re-engage him in comparable employment pending the determination of his complaint at the subsequent full tribunal hearing).

- An application for interim relief in the circumstances described *must* be submitted to an employment tribunal within seven days of the effective date of termination of the employee's contract of employment.

- An employment tribunal must hear an application for interim relief as quickly as possible, but not before sending the employer a copy of the employee's application and giving the employer at least seven days' advance written notice of the date, time and place of the hearing.

- If, on hearing the employee's application for interim relief, the tribunal agrees that there is a likelihood that the complaint will be upheld at a full tribunal hearing (that may not take place until several weeks or months later), it will order the employer to reinstate or re-engage the employee until the date set for the full hearing. If the employer fails to attend the interim hearing or has made it clear that he has no intention either of reinstating or re-engaging the employee, the tribunal will make an order for the continuation of the employee's contract of employment. This means, in effect, that the employer must continue to pay the employee his or her normal wages or salary (less any reduction in respect of payments already made) until the employee's complaint is finally heard and decided. A failure to comply with the terms of a 'continuation order' will likewise attract an award of compensation that, if need be, will be enforced by the ordinary courts.

  See also **Dismissal for asserting a statutory right**, **Time off work: Pension scheme trustees**, and **Victimisation** elsewhere in this handbook.

DISMISSAL OF AN EMPLOYEE OR WORKFORCE REPRESENTATIVE

Key points

- Employee and workforce representatives appear in a variety of situations involving negotiations or consultations with employers. Thus, an employer is legally bound to consult appropriate representatives when planning 20 or more redundancies or when proposing the sale or transfer of his (or her) business (or part of the business) or the purchase of another business (and is liable to heavy penalties for failing to do so).

- The term 'appropriate representatives', in the context of collective redundancies and business transfers, means trade union appointed representatives or, where there is no trade union representation, employees elected by their peers to represent their interests. If there are no elected employee representatives, the employer must allow sufficient time, and provide appropriate facilities, for the election of those employees who have put their names forward as candidates (per sections 188 and 188A of the Trade Union & Labour Relations (Consolidation) Act 1992 and regulations 10 and 10A of the Transfer of Undertakings (Protection of Employment) Regulations 1981.

Workforce representatives

- Under the Working Time Regulations 1998, certain provisions in the Regulations may be modified or excluded by a workforce or collective agreement. There are similar provisions in the Fixed-term Employees (Prevention of Less Favourable Treatment) Regulations 2002. The term 'workforce agreement' means a written and signed agreement between an employer and his (or her) workers or their representatives. If there are no workforce representatives elected to represent the interests of workers (or a group of workers) whose terms and conditions are not otherwise provided for in a collective agreement, the employer must provide the time and facilities needed for an election to take place. The employer must also allow sufficient time for candidates to put their names forward and for votes to be cast and counted. Although the employer may limit the number of representatives to be elected, he (or she) does not have the right to exclude or prevent any worker putting his (or her) name forward as a candidate.

Dismissal of an employee or workforce representative

- If an elected employee or workforce representative (or a candidate for election as such a representative) is dismissed (or selected for redundancy) for performing (or proposing to perform) any of the functions or activities properly concerned with his (or her) role as such a representative (or candidate), the dismissal will be held to have been inadmissible and unfair. In short, an employee or workforce representative (or candidate) has the right to present a complaint to an employment tribunal, regardless of his age or length of service at the material time (sections 101A(d), 103, 105(4A) and (6),108 and 109, Employment Rights Act 1996). The complaint must, however, be presented to the tribunal within three months of the effective date of termination of his contract of employment.

- If the tribunal finds the complaint to be well-founded, it will order the employer either to reinstate or re-engage the dismissed employee or pay him (or her) compensation, which latter will include a minimum basic award of £3,500 (*ibid.* section 120(1)) which latter figure will be increased or decreased by order of the Secretary of State if the retail prices index for September of one year is higher or lower than the index for the previous September. For further information about remedies for unfair dismissal, please turn to the section titled **Dismissal**.

Application for interim relief

- An employee or workforce representative bringing a complaint of unfair dismissal to an employment tribunal, in the circumstances described above, may apply to the tribunal for *interim relief* (briefly, a direction to his (or her) employer or former employer ordering him to reinstate or re-engage the representative pending the determination of his complaint at the subsequent full tribunal hearing). An application for interim relief *must* be submitted to an employment tribunal within seven days of the effective date of termination of the employee's contract of employment (*ibid.* section 128).

- An employment tribunal is duty-bound to hear an application for interim relief as quickly as possible, but not before sending the employer a copy of the employee's application and giving the employer at least seven days' advance written notice of the date, time and place of the hearing.

- If, on hearing the employee representative's application for interim relief, the tribunal agrees that there is a likelihood that the complaint will be upheld at a full tribunal hearing (which may not take place for several weeks or months), it will order the employer to reinstate or re-engage the employee until the date set for the full hearing. If the employer fails to attend the interim hearing or has made it clear that he has no intention of reinstating or re-engaging the employee, the tribunal will make an order for the continuation of the employee's contract of employment. This means, in effect, that the employer must continue to pay the employee his or her normal wages or salary (less any reduction in respect of payments already made) until the employee's complaint is finally heard and decided. A failure to comply with the terms of a *continuation order* will likewise attract an award of compensation that, if need be, will be enforced by the ordinary courts.

See also **Employment tribunals and procedure**, **Dismissal for asserting a statutory right**, and **Victimisation** elsewhere in this handbook.

DISMISSAL ON GROUNDS OF DISABILITY

Key points

- It is unlawful for an employer to discriminate against a disabled person by dismissing him (or her), or subjecting him to any other detriment (section 4(2)(d), Disability Discrimination Act 1995).

- It would be a foolhardy employer indeed who would dismiss a disabled employee (or select him or her for redundancy ahead of other more suitable candidates) because of that employee's disability, and for no other reason. If the purported reason for the dismissal had to do with the employee's conduct, capabilities, attendance record, lack of qualifications, or 'some other substantial reason of a kind such as to justify the dismissal, it will be for the employer to satisfy an employment tribunal that he had acted reasonably and fairly in all the circumstances. In other words, an employer's decision to dismiss a disabled employee is likely to be more closely scrutinised for evidence of unlawful discrimination than would be his decision to dismiss an able-bodied employee. In *British Sugar plc v Kirker* [1998] IRLR 624, EAT it was held that an employee found to have been unlawfully dismissed on grounds of disability, would almost certainly be held to have been dismissed unfairly. However, there might well be circumstances associated with long periods of sickness absence (caused or contributed to by an employee's disability) which might well justify the dismissal of such an employee, so long as the employer can demonstrate that he (or she) had done all that could reasonably be expected of him to accommodate the employee. For further examples of the defence of 'justification' in disability cases, please turn to the section titled **Disabled persons** elsewhere in this handbook.

Complaints to an employment tribunal

- A complaint of unlawful discrimination under the 1995 Act must be presented to an employment tribunal within three months of the alleged unlawful act (*ibid.* section 8). A complaint under the 1995 Act may be brought regardless of the age or length of continuous service of the employee in question.

- To enable a complainant (or would-be complainant) to prepare his (or her) case, the Disability Discrimination (Questions & Replies) Order 1996 provides him with a legal opportunity to question the employer (in the person of the personnel manager or whomever) asking him to explain his apparently unlawful and discriminatory actions in relation to the matter complained of. If dissatisfied with the employer's written explanation (if, indeed, an explanation is offered), the complainant may admit the explanation (or failure to explain) as evidence in any ensuing proceedings before an employment tribunal. The form prescribed for this purpose is Form DL56 which, with its accompanying explanatory notes, is available on request from the Disability Rights Commission on 0870 600 5522.

- If an employment tribunal upholds a complaint of unlawful dismissal on grounds of disability, it will make a declaration to that effect and will order the employer to pay compensation to the employee (that may include compensation for injury to feelings). The amount of the compensation will be calculated by applying the principles applicable to the calculation of damages in claims in tort or (in Scotland) in reparation for breach of statutory duty (*ibid.* section 8(3) and (4)).

- The tribunal may also recommend that the employer take appropriate steps to remedy the situation which prompted the employee to pursue a complaint of unlawful dismissal. Those steps may include adjustments to the workplace; adaptation of, or modifications to, plant and equipment (including means of access and egress); the reallocation of certain duties, and so on. If the employer fails or refuses to comply with any such recommendation, the tribunal may increase the amount of compensation payable to the complainant (*ibid.* section 8).

See also **Disabled persons** elsewhere in this handbook.

DISMISSAL ON GROUNDS OF ILL-HEALTH

Key points

- Lack of *capability* occasioned by illness or injury (physical or mental) is one of several so-called legitimate (or permitted) reasons for dismissal listed in section 98 of the Employment Rights Act 1996. When responding to a complaint of unfair dismissal, an employer must not only explain why he dismissed the complainant but must also satisfy the employment tribunal hearing the complaint that his reason (or, if more than one, the principal reason) for doing so was legitimate – and that he had not been influenced by some ulterior motive.

- Having been satisfied that an employee was dismissed for a reason related to his health (or any other physical or mental quality), a tribunal must then decide whether the dismissal was fair. That, says section 98(4), will depend on whether, in the circumstances (including the size and administrative resources of his undertaking, the employer had acted reasonably in treating illness or injury (and its associated effects) as a sufficient reason for dismissing the employee; and that question 'shall be determined in accordance with equity and the substantial merits of the case'.

Note: In this context, the word *undertaking* means any organisation (firm, company, partnership or business) in which people are employed.

Qualifying period and upper age limit

- To qualify to pursue a complaint of unfair dismissal, an employee dismissed on grounds of illness or injury must have been continuously employed for at least one year at the *effective date of termination* of his (or her) contract of employment, and must have been under *normal retiring age* at that time. Those qualifying conditions apply in all cases of alleged unfair dismissal *unless* an employee is convinced that the real reason for his dismissal was an *inadmissible* or unlawful reason (eg, on grounds of sex, race, disability or pregnancy, or because of his trade union membership and activities, and so on).

- Furthermore, a complaint of unfair dismissal must be presented to the nearest regional office of the employment tribunals within the period of three months beginning with the effective date of termination of the employee's contract of employment. If an employee presents his (or her) complaint 'out of time', it will not be accepted, unless the tribunal is satisfied that it was not reasonably practicable for the employee to have done so within the prescribed three-month period (*ibid.* sections 108, 109 and 111).

Note: An employee in an excluded class of employment at the time of his dismissal is not protected by the 'unfair dismissal' provisions of the 1996 Act. For the meaning of this and other italicised expressions in the previous paragraph, please refer to the section titled **Dismissal**.

Procedural guidelines and the issue of 'reasonableness'

- When asked to state his reasons for dismissing a particular employee, an employer would receive a somewhat peremptory response if he were to inform an employment tribunal that he did so because the employee had bronchitis, asthma, or a heart condition (or whatever), or had caught his or her foot in the power press. What he should say is that (with the best will in the world) he could no longer tolerate a situation in which one of his employees was continually absent from work; that he had a business to run; that work was piling up; that the employee's state of health (or the nature of his or her injuries) prevented him carrying out the work he was paid to do; that the employee posed a risk both to himself and to others within the organisation; and so on. If asked to elaborate, he would point out that the employee was a key worker, or that he had an abysmal attendance record; that he was unlikely to recover (or return to work within the foreseeable future; and that, having discussed the situation with him and investigated all the circumstances (including opportunities for suitable alternative work), he had been left with no alternative but to dismiss.

- A competent employee may be invaluable and irreplaceable while at work, but will be of little benefit to his employer when he is not. And, if he is not at work very often, his employer must, sooner or later, consider the possibility of dismissal. As was indicated earlier, an employee is unlikely to be dismissed simply because of his poor health record but because of the effect his state of health is having on his capabilities as an employee. A poor health record is, more often than not, associated with a poor attendance record. Some illnesses raise issues of safety or hygiene, and fears (many of them groundless) concerning the spread of disease. Furthermore, a disfiguring disease could lead to unseemly and unjustified rejection by fellow employees or resistance from unsympathetic or ill-informed clients and members of the general public. The deciding factor is not only the effect that an employee's state of health has (or may have) on his ability to function in his job, but also the impact on the employer's business. If he is a small employer, his tolerance level will be low. If he is a large employer, his threshold of tolerance will undoubtedly be higher.

- The Department of Trade & Industry (DTI) has produced three guides for employers titled:

AIDS and the Workplace (ref PL 893)

AIDS/Work leaflet (ref PL917)

Drug Misuse in the Workplace (ref PL 880)

Each provides practical guidance for employers uncertain about how to deal with HIV or AIDS-related sickness absence, and problems associated with drug misuse. Booklet PL 893 also gives advice on developing and implementing an AIDS policy to allay any fears and prejudices employees may have about any colleagues who have developed AIDS or who are infected with the HIV virus. Copies of these booklets are available free of charge from:

DTI Publications Orderline
Admail 528
London
SW1W 8YT
Telephone: 0870 1502 500
E-mail orders: publications@dti.gsi.gov.uk

- No fair-minded employer relishes the prospect of dismissing a sick, injured or mentally-incapacitated employee – the more so if the employee has a long and unblemished service record and has never been other than a competent, enthusiastic and loyal member of the workforce. The natural inclination of any reasonable employer faced with the prospect of dealing with an employee who is incapacitated for work, would be to talk to him (or her), to discuss his situation, to explain the problems associated with his continued or repeated absences, to ask his permission to approach his doctor for a prognosis, to obtain a second medical opinion, to explore the possibility of a transfer to less-demanding (including part-time or sedentary) work, to suggest early retirement on health grounds; and so on – anything to avoid the conclusion that dismissal is the only sensible option.

- A decision to dismiss becomes all the more difficult if the employee is chronically ill or disabled within the meaning of the Disability Discrimination Act 1995, or if his state of health is directly attributable either to the type of work on which he (or she) has been engaged or to an injury sustained in the course of his employment. Contemplating an employee's domestic and financial circumstances, and the likelihood of his finding work elsewhere, once his recovery is complete, merely compounds the difficulty.

- Fortunately, the health problems experienced by the vast majority of employees are of a temporary nature. A common cold soon passes, broken limbs are healed, illnesses are cured, permanent disabilities can often be accommodated. Some health problems will take longer to resolve than others. Some lead to sustained absences from work; while others result in intermittent absenteeism (a day or two here, a week or more there). In the meantime, of course, the employer has a business to run.

- Over the past 25 years, case law has demonstrated time and again that the tribunals and courts will rarely condone as *reasonable* an employer's decision to dismiss a sick or injured employee out of hand. In *East Lindsey District Council v Daubney* [1977] IRLR 181, the EAT remarked that there can be no detailed principles to be laid down when an employer is forced to make a decision about the continued employment of a sick or injured employee. 'What will be necessary in one case,' said the EAT, 'may not be appropriate in another. But if, in every case, employers take such steps as are sensible according to the circumstances to consult the employee and to discuss the matter with him, and to inform themselves upon the true medical position, it will be found in practice that all that is necessary has been done.'

- Although every case will turn on its particular circumstances, some of the guidelines put forward by the tribunals and courts are nonetheless worthy of consideration. Thus:

  1. An employer has to know the medical facts, in order to reach a proper decision. With permission, he should either consult with the employee's own doctor or ask for an independent medical opinion (*East Lindsey District Council v Daubney* [1977] IRLR 181).

  2. If a sick or injured employee refuses to cooperate with his (or her) employer in his efforts to establish the medical facts, the employer may be left with no alternative but to dismiss (*Post Office v Jones* [1977] IRLR 422).

  3. Where circumstances permit (given the employee's age, length of service, etc), the employer should consider the possibility of locating the employee in suitable alternative employment (eg, sedentary work or part-time employment). However, he is under no obligation to create another job simply to accommodate the sick employee (*Merseyside & North Wales Electricity Board v Taylor* [1975] IRLR 80, QBD).

  4. An employer has a duty to exercise reasonable care for the safety of his employees. If one employee's state of health is a source of danger to other employees, that can reflect on his *capability* for doing the job he is employed to do and present *some other substantial reason* for his dismissal (*Harper v National Coal Board* [1980] IRLR 260).

  5. The risk of an employee falling ill (eg, having a second or third heart attack) at some future date cannot amount to a ground for dismissing him unless the nature of his job makes it patently unwise to allow him to continue working because of that risk. 'The

case of a sole wireless operator on a sea-going ship, who had the risk of a heart condition, is quite different from the case of a works manager on land in a factory with a heart condition' *(per* the EAT in *Coverfoam (Darwen) Ltd v Bell* [1981] IRLR 195).

- Clearly, it would be insensitive of an employer to issue a strongly-worded warning to a sick or injured employee that he (or she) will be dismissed if his health does not improve or if he is not back at work within a stated number of days or weeks. As was indicated above, an employer must take steps to discuss the situation with the employee or, at the very least, write to him and explain that dismissal may be inevitable if there is no significant improvement in his health within a specified period. Discussions with a sick or injured employee concerning his state of health, the frequency of sick visits, consultations with the employee's doctor (with the employee's written permission) concerning his prospects for recovery, the size of the employer's business, the need for the work to be done – all are factors likely to be taken into account by an employment tribunal when determining the reasonableness or otherwise of the employer's decision to dismiss *(vide Spencer v Paragon Wallpapers Ltd* [1976] IRLR 373).

- Malingerers, who abuse their employers' sick pay schemes, or who routinely use sickness as an excuse to take time off work when it suits them, are guilty of misconduct and should be dismissed for that reason. Fortunately, practised malingerers are usually found out and uprooted long before they earn the right to pursue a complaint of unfair dismissal. But, whatever the apparent circumstances, an employer should never presume to dismiss an employee without first talking to him (or her) (and any available witnesses) and offering him an opportunity to explain his conduct. If an employer has a procedure for dealing with issues affecting the employee's conduct or capabilities (including his state of health), he should follow that procedure to the letter (as was pointed out by the House of Lords in *Polkey v Dayton Services Ltd* [1987] IRLR 503).

Occupational sick pay schemes

- If an employee has a contractual entitlement to a number of weeks or months' paid sick leave under the terms of his (or her) employer's *occupational* sick pay scheme, he should not normally be dismissed on grounds of ill-health until he has exhausted that entitlement. Indeed, not only would his dismissal be held to have been unfair in those circumstances, but it would also afford the employee an opportunity to present a claim to an employment tribunal for damages arising out of that breach of his contractual rights. In *Smiths Industries Aerospace & Defence Systems Limited v Brookes* [1986] IRLR 434, an employee was dismissed before he had exhausted what he believed to be his entitlement to 225 days' paid sick leave in any period of 12 calendar months. An employment tribunal held that the employer had acted in breach of contract and that the dismissal was therefore unfair. Although the decision was reversed by the EAT on a question of interpretation, the tribunal had nonetheless made its point. As a rule of thumb, an employer should think long and hard before dismissing an employee who is still on paid sick leave in accordance with the terms of his contract of employment.

Note: There is a distinction to be drawn between an employee's contractual entitlement to paid sick leave under the terms of an occupational sick pay scheme and his (or her) legal right to payment under the Employer's Statutory Sick Pay Scheme (discussed elsewhere in this handbook in the section titled **Sickness and statutory sick pay**). To dismiss an employee before he has exhausted his contractual entitlement may be a breach of contract as well as unfair. But for an employer to dismiss a sick or incapacitated employee simply to avoid his liability to pay statutory sick pay (and for no other reason) would not only be *prima facie* unfair but pointless. Regulation 4 of the Statutory Sick Pay (General) Regulations 1982 (as amended) cautions that, in such circumstances, the employer must continue to pay the dismissed employee his entitlement to statutory sick pay for so long as his illness and incapacity for work persists.

Permanent health insurance schemes

- A similar dilemma arises when an employee is covered by permanent health insurance (PHI). The generosity of some such schemes can pose a real problem for employers faced with the need to replace a key worker who is still technically employed during an extended (perhaps indeterminate) absence from work. The wording of such schemes should be scrutinised to ensure that the employer is permitted a degree of latitude at such times. Furthermore, if there is an express term in the insurance policy underwriting a PHI scheme that benefits under the scheme would cease once an employee's employment had come to an end, that restriction will have no effect unless replicated by an express term to the same effect in the employee's contract of employment (*Villella v MFI Furniture Centres Limited* [1999] IRLR 468).

Frustration of contract

- It is unwise for an employer to rely on the common law doctrine of frustration of contract as an excuse to terminate the employment of a sick or injured employee who has been absent from work for a prolonged period. In *Harman v. Flexible Lamps Limited* [1980] IRLR 418, the Employment Appeal Tribunal held that:

'where a contract of employment is terminable by notice, there is really no need to consider the question of frustration, and, if it were the law that... an employer was in a position to say "this contract has been frustrated", then that would be a very convenient way in which to avoid the (unfair dismissal) provisions of the [now] Employment Rights Act 1996.'

- Although an employer should consider the opportunities for transferring a sick employee (or one with a poor health and attendance record) to other work within his organisation, involving lighter duties or sedentary work, he is under no obligation to create a new job to accommodate that employee (*Garricks (Caterers) Limited v Nolan* [1980] IRLR 259).

- It is not unreasonable for an employer to ask a sick employee to agree to submit to an independent medical examination by a doctor nominated by the employer; although it *would* be unreasonable to expect him (or her) to pay for that examination. Indeed, this is a common provision in many occupational sick pay schemes. The refusal of a sick employee (or one with an unsatisfactory health and attendance record) to permit such an examination, or to allow the employer to approach his own doctor to discuss his condition, will be an important factor to be taken into account by an employment tribunal when determining the fairness or otherwise of a dismissal in such circumstances. However, an employer wishing to obtain a medical report from an employee's doctor should be aware of the employee's statutory rights under the Access to Medical Reports Act 1988 (discussed elsewhere in this handbook in the section titled **Medical reports, access to**).

Pregnancy and ill-health

- It is important to remember that health problems that attend pregnancy (however disruptive those problems may be) do not of themselves provide grounds for dismissal. Indeed, section 99 of the 1996 Act cautions that an employee will be treated as having been unfairly dismissed if the reason (or, if more than one, the principal reason) for her dismissal was that she was pregnant or any other reason connected with her being pregnant or having given birth to a child or for being absent on (or for having availed herself of the benefits of) maternity leave. For further particulars, see the section titled **Pregnant employees and nursing mothers**.

Note: An employee who is dismissed (for whatever reason) during her pregnancy or after childbirth (before the end of her maternity leave period) is entitled, as of right, to a written statement explaining the reasons for her dismissal. In other words, her employer is duty-bound to provide her with the statement (within 14 days of her dismissal) whether or not she has asked for it (*ibid.* section 92(4)). See **Written reasons for dismissal** elsewhere in this handbook.

Rights during period of notice

- When dismissing an employee on grounds associated with illness or injury, an employer should bear in mind the employee's statutory rights during the notice period. Section 88 of the 1996 Act allows that, if during the period of his notice an employee is incapable of work because of sickness or injury, his employer must nonetheless pay him his normal wage or salary throughout that period. However, this right arises *only* if the period of notice required to be given by the employer under the terms of the employee's contract of employment is the same as that prescribed by section 86 of that Act (or not more than one week more than that statutory minimum period). This requirement is particularly important in the case of an employee who, at the time notice of dismissal was served on him (or her), had exhausted his entitlement to be paid under his employer's sick pay rules (if any). But payments by way of sick pay, statutory sick pay, holiday pay or otherwise (during or in relation to the notice period) will go towards meeting the employer's liability in this regard.

   Note: If an employee who has been employed for one month or more resigns, the same rule applies – unless the notice he is required to give under his contract of employment is more than one week more than the period of notice prescribed by section 86(2) of the 1996 Act. For further details, please turn to the section titled **Notice of termination of employment**, elsewhere in this handbook.

Reinstatement after dismissal

- If an employee is dismissed (or resigns) on grounds of illness or injury and is subsequently reinstated or re-engaged by the same or an associated employer within 26 weeks of the effective date of termination of his employment, the intervening period will count as part of his total period of continuous employment with his employer (*ibid.* section 212(3) and (4)). See also **Continuous employment** elsewhere in this handbook.

   See also **Disabled persons, dismissal on grounds of disability**, and **Sickness and statutory sick pay**.

DISMISSAL ON GROUNDS OF REDUNDANCY

Key points

- Although redundancy is a legitimate and commonplace reason for dismissal, an employee may nonetheless challenge the fairness or legality of his (or her) selection for redundancy before an employment tribunal. To qualify to do so (*unless* selected for an inadmissible or unlawful reason – see below), such an employee must have completed at least one year's continuous service by the effective date of termination of his contract of employment. Furthermore, he must have been under normal retiring age at that time. Every such complaint must be 'presented' within three months. A tribunal will not accept a complaint presented 'out of time' unless satisfied that it was not reasonably practicable for the complainant to have acted sooner. For the meaning of the expressions *effective date of termination and normal retiring age*, please turn to the section in this handbook titled **Dismissal**.

- If an employee's complaint is upheld, the tribunal will order the employer either to reinstate or re-engage the dismissed employee and/or to pay that employee an award of compensation (particulars of which are likewise explained elsewhere in this handbook in the section titled **Dismissal**).

Redundancy and trade union activities

- If an employee can show that he (or she) was one of several employees holding similar positions, who were not made redundant, and that the reason (or, if more than one, the principal reason) for his selection for redundancy was his participation in the activities or membership of, an independent trade union or his refusal to join or remain a member of any trade union or of a particular trade union, his dismissal will be regarded in law as having been inadmissible and unfair (section 153, Trade Union & Labour Relations (Consolidation) Act 1992). Such an employee can pursue a complaint of unfair dismissal before an employment tribunal regardless of his (or her) age or length of service at the material time. For further particulars, see **Redundancy** elsewhere in this handbook.

Other inadmissible reasons

- It is inadmissible, unlawful and unfair to select an employee for redundancy because of his (or her) race, colour, nationality or ethnic origins; or on grounds of sex, marital status or disability; or because the employee (as a shop worker or betting worker) had exercised, or proposed to exercise, his legal right not to work on Sundays; or had attempted or proposed to carry out his legitimate duties as an elected employee representative or as a trustee of a relevant occupational pension scheme; or because he had asserted any other statutory employment right. The same applies to the selection for redundancy of an employee who had carried out (or proposed to carry out) his duties as a safety representative or as a member of a safety committee, or as a *representative of employee safety*, or as a person designated by his employer to maintain a 'watching brief' on health and safety issues, or who had expressed concern about his employer's health and safety arrangements and had taken action to protect himself and others from danger (*ibid.* section 105). Again, an employment tribunal will entertain a complaint of unfair dismissal in such circumstances, regardless of the complainant's age or length of service at the material time.

- An employer who has a policy in place for selecting candidates for redundancy (for example 'last in, first out'), will need to satisfy an employment tribunal that he had sound business reasons for departing from that policy. Although the 'customary arrangement and agreed procedures' provisions of the former Employment Protection (Consolidation) Act 1978 were repealed in 1994, an arbitrary departure from any such arrangement or agreed procedure would be in breach of an employee's contractual rights. In any event, when consulting *appropriate representatives* about 'the proposed method of selecting employees who may be dismissed', the employer must do so with a view to reaching agreement (per section 188(2) and (4)(d), Trade Union & Labour Relations (Consolidation) Act 1992).

See also **Disabled persons, Dismissal, Dismissal of an employee representative, Dismissal of a pension scheme trustee, Dismissal for asserting a statutory right, Dismissal for refusing Sunday work, Dismissal in health and safety cases, Dismissal on grounds of pregnancy or childbirth, Dismissal on grounds of trade union membership** (next section), **Fixed-term employees, Part-time workers, Racial discrimination, Redundancy** and **Sex discrimination** elsewhere in this handbook.

DISMISSAL ON GROUNDS OF TRADE UNION MEMBERSHIP OR NON-MEMBERSHIP
(*or for taking part in trade union activities*)

Key points

- As a rule, a dismissed employee cannot pursue a complaint of unfair dismissal unless he (or she) was under 'normal retiring age' and had been continuously employed for one or more years at the effective date of termination of his contract of employment. However, those qualifying conditions do *not* apply if an employee alleges that he was dismissed because of his trade union membership or activities or because of his refusal to join or remain a member of a particular trade union or of any trade union. Complaints under this heading must be presented within three months of the effective date of termination of the employee's contract of employment. A tribunal will not entertain a complaint presented 'out of time' unless satisfied that it was not reasonably practicable for the complainant to have acted sooner.

Trade union membership and activities

- Section 152 of the Trade Union & Labour Relations (Consolidation) Act 1992 states that the dismissal of an employee will be regarded as inadmissible and unfair if the reason, or principal reason, for the dismissal was:

  (a) that the employee had joined, or had declared his (or her) intention of joining, an independent trade union; or

  (b) that the employee had taken part (or had declared his intention to take part) in the activities of an independent trade union, either outside his normal working hours or during his normal working hours when it is ordinarily permissible (that is to say, with the employer's tacit consent) for such activities to take place; or

  (c) that the employee was not a member of any trade union, or had refused (or had clearly indicated his or her intention to refuse) to join a particular trade union or any trade union.

  An employee who has been dismissed (or believes that he (or she) has been dismissed) for one or other of reasons (a), (b) or (c) above, may present a complaint to an employment tribunal – regardless of his age or length of employment at the effective date of termination of his contract of employment.

Dismissal and the closed shop

- Before 20 July 1988, an employer could justify his decision to dismiss a non-union employee because of the existence of an 'approved' closed shop agreement and the employee's refusal to be or remain a member of one or other of the unions party to that agreement. However, that 'justification' no longer exists. Closed shops no longer have any legal relevance. Nowadays, it is up to the employee to decide whether or not he (or she) wants to be a member of a trade union – closed shop or no closed shop. If any employee is dismissed for refusing to join a trade union or for tearing-up his union card, his dismissal will be held to have been unfair; in which event, a tribunal will order his employer to pay very heavy compensation indeed (as to which, see the section titled **Dismissal** elsewhere in this handbook).

Payments in lieu of union membership

- If an employee cannot lawfully be dismissed for refusing to be or remain a member of a trade union in any circumstances, it follows that he (or she) cannot be dismissed for refusing to make a contribution to a trade union or to some other body (such as a charity) in lieu of trade union membership. The dismissal of an employee for that secondary reason will be regarded in law as having been unfair – irrespective of the existence of any such express or implied requirement in the employee's contract of employment (*ibid.* section 152(3)).

    Note: While an employee might very well agree to make some form of voluntary payment to a charity, trade union, or whatever, in lieu of trade union dues, it is not open to his employer to insist that he does so, or to discipline, victimise or dismiss him for refusing to make any such payment.

Interim relief

- An employee who has complained to an employment tribunal that he (or she) has been unfairly dismissed because of his trade union membership or activities, or because of his non-membership of a trade union or of a particular trade union, may apply to the tribunal for so-called *interim relief* (briefly, a direction to his employer ordering his rein-statement or re-engagement, or the continuation of his contract of employment) pending the determination of his complaint at the subsequent full tribunal hearing (*ibid.* section 161(1)).

- An application for interim relief must be submitted within seven days of the effective date of termination of an employee's contract of employment, and, in a case where he (or she) has been dismissed (or alleges that he has been dismissed) because of his trade union member-ship or activities, must be accompanied by a certificate in writing signed by an authorised official of the independent trade union in question stating that there appear to be reasonable grounds for suppos-ing that the employee had indeed been dismissed for one or other, or both, of those reasons (*ibid.* section 161(2)).

- If the employment tribunal agrees that there is the likelihood of a finding of unfair dismissal when the full tribunal hearing is convened, it will order the employer in question to reinstate or re-engage the employee until the date set for the hearing. If the employer is unwilling to do so, the tribunal will make an order for the continuation of the employee's contract of employment (ie, a direction to the employer to pay the employee his or her normal wages or salary until such time as the question of the fairness or otherwise of the dismissal is finally resolved). A failure to comply with the terms of a 'continuation order' will result in an award of compensation to the dismissed employee – separate from, and additional to, any subsequent award of compensa-tion on a finding of unfair dismissal at the later hearing. If need be, either or both of those awards will be enforced by the courts (*ibid.* sections 164, 165 and 166).

Compensation for unfair dismissal

- The employment tribunals are empowered to impose swingeing penal-ties where an employee has been held to have been unfairly dismissed because of his (or her) non-membership of a trade union, or because of his trade union activities.

  See also **Dismissal for asserting a statutory right, Time off work: trade union members, Time off work: trade union officials, Trade union members, rights of, Trade union membership and activities**, and **Victimisation** elsewhere in this handbook.

DISOBEDIENCE

Key points

- Every employee has an implied contractual duty to co-operate with his (or her) employer, to carry out his duties to the best of his abilities, and to obey the lawful and reasonable orders of his superiors. If he is lazy and insubordinate, and refuses to do as he is told, he is liable to be dismissed.

- This is not to say that an employee can be required by his employer to carry out tasks that he is neither employed nor paid to do; or to work repeated and excessive overtime; or to transfer willy-nilly from one location to another. A great deal will depend on the existence or otherwise of an express or (less frequently) an implied term in the individual contract of employment, and on the circumstances at the relevant time.

- For instance, there may be a customary or long-standing arrangement in certain companies and businesses (notably those dealing directly with members of the public) for employees to share each other's duties or to work overtime during staff shortages or times of seasonal pressure. If an employee refuses to do a particular job, on an isolated occasion, to help his employer over a temporary difficulty, his lack of cooperation will not go unnoticed. Indeed, in time, it could lead to his dismissal. The employment tribunals have long since upheld the prerogative of employers to manage their enterprises to the best of their ability. The dismissal of a disobedient and uncooperative employee will invariably be held to be fair, provided the employer is held to have acted 'reasonably'. At any event, the insubordinate employee is very often found out well before he (or she) earns the right to present a complaint of unfair dismissal to an employment tribunal.

- Whether or not a single act of disobedience is so serious or damaging as to warrant the summary dismissal of an obstinate employee will depend again on the circumstances, including the size and administrative resources of the employer's undertaking. If his (or her) refusal to do as he is told endangers the health and safety of fellow-employees, customers or clients, he should be dismissed 'on the spot', provided he knew exactly what was expected of him and the risks involved. However, he should first be given an opportunity to explain his conduct and be reminded of his right of appeal (see **Disciplinary rules and procedures** elsewhere in this handbook).

- If an act of disobedience does serious and irrevocable harm to an employer's business, threatens his licence, or results in the loss of valued trade, immediate dismissal may also ensue. Once again, the employer should satisfy himself that the employee knew exactly what was expected of him and the implications. A single lapse of memory, or a failure to understand what his employer was saying, may mitigate the seriousness of the offence in the eyes of an employment tribunal and challenge the 'reasonableness' of an employer who reacted over-hastily.

- For the avoidance of doubt, an employer should make it known to all new recruits (either at the interview stage or on their first day of work) that they will, from time to time, be expected to work overtime or to go to the assistance of other employees during busy periods or to cover occasional or unavoidable staff shortages. Thus, a cook in a busy restaurant might reasonably be expected to rinse out the occasional saucepan if the kitchen porter has been rushed off to hospital or has not turned in for work. A bank clerk could be asked to double as cashier during the lunch-time rush hour. A night shift foreman in a factory would be expected to remain at his or her post until the next shift has arrived; and so on. See also **Cooperation, employee's duty of** and **Dismissal** elsewhere in this handbook.

E

EEA NATIONALS, EMPLOYMENT OF

- Although this will not normally be a matter for concern when it comes to employing a national of an EEA Member State, the immigration authorities do have the right to deny entry to the UK to any person (whether an EEA national or otherwise) who is considered to be 'undesirable'. Under section 8 of the Asylum & Immigration Act 1996, which came into force on 27 January 1997), an employer (director, manager or company secretary) commits an offence, and is liable to a fine of up to £5,000, if he (or she) employs any person who is either an illegal immigrant or who does not have the legal and subsisting right to seek or obtain employment during his or her stay in the United Kingdom. For further information, please turn to the opening paragraphs in the section titled **Foreign nationals, employment of** elsewhere in this handbook.

- The following is a summary only of Home Office rules relating to the entry into and stay of persons in the United Kingdom. Those rules are to be found in the *Statement of Changes in Immigration Rules* (HC 395), notably paragraphs 255–262, laid before Parliament on 23 May 1994 under section 3(2) of the Immigration Act 1971. Copies of the *Statement* (ISBN 0 10 239594 2) may be purchased from The Stationery Office (as to which, please turn to page 132). When ordering the *Statement*, readers should take care to ask for copies of all subsequent amending statements.

Key points

- Under European Community law, an EEA national has a right of residence, that is to say, a right to live and work either in the UK or in any other Member State of the European Economic Area (EEA). That same right extends to citizens of Switzerland. To gain entry into the UK, an EEA or Swiss national need only produce a valid passport or national identity card. The person in question has no need of a work permit and (subject to certain rules) may be joined by his (or her) family and dependants once he has obtained employment. That right also extends to citizens of Switzerland who no longer need work permits in order to enter or take up employment in the UK.

- At the present time, the EEA comprises the 15 Member States of the European Union (Austria, Belgium, Denmark, Finland, France, Germany, Greece, the Irish Republic, Italy, Luxembourg, The Netherlands, Spain, Sweden, Portugal and the UK) together with Iceland, Norway and Liechtenstein.

- An EEA or Swiss national, with the right of residence, may remain in the UK for as long as he (or she) pleases and has no need to obtain a residence permit or register with the police. An EEA or Swiss national who chooses to do so may apply to the Immigration & Nationality Directorate (see address below) for a residence permit, although the latter, once issued, is little more than formal confirmation of the applicant's right of residence. A form of application will be supplied on request by the Directorate's Application Forms Unit (AFU) and must be returned to the AFU with two passport-sized photographs. A residence permit is normally valid for five years, but may be issued for a shorter period if the applicant is working or studying in the UK for less than 12 months. A residence permit will not normally be issued if the person has either not found employment at the end of six months or has become a charge on public funds.

- A UK employer may engage the services of an EEA or Swiss national without formality, although he should ask to see the job applicant's passport or national identity card. The employer must not discriminate against any foreign employee by offering him (or her) less favourable terms and conditions of employment or subjecting him to any restriction by virtue of his nationality or national or ethnic origins (see **Racial discrimination** elsewhere in this handbook).

- An EEA or Swiss national may settle his (or her) family and dependants in the UK and is entitled to claim social security benefits, and access to housing and property.

Further information

- Further information about the rights of residence of EEA and Swiss nationals (and their family members) can be obtained by writing to:

Immigration & Nationality Directorate
Block C
Whitgift Centre
Wellesley Road
Croydon
CR9 1AT
Telephone: 0870 241 0645
or by accessing the following website:
www.homeoffice.gov.uk/ind/ eea.htm

Citizens of the Irish Republic

- It should be noted that citizens of the Irish Republic have long since been admitted freely to the United Kingdom, whether coming from within or outside the Common Travel Area (which latter comprises the United Kingdom, the Channel Islands, the Isle of Man and the Irish Republic, collectively). However, there are circumstances in which the Secretary of State may exclude a particular person if the exclusion is conducive to the public good.

  See also **Foreign nationals, employment of** elsewhere in this handbook.

EMPLOYMENT AGENCIES
(and employment businesses)

Key points

- Under the Employment Agencies Act 1973 (as originally enacted), employment agencies and employment businesses could not legally operate without a licence. With the coming into force on 3 January 1995 of the relevant provisions of the Deregulation & Contracting Out Act 1994, that requirement no longer applies. However, the former licensing provisions of the 1973 Act have since been replaced by other statutory controls (as explained later in this section).

- Under the 1973 Act, the term 'employment agency' means one thing; and 'employment business', another (see *Note* below). However, the distinction is of no particular relevance in the present context – the more so as most employers consider themselves to be dealing with an 'employment agency' whether seeking to recruit permanent staff or looking to hire the services of an agency 'temp'. To avoid confusion, the term 'employment agency' is used throughout this section to encompass both employment agencies and employment businesses.

Note: An 'employment agency' is effectively a recruitment agency that is in business to find permanent employment for workers, and permanent workers for employers. A firm of 'headhunters' would usually fall within this category. When publishing advertisements, an employment agency must make it clear that it *is* an employment agency acting on behalf of one or more (albeit unnamed) employers. An 'employment business' (or temporary staff agency), on the other hand, usually recruits its own workers or has a number of workers on standby, hiring them out to client employers on a temporary basis. Employment businesses are commonly associated with the supply of 'temp' secretaries, clerical staff, drivers, etc.

Penalties for infringement of the 1973 Act and its attendant Regulations

- Before the 1973 Act was amended, any employment agency which conducted its business improperly risked forfeiting its operating licence. Nowadays, the Secretary of State may apply to an employment tribunal for an order prohibiting the owner or manager of the agency in question from carrying on (or being concerned with the carrying on of) any employment agency or any specified description of employment agency.

- A prohibition order will either prohibit a person from engaging in an activity altogether (for a period of up to 10 years) or prohibit him (or her) from doing so otherwise than in accordance with conditions specified in the order itself. If the agency has been improperly conducted, each person carrying on (or concerned with the carrying on) of that agency at the time, will be deemed to have been responsible for its actions – unless he (or she) can show that events happened without his (or her) connivance or consent and were not attributable to any neglect on his part. A failure to comply with the terms of a prohibition order (without reasonable excuse) is an offence for which the penalty on summary conviction is a fine of up to £5,000.

  If an employment agency is a company (or body corporate) the company itself may be served with a prohibition order if the employment tribunal is satisfied that:

  (a) any director, secretary, manager or similar officer of the company (or any person who performs the functions of a director, secretary, manager or similar officer on behalf of the body corporate); or

  (b) any person (other than a person giving advice in a professional capacity) in accordance with whose directions or instructions the directors of the company are accustomed to act, is unsuitable, because of his (or her) misconduct (or for any other sufficient reason) to do what the order prohibits.

- A prohibition order may be made in relation to a partnership, if the tribunal is satisfied that any member of the partnership, or any manager employed by the partnership, is unsuitable to do what the order prohibits.

Conduct of Employment Agencies & Employment Businesses Regulations 1976

- The activities of employment agencies are currently regulated by the Conduct of Employment Agencies & Employment Businesses Regulations 1976. However, those Regulations are soon to be revoked, and might well have been revoked and replaced by the time this book goes to press (as to which, see *Recent developments* at the end of this section).

- Under the 1976 Regulations, any employer who approaches an employment agency for help in recruiting permanent employees, or for the *supply* of temporary or casual workers, is entitled to assume that the candidates introduced or the workers supplied have the required qualifications, experience and skills. In other words, an employment agency is duty-bound to interview would-be candidates for employment on behalf of clients, and must make appropriate inquiries concerning their qualifications, experience, etc. If a client is dissatisfied with the capabilities of any job applicant or agency 'temp', he (or she) should refuse to pay any fee charged by the agency in question.

  Note: It is an offence for an employment agency or business to charge a job applicant a fee for finding or attempting to find him (or her) a job. The only exceptions (subject to limitations) relate to the finding of work for fashion or photographic models and entertainers. An employment agency may also charge a fee of up to £40 for finding an au pair work outside the UK – but only if it has used an overseas agent to find a suitable position for that au pair. Even so, the fee cannot be levied until a position has been found and the au pair has accepted that position.

- An employment agency must take all reasonably practicable steps to obtain as much information about the work for which a worker is to be supplied or introduced. This information must be passed on to the worker and must include particulars of the kind of work involved and the minimum rates of pay applicable to that work. An agency or business must take extra care when arranging to send a worker overseas to work for an employer who has no business premises in the UK. No such arrangement should be concluded unless the agency has received satisfactory *written* assurances from the employer (or elsewhere) that the work in question will not be detrimental to the worker's interests. Employment agencies are not permitted to supply temporary workers as replacements for workers who are on strike or otherwise in dispute with their employer. They must also obtain the written consent of a client before supplying any 'temp' who was directly employed by that client within the previous six months.

- If an employment agency has received a fee for introducing a worker to a client, it must not approach that worker at a later date with an offer to find him (or her) work elsewhere.

- An employment agency *must* pay all of its temporary or casual staff on time. The fact that a client employer is late in settling his account is of no relevance, and may not be used as an excuse for delaying payments of wages or salary to any employee hired-out to that employer (*ibid.* regulation 9(10)).

For advice, call the
EMPLOYMENT AGENCIES STANDARDS OFFICE
local-rate helpline on
0845 9 555 105

Information for client employers

- Not later than 24 hours after the first 'temp' has started work with a client, an employment agency must supply the client with particulars of its terms of business – including information about the procedure to be followed if any worker proves to be unsatisfactory. Those particulars must also include information about any fee payable if a client wishes to take a 'temp' into his or her direct employment. It is important to note that employment businesses have no legal right to restrict or prohibit any of their 'temps' in any way from entering the direct employment of a client. Clients must also be told which of the 'temps' supplied are employed by the agency itself, and which of them are self-employed.

Discrimination on grounds of sex or race

- Employment agencies which discriminate against job applicants on grounds of sex, marital status, race, colour, nationality, national or ethnic origins (whether at the direction of a client employer or otherwise) can be 'brought to book' by an employment tribunal and will be ordered to pay compensation to any job applicant held to have been unlawfully discriminated against in this way. Furthermore, there is a risk that the Secretary of State may apply to an employment tribunal for a prohibition order (the effect of which is discussed earlier in this section).

- An employment agency, which has allegedly discriminated against (or denied its services to) any person on grounds of sex or race, may justify its actions if it can satisfy an employment tribunal that its actions were based on an assurance by the client employer that being of a particular gender, colour, race or nationality was a 'genuine occupational qualifi-cation' for the vacancy or position in question.

• These provisions are to be found in sections 15 and 14, respectively, of the Sex Discrimination Act 1975 and the Race Relations Act 1976.

Discrimination on grounds of disability

• Under section 4 of the Disability Discrimination Act 1995 it is unlawful for an employer (or would-be employer) to discriminate against a disabled person:

(a) in the arrangements he makes for determining to whom he should offer employment;

(b) in the terms on which he offers that person employment; or

(c) by refusing to offer, or deliberately not offering, him (or her) employment.

An employer (or would-be employer) discriminates against a disabled person if, for a reason which relates to the disabled person's disability, he treats him (or her) less favourably than he treats or would treat others to whom that reason does not or would not apply; and he cannot show that the treatment in question is justified (*ibid.* section 5). For further information, please turn to the section titled **Disabled persons** elsewhere in this handbook.

• Under Part III of the 1995 Act, it is likewise unlawful for a provider of services (such as an employment agency) to discriminate against a disabled person by refusing to provide (or deliberately not providing) to the disabled person any service which he provides, or is prepared to provide, to members of the public. A claim by a disabled person that another person (such as an employment agency) has discriminated against him, contrary to Part III of the 1995 Act, may be made the subject of proceedings before a county court (or, in Scotland, a sheriff court). Damages awarded by the court in such cases may include compensation for injury to feelings whether or not they include compensation under any other head (*ibid.* section 25). For further particulars, please turn to the sections titled **Racial discrimination** and **Sex discrimination** elsewhere in this handbook.

Note: The Disability Rights Discrimination has published a code of practice titled *Disability Discrimination Act 1995 Code of Practice: Rights of Access, Goods, Facilities, Services & Premises,* copies of which may be obtained from the Stationery Office (Tel: 0870 600 5522) or by email from books.orders@tso.co.uk. A free text version of the code may be downloaded from website www.drc.gov.uk/drc/informationandlegisla-tion/page312.asp. See also **Disabled persons** elsewhere in this handbook.

Discrimination on grounds of trade union membership or non-membership

- Section 138 of the Trade Union & Labour Relations (Consolidation) Act 1992 cautions that it is unlawful for an employment agency to deny its services to any job applicant (whether at the request of a client employer or otherwise):

  (a) because the applicant in question is, or is not, a member of a trade union; or

  (b) because he (or she) is unwilling to accept a requirement to take steps to become or cease to be (or remain or not to become) a member of a trade union.

  Advertisements couched in similar terms are likewise unlawful. Any person who responds to such an advertisement, but is turned away because he (or she) does not satisfy the conditions laid down in the advertisement, will be conclusively presumed to have been refused employment on grounds of his trade union membership (or non-membership) (*ibid.* section 137(3)). See **Advertisements (discriminatory)** elsewhere in this handbook.

- Any person who is discriminated against in this way may complain to an employment tribunal. If his (or her) complaint is upheld, the offending agency will be ordered to pay the complainant compensation of up to £50,000. Complaints of unlawful discrimination on grounds of a person's membership or non-membership of a trade union must be presented within three months of the date on which the conduct complained of occurred (*ibid.* section 139). See also **Trade union membership and activities** elsewhere in this handbook.

Agency 'temps' and the national minimum wage

- Persons working for, or employed by, an employment agency (including persons hired out as 'temps' to client employers) must be paid the appropriate national minimum wage for all hours worked. If, as is usually the case, the agency pays a 'temp's' wages or salary, it is the agency also which must pay the national minimum wage (*per* section 34(1), National Minimum Wage Act 1998). In March 2002, the Commission of the European Communities published a proposal for a directive 'on working conditions for temporary workers'. Adoption of the directive (fiercely resisted by the UK Government) will mean that agency 'temps' will be entitled to the same pay and benefits as those enjoyed by workers doing the same or an identical job in the client organisation. The draft directive may be accessed and downloaded from website europa.eu.int/eur-lex/en/com/pdf/2002/en_502PC0149.pdf.

Agency 'temps' and the Working Time Regulations 1998

- Under the Working Time Regulations 1998, as amended, the term 'worker' applies to an individual who has entered into or works under (or, where the employment has ceased, worked under) a contract of employment *or under any other contract*, whether express or implied and (if it is express) whether oral or in writing, whereby the individual undertakes to do or perform personally any work or services for another party to the contract whose status is not by virtue of the contract that of client or customer of any profession or business undertaking carried on by the individual.

- It follows that the majority of agency 'temps' and freelancers (unless *genuinely* self-employed) are workers for the purposes of the 1998 Regulations, whether employed under a contract of employment or a contract *sui generis* (of its own kind), so long as it is the agency which provides them with work, and deducts tax and national insurance contributions from their pay. For further particulars, please turn to the sections titled **Holidays, annual**, **Rest breaks and rest periods** and **Working hours**, elsewhere in this handbook

Recent developments

- Section 37 and Schedule 7 to the Employment Relations Act 1999 amends section 5(1) and 6(1) of the Employment Agencies Act 1973 by further empowering the Secretary of State to make regulations restricting the services which may be provided by employment agencies (and businesses), regulating the way in which (and the terms on which) those services are provided, and restricting or regulating the charges of fees by persons carrying on such agencies (and businesses).

- In May 1999, the Department of Trade & Industry (DTI) published a consultation document titled *Regulation of the Private Recruitment Industry* in which it sought the views of interested parties on an overhaul of regulations to be made under the amended sections 5(1) and 6(1) of the 1973 Act. On 23 July 2002, following lengthy consultations with interested parties, notably bodies representing the interests of employment agencies, the DTI launched a second consultative document accompanied by draft new Conduct of Employment Agencies & Employment Businesses Regulations 2002.

- Under those regulations, employment agencies, involved in placing temporary workers with client employers, must not only ascertain the nature of the work which those workers will be required to do, but must also ascertain the desired levels of experience, training and quali-fications, and obtain details of any associated health and safety risks. They must also consider the suitability of individual workers for the work in question. The agency must relay this information in writing both to the 'temps' it intends to supply and to the relevant client employers. Furthermore, the agency must inform the client employer whether the 'temps' it supplies are employed by the agency itself under contracts of service (or employment) or whether they are self-employed. The latter measure is intended to resolve the long-standing confusion over the contractual status of agency 'temps'.

- The Regulations are also designed to resolve the issue of 'temp to perm' fees. Under existing legislation, it is unlawful for an employment agency to impose any restriction or prohibition designed to deter any of its workers from taking up permanent employment with a client employer. However, there is nothing in those Regulations that makes it unlawful for an agency to charge a so-called 'temp to perm' fee when this happens. What this means is that employment agencies are currently free not only to impose 'temp to perm' charges but also to set those charges at any level they choose. This practice, said the Government, not only acts as a restriction on the labour market and a deterrent to client employers (many of whom simply cannot afford to pay such a fee or are disinclined to do so), but also undermines the effectiveness of regulation 9(9) of the 1976 Regulations.

- To resolve this problem, the draft 2002 Regulations state that client employers seeking to take agency temps into their direct employment have one of two options. They may either agree to pay a reasonable 'temp to perm' fee to the agency in question or serve notice on the agency that they propose to extend the hiring arrangement for an agreed further period. At the end of that agreed further period, they can take the 'temp' into their direct employment without having to pay any fee for doing so. Indeed, any term in a contract between an employment agency and a client employer for the hire of a temporary worker will be unenforceable if it does not include a provision to that effect. However, to avoid possible abuse of this arrangement, the draft Regulations propose that a client employer need not pay a 'temp to perm' fee to an employment agency (regardless of any contractual term to the contrary) so long as the employer does not take a 'temp' into his or her direct employment before the end of what the Regulations refer to as 'the relevant period'. For these purposes, the relevant period will be either the period of eight weeks commencing on the day after the day on which the contract between the employer and the agency for the supply of the 'temp' in question came to an end or the period of 14 weeks commencing on the first day on which the 'temp' first started work with the client employer under that contract, whichever of those periods ends later – discounting any break of more than six weeks between the end of one hire contract and the beginning of the next. The new Regulations (once approved) are expected to come into force in mid-2003.

- Copies of the consultation document and the accompanying draft Regulations may be accessed and downloaded from website www.dti.uk/er/agency/newregs.htm.

EMPLOYMENT APPEAL TRIBUNAL

Key points

- The Employment Appeal Tribunal (or EAT) was first brought into being by the Employment Protection Act 1975. The relevant provisions are now to be found in Part II (sections 20 to 37) of the Employment Tribunals Act 1996. The EAT comprises a panel of High Court and Court of Appeal judges, at least one judge of the Court of Session appointed (after consultation with the Lord President of the Court of Session) by the Lord Chancellor, plus a number of lay members (appointed by the Lord Chancellor and the Secretary of State) with specialist knowledge and experience of industrial relations matters.

- The EAT is a superior court of record. It has its central office in London, but may sit anywhere in the country. One or more divisions of the EAT may sit at the same time. Appeals from a decision of the EAT on points of law will lie to the Court of Appeal (in Scotland, the Court of Session) and, ultimately, to the House of Lords (with leave). See also the next section titled **Employment tribunals and procedure**.

Appeal procedure

- An appeal from a decision of an employment tribunal must be served on the EAT within 42 days of the date on which the document recording the decision appealed against was sent to the putative appellant (employee or employer). A copy of the *extended* written reasons for the tribunal's decision (not the *summary*) must accompany the Notice of Appeal (which latter must be in, or substantially in, accordance with Form 1 in the Schedule to the Employment Appeal Tribunal Rules 1993.

Copies of the Notice of Appeal may be obtained from any local office of the Employment Service.

Note: An appeal from a decision of an employment tribunal concerning the service of an improvement or prohibition notice (issued under the Health & Safety at Work etc Act 1974) will lie to the Court of Appeal (or, in Scotland, the Court of Session) and not to the Employment Appeal Tribunal.

Proceedings before the EAT

- Proceedings before the EAT will ordinarily be heard by a judge and either two (or four) appointed (ie, lay) members, one (or two) of whom will have knowledge or experience of industrial relations as representatives of employers and the same number with knowledge or experience as representatives of workers. However, with the consent of the parties, proceedings before the EAT may be heard by a judge and one lay member or by a judge and three lay members.

Jurisdiction of the EAT

- The EAT hears appeals on any question of law arising from any decision of an employment tribunal under or by virtue of:

  (a) the Equal Pay Act 1970;

  (b) the Sex Discrimination Act 1975;

  (c) the Race Relations Act 1976;

  (d) the Trade Union & Labour Relations (Consolidation) Act 1992;

  (e) the Disability Discrimination Act 1995;

  (f) the Employment Rights Act 1996;

  (g) the National Minimum Wage Act 1998;

  (h) the Tax Credits Act 2002;

  (i) the Employment Tribunals Act 1996;

  (j) the Working Time Regulations 1998;

  (k) the Part-time Workers (Prevention of Less Favourable Treatment) Regulations 2000; and

  (l) the Fixed-term Employees (Prevention of Less Favourable Treatment) Regulations 2002

  (section 21, Employment Tribunals Act 1996, as amended).

It also hears appeals on questions of fact or law arising from any decision of an employment tribunal under section 174 of the Trade Union & Labour Relations (Consolidation) Act 1992 (unreasonable exclusion or expulsion from a trade union) (*ibid.* section 291).

- The EAT also has jurisdiction under section 9 of the Trade Union & Labour Relations (Consolidation) Act 1992 Act to hear appeals:

    (a) from an organisation aggrieved by the refusal of the Certification Officer to enter its name in the list of trade unions, or by a decision of his to remove its name from that list; or

    (b) from a trade union aggrieved by the refusal of the Certification Officer to issue it with a certificate of independence or by a decision of his to withdraw its certificate.

    The rights of appeal to the EAT in such circumstances extend to any questions of fact or law arising in the proceedings before (or arising from the decision of) the Certification Officer.

Other jurisdiction

- The EAT has jurisdiction also in respect of matters other than appeals, which is (or may be) conferred on it by or under the Trade Union & Labour Relations (Consolidation) Act 1992, the Employment Tribunals Act 1996, or any other Act (per section 21(4) of the Employment Tribunals Act 1996, as inserted by Schedule 1, paragraph 17 to the Employment Rights (Dispute Resolution) Act 1998). For example, an appeal lies to the Employment Tribunal arising out of an employer's failure (in prescribed circumstances) to establish a European Works Council (per the Transnational Information and Consultation of Employees Regulations 1999).

EMPLOYMENT TRIBUNALS AND PROCEDURE
(*Constitution, jurisdiction, etc*)

Key points

- Employment tribunals were first established by section 12 of the Industrial Training Act 1964 to hear appeals by employers against any notice of assessment to levy (the training levy) imposed by industrial training boards under section 4 of that Act.

- The law relating to the composition and jurisdiction of employment tribunals (and of the Employment Appeal Tribunal) is presently to be found in the Employment Tribunals Act 1996 and in regulations made under (or saved by) that Act. In short, proceedings may be brought before an employment tribunal on a complaint or reference under a variety of statutes and regulations, notably the:

  - Equal Pay Act 1970;

  - Sex Discrimination Acts 1975 and 1986;

  - Race Relations Act 1976;

  - Transfer of Undertakings (Protection of Employment) Regulations 1981;

  - Trade Union & Labour Relations (Consolidation) Act 1992;

  - Pension Schemes Act 1993;

  - Disability Discrimination Act 1995;

  - Employment Rights Act 1996;

  - Working Time Regulations 1998;

  - National Minimum Wage Act 1998;

  - Employment Tribunals Act 1996;

  - Part-time Workers (Prevention of Less Favourable Treatment) Regulations 2000;

  - Tax Credits Act 2002;

  - Fixed-term Employees (Prevention of Less Favourable Treatment) Regulations 2002.

  An appeal from any decision of an employment tribunal under (or by virtue of) the Acts or Regulations listed above lies to the Employment Appeal Tribunal alone (EAT) (per section 21, Employment Tribunals Act 1996).

Constitution of employment tribunals

- An employment tribunal ordinarily consists of a Chairman (a barrister or solicitor of at least seven years' standing) and two lay members drawn from two panels of members appointed by the Secretary of State for Employment – one, after consultation with employers' organisations; and the other, after consultation with employees' organisations (ie, the trade unions). Most originating applications (or complaints) are heard by a three-member tribunal. However, with the 'appropriate consent' (that is to say, consent given at the beginning of a tribunal hearing by such of the parties as are then present in person or represented, or consent given by each of the parties) proceedings before an employment tribunal may be heard by the chairman and just one lay member (*ibid.* section 4(1), as amended by section 4 of the Employment Rights (Dispute Resolution) Act 1998).

Note: When cases are brought under the Equal Pay Act 1970, or the Sex Discrimination Act 1975, one member of the three-member tribunal will usually be a woman, although this is not mandatory. Similarly, in cases alleging unlawful discrimination under the Race Relations Act 1976, one of the tribunal members will ordinarily be a person with special experience in race relations.

- All tribunal hearings take place in public unless a Minister of the Crown has directed a tribunal to sit in private on grounds of national security. A tribunal may also sit in private to hear evidence that consists of:

  - information that a person giving that evidence could not otherwise disclose without contravening a prohibition imposed by or under any enactment; or

  - information that has been communicated to that person in confidence or which that person has otherwise obtained in consequence of the confidence reposed in him or her by another person; or

  - information the disclosure of which would cause substantial injury to a person's business or the business or organisation for which he or she works, for reasons other than its effect on negotiations with respect to a trade dispute (as to which, see **Trade disputes** elsewhere in this handbook).

Hearings by a chairman sitting alone

- A tribunal chairman sitting alone may hear proceedings:

  (a) on a complaint (or an application) under section 68A of the Trade Union & Labour Relations Act 1992 (relating to the deduction of unauthorised or excessive 'union dues');

  (b) on a complaint (or an application) under *ibid.* section 87 (noncompliance by the employer with a tribunal order under (a) above);

  (c) on a complaint under *ibid.* section 192 (employer's failure to pay remuneration under a protective award);

  (d) on an application under *ibid.* section 161 for interim relief in consequence of a complaint by an employee that he (or she) had been unfairly dismissed on grounds related to his trade union membership or activities (see **Dismissal on grounds of trade union membership** elsewhere in this handbook);

(e) on an application under *ibid.* section 165 for the variation or revocation of an order for interim relief under (d) above;

(f) on an application under *ibid.* section 166 concerning an employer's non-compliance with the terms of a tribunal order for the reinstatement or re-engagement of an employee;

(g) on a complaint under section 126 of the Pension Schemes Act 1993 (failure of Secretary of State to pay a sum equivalent to unpaid pension contributions into an occupational pension scheme when the employer is insolvent);

(h) on a reference under section 11 of the Employment Rights Act 1996 concerning an employer's failure to provide a written statement of employment particulars (or a statement of changes in the particulars to be included in such a statement) or an itemised pay statement;

(i) on a reference by an employee under section 163 of the 1996 Act concerning his (or her) right to a redundancy payment or the amount of a redundancy payment;

(j) on an application by an employee under *ibid.* section 170 concerning the Secretary of State's alleged failure to pay (out of the National Insurance Fund) the whole or part of a statutory redundancy payment owed to the employee by his (or her) insolvent employer;

(k) on a complaint by an employee under *ibid.* section 23 that his (or her) employer has made one or more unauthorised deductions from his wages, or has demanded (and received) one or more unauthorised payments (see **Deductions from pay** elsewhere in this handbook);

(l) on a complaint by an employee under *ibid.* section 34 concerning his (or her) employer's failure to pay the whole or any part of a guarantee payment to which the employee is entitled;

(m) on a reference under *ibid.* section 188 concerning the Secretary of State's alleged failure to pay (out of the National Insurance Fund) arrears of pay, accrued holiday pay, money in lieu of notice, etc, owed to an employee by his (or her) insolvent employer (see **Insolvency of employer** elsewhere in this handbook);

(n) on a complaint by an employee under *ibid.* section 70 relating to the employer's failure to pay the whole or any part of the remuneration to which the employee was entitled while suspended from work on medical grounds (see **Suspension on medical grounds** elsewhere in this handbook);

(o) on an application under *ibid.* section 128 for interim relief by an employee who has presented a complaint to an employment tribunal that he (or she) had been unfairly dismissed for carrying out (or proposing to carry out) his functions or activities as:

- a trade union-appointed safety representative,

- an employee-elected safety representative,

- a member of a safety committee, or

- a person designated (or acknowledged) by his employer as having responsibility for health and safety matters (as to which, see **Dismissal in health and safety cases** elsewhere in this handbook);

(p) on an application under *ibid.* section 128 for interim relief by an employee-elected *workforce representative* (or by a candidate for election as such a representative), under the Working Time Regulations 1998, who has presented a complaint to an employment tribunal that he (or she) had been unfairly dismissed for performing (or proposing to perform) any functions or activities as such a representative (or candidate);

(q) on an application under *ibid.* section 128 for interim relief by a *trustee of a relevant occupational pension scheme* following a complaint that he (or she) had been unfairly dismissed for performing (or proposing to perform) his functions as such a trustee (see **Dismissal of a pension scheme trustee** elsewhere in this handbook);

(r) on an application under *ibid.* section 128 for interim relief by an employee who has presented a complaint to an employment tribunal alleging that he had been unfairly dismissed for performing (or proposing to perform) his functions or activities as an *employee representative* or as a candidate for election as such a representative (for the purposes of Chapter 11 of Part IV of the Trade Union & Labour Relations (Consolidation) Act 1992 (collective redundancies) or regulations 10 and 11 of the Transfer of Undertakings (Protection of Employment) Regulations 1981) (see **Dismissal of an employee representative** elsewhere in this handbook);

(s) on an application under *ibid.* section 128 for interim relief by an employee who has presented a complaint to an employment tribunal alleging that he had been unfairly dismissed for having made a 'protected disclosure' (within the meaning of the Public Interest

Disclosure Act 1998) (see **Public interest disclosures** elsewhere in this handbook);

(t) on an application under *ibid.* section 131 (by an employer or employee) for the variation or revocation of an order for interim relief on the ground of a relevant change of circumstances since the making of the order under paragraphs (o) to (s) above;

(u) on an application under *ibid.* section 132 concerning an employer's failure to comply with the terms of an order for the reinstatement or re-engagement of an employee pending the determination or settlement of the employee's complaint that he or she had been unfairly dismissed for one or other of the reasons specified in paragraphs (o) to (s) above;

(v) for the appointment of an 'appropriate person' to institute or continue with any tribunal proceedings on behalf of a deceased employee arising (where there is no personal representative to represent the interests of that employee) (*ibid.* section 206(4));

(w) in breach of employment contract cases in respect of which an employment tribunal has jurisdiction by virtue of Regulations made under (or saved by) section 3 of the Employment Tribunals Act 1996 (see **Contract of employment** and **Wrongful dismissal**);

(x) in which the parties have given their written consent to the case being heard by a chairman sitting alone (whether or not they subsequently withdraw that consent);

(y) in a case in which the person bringing the proceedings has withdrawn his complaint; and

(z) in a case in which the person (or each of the persons) against whom the proceedings were brought no longer wishes to contest it.

Under the 'Collective Bargaining: Recognition' of the Trade Union & Labour Relations (Consolidation) Act 1992, an employee who is unfairly dismissed for acting to obtain or prevent recognition of a union, or for supporting or not supporting recognition, or for voting or not voting in a ballot for recognition, or for influencing or seeking to influence the way in which votes are cast, etc, will have the right to apply to an employment tribunal for interim relief pending the full hearing of his complaint (per section 128(1) of the Employment Rights Act 1996, and paragraph 161(2) of Schedule A1 to the Trade Union & Labour Relations (Consolidation) Act 1992). For further particulars, please turn to the section titled **Trade union recognition** elsewhere in this handbook.

- An application for interim relief may also be made by a worker who has presented a complaint to an employment tribunal that he (or she) had been unfairly dismissed for exercising or seeking to exercise his right to be accompanied at a disciplinary or grievance hearing by a trade union official or fellow employee, or for seeking to postpone the hearing for up to five working days to enable his chosen companion to attend the hearing (*per* section 12(5), Employment Relations Act 1999, not yet in force).

- Although a tribunal chairman has the right to hear proceedings under (a) to (z) above sitting alone, he may decide that it is more desirable for a particular case to be heard by the standard three-member tribunal. A chairman may do so (either before or at any time during the proceedings) if the facts of the case are likely to be disputed by one or other of the parties or if there is an important issue of law to be aired. In making his decision, the chairman will consider the views of the parties concerned.

Rules of procedure

- The rules of procedure for tribunal hearings in England and Wales are laid down in the Employment Tribunals (Constitution & Rules of Procedure) Regulations 2001, which came into force on 18 April 2001. For Scotland, the rules of procedure are as laid down in the eponymous (Scotland) Regulations, which came into force on the same date. The rules of procedures contained in Schedules 1,2,3,4, 5 and 6 to those Regulations may be referred to, respectively, as:

   (a) the Employment Tribunals Rules of Procedure 2001;

   (b) the Employment Tribunals (National Security) Complementary Rules of Procedure 2001;

   (c) the Employment Tribunals (Equal Value) Complementary Rules of Procedure 2001 – which complement the rules in (a) above and apply to proceedings involving claims for equal pay for work of equal value under the Equal Pay Act 1970;

   (d) the Employment Tribunals (Levy Appeals) Rules of Procedure 2001 – which apply to appeals against assessments to industrial training levy under the Industrial Training Act 1982;

   (e) the Employment Tribunals (Improvement & Prohibition Notices Appeals) Rules of Procedure 2001 – which apply to appeals against improvement and prohibition notices served under the Health & Safety at Work etc Act 1974; and

(f) the Employment Tribunals (Non-Discrimination Notices Appeals) Rules of Procedure 2001 – which apply to appeals against non-discrimination notices served under the Sex Discrimination Act 1975, the Race Relations Act 1976 or the Disability Discrimination Act 1995.

Note: This section of the handbook concentrates on the Employment Tribunals Rules of Procedure 1993 (as outlined in Schedule 1 to the 2001 Regulations). Most tribunal hearings are conducted in accordance with those rules.

Infringements of statutory employment rights

- The Employment Tribunals Rules of Procedure 2001 apply to proceedings relating to applications, complaints or references under the enactments and regulations listed at the beginning of this section (as well as under the Health & Safety at Work etc Act 1974).

- In July 1994, the jurisdiction of the employment tribunals was extended to include all breach of employment contract cases except for personal injury claims, which latter remain a matter for the civil courts. However, there is an upper limit of £25,000 on the amount a tribunal may award in breach of employment contract cases. A claimant seeking higher damages should do so through the civil courts (which latter retain concurrent jurisdiction) (*per* section 3, Employment Tribunals Act 1996).

- The procedure for the bringing and hearing of an appeal against an improvement or prohibition notice under the Health & Safety at Work etc Act 1974 is explained in the notice itself (and in our companion handbook, *An A-Z of Health & Safety Law*). The same is true of appeals against 'Non-Discrimination Notices' served on an employer by either the Equal Opportunities Commission, the Commission for Racial Equality or the Disability Rights Commission (as to which, please turn to the sections titled **Disabled persons**, **Racial discrimination** and **Sex discrimination** elsewhere in this handbook). For a summary of the procedure in equal value claims under the Equal Pay Act 1970, please refer to the section titled **Equal pay and conditions**.

- Most complaints dealt with by the employment tribunals are presented by employees seeking remedies for alleged infringements of their statutory rights in employment – in particular, the right not to be unfairly dismissed. In this respect, it is important to point out that – except in a case of alleged unfair dismissal or a claim for damages arising out of a wrongful dismissal, in which termination will have already occurred – an employee does not have to terminate his (or her) employment in order to complain to a tribunal about an alleged infringement of his statutory employment rights, eg his right to be given a written statement containing particulars of the terms and conditions of his employment or to receive an itemised pay statement. Indeed, if an employee is dismissed either for asserting one or other of his statutory employment rights or for complaining to an employment tribunal that his employer has infringed such a right, his dismissal will be held to have been unfair – even if the evidence later shows that the employee was not entitled to the right he claims was infringed. See **Dismissal for asserting a statutory right** elsewhere in this handbook.

The procedure in operation

Originating application (Form IT1)

Note: An employee who has signed a legally-binding COT 3 agreement, or a valid compromise agreement, or who has agreed in writing to submit a dispute to arbitration under an approved ACAS arbitration scheme thereby forfeits his right to institute or continue with the proceedings to which the agreement relates. For further particulars, please turn to the sections titled **Compromise agreements** and **Conciliation officers**.

- Proceedings for the determination of any complaint by an employment tribunal are begun by the applicant or complainant (usually an employee or former employee) forwarding an originating application to the Secretary to the Employment Tribunals. In practice, the application should be sent to the applicant's nearest regional (or other) office of the employment tribunals (ROET or OET). The form recommended for that purpose is Form IT1 (*Originating Application to an Employment Tribunal*) (in Scotland, Form IT1 (Scot)), copies of which will be supplied by any job centre or office of the Employment Tribunals Service. The information pack accompanying Form IT1 will indicate the address of the ROET or OET to which the applicant or complainant should send the form once completed.

Note: A person who presents a complaint to an employment tribunal is referred to as the *applicant* or the *complainant*. The person against whom the complaint is made is known as the *respondent*. If either party appeals to the EAT or a higher court against the decision of a tribunal, he or she) becomes the *appellant*, and the other party, the *respondent*. To avoid confusion, the text in this section uses the more familiar terms *employee and employer*. The parties to a tribunal hearing will be either of the employer or the employee (or both) and any other person (eg, a trade union representative) joined (or both) as a party to the proceedings.

- Although use of Form IT1 is not mandatory, the form does require the complainant to provide all the information needed by the Secretary to the Tribunals to enable him to decide whether or not the matters raised in the application are within the jurisdiction of the tribunals. If a complainant is unable to obtain a copy of Form IT1, a letter will suffice.

But there may be a further exchange of correspondence before the complainant's originating application is accepted and formally 'registered' (see next paragraph).

- Most complaints or references to a tribunal must be submitted to the Employment Tribunals Service within three months of the alleged infringement or within three months of the *effective date of termination* of the employee's (the complainant's) contract of employment. Nowadays, tribunals are reluctant to hear complaints presented 'out of time' – although they will do so if satisfied that it was not reasonably practicable for the complainant to have submitted his originating application before the three-month deadline. For the meaning of the expression *effective date of termination*, please turn to the section titled **Dismissal**. See also *Future developments* at the end of this section.

Action upon receipt of an originating application (or complaint)

- Within 28 days of receiving an originating application, the Secretary to the Tribunals must enter the relevant particulars in the Register of Applications, Appeals & Decisions. If the application appears to involve allegations of the commission of a sexual offence, the Secretary has a duty to omit information that could lead members of the public (or the media) to identify the person or persons making those allegations or affected by them.

  Note: The Secretary will send copies of most originating applications to a conciliation officer of the Advisory, Conciliation and Arbitration Service (ACAS). It is the job of a conciliation officer to try to assist the parties to reach a settlement before the complaint goes to a full tribunal hearing. This procedure does not delay arrangements for the tribunal hearing; nor is anything said to or by the conciliation officer admissible in evidence at the subsequent tribunal hearing without the express permission of the parties concerned, For further particulars, see **Conciliation officers** elsewhere in this handbook. See also **Compromise agreements**.

- If the Secretary considers that an originating application does not seek or (on the facts stated in the application) cannot entitle the employee to a relief that an employment tribunal is empowered to give, he will write to the employee giving his reasons for that view and informing the employee that his (or her) application will not be registered until he confirms in writing that he still wishes to proceed with it.

  Note: For example, it may be obvious to the Secretary (from the information provided in the originating application) that the employee is not qualified to register a complaint – perhaps because he (or she) does not seem to have been employed for long enough to qualify for the right he claims has been infringed. In such a case, the Secretary will inform the employee of his opinion and will ask him to confirm that he still wishes to proceed. However, it is as well to point out that the Secretary cannot refuse to accept an originating application. If the employee insists on proceeding, the Secretary must register the application and progress it in the normal way. But see *Pre-hearing review* below.

- Once he has registered an originating application, the Secretary will send a copy to the respondent employer – together with a *Notice of appearance* (Form IT3) – asking him if he intends to contest the employee's complaint and, if so, to give particulars of his grounds for doing so. If the employer does not enter an appearance within 21 days (without good reason), he will not normally be entitled to take any part in the later proceedings (other than to receive a copy of the tribunal's decision), although he may be called as a witness. If the employer *does* enter a *Notice of appearance*, a copy will be sent to the employee.

Notice of hearing

- Except in the case of an application for interim relief (which must be presented within seven days and heard as soon as possible), the Secretary will give the parties concerned at least 14 days' advance written notice of the date, time and place fixed for the tribunal hearing. The notice will also include information and guidance about the hearing itself, the attendance of witnesses, the documents (if any) that must be produced, the right of either party to representation by another person, and affidavits.

Pre-hearing review

- Before the date fixed for the tribunal hearing, a tribunal may call for a pre-hearing review (either of its own motion or on the application of one or other of the parties) to consider the contents of the (employee's) originating application and the (employer's) notice of appearance, as well as any written representations and any oral argument advanced by either party.

  Note: Before a pre-hearing review, the Secretary of the Tribunals will write to the parties telling them that there is to be a pre-hearing review on such-and-such a date and inviting them to submit written representations and to attend and speak at the review if they so wish.

- If, at the end of a pre-hearing review, the tribunal decides that the employee's complaint (or the employer's response) has no reasonable prospect of success, it will order the employee (or the employer, as the case may be) to pay a deposit of up to £500 as a condition of being permitted to take the issue before a full tribunal hearing. The tribunal will also caution that party that he (or she) could forfeit his deposit if he loses his case at the full hearing and could have an order for costs made against him. If the deposit is not paid within 21 days (or within such further period not exceeding 14 days, as the tribunal may allow, in the light of representations made by the party in question) the tribunal will strike out the originating application or notice of appearance of that party. It is as well to point out that, in determining the amount of any deposit to be paid, an employment tribunal must take reasonable steps to ascertain the ability of the party to pay that deposit (*ibid*. Rule 7).

- To avoid the risk of bias, Rule 7(9) of the 2001 Rules of Procedure states that no member of a tribunal which has conducted a pre-hearing review may be a member of the tribunal at the subsequent full tribunal hearing. In other words, the full hearing must be conducted by a newly-constituted tribunal.

Note: The opportunity for a pre-hearing review (previously referred to as a 'pre-hearing assessment') was first introduced by the Employment Tribunals (Rules of Procedure) Regulations 1980 (since overtaken by the 2001 Rules of Procedure. The purpose of a pre-hearing review is to discourage a time-consuming and costly tribunal hearing whose outcome is predictable. If an employee insists on pursuing a complaint that he has little prospect of winning, he will not only have to pay a deposit of up to £150 (which he must well forfeit) but could also be ordered to pay the other party's costs on top of his own. The same will be true of a respondent (usually the employer) who presses ahead with a case that he is almost certain to lose.

Restriction on 'vexatious' proceedings

- Section 33 of the Employment Tribunals Act 1996, empowers the Employment Appeal Tribunal (EAT) to make a 'restriction of proceedings' order against any person who habitually, persistently and without reasonable grounds institutes vexatious proceedings (or makes vexatious applications) in an employment tribunal or before the EAT. Such an order (which will not be made until the person concerned has been given an opportunity to put his or her point of view) is designed to prevent a known litigious applicant from pursuing spurious complaints and appeals anywhere in Great Britain – without the leave of the EAT.

- A copy of a restriction of proceedings order (which will remain in force indefinitely, unless stated otherwise) will be published in the *London Gazette* and in the *Edinburgh Gazette*.

Witnesses and documentary evidence

- Each of the parties to a tribunal hearing (including any person joined or sisted as a party to the proceedings) has the right to arrange for witnesses to attend the hearing to give evidence on his (or her) behalf. The tribunal can order the attendance of (possibly reluctant) witnesses and can require the production of any document relating to the issues under consideration. Any person who fails to comply with either requirement, without reasonable excuse, is guilty of an offence and liable on summary conviction to a fine of up to £1,000.

- A tribunal can order the attendance of witnesses or the production of documents either before the date set for the hearing, or at the hearing itself. An employee may, for example, apply to the tribunal for an order directing his (present or former) employer to supply copies of documents that he considers pertinent to his case.

- All documents that a tribunal considers to be relevant to the issues under consideration must be produced at the tribunal hearing. These will usually include (in the appropriate cases):

    - the employee's contract of employment (or the written statement of terms and conditions of employment required by section 1 of the Employment Rights Act 1996);

    - the employee's job description, copies of collective agreements, disciplinary rules and procedures, performance appraisals, etc;

    - pay statements, wage records, details of bonus earnings and commissions paid;

    - documents relating to other benefits received, eg travelling expenses, car allowance, board and lodging, pension scheme, etc;

    - details of any severance or redundancy payment, money in lieu of notice, etc, paid to an employee on the termination of his employment; and

    - evidence of verbal and written warnings, details of disciplinary and disciplinary appeal hearings; and so on.

- Also admissible in evidence are an employer's replies (or failure to reply) to questionnaires sent to him by a complainant (or would-be complainant) under the 'Questions & Replies' procedure laid down in the Sex Discrimination Act 1975, the Race Relations Act 1976, and the Disability Discrimination Act 1995 – as to which, please turn to the 'questions and replies' entry in the Index or to the sections titled **Disabled persons, Racial discrimination** and **Sex discrimination** elsewhere in this handbook.

- Copies of the documents that an employer intends to produce in evidence at a tribunal hearing must be sent to the employee (and *vice versa*) well in advance of the date fixed for the tribunal hearing.

- If a tribunal hearing has to be adjourned or postponed because of an employer's failure to produce documents necessary for the determination of an award of compensation (*if* such an award is to be made), the employer may be ordered to pay the costs associated with that adjournment or postponement.

Procedure at the hearing

- The procedure at a tribunal hearing is orderly, but simple and flexible. According to Rule 11 of the 2001 Rules of Procedure (*qv*): 'The tribunal shall, so far as it appears to it appropriate, seek to avoid formality in its proceedings and shall not be bound by any enactment or rule of law relating to the admissibility of evidence in proceedings before the courts of law. The tribunal shall make such enquiries of persons appearing before it and witnesses as it considers appropriate and shall otherwise conduct the hearing in such a manner as it considers most appropriate for the clarification of the issues before it and generally to the just handling of the proceedings.'

- Either party may give evidence, may call witnesses to give evidence, and may question both his (or her) own witnesses and those brought by the other party. The order in which evidence is given may be varied at the discretion of the tribunal. However, it is customary for the party on whom the burden of proof rests (eg, the respondent employer in unfair dismissal cases) to begin the proceedings by making an opening statement and calling his evidence. Either party may present his case in person or be represented by any person whom he has asked to represent him and who has agreed to do so.

- The tribunal clerk will normally advise the parties about procedure before the case begins and is available to give information about the arrangements. If need be, the tribunal will give guidance on procedure to a party during the presentation of his (or her) case. Tribunal members may themselves ask questions of parties or witnesses in order to obtain relevant facts.

- If one of the parties is not present or represented at the hearing, the tribunal may decide the case in his (or her) absence. If, as sometimes happens, the applicant fails to attend without explanation, and the tribunal cannot reach a decision in his absence, his application (or complaint) may be dismissed.

- As was indicated earlier, tribunal hearings are normally open to the public, including representatives of the Press (but see *Restricted report-*

ing orders below). A tribunal will agree to a private hearing if satisfied that the evidence to be produced at the hearing is likely to contain information whose disclosure would cause substantial injury to any business or undertaking, or information that could not be disclosed by a person in public without contravening a prohibition imposed by or under any enactment.

Restricted reporting orders

- In any case involving allegations of sexual misconduct or unlawful discrimination on grounds of disability (when evidence of a personal nature is likely to be heard), a tribunal may make a restricted reporting order, either before the hearing begins or at any time before it promulgates its decision. It may make an order either on the application of one of the parties (to the Secretary of the Tribunals) or of its own motion. However, before doing so, the tribunal will give each party an opportunity to 'advance oral argument' at the hearing, 'if they so wish'.

  Note: 'Promulgation' of an employment tribunal's decision occurs on the date recorded as being the date on which the document recording the determination of the originating application was sent to the parties. This may be some weeks after the oral decision announced by the tribunal chairman at the conclusion of the hearing.

- A restricted reporting order will specify the person (or persons) who may not be identified either by the media or by any other person. Unless revoked earlier, the order will remain in force until the tribunal promulgates its decision. If an order is made, a notice of that fact will be displayed both on the tribunal notice board (alongside a list of the proceedings taking place before the tribunal) and on the door of the room in which the relevant tribunal hearing is in progress or about to take place.

  Note: In appeals to the Employment Appeal Tribunal (EAT) in cases involving allegations of sexual misconduct or unlawful discrimination on grounds of disability, where the appeal is against an employment tribunal's decision or refusal to make a restricted reporting order (or against an interlocutory decision by a tribunal in a case which is the subject of a restricted reporting order, that has not been revoked), the EAT can make a restricted reporting order of its own. The order lapses once the EAT promulgates its decision or revokes the order (whichever occurs sooner). In such cases, the EAT is also able to remove permanently from its decisions and other documents open to the public any information capable of identifying the person or persons making (or affected by) allegations of sexual misconduct or disability discrimination.

- If any identifying matter is published by a newspaper, radio or television programme (or the like), in contravention of a restricted reporting order, the person responsible (proprietor, publisher, editor) and/or the relevant body corporate will be guilty of an offence and liable on summary conviction to a fine not exceeding Level 5 on the standard scale (currently £5,000).

The decision of the tribunal

- Once the hearing is concluded, the tribunal will withdraw to consider its decision. A decision of the tribunal may be taken by a majority. In other words, it is quite possible for the chairman to be overruled by the two lay members (although this rarely happens on a point of law). On occasion, a tribunal hearing may take place with just the chairman and one of the lay members present; in which event, the chairman will have a second or casting vote. However, as was mentioned earlier, a two-member tribunal may only proceed to deal with a complaint (application or reference) with the 'appropriate consent' (that is to say, with the consent given at the beginning of the hearing by such of the parties as are then present in person or represented, or with the consent of each of the parties). See also *Hearings by a chairman sitting alone* above.

- An employment tribunal will usually announce its decision, and the reasons on which it is based, at the close of the hearing. In some cases, the decision and/or the reasons for it will be 'reserved' and announced to the parties at a later date. The decision is recorded in summary or extended form in a document signed by the chairman, which is then sent to the Secretary of the Tribunals. The decision will usually be given in summary form unless the case involved the determination of an issue arising under or relating to the Equal Pay Act 1970, the Sex Discrimination Acts 1975 or 1986, or the Race Relations Act 1976. One or other of the parties to the tribunal hearing may request a decision in extended form either orally, at the hearing itself, or in writing (to the Secretary of the Tribunals) not later than 21 days after the date on which the tribunal's summary decision was sent to the parties (see next paragraph). If an employer or employee wishes to appeal to the EAT from a decision of an employment tribunal, he (or she) will need to secure a copy of the tribunal's written decision in its extended form (see *Appeal to the Employment Appeal Tribunal* below).

- Once the Secretary to the Tribunals has entered the decision of an employment tribunal in the Register of Applications, Appeals and Decisions, he (or she) will send a copy of that entry to the parties concerned (employer and employee) and to the persons who were entitled to appear and did appear at the hearing. If a case involved allegations of a sexual offence, the Secretary will register the tribunal's decision with such deletions or amendments as may be necessary to conceal the identity of the person or persons who made or were affected by those allegations.

- An employment tribunal's decision is binding once it has been entered in the Register of Applications, Appeals and Decisions and copies have been sent to the parties concerned. If the tribunal has made an award of compensation (eg, to an employee who has been unfairly dismissed or who has been denied one or other of his statutory rights in employment), that award must be paid within 42 days (but see next paragraph) and directly to the person concerned. The issue of compensation (and the limits on the amount of compensation that may be awarded) is discussed at length elsewhere in this handbook in the section titled **Dismissal**.

Note: Awards of compensation will carry simple interest if still unpaid 42 days after the document containing the tribunal's decision is sent to the parties. A notice specifying the date from which interest will begin to accrue, and the rate at which it accrues, will accompany the tribunal's decision.

Recoupment notices

- An employer must withhold payment of a tribunal award of compensation until such time as the Department for Work & Pensions (DFWP) has served him with a *recoupment notice* directing him to deduct a specified sum in respect of any jobseeker's allowance or income support paid to the employee pending the hearing of his application by the employment tribunal (*per* sections 16 to 18, Employment Tribunals Act 1996 and the Employment Protection (Recoupment of Jobseeker's Allowance & Income Support) Regulations 1996).

- A recoupment notice (which may constitute a 'nil return') will be issued either within 21 days of the conclusion of the tribunal hearing, or not later than 21 days after the date on which the written decision of the tribunal was sent to the parties. The amount (if any) specified in the recoupment notice must be deducted from the award of compensation before that award is paid to the employee. The issue of compensation is dealt with in greater detail elsewhere in this handbook in the section titled **Dismissal**.

Award of costs or expenses

- An employment tribunal will not normally make an award in respect of any costs or expenses incurred by a party to the proceedings. Win or lose, each will usually be expected to meet his or her own expenses. However, if the tribunal is of the opinion that one of the parties has acted vexatiously, abusively, disruptively or otherwise unreasonably in bringing or conducting the proceedings, it may order that party to pay a specified sum not exceeding £10,000 in respects of part or all of the costs and expenses of the other party, including any travelling costs, subsistence allowance or compensation for loss of earnings (or National Insurance benefit) paid to witnesses who attended the hearing. Such an order may be made even if the originating application has been withdrawn and the case did not proceed to a full hearing. See also *Pre-hearing review* above.

- If a tribunal hearing was needlessly adjourned or postponed because of a failure by either the employer or the employee (or, perhaps, a trade union representative) to produce or adduce evidence needed to bring the hearing to a satisfactory conclusion, the tribunal may order the person concerned to pay any costs and expenses incurred as a result of his intransigence or forgetfulness.

Appeal to the Employment Appeal Tribunal

- An appeal on a question of law arising from any decision of an employment tribunal will lie to the Employment Appeal Tribunal (EAT). The EAT will also hear appeals *on questions of law or fact* arising from any decision of an employment tribunal under section 174 of the Trade Union & Labour Relations (Consolidation) Act 1992 (unreasonable exclusion or expulsion from a trade union) (*ibid.* section 291). For further particulars, please turn to the previous section titled **Employment Appeal Tribunal**.

Appeal procedure

- An appeal from a decision of an employment tribunal must be served on the EAT within 42 days of the date on which the document recording the decision appealed against was sent to the putative appellant (employee or employer). A copy of the *extended* written reasons for the tribunal's decision (not the *summary*) must accompany the Notice of Appeal (which latter must be in, or substantially in, accordance with Form 1 in the Schedule to the Employment Appeal Tribunal Rules 1993). Copies of the Notice of Appeal may be obtained from any local office of the Employment Service.

Note: An appeal from a decision of an employment tribunal concerning the service of an improvement or prohibition notice (issued under the Health & Safety at Work etc Act 1974) will lie to the Court of Appeal (or, in Scotland, the Court of Session) and not to the Employment Appeal Tribunal.

- Appeals from judgments of the EAT may be brought, with leave, to the High Court, the Court of Appeal and, ultimately, the House of Lords. In some instances, the House of Lords will reserve judgment pending a determination by the European Court of Justice.

Discretion to extend time limits

- Most complaints (applications or references) to an employment tribunal must be presented within three months of the effective date of termination of an employee's contract of employment (if no longer employed) or within three months of the act or failure to act complained of. The tribunals do have the power to entertain complaints, applications or references presented 'out of time' if, but only if, satisfied that it was not reasonably practicable for such applications to be presented within the prescribed time limits. However, such discretion is not exercised lightly.

Future developments

- Once Parts 2 and 3 of the Employment Act 2002 come into force (in late 2003?), the Employment Tribunals Act 1996 will be amended to empower the employment tribunals to postpone the fixing of a time and place for a hearing in order for the proceedings to be settled by conciliation. Proceedings may also be delayed to allow time for the parties to a dispute to follow the then newly-introduced statutory dismissal and disputes procedure (DDP) or statutory grievance procedure (GP) to be imported as an implied term of every contract of employment between an employer and an employee. Once section 31 of the 2002 Act comes into force, the employment tribunals will be required to vary compensatory awards by between 10 and 50 percent for failures (by employers or employees) to use those statutory procedures. For further information, please turn to the sections on **Disciplinary rules and procedure** and **Grievances and procedure**, elsewhere in this handbook.

    See also **Conciliation officers, Continuity of employment, Dismissal, Employment Appeal Tribunal**, and **Sunday working**.

EQUAL OPPORTUNITIES COMMISSION

Key points

- The Equal Opportunities Commission (EOC) was established under the Sex Discrimination Act 1975 to review the working of that Act (and the Equal Pay Act 1970), to work towards the elimination of discrimination in employment and other fields, and to promote equality of opportunity between men and women generally.

- The Commission may issue codes of practice containing practical guidance for employers and employees alike. It may conduct a formal investigation of an employer's activities if it has reason to suspect that he is contravening either the Sex Discrimination Act 1975 or the Equal Pay Act 1970. It may require an employer to produce documentary evidence of his employment policies and practices.

- *The Code of Practice for the Elimination of Discrimination on the Grounds of Sex and Marriage, and the Promotion of Equality in Employment* came into effect on 30 April 1985, and is available from the Stationery Office (see page 132). The code gives guidance on steps to be taken in areas such as the recruitment, selection, training, transfer and promotion of employees, and urges employers to formulate and administer equal opportunities policies within their organisations. A more recent *Code of Practice on Equal Pay* came into force on 26 March 1997.

- If satisfied that an employer has contravened the law, the Commission may serve a so-called Non-Discrimination Notice on that employer requiring him to cease his unlawful practices and to furnish evidence of his compliance with the terms of the Notice over a period of five years.

- Should the employer continue to contravene the terms of a Non-Discrimination Notice, the Commission may seek a finding from an employment tribunal and, ultimately, an injunction from a county or sheriff court. An employer has six weeks within which to appeal to an employment tribunal against the service of a Non-Discrimination Notice.

- The EOC also deals with discriminatory advertisements placed in newspapers and other media. It may either investigate an alleged unlawful advertisement and serve a Non-Discrimination Notice on the offender (whether employer or publisher) or apply to a county court (or sheriff court) for an injunction to prevent any further contravention of the 1975 Act.

- The Commission may also (and often does) provide assistance to individual employees who are contemplating making a complaint to an employment tribunal. In some cases, it will represent those employees before an employment tribunal.

Addresses

- The Head Office of the EOC is in Manchester, at:

Equal Opportunities Commission
Arndale House   Telephone: 0161 833 9244
Arndale Centre   Fax: 0161 838 8312
Manchester   Website: www.eoc.otg.uk
M4 3EQ   Email: info@eoc.org.uk

Also at:

EOC Scotland (Tel: 0141 248 5833)
EOC Wales (Tel: 029 2034 3552

See also the sections titled **Advertisements, Disabled persons, Equal pay and conditions** (next section), **Sex discrimination**, and **Women and young persons, employment of**.

EQUAL PAY AND CONDITIONS

Key points

- Article 141 (formerly Article 119) of the Treaty of Rome (which became part of the law of the United Kingdom on 1 January 1973) and EC Regulations and Directives made under that Treaty oblige each Member State of the European Community to 'ensure and maintain the application of the principle that men and women should receive equal pay for equal work'. As was pointed out by the Court of Appeal in *Shields v Coombes (Holdings) Ltd* [1978] ITR 473, European law takes precedence over UK legislation. In short, UK courts and tribunals must not follow domestic legislation if it conflicts with European law.

  Note: The Treaty of Amsterdam with its consequent amendments to, and renumbering of, Articles in the Treaty of Rome, came into force on 1 May 1999.

- In Great Britain, this principle is embodied in the Equal Pay Act 1970, as amended by the Equal Pay (Amendment) Regulations 1983, and the Sex Discrimination Act 1986. The purpose of the 1970 Act is 'to prevent discrimination, as regards terms and conditions of employment, between men and women'. The Act is not solely concerned with the question of equal pay (in spite of its title). An employee may exercise her (or his) right to equal pay and conditions under the terms of an equality clause implicitly incorporated in every contract of employment. Thus, a woman may legitimately lay claim to the same holiday and sickness benefits as a man in the same employment (if employed by the same or any associated employer, even if employed in different premises or at a different location), as well as equal access to her employer's occupational pension scheme, the same working hours (unless these are otherwise regulated by statute), the same fringe benefits, the same opportunities for promotion and further training, and so on.

- In *Leverton v Clwyd County Council* [1989] IRLR 28; [1989] ICR 33, a nursery nurse sought to compare her value with that of 11 male workers employed by the council at different locations in a variety of occupations – from clerks to caretakers. The House of Lords held that, although the nurse and her 11 'comparators' were all employed under essentially the same terms of employment (laid down in the Council's 'Purple Book') the difference between her annual rate of pay and theirs was due to a 'genuine material factor'. She worked for fewer hours every week and enjoyed longer annual holidays.

- A woman may exercise her right to equal treatment by demonstrating to an employment tribunal either that she is employed on *like work* with a man in the same employment, or on *work rated as equivalent* under some form or other of job evaluation or job grading scheme, or that she is employed on work that is of *equal value* to that of a man in the same employment. A man may also exercise those rights if he believes that he is being treated less favourably than a woman in the same employment.

'Like work'

- The expression *like work* means work of the same or a broadly similar nature; in other words, work that is either identical to that undertaken by a man or that contains differences that are of no practical importance. For example, a woman may now and then need help in lifting and carrying the occasional heavy load, whereas a man in the same job may be able to cope without help. If, in most other respects, the two jobs are identical, the pay and conditions of each should also be the same.

'Work rated as equivalent'

- If two distinct jobs have been *rated as equivalent* under a job evaluation scheme (using criteria such as skill, qualifications, effort, responsibilities, etc), then men and women filling those jobs should enjoy the same pay and conditions or, at the very least, be on the same pay scales. In disputed cases, the tribunals will certainly want to examine the method of job evaluation employed and the criteria applied. Pay differentials based solely on merit or ability are justifiable if the employer can demonstrate that these are applied fairly and equitably irrespective of sex.

'Work of equal value'

- A woman who is neither employed on like work nor on work rated as equivalent to that of a man in the same employment may, nonetheless, claim that she is employed on work of *equal value*; that is to say, equal value in terms of the demands made on her (for instance, under such headings as effort, skill and decision). If there is any dispute, the matter may be referred to conciliation by a conciliation officer of ACAS and/or to an employment tribunal for a decision. In the latter instance, a tribunal will commission a report from an impartial and independent expert as to whether the two jobs are or are not of *equal value*.

Note: The rules applicable to tribunal proceedings involving a claim for equal pay for work of equal value under the Equal Pay Act 1970 are as laid down in Schedule 2 to the Employment Tribunals (Constitution & Rules of Procedure) Regulations 2001, which came into force on 18 April 2001. The rules in Schedule 3 are complementary to those in Schedule 1 which also apply to such proceedings.

Jobs previously filled by a man/woman

- A female employee, who occupies a job previously filled by a man, is entitled to be paid the same as her predecessor in that job. Any differential between her pay and conditions of employment and those of her predecessor must be justifiable on grounds other than those of sex (eg, length of experience, qualifications, length of service) (see *Macarthys Limited v Smith* [1980] IRLR 211). The same approach must, of course, be adopted in the case of a man who is appointed or promoted to a job recently vacated by a woman.

- A pay scale consisting of a series of incremental advances based on length of service and/or experience will justify a difference between the rate of pay received by a woman appointed to a job previously filled by a man if that same rate of pay would have been offered to a man with essentially the same qualifications, skills and experience as her own. The same rule can be applied if longer annual holidays and more generous sickness benefits are available to employees who have worked for their employer for a specified period (regardless of sex).

Meaning of 'in the same employment'

- An employee may only compare her (or his) job with that held by a man (or, if male, a woman) *in the same employment*. Comparisons with the pay and conditions of persons employed by another employer or by a different company will not be entertained by the employment tribunals. However, an employee is perfectly entitled to make comparisons with the pay and conditions of persons employed by his or her employer (or by any associated employer) in other establishments and towns within Great Britain (eg, if the employer owns and operates a chain of restaurants).

Collective agreements and sex discrimination

- Under the Sex Discrimination Act 1975, any term in a *legally binding* collective agreement is void if it discriminates directly or indirectly against an employee on grounds of sex or marital status. With the coming into operation on 7 February 1987 of the Sex Discrimination Act 1986, the same rule applies to *every* collective agreement – whether or not that agreement is legally enforceable. A discriminatory term in a collective agreement is one that presumes to treat one sex less favourably than the other, either in terms of the number of hours a person is required to work, fewer holidays for female employees *vis à vis* their male colleagues in the same department, the exclusion of part-time workers from certain benefits available to full-time employees, different retirement ages for men and women; and so on.

- As the terms of a collective agreement are usually imported into an individual employee's contract of employment, employers should long since have amended those contracts of employment to eliminate any discriminatory terms. If they have not done so, any employee (male or female) who is adversely affected by such a term may refer the matter to an employment tribunal and seek compensation for any resultant loss of pay or benefits.

Exceptions: pregnancy, childbirth, etc

- An employer is entitled to treat a female employee more favourably in relation to pregnancy or childbirth (eg, time off with pay to attend an ante-natal clinic). However, with the coming into operation on 7 February 1987 of the Sex Discrimination Act 1986, a female employee must be permitted to retire at the same age as a man in the same employment, notwithstanding any contrary provision either in her contract of employment or in the rules of the pension scheme to which she contributes (*ibid.* section 2).

Presumed 'equality clause' in contract of employment

- As was mentioned earlier, an employee may enforce her (or his) right to equal treatment through a presumed equality clause in her contract of employment. If an employment tribunal upholds a complaint of unfair or unequal treatment, it may order the employer to pay backdated arrears of remuneration for a period of up to six years.

- Alternatively the employee may be awarded damages for breach of the equality clause which, in all respects, is a breach of a term of her contract of employment. In any proceedings of this nature, the burden of proof rests with the employer. He will need to show that the advantage enjoyed by a male employee over a female counterpart (or *vice versa*) is genuinely due to a material difference (other than that of sex) between her case and his (or, as the case may be, between his case and hers).

Occupational pension schemes

- Under the Pensions Act 1995, occupational pension schemes that do not contain an *equal treatment rule* will be treated as including such a rule. An equal treatment rule is a rule that relates to the terms on which (a) persons become members of the scheme, and (b) members of the scheme are treated. In short, if a woman is employed on like work, or work rated as equivalent to, or work of equal value to, that of a man in the same employment, any term in an occupational scheme that is (or becomes) less favourable to the woman than it is to the man, shall be treated as so modified as not to be less favourable (*ibid.* section 62). There are exceptions to the equal treatment rule, that will be familiar to the trustees of occupational pension schemes and are beyond the scope of this handbook.

Equal pay questionnaires

- Once section 42 of the Employment Act 2002 comes into force, any person, who considers that she (or he) may have a claim under section 1 of the Equal Pay Act 1970, may submit a questionnaire to her employer (in a yet-to-be-prescribed form) asking for an explanation. Her employer's refusal or failure to complete the questionnaire within a prescribed period (eg, 56 days) will be admissible in evidence in any subsequent proceedings before an employment tribunal – as will the contents of the completed questionnaire and any answers that are evasive or equivocal. The procedure will undoubtedly be similar to that available to employees and other workers under the Sex Discrimination Act 1975, the Race Relations Act 1976 and the Disability Discrimination Act 1995 (as to which, see the sections on **Disabled persons**, **Racial discrimination** and **Sex discrimination** elsewhere in this handbook.

For information about the activities of the **Equal Opportunities Commission** and current **Codes of practice** issued by the Commission, please turn to those sections elsewhere in this handbook.

EUROPEAN WORKS COUNCILS

Key points

- UK-based multinational companies with 1,000 or more employees 'on the payroll' (of whom 150 or more are employed in each of at least two EEA Member States) must respond positively to a valid request for the establishment of a European Works Council (EWC) or for a European-level 'information and consultation procedure'. This requirement is to be found in the Transnational Information & Consultation of Employees Regulations 1999, implementing Council Directive 94/45/EC 'on the establishment of a European Works Council or a procedure in Community-scale undertakings and Community-scale groups of undertakings for the purposes of informing and consulting employees'. For convenience, the Regulations are referred to throughout this section as 'the 2000 Regulations' or by their acronym 'TICER'.

Note: Directive 94/45/EC was adopted by all other EU Member States on 22 September 1994 under Article 2(2) of the so-called Social Chapter and was later extended to cover Norway, Liechtenstein and Iceland (which latter, together with the EU Member States, comprise the European Economic Area, or EEA). The deadline for national implementation within the EEA was 22 September 1996. Originally rejected by the then UK government when it opted-out of the Social Chapter, the original directive was formally extended to the UK by EU Directive 97/74/EC of 15 December 1997. Strictly speaking, the deadline for implementation within the UK was 15 December 1999, although CER did not officially come into force until a month later, on 15 January 2000.

- Multinational companies in the UK, which had voluntarily established their own EWCs or European-level information and consultation procedures – either before 22 September 1996 (under Article 13 of Directive 94/45/EC) or before 15 December 1999 (under Article 3 of Directive 97/74/EC) – are not bound by TICER so long as the EWCs and procedures in question cover the entire workforce in each case. Nor do the 2000 Regulations apply to the UK-based subsidiaries of a multinational company established elsewhere in the EEA which had already been voluntarily included in EWC arrangements established by the company's central management.

- Council Directive 94/45/EC (or, as appropriate, extending Directive 97/74/EC) applies equally to any foreign-owned multinational company whose head office or central management is outside the EEA (eg, in Japan or the USA) – so long as the company in question employs 1,000 or more people within the EEA, and has at least 150 personnel in each of at least two EEA Member States. In short, the company's 'designated EEA representative' (or, if the company has not designated any such representative, the central management of its largest EEA-based undertaking) must respond to a valid employee or employee-sponsored request for the establishment of an EWC (or information and consultation procedure) for its EEA workforce.

Information about employee numbers

- Any UK-based employees of a multinational company (or their appointed or elected representatives), who are minded to submit a request to their employer for the establishment of an EWC (or European-level information and consultation procedure), have the legal right under TICER to seek and obtain data from local or central management about the number of persons employed by the company both within the UK and in every other EEA member state in which the company has operations.

- Should the company refuse or fail to provide that data within one month of receiving such a request (or provide information suspected of being false or incomplete), the matter may be referred to the Central Arbitration Committee (CAC) which, if it upholds the employees' complaint, will order the company either to provide that information by a specified date or face an action for contempt of court. The CAC may decide, on the other hand, from the evidence before it, that the company in question is, or is part of, a multinational company employing 1,000 or more employees within the EEA (with 150 or more employees in each of at least two EEA Member States), and will make a declaration to that effect. In the latter instance, the employees may rely on that declaration when submitting a request for the establishment of an EWC or European-level information and consultation procedure.

Calculating the number of people employed

- Each EEA Member State has its own rules for calculating the number of people employed by a multinational company within its territory. For UK-based employees, the total number of persons employed by the company in the UK are to be ascertained by adding together the numbers employed in each of the 24 months immediately preceding the date on which the request to establish an EWC (or alternative procedure) was received (whether the employees in question were employed throughout the month or not), and by dividing the resultant figure by 24. Part-time employees working, or contracted to work, fewer than 75 hours a month (excluding overtime hours), may be counted as half-units, if the company so chooses.

Meaning of valid request

- A request for the establishment of an EWC (or some other form of European-level information and consultation procedure) is valid for the purposes of TICER if it comprises:

  - a single request *in writing* by 100 or more employees (or by their elected or appointed representatives) in at least two undertakings or establishments in at least two EEA Member States; or

  - one or more separate requests *in writing*, on the same or different days, by employees or their representatives, which, when taken together, mean that at least 100 or more employees in at least two undertakings or establishments in at least two different Member States have made requests.

  Each request must be sent to the undertaking's central or local management and must specify the date on which it was sent.

- A UK-based multinational company contesting the validity of a request for the establishment of an EWC (or a European-level information and consultation procedure) may apply to the Central Arbitration Committee (CAC) for a declaration on the matter. It cannot reject the request out of hand and must put its case to the CAC within three months of the date on which the request was made (or within three months of the last request, if that is the one that brings the numbers up to 100). If the CAC upholds the validity of the employees' request (or requests), the company's central management must begin negotiations for the establishment of an EWC (or alternative information and consultation procedure).

Negotiations for the establishment of an EWC

- Once it has received a valid request for the establishment of an EWC (or alternative information and consultation procedure), the company in question has six months within which to begin negotiations with employees or their representatives. This entails setting up a 'special negotiating body' (SNB) comprising employee-elected or appointed representatives drawn from each of the EEA Member States in which the company has operations. If the company fails or refuses to begin negotiations within that six-month period, it will have no choice but to accept the statutory or fallback EWC set out in the Schedule to TICER (see *The statutory EWC* below).

  Note: The central managements of multinational companies, which fall within the scope of TICER, are under no statutory obligation to initiate negotiations for the establishment of an EWC or a European-level information and consultation procedure.

Composition of the SNB

- The SNB must comprise at least one, but no more than four, representatives from each of the relevant EEA Member States. If between 25 and 50 per cent of the company's total workforce works in a particular Member State, one additional member must be elected or appointed to the SNB; if 50 per cent or more, but less than 75 per cent, two additional members; and, if 75 per cent or more, three additional members.

- The UK members of the SNB must be elected by a secret ballot of the entire UK workforce, unless there is already a standing consultative committee in existence whose members were themselves elected by a ballot of the entire UK workforce. In the latter case, it will be for the committee itself to nominate one or more of its members to represent the interests of employees on the SNB. What is important is that the persons elected or appointed to the SNB represent the interests of all employees, not just a particular group or sector of employees.

- If there is to be a ballot of the entire workforce, every UK employee must be afforded the right and opportunity to vote, and must be permitted, without hindrance, to put his or her name forward as a candidate for election as an SNB member. The company's UK central management must discuss its arrangements for the conduct of the ballot with existing employee representatives and must appoint one or more 'independent ballot supervisors' to ensure that workplace ballots are conducted in secret and that the votes cast are counted fairly and accurately.

- Similar procedures apply for the election or appointment of SNB members from each of the other EEA Member States in which the company has operations. Those procedures will be as laid down in the national legislation of the Member States in question.

Negotiations with the SNB

- Once an SNB has been established, it is up to the company's central management to begin negotiations with the SNB for the establishment of an EWC or information and consultation procedure, and to inform local managements accordingly. The 2000 Regulations stress that the central management of a multinational company and the SNB are 'duty-bound to negotiate in a spirit of cooperation with a view to reaching a written agreement on the detailed arrangements for the information and consultation of employees' throughout the organisation. During negotiations, the SNB will take decisions by a majority of the votes cast by its members (with each member being entitled to one vote).

- The role of the SNB is to determine, with central management, by written agreement, the scope, composition, functions and term of office of an EWC. The parties may agree to adopt the statutory or fall-back EWC (outlined in the Schedule to TICER) or one tailored to their own needs (see *The statutory EWC* below). They may decide, on the other hand, in writing, to establish an information and consultation procedure instead of an EWC.

- If the parties decide to proceed with the establishment of an EWC the agreement establishing it must:
  - identify each of the company's EEA operations covered by the agreement;
  - specify the number of members to be elected or appointed to the EWC (by whatever means), the allocation of seats, and the terms of office of the members;
  - explain the EWC's functions, and the procedures for information and consultation;
  - specify the location, frequency and duration of EWC meetings; and what funding and other resources are to be allocated to the EWC to enable it to carry out its functions; and

    – determine the duration of the agreement and the procedure for its renegotiation.

The parties to the agreement must decide on the method to be employed for the election or appointment of EWC members from each of the EEA Member States in which the company has operations. Those members may be elected by a workforce ballot in each of the Member States in question or be appointed by a standing consultative committee from amongst its own members.

- If the parties decide to establish an information and consultation procedure instead of an EWC, the agreement establishing the procedure must specify a method by which the information and consultation representatives are to enjoy the right to meet and discuss the information conveyed to them; the latter must relate in particular to questions which significantly affect the interests of employees throughout the EEA. The information and consultation representatives may be either elected or appointed in accordance with the terms of the agreement.

- Central management must pay for (or reimburse) all legitimate expenses incurred by the members of the SNB (travelling, accommodation, meals, etc) during negotiations for the establishment of an EWC or an information and consultation procedure.

- Once agreement has been reached on the establishment of an EWC (or an information and consultation procedure), it is up to the central management of the company in question to implement that agreement. If it fails to do so, it will be ordered by the EAT to take such steps as are necessary to establish the EWC (or procedure) or face proceedings for contempt of court. The central management will also be ordered to pay the Secretary of State for Trade & Industry a penalty of up to £75,000.

Subsidiary requirements

- A company's central management which refuses (within six months of receiving a valid request) to commence negotiations for the establishment of an EWC (or for an information and consultation procedure) will be ordered by the EAT to adopt the fall-back or statutory EWC outlined in the Schedule to the 2000 Regulations (*see Statutory EWC* below) or face an action for contempt of court. When making that order, the EAT will also order the central management to pay a penalty of up to £75,000.

- If the negotiating parties fail to agree on the establishment of an EWC (or alternative information and consultation procedure) within three years of the date on which a valid request for the establishment of such an EWC or procedure was made, the parties will have no choice but to adopt the fall-back or statutory EWC outlined in the Schedule to TICER.

Functions of an EWC

- Neither TICER nor the originating EC Directive offer any advice as to the information that must be, or need not be, relayed to the members of an EWC (or to information and consultation representatives) by the central management of a multinational company. That is a matter for negotiation and agreement. However, the fall-back or statutory EWC described in the Schedule to Directive 94/45/EC provides several clues. The statutory EWC (which may be imposed on the central management of any multinational company which refuses or fails to negotiate for the establishment of an EWC or a European-level information and consultation procedure) states that an EWC has 'the right to meet with the central management once a year, to be informed and consulted, on the basis of a report drawn up by the central management, on the progress of the business...'.

- Furthermore, 'the meeting shall relate in particular to the structure, economic and financial situation, the probable development of the business and of production and sales, the situation and probable trend of employment, investments, and substantial changes concerning organisation, introduction of new working methods or production processes, transfers of production, mergers, cut-backs or closures of undertakings, establishments or important parts thereof, and collective redundancies'. See also *Compliance and enforcement* below.

Confidential information

- Both the originating Directive and TICER acknowledge that the central management of a multinational company has the right to withhold from the members of an EWC (or from information and consultation representatives) any information or document which would, if disclosed, do serious harm or be prejudicial to the company's legitimate business interests. Central management has the right also to insist that certain documents or information entrusted to an EWC (or to information and consultation representatives) be held by them in confidence – although the members or representatives in question may apply to the CAC for a declaration as to whether it was reasonable for the central management to impose such a requirement.

- If the CAC considers that the release or disclosure of allegedly confidential information is unlikely to prejudice or cause serious harm to the company's business interests, it will make a declaration to that effect. In short, the CAC will either order the central management to disclose documents or information previously withheld from an EWC (or from information and consultation representatives) or will release members of the EWC (or the representatives in question) from any obligation imposed on them by central management to hold certain information or documents in confidence – subject to any conditions which the CAC considers appropriate in the circumstances.

Protection for members of an EWC, etc

- Under the original Directive and TICER, any employee of a qualifying multinational company who is:

  - a member of an SNB or EWC;

  - an information and consultation representative; or

  - a candidate for election as a member of an SNB or EWC, or as an information and consultation representative,

  has the right to be permitted by his (or her) employer to take a reasonable amount of paid time off during normal working hours in order to perform his functions as such a member, representative or candidate.

- An employer who refuses to allow time off in the circumstances described above, or who fails to pay the employee his (or her) normal wages or salary during such time off, will be ordered by an employment tribunal to pay the employee an amount equal to the remuneration to which he would have been entitled but for the employer's refusal or failure.

Victimisation or dismissal

- An employee who is a member of an EWC or SNB (or an information and consultation representative) or a candidate for election as such a member of representative, has the right also not to be disciplined, dismissed, selected for redundancy or subjected to any other detriment (eg, denial of a promotion, transfer, opportunities for training, a promised pay rise, etc) for exercising his (or her) statutory rights under TICER or for performing his functions as such a member, representative or candidate.

- That same protection extends to employees who have challenged their employer's refusal or failure to acknowledge their statutory rights under TICER or who have brought proceedings before the CAC, the EAT or an employment tribunal to enforce or secure any entitlement conferred on them by TICER. Employees have the right also not to be victimised, disciplined, dismissed or selected for redundancy for seeking information about the number of persons employed by their employer, or for influencing or seeking to influence the voting intentions of other employees (in a ballot for the election of SNB or EWC members or for information and consultation representatives), or for voting in such a ballot, or for expressing doubts about the conduct or outcome of the ballot.

Complaint to an employment tribunal

- An employee who is dismissed or selected for redundancy for exercising his (or her) statutory rights under TICER (whether before an employment tribunal or otherwise) may complain to an employment tribunal regardless of his age or length of service at the material time. The amount of compensation that may be awarded in such cases is substantial. An employee who is victimised, disciplined or subject to any other form of detriment for presuming to assert those same statutory rights has no need to resign in order to seek redress before an employment tribunal, and will be awarded such compensation as the tribunal considers 'just and equitable' in the circumstances. For further information, please turn to the sections titled **Dismissal, Dismissal for asserting a statutory right** and **Victimisation** elsewhere in this handbook.

Disclosure of confidential information

- Any member of an SNB or EWC (or an information and consultation representative) who is dismissed, selected for redundancy or otherwise disciplined for unlawfully disclosing information or the contents of any document entrusted to him (or her) in confidence, thereby forfeits the protection otherwise available to such employees under TICER – unless the disclosure amounts to a 'protected disclosure' as defined by section 43A of the Employment Rights Act 1996 (as to which, please turn to the section titled Public interest disclosures elsewhere in this handbook).

Compliance and enforcement

- Complaints about the failure of a company's central management to respond positively to a valid request for, or to implement an agreement for, the establishment of an EWC (or an information and consultation procedure), may be presented to the Employment Appeal Tribunal by an employee, employee representative or member (or former member) of an SNB. If such a complaint is upheld, the EAT will order the central management of the company in question to take such steps as are necessary to establish the EWC or procedure in accordance with the terms of the agreement concluded with the SNB or, if there is no such agreement, to establish an EWC in accordance with the Schedule to TICER. When making such an order, the EAT will also issue a written penalty notice to the central management of the multinational company in question requiring it to pay to the Secretary of State for Trade & Industry a penalty of up to £75,000 in respect of that failure.

- In determining the amount of the penalty payable by a defaulting company's central management, the EAT will take into account the gravity of the failure, the period of time over which the failure occurred; the reason for that failure, the number of employees affected by the failure, and the number of persons employed by the company throughout the EEA.

The statutory EWC

- The statutory (or fall-back) EWC referred to in the text above will be imposed by the EAT on the central management of a company which has disregarded a valid request for the establishment of an EWC (or information or consultation procedure) and has refused to commence negotiations within six months of the date on which that request was made. The statutory EWC is also likely to be imposed if the negotiating parties are deadlocked and fail to reach agreement within three years of that date. It is as well to add that the negotiating parties are free to adopt the statutory EWC, if that is what they have agreed to do.

Composition of the statutory EWC

- The statutory EWC must comprise a minimum of three and a maximum of 30 members, with at least one member from each of the EEA Member States in which the company has operations. If between 25 and 50 per cent of the company's total EEA workforce works in a particular Member State, one additional member must be elected or appointed to represent the interests of employees in that Member State – rising to two additional members from a Member State in which 50 per cent or more but less than 75 per cent of the workforce is employed; and three additional members from a Member State in which the numbers employed account for 75 per cent or more of the company's total EEA workforce.

Appointment or election of UK members of the statutory EWC

- The UK members of the statutory EWC may be elected or appointed by the members of an existing negotiating committee (representing the interests of the entire UK workforce for the purposes of collective bargaining) or, if there is no such committee, by a secret ballot of the entire UK workforce (similar to the balloting procedures described earlier in this section). Every employee must be afforded an opportunity to vote in the ballot and to put his or her name forward as a candidate for election as a member of the EWC.

Information and consultation meetings

- The statutory EWC has the right to meet with central management once a year in an information and consultation meeting, on the basis of a report drawn up by the central management on the progress of the business and its prospects. Additional meetings should take place if there are exceptional circumstances directly affecting the employees' interests (eg, collective redundancies, the closure of certain establishments, etc).

- Furthermore, EWC meetings 'must relate in particular to issues such as the company's structure, economic and financial situation; its probable future development (including production and sales plans); employment trends; likely future investments; proposed organisational changes; the planned introduction of new working methods or production processes; transfers of production; mergers, cut-backs or closures of undertakings or establishments; collective redundancies', etc.

Procedures

- The statutory EWC may adopt its own rules of procedure. It has the right also to conduct its own meeting before joining central management at the formal information and consultation meeting; and may be assisted in its deliberations by one or more experts of its own choosing. Once discussions with management have ended, the EWC must take steps to inform the workforce (or their representatives) of the content and outcome of the information and consultation procedure.

- Central management is duty-bound to pay the EWC's travel and accommodation costs, as well as any cost involved in organising meetings and arranging for interpretation facilities (although it need not pay the expenses of more than one expert appointed by the EWC to assist it in carrying out its tasks). Central management must ensure that EWC members have whatever financial and material support they may need to enable them to carry out their duties in an appropriate manner.

F

FIDELITY AND TRUST, EMPLOYEE'S DUTY OF
(Confidential information, etc)

Key points

- When a job applicant accepts an offer of employment, he (or she) does so on the tacit understanding that he will be diligent and efficient in the performance of his duties, will behave responsibly and safely, and do nothing to damage his employer's property, goodwill or business interests. If he later proves to be unpunctual, dilatory, inept, perverse or unruly, he knows full well (or should do) that he is putting his job 'on the line' and will be dismissed if he does not mend his ways. If he deliberately or carelessly discloses information about his employer's business methods, trade secrets, chemical formulae, pricing policy, customer lists, marketing strategy, and the like, he not only risks losing his job but could also be restrained by the courts (as could any third party to whom he has relayed sensitive information) and may be ordered to compensate his employer for the damage he has done.

- The employee who is wilfully wasteful of company property, or who directs potential customers to cheaper and more reliable products elsewhere, or who claims longer hours than he actually works, or who rings-up an incorrect amount on a cash register (and pockets the difference), or who accepts a bribe from a client in return for special treatment, is also in breach of his implied duty of fidelity and honesty and is liable to be dismissed without notice.

- However, the common law right of an employer to dismiss the indiscreet or dishonest employee is nowadays modified by the statutory right of an employee not to be unfairly dismissed (Part X, Employment Rights Act 1996). An employee has the right to be given an opportunity to explain his (or her) conduct and to be represented at any disciplinary hearing by a shop steward or colleague of his own choosing. This procedure is particularly relevant when dishonesty or fraud is alleged to have taken place. Unless the employer undertakes a complete investigation of all the circumstances, his decision to dismiss such an employee may be challenged by an employment tribunal, although he need only satisfy the tribunal that he had reasonable grounds for believing that the employee had indeed committed the offence in question.

- A case in point is that of *Trust House Forte Ltd v D J Murphy* [1977] IRLR 187, when the night porter in a hotel was unable to explain a £10.07 deficiency from the proceeds of liquor sales to guests. After a thorough investigation, he was summarily dismissed. The Employment Appeal Tribunal held that, so long as an employer in such a case had investigated the circumstances fully, and had reasonable grounds for suspecting the employee of theft, he was fully entitled to dismiss him without warning. In a similar case, that of *British Home Stores Limited v Burchell* [1978] IRLR 379, the Employment Appeal Tribunal held that 'where an employee is dismissed because the employer suspects or believes that he or she has committed an act of misconduct, in determining whether that dismissal is fair, an employment tribunal has to decide whether the employer entertained a reasonable suspicion amounting to a belief in the guilt of the employee'. It is not, said the EAT, the role of an employment tribunal to establish the employee's guilt or innocence. What is important is whether the employer acted 'reasonably' (*Harris (Ipswich) Limited v Harrison* [1978] IRLR 382).

The employee's duty of confidentiality

- Every employee has a common law (and, hence, an implied contractual) duty not to divulge or misuse confidential information acquired by, or given to, him in the course of his employment. If his duties are such that he is unlikely to come across any information that he could possibly use, or misuse, to his advantage, his employer may not consider it important enough to remind him that he 'must not talk to strangers'. If, on the other hand, he occupies a responsible position or does a job in which he is routinely or even occasionally exposed to sensitive or confidential information, it would be tempting fate for an employer not to insert a clause in his contract of employment pointing out (or reminding the employee), in terms perhaps similar to the following, that he must not, during his employment by the company, or thereafter:

  > 'misuse, communicate or divulge to any person (except to those officials of the Company whose province it is to know the same), any confidential information relating to the business affairs, processes or trade secrets of the Company or of any associated employer'.

Such a clause in an employment contract should at least prompt the employee to think twice before doing anything (or embarking on any project) likely to do harm to his or her (former) employer's business interests.

Note: As was pointed out by the Court of Session in *Dalgleish & Others v Lothian & Borders Police Board* [1991] IRLR 422, employers also have a duty to preserve the confidentiality of personal or related information conveyed to them by their employees. For example, an employer should not give out an employee's address or telephone number to a third party without the express permission of the employee concerned. Nor should an employer lose sight of his duties under the Data Protection Act 1998 in relation to information about employees that he holds on computer. Such data must not be used or disclosed in any manner incompatible with the purpose for which it is held. See **Data protection** elsewhere in this handbook.

- In *Faccenda Chicken Limited v Fowler & Others* [1986] IRLR 69, Lord Justice Neill observed that the courts will intervene speedily to enforce an employee's implied duty of confidentiality so long as he remains in the employment of his employer. But, he added, the courts will be decidedly more cautious when responding to a motion for an injunction restraining his activities after his employment has ended. 'It is clear,' he said, 'that (an employee's) obligation not to use or disclose information may cover secret processes or manufacture, such as chemical formulae, designs or special methods of construction, and other information that is of a sufficiently high degree of confidentiality as to amount to a trade secret. The obligation does not extend, however, to cover all information that is given to or acquired by the employee while in his employment and, in particular, may not cover information that is only "confidential" in the sense that an unauthorised disclosure of such information to a third party while the employment subsisted would be a clear breach of the duty of good faith.'

- Similar sentiments were expressed by Mr Justice Cross in *Printers & Finishers Ltd v Holloway* [1965] RPC 239. 'One must bear in mind,' he said, 'that not all information which is given to a servant in confidence, and which it would be a breach of duty for him to disclose to another person during his employment, is a trade secret which he can be prevented from using to his own advantage after the employment is over, even though he has entered into no express covenant with regard to the matter in hand.'

Note: In *Stephenson Jordan & Harrison Ltd v MacDonald & Evans* [1952] 1 TLR 101, CA, Lord Justice Denning (as he then was) remarked that 'a servant cannot help acquiring a great deal of knowledge of his master's methods of business, and of the science which his master practises. The servant, when he leaves, cannot be restrained from using the knowledge so acquired, so long as he does not take away trade secrets or lists of customers.'

The nature of 'confidential' information

- In my view, said Neill LJ in the *Faccenda case* (*qv*), there are three categories of information (some or all of it labelled as 'confidential' but not the subject of any relevant express agreement) which an employee can acquire in the course of his employment. These are:

   (a) Information of a trivial nature, readily accessible from public sources, which would not be regarded by reasonable persons, or indeed by the courts, as being remotely confidential. An employee is quite at liberty to disclose that information to any person either during his employment or afterwards.

   (b) Information that an employee must treat as confidential, either because he has been told it is confidential or because it is obviously so. Once an employee absorbs this information, it becomes part of his acquired skill and knowledge that he is expected to put to effective use in the performance of his duties. So long as he remains in the same employment, he must not misuse or divulge that information to any unauthorised person or company. If he does so, he is in breach of his duty of confidentiality. But, once he has left his employer's service, the law allows him to use his full skill and knowledge, either by competing directly with his former employer or by accepting a position with a rival employer, even though the latter involves disclosure and not mere personal use of that information. If an employer wants to protect information of this kind, he can do so by an express term in the employee's contract restraining him from competing with him (within reasonable limits of time and space) after the termination of his employment.

   (c) Specific trade secrets, chemical formulae, manufacturing processes, special methods of construction, and the like, that are so confidential that an employee cannot lawfully use or divulge them (before or after the termination of his employment) even though he may have committed that information to memory.

The implications are clear. Reliance on an employee's *implied* duty of confidentiality is fine, so long as that employee remains in his (or her) employer's service. But, if the employer wishes to ensure a continuation of that duty, after the employee has left his employment, he would be well-advised to insert an *express* term to that effect in the employee's contract – preferably when his employment begins – or, at the very least, require him to sign a document (or covenant) restraining him from misusing or divulging confidential information during his employment and for a reasonable period afterwards. But, as Lord

Justice Neill remarked in the *Faccenda* case, a restrictive covenant (or express term) will not be upheld unless the information that it seeks to protect can properly be regarded as a trade secret or the equivalent of a trade secret or, as Lord Waddington made clear in *Herbert Morris Ltd v Saxelby* [1916] 1 AC 688, unless the protection sought is reasonably necessary to protect a trade secret or to prevent some personal influence over customers being abused in order to entice them away.

Status of restrictive covenants

- As a rule, any clause in a contract of employment (or similar document signed or accepted by an employee), that purports to restrict an employee's activities after his or her employment has ended, is in restraint of trade at common law and *prima facie* void. And, as was indicated earlier, such a clause will only be upheld by the courts if considered reasonable and not contrary to the public interest (*Nordenfelt v Maxim Nordenfelt Guns & Ammunition Co Ltd* [1894] AC 535; [1893] 1 Ch 630. A restrictive covenant must be for a specified period and cover a specified geographical area and it must, for the most part, be designed to protect the employer's legitimate interests. If a covenant is couched in vague terms or 'casts too wide a net' it will almost certainly be declared invalid and unenforceable. Given that it is up to an employer to justify a restrictive covenant, he would be well-advised to seek legal advice to ensure that it is properly drafted.

Wrongful or 'constructive' dismissal

- In *Rex Stewart Jeffries Parker Ginsberg Ltd v Parker* [1988] IRLR 483, the Court of Appeal held that an employer cannot enforce a restrictive covenant in the contract of employment of an employee who has been wrongfully dismissed. In other words, an employer cannot benefit from his own wrongdoing. The same rule applies, said the House of Lords in *General Bill Posting v Atkinson* [1909] AC 118, when an employee resigns, when he has every right to do so because of his employer's repudiatory conduct (nowadays referred to as a 'constructive' dismissal).

Searching employees

- An employer does not have the automatic right to search the persons or property of his employees without their consent. Any such right must have been conceded by the individual at the time he (or she) started work with his employer and should be incorporated as an express term in his contract of employment, eg by inclusion in the written statement of terms of employment, in a staff handbook, a disciplinary code, or whatever. Nor can an employee be forced to submit to a search of his or her person or belongings. If he refuses, he could be held to be in breach of contract and, therefore, liable to dismissal. Alternatively, his employer may exercise reasonable force to detain the employee pending the arrival of the police, provided he has reasonable cause for suspecting that the employee is in possession of stolen property.

Note: For obvious reasons, a search of an employee's person, clothing or belongings (including the search of a locker or desk) must always be carried out in the presence of a witness. In appropriate cases, the employee should also be invited to be present. It goes without saying, that a body search should only be carried out by a person (and in the presence of persons) of the same sex. A forced body search constitutes an unlawful trespass (or, in certain cases, an assault) and is best left to a police officer.

'Moonlighting' by employees

• An employer does not have a great deal of control over the spare-time activities of his employees. Indeed, few employees would accept a term in their contracts that forbids them doing part-time work outside their normal working hours. However, as has been suggested elsewhere in this handbook, the tribunals have long since acknowledged the right of an employer to manage his business to the best of his abilities. The employee who comes to work in the mornings tired and worn-out, after working through the night for another employer, will be unable to devote his (or her) full attention and energies to his 'regular' job. Given the nature of his work, he might well pose a safety risk to himself and other employees. Indeed, after due warning, he could be fairly dismissed – either on grounds of misconduct (eg, falling asleep at his desk, or being rude to clients), incompetence (eg, making inexcusable mistakes and errors of judgement) or safety, hygiene or security.

Note: An employee who 'moonlights' (ie, who takes on part-time work in his spare time to supplement his regular income) cannot be said to be in breach of his implied duty of fidelity to his principal employer unless, to paraphrase the then Master of the Rolls in *Hivac Ltd v Park Royal Scientific Instruments Ltd* [1946] 1 All ER 350, CA, he knowingly, deliberately and secretly sets out to do something in his spare time which would inflict great harm on his employer's business.

• An express term in a contract of employment, forbidding spare time employment – either in the interests of health, safety and efficiency, or to prevent employees 'moonlighting' with a specific rival employer – is more likely to impress a tribunal or court than a 'catch-all' and unexplained blanket prohibition on all forms of spare time work. If an otherwise satisfactory employee is peremptorily dismissed on discovery that he (or she) has been pulling pints for three or four hours every evening at the local pub, a tribunal is almost certain to challenge the reasonableness of a rule that imposes a seemingly arbitrary prohibition on all spare time work. If there is nothing to show that the employee's extracurricular activities adversely affected his capabilities as an employee, the dismissal may well be held to have been unfair.

- In some situations, an employer may be prompted to apply to the courts for an injunction restraining a rival employer from employing his employees during their spare time. However, the employer would need to show that his own business would suffer as a consequence of his employees' out-of-hours activities with the rival employer.

See also **Cooperation, employee's duty of**, **Inventions, patents and copyright** and **Public interest disclosures** elsewhere in this handbook.

FIXED-TERM EMPLOYEES

Key points

- With the coming into force on 1 October 2002 of the Fixed-term Employees (Prevention of Less Favourable Treatment) Regulations 2002, employees on fixed-term or task-related contracts, or on contracts intended to come to an end on the occurrence or non-occurrence of a particular event, have the right not to be treated less favourably than comparable permanent employees working in the same establishment. In short, they have the right to be paid the same as those employees and to enjoy equivalent terms and conditions of employment (albeit, in appropriate circumstances, on a *pro rata* basis) including equal access to their employers' occupational pension schemes.

- Fixed-term employees have the right also to be afforded equal access to opportunities for transfer, promotion or developmental training, and must be informed of any suitable vacancies that may arise within the establishment in which they work. On completion of four year's continuous employment under one or a series of consecutive fixed-term contracts, a fixed-term employee automatically acquires permanent status when that or the last of those contracts is renewed, unless their employers have objective reasons for continuing to employ that employee on a fixed-term basis. Amendments to the Social Security Contributions & Benefits Act 1992, and the Employment Rights Act 1996, mean that fixed-term employees engaged on contracts lasting (or expected to last for three months or less) now have access to certain rights previously denied to them under those statutes. Finally, the insertion of redundancy waiver clauses in fixed-term contracts of two years or more is no longer permissible.

- The 2002 Regulations, which implement EU Council Directive 99/70/EC of 28 June 1999 'concerning the framework agreement on fixed-term work', give employees on fixed-term or task-related contracts the right to compare the terms and conditions on which they are employed with those enjoyed by comparable permanent employees working in the same establishment; to seek a written explanation from their employers for what they perceive to be less favourable treatment; and to refer the issue to an employment tribunal if dissatisfied with the explanation proffered by their employers. On completion of four years' continuous under one or more consecutive fixed-term contracts, an employee automatically acquires permanent status within the employing organisation.

Regulations apply only to 'employees'

- The reader should note that the 2002 Regulations apply to those workers only who are 'employees' in the strict legal sense of the word, that is to say, to persons employed under contracts of employment or service. They do *not* apply to workers who are hired on an 'as and when required' basis, who are free, without penalty, to accept or reject any offer of occasional or short-term work that happens their way. Nor do the regulations apply to students undergoing work experience, or to agency 'temps', to persons employed under fixed-term contracts that are contracts of apprenticeship; or to persons who are genuinely self-employed. That said, it is arguable that the majority of people (notably youngsters paying their way through college or university) who are engaged to work in factories, offices, supermarkets, department stores, shops, hotels, restaurants, and the like, for an agreed number of weeks or months (or, in some instances, years) are not only employees, but fixed-term employees, given the clear evidence of mutuality of obligation and control that is characteristic of a contract of employment. The same applies to people engaged to replace permanent employees who are absent on maternity, parental or sick leave; and to employees hired to complete a particular task or project (for however short or long a period).

Meaning of 'fixed-term' contract

- A 'fixed-term contract is a contract of employment that, under its provisions, is intended to terminate:

(a) on the expiry of a specific term (one, two, three months, or what-ever);

(b) on the completion of a particular task (eg, the installation and testing of a new computer system);

(c) on the occurrence or non-occurrence of any other specific event (other than the achievement of normal retiring age) – such as the return to work of an employee after extended sick, maternity or adoption leave or (in the case of the non-occurrence of a specific event), the cancellation of a contract for goods or services.

Meaning of 'comparable permanent employee'

- An employee is a comparable permanent employee in relation to a fixed-term employee if, at the time when the treatment that is alleged to be less favourable to the fixed-term employee takes place, both employees are employed by the same employer and are engaged in the same or broadly similar work (having regard, where relevant, to whether they have a similar level of qualifications and skills). Further, the permanent employee must either work or be based at the same establishment as the fixed-term employee or (if there is no comparable permanent employee working at that establishment who satisfies those requirements) works or is based at a different establishment within the same organisation and satisfies those requirements.

Objective grounds for less favourable treatment

- As was indicated in the preamble to this section, fixed-term employees have the right to be paid the same as comparable permanent employees working in the same establishment and to be employed on the same terms and conditions as those other employees albeit, in appropriate circumstances, on a pro rata basis. If, for example, a comparable permanent employee has the right under his (or her) contract to six weeks' paid annual holidays, a fixed-term employee employed for just three months, would be entitled to one-and-a-half weeks' holidays during that three-month period. The same pro rata principle would need to be applied in relation to other benefits (such as the use of a company car, free medical insurance, permanent health insurance, access to an occupational pension scheme, annual rail season tickets, clothing allowances, low-interest loans, and so on).

- Employers may justify the less favourable treatment of fixed-term employees if they can demonstrate to the satisfaction of an employment tribunal that there are objective grounds for such treatment, eg. if

the cost of offering a fixed-term employee a particular benefit is dispro-
portionate when compared to the benefit the employee would receive,
or that there is no practical way of offering the same benefits to a fixed-
term employee on a pro rata basis. For example, an employer may be
able to justify a refusal to offer a company car to a fixed-term employee
on a three-month contract (whose comparator has a company car) if the
cost of doing so is high and the employee's need to travel on business
can be accommodated in some other more cost-effective way.
Alternatively, less favourable treatment may be acceptable under the
2002 Regulations if the terms of a fixed-term employee's contract of
employment, taken as a whole (or as a 'package'), are at least as
favourable as those enjoyed by a comparable permanent employee
working at the same establishment. In the final analysis, it will be for an
employment tribunal to determine whether a fixed-term employee has
been treated less favourably than a comparable permanent employee
working in the same establishment. See also *Further information* below.

Complaints of less favourable treatment

- Fixed-term employees have the right under the 2002 Regulations to
  challenge their employers' refusal or failure to acknowledge their
  rights under those Regulations by demanding a written statement from
  their employers asking the latter to explain why they are being treated
  less favourably than comparable permanent employees. An
  employer's refusal or failure (without reasonable excuse) to provide
  that statement within the next 21 days, as well as the contents of any
  statement that *is* provided, is admissible in evidence in proceedings
  before an employment tribunal.

Amendments to primary legislation

- Until 1 October 2002, access to certain statutory rights (payments under
  the Employers' Statutory Sick Pay Scheme) was denied to employees
  on fixed-term contracts lasting or expected to last for three months or
  less. With the concomitant repeal of these and related provisions in
  both the Social Security Contributions & Benefits Act 1992 and the
  Employment Rights Act 1996, all fixed-term employees, regardless of
  the duration (or expected duration) of their contracts, are now entitled
  (subject to the usual qualifying conditions) to statutory sick pay (SSP)
  when incapacitated for work; guaranteed payments in respect of workless days; and payment of their normal wages or salary if suspended
  from work on medical grounds. Furthermore, they are henceforth
  required to give and are entitled to receive the prescribed minimum
  statutory notice to terminate their contracts of employment.

Redundancy waiver clauses no longer permissible

- Section 197 of the 1996 Act has also been repealed. What this means is that the insertion of a redundancy waiver clause in a fixed-term contract lasting or expected to last for two or more years will be void and unenforceable unless the contract in question (or, in the case of successive renewals, the most recent renewal of that fixed-term contract) was agreed before 1 October 2002, and the agreement to exclude any right to a statutory redundancy payment was entered into and took effect before 1 October 2002.

Right to be informed of suitable vacancies

- Fixed-term employees working alongside comparable permanent employees in the same establishment have the right to compete on equal terms when vacancies are advertised or posted on company notice boards. To that end, their employers are duty-bound to inform fixed-term employees (eg, by email or internal memos) of suitable available vacancies within their establishments, and at the same time as those details are circulated or made available to permanent employees.

Acquiring permanent status

- Under the 2002 Regulations, the use of successive fixed-term contracts will be limited to a maximum of four years. If a fixed-term contract (which may be a stand-alone contract or one of a succession of fixed-term contracts) is renewed after that four-year period (ignoring any period of continuous employment that began before 10 July 2002 – being the date on which the UK Government should have implemented Council Directive 99/70/EC), it will be treated in law as a permanent contract, unless its use for a longer period can be objectively justified. In such circumstances, the employee in question may write to his (or her) employer asking for written confirmation that he (or she) is now in permanent employment or setting-out objective reasons for his continued status as a fixed-term employee. If the employer does not respond in writing within the next 21 days, the employee may refer the matter to an employment tribunal for adjudication, without having to resign in order to do so.

- With a view to preventing fixed-term employees building up sufficient service to qualify for statutory rights otherwise dependent on qualifying periods of continuous employment (eg, the right not to be unfairly dismissed) many employers operate a system of successive fixed-term contracts, with breaks of one or more weeks between each, in the (often mistaken) belief that this tactic destroys continuity of service. Section 212(3) of the Employment Rights Act 1996 clearly states that continuity is preserved if an employee is absent from work in circumstances such that, by arrangement or custom, he (or she) is regarded as continuing in the employment of his employer for any purpose. In *Ford v Warwickshire County Council* [1983] IRLR 126, the House of Lords held that the interval between the termination of a teacher's fixed-term contract at the end of every summer term and its renewal at the beginning of the autumn term did not break the continuity of his period of employment. If a fixed-term employee is informed (or is given to understand) on the termination of his contract that he will be re-engaged under a second fixed-term contract in (*sic*) 'one or two weeks' time', the likelihood is that there will be no break in the continuity of his period of employment; the more so, if this happens more than once.

- Notwithstanding the foregoing, the 2002 Regulations allow that, in certain situations, fixed-term employees will not acquire permanent status on completion of four years' continuous service under one or more fixed-term contracts if, under the terms of a collective or workforce agreement they and their employers accept that there are objective reasons for continuing to employ them under fixed-term or task-related contracts. Guidance notes produced by the Department of Trade & Industry (see *Further information* below) suggest that such an agreement would be appropriate in the case of actors, professional sports people, and similar, who are traditionally employed under a series of fixed-term contracts.

Termination and non-renewal of a limited-term contract

- Section 95 of the Employment Rights Act 1996, as amended by the 2002 Regulations, states that the expiry and non-renewal (under the same contract) of a 'limited-term' contract – which is the collective term for a fixed-term contract, a 'task-related contract', and a contract that provides for its termination on the occurrence or non-occurrence of a particular event – is a dismissal in law. Subject to the usual age and service qualifications (ie, one year's continuous service and under normal retiring age at the effective date of termination), a person employed under a limited-term contract, that expires without being renewed (whether under the same contract or otherwise), may not only challenge the fairness of his or her dismissal before an employment tribunal but may also (in accordance with section 92 of the 1996 Act) request a written statement of reasons for dismissal, which latter must be supplied within the 14 days. It is as well to add that no such qualifying conditions apply if a fixed-term employee is dismissed or selected for redundancy simply for being a fixed-term employee or for presuming to assert his or her statutory rights under the 2002 Regulations.

Unfair dismissal and the right not to be subjected to a detriment

- Fixed-term employees, who are dismissed, selected for redundancy, disciplined, victimised, or subjected to any other detriment, for asserting their rights under the 2002 Regulations, or for questioning or challenging any alleged infringement of those rights (either before an employment tribunal or otherwise), may complain (or yet again complain) to an employment tribunal and will be awarded appropriate compensation should their complaints be upheld. Such complaints must be presented within three months of the effective date of termination of their contracts.

Written statement of employment particulars

- Readers should note that the written statement of initial employment particulars (or 'contract') necessarily issued to every new employee under sections 1 to 7 of the Employment Rights Act 1996 must, if the employment is not intended to be permanent, specify the period for which the employee's employment is expected to continue or, if it is for a fixed term, the date when it is to end. See **Written statement of employment particulars** elsewhere in this handbook.

Further information

- A detailed Guide to the 2002 Regulations (including further guidance on the pro rata principle and advice on what may or may constitute objective grounds for the less favourable treatment of fixed-term employees) may be accessed and downloaded from website www.dti.gov.uk/er/fixed/fixed-pl512.htm. The Guide in booklet form (Ref. PL512) may also be obtained from the DTI Publications Orderline on 0870 1502 500, or by email from publications@dti.gsi.gov.uk.

  See also **Part-time workers** and **Continuous employment**, elsewhere in this handbook.

FLEXIBLE WORKING

Key points

- Although employees returning to work after maternity leave have no statutory right to do so on a part-time or job-sharing basis, recent amendments to the Employment Rights Act 1996 mean that the parents (or adoptive parents) of children under the age of six, or of disabled children under the age of 18, who have been continuously employed for 26 or more weeks, now have the right (without penalty) to *apply* to their employers for a more flexible pattern of working hours. In short, they have the right to seek to vary their contracts of employment so as to enable them to spend more time with their children. Their employers may not reject any such application 'out of hand', but must consider the implications and be prepared to offer sound business reasons if they decide to reject it. If, on the other hand, an employer agrees to accommodate the employee's request, the variation in the employee's terms and conditions will be permanent and irreversible.

- It is as well to point out that the right to apply for flexible working is restricted to parents, foster parents, etc who are 'employees' in the strict legal sense of the word; that is to say, to persons employed under contracts of employment or service. For the time being at least, agency workers (or 'temps'), who are supplied by employment agencies to client employers, have no right to request a more flexible pattern of working hours.

- The relevant legislation is to be found in sections 80F to 80I of the Employment Rights Act 1996 (as inserted by section 47 of the Employment Act 2002). The legislation, which came into force on 6 April 2003, is supported by the Flexible Working (Eligibility, Complaints & Remedies) Regulations 2002, and the Flexible Working (Procedural Requirements) Regulations 2002.

Meaning of 'flexible working'

- Section 80F of the Employment Rights Act 1996 defines an application for 'flexible working' as meaning a request for a change in an employee's terms and conditions of employment involving staggered daily starting and finishing times (or flexi-time), shorter working hours, a shorter working week, a system of annualised hours, job sharing, term-time working, self-rostering, and so on. The legislation also allows that, in appropriate circumstances (given the nature of their work), employees may ask to work from home.

Eligibility

- However, the right to apply for a more flexible pattern of working hours (or more flexible working arrangements) is restricted to those individuals who are the parents, adopters, guardians or foster parents of children under the age of six (or 18, in the case of children who have been awarded a disability living allowance) or who are either married to or the partners of such persons.

- An employee who is the parent or guardian, etc of a child under the age of six (or 18) will not be eligible to submit an application for flexible working unless he or she:

  (a) has been continuously employed by his or her employer for at least 26 weeks at the time the application is made;

  (b) submits that application at least two weeks before the child's sixth birthday (or the child's 18th birthday, if disabled);

  (c) has or expects to have responsibility for the child's upbringing;

  (d) has a genuine need to work more flexibly in order to have more time to care for the child; and

  (e) has not submitted an earlier application to work flexibly within the previous 12 months.

Contents of Employee's Application

- Applications for flexible working must be submitted in writing and must:

  (a) state that it is such an application;

  (b) specify the change applied for and the date on which it is proposed the change should become effective;

  (c) explain what effect (if any) the employee thinks making the change applied for would have on his (or her) employer and how, in the employee's opinion, any such effect might be dealt with; and

  (d) explain his or her relationship to the child in question.

  Employees applying for flexible working should be given to understand that any resultant and agreed variation in their terms and conditions of employment will be permanent and irreversible. In other words, they may not later change their minds, even if no longer responsible for the care and upbringing of the child or children in question. To that end, they should consider the financial implications (eg, a drop in pay, if their applications are accepted).

Procedure

- On receipt of an employee's written application for flexible working, an employer has 28 days within which to accept that application or to arrange a meeting with the employee. The purpose of the meeting is to consider the employee's application and its implications, and to discuss any compromise arrangements. The employee has the right to be accompanied at the meeting by a working colleague of his or her own choosing, or by a shop steward or full-time trade union official. The meeting must be postponed if the employee is absent on holidays or sick leave, or for up to five days if the person nominated to accompany the employee at the meeting is temporarily unavailable.

- Within 14 days of the meeting, the employer must write to the employee either

  - agreeing to the proposed new work pattern and its start date; or

  - confirming any compromise arrangement discussed and agreed at the initial meeting; or

  - explaining in precise terms why his or her application has been rejected.

  If the application is rejected, the employee should be reminded of his or her right of appeal against that decision, and the procedure for doing so. An employee who chooses to appeal must do so in writing within 14 days of receiving the employer's letter. The appeal must be heard within the next 14 days. At the appeal hearing, the employee again has the right to be accompanied by a fellow-employee of his or her own choosing, or by a shop steward or full-time trade union official. Within 14 days of the appeal hearing, the employer must convey his decision to the employee in writing. If the appeal has been upheld, the employer's letter must specify the contract variation agreed to and the date from which it is to take effect. If the employee's appeal has been dismissed, the letter must set out the grounds on which the dismissal is based.

Grounds for rejecting an application for flexible working

- Section 80G of the Employment Rights Act 1996 states that an employer who has received an application for flexible working may only refuse the application for one or more of the following reasons:

  (a) the burden of additional costs;

(b) detrimental effect on the ability to meet customer demand;

(c) inability to re-organise work among existing staff;

(d) inability to recruit additional staff;

(e) detrimental impact on quality or performance;

(f) insufficiency of work during the periods the employee proposes to work;

(g) planned structural changes; or

(h) such other grounds as may be specified in regulations made by the Secretary of State;

and must be prepared to explain those reasons before an employment tribunal should the need arise.

Complaints to an employment tribunal

- An employee whose application for more flexible working has been rejected out of hand (without the benefit either of an initial meeting or an appeal hearing), or if the employer has been dilatory in dealing with the employee's application (or has made it plain that he is not prepared to discuss it), or if the employee believes that the employer's dismissal of the application was based on grounds other than those listed in the preceding paragraph (eg, on grounds of sex, race, disability or trade union membership) may complain to an employment tribunal, but must do so within three months of the employer's rejection or refusal to entertain the application.

- If an employment tribunal finds such a complaint to be well-founded, it will make a declaration to that effect and may order the employer both to reconsider the employee's application and to pay such compensation to the employee as the tribunal considers to be just and equitable in all the circumstances (subject to a maximum of eight weeks' pay).

- An eligible employee who is be dismissed, selected for redundancy, victimised or subjected to any other detriment by his (or her) employer for presuming to exercise or assert his right to apply for flexible working, or for challenging or questioning any alleged infringement of those rights (whether before an employment tribunal or otherwise) may apply (yet again) to an employment tribunal and will be awarded substantial compensation if that complaint is upheld,

See also **Adoption leave, Dismissal for asserting a statutory right, Parental leave, Paternity leave** and **Maternity rights**, elsewhere in this handbook

FOREIGN NATIONALS, EMPLOYMENT OF

Key points

- Under section 8 of the Asylum & Immigration Act 1996 (which came into force on 27 January 1997), employers are liable to fines of up to £5,000 (for each offence) if they employ persons aged 16 or over who are either illegal immigrants or who do not have a legal and subsisting right to seek and obtain employment during their stay in the UK.

  Note: Prosecutions will be brought not only against the body corporate but also against the individual director, personnel manager, company secretary, or other manager or supervisor identified as having been directly responsible for recruiting any such person.

- In short, employers are nowadays duty-bound to check the P45, (which will include a successful job applicant's permanent National Insurance number), or the birth certificate, passport, identity card, certificate of registration or naturalisation as a British Citizen, a letter from the Home Office, or any other document containing a National Insurance number of any person aged 16 or over applying for work under a contract of service (ie as an employee) to ensure that he (or she) has been granted leave to enter or remain in the United Kingdom and that there is no current restriction preventing that person from taking up employment in the UK *(per* the Immigration (Restrictions on Employment) Order 1996). A Home Office booklet titled *Prevention of Illegal Working – Guidance for Employers* is available on enquiry to the Home Office Public Enquiry Point. Employers wary of the validity of any documents presented by a foreign national can obtain further advice by telephoning the Home Office's Immigration & Nationality Directorate Helpline on 020 8649 7878.

- To avoid a complaint of unlawful discrimination on racial grounds, an employer would be well-advised to modify his recruitment procedures to ensure that similar checks are made for *every* successful job applicant and that copies of the relevant documents are made and retained on file for so long as a successful job applicant continues to be employed. Section 8 of the 1996 Act is not retrospective and does *not* apply to persons employed before 27 January 1997. However, it does apply to any such employee who resigns or is dismissed and subsequently reapplies for work for the same organisation. Section 8 does not apply to self-employed persons (who work under contracts for services).

Note: The Commission for Racial Equality (CRE) has published guidance notes for employers titled *The Asylum & Immigration Act 1996: Implications for Employers*, copies of which are available on request from Central Books, 99 Wallis Road, London E9 5LN (Tel: 020 8986 4854).

Codes of practice

- Under Section 8A of the 1996 Act, the Home Secretary is duty-bound to issue a code of practice as to the measures which employers should take (or not take, as the case may be) in order to avoid allegations of unlawful discrimination when establishing the legal right of any job applicant 'subject to immigration control' to enter (or remain) in the UK or to take up employment while in the UK.

- In preparing a draft of the code, the Home Secretary must consult the Commission for Racial Equality (CRE) or (in Northern Ireland) the Equality Commission, and such organisations and bodies as he considers appropriate. The draft must then be laid before both Houses of Parliament, after which the Secretary of State may bring the code into operation by an order made by statutory instrument.

- The Home Office has since produced a draft Code of Practice 'for all employers on the avoidance of race discrimination in recruitment practice, while seeking to prevent illegal working'. The draft code (which may or may not be in force by the time this edition goes to press) may be accessed and downloaded from website www.ind.homeoffice.gov.uk/default.asp?pageid=270. The draft code draws heavily on the Commission for Racial Equality's Guide (*Racial Equality and the Asylum & Immigration Act 1996: A guide for employers on compliance with the Race Relations Act 1976*) (ISBN 1 85442 191 3), copies of which are available free of charge from CRE Customer Services, PO Box 29, Norwich NR3 1GN (tel: 0870 240 3697; fax: 0870 240 3698, email: CRE@tso.co.uk).

Immigration rules

- Home Office rules relating to the entry into and the stay of persons in the United Kingdom are to be found in the *Statement of Changes in Immigration Rules* (HC 395) laid before Parliament on 23 May 1994 under section 3(2) of the Immigration Act 1971. The *Statement* (ISBN 0 10 239594 2) may be obtained from The Stationery Office (as to which, please turn to page 132). When ordering the *Statement*, readers should take care to ask for copies of all subsequent amending statements.

Work permits and procedure

- As a rule, foreign nationals subject to immigration control will not be permitted to enter the UK to seek or take up employment unless they have valid work permits issued to prospective UK employers on their behalf.

- That said, work permits are not needed for:
  - nationals of Member States of the European Economic Area (EEA) (see **EEA nationals, employment of** elsewhere in this handbook);
  - citizens of Switzerland;
  - citizens of British Overseas Territories (ie, Anguilla, Bermuda, British Antarctic Territory, British Indian Ocean Territory, British Virgin Islands, Cayman Islands, Falkland Islands, Gibraltar, Monserrat, Pitcairn Islands, St Helena and Dependencies, South Georgia and the South Sandwich Islands, and the Turks and Caicos Islands) – except those from Sovereign Base Areas in Cyprus;
  - Commonwealth citizens given leave to enter or to remain in the UK on the basis that a grandparent was born in the UK; and
  - spouses and dependent children of existing work permit holders, and of any of the above – provided that the endorsement in their passports places no restriction on their employment in the UK.

  Nor are work permits required by certain foreign nationals coming to the UK for employment in their own fields (eg, doctors, dentists, journalists, etc) all of which is explained in the current *Statement of Changes* document referred to above.

  Note: A Commonwealth citizen who has been given limited leave to enter the UK may later establish a claim to the right of abode. If he (or she) can show that, immediately before the commencement of the British Nationality Act 1981, he was a Commonwealth citizen born to a parent who, at the time of the birth, had citizenship of the United Kingdom and Colonies by his birth in the UK or in any of the islands, the time limit on his stay in the UK should be removed.

Restrictions on the issue of work permits

Work permits will be issued only for work requiring people in the following categories:

- those with recognised degree level or equivalent professional qualifications;
- senior executive staff;
- highly qualified technicians with specialised experience;
- senior employees in multi-national companies transferring to the UK office for periods of career development;
- entertainers, sports persons and models; and
- others whose employment is, in the opinion of the Secretary of State, in the national interest.

- 'Key workers' (so-called) are overseas nationals having technical or specialised skills and expertise essential to the day-to-day operation of the organisation by which they are to be employed. They need not hold high academic or professional qualifications, but they must possess specialised knowledge or experience not readily available in the UK or in the European Community (EC). Furthermore, their employer must demonstrate that the jobs of others depend on them.

  Employees who have extensive knowledge of languages and cultures not readily available in the UK or EC, and whose jobs involve spending at least 60 per cent of their time in contact work using that knowledge, may also qualify as 'key workers'.

Short-term low skilled work permits

- On 7 October 2002, the Home Secretary announced that from early 2003, two new managed migration schemes will be introduced to allow employers in the food manufacturing and hospitality industries to recruit short-term low-skilled workers from overseas to help ease recruitment difficulties. More information about the proposed new schemes can be obtained by emailing WP(UK) on managed-migration.workpermits@wpuk.gov.uk.

Work permit procedure: overview

- UK employers seeking to employ a foreign national subject to immigration control, who needs permission to work in the UK must apply for a so-called 'business and commercial' work permit from Work Permits (UK) a branch of the Home Office's Immigration & Nationality Directorate. Applications may be submitted by post or electronically (ie, by email). The prescribed form for these purposes is form WP1, copies of which can be obtained either by downloading them from website (www.workpermits.gov.uk) or by telephoning WP(UK)'s distribution centre on 08705 210224. Applications for permits to work in the Isle of Man, Jersey and the Channel Islands must be sent to the relevant agencies in those areas (listed at the end of this section). Form WP1 makes provision for two types of application: a Tier 1 application or a Tier 2 application. The criteria for each type of application are discussed later in this section. Applications to extend existing work permits must be submitted on Form WP1X.

Note: Employers wishing to provide a foreign national with work experience or training leading to a recognised professional qualification must apply for a Training & Work Experience Scheme (TWES) permit (discussed later in this section).

- It is important to note that it is the would-be employer who must apply for a work permit (not the foreign national) and it is the putative employer who will be issued with the work permit and who must forward it to the person named in the permit in his or her country of residence. Possession of a work permit does not override the foreign national's need (if any) to obtain a visa before entry to the UK. Work permits are not transferable and will not enable the holder to work for any other employer in the UK unless that other employer applies for a work permit on the existing permit holder's behalf. A move to a different job within the same organisation will also require a fresh WP1 application to WP(UK). A person who has remained in the UK for four years under a full business and commercial work permit may apply to the Home Office for leave to remain in the UK indefinitely. Applications for extensions to existing work permits must be submitted on Form WP1X.

First-time applications

- UK employers who have not previously applied for work permits (or have not done so within the previous four years) will be asked to supply copies of their latest audited accounts or their latest annual reports. If neither of those is available, they must produce documents that show that they are trading in the UK or are under contract to do so. Those who are in a professional partnership will need to produce a copy of one of the partner's registration with the appropriate professional body.

Postal applications

- An application for a work permit submitted by post will normally be acknowledged within five working days, giving the name, telephone number or email address of the person or team with WP(UK) who will be dealing with that application. Most work permit applications will be decided within a week, unless the application form has not been correctly filled-in or is not accompanied by the necessary supporting documentation. Postal application for permits to work in Great Britain and Northern Ireland should be sent to the appropriate business team at the address given at the end of this section. See *Further information*.

  Applications for permits to work in the Isle of Man or the Channel Islands should be sent to the addresses given at the end of this section (see *General Information*).

Electronic applications

- Employers with access to the Internet may e-mail their work permit applications to WP(UK). As electronic applications cannot be 'signed' in the usual manner, applicants who have not already done so must first register their details electronically with WP(UK) in exchange for a unique eight-character Personal Identification Number (or PIN). This will be acknowledged within 30 minutes, followed within the next 30 minutes by confirmation of the applicant's company or business name, postcode and PIN. The PIN acts as a signature and must be entered on every email application. The electronic version of Form WP1 is 'smart', in the sense that certain questions on the form will appear or disappear in response to the applicant employer's answers. The form has been designed in such a way as to enable it to be saved and despatched to WP(UK) as an email attachment. Scanned images of supporting documents, such as certificates confirming the relevant foreign national's education and qualifications can also be sent by email. However, passports and police registration certificates (if required) must still be sent by post to reach WP(UK) within five days of the emailed application. For extensions to existing work permits, the prescribed electronic form is Form WP1X.

Criteria for work permit applications

- There are two main types of work permit application – Tier 1 and Tier 2 applications. Tier 1 applications, which are quicker and easier to process than Tier 2 applications, are reserved for multi-national companies with offices in the UK who wish to transfer senior employees with specialist skills, knowledge or experience to the UK or who wish to relocate more junior members of staff (with degree level qualifications and at least 12 months' experience in their jobs) for career development purposes. A Tier 1 application is also required when an overseas national is appointed to the board of a UK company or where the employment of an overseas national in the UK will result in inward investment of at least £250,000 and the creation of jobs for EEA nationals. UK employers may also submit Tier 1 applications in respect of so-called 'shortage occupations' (see below) for which WP(UK) acknowledges that there is an insufficient number of suitably-qualified resident workers within the EEA. However, WP(UK) will not consider Tier 1 applications under the 'shortage occupation' category (requiring a rare level of skills, knowledge and experience) if the occupation itself is not in short supply. In the latter situation, the employers in question will need to submit a full Tier 2 application.

- All other work permit applications will be considered under Tier 2. Employers submitting Tier 2 applications for the employment of foreign nationals subject to immigration control will need to explain why they have been unable to recruit suitably-qualified resident workers to fill the vacancies in question. They must also give details of their recruitment methods, explain their reasons for rejecting otherwise qualified job applicants from within the EEA, including those amongst them who might well have been capable of doing the job with a little extra training. To that end, they must not only provide copies of job advertisements placed in EEA national newspapers or professional journals (or on the Internet) but must also must satisfy WP(UK) that the prominence given to those advertisements truly reflected the level and nature of the vacancies in question. An application for a Tier 2 business and commercial work permit will normally be refused if the applicant employer is unable to satisfy WP(UK) concerning the non-availability of a suitably qualified 'resident' or 'settled' worker' In short, employers will need to satisfy WP(UK) that their attempts to recruit suitably-qualified candidates from within the EEA have been unsuccessful.

- Work permit applications are considered against four basic criteria. These are:
  - whether the vacancy for which the permit is required is a genuine vacancy;
  - the skills, qualifications and experience needed for the job;
  - whether the person named in the application is suitably qualified or experienced; and
  - whether there are suitably qualified or experienced 'resident workers' available to fill the vacancy in question.

For these purposes, the term 'resident worker' means a person who is an EEA national, citizen of Switzerland, a citizen of a British Territory Overseas, or who has settled status in the UK within the meaning of the Immigration Act 1971.

Skills, qualifications and experience criteria

- To qualify for a work permit, the job must require the intended occupant to have:

  - a UK-equivalent degree level qualification; or

  - a Higher National Diploma (HND) level qualification which is relevant to the post on offer; or

  - a HND level qualification which is not relevant to the post on offer, plus one year of relevant work experience, or

  - three years' experience of using specialist skills acquired through doing the job for which the permit is sought, at National/Scottish Qualification (N/SVQ) level 3 or above.

  Furthermore, the person for whom a work permit is sought should have the skills, qualifications and experience to do the job in line with those criteria. WP(UK) will not take account of any experience gained by a foreign national while working illegally in the UK.

- WP(UK) does not issue work permits for low level or unskilled jobs (eg, manual, clerical, secretarial or similar) or for domestic work, such as nannies or housekeepers. Nor does it issue work permits for self-employment if the person in question will be self-employed on his or her own, or in a partnership or by joining an existing business. Nor will persons qualify for a work permit simply because they have, or have had, a significant shareholding or beneficial interest in the UK company for whom they intend to work, or in a connected business.

Shortage occupations

- As indicated earlier, employers may submit Tier 1 applications in respect of so-called 'shortage occupations' for which WP(UK) acknowledges that there are acute shortages of suitably qualified and skilled workers within the resident labour market. The current approved list of shortage occupations includes electronic engineers and physicists of IENG (or equivalent level in cellular phones systems development, integrated circuit design, opto-electronics, photonics, systems integration, telecommunications systems development, video and audio systems development, radio frequency and microwave system and component design, and design and development of electronic systems with embedded software. The list also includes railway planners or engineers, etc (with engineering degrees and at least two years' relevant experience from a civil, structures or electrical background); structural and bridge engineers; transportation and highways engineers; consultants, doctors, nurses, physiotherapists, dieticians, etc; actuaries, CAA licensed aircraft engineers, teachers, and veterinary surgeons. The list of 'shortage occupations' is amended and updated regularly on website www.workpermits.gov.uk/default.asp?pageid=3019 or may be obtained by telephoning WP(UK) on 0114 259 4014.

Changing employers and occupations

- It should be stressed that a work permit is issued for a specific job with a specific employer. A work permit does not constitute a contract of employment between an employer and an overseas worker. It does not authorise the employer to retain the overseas national in employment if that person does not wish to remain, nor does the employer require permission to terminate the employment. Similarly, an overseas worker is not permanently restricted to the particular job for which the work permit was originally issued. However, he will be expected to remain in the same occupation and will not be permitted to start work with another UK employer unless that second employer applies to the Employment Department for a work permit using Form WP1. In other words, the whole process must begin again.

- The same rule applies if an employer wishes to employ an overseas national in a different capacity to the one for which the work permit was originally issued. He must apply again on Form WP1.

Training and work experience scheme

- The Training and Work Experience Scheme (TWES) is a scheme operated by the Department for Education & Skills (DfES). Its primary purpose is to help developing countries by allowing their citizens to receive training in the United Kingdom that is not readily available to them at home. However, the Department will also consider applications for overseas nationals who do not come from a developing country. Permits may be issued for an initial period of up to three years. The scheme also allows young overseas nationals of non-EEC countries to come to the UK for short periods of employment intended only to broaden their industrial or commercial experience and, if appropriate, to improve their knowledge of English. Approval will not ordinarily be given for training or work experience leading to employment in the UK. Applications for work permits under TWES may be submitted either electronically or by post, on Form WP1.

Working holidays

- Young Commonwealth citizens, aged 17 to 27 inclusive, who satisfy the immigration officer at the port of entry that they are coming to the UK for an extended holiday before settling down in their own countries, and that they intend to take only employment which will be incidental to their holiday, may be admitted for up to two years provided that they have the means to pay for their return journey and on the strict understanding that they will not have recourse to public funds during their stay. Work deemed 'incidental' to a holiday is defined as engaging in full-time employment (ie, for more than 25 hours a week) for 50 per cent or less of the working holiday. Alternatively, working holidaymakers may engage in part-time work for more than 50 per cent of their stay in the UK on the understanding that they must have a holiday period at some point. For up-to-date information on the Working Holidaymaker Scheme, the reader is commended to website www.workpermits.gov.uk/default.asp?pageid=2907.

General information

- For permits to work in the Isle of Man, prospective employers should write to:

Overseas Labour Section
Employment Division
Department of Industry
Division House
31 Prospect Hill
Douglas
Isle of Man
IM1 1QS
Tel: 01624 687025
Fax: 01624 685682

- For permits to work in Jersey, prospective employers should write to:

  Chief Inspector of Immigration
  Immigration & Nationality Department
  Maritime House
  La Route du Port Elizabeth
  Jersey
  JE1 1JD
  Tel: 01534 838838
  Fax: 01534 838839
  Email: immnatjy@super.net.uk
  Website: www.jersey.gov.uk/immigration

- For permits to work in Guernsey, prospective employers should write to:

  Chief Immigration Officer
  Immigration & Nationality Department
  White Rock
  New Jetty
  St Peter Port
  Guernsey
  GY1 3WJ
  Tel: 01481 726911
  Fax: 01481 712248

Further information

- Applications by UK employers for business and commercial work permits are dealt with by the following business teams at WP(UK). The alphabetical letters (shown in brackets alongside each of the business teams) refer to the first letter of the employing company or organisation. For example, an application by a business or company whose name begins with 'F' should be sent to Business Team 4 (or BT4).

  Business Team 1 – (Employers A & Teaching)
  bt1.workpermits@wpuk.gov.uk
  Tel: 0114 259 4425
  Fax: 0114 259 4073

  Business Team 2 – (Employers B & D)
  bt2.workpermits@wpuk.gov.uk
  Tel: 0114 259 6665
  Fax: 0114 259 6668

Business Team 3 – (Employers C & E)
bt3.workpermits@wpuk.gov.uk
Tel: 0114 259 3290
Fax: 0114 259 3345

Business Team 4 – (Employers F to H)
bt4.workpermits@wpuk.gov.uk
Tel: 0114 259 4810
Fax: 0114 259 4775

Business Team 5 – (Employers I to L)
bt5.workpermits@wpuk.gov.uk
Tel: 0114 259 3322
Fax: 0114 259 3324

Business Team 6 – (Employers M & N)
bt6.workpermits@wpuk.gov.uk
Tel: 0114 259 3150
Fax: 0114 259 3620

Business Team 7 – (Employers O to R)
bt7.workpermits@wpuk.gov.uk
Tel: 0114 259 4071
Fax: 0114 259 3707

Business Team 8 – (Employers S & T)
bt8.workpermits@wpuk.gov.uk
Tel: 0114 259 1110
Fax: 0114 259 1245

Business Team 9 – (Employers U to Z)
bt9.workpermits@wpuk.gov.uk
Tel: 0114 259 3664
Fax: 0114 259 3946

The following team deals with the Passport aspects of the work permit scheme.

Passports Team
passports.workpermits@wpuk.gov.uk
Tel: 0114 259 1001
Fax: 0114 259 1140

The following team deals with appeals against decisions on the work permit criteria; although the appeal must in the first instance be sent to the original team that dealt with the employer's application.

Appeals Team
appeals.workpermits@wpuk.gov.uk
Tel: 0114 259 5880
Fax: 0114 259 5566

The following team deals with allegations of abuse of the work permit scheme.

Allegations Team
allegations.workpermits@wpuk.gov.uk
Tel: 0114 279 3480

The following team deals with applications from the Highly Skilled Migrant Programme (HSMP).

Highly Skilled Migrant Programme
hsmp.workpermits@wpuk.gov.uk
Tel: 0114 259 1113

The following team provides effective policy development and advice to internal and external customers.

Policy Team
policy.workpermits@wpuk.gov.uk
Tel: 0114 259 3792
Fax: 0114 259 3776

The following team deals with all other queries relating to the administration of the work permit scheme.

Customer Relations Team
customrel.workpermits@wpuk.gov.uk
Tel: 0114 259 4074
Fax: 0114 259 3776

Postal applications

- Postal applications for business and commercial work permits (for employment in Great Britain or Northern Ireland) should be sent to the relevant business team (eg, Business Team 5) at the following address:

(Team Name)
Work Permits (UK)
Integrated Casework Directorate (Sheffield)
Home Office
Level 5
Moorfoot
Sheffield
S1 4PQ

Please refer also to the section titled **EEA nationals, employment of** elsewhere in this handbook.

FRUSTRATION OF CONTRACT

Key points

- At common law, a contract of employment is said to have been frustrated when one of the parties, usually the employee, is unable to comply with his contractual obligations – either through death, a prolonged or permanent illness or disability, or a sentence of imprisonment. The winding-up of a company, the appointment of a receiver, or the dissolution of a partnership will result in most, but not all, cases in the automatic termination of the contracts of employment of the relevant employees. In theory at least, the employer is under no obligation to terminate the contract formally or give notice to such an employee that he is no longer employed. In practice, the prudent employer will be a little more cautious before treating a contract of employment as no longer subsisting.

- In the case of a prolonged illness, a contract cannot be frustrated so long as the employee has not exhausted his (or her) right to paid sick leave under the terms of that contract. Once the employee has reached the point beyond which no further sick pay is payable, the employer will need to consider other factors, such as the nature of his employment (is the employee a key worker or one of many doing similar jobs?), his length of service (how long has he been employed and might he have expected to remain with his employer until normal retirement age?), the nature of his illness or injury (how long has he been ill and what are his chances of recovery in the immediate or short-term future?), and so on. The burden of proof in frustration rests with the employer. In some situations, it will be difficult for the employer to argue frustration of contract if he still retains the employee's 'cards' or continues to pay pension contributions on his behalf.

- In *Harrison v George Wimpey & Company Limited* [1972] 7 ITR 438, the judgment of the National Industrial Relations Court included the following: 'We wish to affirm that it is an employee's duty, when he is away sick, to keep his employer fully informed as to the progress he is making towards recovery, in order that the employer may know that his employee intends to return for further work. Equally, we regard it as very important that an employer who is minded to treat the employment as having come to an end for any reason, should communicate so far as he can with the employee, stating his intentions.'

- With the appearance of unfair dismissal legislation (now to be found in the Employment Rights Act 1996), it would be unwise of an employer to rely on the doctrine of frustration when considering the position of a sick employee. See **Dismissal on grounds of ill-health** and **Disabled persons** elsewhere in this handbook.

- Frustration of contract does not necessarily occur if an employee is remanded in custody for an alleged offence and is awaiting a court hearing. Again, the employer will need to consider the employee's past employment record, his length of service, the size of his business, and how long he can reasonably expect to hold the employee's job open for him. He may dismiss the employee if the offence was committed on his own premises and he has reasonable grounds for believing that the employee is guilty – whether or not he has been remanded in custody and whether or not he is subsequently convicted. If he has held the employee's job open for him pending the outcome of the trial, he will almost certainly be justified in treating the contract of employment as having been frustrated if the employee is convicted and sentenced to a term of imprisonment.

- Paragraph 26 of ACAS Code of Practice 1 (*Disciplinary and Grievance Procedures*) advises that criminal offences outside employment 'should not be treated as automatic reasons for dismissal, regardless of whether the offence has any relevance to the duties of an individual as an employee. The main consideration', says the Code, 'should be whether the offence is one that makes the individual unsuitable for his or her type of work, or unacceptable to other employees. Employees should not be dismissed solely because a charge against them is pending or they are absent through having been remanded in custody.' The small businessman, with but a handful of employees, may be obliged to take a contrary view if any such employee occupies a key post that must be filled without delay. So long as an employer in that situation has considered the pros and cons in a careful and reasoned manner, the tribunals are unlikely to challenge his decision to terminate the employee's contract of employment.

Please see also the sections titled **Contract of employment** and **Disciplinary rules and procedure** elsewhere in this handbook.

G

GRIEVANCES AND PROCEDURE
(*Employee complaints*)

Key points

- Most employees have the right to receive a written statement from their employer explaining the principal terms and conditions of their employment. The statement must be issued within two months of the date on which the employee's employment began, and must, in every case, contain a note giving the name and/or job title of the person to whom the employee can apply for the settlement of any problem or grievance arising out of his employment, and the manner in which any such application should be made. Furthermore, if an employee can appeal to progressively higher levels of management until his grievance is resolved, the written statement must explain those steps or, at the very least, refer the employee to some other document that is reasonably accessible to him, and explains them (sections 1 and 3, Employment Rights Act 1996). But see *Future developments* at the end of this section.

  Note: The written statement of employment particulars referred to above must be issued to every employee, regardless of the number of hours he (or she) is required to work each week.

- Section 2 of ACAS Code of Practice 1 on *Disciplinary & Grievance Procedures* contains a model procedure for the resolution of employee grievances and advises employers to establish a procedure for the fair and speedy settlement of employee grievances. The procedure, says the Code, should be in writing and should provide:

  (a) that a grievance should normally be discussed first between the employee and his immediate supervisor or manager;

  (b) that the employee should be accompanied by a colleague or shop steward at the second and subsequent stages of the procedure; and

  (c) that the employee be given the right of appeal.

- Under section 10 of the Employment Relations Act 1999, a worker (whether employee or otherwise) has the statutory right to be accompanied at a grievance hearing by a fellow-worker or shop steward or full-time trade union official. A worker must not be subjected to any detriment for exercising that right, nor may he (or she) lawfully be dismissed (or selected for redundancy) for that reason. The accompanying worker is similarly protected and is entitled also to be paid time off work when accompanying a worker at a grievance hearing.

- Where trade unions are recognised, management should establish with them a procedure for settling collective disputes. The procedure should also be in writing and may include a procedure for dealing with any individual grievance that could develop into a dispute. The ACAS *Code of Industrial Relations Practice*, referred to earlier, identifies (at paragraph 126) two types of collective disputes. These are:

   (a) disputes of right, that relate to the application or interpretation of existing collective agreements or contracts of employment; and

   (b) disputes of interest, that relate to claims by employees, or proposals by management, about terms and conditions of employment.

- The procedure should state the level at which an issue should be raised; time limits for each stage of the procedure; and a clause that precludes a strike, lockout, or other form of industrial action, until all stages of the procedure have been exhausted.

- At each stage in the procedure, progressively higher levels of management should become involved. The trade unions, for their part, may seek the intervention of full-time officials and, ultimately, a national officer.

- Some procedure agreements will call for the intervention and assistance of a conciliation officer of the Advisory, Conciliation and Arbitration Service (ACAS) whose decision will be accepted as final and binding on all parties (see **Advisory, Conciliation & Arbitration Service** and **Conciliation officers**, elsewhere in this handbook).

Future developments

- Once section 29 and Schedule 2 of the Employment Act 2002 come into force (probably in the second half of 2003), all employers (regardless of the number of people they employ) will be required to adopt statutory grievance procedures (GPs), as well as statutory dismissal and disciplinary procedures (DPPs) which may or may not fall short of employers' existing procedures for dealing with workplace grievances, disciplinary issues, and the like. Furthermore, those statutory procedures are to be imported as implied terms in every contract of employment. The planned statutory GP comprises a three-step procedure; and the modified version, a two-step procedure (similar to the proposed statutory DPP, as to which, see page 142 of this handbook).

- Regulations to be made under Part III of the 2002 Act will outline the circumstances in which either of these procedures is to be applied. Section 31 of that Act allows that a failure to follow those minimum procedures will result in tribunal awards of compensation for unfair dismissal being increased or reduced by between 10 and 50 per cent. The award will be increased by between 10 and 50 per cent if the failure is attributable to inaction on the part of a respondent employer, or reduced by between 10 and 50 per cent if attributable to a refusal or failure by the complainant employee to comply with a requirements of either procedure or to exercise his or her right of appeal under that procedure.

See also **Written statement of employment particulars** elsewhere in this handbook.

SAMPLE GRIEVANCE PROCEDURE

Note: There are no hard-and-fast rules about the lengths to which an employer should go when attempting to resolve employee complaints. A great deal will depend on the size and nature of the employing organisation. In the smaller business, two stages may be the best that can be managed. In the larger organisation, a complaint, say, by a factory operative might first be referred to the manager of his department, then to the personnel manager and then, perhaps, to the general manager or managing director. What is important is that an employee should be encouraged to air any complaint or grievance he may have without being given the impression that he could be putting his job on the line or that his card will be marked as a potential 'trouble-maker'.

The following is an example of a typical grievance procedure. Employers who choose to adopt or adapt this procedure to their own requirements should bear in mind that, once section 29 and Schedule 2 to the Employment Act 2002 come into force (in the second half of 2003?), their procedures for dealing with workplace grievances may need to be modified to ensure that they comply with the minimum statutory grievances procedures (GPs) outlined in that Act and in any associated orders or regulations (see *Future developments* above).

STAGE 1

If you have a grievance or complaint about your work or related issues, please talk the matter over with your immediate supervisor on an informal and confidential basis. Your complaint may have to do with a misunderstanding about your duties, your working hours, rate of pay, holiday entitlement, issues of hygiene or safety, any perceived infringement of your statutory employment rights, and so on. Or, it may have to do with your treatment at the hands of your supervisor himself (including verbal abuse, victimisation, sexual or racial harassment, disability discrimination, etc). If you prefer to put your complaint on a more formal footing, please write to your supervisor, explaining the nature of your grievance, and ask for a meeting in his (or her) office.

If your supervisor cannot resolve your difficulty within THREE working days, or you tell him (or her) that you are unhappy with his decision, you may appeal in writing to your head of department.

STAGE 2

On receipt of your complaint or appeal, your head of department must deal with your problem and make his (or her) decision within the next FIVE working days. If you are still unhappy, you should ask him to send a copy of his written decision to the Managing Director within the next FIVE working days, together with your notice of appeal and a copy of your original complaint.

STAGE 3

The Managing Director will discuss your grievance with you in private, will speak to your supervisor and the head of your department, and will give you his decision in writing within the next SEVEN working days. The Managing Director's decision will be final.

Note: If your grievance has to do with an alleged infringment of your statutory employment rights, and is not resolved to your satisfaction at the end of the 3-stage procedure described above, the company acknowledges your right (subject to any related qualifying conditions) to refer the matter for adjudication by an employment tribunal, without having to resign in order to do so.

IMPORTANT

Please note that you have the right, at each stage of the Grievance Procedure, to be accompanied by a working colleague, your shop steward or full-time trade union official who may address the hearing but not answer questions on your behalf. You also have the right to produce documents and other evidence in support of your complaint.

GUARANTEE PAYMENTS

Key points

- Section 28 of the Employment Rights Act 1996 states that an employee is entitled to a guarantee payment if his (or her) employer does not provide him with work *throughout a day* on which he would normally expect to work under the terms of his contract of employment. Such a day is referred to in the 1996 Act as a *workless day*. It should be stressed at this point that, in the absence of any contractual right to do so, an employer does not have any automatic right to lay-off his employees (whatever the circumstances). To do otherwise is a breach of contract – as to which see **Lay-offs and short-time working** elsewhere in this handbook.

- At present (March 2003), the maximum guarantee payment is £17.30 a day. This figure will be increased or decreased in February of each year in line with the previous September-on-September changes in the retail prices index. If an employee's average daily earnings are less than £17.30, his employer need only pay him the lesser amount. Finally, guarantee payments are payable for a maximum of five workless days only in any period of three consecutive months (*ibid.* sections 29 to 35). See also *Qualifying conditions* below.

- The expression *throughout a day* in the paragraph above means the whole of an employee's normal working day or shift. An employee who is sent home after he has 'clocked-in' for work is not entitled to a guarantee payment in respect of the remainder of that working day or shift. The word *day* for these purposes means the 24-hour period between midnight and midnight. However, if a nightshift worker's usual shift begins before midnight and ends in the early hours of the following morning, his (or her) period of employment will be treated as falling wholly on the day on which the major portion of the shift falls. If, for instance, a shiftworker is not provided with work throughout a shift that normally begins at 10:00 pm on Monday and ends at 6:00 am on Tuesday, the *workless day* in relation to that shift is Tuesday. If his shift normally begins at 7:00 pm on Monday and ends at 3:00 am on Tuesday, the workless day will be Monday. If the number of working hours is the same, before and after midnight, the workless day will be the day on which the shift ends.

- An employer's inability to provide an employee with work *must be due to factors beyond his control* – such as a power failure, a fire or flood, the sudden cancellation of an important contract or order, a major equipment breakdown, the non-delivery of essential raw materials, and so on. But, guarantee payments are not payable if an employer's inability to provide some of his employees with work is due to a strike or other industrial action involving other employees within the same organisation or employees employed by an associated employer (*ibid.* section 29(3)).

For example, a laboratory technician is not entitled to guarantee payments if his employer instructs him to stay at home for a day or two because of industrial action on the shopfloor. But, he *would* be entitled to a guarantee payment if he was told to stay away from work because of damage caused by a fire or explosion in the laboratory or elsewhere in the same premises.

Qualifying conditions

- To qualify for a guarantee payment in respect of a workless day, an employee:
  - must have been continuously employed for a period of at least one month ending with the day before that in respect of which the guarantee payment is claimed;
  - must not unreasonably refuse an offer by his employer of suitable alternative work, even though the work in question may not be of a kind which the employee is normally required or paid to do; and
  - must comply with any reasonable request by his or her employer to keep himself available for work against the possibility that his employer may find suitable alternative work for him to do.

Meaning of 'continuous employment'

- A week counts as part of a period of continuous employment if, during the whole or part of that week, his (or her) relations with his employer are governed by a contract of employment. In short, a period of continuous employment begins with the day on which an employee started work with his (or her) employer and ends with the day by reference to which the length of his period of continuous employment is to be ascertained. In the present context, that day is the day immediately preceding that in respect of which a guarantee payment is claimed (*ibid.* section 29(1)).

- For further particulars, including information about intervals in employment (eg, absences from work occasioned by industrial disputes), please turn to the section titled **Continuous employment** elsewhere in this handbook.

Contractual and statutory rights

- An employee who has a *contractual* right to be paid part or all of his (or her) normal wages or salary, when his employer fails to provide him with work, is not entitled to be paid a statutory guarantee payment in addition to that payment. But if the contractual remuneration paid to an employee falls short of the minimum guarantee payment to which he would otherwise be entitled under the 1996 Act, his employer must make up the difference. As we have seen, the present (2003/04) maximum guarantee payment is £17.30 in respect of any one workless day.

Collective agreements

- Nowadays, most collective agreements between employers (or employers' associations) and representative trade unions include provisions for guaranteed minimum remuneration on workless days. The parties to any such agreement may, if they wish, apply to the Secretary of State for Education & Employment for an order exempting the employees specified in the agreement from any entitlement to a guarantee payment under the 1996 Act. The Secretary of State will not make an exemption order unless satisfied that the collective agreement incorporates safeguards for the protection of the employees covered by the agreement, or that the agreement provides for disputes to be referred for determination by an independent referee or an employment tribunal. As the terms of a collective agreement are usually imported or 'read into' the individual employee's contract of employment, any payment made under the agreement in respect of a workless day may be offset against any statutory payment made under section 28 of the 1996 Act.

Complaint to an employment tribunal

- An employee may complain to an employment tribunal that his (or her) employer has failed to pay the whole or part of a guarantee payment to which he believes he is entitled. The complaint must be presented within three months of the alleged failure. If a tribunal upholds the employee's complaint, it will order the employer to pay the amount of the guarantee payment due.

Industrial disputes

- As was mentioned earlier, an employer is not obliged to pay a guarantee payment to an employee if his (or her) inability to provide that

employee with work is the direct result of an industrial dispute initi-
ated by the employee himself (or herself) or by other employees within
his organisation (including persons employed by an associated
employer). If, for instance, a strike or 'go-slow' in one area of a factory
results in employees being laid-off in another area or department of the
same factory (or in other premises owned or managed by the same or
an associated employer), those employees have no legal right to a guarantee payment – even though they are not involved in any way in the
industrial action which gave rise to their being laid off.

- It follows that an employer must pay guarantee payments to those of
  his employees who are laid off because of an industrial dispute within
  another (wholly unrelated) organisation, eg within a company which
  supplies the bulk of the employer's raw materials.

See also the sections titled **Lay-offs and short-time working** and
Redundancy, elsewhere in this handbook.

H

HOLIDAYS, ANNUAL
(and the Working Time Regulations)

Key points

- The Working Time Regulations 1998 (as amended) implement Council Directives 93/104/EC (concerning certain aspects of the organisation of working time) and 94/33/EC (on the protection of young people at work). The Regulations, which came into force on 1 October 1998, contain provisions relating to maximum working hours, night work, rest breaks and annual holidays. This section deals with a worker's legal right to four weeks' paid annual holidays.

Meaning of 'worker'

- The reader will note that the 1998 Regulations apply to 'workers', which expression encompasses workers who are employees (ie, people employed under contracts of employment) but also individuals (such as casual and seasonal workers, agency 'temps' and so-called 'freelancers') who undertake to do or perform personally any work or services for an employer, whether the contract under which they are employed or engaged is verbal or written, express or implied. The Regulations do not, however, apply to persons who are *genuinely* self-employed, nor do they apply to workers in the air, rail, road, sea, inland waterway and lake transport sectors (or to ancillary workers in those sectors); or to fishermen and others engaged in work at sea; or to the activities of doctors in training.

Note: In a consultation document published on 31 October 2002, the Secretary of State for Trade & Industry outlined the Government's proposals for implementing a further working time directive (2000/34/EC), known as the Horizontal Amending Directive (HAD), which was adopted by the European Parliament and Council on 1 August 2002. Once amending legislation comes into force (on a date yet to be specified), the 1998 Regulations will be amended to encompass mobile and non-mobile workers in transport and related industries (as well as off-shore workers and junior doctors). Copies of the consultation document (Ref. URN 02/1424) may be accessed and downloaded from website www.dti.gov.uk/er/work_time_regs/hadconsult.htm, or can be obtained from the DTI's Publications Orderline on 0845 6000 925. The consultation period ended on 31 January 2003.

Entitlement to paid annual holidays

- Every worker in the UK (unless employed in one or other of the excluded sectors referred to in the previous paragraph) is entitled to a minimum of four weeks' paid holidays in every holiday year. It is important to note that, with the coming into force on 25 October 2001 of the Working Time (Amendment) Regulations 2001 (and the abolition of the former 13-week qualifying rule), workers begin to accrue an entitlement to paid holidays from day one of their contracts and must be paid holiday pay even if they resign or are dismissed within a day or two of starting work. It is as well to add that a worker does not forfeit his (or her) entitlement to accrued statutory holiday pay on the termination of his employment, even if summarily dismissed for gross misconduct. Any term in a contract of employment (or related contract) that purports to undermine or override a worker's entitlement to four weeks' paid annual holiday is void and unenforceable.

- The Regulations allow that bank and public holidays may form part of a worker's statutory entitlement to paid annual holidays – *unless* there is a term to the contrary in the worker's contract or the worker in question has traditionally or customarily enjoyed the right to bank and public holidays in addition to any contractual entitlement to holidays and holiday pay (as to which, see *Written statement of employment particulars* below). Employers who take it upon themselves to override any such contractual or customary arrangement, without the express permission of the workers in question, are liable to face county court proceedings for breach of contract or (if their employment has come to an end) proceedings for breach of contract before an employment tribunal.

Meaning of 'holiday year'

- The expression 'holiday year' means the period of 12 consecutive months beginning each year on an agreed date (eg, 1 January); or as already specified in a worker's contract of employment; or (by default) the period of 12 consecutive months beginning each year on 1 October (ie, the date on which the Regulations came into force); or, if a worker's employment began after 1 October 1998, the date on which the employment began and each subsequent anniversary of that date. In most organisations, the holiday year has long since been established, either by custom and practice or (more usually) by an express term in an employee's contract of employment.

Notification of intention to take holidays

- The 1998 Regulations state that, in the absence of any contractual or long-established procedure in relation to the taking of annual holidays, a worker wishing to take some or all of his (or her) holiday entitlement during a particular holiday year must give advance notice to his employer equal to twice the required holiday period. Thus, a worker wanting to take two weeks' paid holiday must give his employer at least four weeks' advance notice of the date on which he intends those holidays to start. Should the employer be unable to accede to the worker's request (perhaps for operational reasons, or because too many people have asked to take their holidays at the same time) he must give the worker at least two weeks' notice of his refusal to allow that worker to begin his holidays on the date in question (ie, notice equivalent to the number of days or weeks' leave requested by the worker in the first place). An employer who postpones a worker's requested period of leave must nonetheless see to it that the worker is permitted to take that leave (and any remaining leave due to him) before the end of the relevant holiday year.

- In practice, most employers have well-developed procedures relating to the notification and timing of annual holidays. To avoid the inevitable disruption caused by people wishing to take their holidays (or part of their holidays) at the same time, employers will often draw up their holiday rosters at the beginning of a holiday year. Employers also have the right to limit the number of days' or weeks' holidays that their workers may take at any one time, subject to the proviso that their workers must be permitted to take their full statutory entitlement to paid holidays in the holiday year in which they fall due.

Holidays during the first year of employment

- Under the 1998 Regulations, as originally enacted, a worker whose period of employment began *before* 25 October 2001, and part-way through a holiday year, was entitled to anticipate the holidays to which he (or she) was entitled during the remainder of that holiday year, on the assumption that he would remain in his employer's employment until the end of that holiday year. After having taken that full entitlement, any overpayment would be recovered from his final pay cheque.

- However, with the coming into force on 25 October 2001 of the Working Time (Amendment) Regulations 2001, the rules have changed. Under the 1998 Regulations, as now amended, a worker's entitlement to paid holidays during his (or her) first year of employment may be calculated *monthly in advance*; that is to say, at the rate of one-twelfth of the worker's full statutory entitlement to four weeks' paid holidays during a complete holiday year (with fractions of a day rounded-up to the nearest half day). In short, during their first year of employment, workers may only take the holidays that have accrued due to them, at the time they choose (or are permitted) to take those holidays (unless their contracts state otherwise).

- For example:

    – A full-time worker, working a five-day week, who is in his or her fifth month of employment, will have built up an entitlement to 8.5 days' leave, ie, his or her annual entitlement of 20 days' paid holiday (four weeks times five days a week) multiplied by 5/12, equals 8.33 days (which is rounded up to 8.5 days).

    – A full-time worker (working a six-day week), who is in his or her seventh month of employment, will have built up an entitlement to 14 days' leave, ie, his or her annual entitlement of 24 days' paid holiday (four weeks times six days a week) multiplied by 7/12, equals 14 days.

    – A part-time worker (working a three-day week), who is in his or her second month of employment, will have built up two day's leave, ie, his or her annual entitlement of 12 days' paid holiday (four weeks times three days a week) multiplied by 2/12, equals two days.

- It is as well to point out that rounding-up a worker's entitlement to the nearest half-day should only occur when the worker in question actually takes the whole (or part) of his or her accrued holiday entitlement. The rounded-up element may then be carried forward and deducted when the worker takes his (or her) next tranche of holidays during the remainder of that same first year of employment (before rounding again takes place in respect of that second or subsequent tranche of leave). However, there should be no rounding-up when calculating a worker's entitlement to accrued holiday pay on the termination of his or her employment (whether termination occurs during the worker's first or any subsequent year of employment); in which event, the amount of (rounded-up) leave actually taken before termination should be deducted from the worker's entitlement to leave (calculated, if need be, to two or three decimal places) at the time termination occurs. These provisions are to be found in un-amended regulation 14 of the 1998 Regulations; as to which see *Accrued holiday pay on termination* (below).

- The 'monthly in advance' procedure (described above) for calculating the holiday entitlement of workers during their first year of employment is unlikely to appeal to employers whose holiday years run from, say, 1 January to 31 December. Rather than adopt that procedure in their entirety, there is nothing in the 1998 Regulations (as amended) to prevent an employer adopting the same or a similar piecemeal approach to holidays for new recruits during the remainder of the employer's holiday year (rather than the 12-month period that constitutes the work's first year of employment).

No 'roll-over' or money in lieu

- The statutory minimum four weeks' paid annual holidays must be taken in full in the holiday year in which they fall due. They may not be 'rolled-over' into the next holiday year nor may a worker accept (or an employer insist on a worker accepting) an offer of money in lieu of those holidays. Money in lieu of unused holidays is payable if, but only if, a worker resigns or is dismissed part-way through a holiday year. In the case of workers who are entitled under their contracts to more than four weeks' paid holiday, the prohibition on 'roll-overs' and money in lieu of unused holidays applies only to the four-week minimum statutory entitlement.

A refusal to take paid holidays?

- It is a moot point whether a worker can refuse to take the paid annual holidays, to which he or she is entitled under the 1998 Regulations. Although the Regulations do not allow of any derogation from a worker's entitlement to paid annual holidays (whether that worker be a post-room clerk or the managing director), they do not address the situation that may arise when a worker simply refuses to take any annual holidays. Apart from the fact that such a refusal is tantamount to insubordination giving rise to disciplinary action (and, possibly, dismissal), it should be remembered that the EU's Working Time Directive was introduced and adopted (controversially) as a 'health and safety measure' under Article 118a of the Treaty of Rome.

- It would be contrary to the spirit of the Directive for employers to permit any persons in their employ to forego their statutory entitlement to paid holidays under the 1998 Regulations. Indeed, an employer's failure to insist on a worker taking the annual holidays to which he (or she) is entitled would be admissible as evidence in a tribunal or court in the event of a complaint of unfair dismissal for lack of capability (eg, due to a stress-related illness) or a civil action for damages brought by a worker taken ill or injured as a direct consequence of the employer's negligence or breach of a statutory duty.

- If, towards the end of a holiday year, a worker has shown little sign of wanting to take annual holidays, or has made no arrangements for taking those holidays, or has used only part of his (or her) statutory entitlement, the employer has the right to insist that the employee takes all of his entitlement before that holiday year ends. The notice required to be given by an employer in such circumstances is twice the period of holidays to be taken.

Holidays during extended sick leave or maternity leave

- Strictly speaking, a worker forfeits his (or her) entitlement to paid annual holidays if he (or she) is unable to take his full statutory entitlement due to illness or injury which unavoidably keeps him away from work for the whole or major portion of the relevant holiday year. However, as was pointed out by the Employment Appeal Tribunal (EAT) in *Kigass Aero Components v Brown* (EAT/481/00), there is nothing in those Regulations to prevent workers on extended sick leave (maternity leave, adoption leave, or whatever), taking their statutory entitlement to four weeks' paid annual holidays (or money in lieu of those holidays) during their enforced absences from work, the more so if they would otherwise be unable to take those holidays (or what remains of those holidays) in the holiday year in which they fall due.

- The only requirement, said the EAT in *Kigass*, is that the workers in question give their employers the required advance notice of the date (or dates) on which they intend those holidays to start, whether or not they actually take those holidays or are physically in any condition to do so (as to which, see *Notification of intention to take holidays* earlier in this section). The fact that a worker on extended sick leave may or may not have exhausted his or her entitlement to SSP or occupational sick pay, said the EAT, is irrelevant.

- Readers should note that absentee workers (notably employees) continue to accrue an entitlement to four weeks' paid annual holidays so long as they remain in their employers' employment. This is as true of employees on extended sick leave (as in the *Kigass* case above) as it is of employees on maternity leave, adoption leave, or on extended leave of absence without pay (eg, study leave). If their absences from work during the whole or major part of a holiday year would prevent them taking the statutory holidays otherwise due to them in that holiday year, they too would be entitled to lay claim to holiday pay before their return to work. The only requirement is that they serve notice on their employers of the date or dates on which they intend their holidays to start – the amount of notice in such cases being the notice required by their contracts of employment or, in the absence of any collective of workforce agreement to the contrary, the notice prescribed by Regulation 15(4) of the 1998 Regulations (see, again, *Notification of intention to take holidays* earlier in this section). So far as maternity leave is concerned, the reader will be aware that a woman who qualifies for both ordinary and additional maternity leave might well be absent from work for up to 52 weeks, even longer if she chooses to take up to four weeks' unpaid parental leave at the end of her additional maternity leave periods – and longer still if illness or injury intervenes to prevent her returning to work on the due date. That same right would apply to an employee who is exercising his or her right to take up to 52 weeks' adoption leave.

Incorporating holiday pay in a worker's wages

- The practice adopted by many employers of incorporating an element for statutory holiday pay in a worker's wages or salary, and then paying them nothing when they physically take their holidays, quit their jobs or are dismissed, was castigated recently by the EAT in *MPB Structure Ltd v Munro* (EAT/1257/01) as being contrary to the spirit of the 1998 Regulations, and void. 'It is clear to us', said the EAT, 'that the basic theme or aim of the Regulations is to ensure that workers obtain appropriate holiday leave and to do so they must have the necessary funds. We consider that, by placing the onus of retaining the funds from week to week for holiday purposes [on the worker], there may well arise the problem of adequate funding at the time of the holiday leave being taken. This could become compounded if sufficient service in any one year had not been served so as to build up a sufficient entitlement to be paid the equivalent of a week's pay during the holiday period. We consider that the only way that the provisions of the 1998 Regulations and, indeed, their spirit can be met, is for holiday pay to be paid as and when the holiday is taken, at the appropriate rate'.

- In light of the EAT's decision in *MPB Structure Ltd v Munro*, which (at the time of writing) remains unchallenged, employers contemplating incorporating an element for statutory holiday pay in a worker's wages or salary should think again. Furthermore, as was pointed out by the Court of Appeal in *Blackburn & Others v Gridquest Ltd* [2002] IRLR 604, an employer cannot unilaterally decide that a week's pay is a payment not only for the hours worked during a week but also includes an element for holiday pay. 'The weekly payment', said the CA, 'can only be held to include an amount for something else, such as holiday pay, if that is agreed between employer and employee. The claim [by the employers in the present case] that holiday pay was in fact paid amounts to an assertion that the employer can decide unilaterally what is included in the weekly payment. Regulation 16(5) [of the Working Time Regulations 1998] does not confer that right upon an employer'. In reaching its judgment in the *Blackburn* case, the CA declined to address that of the EAT in *MPB Structure Ltd v Munro (qv)*, as there was no reference in that earlier judgment to Regulation 16(5) of the 1998 Regulations.

- Given the circumstances that prompted the EAT's ruling in *MPB Structure Ltd v Munro*, it may be (repeat, may be) acceptable to incorporate an element for holiday pay (sick pay, or whatever) in the wages of those casual, seasonal or temporary workers who rarely spend more than two or three days at a time working for a particular employer. However, in light of the CA's decision in the *Blackburn* case (see previous paragraph), they should see to it that the workers in question are made aware of (and accept) that arrangement before they actually start work. Ideally, this should be done in writing. Furthermore, to avoid a situation in which workers make unfavourable comparisons with the wages paid to other workers doing the same or similar work within the same organisation, employers should make it clear to those casual workers (again, preferably, in writing) precisely what percentage or element of their hourly or daily rate of pay constitutes a payment in respect of holiday pay. That element should not be less than 8.33%. In other words, if the standard rate of pay for a particular job is, say, £5 an hour, a casual worker doing the same job, whose wages include an element for statutory holiday pay, should be paid a minimum of £5.42 an hour.

Part-time workers

- It should, perhaps, be pointed out that the 1998 Regulations make no distinction between part-time and full-time workers. Each has the right to four weeks' paid annual holidays (ie, which is tantamount to a right to be physically absent from the workplace for four weeks), regardless of the number of hours or days they actually work, or are contracted to work, in each week. The difference lies in the amount of a week's pay. For example, a part-timer who works two days a week is still entitled to be absent from work for four weeks in each holiday year, but will not be entitled to more than eight days' holiday pay. Employers should also be mindful of the now legal right of part-time workers not to be treated less favourably than comparable full-time workers working in the same establishment; as to which, please turn to the section on **Part-time workers** elsewhere in this handbook.

Calculating holiday pay

- Simply stated, a week's holiday pay for a worker who is contracted to work a fixed number of hours each week, is the amount he (or she) would normally expect to earn in that week. For a worker, whose working hours vary from week to week, it is the average of that worker's earnings over the 12-week period immediately preceding the week in which the worker elects to take some or all of his holidays. Although overtime hours must be included in calculations, overtime premium payments need not – unless the worker's contract states otherwise or the employer is contractually-bound to provide a specified number of overtime hours each week and the worker is obliged to work those additional hours. If, for one reason or another, a worker has not received any pay during one or more weeks in that 12-week period, account should be taken of earlier paid weeks in order to bring the aggregate up to 12. A day's holiday pay for a worker would be his normal (or average) week's pay divided by the number (or average number) of hours worked in a week.

- Salaried workers do not normally receive their holiday pay in advance – their salaries usually being paid seamlessly into their bank or building society accounts at the end of each month. Should the issue arise, a week's pay for a salaried worker is his or her annual salary divided by 52; and a day's pay, a week's pay divided by the number of days the worker is contractually required to work in a week.

Accrued holiday pay on termination

- A worker who resigns or is dismissed part-way through a holiday year is nonetheless entitled to money in lieu of the holidays that have accrued due to him (or her) at the time his employment comes to an end, less a deduction in respect of any paid holidays taken by the worker during that same holiday year. If the worker has taken more paid holidays than those to which he is entitled, his employer may either require him to repay the excess amount or deduct the excess from the worker's final pay packet. However, as was pointed out by the EAT in *Hill v Chappell* (EAT 1250/01) (see next paragraph), an employer has no right to deduct excess holiday pay from a worker's final payment of wages or salary (or to demand a repayment) unless there is an express term to that effect in the worker's contract (or in a collective or workforce agreement imported into that contract). That said, the correct formula for calculating a worker's entitlement to accrued holiday pay on the termination of his employment is $A \times B - C$, where **A** is the period of leave to which the worker is legally entitled during a full holiday year (ie, four weeks); **B** is the proportion of the holiday year that expired before the date on which the worker's employment came to an end; and **C** is the period of leave already taken by the worker between the beginning of the holiday year and the termination date.

- The assumption by many employers that they have a common law, if not a statutory, right to 'claw back' overpaid holiday pay when one or other of their workers resigns or is dismissed part-way through a holiday year is misconceived. So said the Employment Appeal Tribunal (EAT) in the *Hill v Chappell* case referred to in the previous paragraph. Unless there is an express term to that effect in an employee or worker's contract, said the EAT, such a deduction is unlawful. In the *Hill* case, an employee with six months' service quit her job and sued her employers for breach of contract arising out of their failure to pay her any salary for two consecutive months. An employment tribunal awarded her damages equivalent to two months' salary, less one week's pay in respect of overpaid holiday pay. In evidence it was revealed that, prior to the termination of her employment, Miss Hill had taken three weeks' paid holidays – one week more than her statutory entitlement, given that she had completed only six months' service when she resigned. At the appeal hearing, the EAT pointed out that an employer has no legal right to deduct overpaid holiday pay from a worker's final pay packet unless, consistent with regulation 14(4) of the Working Time Regulations 1998 (see *Note* below), there is an express term to that effect either in the worker's contract or in a workforce or collective agreement imported into that contract. Nor, contrary to the argument, advanced by Miss Hill's former employers, did the deduction amount to a lawful deduction under section 14(1) of the Employment Rights Act 1996.

Note: Regulation 14(4) of the Working Time Regulations 1998 reads as follows: 'A relevant agreement may provide that, where the proportion of leave taken by the worker exceeds the proportion of the leave year which has expired, he shall compensate his employer, whether by a payment, by undertaking additional work or otherwise'.

- In the *Hill* case, the EAT acknowledged that section 14(1) of the 1996 Act does indeed authorise the deduction of any overpayment of wages or salary from a worker's pay packet without the worker's prior consent. However, Miss Hill's excess holiday pay was *not* an 'overpayment', said the EAT. She had applied for, and been granted, three weeks' holidays. She was legally entitled to be paid for those holidays when she took them. However, her employers had neglected to include a term in her contract authorising them to recover any overpaid holiday pay should she resign or be dismissed. That had been their undoing.

Victimisation or dismissal

- A worker who does not receive the paid annual holidays to which he (or she) is entitled under the Working Time Regulations 1998 may refer the matter to an employment tribunal. If the complaint is upheld, the employer will be ordered to pay compensation. A worker who is dismissed, selected for redundancy or subjected to any detriment (by any action or inaction on the part of his employer), for having challenged his employer's conduct or for asserting his statutory right to paid annual holidays, may complain to an employment tribunal. If that complaint is upheld, the employer will be ordered to pay the worker a substantial amount of compensation (as to which, please turn to the sections titled **Dismissal** and **Victimisation** elsewhere in this handbook) (*per* sections 45A, 101A, 104 and 105(4A), Employment Rights Act 1996).

- A worker in these circumstances may complain to an employment tribunal regardless of his (or her) age or length of service at the material time. The complaint must be presented within three months of the alleged unlawful action or, if the worker has resigned or been dismissed, within three months of the effective date of termination of his contract of employment.

Written statement of employment particulars

- Every worker (*qua* employee) has the legal right, under sections 1 to 7 of the Employment Rights Act 1996, to be issued with a written statement outlining the principal terms and conditions of his (or her) employment. The statement (often, if not entirely accurately, referred to as 'the contract of employment') must be issued within the first eight weeks of employment and must include information about the employee's job title, rate of pay, sickness benefits, and the like. It must also explain the employee's entitlement to paid annual holidays, including public and bank holidays. As the law now stands, those written statements need not be issue to workers who are not 'employees' in the strict legal sense of the word.

  Note: Once section 38 of the Employment Act 2002 comes into force (probably in the second half of 2003), awards of compensation arising out of a breach of the employee's statutory employment rights will be increased by the equivalent of up to four weeks' pay if the evidence before an employment tribunal reveals that the respondent employer had refused or failed to provide the complainant with a written statement of initial employment particulars, or had provided a statement that was inaccurate or incomplete.

- The information in the written statement concerning paid annual holidays must be sufficiently detailed so as to enable the employee in question to calculate his (or her) entitlement to accrued holiday pay on the termination of his employment (*ibid.* section 1(4)(d)(i)). In light of the Working Time Regulations 1998, the statement should also acknowledge the employee's statutory right to a minimum of four weeks' paid annual holidays and the right to accrued holiday pay on the termination of his employment. Any term in the written statement, or in a contract of employment, that purports to override or undermine those rights, is void and unenforceable.

- Furthermore, the information about paid annual holidays must be given in the written statement itself. It is not permissible for the statement to refer an employee to a collective agreement or some other document for information about his (or her) holiday entitlements – however accessible that other document may be (*ibid.* section 2(4)).

- If an employee is dismissed or selected for redundancy (either for questioning his (or her) employer's failure to comply with section 1 of the 1996 Act or for referring the matter to an employment tribunal), that dismissal will be held to have been unfair and compensation will be awarded (*ibid.* sections 104 and 105(7)). An employee may present a complaint of unfair dismissal in such circumstances (including a claim for damages arising out of any breach of contract), regardless of his age or length of service at the material time. But the complaint must be presented within three months of the effective date of termination. If the complaint is upheld, the employer will be ordered to pay compensation. For further details, see **Dismissal for asserting a statutory right**, elsewhere in this handbook.

- An employer's failure to provide an employee with a written statement (or to provide a statement that includes particulars about an employee's entitlement to paid annual holidays) may be referred to an employment tribunal for adjudication. Should the employee's complaint (or reference) be upheld, the tribunal will order the employer either to set matters to rights or to accept such terms and conditions as the tribunal considers to be appropriate in the circumstances.

Further information

- The Department of Trade & Industry has published *A Guide to the Working Time Regulations* (Ref URN 98/894), copies of which are available on request by telephoning 0845 6000 925. The *Guide* includes the telephone numbers of all ACAS Public Enquiry Points for those employers who need further assistance on matters relating to paid annual holidays, rest periods and in-work rest breaks. See also **Rest breaks and rest periods** and **Working hours** elsewhere in this handbook.

See also **Bank and public holidays, Deductions from pay,** and **Written particulars of terms of employment.**

I

INDEPENDENT TRADE UNION

Key points

The expression *independent trade union* is the term used to describe a trade union that:

(a) is not under the domination or control of any one employer, or of a group of employers, or of one or more employers' associations; and

(b) is not liable to interference by an employer or any such group or association (arising out of the provision of financial or material support or by any other means whatsoever) tending towards such control;

and, in relation to a trade union, the word *independent* must be construed accordingly (section 5, Trade Union & Labour Relations (Consolidation) Act 1992).

Certification as independent trade union

- Furthermore, in order to take advantage of the statutory rights available to trade unionists (officials as well as members) under current industrial relations legislation, a trade union must apply to the Certification Officer (who fulfils the functions of the former Chief Registrar of Friendly Societies) for a certificate that it is 'independent' – which application must be accompanied by the prescribed fee (*ibid.* section 6).

- The Certification Officer will not come to a decision on the application before the end of the period of one month after it has been entered on the record. Before he does make a decision, he will make such enquiries as he thinks fit (taking into account 'any relevant information submitted to him by any person') (*ibid.* section 6(4)).

- Once issued, a certificate of independence will (for all purposes) be conclusive evidence that the recipient trade union is indeed *independent*. If the Certification Officer refuses to issue (or subsequently withdraws or cancels) a certificate of independence, the trade union in question may appeal to the Employment Appeal Tribunal to have that decision reversed. However, a trade union has no legal right to challenge a decision by the Certification Officer to issue a certificate of independence to another trade union (such as a staff association), however much it may disagree with that decision. See *General & Municipal Workers Union v Certification Officer* [1977] ICR 183.

Relevance of certificate of independence

- A trade union that has been certified as *independent* by the Certification Officer has access to the statutory rights listed in the following paragraphs.

- For example, any term in a collective agreement, that purports to exclude or restrict the right of employees to engage in a strike or other form of industrial action, will be invalid and unenforceable unless each trade union party to that agreement is an independent trade union *(ibid.* section 180).

- An employer is not duty-bound to disclose information to a trade union for the purposes of collective bargaining (ie, information without which a representative of that union would be impeded to a material extent in negotiations with that employer) unless the trade union in question is an independent trade union *(ibid.* section 181).

- A trade union representative has no legal right to be consulted in advance concerning proposed redundancies unless the trade union he or she represents is independent *(ibid.* section 188).

- An employee, who is victimised or otherwise discriminated against by his (or her) employer, with a view to preventing or deterring him from joining a trade union, or from taking part in the activities of a trade union, may apply to an employment tribunal for compensation, provided that the union in question is independent *(ibid.* section 146).

- An official of a trade union has no legal right to take paid time off work to carry out his functions, unless the trade union he or she represents is an independent trade union *(ibid.* section 168).

- Likewise, the right of a member of a trade union to take time off work (albeit unpaid), in order to participate in the activities of that trade union, does not arise if the trade union in question is not independent *(ibid.* section 170).

- The dismissal of an employee for being or proposing to become a member of a trade union, or for taking part in trade union activities, is *inadmissible* (that is to say, automatically unfair) only if the trade union in question is an independent trade union (*ibid.* section 152).

  See also the sections in this handbook titled **Closed shop; Dismissal on grounds of trade union membership; Time off work: trade union officials; Time off work: trade union members;** and **Trade union membership and activities.**

INDUCTION TRAINING

Key points

- The term 'induction training' is generally understood to mean the process by which a new employee is informed about his (or her) employer's business, the terms and conditions of his employment and his new duties and responsibilities – complemented by an introduction to the people with or for whom he will be working, the materials, machines, plant or equipment he will be expected to use, information and training about safe working methods, (hazardous substances, and the like), fire precautions and fire evacuation procedures; and so on.

- In the smaller organisation, such as a light engineering works, depot, garage, workshop, retail outlet, restaurant, insurance office, public house, etc, induction training may consist of a brief chat with the immediate supervisor followed by an introduction to another employee who will 'show him the ropes'. In larger premises, such as factories, major manufacturing plants, chemical works or headquarters buildings, a more systematic approach may be adopted. The new employee may be required to spend a certain amount of time with several supervisors or managers, will be issued with a job description and a staff or training handbook, and will be expected to attend a series of lectures and discussion groups designed to explore every facet of his (or her) employer's business and his own role within the organisation.

Health and safety at work

- Although an employer is under no strict legal obligation to provide induction training as such, he does have a duty under section 2(2)(c) of the Health and Safety at Work etc Act 1974 (and under Regulations made under, or saved by, that Act) to provide 'such information, instruction, training and supervision as is necessary to ensure, so far as is reasonably practicable, the health and safety at work of his employees'. Should a new recruit be injured in the course of his (or her) employment, the employer's failure to provide suitable training before setting the employee to work will be an important factor in any subsequent civil proceedings for damages. It may prompt a health and safety inspector to institute criminal proceedings. The penalty on conviction is a fine of a maximum of £20,000 and, on conviction on indictment, a fine of an unlimited amount (*ibid.* sections 33(l)(a) and 33(3)).

- The prudent employer will interpret his obligations under the 1974 Act as meaning a duty to provide exhaustive training to every new recruit before setting him to work in any area where inexperience and lack of instruction could lead to injury to himself and others.

The Management of Health & Safety at Work Regulations 1999

- Regulation 13 of the Management of Health & Safety at Work Regulations 1999 – which apply to every employer (and to every self-employed person), regardless of the type of business in which he (or she) is engaged, the size of his premises, or the number of people he employs – cautions that, when entrusting tasks to his employees, *every* employer must take into account the capabilities of those employees as regards health and safety. Furthermore, every employer must ensure that his employees receive adequate health and safety training:

  (a) when first recruited; and

  (b) when exposed to new or increased risks following a promotion or transfer, or when introduced to new or amended systems of work, new technology, or new or modified plant and equipment.

- Furthermore, all such training must take place during normal working hours, must be repeated periodically (where appropriate), and must be adapted to take account of any new or changed risks to the health and safety of the employees concerned.

  Note: Similar provisions relating to training are to be found in the Control of Asbestos at Work Regulations 2002; the Health & Safety (Display Screen Equipment Regulations 1992; the Control of Lead at Work Regulations 2002; the Provision & Use of Work Equipment Regulations 1998; the Control of Substances (Hazardous to Health) Regulations 2002; and so on.

- Under the Health & Safety (Young Persons) Regulations 1997, which came into force on 3 March 1997 (and are now incorporated in the

Management of Health & Safety at Work Regulations 1999 (*qv*)), the risk assessment exercise every employer is obliged to carry out must take particular account of the inexperience of young persons, as well as their immaturity, and ignorance about the risks they may face. In short, employers must take particular care to train young persons thoroughly before exposing them to such risks.

Fire prevention and training

- A fire certificate issued in accordance with the provisions of the Fire Precautions Act 1971 (as amended) will impose requirements 'for securing that persons employed to work in the premises receive appropriate instruction or training in what to do in case of fire, and that records are kept of instruction or training given for that purpose' (*ibid.* section 6(2)(c)). The following extract from a fire certificate is quite specific:

  'All members of the staff shall each receive a personal copy of prepared written instructions (on fire prevention and evacuation procedures), and shall initially receive two periods of at least half an hour of verbal instruction given by a competent person. Such instructions shall include details of how to call the Fire Brigade. These two periods shall be given within one month. In the case of newly-engaged staff, this shall be as soon as possible after engagement.'

- The penalty for contravening any requirement of a fire certificate is a fine, on summary conviction, of a maximum £20,000 and, on conviction on indictment, a fine or imprisonment for a term not exceeding two years, or both (*ibid.* section 7(4)).

- In premises that do not require a fire certificate, the occupier nonetheless has a duty to provide 'such information, instruction, training and supervision as is necessary to ensure, so far as is reasonably practicable, the health and safety at work of his employees' (section 2(2)(c), 1974 Act) (see above), a duty that should not lightly be set aside. See also **Training of employees** and **Trade union recognition** elsewhere in this handbook.

INSOLVENCY OF EMPLOYER
(*Rights of employees*)

Key points

- For many years, wages or salaries owed to employees by an insolvent employer have been treated in law as 'preferential debts'. However, that preference is accorded only to the first £800 of any claim in respect of wages earned during the four months preceding the date of the receiving order or of the appointment of the provisional liquidator. Amounts in excess of £800 (or for periods longer than four months), and other monies owed to an employee at the time his employer became insolvent, rank as ordinary debts (*per* Insolvency Act 1986, Schedule 6).

- In recognition of the fact that it could take years for employees to recover unpaid wages or salaries, let alone any other monies owed by an insolvent employer, sections 182 to 190 of the Employment Rights Act 1996 empower the Secretary of State for Trade & Industry to borrow from the National Insurance Fund and to pay some or all of those monies on the employer's behalf. The Secretary of State would then assume the role of preferred and ordinary creditor in an attempt to recover part at least of that money from the employer's remaining assets.

Note: The Secretary of State will not normally pay monies from the National Insurance Fund, in respect of an amount owed by an insolvent employer, until the relevant liquidator, receiver, manager or trustee in bankruptcy confirms in writing that the employee in question is entitled to that amount. If that information is not forthcoming within six months of an employee's application to him, the Secretary of State may decide to pay the employee out of the Fund if he is satisfied that a further delay appears likely and that the employee's claims are genuine.

Eligible debts and upper limits

- There are limits on the amounts payable from the National Insurance Fund and the debts to which they relate. Section 184 of the 1996 Act empowers the Secretary of State (in practice, the Employment Department) to pay an employee:

  (a) arrears of pay (see *Note* below) for a period not exceeding eight weeks at a maximum £260 per week;

  (b) unpaid pay in lieu of the statutory minimum period of notice due (again subject to a maximum of £260 per week);

(c) up to six weeks' holiday pay in respect of a period or periods of holidays to which the employee became entitled during the 12 months ending with the date on which the employer became insolvent (at a maximum £260 per week); and

(d) any basic award of compensation for unfair dismissal or so much of an award under a designated dismissal procedures agreement as does not exceed any basic award of compensation for unfair dismissal to which the employee would be entitled but for the agreement;

(e) where appropriate, any reasonable sum by way of reimbursement of the whole or part of any fee or premium paid by an apprentice or articled clerk.

Note: For these purposes, the expression *arrears of pay* (see paragraph (a) above) includes not only unpaid wages, salaries, overtime earnings, commissions, and the like, but also statutory guarantee payments, remuneration on suspension on medical or maternity grounds, payment for time off work, statutory sick pay, and remuneration under a protective award made by an employment tribunal in consequence of an employer's failure to consult trade union representatives about his redundancy proposals (*ibid.* section 184(2)). These matters are dealt with elsewhere in this handbook under the relevant subject heads.

- The current (2003/04) upper limit of £260 on the amount of a week's pay for these purposes will in future be increased (or reduced) by order of the Secretary of State, in line with the September-on-September rise or fall in the retail prices index.

- Statutory Maternity Pay (SMP) owed to an employee at the time her employer became insolvent is the responsibility of the Department for Work & Pensions. SMP due and payable after that date becomes the responsibility of the Secretary of State. See also **Pregnancy and maternity rights** elsewhere in this handbook.

- If an employee is denied the whole or part of any statutory redundancy payment due to him (or her) because of his employer's insolvency, the Secretary of State will pay the amount due out of the National Insurance Fund (*ibid.* section 189). See also **Redundancy** elsewhere in this handbook.

Procedure

- To set matters in motion, an employee owed money by his (or her) insolvent employer on the termination of his employment should complete Form IP1 – available from the employer's representative or *relevant officer* (see *Note* below) – and return it to him as soon as possible.

If he wishes to apply for a payment to compensate him for not receiving the correct *statutory* notice of the termination of his employment, he will also need to complete and return Form IP2. The relevant officer will deal directly with the Department for Work & Pensions (DfWP) on the employee's behalf.

Note: The *relevant officer* is a person appointed in connection with an employer's insolvency, that is to say, a trustee in bankruptcy, a liquidator, administrator, a receiver or manager, or a trustee under a composition or arrangement between the employer and his creditors or under a trust deed for his creditors executed by the employer. In this connection, trustee, in relation to a composition or arrangement, includes the supervisor of a voluntary arrangement proposed for the purposes of, and approved under, Part I or VIII of the Insolvency Act 1986.

Unpaid contributions to a pension scheme

- The trustees of an occupational pension scheme may apply in writing to the Secretary of State for Employment claiming that an insolvent employer has failed to pay pension contributions (either on his own account or on behalf of the employee) into the scheme during the 12 months preceding the date on which he became insolvent (*per* section 124, Pension Schemes Act 1993).

- Subject to certain conditions (that are not explored here), and once satisfied that there are unpaid contributions, the Secretary of State will withdraw the money from the National Insurance Fund and pay it into the resources of the occupational pension scheme.

Complaints

- Should the Secretary of State decline or fail to pay any of the amounts referred to in the preceding paragraphs, the affected employee may refer the matter to an employment tribunal for determination. Any such complaint must be lodged within three months of the alleged failure to pay.

- If an employment tribunal finds that the Secretary of State ought to have made those payments, it will make a declaration to that effect and will also declare the amount of any such payment that it finds the Secretary of State ought to make (*ibid.* section 188).

INVENTIONS, PATENTS AND COPYRIGHT

Key points

- Although not a matter that is likely to be of particular concern to *every* employer, there will be occasions when an employee invents a machine, product or process that is new and capable of industrial application.

- The question may arise as to the ownership of such an invention. That question has largely been resolved by sections 39 to 43 of the Patents Act 1977 in respect of inventions made after 1 June 1978.

- Section 39 of the 1977 Act states that an invention made by an employee will be taken to belong to his employer if:

  (a) it was made in the course of the normal duties of the employee in circumstances such that an invention might reasonably be expected to result from the carrying out of those duties; or

  (b) it was made in the course of the duties of the employee, and the nature of those duties and his particular responsibilities were such that he had a special obligation to further the interests of his employer's undertaking.

  In any other circumstances, an invention made by an employee is his own property.

- There are very few people who are employed specifically to invent tools, plant, machinery or equipment. If a kitchen porter in a hotel designs a new type of dishwashing machine, his (or her) employer would be hard put to it to convince a court that doing so was within the scope of the porter's normal duties.

- If the ownership of an invention clearly vests in an employee, he (or she) has the right to apply for and obtain a patent and to be named as the inventor. The form of application to be used is Patents Form 2/77. The inventor may subsequently grant a licence or licences to another person or persons (including his employer, if he chooses) to supply the product or work the invention, as the case may be, on reasonable terms.

- If an employer owns an invention produced by one of his employees, that need not be an end to the matter. Once a patent has been granted, the inventor has every right to apply to the Comptroller-General of

Patents, Designs and Trade Marks or, if need be, to the High Court (or the Court of Session) for an award of compensation – that is to say, a fair share of the benefit that his employer has derived, or may reasonably expect to derive, from the patent. In determining what constitutes a 'fair share', the court or the comptroller will, among other things, take into account:

(a) the nature of the employee's duties, his remuneration and any other advantages he derives, or has derived, from his employment;

(b) the effort and skill that the employee has devoted to making the invention;

(c) the effort and skill that any other person has devoted to making the invention jointly with the employee concerned and other assistance contributed by any other employee who is not a joint inventor of the invention; and

(d) the employer's contribution to the making, developing and working of the invention, eg by giving advice, by providing the necessary facilities and other technical assistance, and by offering his managerial and commercial skills.

An order directing an employer to pay compensation to the employee may be an order for the payment of a lump sum or for periodical payments, or for both.

- An employee's application to the Comptroller-General for an award of compensation must be made on Patents Form 26/77, accompanied by one copy of the Form and a statement in duplicate setting out fully the facts relied on. The application may be submitted at any time after the relevant patent is granted to the employer, but not later than one year after the patent ceases to have effect.

Contract of employment

- Any term in a contract of employment that purports to diminish an employee's statutory rights in inventions of any description made by him, or in or under patents for those inventions (or applications for such patents), is void and unenforceable. Notwithstanding such a term in his contract, the employee may still pursue his claim for ownership of an invention, or an award of compensation, as the case may be. His right to do so does not, on the other hand, derogate from any duty of confidentiality that he may owe to his employer by virtue of his contract of employment.

Collective agreement

- If a collective agreement between a trade union and an employer, provides for the payment of compensation in respect of employee inventions, the relevant terms of that agreement will supersede the rights of the individual employee under sections 39 to 43 of the 1977 Act. However, the agreement must encompass all employees of the same description as that employee, and must envisage inventions of the same description as the invention produced by the employee. In the event of a dispute, it will be for the courts to determine the issues.

Copyright

- Under section 11 of the Copyright, Designs & Patents Act 1988, the copyright in any literary, dramatic or artistic work produced by an employee in the course of his (or her) employment (that is to say, arising out of the duties of his employment) belong to his employer – unless there is an agreement to the contrary.

  Note: Section 11 of the Copyright, Designs & Patents Act 1988 reads as follows: '(1) The author of a work is the first owner of any copyright in it, subject to the following provisions. (2) Where a literary, dramatic, musical or artistic work is made by an employee in the course of his employment, his employer is the first owner of any copyright in the work subject to any agreement to the contrary...'

- Thus a public relations executive (as an employee) cannot claim ownership of any material written by him for the purposes of advertising or promoting his employer's business. That is what he is paid to do. On the other hand, a security guard in a factory, who writes a best-selling book when he should have been patrolling his employer's premises, may be dismissed for gross misconduct but would retain the ownership of the copyright in his book (section 11, Copyright, Designs & Patents Act 1988).

  Note: Under UK law, copyright comes into existence when an original literary, dramatic or artistic work is produced. There is no formal procedure for registering the ownership of the copyright in any such work. Copyright protection persists tor the lifetime of the copyright owner and for 75 years after his (or her) death (increased from 50 years on 1 July 1995, to accommodate EC legislation).

- Employers all too often lose sight of the fact that many of their personnel (eg, computer programmers, research chemists, public relations experts, advertising managers, copywriters, training officers, personnel executives, and the like) are routinely employed to write software programs, reports, statistical analyses, advertising and promotional copy, training manuals, etc, that should not be published or divulged to unauthorised third parties. So far as the issue of copyright ownership is concerned, employers should perhaps insert a clause in the contracts of employment of such persons to the effect that 'any publicity material, brochures, training manuals, software programs, research reports or documents [etc] produced or prepared by you in the course of your employment by the company shall be the sole copyright of the company'.

- If need be, personnel engaged in sensitive work should also give a written undertaking to submit the manuscripts of magazine articles, theses, etc, for scrutiny by a senior member of management (or by the company's solicitors or legal department) before that material is released for publication.

- Contracts of employment should likewise remind employees of their common law duty to return all company property in their possession (documents, notes, manuals, computer discs, etc) on the termination of their employment. They should, at the same time, be asked to sign a form accounting for any readily-identifiable property known to be in their possession, as well as a declaration to the effect that they have not retained any other documents, copies of software programs, etc, that are properly their employer's property.

Note: It is curious that while an employer is legally entitled to a fair share of any benefit that accrues to his (or her) employer from an invention he has made in the course of his employment, there is no equivalent provision in the 1988 Act that gives an employee the legal right to claim a share of the royalties earned by his employers from the sale of a book which the employee has researched and written on their behalf (although there is nothing to prevent some contractual provision to that effect).

See also **Cooperation, employee's duty of** and **Fidelity and trust, employee's duty of** elsewhere in this handbook.

ITEMISED PAY STATEMENT
(Employer's duty to provide)

Key points

- An employee has the right to be given by his employer, at or before the time at which any payment of wages or salary is made to him, a written itemised pay statement (section 8, Employment Rights Act 1996).

- This right extends not only to employees who are paid in cash but also to those employees whose wages or salaries are paid by cheque or by credit transfer to their bank or building society accounts.

  Note: This right does not extend to merchant seaman or share fishermen, or to any employee who (under his contract of employment) ordinarily works outside Great Britain (*ibid*. sections 196 and 199).

Information to be included in the statement

- An itemised pay statement must include the following particulars:

  (a) the gross amount of the wages or salary payable to the employee on that occasion;

  Note: Curiously, an itemised pay statement need not show how the employer arrived at the gross amount or what that amount comprises. However, it is unlikely that any self-respecting employee will for long tolerate a system that denies him an opportunity to challenge the accuracy of a gross figure that purports to include his (or her) overtime earnings, any bonus, commission or shift allowance payments that are his due.

  (b) the amount of any fixed deductions and the purposes for which they are made;

  Note: Fixed deductions are those amounts specifically authorised in writing by an employee. They include contributions to a National Savings Scheme (SAYE) or sports & social club, private or company-sponsored medical plan (eg, BUPA or PPP), trade union dues, etc. The alternative to an itemised account of fixed deductions is a *Standing Statement of Fixed Deductions* (discussed below).

  (c) the amount and purposes of any variable deductions; and

  Note: Variable deductions are deductions which vary from week to week or from month to month (or whatever), such as income tax (PAYE), National Insurance Contributions (NIC), contributions to an occupational pension scheme, or payments to the court under an attachment of earnings order.

  (d) the net amount of the wages or salary payable on that occasion.

  Note: If an employer has agreed to pay part of an employee's wages or salary in cash (or by some other means) and part, perhaps, by cheque or by credit transfer to the employee's bank or building society account, the itemised pay statement must list the amounts in question and the methods by which they are paid.

Tax credits also to be recorded on the itemised pay statement

- With the coming into force on 1 March 2003 of the Working Tax Credit (Payment by Employers) Regulations 2002, employers are liable to pay Child Tax Credits and Working Tax Credits *through the payroll* to the nominated employee, and when as instructed to do so by the Tax Credits Office (TCO). Every such payment must be recorded as a 'tax credit' on the itemised pay statement (or payslip) issued to such employees (*ibid.* regulation 9(4)).

Standing statement of fixed deductions

- There will be occasions when the sheer number of fixed deductions authorised by an employee make it administratively impossible for an employer to itemise each of those deductions on a pay packet or payslip every time that employee is paid his wages or salary. To overcome that problem, the employer may (if he chooses) simply aggregate those fixed deductions on the itemised pay statement (without explaining their purpose) so long as he supplies the employee in question with a so-called Standing Statement of Fixed Deductions.

- A Standing Statement must be issued on or before the date on which an employee receives his (or her) first payslip or pay packet showing only the aggregate amount of fixed deductions from his wages or salary. The Statement becomes effective on the date of issue and is valid for 12 months. However, it must be amended and re-issued every time one or other of those fixed deductions is adjusted or stopped. An amended Statement, in its turn, is valid for 12 months, provided no other changes occur in the interim.

A refusal or failure to comply

- An employee may require a reference to be made to an employment tribunal if:

  (a) his (or her) employer has refused or failed to supply him with an itemised pay statement; or

  (b) the statement he gives does not comply with sections 8 or 9 of the 1996 Act.

  The complaint or reference must be presented within three months of the alleged refusal or failure to comply or (if the employee is no longer employed) before the end of the period of three months beginning with the date on which his or her employment ended (*ibid.* section 11(4)).

- A conciliation officer of the Advisory, Conciliation and Arbitration Service (ACAS) will ordinarily be informed about a complaint or reference arising out of an alleged breach of an employee's rights under section 8 of the 1996 Act and will offer to mediate with a view to resolving the dispute amicably and informally. Should he fail to do so, the matter will proceed to a full tribunal hearing.

- If an employment tribunal upholds the employee's complaint, it will make a declaration to that effect and will instruct the employer to set matters to rights. If it finds that any unnotified deductions have been made from the employee's pay during the period of 13 weeks preceding the date on which the employee made his complaint (whether or not the deductions were made in breach of the employee's contract of employment), it will order the employer to pay the employee a sum not exceeding the aggregate of the unnotified deductions so made (*ibid.* section 12(4)). For these purposes a deduction will be treated in law as 'unnotified' (even if agreed to by the employee) unless declared on the employee's pay packet or payslip in the form of an itemised pay statement.

See also **Conciliation officers, Deductions from pay, Employment tribunals and procedure**, and **Wages, payment of** elsewhere in this handbook.

J

JOB TITLE

Key points

- The written statement of terms of employment issued to a new employee (as well as any amended statement issued to an existing employee) must contain – in the principal statement itself – particulars of 'the title of the job which the employee is employed to do or a brief description of the work for which the employee is employed' (section 1(4)(f), Employment Rights Act 1996).

- Section 235(1) of the 1996 Act defines 'job', in relation to an employee, as meaning 'the nature of the work which he is employed to do in accordance with his contract and the capacity and place in which he is so employed'.

- It follows that a newly-recruited employee (as well as one who has been newly-promoted or transferred) has the legal right to be told about the work he (or she) has been employed to do, his duties and responsibilities, the limits of his authority, the place where he works, and his duty (if any) to accept a transfer from one department or location to another when instructed to do so by his employer.

Job description?

- Although an employer is not duty-bound to provide his employees with job descriptions as such, he has little to gain by denying an employee his (or her) implied contractual right to be informed about the nature and extent of his duties and responsibilities. Furthermore, such an employer could be prosecuted under section 2(2)(c) of the Health & Safety at Work etc Act 1974 for failing in his general duty to provide his employees with the information, instruction and training they need to ensure their health and safety at work. He could also be held vicariously liable under section 36 of that Act for an offence unwittingly committed by an employee who was misinformed (or not informed at all) about the true nature of his job and the precautions needed to carry out his duties safely. Section 2 of the 1974 Act is reinforced by the Management of Health & Safety at Work Regulations

1992 which, *inter alia*, requires employers to assess the risks to the health and safety of their employees and to provide them with 'comprehensible and relevant' information on those risks and the preventive and protective measures that have been put in place to minimise or eliminate those risks.

Dismissal for misconduct

- The employee who is dismissed for misconduct may be able to persuade an employment tribunal that he (or she) had been misinformed about the true nature of his job and had never agreed to undertake the additional duties demanded of him at the time of his dismissal. The redundant employee may claim that there had been no cessation or diminution of the work he was employed to do, or that he was unfairly selected for redundancy, given that other persons similarly employed were not made redundant. The female employee, who has exercised her right to return to work after childbirth may complain that, on her return to work, she was relocated in a job which bore little (if any) resemblance to the type of work she had been doing (and had been employed to do) before her maternity leave period began. There are other examples in which the nature and capacity of an employee's job will be an important and, in many cases, determining factor – on a reference or complaint concerning a breach of an employee's statutory rights or in proceedings arising out of an alleged breach of contract.

- In a small organisation, with few employees, it makes sense for an employer to expect a degree of flexible working from his staff. Indeed, the employment tribunals have long since recognised and upheld the employer's right to manage his business to the best of his ability. In many situations, the dismissal of an uncooperative employee will be held to be fair. However, the tribunals also recognise an employee's right to be told what is expected of him (or her) when carrying out the work he has been employed to do. Accordingly, it makes sense to forewarn employees, particularly in the small organisation, that they will be expected to work overtime during busy periods, or to 'double-up' or help out in other departments when there are staff shortages or other unforeseen problems. If a degree of job flexibility or mobility is required, that requirement should be spelled-out either in the individual 'contract of employment' (ie, the written statement of particulars of employment) or in a related document (such as a job description or letter of appointment) handed to a new employee when he first takes up his duties.

See also the sections in this handbook titled **Contract of employment, Cooperation, employee's duty of, Disobedience,** and **Written particulars of terms of employment.**

JURY SERVICE

Key points

- Section 1 of the Juries Act 1974 (as amended by the Criminal Justice Act 1988) states that 'every person shall be qualified to serve as a juror in the Crown Court, the High Court and county courts and be liable accordingly to attend for jury service when summoned under this Act, if:

  (a) he is for the time being registered as a parliamentary or local government elector and is not less than eighteen nor more than sixty-five years of age; and

  (b) he has been ordinarily resident in the United Kingdom, the Channel Islands or the Isle of Man for any period of at least five years since attaining the age of thirteen,

  but not if he is for the time being ineligible or disqualified for jury service'.

- This means, in effect, that every person between the age of 18 and 65, who is on the electoral roll (and not otherwise ineligible or disqualified), may be summoned to attend as a juror in court proceedings. Furthermore, he (or she) must attend in court for as many days as may be directed in the summons.

Persons excused, ineligible or disqualified from/for jury service

- The following persons may be excused from jury service:

  (a) any person who can satisfy the court that he (or she) has served on a jury at any time during the preceding period of two years;

  (b) any person who, on account of physical disability or insufficient understanding of English, is considered unlikely to act effectively as a juror; and

  (c) any person who can satisfy the court that there is good reason why he (or she) should be excused from attending.

- There are also persons who are excusable as of right. These are:

  (d) peers and peeresses, members of the House of Commons, officers of the House of Lords, and officers of the House of Commons;

  (e) full-time serving members of any of Her Majesty's naval, military or air forces (including any Voluntary Aid Detachment serving with the Royal Navy); and

(f) medical practitioners, dentists, nurses, midwives, veterinary surgeons and veterinary practitioners, and pharmaceutical chemists, if they are actually practising their respective professions and are registered, enrolled or certified under the enactment relating to those professions.

- Persons ineligible for jury service include:

    (g) barristers or solicitors, whether or not in actual practice as such; solicitors' articled clerks, barristers' clerks and their assistants, legal executives in the employment of solicitors, and others (including judges and justices of the peace) employed by the judiciary or concerned with the administration of justice;

    (h) the clergy (including avowed members of any religion order); and

    (i) any person who suffers or has suffered from mental illness, subnormality, severe subnormality or a psychopathic disorder.

- Also disqualified from jury service is any person who has, at any time, been sentenced in the United Kingdom, the Channel Islands or the Isle of Man, to custody for life or to a term of imprisonment or youth custody for five years or more; or who, at any time in the last 10 years, has served any part of a sentence of imprisonment or detention (being a sentence for a term of three months or more), or been detained in a youth custody centre.

Offences and penalties

- Any person who fails to comply with a summons for jury service, or who is unfit for service by reason of drink or drugs, shall be liable to a fine not exceeding £1,000, unless, in the case of a failure to comply, he (or she) can show some reasonable cause for that failure. A person who makes a false representation, or gives false information, with the intention of evading jury service, is liable on summary conviction to a fine of up to £5,000. A person who serves on a jury when disqualified is liable to a fine of up to £1,000.

Payment for jury service

- A person who serves as a juror is entitled to receive payments for travelling and subsistence; and an allowance for loss of earnings or social security benefit (*ibid.* section 19).

At present (2003), the following allowances are payable:

(a) full bus and tube fares; second class rail fares; and taxi fares (if no public service transport is reasonably available);

(b) if a private motor car is used, a mileage allowance of a maximum 25.3p per mile (each way), although this may increase to 38.4p per mile if use of a private car results in a substantial saving in time;

(c) parking fees necessarily incurred by a juror who travels in his (or her) own car (unless it would have been cheaper for him/her to have used public transport);

Note: If fellow jurors are carried as passengers in the same car, a supplement of 2p per mile is payable in respect of the first passenger and 1p per mile for each additional passenger.

(d) if a juror travels by private motorcycle, he is entitled to a mileage allowance of 25.3p per mile (regardless of engine capacity) or 26.4p per mile if using a motorcycle saves time;

plus:

(e) a subsistence allowance to meet the extra expenses of meals and other incidental expenses incurred while attending court – the amount of which will depend on the length of time for which a juror is necessarily away from his or her home or place of business, as follows:

not exceeding 5 hours	£2.22
between 5 and 10 hours	£4.51
more than 10 hours	£9.86

(f) a loss of earnings or benefits allowance of £26.32 a day if a juror loses earnings, or social security benefits or has other expenses during a part of a day that is *up to and including four hours* in the first 10 days of jury service, or £52.63 a day during a part of a day that is *up to and including four hours* on the 11th and subsequent days of jury service;

or:

(g) a loss of earnings or benefits allowance of £52.63 a day if a juror loses earnings, social security benefits or has other expenses during a part of a day that is *more than four hours* in the first 10 days of jury service, or £105.28 a day during a part of a day that is *more than four hours* on the 11th and subsequent days of jury service.

Note: A juror claiming a loss of earnings or benefits allowance must produce a certificate completed and signed by his or her employer or local benefit office confirming the loss of earnings or benefits.

- An allowance is also payable in respect of overnight accommodation – £72.58 a day, if the accommodation is within a five-mile radius of Charing Cross in London; and £66.91 a day, if elsewhere.

National Insurance contributions

- An employee, whose earnings during jury service fall below the 'lower earnings limit' for the payment of National Insurance contributions, will be entitled to NI contribution credits for each week or part-week in which that situation arises – as if his (or her) earnings were equal to that lower limit. The allowances described above do not count as 'earnings' for this purpose. To apply for those NI credits, the juror must write to his local social security or benefit office before 1 January of the year immediately following the end of the tax year in which the jury service occurred. These credits are not available to married women and widows who have elected to pay reduced NI contributions.

Duties of employer

- An employer is under no legal obligation to continue to pay an employee his (or her) normal wages or salary during any absence from work on jury service. But it would be unwise of an employer to dismiss an employee who is necessarily absent from work for that reason – given that the employee is under a legal obligation to comply with a jury summons and that the reason for his absence from work could not normally be said to amount to 'some other substantial reason of a kind such as to justify the dismissal of an employee holding the position which that employee held' (section 98(1)(b) of the Employment Rights Act 1996).

- Even if the employee is (or was) a key worker, the employer would need to satisfy an employment tribunal that he had acted reasonably in treating the employee's absence on jury service as a reason for dismissing him (or her). The tribunal might well need answers to the following questions: How long was the employee likely to be absent from work? Could not the employer have found a suitable replacement to cover for the employee during his absence? Did the employer write to the court asking for the employee to be excused from jury service? And so on.

L

LAY-OFFS AND SHORT-TIME WORKING

Key points

- In some situations, an employer will prefer to lay-off his employees or place them on short-time working rather than make them redundant. One or other of those options will usually be considered when the employer is in financial difficulties (or has related business problems, such as the non-delivery of essential raw materials) and believes that those problems are likely to be short-lived.

- However, whatever his difficulties, an employer does *not* have the right either to lay-off any employee or keep him (or her) on short-time working unless there is an express term to that effect in the employee's contract of employment. If he takes unilateral action (that is to say, in the absence of any such express term), he is in breach of contract and could force the employee to resign and pursue a complaint of unfair constructive dismissal (including a claim for damages for breach of contract).

- There is, of course, nothing to prevent an employee agreeing to accept a cut in pay or a reduction in working hours if persuaded by his employer that the only other alternative is redundancy. But that would be a matter for discussion and formal agreement.

Meaning of 'lay-off' and 'short-time working'

- An employee will be held to have been *laid-off* by his (or her) employer for a week, if:

  (a) his contract of employment states that he will be paid only if he is provided with work of the kind that he is employed to do; but

  (b) he earns no pay at all in respect of that week because his employer has not provided him with any such work to do.

- An employee will be treated as having been kept on *short-time working* for a week if his employer gives him some work to do during that week (being work of the kind that he is employed to do), but the money he earns as a result is less than half a week's pay (section 147, Employment Rights Act 1996).

Guarantee payments

- In the absence of any term in an employment contract or collective agreement, that provides for a fall-back or guaranteed minimum payment on such occasions, an employee who is not provided with *work throughout a day* on which he (or she) is normally required to work may nonetheless be entitled to be paid a statutory guarantee payment of a specified minimum amount for each of a maximum five *workless days* in any period of three consecutive months. But, to qualify for a guarantee payment, an employee must have been employed for a continuous period of at least one month ending with the day immediately preceding the relevant workless day. For further details, please turn to the section of this handbook titled **Guarantee payments**.

Lay-offs, short-time working and redundancy

- An employer may face a claim for a statutory redundancy payment if he repeatedly lays off one of his employees or keeps him (or her) on short-time working (even if he has the contractual right to do so or the employee in question has agreed to those arrangements). Section 148(2) of the 1996 Act (*qv*) states that an employee who is laid off or kept on short-time working for four consecutive weeks (or for a series of six or more weeks, of which not more than three were consecutive, within a period of 13 weeks) – discounting any weeks where the lay-off or short-time was attributable to a strike or lock-out – may write to his employer announcing his intention to claim a redundancy payment. However, he must do so not later than four weeks after the end of the last week on which he was laid off or kept on short-time working. He must also (either at the same time or not later than three weeks afterwards) give his employer one week's written notice of his intention to terminate his employment (or such longer period of notice as he is required to give under his contract of employment) (*ibid.* section 150).

- When served with an employee's written notice of intention to claim a redundancy payment, an employer may respond in one of two things. He may:

  (a) either dismiss the employee and face the likelihood of a claim for a redundancy payment arising out of that dismissal; or

  (b) write to the employee within the next seven days declaring his intention to contest any liability to pay him (or her) a redundancy payment and inviting him to withdraw his notice of intention to claim.

However, the employer would be ill-advised to serve the counter-notice in (b) above unless he reasonably expects to provide the employee in question with at least 13 weeks of employment (during which the employee would not be laid off or kept on short-time working) beginning not later than four weeks after the date on which the employee served his notice of intention to claim. But if, during that four-week period, the employee is again laid off or kept on short-time working for each of those weeks (discounting any weeks where the lay-off or short-time was attributable to a strike or lock-out), it will be presumed *without more* that the employer is (or was) unable to comply with his commitment to provide those 13 consecutive weeks of uninterrupted employment (*ibid.* section 152).

- If an employee declines to withdraw his notice of intention to claim (in spite of having received a counter-notice from his employer contesting any liability to pay him a redundancy payment), he must (if he has not already done so) write to his employer within the next three weeks terminating his employment by a week's notice or by such longer period of notice as he is required to give under his contract of employment (*ibid*).

- In the final analysis, it will be for an employment tribunal to decide whether or not an employee, who has terminated his employment in the circumstances described above, is entitled to a redundancy payment.

- It should be pointed out that a redundant employee will not qualify for a statutory redundancy payment unless employed for a continuous period of two or more years (excluding any period of employment that began before his or her 18th birthday) and under *normal retiring age* or 65 (whichever is the later) at the *effective date of termination* of his contract of employment.

For further particulars, please turn to the section titled **Redundancy**, elsewhere in this handbook.

LOCK-OUTS

Key points

- Section 235(4) of the Employment Rights Act 1996 defines *lock-out* as meaning 'the closing of a place of employment, or the suspension of work, or the refusal by an employer to continue to employ any number of persons employed by him in consequence of a dispute, done with a view to compelling those persons, or to aid another employer in compelling persons employed by him, to accept terms or conditions of or affecting employment'.

- Section 238 of the Trade Union & Labour Relations (Consolidation) Act 1992 cautions that an employment tribunal will not entertain a complaint of unfair dismissal from any employee if, at the time of his (or her) dismissal, his employer was conducting a lock-out affecting him and other workers unless the employee can show that one or more relevant workers had not been dismissed, or that one or more of them had been offered their jobs back within three months of his own dismissal, but that a similar offer had not been made to him.

- This means, in effect, that the only way an employer can avoid a complaint (or complaints) of unfair dismissal in such circumstances is to dismiss every worker involved in the dispute that prompted the lock-out and not to re-employ any of those workers within three months of the date on which the last worker was dismissed. For further details, see **Dismissal for taking industrial action** elsewhere in this handbook.

- However, it must be remembered that, in order to bring a complaint of unfair dismissal, an employee must have been employed for a continuous period of one year or at the effective date of termination of his (or her) contract of employment. He must also have been under normal retiring age at that time. There are, on the other hand, circumstances in which an employee can pursue such a complaint regardless of his or her age or length of service at the material time, as to which, please turn to the section titled **Dismissal** and the paragraphs headed *Unlawful and inadmissible reasons for dismissal*. The meaning of the terms 'effective date of termination' and 'normal retiring age' are also explained in that section.

Lock-outs and continuity of employment

- Absence from work because of a lock-out does not break the continuity of a period of employment. However, days 'lost' because of a lock-out (ie, the number of days lost between the last working day before the lock-out began and the day on which work was resumed) must be discounted when computing an employee's total period of continuous employment. This is done by postponing the beginning of the employee's period of continuous employment (that is to say, the date on which employment began) by the number of days falling within that intervening period (1996 Act, sections 211(3) and 216(3)). See also the sections titled **Dismissal for taking industrial action** and **Continuity of employment** elsewhere in this handbook.

M

Key points

Overview

- Legislation governing the rights of employees before and after child-birth is currently to be found in Part VIII of the Employment Rights Act 1996, as substituted by section 7 and Schedule 4 (Part 1) of the Employment Relations Act 1999 and 'fleshed out' by the Maternity & Parental Leave etc Regulations 1999, which latter were amended (on 24 November 2002) by the Maternity & Parental Leave (Amendment) Regulations 2002. The law regulating an employee's entitlement or otherwise to statutory maternity pay (SMP) or the state maternity allowance (MA) is to be found in Parts II and XII of the Social Security Contributions & Benefits Act 1992 (referred to in this section as 'the 1992 Act'), and in Regulations made under (or saved by) that Act. The 1992 and 1996 Acts apply to persons employed in England, Scotland and Wales. Cognate legislation covers persons employed in Northern Ireland.

The old and the new

- This section is concerned solely with the right of a pregnant employee, whose expected week of childbirth (EWC) begins on or after 6 April 2003, to take up to 52 weeks' maternity leave and her (new) right to be paid up to 26 weeks' Statutory Maternity Pay (SMP) during her ordinary maternity leave period. In the interests of space, the rights of employees whose EWCs occur (or occurred) before 6 April 2003 are not discussed in this section. Suffice to say that a pregnant employee whose EWC begins before 6 April 2003 is restricted to the former maximum of 18 weeks' ordinary maternity leave, supplemented (if she qualifies) by up to 29 weeks' additional maternity leave starting with the Sunday of the week in which childbirth occurred. In her case, the former rules prevail, even if she gives (or gave) birth on or after 6 April 2003.

- Other rights in relation to pregnancy and childbirth are examined else-where in this handbook in the sections titled **Parental leave, Pregnant employees and nursing mothers, Suspension from work on maternity grounds, Time off for dependants, Time off work: pregnant employ-ees**, and **Written reasons for dismissal**

Ordinary and additional maternity leave periods

- Subject to certain procedural requirements (discussed later in this section), every pregnant employee whose expected week of confine-ment (or childbirth) (EWC) begins on or after 6 April 2003 has the legal right to a minimum 26 weeks' *ordinary maternity leave*, regardless of her working hours or length of service. If she has been continuously employed for 26 or more weeks by the end of the 15th week before her EWC, she is entitled also to take up to 26 weeks' additional maternity leave. The additional maternity leave period begins on the day imme-diately following the day on which the employee's ordinary maternity leave period ends.

Statutory maternity pay (SMP)

- A pregnant employee who has worked for her employer for 26 weeks or more by the end of the 15th week before her EWC and who has average weekly earnings equal to or greater than the current 'lower earnings limit' for National Insurance purposes (ie, £77), is entitled to be paid up to 26 weeks' statutory maternity pay (SMP) during her maternity pay period. The 'maternity pay period' is the period of up to 26 weeks that begins on the day immediately following the day on which an employee began her ordinary maternity leave, and ends with the payment week immediately preceding the date on which she returned to work. An employee who does not qualify for SMP, may be entitled to receive the state maternity allowance (MA) or a payment from the Social Fund. SMP is discussed in more detail later in this section.

Recovery of SMP

- An employer who has lawfully paid SMP to an employee can recover 92 per cent of the gross amount paid by deducting that amount from the total amount of employees' and employers' National Insurance contributions payable (together with income tax) to the Collector of Taxes within 14 days of the end of each income tax month. An employer who qualifies for Small Employer's Relief can recover 100 per cent of the gross amount of SMP payments made, plus an additional 4.5 per cent as compensation for National Insurance contributions paid on SMP (*vide* the Statutory Maternity Pay (Compensation of Employers) Amendment Regulations 2002). See below for further details.

Return to work after childbirth

- A woman returning to work after her ordinary maternity leave period is entitled to do so in the job in which she was employed before her absence began. A woman who takes additional maternity leave is also entitled to return to work in the job in which she was employed before her absence, or, if it is not reasonably practicable for her employer to permit her to return to that job, to another job which is both suitable for her and appropriate for her to do in the circumstances. But see **Parental leave**.

   Note: An employee entitled to additional maternity leave is no longer obliged to inform her employer in advance that she intends to exercise her right to return to work on completion of that period of leave; nor does her employer have any right to insist that she does so. Nor may her employer write to her (as was previously the case) before the end of her ordinary maternity leave, asking her to confirm whether or not she intends to return to work at the end of the additional maternity leave period.

Meaning of 'childbirth'

- Section 235(1) of the 1996 Act defines *childbirth* as meaning the birth of a living child or the birth of a child whether living or dead after 24 weeks of pregnancy. The *expected week of childbirth* is the week, beginning at midnight between Saturday and Sunday and ending at midnight on the following Saturday, in which it is expected that childbirth will occur. The word *confinement* no longer appears in the 1996 Act. However, it is still used in the social security legislation (and means exactly the same as *childbirth*).

Interaction of contractual and statutory rights

- An employee who has a contractual as well as a statutory right to maternity leave may take advantage of whichever of those rights is the more favourable to her (not both). The same applies if she has a contractual right to be paid the whole or part of her normal wages or salary during her ordinary maternity leave period. In that event, her employer may offset SMP (if any) paid to that employee against the amount paid under her contract (and *vice versa*), but only in respect of weeks in which both the contractual and statutory amounts are due. For example, an employee may be entitled under her contract to 32 weeks' paid maternity leave, but her employer cannot insist that she delay her return to work until the end of that contractual entitlement, as that would deny her her legal right to return to work (on full pay) at the end of her 26-week ordinary maternity leave period.

Change of employer

- If there has been a change of employer (for example, in circumstances in which there is no break in the mother-to-be or new mother's period of continuous employment), the new employer (who may be an associate or successor employer) inherits her former employer's contractual and statutory obligations in relation to that employee including her right to maternity leave and pay, and her right to return to work after childbirth. If her former employer had started paying her SMP before the change in ownership, her new employer must continue paying SMP until her maternity pay period ends.

Ordinary maternity leave

- Every pregnant employee expecting a baby on or after 6 April 2003 is entitled to take up to 26 weeks' ordinary maternity leave, whether she is in full-time or part-time employment and regardless of her length of service at the material time. If she is healthily pregnant, she has the right also to decide when her maternity leave period is to begin (subject to the proviso that, unless she gives birth prematurely, she may not begin her maternity leave before the beginning of the 11th week before her EWC. Furthermore, her maternity leave period begins immediately if she is absent from work with a pregnancy-related illness at any time during the four weeks immediately preceding her EWC (see *Pregnancy-related illnesses* below).

Notification procedure

- Once she has made up her mind, a pregnant employee must inform her employer by the end of the 15th week before her EWC of the date on which she intends her maternity leave period to begin (in writing, if her employer insists). At the same time, she must specify her EWC and (if asked to do so) produce for her employer's inspection a certificate of expected confinement (Form MatB1 or the equivalent) signed by her doctor or registered midwife. If for one reason or another, the employee is unable to give the required advance notice by the end of that 15th week, she must do so as soon as is reasonably practicable. If she later changes her mind about the date on which she intends to start her maternity leave, she must give her employer at least 28 days' advance notice of the revised start date. The employee's maternity leave period begins on the notified date, unless she gives birth or is taken ill with a pregnancy-related illness before that notified date, as to which see *Premature birth* and *Pregnancy-related illnesses* below.

Note: Form Mat B1 (*Maternity Certificate*) is the standard form of certificate issued by doctors and midwives, although any form of certificate signed by a doctor or registered midwife, and couched in similar terms, will satisfy the legal requirement. A doctor or midwife will not normally issue Form Mat B1 until the beginning of the 14th week before the expected week of childbirth. Form Mat B1 is in two parts. Part A nominates the week in which childbirth is expected to occur; while Part B (Mat B2) certifies the date on which childbirth actually occurred.

- An employee, who neglects (or wilfully refuses) to give the prescribed advance notice of the date on which she intends to start her maternity leave, runs the risk of forfeiting her right to maternity leave and, very possibly, her right (if any) to SMP.

- An employer who has been correctly informed of an employee's pregnancy and EWC, and of the date on which she intends to start her maternity leave, must respond in writing within the next 28 days. In doing so, he must inform her of the date on which her full entitlement to maternity leave ends. By 'full entitlement' is meant her entitlement to ordinary maternity leave or, where appropriate, her entitlement to both ordinary and additional maternity leave). If he fails to reply in those terms within that 28-day period, he may not prevent her returning to work sooner than the due date and may not legitimately dismiss or discipline her for returning to work later than expected. The reader should note also that, with the coming into force on 6 April 2003 of the Maternity & Parental Leave (Amendment) Regulations 2002, an employer may no longer write to an employee towards the end of her ordinary maternity leave period asking her to confirm whether or not she intends to return to work at the end of her additional maternity leave period.

Premature birth

- If an employee gives birth prematurely (that is to say before her EWC and before the date on which she intended to begin her maternity leave, whether or not she had already notified her employer of that intended start date), her ordinary maternity leave period begins with the day on which childbirth occurs. But she risks forfeiting her entitlement to ordinary maternity leave (and, where appropriate, SMP) unless she informs her employer as soon as is reasonably practicable that she gave birth on such-and-such a date.

- If she has not done so already, she must also inform her employer of her EWC (supported by a Form Mat B1, if her employer asks her to produce that document or its equivalent), bearing in mind that it is her EWC, not the actual date of birth, which determines her entitlement, if any, to SMP and additional maternity leave. It is useful to note that one side of Form Mat B1 is a 'Certificate of Expected Confinement'; the other, a 'Certificate of Confinement'. If an employee gives birth prematurely, she should ask her doctor or midwife to sign both sides of the form before sending it off to her employer.

Note: An employee whose baby is stillborn within the first 24 weeks of pregnancy has no legal right to maternity leave (but will usually qualify for statutory sick pay (SSP) and, very likely, occupational sick pay, for so long as it takes for her to recover and return to work). But, if the stillbirth occurs *after* 24 weeks of pregnancy, she retains her right to ordinary maternity leave and, if she qualifies, to additional maternity leave also.

Pregnancy-related illnesses

- If a pregnant employee falls ill (or is still ill) with a pregnancy related illness at any time on or after the beginning of the fourth week before her EWC, her ordinary maternity leave period must begin immediately (regardless of the date on which she had otherwise intended to start her leave). If she has been receiving SSP in respect of her illness, those payments must cease, to be replaced (if she qualifies) by SMP. No further payments of SSP are permissible during the maternity leave period, even if the employee does not qualify for SMP during that period. In these circumstances also, she must notify her employer as soon as is reasonably practicable that she is absent from work wholly or partly because of pregnancy.

Note: A pregnant employee who is on sick leave (because of an illness or injury that has nothing to do with her being pregnant) may continue to draw statutory sick pay or invalidity benefit until her *notified leave date* (ie, the date on which she intended her maternity leave period to begin) or until her baby is born, whichever occurs sooner.

Application of terms and conditions during ordinary maternity leave

- An employee who takes ordinary maternity leave is entitled, during that period of leave, to the benefit of all the terms and conditions of employment that would have applied but for her absence (other than her right to be paid her normal wages or salary), and is bound, during that period, by any obligations arising under those terms and conditions.

- If, for example, an employee's entitlement to paid annual holidays or occupational sick pay (or, indeed, a pay rise) is determined by reference to her length of service, her absence on maternity leave counts as part of her total period of continuous employment. If her employer pays pension contributions while she is at work, he must continue to pay those contributions at the same level while she is absent on ordinary maternity leave (that is to say, based on her normal wages or salary). However, unless she volunteers otherwise, her own pension contributions must be based only on the amount of any contractual remuneration or SMP actually paid to her during her maternity leave (*per* section 23 and Schedule 5 to the Social Security Act 1989). The point is that, save for the suspension of her right to be paid her normal wages or salary, an absentee employee's remaining terms and conditions of employment (as well as her statutory right to four weeks' paid annual holidays) prevail throughout her ordinary and additional maternity leave periods.

Return to work after ordinary maternity leave

- An employee returning to work after her ordinary maternity leave has the right to do so in the job she occupied before that period of leave began (that is to say, in her original job) – unless, as is explained below, she takes four or more weeks' parental leave before returning to work. If she intends to return to work on the day following the day on which her ordinary maternity leave period comes to an end, she need do no more than turn up for work on the day in question. However, different rules apply if she wishes to return to work sooner than expected (see *An early return to work?* below). While it would be sensible for an employee approaching the end of her ordinary maternity leave period to keep in touch with her supervisor or head of department, to ensure that everything is in readiness for her return to work, this is by no means a legal requirement. A woman who does not intend to return to work after her ordinary (or additional) maternity leave period must give her employer the notice of termination required by her contract of employment.

- A woman who takes up to four weeks' parental leave immediately after the end of her ordinary maternity leave period retains her right to return to work in her original job on the same terms and conditions as if she had not been absent. But, if she takes more than four weeks' parental leave at that time, she may have to forego that right and accept an offer of suitable alternative employment if it is not reasonably practicable for her employer to permit her to return to her original job. It is as well to point out that a woman who wishes to take a period of parental leave immediately after her ordinary (or additional) maternity leave period must apply to take that leave at least 21 days before the end of her maternity leave period. A woman does not qualify to take a period of parental leave, of whatever duration, at the end of her ordinary maternity leave (or at any other time) unless she has completed one or more years' continuous service by the time the requested period of parental leave is set to begin (as to which, see **Parental leave** elsewhere in this handbook).

- A woman's ordinary maternity leave period will usually end after 26 weeks (unless she has a contractual right to a longer period of leave), but must continue for so long as may be necessary to accommodate the 'compulsory maternity leave period' referred to in the next paragraph. If she is prevented by illness from returning to work at the end of her ordinary maternity leave, she must comply with such procedures for notifying sickness absence as are laid down in her contract of employment or in any associated document. An employer does not have the right to postpone an employee's return to work after the end of her ordinary (or, indeed, her additional) maternity leave period (*ibid.* regulation 11).

An early return to work?

- But if an employee plans to return to work early – bearing in mind that she may not lawfully do so within the compulsory maternity leave period, that is to say, within two weeks of giving birth (or within four weeks of that date if she works in a factory (*per* section 205, Public Health Act 1936) – she must give her employer at least 28 days' notice of her intentions, although there is no need for her to do so in writing. If she returns to work unannounced and earlier than the due date, or after having given less than 28 days' notice, her employer has every right to send her home and to insist that she delay her return to work until those 28 days have elapsed or until the end of her ordinary maternity leave period, whichever occurs sooner. An employer has no right to delay an employee's return to work beyond the end of her ordinary maternity leave period. An employee who is denied her right to return to work after that period will be treated in law as having been unfairly dismissed and may pursue the matter before an employment tribunal.

Dismissal during ordinary maternity leave

- Section 99 of the 1996 Act (supported by Regulation 20 of the Maternity & Parental Leave etc Regulations 1999 (*qv*)) cautions employers that it is unlawful and automatically unfair to dismiss an employee (or select her for redundancy) during her ordinary (or additional) maternity leave period if the reason (or, if more than one, the principal reason) for her dismissal or selection is that she is (or was) pregnant or had given birth to a child, or because she had exercised her statutory rights in relation to pregnancy and childbirth. See also *Written statement of reasons for dismissal* later in this section.

Redundancy during ordinary maternity leave

- If an employee is made genuinely redundant during her ordinary maternity leave, her employer is nonetheless duty-bound to offer her suitable alternative employment before her employment under her old contract comes to an end. The alternative employment must begin on the day following the day on which her previous employment ended and, to be 'suitable', must involve work that is both suitable and appropriate for her to do in the circumstances (given her qualifications, experience and skills) and on terms and conditions of employment not substantially less favourable to her than those that would have applied had she continued to be employed in her original job. In short, she should enjoy the same or equivalent status or seniority under the new contract, work in the same location (if not in the same department or section), receive the same or a comparable rate of pay, and be entitled to the same annual holidays, the same sickness benefits; and so on (*ibid.* regulation 10).

- If an employee is made redundant during her ordinary maternity leave period without being offered suitable alternative employment, or without being consulted about the suitability of any available vacancies, her dismissal will be held to have been unfair. If she believes that she has been unfairly treated, she has the right to pursue her case before an employment tribunal. If the tribunal finds in her favour or believes that she was selected for redundancy principally because she was pregnant or because she had given birth to a child (or for a connected reason), it will order her employer to pay a substantial award of compensation – the more so if she elects to pursue her complaint under the Sex Discrimination Act 1975.

- If the employer's defence is that there was no suitable alternative employment to offer the employee, or that she had unreasonably refused an offer of what would ordinarily be considered to be suitable alternative employment, or that there was nothing untoward about the employer's motives in selecting her for redundancy, the case will be decided on its merits.

- An employer should be extremely cautious about dismissing an employee (for a reason other than redundancy) during her ordinary (or additional) maternity leave period – bearing in mind that her contract of employment subsists during her absence and that she is accordingly entitled to the same consideration as any person who is absent from work on holidays or sick leave. To dismiss an employee *in absentia* will usually be held unfair – the more so if the evidence shows that she was not told about the reasons for her dismissal, had not been forewarned of the likelihood of her being dismissed, and not been afforded an opportunity either to put her side of the case or to appeal against her employer's decision to dismiss her – issues of procedural fairness re-emphasised by the House of Lords in *Polkey v Dayton Services Limited* [1987] IRLR 503.

Note: Unless dismissed for an unlawful or inadmissible reason (or for a reason connected with her having been pregnant or given birth to a child), an employee dismissed during her maternity leave period for a reason other than redundancy (eg, misconduct) will not normally qualify to bring a complaint of unfair dismissal unless employed by her employer for a continuous period of at least one year ending with the effective date of termination of her contract of employment. However, there is nothing to prevent her pursuing her complaint (regardless of her length of service) if she is convinced that the real reason for her dismissal was an unlawful or inadmissible reason; as to which latter, please turn to the section titled **Dismissal** elsewhere in this handbook (notably the paragraphs headed *Inadmissible and unlawful reasons for dismissal*).

Additional maternity leave

- In addition to her right to a minimum of 26 weeks' ordinary maternity leave, a woman who has been continuously employed for 26 weeks or more by the end of the 15th week before her EWC, is entitled to 26 weeks' additional maternity leave beginning on the day immediately following the day on which her ordinary maternity leave period ends. Furthermore, she has the right to return to work at the end of (or, subject to certain conditions, during) that additional maternity leave period.

Note: For the meaning of the expression continuously employed, please turn to the section titled **Continuous employment**, elsewhere in this handbook.

Notification procedure

- An employee who has the right to take additional maternity leave has no need to inform her employer in advance that she intends to take advantage of that right; nor need she inform her employer (as was the case under the previous regime) that she intends to exercise her right to return to work after her additional maternity leave period ends. As was explained earlier, the only advance notice she need give her employer (before the end of the 15th week before her EWC) is notice confirming that she is pregnant (with supporting documentation) and specifying the date on which she intends to start her maternity leave. Her additional maternity leave period commences automatically on the day immediately following the day on which her ordinary maternity leave period ends.

Contractual rights during additional maternity leave

- The Maternity & Parental Leave etc Regulations 1999 (as amended) make it clear that an employee's contract of employment continues during her additional maternity leave period although not necessarily to the same extent as her contractual rights during her ordinary maternity leave period.

- Regulation 17 of the 1999 Regulations states that, during her additional maternity leave, an employee is entitled to the benefit of her employer's implied obligation to her of trust and confidence and to any terms and conditions relating to:

  (a) notice to terminate her employment;

  (b) compensation in the event of redundancy; or

  (c) disciplinary and grievance procedures.

  In short, if she is dismissed during her additional maternity leave, she must be paid her normal wages or salary during the notice period (or money in lieu of notice), as well as any accrued entitlement to holiday pay. If she is made redundant, she must also be paid any entitlement to statutory redundancy pay, plus any 'top up' payment by way of severance pay (to which she would otherwise be entitled but for her absence). If she is to be dismissed, or has a grievance against her employer, she is entitled to be treated in the same way as any other employee facing dismissal or intent upon pursuing any such grievance.

- For her part, an employee intent on resigning during her additional maternity leave, must give her employer the prescribed notice to terminate her contract of employment; must not disclose to an unauthorised third party any confidential information concerning her employer's business affairs (trade secrets, pricing policy, marketing strategy, etc); must not accept any gifts or benefits in breach of her implied contractual duty of trust and confidence; and must not participate in any other business in competition with her employer.

Dismissal during additional maternity leave

- Section 99 of the 1996 Act (supported by Regulation 20 of the now amended Maternity & Parental Leave etc Regulations 1999 (*qv*)) cautions employers that it is unlawful and automatically unfair to dismiss an employee (or select her for redundancy) during her additional (or ordinary) maternity leave period if the reason (or, if more than one, the principal reason) for her dismissal or selection is that she had given birth to a child, or because she had exercised any of her statutory rights in relation to pregnancy and childbirth (including her right to ordinary or additional maternity leave). For further particulars, please turn to the section titled **Dismissal** and the paragraphs in that section titled *Inadmissible and unlawful reasons for dismissal*. See also *Written statement of reasons for dismissal* below.

- If an employee is dismissed during her additional period maternity leave (for a reason other than redundancy), it will be for an employment tribunal to decide whether her dismissal was fair bearing in mind that the tribunal is likely to question her employer's motives in dismissing her *in absentia* and his (or her) failure to follow the correct procedure when doing so. If the tribunal finds that the employee was dismissed for an unlawful or inadmissible reason, it will make a declaration to that effect and will order the employer either to reinstate or reengage the employee in her old job or pay her an additional award of compensation (over and above the amount of the basic and compensatory awards of compensation for unfair dismissal) (as to which latter, see **Dismissal** elsewhere in this handbook).

Redundancy during additional maternity leave

- An employee made redundant during her additional maternity leave period is entitled to the same consideration as an employee made redundant during her ordinary maternity leave period. In short, she is entitled to be offered suitable alternative employment beginning on the day immediately following the day on which her previous employment ended, and on terms and conditions of employment not substantially less favourable to her than those that would have applied had she continued to be employed in her original job – as to which, see *Redundancy during ordinary maternity leave* above.

Right to return to work after additional maternity leave

- When an employee returns to work after her additional maternity leave period, she is entitled to do so in the job in which she was employed before her ordinary maternity leave period began – unless it is not reasonably practicable for her employer to permit her to return to work in that job, in which case she is entitled to return to work in another job which is both suitable for her and appropriate for her to do in the circumstances. Whether she returns to work in her original job or in a 'suitable and appropriate' alternative job, she must be permitted to do so:

(a) on a salary or wage (or rate of pay) not less favourable to her than the remuneration that would have been applicable to her had she not been absent from work at any time since the commencement of her ordinary maternity leave period;

(b) with her seniority, pension rights and similar rights as they would have been if the period (or periods) of her employment prior to her additional maternity leave period were continuous with her employment following her return to work; and

(c) otherwise on terms and conditions no less favourable than those that would have applied to her had she not been absent from work after the end of her ordinary maternity leave period *(ibid.* regulation 18).

- An employee who takes a period of parental leave of four weeks or less, immediately after the end of her additional maternity leave, retains her right to return to work in her original job unless it would not have been reasonably practicable for her to have returned to that job at the end of her additional maternity leave period and it is still not reasonably practicable for her to do so. If she takes more than four weeks' parental leave immediately after the end of her additional maternity leave, she is entitled to return to her original job or, if that is not reasonably practicable, to a similar job on terms and conditions no less favourable to her than those to which she was entitled in her original job. For further particulars, please turn to the section on **Parental leave** elsewhere in this handbook.

Exercise of right to return to work after additional maternity leave

- An employee who intends to return to work at the end of her additional maternity leave period need do no more than turn up for work on the due date. However, if she intends to return to work early, that is to say, *before* the end of that period, she must notify her employer at least 28 days beforehand that she intends to return to work on that earlier date. If an employee's return to work is delayed because of illness or injury, she need do no more than inform her employer of that fact (in accordance with her employer's rules in relation to sickness absence) and provide the necessary evidence of incapacity.

Note: Employers should note that they no longer have the statutory right to delay an employee's return to work after childbirth (for whatever reason); nor do would-be-returning employees forfeit their right to return to work if illness or injury intervenes to prevent them doing so within four weeks of the notified date. Those provisions of the Employment Rights Act 1996 have long since been repealed.

- If an employee returns to work early and unannounced, without having given the prescribed 28 days' advance notice, her employer has every right to send her home and to insist that she delay her return until those 28 days have elapsed or until the end of her ordinary maternity leave period, whichever occurs sooner. She has no right to be paid if she ignores her employer's instructions and remains at work during the notice period.

Failure to permit a return to work treated as a dismissal

- An employee who is denied her statutory right to return to work after either of her ordinary or additional maternity leave periods will be treated in law as having been unfairly dismissed if her dismissal is solely or mainly attributable to the fact that she exercised her right to maternity leave or took advantage of the benefits of her terms and conditions of employment to which she was entitled during that leave. In short, her employer will need to satisfy an employment tribunal that he (or she) had a legitimate reason for dismissing the employee (unconnected with her having taken advantage of statutory maternity rights) and had acted fairly and reasonably in doing so.

- If an employer can satisfy an employment tribunal that the employee's original job was no longer available because of redundancy and that he (or she) had acted fairly and lawfully in selecting her for redundancy – there being no suitable available vacancy to offer her, or that she had been offered suitable alternative employment by an associated employer which she had either accepted or unreasonably refused – her dismissal will be held to have been fair (*ibid.* section 81).

Note: If the evidence before an employment tribunal shows that the employee was selected for redundancy for an inadmissible reason (eg, because of her sex or for reasons connected with her having taken advantage of her statutory rights in connection with pregnancy or childbirth, including her right to maternity leave), her dismissal will be held to have been inadmissible and unfair (*ibid.* regulation 20(2)).

- Finally, an employee who has been denied her right to return to work after additional maternity leave will not be held to have been unfairly dismissed:

(a) if, immediately before the end of her additional maternity leave period (or immediately before her dismissal, if her additional maternity leave ended with her dismissal) the number of persons employed by her employer (including the employee herself, added to the number employed by any associated employer, did not exceed five; and

(b) her employer (who may be the same employer or a successor) can satisfy the tribunal that it was not reasonably practicable either to permit her to return to work in her original job or to offer her suitable alternative employment or for an associated employer to offer her a job of that kind (*ibid.* section 96(2)).

As was indicated earlier, the alternative employment (or job) offered to an employee who has been denied her right to return to work in her original job, must involve work that is both suitable and appropriate for her to do (given her qualifications, experience and skills) and must be on terms and conditions of employment not substantially less favourable to her than those that would have applied had she been permitted to return to work in her original job. In short, she should enjoy the same or equivalent status or seniority, be employed in the same place (if not in the same department or section), receive the same or a comparable rate of pay, and be entitled to the same annual holidays, the same sickness benefits; and so on.

Written statement of reasons for dismissal

- An employee who is dismissed (for whatever reason), either while pregnant or after having given birth (in circumstances in which her ordinary or additional maternity leave period ends by reason of the dismissal) must be provided by her employer with a written statement explaining the reasons for her dismissal – regardless of her working hours or length of service at the relevant time and regardless of whether she has asked to be issued with such a statement. Furthermore, the statement must be given or sent to the employee within 14 days of the date on which her dismissal took place (*ibid.* section 92(4)).

- On a complaint to an employment tribunal, an employer who has refused or failed to provide the written statement, or has failed to do so within the prescribed 14 days, or provides a statement containing information that is inadequate or untrue, will be ordered by the tribunal to pay the employee a sum equivalent to two weeks' pay. Where appropriate, the tribunal will also make a declaration as to what it finds the employer's real reasons were for dismissing the employee – bearing in mind that a complaint arising out of an employer's failure to provide a written statement will very likely be heard at the same time as a complaint of unfair or unlawful dismissal (*ibid.* section 93).

The written statement of reasons for dismissal referred to in the previous paragraph is admissible in evidence in proceedings before a tribunal or court (*ibid.* section 92(5)).

Statutory maternity pay (SMP)

Summary

- A pregnant employee who has been employed by her employer for a continuous period of at least 26 weeks by the end of the 15th week before her EWC, and has average weekly earnings of £77 or more per week – the current (2003/04) 'lower earnings limit' for NI contributions purposes – is entitled to be paid SMP for a period of up to 26 weeks during her ordinary maternity leave period. SMP is payable in weekly amounts only (a week, for these purposes, being a period of seven consecutive days, eg, Wednesday/Tuesday). Unlike statutory sick pay (SSP), there is no equivalent daily rate of SMP.

- An employee's maternity pay period cannot begin before the Sunday of the 11th week before her EWC, unless she gives birth before the beginning of that 11th week, in which event it will start on the day after the day on which childbirth occurs. If a pregnant employee is absent from work wholly or partly because of a pregnancy or confinement, on or after the beginning of the fourth week before her EWC (but not later than the week immediately following the week in which childbirth occurs) the first week of her maternity pay period is the period of seven consecutive days that begins on the day immediately following the day on which she is so absent.

- The period during which SMP is payable is referred to as the 'maternity pay period'. An employee's right to be paid SMP persists if she leaves her employment at any time after the beginning of the 11th week before her EWC and before the start of her maternity pay period, but not later than the week immediately following the week in which she gives birth. In that situation, the first week of her maternity pay period is the week after the week in which her employment ends. In this situation only, a 'week' is the period of seven consecutive days that begins on a Sunday and ends on the following Saturday.

- An employee with eight or more weeks' continuous service, who is dismissed by her employer solely or mainly for the purpose of avoiding liability for SMP, will retain her right to SMP if, but for her dismissal, she would have completed 26 weeks' service by the end of the 15th week before her EWC (*per* regulation 3, Statutory Maternity Pay (General) Regulations 1986 (discussed later in this section)).

SMP rights on resignation or dismissal

- The maternity pay period for an employee entitled to SMP, who resigns or is dismissed (for whatever reason) after the beginning of the 15th week before her EWC, but before the beginning of the 11th week before her EWC, begins on the Sunday of that 11th week, not on the day immediately following the day previously notified as the day on which she intended her maternity leave period to begin.

- The maternity pay period for an employee entitled to SMP, who resigns or is dismissed, on or after the beginning of the 11th week before her EWC but before the day previously notified as the day on which she intended to begin her maternity leave (the notified date), begins on the day immediately following the day on which her employment came to an end.

- A woman who resigns or is dismissed on or after the beginning of her maternity pay period must continue to be paid SMP by her (former) employer until the payment period ends. However, if she starts work for another employer during what remains of her maternity pay period, she must notify her former employer of that fact – in which event, her maternity pay period ends with the last weekly payment before the date on which she started work with that other employer (as to which, see *When SMP must stop* below).

SMP rates

- There are two rates of SMP: the higher rate and the lower rate. The higher rate, which is equal to nine-tenths of an employee's average weekly earnings (see below), is paid for the first six weeks of the maternity pay period. The lower rate is payable for the remainder of that period, but not for more than 20 weeks. From 6 April 2003, the lower rate of SMP is £100 a week or 90 per cent of the employer's average weekly earnings, whichever is the lesser of those amounts.

  Note: An employer can recover 92 per cent of the gross amount of SMP due and paid to an employee by deducting the amount in question from the total of the employers' and employees' Class 1 national insurance contributions payable (together with income tax) to the Inland Revenue accounts office at the end of each month. If he (or she) is entitled to Small Employers' Relief, he can recover 100 per cent of the SMP due plus a further 4.5 per cent in compensation. See *Recovering SMP* below.

- As is the case with payments under the employers' statutory sick pay (ESSP) scheme, all payments of SMP are subject to the deduction of income tax (PAYE) and National Insurance Contributions (NIC). Attachment of earnings orders do *not* apply to payments of SMP, but other amounts normally deducted from an employee's pay, such as pension contributions, are permitted (but see *Application of terms and conditions during ordinary maternity leave* above).

- SMP should be paid on a normal payday, using the method of payment normally used for paying wages and salaries. SMP must not be paid in kind. Nor may it be paid in the form of board or lodgings or by way of a service. If an employee normally collects her wages in cash (eg, from the wages office), she should talk to her employer about a more convenient way of receiving her SMP, or arrange to have a relative or friend collect the money on her behalf.

Qualifying conditions for SMP

- To qualify for SMP, an employee:

  (a) must have been employed (or be deemed to have been employed) by her employer for at least 26 weeks up to and into the 15th week before her EWC;

  (b) must have 'average weekly earnings' equal to or higher than the current earnings threshold for SMP purposes (ie, £77 a week) – which average weekly earnings are to be calculated over the eight-week period ending with her last payday before the end of that 15th week;

  (c) must either still be pregnant at the beginning of the 11th week before her EWC or have already given birth.

  Note: If an employee's baby is stillborn before the beginning of the 16th week before the EWC, the mother will not be entitled to SMP (but should qualify for either or both of statutory or occupational sick pay). But, if her baby is born (alive or dead) after the beginning of that 16th week, she will still qualify for SMP if she has average earnings equal to or higher than the then current 'lower earnings limit' for National Insurance contributions and would have satisfied the 26-week rule but for the premature birth.

- To exercise her right to be paid SMP during her absence on maternity leave, an employee must serve notice on her employer (in writing, if he insists) of the date from which she expects his liability to pay her SMP to begin, so long as she does so at least 28 days before that date or, if that is not reasonably practicable, as soon as is reasonably practicable.

The 26-week rule

- The first and, perhaps, most important condition for entitlement to SMP is the so-called '26 week rule', which states that a pregnant employee will not qualify for SMP unless she has been (or is deemed to have been) employed for a period of at least 26 consecutive weeks up to and into the 15th week before the expected week of her confinement (the 'qualifying week').

  Note: If there has been a change of employer or if an employer's business or undertaking is sold as a going concern, the new owner (employer) inherits the contracts of employment of the persons employed in that business or undertaking at the time of the transfer or sale (*vide* regulation 5, Transfer of Undertakings (Protection of Employment) Regulations 1981). He also inherits the former employer's duty to pay or to continue to pay SMP to an employee who satisfies the qualifying conditions for the payment of SMP (or would have done so had the transfer or sale not intervened). Regulation 14 of the Statutory Maternity Pay (General) Regulations 1986 provides that, when a business is transferred as a 'going concern', an employee's employment with her former employer (the transferor) must be treated (for SMP purposes) as continuous with her employment with her new employer (the transferee). When deciding whether or not an employee is entitled to SMP, the transferee employer must (if need be) take into account her earnings and period of employment with her former employer. See also *Change of employer* earlier in this section.

- Certain breaks in employment can count as periods of employment for SMP purposes. If, for example, an employee had previously resigned or been dismissed because of ill-health or injury, each of the intervening weeks of absence will count as a period of employment so long as she is re-employed by the same employer (or a successor of his) within 26 weeks of that resignation or dismissal. The same 'rule of thumb' applies to gaps in employment occasioned by the seasonal nature of an employee's work or by some unexpected occurrence (such as a fire or flood) that results in the termination of her employment – so long as she has been given to understand that she would be re-hired (and is re-hired) at the start of the new season or on completion of renovations, or whatever (as to which, please turn to the section titled **Continuous employment** elsewhere in this handbook).

- If an employee has been unfairly dismissed and subsequently reinstated or re-engaged, the period between the date on which her dismissal took effect and the date on which she was reinstated or reengaged counts as part of her period of continuous employment for SMP purposes.

- A week during the whole or part of which a woman does no work because of a stoppage of work due to a trade dispute does not break the continuity of her employment. However, that week must be discounted when computing her total period of employment for SMP purposes – unless she can prove that at no time did she have a direct interest in the trade dispute in question (regulation 13, Statutory Maternity Pay (General) Regulations 1986). For example, a pregnant employee, who had otherwise worked for her employer for, say, 28 weeks by the end of the 15th week before her EWC, would forfeit her right to SMP during her maternity leave period if her employer's records reveal that a trade dispute had prevented her from working during three of those 28 weeks, unless she can satisfy her employer (or, indeed, an Inland Revenue 'decision-maker') that she had no direct interest in the dispute in question. However, if not entitled to SMP, she might well qualify for the state maternity allowance (MA) discussed at the end of this section.

- There are two points to be emphasised in relation to the 26-week rule. First, a pregnant employee will not satisfy that rule (and will not, therefore, qualify for SMP) unless she continues to be employed by her employer up to and into the 15th week before the expected week of childbirth. If she is employed for at least one day in that 15th week, the whole of that week will count in computing her length of service for SMP purposes. She will also satisfy the 26-week rule if she gives birth (unless her child is stillborn within the first 24 weeks of pregnancy) before the beginning of that week if, but for that event, she would have completed 26 weeks' service by the end of that 15th week. However, she will not be entitled to SMP if she resigns or is dismissed before the beginning of the 15th week, regardless of her length of service at that time (unless, of course, her employer dismissed her simply in order to avoid having to pay SMP, as to which, see the paragraph titled *Disagreements between employers and employees* later in this section).

- To qualify for SMP an employee must not only satisfy the 26-week rule but must also have average earnings equal to or higher than the current earnings threshhold for SMP purposes. From 6 April 2003, that threshold is £77 per week.

- For SMP purposes, the expression 'earnings' means a woman's gross wages or salary derived from her employment, plus any and all overtime payments, bonuses, fees, commission, holiday pay, payments received under an occupational sick pay scheme, and statutory sick pay (SSP). Earnings in this context also include any sum payable by way of arrears of pay, or remuneration under a protective award in pursuance of an order by an employment tribunal under the provisions of the Employment Rights Act 1996. For a more exhaustive definition, the reader should consult the current DSS leaflet NP15: *Employer's Guide to National Insurance Contributions*.

- If an employee is paid a salary of £10,000 a year, her employer should not have to reach for his pocket calculator to confirm that she earns an average of £77 or more a week. A calculator will only be needed if an employee's gross weekly earnings vary with the amount of work done and occasionally dip below that 'lower earnings limit'. Average weekly earnings are calculated by adding together the gross amounts paid to an employee over the period of eight consecutive weeks up to and including the last payday immediately preceding the end of the 15th week before the expected week of childbirth.

  Note: If an employee gives birth before or during the 15th week before the *expected* week of childbirth, her average weekly earnings must be calculated over the period of eight weeks ending with the last payday before the baby was born.

- If an employee is paid weekly on or about the same day of the week, her average weekly earnings will be one-eighth of the aggregate of the gross amount paid on each of the eight paydays preceding the Saturday of the 15th week before her expected week of childbirth. If she is paid monthly (eg, on or about the last working day of the month), her average weekly earnings will be calculated (i) by adding together the gross amount paid to her on the last payday before the end of that 15th week and all gross payments made to her during the eight weeks preceding that payday, (ii) then by multiplying the total by six, and finally (iii) by dividing the resultant figure by 52.

Excluded categories

- An employee is excluded from entitlement to SMP, whatever her earnings or length of employment, if, at any time during the week in which her maternity pay period begins she is in (or is taken into) 'legal custody' (that is to say, is detained by the police, arrested, or in prison).

- Also excluded from SMP is any foreign-going mariner employed by a UK employer while under contract for which her employer pays a special rate of National Insurance contributions.

- The steps to be taken when an employee is excluded from SMP are outlined in *Procedure when SMP stops* later in this section. It is important to stress that, once an employee is *excluded* from SMP, the exclusion persists throughout the remainder of the relevant maternity pay period.

When SMP must stop

- In the normal course of events, an employer must stop paying SMP to an employee once she has been paid her full 26-week entitlement or when she returns to work, whichever occurs sooner. As SMP payments are for calendar weeks only, payments must end with the last weekly payment *immediately preceding the date on which the employee returned* to work. If an employee occasionally interrupts her maternity pay period to help out in the office (or wherever) for a day or two (in one week) or for several days (spanning two or more weeks), she cannot lawfully be paid SMP for any such week. Although SMP payments can restart for weeks in which she does no work, her maternity pay period cannot be extended to compensate for the loss of SMP for any intervening weeks.

- There are a number of other circumstances that will bring an abrupt end to SMP payments – whether or not the employee in question has received her maximum SMP entitlement. Thus, SMP payments must stop (and stop altogether):

  (a) if the employee dies – in which event her last weekly payment of SMP will be for the payment week ending with the week in which death occurred;

  (b) if she is taken into legal custody – in which case, her employer's SMP liability ends with the last weekly payment before the date on which she was taken into custody;

  (c) if she starts work for another employer during her maternity pay period – in which event, her (former) employer's liability to pay SMP, ends with the last weekly payment immediately preceding the day on which her new employment began.

It follows that an employee, who has not exhausted her full entitlement to SMP, must inform her (erstwhile) employer if she starts work with another employer, or if she is taken into legal custody during her maternity pay period. A woman is said to be in legal custody if she is arrested by the police, but not if she is voluntarily helping the police with their enquiries.

Procedure when SMP stops: Form SMP1

- Employers who cannot pay (or are obliged to cease paying) SMP to an employee because she is either in an excluded category or is in (or has been taken into) legal custody, must complete and sign form SMP1 (available from local Benefits Agency offices) and send it to the employee within seven days of deciding that she is not entitled to SMP or within seven days after the end of the week for which the last payment of SMP was made. If they have not already done so, they must also return the original of the employee's Certificate of Expected Confinement (Form Mat B1 or its equivalent). The employee will need that certificate in support of her claim for the state maternity allowance (MA) discussed at the end of this section. The employer should first make photocopies of Forms SMP1 and Mat B1, to be kept on on file for a period of at least three years from the end of the tax year in which they were issued. See *Mandatory and voluntary SMP records* below.

Disagreements between employers and employees

- The very complexity of the SMP scheme suggests that employers have a moral obligation (if not an implied duty in law) to ensure that female employees are aware of their rights under that scheme. To encourage or pressurise a pregnant employee into resigning, before she has satisfied the 26-week rule, could be construed by an adjudication (or decision-making) officer of the Inland Revenue (or, indeed, by an employment tribunal) as an attempt by her employer (albeit fruitless) to avoid liability for SMP. A dismissal for that reason alone would also be self-defeating. In either situation, the employer would almost certainly be ordered to pay SMP to the employee or face prosecution and a heavy fine.

Instruction and training

- In organisations employing sizeable numbers of women, the personnel and training departments may take it upon themselves to conduct a series of in-house seminars – not only for the benefit of pregnant employees and those of 'reproductive capacity' (to borrow a phrase from the Management of Health & Safety at Work Regulations 1999), but also as a means of ensuring that managers and supervisors are well-placed to counsel (and not inadvertently to mislead) such employees about their maternity rights should they become pregnant, and to instruct them about the correct procedures for securing those rights. In smaller companies (that may or may not have a personnel function), the company secretary or site manager should nonetheless encourage pregnant employees to discuss their situation with him (or her) in confidence to determine what they need to do to secure and protect those rights.

Explanation and written statement

- If an employer is of the opinion that a particular employee does not qualify for SMP, or that SMP payments must stop at a certain point during an employee's maternity pay period (eg, before she had been paid her full entitlement to SMP), he should explain his reasons to that employee (preferably in person) before issuing Form SMP1. There may, for instance, be disagreement about the method used to calculate the employee's average weekly earnings or her total period of employment, and so on. Such issues may be explored and possibly resolved using normal grievance procedures. But if, in the event, the employee is still unhappy about her employer's decision, she has the legal right to insist on a written statement containing the following particulars:

- the reasons why the employer considers that the employee is no longer entitled to SMP or why SMP payments must end;

- the weeks when SMP can be paid, and the weeks for which the employer disclaims any liability to pay SMP; and

- the amount (if any) of SMP payable during specified weeks.

An employer must respond to the employee's request for a written statement within a reasonable time. Given that he (or she) must issue Form SMP1 not later than seven days after his decision not to pay (or to cease paying) SMP, it is suggested that he would be acting unreasonably if he failed to provide an accompanying written statement within that same seven-day period.

Intervention of 'decision maker'

- If, having received a written statement from her employer that he is unable to pay (or is about to cease paying) SMP, the employee concerned is still unhappy about his (or her) decision, she may apply to an officer of the Inland Revenue (the 'decision maker') and ask for her complaint to be investigated.

  Note: An employer is not free to approach an officer of the Inland Revenue concerning his (or her) decision to pay or not to pay SMP. Such an approach can only be made by an employee or by the Secretary of State (*per* the Statutory Sick Pay & Statutory Maternity Pay (Decisions) Regulations 1999.

- On receipt of a complaint about the amount of SMP paid, or about an employer's decision not to pay (or to cease paying) SMP, the decision maker will ask for further written particulars from both parties, together with any evidence to support their respective points of view. However, neither party will be asked to appear before the officer. Nor will there be an exchange of evidence between the parties unless the officer's decision is appealed to a Social Security Appeals Tribunal. The officer will convey his (or her) decision to both the employer and the employee.

- If it is decided that SMP should be (or should have been) paid, the employer must comply with that decision within a specified period –

unless he (or she) decides to appeal. If it is decided that SMP is not payable (or that the amount paid *is* correct), the employee may either accept that decision or register an appeal with the same appeals tribunal. The procedure for doing so (and the time limits for registering an appeal) will accompany the decision maker's decision.

Appeals

- In most cases, the decision of the Social Security Appeals Tribunal will be final and binding on both parties. In some circumstances there will be a further right of appeal to a Social Security Commissioner. An employer who fails or refuses to pay SMP, when ordered to do so, is guilty of an offence and liable on conviction to a fine of up to £1,000.

Recovering SMP

- Briefly, an employer can recover 92 per cent of the gross amount of any SMP due and paid to a *qualified* employee by deducting that amount from the total amount of employees' and employers' National Insurance contributions payable (together with income tax) to the Collector of Taxes within 14 days of the end of each income tax month. An employer who qualifies for Small Employer's Relief may recover 100 per cent of the gross amount of SMP payments made, plus a further 4.5 per cent as compensation for National Insurance contributions paid on SMP.

  Note: An employer qualifies for Small Employer's Relief in 2003/04 if he (or she) paid less than £40,000 total gross Class 1 National insurance contributions in 2002/03. The figures are routinely reviewed/adjusted each year.

- While an employer is free to recover 92 per cent or more of the SMP he (or she) has paid, either at the end of the tax month in which the SMP was paid or at the end of any subsequent tax month, he should endeavour to recover the full amount due by the end of the relevant tax year. If he is unable to do so, he should seek the advice of his local Benefits Agency office before taking any action to recover the amount outstanding.

  Any reader directly involved in the recovery of SMP will find the procedure fully explained in the *Employer's Helpbook* (Ref. E15(2003)) copies of which are available on request from the Employer's Orderline on 0845 7 646 646.

Mandatory and voluntary SMP records

- The Statutory Maternity Pay (General) Regulations 1986 (as amended) require employers to maintain specified records associated with the payment of SMP. Furthermore, those records must be kept for a period of at least three years after the end of the tax year to which they refer. The penalty for non-compliance is a fine of up to £1,000, plus a further fine of up to £40 for each day of continued non-compliance.

  SMP records that must be maintained are:

  - a record of the date notified by a pregnant employee as being the date on which she intends her maternity leave period to begin;

  - a record of any week (or weeks) within the maternity pay period for which SMP was not paid, and the reasons for non-payment; and

  - the original of Maternity Certificate Form Mat B1 (or its equivalent) provided by an employee who has been paid SMP;or a copy of that certificate (or its equivalent) if the original was (necessarily) returned to the employee, eg when the employer's liability to pay SMP ended.

  An employer may keep SMP records in whatever form he chooses, so long as they are conveniently accessible and contain the required information. However, the Inland Revenue has produced an information sheet (Form SMP2) which most employers will find helpful. Supplies of these forms are available on request from the Employer's Orderline on 0845 7 646 646.

- Inland Revenue inspectors have the right to enter an employer's premises and to insist on the production of SMP records in pursuit of their investigations into the payment (or non-payment) of SMP. It is an offence for an employer to fail to maintain or produce such records. The production of false or 'doctored' records could lead to prosecution and a fine of up £5,000 and/or imprisonment for a term of up to three months.

Suggested additional records

- An employer has the right to decide how a pregnant employee should notify him (or her) about her intended absence on maternity leave. If he wants notification to be given in writing (perhaps on a form he has designed and provided for that purpose), it follows that he must see to it that his (female) employees know and understand what procedure to follow should they become pregnant. Furthermore, he should keep details of his 'notification' rules (and evidence as to how those rules were promulgated) on file, to be produced for inspection by Inland Revenue inspectors should an employee decide to challenge her employer's decision not to pay SMP.

- Other useful records will include the employer's calculation of an employee's *average weekly earnings* for SMP purposes and details of the periods of employment (including employment with a previous or associated employer) which were taken into account when determining an employee's entitlement (if any) to SMP.

Dealing with mistakes

- If an employer has paid too much or too little SMP; or pays SMP to an employee who is not entitled to receive it; or mistakenly issues form SMP1 when SMP should have been paid; or makes too great or too small a deduction from his end of month NIC payments to the Collector of Taxes, he should act quickly to remedy the situation.

- If an employer has overpaid SMP, he (or she) may or may not consider it appropriate to recover the overpayment from the employee herself. But if, as seems likely, he has deducted too great an amount from moneys otherwise payable to the Collector of Taxes at the end of the relevant tax month, he must restore the amount overpaid at the end of the following tax month. If the error is not discovered until after he has sent his end-of-year return to the Inland Revenue, and the return is no longer held by his local tax office, he should contact his local Social Security office for advice on what to do next.

- If an employer has underpaid SMP to an employee, he (or she) need not raise the matter with the employee's local DSS office unless he has also incorrectly issued Form SMP1. However, the underpayment must be made good to the employee at the earliest opportunity.

- If an employer discovers that he (or she) has mistakenly withheld SMP from any employee (having already issued her with Form SMP1), he should notify her of his error and commence SMP payments immediately. At the same time, he must contact the employee's local benefits office to prevent (or halt) any payments of the state maternity allowance (MA).

- SMP payments should ordinarily be made on the employee's usual pay day. While there is nothing in law to prevent an employer paying the full amount of SMP due in a lump sum at the beginning of an employee's maternity pay period, he (or she) could face problems recovering part of that amount if the employee dies or starts work with another employer before the expected 26-week maternity pay period has run its course. Whether or not an employer in such a situation manages to retrieve the amount of SMP overpaid, he will still be liable to pay back to the Collector of Taxes the amount wrongly deducted from his monthly NIC payments.

FREE PHONE ADVICE FOR EMPLOYERS

Employers needing advice on how to operate the statutory maternity pay scheme can now call the DSS on 0845 7 143 143 (ask for Contributions Agency). These calls are charged at local rate.

Maternity Allowance (MA)

- The State Maternity Allowance (MA) is a weekly benefit payable for a period of up to 26 weeks to employees who do not qualify for SMP. The allowance is also available to self-employed women and to women who have recently been employed. There are two rates of MA. To qualify for MA, a woman must have been employed or self-employed in at least 26 of the 66 weeks ending with the week before her EWC (the test period). There are two rates of MA: the standard rate and the lower rate. The standard rate is £100 a week (or 90 per cent of average weekly earnings, if these are less than £100) payable to a woman with average earnings at least equal to the current MA threshhold limit of £77 a week. Women whose average weekly earnings are less than £77, but at least £30, will receive 90 per cent of their average weekly earnings during that 26-week period, subject to a maximum of £100 a week. A woman who does not qualify for MA, may be entitled to a maternity payment from the Social Fund (using Form SF 100).

- MA is not payable until an employee either stops work or begins her ordinary maternity leave – bearing in mind that an employee who does not qualify for SMP does not thereby forfeit her right to ordinary or additional maternity leave. An employee who is in receipt of MA must notify the DSS if she is taken into legal custody, as this may affect her continued entitlement to the allowance.

SSP and SMP

- As was indicated earlier in this section, an employee cannot legally be paid statutory sick pay (SSP) and SMP in respect of the same week. Unlike SSP, which can be paid for a single qualifying day of sickness absence, SMP is payable in respect of whole weeks only. Accordingly, once the maternity pay period begins, payments of SSP must end. The same rule applies once an employee who is not entitled to SMP begins her ordinary maternity leave period (in respect of which period, she might well qualify for the MA. See **Statutory sick pay** elsewhere in this handbook.

  See also **Adoption leave and pay, Parental leave, Paternity leave**, and **Time off for dependants**, elsewhere in this handbook.

MEDICAL REPORTS, ACCESS TO

Key points

- An employer will often ask an employee – or a job applicant – for permission to approach his (or her) family doctor (or GP) for a report on his recent medical history and current state of health. This is acceptable so long as the employer first informs the person concerned of his (or her) statutory rights under the Access to Medical Reports Act 1988.

- An employer may have a number of reasons for wanting to see a medical report on an employee (or prospective employee). Very often, an offer of employment will be subject to the receipt of a satisfactory medical report. It could be that a job applicant has an unsatisfactory health or attendance record. If an employer has it in mind to dismiss a long-serving employee on health grounds, he should not take the matter further without first obtaining a report from the employee's doctor (see **Dismissal on grounds of ill-health** elsewhere in this handbook). Furthermore, there are certain industries or processes where people with specific health problems (eg, asthma or dermatitis) should not be engaged in work involving exposure to hazardous substances.

- It has always been an employee's (or job applicant's) prerogative to refuse to allow his (or her) employer (or putative employer) to make any direct approach to his doctor. A doctor will not willingly disclose information about a patient without that person's express permission.

- The whole business of seeking and obtaining a report on an employee's state of health was put on a statutory footing on 1 January 1989 when the Access to Medical Reports Act 1988 came into force.

- In broad terms, the Act gives any person applying for a job, and any person already in work, the right:

  (a) to agree or to refuse to allow his (or her) employer (or prospective employer) permission to approach his doctor for a medical report on his state of health;

  (b) to intercept any medical report prepared by his doctor for employment purposes;

  (c) to challenge the accuracy or relevance of any of the information given in the medical report;

  (d) to attach a statement of his own views to the medical report (if, in the event, his doctor refuses to amend it) before it is sent to the employer;

  (e) to refuse to allow the medical report to be sent to the employer; and

  (f) to be given access to any medical report supplied for employment purposes during the previous six months.

Meaning of 'medical report'

- Under section 2(1) of the Act, a *medical report* is a report on the physical or mental health of an individual prepared by a doctor or physician who is or has been responsible for his or her clinical care. In this context, the word *care* means any 'examination, investigation or diagnosis for the purposes of, or in connection with, any form of medical treatment' (*ibid.*).

- For most people in employment, their family doctor or GP is the doctor normally responsible for their clinical care. Company doctors, and other doctors specifically nominated by an employer, may carry out routine or occasional medical examinations of employees when asked to do so. But they are not responsible for the clinical care of the employees they examine. If they diagnose a health problem in a particular employee (or job applicant) they will urge that person to make an appointment to see his or her own doctor. A company doctor will not willingly intrude on the relationship which exists between a patient and his usual doctor.

- It follows that a medical report prepared by a company doctor will not normally fall within the scope of the Access to Medical Reports Act

1988. An employee or job applicant will have no statutory right of access to that report and no right to stop the report being sent forward to his or her employer or would-be employer.

- An employer cannot compel an employee (or job applicant) to submit to a medical examination for employment purposes. But he *can* refuse to engage any person who refuses to attend a pre-employment medical examination. Indeed, he may have no choice but to dismiss an existing employee who unreasonably refuses to be medically examined either by his or her own doctor or one nominated by (and paid for) by the employer. Contemporary health and safety legislation often includes provision for the routine health surveillance of employees engaged in hazardous work. Thus, regulation 6 of the Management of Health & Safety at Work Regulations 1999 imposes a duty on every employer to provide his employees with such health surveillance as is appropriate 'having regard to the risks to their health and safety'. Paragraph 30 of the accompanying Approved Code of Practice adds that health surveillance procedures can include 'clinical examination and measurements of physiological or psychological effects by an appropriately qualified practitioner'.

The contents of medical reports

- While the Access to Medical Reports Act 1988 accepts that an employer may have good reason for wanting a medical report on an employee's state of health, it recognises also that some medical reports may contain information which could prejudice a person's chances of finding and keeping work.

- Does an employer really need to be told that a job applicant is homosexual or that he once had a sexually-transmitted disease? Should a doctor tell an employer that one of his staff has the HIV virus or an alcohol or drug-related problem?

   Note: Principle 5 of the data protection principles in the Data Protection Act 1998 states that personal data must not be processed (eg kept on file) for longer than is necessary, given the reason for securing that data in the first place. Information which relates to an employee's physical or mental health or condition or his sexual life falls within the category of 'sensitive personal data' and should not be processed other than in accordance with the 1998 Act (as to which, see **Data protection** elsewhere in this handbook).

- In the final analysis, it is up to an employee's (or job applicant's) own doctor to decide whether such information should be supplied – given the nature of the employee's job and the questions raised by the employer. What the 1988 Act does is give an employee the right to intercept his (or her) doctor's medical report, to challenge the relevance or accuracy of some of the information contained in the report, to ask his doctor to remove any prejudicial or irrelevant information, to add his own comments and, as a last resort, to refuse to allow the report to go forward.

Procedure

- In the text that follows, the expression *employee* should be taken to include job applicant; and the expression *employer* to include *prospective employer.*

  If an employer wishes to apply to an employee's own doctor for a report on his recent medical history and current state of health he must:

  (a) notify the employee in writing that he wishes to make the application;

  (b) obtain the employee's written consent (reminding him at the same time that he has the right under the 1988 Act to withhold that consent);

  (c) advise the employee (again in writing) that he has the right also to see the medical report before it is supplied (even if he has previously indicated that he does not wish to see it); to ask his doctor to amend any part of the report which he considers to be inaccurate, misleading or irrelevant; to attach his own written comments to the report if his doctor is unwilling to alter the report; and (in the final analysis) to refuse to allow the report to go forward;

  (d) make sure that the employee understands that it is his responsibility (and his alone) to approach his doctor and arrange with him to see or take a copy of the medical report before it is sent forward, emphasising that he must do so within 21 days after the date of the employer's application.

  When applying to an employee's doctor for a medical report, the employer should not only confirm that the employee has consented to his doing so, but must also indicate whether the employee wishes to be given access to the report before it is sent.

- If the employee does not exercise his (or her) statutory right to see the report within 21 days after his employer's application to his doctor, the doctor need wait no longer and can send the report to the employer. If the doctor has been told that the employee does *not* wish to preview the report, he (or she) is free to send it as soon as it is ready. The employee can change his mind about not wanting to see the report. But he will need to act swiftly if he is to have any chance of intercepting the report before his doctor mails it to the employer.

Exceptions

- The 1988 Act recognises that a doctor may be reluctant to show some parts of his (or her) medical report to a patient if doing so would cause distress. The medical report may, for example, indicate that the man or woman is suffering from an incurable illness or that major surgery is required. In those circumstances, the doctor may either withhold the report from the employee altogether or allow him or her to see only parts of it. If he adopts either course, he must write to the employee explaining what he has done and his motives for doing so. At this point the employee may refuse to allow the report to go forward.

Enforcement of the 1988 Act

- If an employee or job applicant is denied (or seems likely to be denied) his (or her) statutory rights under the 1988 Act, he may apply to the county court (or sheriff's court in Scotland) for an order directing his employer or doctor to comply with the relevant requirement of the Act. A refusal to comply with the terms of any such court order would be a contempt of court.

N

NATIONAL MINIMUM WAGE

Key points

- Since the coming into force on 1 April 1999 of the National Minimum Wage Regulations 1998 (as amended), every UK worker aged 18 and over now has the statutory right to be paid no less than the national minimum wage (NMW) appropriate to his or her age.

- From 1 October 2002 to 30 September 2003, the NMW for workers aged 22 and over is £4.20 an hour. For workers aged 18 to 21, inclusive, it is £3.60 an hour. And, for workers aged 22 and over who are in receipt of 'accredited training' (on at least 26 days in their first six months of employment) it is also £3.60 an hour. At present, there is no NMW for workers under the age of 18. Certain payments made to workers (such as overtime premium payments, shift allowances, cost of living allowances, and the like) do not count towards the NMW; nor do most benefits in kind. Some deductions from pay also do not count. Deductions and payments which do or do not count towards the NMW are discussed later in this section.

  Note: The term 'accredited training' means training undertaken with a *new* employer during normal working hours (at or away from the workplace) which leads to a vocational qualification approved by the Secretary of State for Education. It does *not* apply to in-house training devised and provided by employers. At present, there is no NMW for workers aged 16 and 17 (see also *Excluded categories* below).

- A refusal or failure to pay the appropriate NMW is an offence, the penalty for which, on summary conviction, is a fine of up to £5,000 for each offence. Inland Revenue enforcement officers have the right to enter an employer's premises and to inspect wage records. A failure to keep adequate or accurate records, or an attempt to obstruct inspectors in the exercise of their functions, will also lead to prosecution and a fine of up to £5,000.

- Workers who are dismissed, selected for redundancy, or subjected to any other detriment, for questioning or challenging their employer's refusal or failure to pay the NMW, or for bringing proceedings before a tribunal or court, will likewise be entitled to compensation. Indeed, a worker who suspects that he or she is being paid less than the NMW may write to his or her employer demanding to see the relevant wage records, and must be supplied with those records within 14 days. An employer who fails to comply with such a request will be ordered to pay the worker in question the sum of £288 (that is to say, 80 times the level of the NMW), as well as compensation for the shortfall in pay.

Practical guidance

Meaning of 'worker'

- A 'worker' is a person who does work for an employer, either under a contract of employment or under a contract *sui generis* (that is to say, of its own kind). In short, the term encompasses employees, seasonal and casual workers, freelances, agency 'temps', pieceworkers (or output workers), workers paid entirely on commission, and homeworkers. All such workers must be paid no less than the appropriate NMW rate. As a 'rule of thumb', a worker's employer is the person (or organisation) who (or which) pays the worker's wages or salary, and deducts payments in respect of PAYE tax and NI contributions. It is important to stress that workers over normal retiring age or the state pension age (60 or 65, as the case may be) must be paid the appropriate NMW rate if they are workers.

- The only category of person who is not a 'worker' in this sense, and who does not qualify for the NMW, is the self-employed person. The genuinely self-employed person is engaged under a contract for services to carry out a specific task or activity in return for an agreed fee. The self-employed person prepares his (or her) own annual accounts for submission to the Inland Revenue, pays his own taxes and National Insurance contributions, submits his own invoices (preferably on a preprinted form), is (where appropriate) registered for VAT, provides his own tools and equipment, and is not under the direction or control of any other person. An employer would be well-advised to demand proof of 'self-employed' status from any person who holds himself out to be self-employed.

- Employers who choose to categorise some or all of their workers as 'self-employed', in order to avoid paying the appropriate NMW rate, are liable to prosecution and heavy fines – unless they are in a position to convince Inland Revenue enforcement officers that the workers in question are indeed self-employed.

- Agency 'temps' are usually employed by the employment business which hires them out to client employers. It is the employment business (not the client employer) that is responsible both for paying a temp's wages (within clearly defined time limits) and for ensuring that their workers are paid the appropriate NMW rate.

Excluded categories

- The NMW need not be paid until their 19th birthdays to 18-year-old apprentices who began their apprenticeships at 16 or 17. Nor need it be paid to apprentices age 19 and over during the first 12 months' of their apprenticeships or until their 26th birthdays, whichever occurs sooner. An 'apprentice', for these purposes, is a person who is either employed under a contract of apprenticeship or who is taking part in the Government's Modern Apprenticeship programme.

- Also excluded from the NMW during their placements with employers are 'sandwich course' students, students obtaining work experience, teacher trainees, and trainees on Government-funded schemes (such as the 'New Deal', 'Work-based learning for adults', and so on).

  Note: Also excluded are members of the armed forces, share fishermen, voluntary workers (who receive no pay for their time apart from genuine expenses), and prisoners.

- But those exclusions do *not* apply to students taking a 'gap year' between school (or college) and university. Nor do they apply to students undertaking post-graduate studies (whether taking up employment independently or as an adjunct to their studies). All such people must be paid no less than the appropriate NMW rate during their employment.

Deductions and payments that do or do not count towards the NMW

- As was mentioned above, there are some payments included in a worker's gross wages or salary (such as overtime premium payments and shift allowances) which do *not* count towards the NMW; and there are others which do. Likewise, there are certain benefits in kind and deductions from pay (or payments made to an employer) which must be excluded from calculations. There is, for example, no upper limit on the amount of rent that an employer may charge a worker for 'live-in' accommodation (a not uncommon feature of employment in the hotel and leisure industries). However, as is explained below (see *Live-in accommodation*) that portion of the rent paid by a worker, which exceeds a specified hourly, daily or weekly amount, does not count towards the

NMW. In short, the excess amount must be deducted from the worker's gross wages or salary in order to establish whether the worker in question is being paid the appropriate NMW rate.

- Other deductions (or payments by a worker) that do not count include deductions in respect of meals compulsorily purchased by a worker from his or her employer; and deductions in respect of uniforms or protective clothing and equipment. The object of the exercise here is to ensure that employers do not use deductions from pay (or demands for certain payments from workers) as a means of 'clawing-back' (or reducing the effect of) the NMW.

Deductions and payments that do not count

- The following components of a worker's gross wages or salary in a particular pay reference period (week, fortnight or month) do *not* count as part of the NMW:

  - overtime premium payments;
  - shift allowances;
  - premium payments for work carried out on a bank or public holiday;
  - unsociable hours payments;
  - danger money;
  - standby or on call allowances;
  - travel allowances;
  - cost of living allowances (eg 'London weighting' payments); and
  - payments carried forward from a previous pay reference period.

  Benefits in kind provided by an employer (whether taxable or not) do *not* count towards the NMW. These include:

  - a company car;
  - petrol, oil and lubricants;
  - meals (or the notional value of such meals) if, as is unlikely, a worker is required by his (or her) contract to take his meals in a staff or works canteen;
  - luncheon vouchers (or the notional value of such vouchers);
  - the employer's contributions to an occupational pension plan;

- relocation expenses;

- free health insurance; and

- that part of the rent charged by an employer for live-in accommo-dation which exceeds a specified hourly, daily or weekly amount (see *Live-in accommodation below*).

Furthermore, tips paid directly to a worker (or distributed amongst fellow workers), which are not paid through the payroll, do not count towards the NMW. The same applies to deductions from pay (or payments made to an employer) in respect of protective clothing and equipment, uniforms, dry cleaning or laundry costs, tools, etc.

Deductions and payments that count towards the NMW

Deductions or payments that do count towards the NMW include:

- incentive payments, bonuses, commission;

- tips, gratuities and service charges collected centrally by the employer and distributed to a worker through the payroll (but not otherwise);

- deductions in respect of PAYE tax and NI contributions;

- a worker's pension contributions;

- fine imposed in accordance with a worker's contract for miscon-duct (including authorised deductions in respect of cash shortages or stock deficiencies);

- deductions in respect of overpaid wages or salary (or overpaid expenses);

- deductions (or payments) in respect of live-in accommodation up to a prescribed maximum (see *Live-in accommodation* below);

- voluntary deductions in respect of trade union dues, private health insurance, membership of a social club;

- deductions or payments in respect of meals voluntarily purchased by a worker from a staff or works canteen; and

- deductions in respect of goods and services *voluntarily* purchased by a worker from his or her employer.

Live-in accommodation

- Live-in accommodation is a common feature of employment in the hotel and leisure industry, both for the convenience of employers and that of workers. Although technically there is no upper limit on the amount of rent that a worker may be required to pay for live-in accommodation, the 1998 Regulations make it clear that employers will not lessen the effect of the NMW Regulations by charging more than a prescribed amount for such accommodation.

- The most that an employer may offset against the NMW by way of accommodation charges is 57 pence for each hour of a worker's contractual weekly hours or £19.95 a week, whichever is the lower of those two amounts. In short, the maximum that may be offset against the NMW is £22.75 a week. If a worker works a 35-hour week, the maximum that may be offset against his or her NMW is £19.95 a week; if a 30-hour week, £17.10; and so on.

- If a worker occupies live-in accommodation for less than a whole week (eg, five days a week), the maximum daily amount that may be offset against the NMW is whichever is the lower of 57p per hour for each of the worker's contracted (or average) daily hours or £3.25. A day for these purposes is the period from midnight to midnight.

Categories of worker

- Most workers in industry and commerce can be categorised as salaried or hourly-paid. Other categories include seasonal workers, casual workers, workers paid wholly or mainly by commission, agency 'temps', and homeworkers.

Salaried workers

- The ranks of salaried workers traditionally include senior executives, managers, accountants, clerks, secretaries, etc, most of whom are paid at regular monthly intervals by cheque or credit transfer to their bank accounts. A salaried worker's pay usually remains the same month after month (unless absent from work because of illness or injury or on maternity or parental leave, or on approved leave of absence without pay). A salaried worker's pay will also encompass meal and rest breaks, and annual holidays.

- Many salaried workers (especially those in the middle and higher echelons of management) are not paid for overtime working, it being a feature of their contracts that they work such additional hours as may be necessary for the more efficient performance of their duties. Given that salaried jobs are no longer the exclusive preserve of 'white-collar' workers, there will, of course, be salaried workers who are relatively lowly-paid (eg, in the region of £8,000 to £10,000 per annum), whose hourly rate of pay in a particular pay reference period may dip below the appropriate NMW rate – the more so if any such worker routinely works overtime hours (paid or otherwise) or is paying more than £22.75 a week in rent for 'live-in' accommodation provided by his or her employer. As was explained earlier, there are a number of payments or deductions from pay that do *not* count towards the NMW.

Note: The term 'pay reference period' means the period (not exceeding one month) in respect of which wages or salary are normally paid (monthly, weekly, fortnightly, etc). Workers who are paid weekly have a pay reference period of one week. Those who are paid monthly have a pay reference period of one month. Some workers, notably casual workers will have a pay reference period of one day. Workers who are paid less frequently than once every month (eg every three months) nonetheless have a pay reference period of one month. In short, the maximum pay reference period for any worker (under the 1998 Regulations) is one month.

Example

- 24-year-old Mary Brown works as an Assistant Manager at a small London hotel. She earns a salary of £9,600 per annum, and is contracted to work a 5-day, 40-hour week (including meal and rest breaks). She is paid monthly, receives all her meals free of charge, but occupies 'live-in' accommodation, provided by her employer, for which she pays rent of £200 a month. Mary often works more than 40 hours a week when the hotel is busy or there are staff shortages. She is paid time-and-a-half for all hours worked in excess of 173 hours a month.

- Mary's gross salary for June 2003 (before the deduction of PAYE tax and NI contributions) was made up as follows:

Monthly pay (£9,600, divided by 12):	£800.00
Overtime pay (23 hours @ £6.92/hour):	£159.16
Gross pay:	**£959.16**
less rent of £200:	£639.38

Was Mary paid less than the NMW for June 2003? To answer that question, Mary's overtime premium payments (£53.05) must be disregarded, as must all rental payments in excess of £22.75 a week (or £98.58 a month) (ie, £101.42). These 'specified reductions' effectively reduce Mary's gross pay for May 2000 from £959.16 to £804.69. As Mary worked a total of 196 hours during May, her hourly rate of pay for that month was £4.11, that is to say, £0.09 per hour less than the NMW of £4.20 for her age. It follows that Mary's employer must pay her an additional £17.64 for June 2003.

Hourly-paid workers

- As the term implies, hourly-paid workers are paid for the number of hours they work each week or month (whatever the pay reference period). They are traditionally paid overtime for all hours worked in excess of their standard (or contractual) working hours, but are not normally paid for meal and rest breaks. If they work a system of shifts, they may be paid a shift allowance. If they work normally on a bank or public holiday, or on a rest day, they may be paid at a higher hourly rate for such work or they may have a contractual right to an equivalent amount of paid time off work to be taken at an agreed later date. If employed under a contract of employment, their terms and conditions of employment (including working hours, rate of pay, shift allowances, overtime premium payments, and the like) must be explained in the written statement of employment particulars necessarily issued to each of them within two months of the date on which their employment began.

- Hourly-paid workers must be paid no less than the appropriate NMW rate for all hours worked in the standard pay reference period. Working hours do not include recognised meal and rest breaks (even if the worker is paid during such breaks, or works throughout a recognised meal or rest-break), absences from work occasioned by annual holidays, sick leave, maternity leave, parental leave, time off for dependants, and so on. Nor do they include time when a worker is engaged in a strike or other form of industrial action (including a 'go slow' or 'work to rule'). Whether or not a worker is entitled to be paid all or part of his (or her) wages when sick or injured will depend on the terms of his contract (although he will have the qualified right to be paid statutory sick pay at such times). Payments in respect of maternity leave and annual holidays are regulated by statute (notably the Employment Rights Act 1996 and the Working Time Regulations 1998, discussed elsewhere in this book).

- An hourly-paid worker who is on standby or 'on-call', at or near his (or her) workplace (or who is at work, as required, but is not actually provided with work, or is unable to work because of a machine or plant breakdown) must be paid no less than the NMW for that time. The same applies when a worker is travelling between jobs, but not when he is travelling from and to his home and place of work.

Piece-workers and 'output' workers

- There are workers who do not receive a basic wage, but are paid entirely on the basis of the work they do, the sales (or number of telephone calls) they make or the goods they produce. Such people may work from home or in premises provided by their employer. Unless (as is unlikely) they are genuinely self-employed, every such worker must be paid no less than the appropriate NMW wage rate for every hour worked (based on what their employer agrees is a fair estimate of the hours they work). The NMW rules for pieceworkers, output workers, and the like, are complicated. Interested employers are advised to acquire a copy of the DTI's *Detailed Guide to the National Minimum Wage* (Ref URN 99/662), copies of which are available from the address given at the end of this section.

Records

- Regulation 38 of the 1998 Regulations imposes a duty on employers to keep records 'sufficient to establish that he is remunerating [workers] at a rate at least equal to the national minimum wage'. Those records must be kept in a form which enables the information about a worker in respect of any one reference period to be produced in a single document. Furthermore, the employer must keep those records (either in paper form or on a computer or computer disk) for a rolling three-year period and must make those records available either to a worker (on request) or an Inland Revenue enforcement officer (on demand). An employer who fails to keep such records, or who keeps or produces false or inaccurate records, is guilty of an offence and liable on summary conviction to a fine of up to £5,000 – for each and every such offence.

Enforcement and penalties for non-compliance

- As was mentioned above, the National Minimum Wage Act 1998 and its accompanying regulations are policed and enforced by Inland Revenue enforcement officers. Section 14 of the 1998 Act cautions employers that enforcement officers have the power to enter an employer's premises (at reasonable times), to inspect and take copies of pay records, to require an explanation of any such records, to ask questions, and to talk to workers. Enforcement officers can also issue enforcement notices requiring an employer to pay the appropriate rate of NMW to identified workers or to make up the shortfall between the NMW and the wages actually paid to those workers (backdated as appropriate). A failure to comply with the terms of an enforcement notice will prompt the issue of a penalty notice requiring the recalcitrant employer to pay £7.40 a day to each affected worker for every day of continued noncompliance.

- There are a number of criminal offences under the 1998 Act, each of which attracts a penalty of up to £5,000 for each offence. These are:

  - a refusal or wilful neglect to pay the appropriate NMW rate;

  - a failure to maintain adequate and accurate payroll records and time sheets;

  - keeping false or inaccurate records;

  - intentionally obstructing an Inland Revenue enforcement officer in the exercise of his or her authority; and

  - refusing or neglecting to give information to an Inland Revenue enforcement officer.

Complaints by workers

- Workers who know (or suspect) that they are not being paid the appropriate NMW rate have the right to ask to see their payroll records. Any such request must be made in writing. An employer who fails or refuses to produce those records within 14 days, or who prevaricates or refuses to make those records available, will be ordered by an employment tribunal to pay the worker in question an amount equal to 80 times the appropriate NMW rate. A worker may also apply to a tribunal or county court for the recovery of any amount of wages or salary which fell short of the NMW. Any such application must be lodged with the nearest Regional Office of the Employment Tribunals on Form IT1 within three months of the employer's alleged refusal or failure.

- Workers have no need to resign in order to pursue their statutory rights before an employment tribunal. If denied their right to be paid no less than the appropriate NMW rate, they may complain to an employment tribunal and/or invoke the assistance of an Inland Revenue enforcement officer. An employer who dismisses such a worker, or selects him (or her) for redundancy, or subjects him to some other detriment (eg, by demoting or transferring him, withholding a promised pay rise, or by denying opportunities for overtime, etc) for challenging or questioning the employer's refusal or failure to pay the NMW (before a tribunal or court, or otherwise), or for asserting his statutory rights, will be ordered to pay the worker a substantial amount of compensation. In such situations, workers may pursue their rights before the tribunals regardless of their age or length of service at the material time.

Further information

- The Department of Trade & Industry's (DTI) *Detailed Guide to the National Minimum Wage* (Ref URN99/662) may be obtained without charge from the DTI Publication Orderline, ADMAIL 528, London, SW1W 8YT (Telephone: 0870 1502 500; fax: 0870 1502 333; or email: publications@dti.gsi.gov.uk).

  For further assistance on the national minimum wage, employers may call NMW Enquiries on **0845 6000 678** or write to the following address:

  NMW Enquiries
  Freepost PHQ1
  Newcastle upon Tyne
  NE98 1ZH

NOTICE OF TERMINATION OF EMPLOYMENT
(Statutory minimum notice)

Key points

- The written statement of employment particulars (often referred to as the 'contract of employment'), given to an employee when he (or she) first starts work with an employer, must include particulars of 'the length of notice which the employee is obliged to give and entitled to receive to determine his contract of employment' (section 1(4)(e), Employment Rights Act 1996).

Notice to be given by the employer

- By section 86(1) of the 1996 Act, a person who has been continuously employed for a period of *one month or more* is entitled to receive the following minimum notice from his employer to terminate his (or her) contract of employment:

  (a) at least one week's notice of termination if he has been continuously employed for less than two calendar years;

  (b) at least one week's notice of termination for each complete calendar year of continuous employment, if he has been continuously employed for two years or more but less than 12 years; and

(c) at least 12 weeks' notice of termination if he has been continuously employed for 12 years or more.

So far as the term 'continuous employment' is concerned, an employee is deemed to be in continuous employment if he (or she) is employed under a contract of employment. This means that every employee (regardless of the number of hours he normally works in a week) is entitled to notice to terminate his employment, as described above, so long as he has been continuously employed for the requisite period. For further information, please turn to the section titled **Continuous employment** elsewhere in this handbook.

Notice to be given by the employee

• Unless his (or her) contract specifies a longer period of notice, an employee who has been continuously employed for one month or more need only give his employer a minimum of one week's notice to terminate his contract of employment. That minimum notice period of one week does not increase with length of service (*ibid.* section 86(2)).

Summary dismissal

• Any employee, who is summarily dismissed for gross misconduct (which is effectively a repudiation of his (or her) contract of employment), thereby forfeits his entitlement to notice (statutory or contractual). See **Disciplinary rules and procedure** elsewhere in this handbook.

Waiver of right to notice

• There is nothing in law to prevent either party to a contract of employment (whether employer or employee) waiving his or her right to notice on any occasion, or from accepting a payment in lieu of notice. For instance, an employer may agree to allow an employee (who has resigned) to quit his job earlier than the date on which the employee's notice expires. However, it is unlikely that he can insist on his doing so. If the employee agrees to leave early, his employer must nonetheless pay him money in lieu of wages or salary for the whole (or the remainder) of the notice period. Likewise, an employee, who has been dismissed, in circumstances which do not warrant summary dismissal, is under no obligation to accept an offer of money in lieu of notice (unless the contract of employment stipulates otherwise) and may insist on working out his notice period. Finally, if an employer's conduct is such that an employee is entitled to terminate his contract of employment without notice, the employee may do so either with or without notice (as to which, see **Constructive dismissal** elsewhere in this handbook) (ibid. sections 86(6) and 95(l)(c)).

Rights of employee during notice period

- If, during his (or her) period of notice (whether given by the employer or the employee), an employee has normal working hours and during any part of those normal working hours he (or she) is ready and willing to work, but no work is provided for him (or her) to do, or he is incapable of work because of illness or injury, or he is absent from work on approved holidays, parental leave, or wholly or partly because of pregnancy or childbirth, his employer must pay him his normal remuneration during that notice period (but see *Exceptions to the rule* below). However, that right arises if (but only if) the period of notice required to be given by the employer under the terms of the employee's contract of employment is the same as (or not more than one week more generous than) the statutory minimum notice required by section 86(1) (*ibid.* sections 88 and 89, as amended by Schedule 4, Part III, paragraphs 10 and 11, Employment Relations Act 1999).

  Note: Any payment already made by the employer to the employee during the relevant part of the notice period (whether by way of sick pay, statutory sick pay, maternity pay, statutory maternity pay, holiday pay, or otherwise) will go towards discharging the employer's liability under sections 88 or 89, and 90, of the 1996 Act.

- For example, an employee with 10 years' continuous service, who is dismissed while absent from work on sick leave, will be entitled to be paid his (or her) normal wages or salary while serving out his notice (so long as the notice to which he is entitled under his contract of employment does not exceed 11 weeks) – even if he has long since exhausted any contractual or statutory entitlement to sick pay. An employee who resigns during a period of sick leave is likewise entitled to be paid a week's pay (in respect of the period of notice prescribed by *ibid.* section 86(2)) so long as the notice which he is entitled to receive from his employer does not exceed the prescribed statutory minimum by more than one week).

- The same general rules apply to the employee who has no normal working hours under the contract of employment in force during the notice period. Subject to the proviso that the notice required to be given by the employer to **terminate** the contract must not be more than one week more generous than the statutory minimum period of notice, an employee who resigns or is dismissed must be paid his or her normal remuneration during that statutory notice period. However, the employer's liability to pay in these circumstances is conditional on the employee being ready and willing to do work of a reasonable nature and amount to earn a week's pay *(ibid.* section 89(1)).

Exceptions to the rule

- However, no payment is due in consequence of a notice to terminate given by an absentee employee if, after the notice is given and before that notice expires, he (or she) takes part in a strike or other industrial action against his employer *(ibid.* section 91(2)). The same rule applies if the employee breaks the contract by failing to serve out his full notice period. Indeed, where the notice was given by the employee, the employer's liability to pay does not arise until that notice period expires *(ibid.* sections 88(3) and 89(3)).

- Nor is there any entitlement to payment in respect of a period during which the employee is absent from work either with his (or her) employer's permission (eg, approved leave of absence without pay) or in consequence of a request for time off work (within the meaning of Part VI of the 1996 Act or sections 168 to 170 of the Trade Union & Labour Relations (Consolidation) Act 1992: time off for trade union duties and activities).

- Likewise, if an employee who has resigned or been dismissed breaks his (or her) contract of employment and is summarily dismissed for gross misconduct while serving out his notice period, his employer may lawfully withhold any amount otherwise payable to the employee in respect of that part of the notice period which falls after the date on which that summary dismissal took place *(ibid.* section 91(4)).

  See also the sections titled **Dismissal, Employment tribunals and procedure**, and **Written particulars of terms of employment** elsewhere in this handbook.

Wrongful dismissal

- An employee who is wrongfully dismissed (ie, without benefit of the notice to which he (or she) is entitled under his contract of employment, or in law) may nowadays pursue a claim for damages before an employment tribunal. But, if the amount he is claiming exceeds £25,000, he would be best-advised to pursue his case through the civil courts which have concurrent jurisdiction in these matters. See **Employment tribunals and procedure** and **Wrongful dismissal** elsewhere in this handbook.

Note: The jurisdiction of the employment tribunals was extended on 12 July 1994 to include all breach of employment contract disputes which arise or are still unresolved at the end of a period of employment. The relevant statutory orders, saved by section 3 of the Employment Tribunals Act 1996, are the Employment Tribunals Extension of jurisdiction (England & Wales) Order 1994, and the Employment Tribunals Extension of jurisdiction (Scotland) Order 1994.

O

OVERTIME EMPLOYMENT
(*Statutory restrictions*)

Key points

- Until the coming into force, on 1 October 1998, of the Working Time Regulations 1998, there were few legal restrictions in the UK on the number of hours which an employee could be required to work. The 1998 Regulations, which extend to Great Britain only (there are cognate provisions in Northern Ireland legislation) implement Council Directive 93/104/EC of 23 November 1998 'concerning certain aspects of the organisation of working time'. They also incorporate Council Directive 94/33/EC of 22 June 1994 'on the protection of young people at work'.

- The reader will note that the protection afforded by the 1998 Regulations extends to all workers, and not just to those who are employees in the strict legal sense of the word. In short they apply to any person (casual, seasonal, freelance, trainee on work experience, agency 'temp', and so on) who undertakes to do or perform personally any work or service for an employer – whether for a day or two here an there, for a couple of weeks, or whatever. However, they do *not* apply to persons who are genuinely self-employed. An employer should not accept at face value any statement by a worker that he (or she) is self-employed. There must be documentary evidence to support such a claim (eg, business accounts, letterhead, pre-printed invoices, VAT registration, etc). In doubtful cases, an employer should always seek the advice of the Inland Revenue.

The 48-hour week

- Under the 1998 Regulations (as amended by the Working Time Regulations 1999 and the Working Time (Amendment) Regulations 2002) adult workers (ie, workers aged 18 and over) cannot be required to work more than an average 48 hours a week (including overtime hours), calculated over a rolling or fixed reference period of 17 weeks. That reference period may be extended in prescribed circumstances to 26 or 52 weeks. However, there is no provision for averaging in the case of young workers under the age of 18, who have legally left school. A worker under the age of 18 cannot lawfully work, or be required to work for more than 8 hours a day or for more than 40 hours a week. See also **Women and young persons, employment of** elsewhere in this handbook.

- However, there is an opt-out facility that enables an adult worker to agree to work more than that average 48 hours, so long as he (or she) does so individually, voluntarily and in writing. That option is not, repeat, is not, available to workers under the age of 18. A purported general opt-out for the adult workers at large or for a particular group of workers, under the terms of a workforce or collective agreement, is void and unenforceable. The same applies to any term in a contract of employment that presumes to override a worker's rights under the 1998 Regulations. Furthermore, the opt-out agreement signed personally by an adult worker must remind that worker of his (or her) right to cancel the agreement on giving a specified period of notice (not exceeding three months). If the opt-out agreement makes no mention of the worker's right to change his mind, it may be cancelled by the worker giving his employer seven days' advance written notice of that decision (*ibid.* regulations 4 and 5).

- Any attempt on the part of an employer to pressurise a worker into opting out of the 48-hour week will not only invalidate the agreement but could also lead to criminal prosecution and a fine of up to £5,000, or more if a conviction is obtained on indictment. See also *Complaints to an employment tribunal* below.

Exceptions to the 48-hour rule

- The upper limit on working hours does not apply to managing executives and other persons with autonomous decision-making powers; nor does it apply to people whose working time is not measured or predetermined by their employers **or** who determine their own patterns of work (*ibid.* regulation 20(1)).

- The exception also applies to workers (such as travelling salesmen, repairmen, etc) whose working time is partly measured, predetermined or determined by the worker, and partly not. In such cases, the provisions in the 1998 Regulations which relate to weekly working time and night work apply only in relation to that part of the worker's work which is measured, predetermined or cannot be determined by the worker himself (or herself) (*ibid.* regulation 20(2), as inserted (with effect from 17 December 1999) by regulation 4 of the Working Time Regulations 1999).

Extending the reference period

- The standard reference period of 17 weeks, over which an adult worker's average weekly hours (including overtime hours) are calculated, may be extended (in special cases) to up to 26 weeks by an employer, or up to 52 weeks under the terms of a collective or workforce agreement – so long as the extension is for objective or technical reasons or reasons concerning the organisation of work. However, no collective or workforce agreement can override an adult worker's statutory right not to work more than an average 48-hour week. As was explained earlier, that is entirely a matter for the individual. The opt-out option is not available to workers under the age of 18, however willing a 16 or 17-year-old may be to work more than 48 hours in any week.

Work at night

- An adult worker (aged 18 and over) whose contract requires him or her to work at night (ie, for seven or more hours, including the period between midnight and 5:00 am) cannot legally be required to work more than an average eight hours in any 24-hour period calculated over a static or rolling reference period of 17 consecutive weeks. That said, employers must nonetheless see to it that adult night workers engaged in work involving special hazards or heavy physical or mental strain do not work at night for more that eight hours in any period of 24 consecutive hours.

- With the coming into force on 6 April 2003 of the Working Time (Amendment) Regulations 2002, young workers under the age of 18 must not be employed between 10:00 pm and 6:00 am or, where their contracts require them to work after 10:00 pm, between the hours of 11:00 pm and 7:00 am. However, those restrictions do not apply to young workers employed in hospitals or similar establishments or in connection with cultural, artistic, sporting or advertising activities. Young workers employed in agriculture, retail, hotels, bakeries, postal or newspaper deliveries or in catering activities (including bars and restaurants) may be employed up to midnight or after 4:00 am (but not between those hours) so long as they are given an opportunity of a free assessment of their health and capacities before being assigned to such work.

Enforcement

- Responsibility for enforcing the upper limits on working time (and night work) rests with health and safety inspectors and local authority environmental health officers. The latter have sweeping powers to enter an employer's premises, examine records, and talk to workers. Evidence of non-compliance could lead to prosecution and a heavy fine. A failure to maintain appropriate records or to obstruct an inspector in the exercise of his (or her) functions is also a serious matter which will attract swingeing penalties under the Health & Safety at Work etc Act 1974.

Complaints to an employment tribunal

- A worker may complain to an employment tribunal that he (or she) has been disciplined, dismissed, selected for redundancy, or subjected to some other detriment (eg, denial of overtime, forfeiture of a promised pay rise, etc) for challenging his employer's failure to comply with his rights under the 1998 Regulations, or for refusing to forego those rights, or for asserting those rights before a tribunal or court. If such a complaint is upheld, the employer will be ordered to pay the employee a substantial (or further substantial) award of compensation (*per* sections 45A, 48(1ZA), 49(5A), 101A, 104(4)(d) and 105(4A), Employment Rights Act 1996).

- It is as well to point out that a worker (whether employee or otherwise) has no need to resign in order to pursue his (or her) statutory rights before an employment tribunal, so long as the complaint is presented within three months of the employer's refusal or failure to comply. If the worker has resigned or been dismissed, the complaint must be presented within three months of the effective date of termination of his contract of employment or within such further period as the tribunal considers reasonable in the circumstances.

Written statement of employment particulars

- A worker who is an employee, in the strict legal sense of the word, has the legal right to be issued with a written statement explaining the principal terms and conditions of his (or her) employment. The statement must include information about any terms and conditions relating to hours of work (including any terms and conditions relating to normal working hours, night work and, by definition, time off for meals or rest) (per section 1, Employment Rights Act 1996). Any written statement (often inaccurately referred to as the 'contract of employment') which purports to override or undermine the employee's rights under the Working Time Regulations 1998 is void and unenforceable.

Note: The fact that the right to be issued with a written statement of employment particulars is restricted to workers who are employees (as distinct from workers who are not
employees), does not undermine the protection afforded to every worker under the
1998 Regulations.

Overtime premium payments

- Until the repeal on 30 August 1993 of Part II of the Wages Act 1986,
  wages councils were the only statutory bodies with the legal authority
  to require employers to pay premium payments to employees who
  work more than a specified number of hours a week.

- Blue collar workers, shop assistants, restaurant and hotel workers, clerical, administrative and secretarial staff, ordinarily expect to be paid at
  premium rates if they agree to work hours in excess of their normal
  weekly hours, or if their contracts of employment require them to do so
  – but they have no statutory right to such payments. Overtime
  premium payments are less likely to be paid to professional and managerial staff and are almost unheard of in the ranks of senior managers
  and company directors. Much will depend on what is written into an
  employee's contract of employment, bearing in mind that the written
  statement issued under Part I of the Employment Rights Act 1996 (see
  above) *must* include particulars of 'any terms and conditions relating to
  hours of work (including any terms and conditions relating to normal
  working hours)' (*ibid.* section 1(4)(c)).

- Collective agreements drawn up between employers and representative trade unions, and 'imported into' a worker's contract, usually
  specify overtime premium payments for all hours worked in excess of
  the standard working week. Workers in certain industries are traditionally paid double time for overtime hours on Sundays and bank holidays, supplemented in some cases (eg, in the hotel and catering
  industry) by equivalent paid time off work to be taken at a later date.

  Note: The Sunday Trading Act 1994 and the Betting, Gaming & Lotteries Act 1963 (as
  amended) gave shop workers and betting workers the right to opt-out of Sunday work.
  But neither of those enactments (the relevant provisions of which are now to be found
  in the Employment Rights Act 1996) requires employers to pay premium rates for overtime working. See **Sunday work** elsewhere in this handbook.

Compulsory and voluntary overtime

- Whether or not an employee can be fairly dismissed for refusing to
  work overtime will depend, in large part, on any related express or
  implied term in his (or her) contract of employment. If an employee's
  contract requires him to work a minimum of 10 overtime hours a week,
  he must work those hours (subject, of course, to any overriding legal

restriction on the maximum number of weekly hours (including over-time hours) under the 1998 Regulations, discussed earlier in this section). If, having accepted employment on those terms he then refuses to work any overtime at all, let alone 10 hours a week, he will have repudiated a fundamental term in his contract of employment and can be dismissed with impunity bearing in mind that difficulties of this sort will ordinarily be identified, discussed and resolved long before any such employee qualifies to pursue a complaint of unfair dismissal.

- If the same employee decides after one or more years' service that he is unhappy about working 10 hours' overtime a week, his dismissal for refusing to comply with the terms of his contract will still be held to have been fair so long as his employer can satisfy an employment tribunal that he had acted reasonably in treating the employee's refusal to work overtime (and his reasons for doing so) as a sufficient reason for dismissing him. See **Dismissal** elsewhere in this handbook.

- If an employee's contract is silent on the question of overtime, or simply states that overtime hours will be remunerated at such-and-such a rate, his (or her) refusal to work overtime on a single occasion is likely to be less damaging to his prospects of survival than his refusal to work overtime on any occasion. A great deal will depend on the partic-ular circumstances and the employee's general attitude to his work – an issue which is explored elsewhere in this handbook in the section titled **Cooperation, employee's duty of**.

Complaint to an employment tribunal

- On the termination of his (or her) employment, a worker (*qua* employee) can bring a 'breach of contract' claim before an employment tribunal if his employer had denied him his contractual right to work a specified number of overtime hours each week, and/or (provided that he had been continuously employed for one year or more) a complaint of unfair dismissal if dismissed for refusing to work overtime. Unfair dismissal and 'breach of contract' claims must be presented to a tribu-nal within three months of the effective date of termination of the employee's contract of employment. If such a complaint is upheld, the tribunal will make a declaration to that effect and will order the employer to pay damages or compensation (and/or, in the case of a dismissal) to reinstate or re-engage the employee in his original (or in an equivalent) job; as to which, please turn to the sections titled **Contract of employment** and **Dismissal** elsewhere in this handbook.

P

PARENTAL LEAVE

Key points

- Legislation giving employees (in their capacities as parents or adoptive parents) to be granted up to 13 weeks' unpaid parental leave (18 weeks, in the case of a child awarded a disability living allowance) is to be found in Part III of the Maternity & Parental Leave etc Regulations 1999, as amended by the Maternity & Parental Leave (Amendment) Regulations 2001, implementing Council Directive 96/34/EC of 3 June 1996 'on the framework agreement on parental leave'. Before the 1999 Regulations were amended, the right to take a period of unpaid parental leave was restricted to the parents of children born to (or placed with them for adoption) on or after 15 December 1999. Following a challenge mounted by the TUC, and the likelihood of proceedings before the European Court of Justice (ECJ), the UK Government conceded that the right to parental leave should have been made available to all employed parents with children under the age of five on 15 December 1999 as well as to adoptive parents of children under the age of 18, who were placed with them for adoption before that date (see *Rights of disenfranchised parents* at the end of this section).

- The right to parental leave is available only to those employees who have been continuously employed with their respective employers for a period of one year or more and who are either the parents of a child under the age of five (or under the age of 18, if the child has been awarded a 'disability living allowance') or who adopted a child on or after that date.

Nature of the right

- The natural or biological parents of a child born under the age of five may (as employees) each take up to 13 weeks' unpaid leave during the first five years of the child's life (that is to say, up to and including the child's fifth birthday). If the mother gives birth to twins, the entitlement applies to each of those children.

- The parents of a child placed with them for adoption may likewise (as employees) each take up to 13 weeks' unpaid parental leave during the first five years following the adoption or until the child turns 18, whichever occurs sooner.

- The parents of a disabled child (that is to say, a child who has been awarded a disability living allowance) may each take up to 18 weeks' unpaid parental leave until the child's 18th birthday.

- A week's leave, for these purposes, is a period of absence from work which is equal in duration to the period for which an employee is normally required to work in any week. For an employee whose working hours (under his or her contract) vary from week to week, a week's parental leave is a period of absence from work which is equal in duration to the total of the employee's contractual working hours in any one year divided by 52. An employee who takes parental leave for a day or two at a time, will have taken a full week's parental leave when the aggregate of those days equates to the number (or average number) of days in a week in which he or she is normally required to work. Overtime hours should not be included in calculations unless an employee is required under his or her contract to work a specified number of overtime hours each week.

- When dealing with a first request for parental leave, an employer has the right to ask for documentary evidence of parental responsibilities in the form of a birth certificate or adoption papers, or (in the case of a disabled child) evidence that a child has been awarded a disability living allowance. An employer may decline a request for parental leave until such time as that evidence is produced for his inspection.

How much leave can be taken at a time?

- The amount of parental leave that can be taken at any one time is a matter for negotiation and agreement between employees and their employers. If there is nothing in an employee's contract of employment (eg, in the written statement of employment particulars, a staff or works handbook, or in a company policy document) concerning an employee's right to parental leave – including the amount of parental leave that may be taken at any one time – the default (or fallback) provisions outlined in Schedule 2 to the 1999 Regulations will apply (see *The fallback scheme* below).

- Collective and workforce agreements can also be used to determine procedures for dealing with requests for parental leave, the amount of leave that may be taken at any one time; and so on. If an employee's terms and conditions of employment are determined by a collective agreement between the employer and a recognised independent trade union (and those terms are imported into each employee's contract of employment), that same forum may be used to give practical effect to an employee's statutory right to parental leave. A workforce agreement may be used for parental leave purposes if the terms and conditions of employees (or certain identifiable groups of employees) are not otherwise determined by agreement with a recognised independent trade union.

• An employer wishing to conclude a workforce agreement on parental leave must oversee the conduct of a secret ballot for the election of an appropriate number of employee representatives to negotiate the agreement with him. The number of representatives to be elected is a matter for the employer, depending on the size of the workforce or of the group of employees to be covered by the agreement. The employer must ensure that every employee is afforded an opportunity to vote in the ballot and to put his or her name forward as a candidate for election as an employee representative. The employer must provide the necessary facilities and must ensure that votes are counted fairly and accurately.

• To be valid, the resultant workforce agreement must be in writing; must be signed by the negotiating parties; must be shown to all affected employees (together with a guide explaining what the agreement means); and must last for no longer than five years. The agreement should (advisedly) lay down procedures for applying for parental leave, indicate how much leave may be taken at any one time; and, where appropriate, explain the circumstances in which the employer may postpone a request for parental leave (including the employee's right to take that postponed leave at a later date). If negotiations fail to produce a workforce agreement, the fallback parental leave scheme explained below automatically applies.

• Any term in a contract of employment (or in a collective or workforce agreement) that purports to override or undermine an employee's statutory right to parental leave is null and void. However, there is nothing to prevent an employer providing more generous parental leave provisions, including a period of paid parental leave.

Contractual and statutory rights during parental leave

• Although the continuity of a period of employment is not broken by periods of unpaid parental leave, the only contractual rights that prevail during such absences are those relating to notice periods, sever-ance payments (that is to say, payments in excess of statutory redun-dancy pay), and access to the employer's disciplinary or grievance procedures. Both parties to the employment contract are bound by their mutual and implied contractual duty of trust and confidence. From the employee's standpoint, this means that, during any period of parental leave, the employee must not work for any other employer and must not disclose to any unauthorised person confidential infor-mation relating to his (or her) employer's trade secrets, business activi-ties, etc (as to which, please turn to the section titled **Fidelity and trust, employee's duty of** elsewhere in this handbook.

- Apart from the express and implied contractual rights referred to in the previous paragraph, all other terms and conditions of employment (eg, the right to be paid, accrual of occupational sickness benefits, holidays in excess of the statutory minimum, occupational pension rights, etc) are held in suspense when an employee is absent from work on parental leave. An employer may, of course, choose to override these statutory limitations and may, for example, continue to allow an employee the use of a company car or mobile phone during his or her absence on parental leave.

- An employee's statutory rights remain undisturbed during parental leave, including the right not to be unfairly or unlawfully dismissed, the right to be paid a statutory minimum redundancy payment if dismissed for redundancy, and the entitlement to accrue paid annual leave under the provisions of the Working Time Regulations 1998.

Returning to work after parental leave

- An employee who takes parental leave for a period of four weeks or less (other than immediately after taking *additional* maternity leave) is enti-tled to return from leave to exactly the same job that he (or she) held before that period of leave began. That same rule applies if (having completed a minimum of one year's service) a woman takes parental leave for a period of four weeks or less immediately after the end of her *ordinary* maternity leave period.

- An employee who takes parental leave for a period of more than four weeks is likewise entitled to return from leave to the job in which he (or she) was employed before that period of absence began – unless it was not reasonably practicable for his employer to permit him to return to that job; in which case, the employee has the right to return to another job which is both suitable for him and appropriate for him to do in the circumstances. That same rule applies if (having completed one year's service with her employer), a woman takes more than four weeks' parental leave immediately after her *ordinary* maternity leave period.

- A woman who takes parental leave for a period of four weeks or less immediately after her *additional* maternity leave period is entitled to return from leave to the job in which she was employed before her maternity absence began – unless it would not have been reasonably practicable for her to return to that job if she had returned at the end of her additional maternity leave period, and it is still not reasonably practicable to permit her to do so at the end of that period of parental leave.

Note: As is demonstrated elsewhere in this handbook (in the section titled **Maternity rights**), an employee who is made redundant during her ordinary or additional maternity leave periods has the right to be offered suitable alternative employment under a contract that takes effect on the day following the day on which her original contract came to an end. Should she accept such an offer, her right to return to work after her ordinary or additional maternity leave is a right to return to work in that alternative job (not the job she held before her absence began). If the same employee takes parental leave immediately after either of her ordinary or additional maternity leave periods, it is the alternative job (not her original job) to which she has the qualified right to return.

The fallback scheme

- In the absence of any alternative arrangements (negotiated individually or under the terms of a collective or workforce agreement), the fallback scheme outlined in Schedule 2 to the 1999 Regulations comes into play. There is anecdotal evidence that most small- to medium-sized firms have adopted the fallback scheme.

- Under the fallback scheme, an employee may take parental leave in blocks (or tranches) of one week or more, unless the child in question is entitled to a disability living allowance, in which case the leave may be taken in single days or periods of less than one week. No more than four weeks' parental leave may be taken in any one year. For these purposes, a year is the period of 12 months which begins on the date on which the employee first became entitled to take parental leave in respect of the child in question (that is to say, either the day following the date on which the employee completed 12 months' continuous service with his (or her) employer, or the date on which the child was born or placed for adoption, whichever occurs later).

- Employees seeking parental leave under the fallback scheme must (if asked to do so) provide their employer with evidence of parental responsibility (in the form of a birth certificate, adoption papers or evidence that a child has been awarded a social security disability living allowance). Such evidence need only be produced on the first occasion that a parent submits a request for parental leave in respect of a child born or placed for adoption on or after 15 December 1999 (although, strictly speaking, an employer has the right to demand such evidence each time the same employee seeks further tranches of parental leave). The procedure may, of course, be repeated in the case of a second or subsequent child.

- As a rule, a request for parental leave must specify the dates on which the period of leave is to begin and end, and must be submitted to the employer at least 21 days before the date on which the requested period of leave is to begin. If the applicant is a father-to-be, the request for leave must be made at least 21 days before the beginning of the expected week of childbirth (EWC), and must specify that EWC and the duration of the intended period of leave. If a period of parental leave is to begin on the date on which a child is to be placed for adoption with an employee, the request for leave must be submitted at least 21 days before the beginning of the week in which the placement is to occur, and must specify the week in question and the duration of the intended period of leave. An employer's unreasonable refusal to agree to a request for parental leave will very likely be scrutinised by an employment tribunal, the more so if an employee's child was born prematurely or the intended adoption date was unexpectedly brought forward.

- The fallback scheme allows that an employer may postpone the intended start date of a requested period of parental leave for a period of up to six months. This is permissible if the employee's absence from work during that period is likely to cause undue harm to the employer's business. Such a situation might arise if a key worker has asked for parental leave at a very busy time of the year or if a number of employees have asked for overlapping periods of parental leave, leaving the employer seriously understaffed. However, postponement is not permissible if the requested period of parental leave is intended to begin on the day of a child's birth or on the day on which a child is to be placed with an employee for adoption.

- Within seven days of receiving a request for a period of parental leave, an employer intent on postpoing that period of leave must write to the employee explaining his reasons for the postponement and setting out alternative dates for the beginning and end of that leave. Before doing so, the employer must discuss the postponement with the employee and agree alternative start and finishing dates. A postponed period of parental leave must be of the same duration as the period of leave originally requested. An employee may take the postponed period of leave, even if the revised start date occurs after the child's fifth birthday (or after the fifth anniversary of the date on which the child was placed with the employee for adoption; or, in the case of a child entitled to a disability living allowance, after the child's 18th birthday).

Unfair dismissal

- An employee will be treated in law as having been unfairly dismissed if the reason (or principal reason) for the dismissal or selection for redundancy was that the employee had taken (or sought to take) parental leave. The same rule applies if the employee was dismissed or selected for redundancy for refusing to sign a workforce agreement or (as appropriate) for performing or proposing to perform or carry out his (or her) legitimate functions or activities as a workforce representative or as a candidate for election as such a representative. For further particulars, please turn to the section titled **Dismissal** elsewhere in this handbook.

Detrimental treatment

- An employee has the right also not to be punished, victimised or subjected to any other detriment (demotion, transfer, loss of promotion prospects, forfeiture of opportunities for training, etc) for exercising or proposing to exercise his (or her) statutory right to parental leave, or for refusing to sign a workforce agreement, or (where appropriate) for performing or proposing to perform his functions or activities as a workforce representative or as a candidate for election as such a representative. For further particulars, please turn to the section titled **Victimisation** elsewhere in this handbook.

Rights of disenfranchised parents

- As indicated in the preamble to this section, the rights of parents effectively disenfranchised by the 1999 Regulations, as originally enacted (including those who have since changed jobs and are now working for different employers), were reinstated on 10 January 2002 by the Maternity & Parental Leave (Amendment) Regulations 2001. What this means is that the parents of a child born or placed with them for adoption *before* 15 December 1999, and who have (or had) been continuously employed by their present (or a previous) employer for one year or more during the period from 15 December 1998 to 9 January 2002, inclusive, may take the parental leave previously denied to them (so long as they do so by 31 March 2005) – even if (in the case of employees who have since changed employers) they have yet to complete one year's continuous service with their new employers.

- Disenfranchised parents 'deemed' (in the circumstances described) to have worked for their present employers for the minimum qualifying period of one year, will forfeit their restored entitlement to parental leave until and unless they produce the child or children's birth certificates (or adoption papers) and, in the case of a disabled child, confirmation that the child has been awarded a disability living allowance. Disenfranchised parents who resigned or were dismissed from their previous jobs on or after 15 December 1999 must also produce evidence supporting their assertion that they had worked for a previous employer for one year or more during the period from 15 December 1998 to January 9, 2002, inclusive.

Further information

- The Department of Trade & Industry has published a booklet titled *Parental Leave: A Guide for Employers and Employees* (Ref URN 99/1193) copies of which may be obtained (free of charge) from:

  DTI Publications Orderline
  ADMAIL 528
  London
  SW1W 8YT
  Telephone: 0870 1502 500
  Fax: 0870 1502 333
  email: publications@dti.gsi.gov.uk

  See also **Adoption leave, Flexible working, Maternity rights** and **Paternity leave**, elsewhere in this handbook.

PART-TIME WORKERS

Key points

- With the coming into force on 1 July 2000 of the Part-Time Workers (Prevention of Less Favourable Treatment) Regulations 2000, any part-time worker who is treated less favourably (or believes that he (or she) has been treated less favourably) than a comparable full-time worker employed in the same establishment is entitled to demand and receive from his employer a written statement explaining the reasons for such treatment. If dissatisfied with his employer's explanations, the part-time worker may seek redress from an employment tribunal. Any part-timer who is dismissed, selected for redundancy or subjected to any other detriment for exercising or asserting his statutory rights under the 2000 Regulations, or for bringing proceedings before an employment tribunal, may complain (yet again) to an employment tribunal and will be awarded appropriate compensation.

Note: For the meaning of the term 'worker' in this and other contexts, please turn to page 411 under **National Minimum Wage**.

- The 2000 Regulations (as amended by the Part-time Workers (Prevention of Less Favourable Treatment) Regulations 2000 (Amendment) Regulations 2002) implement EC Directive 97/81/EC of 15 December 1997 'concerning the framework agreement on part-time work'.

Rights extended to all workers

- Under the Employment Protection (Part-Time Employees) Regulations 1995 – not to be confused with the Part-time Workers (Prevention of Less Favourable Treatment Regulations 2000 under discussion – part-time employees (as distinct from workers who are not 'employees' in the strict legal sense of the word) have long since enjoyed the same statutory rights as their full-time contemporaries (regardless of the number of hours they work, or are contracted to work, each week). However, the 2000 Regulations add a new dimension to that earlier legislation, by giving all part-time workers (whether 'employees' or otherwise) the right to be treated no less favourably than comparable full-time workers.

Meaning of comparable full-time worker

- For these purposes, a full-time worker is a 'comparable full-time worker' in relation to a part-time worker if, at the time when the allegedly less favourable treatment occurred, both workers are:

  (a) employed by the same employer under the same type of contract (see below);

  (b) are engaged in the same or broadly similar work, having regard, where relevant, to whether they have a similar level of qualifications, skills and experience; and

  (c) work at the same establishment (or, where there is no full-time worker working or based at the same establishment as the part-time worker, work at or are based at a different establishment within the employer's organisation).

Same type of contract?

- Regulation 2(3) of the 2000 Regulations (as amended) states that the following are not to be regarded as being employed under the same types of contract:

  (a) employees employed under a contract of employment, that is not a contract of apprenticeship;

  (b) employees employed under a contract of apprenticeship;

  (c) workers who are not employees;

  (d) any other description of workers that it is reasonable for the employer to treat differently from other workers on the gound that workers of that description have a different type of contract.

  For example, (a) is not the same type of contract as (b), (c) not the same type of contract as (a); and so on. In short, part-time workers who are not 'employees' do not have the right under the 2002 Regulations to compare their terms and conditions of employment with those of their full-time colleagues who *are* employees.

Less favourable treatment of part-time employees

- Part-time workers must not be treated less favourably than comparable full-time workers solely because they work part-time, unless different treatment is justified on objective grounds. For instance, a part-time employee should be paid the same basic rate of pay as a comparable full-time employee, and a part-time worker who is not an employee, the same as a comparable full-time worker engaged in the same or similar work. But a different hourly rate of pay may be justifiable on grounds of performance, so long as levels of performance are measured by a fair and consistently applied performance appraisal scheme.

- It is not uncommon for occupational sick pay schemes to provide more generous benefits to full-time workers (eg, full salary or wages for a period of up to three months in every 12-month period). By the same token, it is not unusual for part-time workers to receive no more than their entitlement to statutory sick pay (SSP) when incapacitated for work on health grounds. Such a sweeping differential is no longer acceptable, or justifiable. Indeed, it could give rise to allegations of unlawful sex discrimination, let alone a complaint to an employment tribunal under the 2000 Regulations. That same general prohibition applies to differential treatment in relation to occupational maternity and parental leave schemes, annual holiday entitlements, unpaid career breaks, access to occupational pension schemes, access to opportunities for training and promotion, redundancy selection criteria, etc (*ibid.* regulation 3).

- To avoid infringing the rights of part-time workers in their employ, employers will need to scrutinise the relative terms and conditions of their full-time and part-time workers and eliminate any discrepancies or anomalies that cannot be justified on objective grounds. In determining whether a part-time worker has been treated less favourably than a comparable full-time worker, the principle of *pro rata temporis* must be applied – unless it is inappropriate. It would be inappropriate, for example, to apply that principle to basic rates of pay (see above), access to pension schemes, opportunities for training, transfer or promotion, career break schemes, contractual maternity or parental leave, or redundancy selection criteria.

Note: The principle of *pro rata temporis* means that where a comparable full-time worker receives (or is entitled to receive) pay or any other benefit, a part-time worker is to receive (or be entitled to receive) not less than the proportion of that pay or other benefit that the number of his (or her) weekly hours bears to the number of weekly hours of the comparable full-time worker (*ibid.* regulation 1(1)).

Exception in relation to overtime payments

- The 2000 Regulations acknowledge that part-time workers have no right to premium payments in respect of overtime work until such time as their working hours (including overtime hours) during a particular pay reference period exceed the number of hours ordinarily worked by comparable full-time workers in that same period. But, once that point is reached, premium payments, for hours worked in excess of those full-time hours, must be the same as those paid to full-time workers (*ibid.* regulation 3(4)).

Written statement of reasons for less favourable treatment

- Any part-time worker, who considers that he (or she) is being treated less favourably than a comparable full-time worker, may ask his employer for a written statement explaining the reasons for that treatment. The employer must provide that statement within 21 days. The written statement is admissible in evidence before an employment tribunal (ibid. regulation 4).

- If an employer deliberately, and without reasonable excuse, fails to provide that written statement, an employment tribunal may draw any inference from that failure that it considers just and equitable (including an inference that the employer has infringed the part-time worker's statutory rights). It may also do so if the written statement is evasive or equivocal (*ibid.*).

Note: There is no need for a separate written statement if a part-time worker (*qua* employee) who has been dismissed has already requested and received a written statement of reasons for dismissal under section 91 of the Employment Rights Act 1996 (as to which, please turn to the section titled **Written reasons tor dismissal** elsewhere in this handbook) (*ibid.* regulation 4(4)).

Unfair dismissal and detrimental treatment

- A part-time employee (who is *not* a worker) and is dismissed or selected for redundancy will be treated in law as having been unfairly dismissed if the reason (or, if more than one, the principal reason) for his (or her) dismissal or selection was that he:

  (a) had complained to an employment tribunal about an alleged infringement of his rights under the 2000 Regulations;

  (b) had asked his employer for a written statement of the reasons for his less favourable treatment;

  (c) had given evidence or information in proceedings before an employment tribunal brought by another worker;

  (d) had alleged (in good faith) that his employer had infringed the 2000 Regulations;

  (e) had refused (or proposed to refuse) to forego a right conferred on him by the 2000 Regulations; or

  (f) that his employer believed or suspected that the employee had done (or intended to do) any of the things mentioned in (a) to (e) above

  (*ibid.* regulation 5(1), (3) and (4)).

  A part-time worker who has been victimised, disciplined or subjected to any other detriment (including dismissal in the case of a worker who is *not* an employee), on any of the grounds (a) to (f) specified above, has the right to refer the matter to an employment tribunal without having to resign in order to do so (*ibid.* regulation 5(2), (3) and (4)).

Complaints to employment tribunals, etc

- A part-time employee (regardless of his or her age or length of service at the material time) may complain to an employment tribunal that his employer has infringed his statutory rights under the 2000 Regulations – either by subjecting him to a detriment or some other punishment, or by dismissing him or selecting him for redundancy. Such a complaint must be presented within three months of the alleged detrimental treatment or, if the employee has been dismissed, within three months of the effective date of termination of the employee's contract of employment. A tribunal may consider a complaint which is out of time if, in all the circumstances of the case, it considers that it is just and equitable to do so.

- If a complaint of unlawful detrimental treatment is upheld, the tribunal will make a declaration to that effect and may order the employer to pay compensation to the worker and/or recommend that the employer take appropriate corrective action (within a specified period) to obviate or reduce the adverse effect on the worker of any matter to which the worker's complaint relates. A failure to take such corrective action will prompt the tribunal either to increase the amount of compensation already awarded to the worker or (if no compensation had previously been awarded) order the employer to pay compensation to the employee. The amount of compensation awarded in such circumstances will be such amount as the tribunal considers just and equitable, and will include compensation for the loss of any benefit which the worker might reasonably be expected to have had but for his employer's infringement of his rights under the 2000 Regulations (or the employer's failure to take the recommended corrective action) (*ibid.* regulation 6).

- A worker (*qua* employee) who has been dismissed (or selected for redundancy), in contravention of the 2000 Regulations, will be treated as having been unfairly dismissed (regardless of his or her age or length of service at the material time) and will be awarded compensation comprising a basic and compensatory award (maximum £7,800 and £53,500, respectively) and, where appropriate, an additional award of compensation of between 26 and 52 weeks' pay (as to which, please turn to the section titled **Dismissal** elsewhere in this handbook) (*ibid.* regulation 5(1)).

See also **Fixed-term employees** elsewhere in this handbook.

PATERNITY LEAVE

Key points

- With the coming into force on 8 December 2002 of the Paternity & Adoption Leave Regulations 2002, the biological father (or the responsible parent) of a child born on or after 6 April 2003 (or expected to be born on or after that date) has the qualified right to take one or two consecutive weeks' paternity leave (either, but not both) within 56 days of the child's date of birth. That same right extends to one or other of the parents of a child notified of having been matched with them for adoption (or placed with them for adoption) on or after that same date. A parent who qualifies for paternity leave (birth or adoption) may also be entitled to statutory paternity pay (SSP) during his or her absence from work.

- To be eligible for paternity leave, an employee must:

  (a) have been continuously employed by his employer for a period of not less than 26 weeks by the beginning of the 14th week before the expected week of the child's birth (or would have been continuously employed for that prescribed minimum 26-week period, but for the fact that the child was either born before the beginning of that 14th week or was stillborn after 24 weeks of pregnancy or has died); or

  (b) in the case of an adopted child, have been continuously employed by his or her employer for 26 or more weeks by the end of the week in which the child was placed with him or her and/or his or her wife or partner for adoption;

  (c) have or expect to have responsibility for the child's upbringing; and

  (d) be the child's biological father; or the mother's husband or partner; or, in the case of an adopted child, the adopter's spouse or partner.

- Employees claiming paternity leave must, if asked to do so by their employers, provide a form of self-certificate as evidence that they meet the eligibility conditions listed above. To that end, employers may either design their own self-certificates or use either of the Inland Revenue's model forms of self-certificate (Form SC3 [birth] or Form SC4 [adoption] available on request from Employer's Orderline on 08457 646 646.

- It is as well to point out that when a child is placed with an individual or with a couple for adoption, only one of them (male or female) is entitled to take up to 52 weeks' adoption leave (discussed elsewhere in this handbook in the section on **Adoption leave**). It is up to the couple in question to decide which of them is to take adoption leave. The other partner will then have the right (if eligible) to take one week or two consecutive weeks' paternity leave.

Timing of paternity leave

- An employee who qualifies for paternity leave must take his or her full entitlement to either one or two consecutive weeks' leave:

  (a) within 56 days of the child's date of birth or, if the child was born prematurely, within the period from the actual date of birth up to 56 days after the mother's expected week of childbirth (EWC); or

  (b) in the case of an adopted child, within 56 days of the date on which the child was placed with him or her and/or his or her partner for adoption (whether that date occurs sooner or later than expected).

  It should be noted that paternity leave can start on any day of the week beginning with the date on which the child is born or placed with the adopter for adoption or from the first day of the expected week of the child's birth, or from a chosen number of days or weeks after the date of the child's birth or adoption (whether this is earlier or later than expected) so long as the selected start date ensures that the full period of leave is completed within the prescribed 56-day period. Only one period of paternity leave is available, regardless of the number of children born or placed with an individual or couple for adoption.

Notification procedure

- To exercise their right to paternity leave, eligible employees must inform their employers of their intentions either by the end of the 15th week before the mother's expected week of childbirth (EWC) or, in the case of an adoptive parent or a couple who are adopting, within seven days of the adopter or adopters being notified by an approved adoption agency that he, she or they have been matched with a child. At the same time, an employee must:

  (a) specify the mother's EWC or the date on which the child is expected to be placed for adoption;

(b) whether he (or she) wishes to take one or two weeks' paternity leave; and

(c) when he (or she) wants that period of leave to start.

Employees who have correctly notified their employers of the date on which they intend to start their paternity leave may change their minds about that start date so long as they inform their employers of that change of mind at least 28 days before the revised start date (or as soon as is reasonably practicable, if circumstances dictate that they are not in a position to give 28 days' advance notice).

Statutory paternity pay

- To qualify for statutory paternity pay (SPP) during the paternity leave period, an eligible employee must have average weekly earnings equal to or greater than the current lower earnings limit for National Insurance purposes. For 2003/04, that lower earnings limit is £77 per week. SPP is payable at the same standard rate as statutory maternity pay (SMP), ie, £100 a week or 90% of the employee's average weekly earnings at the time, whichever is the lower of those amounts. Employers who have lawfully paid SPP to an employee will (as is the case with payments of SMP) be able to recover an amount equal to 92 per cent of the amount paid by deducting it from PAYE tax and NI contributions routinely remitted to the Inland Revenue at the end of each income tax month. Small employers (the total of whose NI contributions did not exceed £40,000 during the preceding tax year) will, on the other hand, be able to recover 100 per cent of the amount of SPP paid, plus a further 4.5 per cent to recoup the additional NI contributions paid on such payments. These figures are reviewed every year.

Return to work after paternity leave

- Employees returning to work after a period of paternity leave have the legal right to do so in the jobs they held immediately before that period of leave began, without any loss of seniority or pension rights, or any other terms and conditions that would have prevailed but for their absences from work.

Claims and remedies

- Eligible employees who are denied their entitlement to paternity leave (paid or otherwise), or who are dismissed, selected for redundancy, victimised, or subjected to any other detriment for asserting their rights under the **Paternity & Adoption Leave Regulations 2002**, may complain to an employment tribunal and will be awarded appropriate compensation if their complaints are upheld.

See also **Adoption leave, Maternity leave, Parental leave** and **Flexible working** elsewhere in this handbook.

PENSION SCHEMES
(Contracting-out certificates, pension scheme trustees, etc)

Key points

- The written statement of employment particulars issued to an employee, when he (or she) first starts work with an employer, must include particulars of any terms and conditions relating to pensions and pensions schemes, and must include a note stating whether a contracting-out certificate under the Pension Schemes Act 1993 is in force for the employment in respect of which the statement is given (sections 1(4)(d)(iii) and 1(5), Employment Rights Act 1996).

Information about pensions and pensions schemes

- If the employer has no occupational pension scheme, the written statement must say as much. If the employer does operate such a scheme, the statement must (a) mention its existence, and (b) indicate whether the employee is eligible to contribute to it, and on what terms. However, the statement need not go into any great detail, so long as it directs the employee to some other document (such as a pensions handbook) which explains what the employer's scheme is about and gives the employee sufficient information so as to enable him (or her) to decide for himself whether or not to join the scheme or take out a pension plan of his own. The employee must either have reasonable opportunities of reading that document in the course of his employment or be afforded reasonable access to it in some other way (*ibid.* section 2(2)).

Note: On 28 September 1994, the European Court of Justice ruled that part-time employees should have the same access to occupational pension schemes as their full-time colleagues. To do otherwise, said the Court, is to discriminate against part-timers, the vast majority of whom (in the UK) are women.

Contracting-out certificate

- A contracting-out certificate will be issued in respect of an occupational pension scheme if the Occupational Pensions Board (OPB) is satisfied that the scheme will provide its members with pension benefits on retirement at least equivalent to the additional pension otherwise available to employees under the State Earnings Related Pension Scheme (SERPS). Furthermore, the employer's scheme must provide a guaranteed minimum pension for widows equal to at least half the additional pension under SERPS, the remaining half being paid by the state. Members of an occupational scheme must also be assured of a preserved pension after two years' pensionable service at least equivalent to the amount which would otherwise have been available to them had they contributed to the state scheme. The decision whether or not to contract-out of SERPS is one for the employer to make. But, before setting up his own pension scheme, he must first consult with his employees and with representatives of any independent trade union recognised by him and with the trustees and managers of the scheme. The rules for contracting-out are quite complicated, and it is not proposed to deal with them here.

Recent developments

- Until recently, employees have had one of two choices. They could either contribute to SERPS or contribute to their employer's occupational pension scheme (either voluntarily or in compliance with a term to that effect in their contracts of employment). With the coming into force of the Social Security Act 1989, employees now have the right to opt out of SERPS and to contribute to a (portable) pension plan of their own choosing. Furthermore, they can leave their employer's pension scheme (regardless of any contrary term in their contracts or in the scheme itself) after only two years' pensionable service (instead of five years, as was previously the case).

Member-nominated trustees

- Section 16 of the Pensions Act 1995 requires the appointment of member-nominated trustees (pension scheme trustees) to represent the interests of their fellow-employees in the administration of the scheme and the funds invested in the scheme for a period of between three and six years. Unless the scheme comprises less than 100 members, there must be at least two member-nominated trustees comprising at least one-third of the total number of trustees. For further information, please turn to the sections titled **Dismissal of a pension**

scheme trustee and **Time off work: pension scheme trustees** elsewhere in this handbook.

The equal treatment rule

- Under the Pensions Act 1995, occupational pension schemes which do not contain an *equal treatment rule* will be treated as including such a rule. An equal treatment rule is a rule which relates to the terms on which (a) persons become members of the scheme, and (b) members of the scheme are treated. In short, if a woman is employed on like work, or work rated as equivalent, or work of equal value, to that of a man in the same employment, any term in an occupational scheme which is (or becomes) less favourable to the woman than it is to the man, shall be treated as so modified as not to be less favourable (*ibid.* section 62). There are exceptions to the equal treatment rule, which will be familiar to the managers and trustees of occupational pension schemes and are beyond the scope of this handbook.

Disabled persons

- Section 17 of the Disability Discrimination Act 1995 cautions that every occupational pension scheme will be taken to include a *non-discrimination rule* relating to the terms on which persons become members of the scheme and on which members of the scheme are treated. The rule will also be taken to impose a duty on the trustees or managers of the scheme to refrain from any act or omission which, if done by an employer in his dealings with his employers, would amount to unlawful discrimination under that Act.

Further information

- As mentioned earlier, the rules about the establishment and management of occupational pension schemes (and the rights of employees in relation to such schemes) are somewhat complicated. However, the DSS has produced two useful books on the subject, which are available on request from most DSS offices. They are titled, respectively, *New Pension Choices: Information for Employers* and *New Pensions Choices: Information for Employees* (ref NP 41). With the coming into force of the Pensions Act 1995, these are likely to have been updated.

See also **Disabled persons, Part-time workers, Fixed-term employees, Transfers of undertakings,** and **Written particulars of terms of employment** elsewhere in this handbook.

PICKETING

Key points

- It is lawful for a person, in contemplation or furtherance of a trade dispute, to attend:

  (a) at or near his own place of work, or

  (b) if he is an official of a trade union, at or near the place of work of a member of that union whom he is accompanying and whom he represents,

  for the purpose only of peacefully obtaining or communicating information, or peacefully persuading any person to work or abstain from work. Picketing is not actionable in tort if it meets these criteria. But it *is* actionable as a form of industrial action if it does not have the support of a ballot or is done in order to put pressure on an employer to dismiss a non-union member (or to discriminate against him) or to 'persuade' him not to hire non-union workers (sections 219, 220 and 222, Trade Union & Labour Relations (Consolidation) Act 1992).

  Note: For these purposes, an *official* of a trade union is a full-time officer of the union or of a branch or section of the union. The term also applies to an employee who has been elected or appointed (in accordance with the rules of the union) to represent fellow-employees in negotiations with his (or her) employer, ie a shop steward. Section 220(4) of the 1992 Act states that a full-time official of a trade union is regarded as representing the interests of all the union's members, whereas a shop steward is treated as representing the interests of only those members who work at his own place of work.

Attendance at or near his own place of work

- The 1992 Act does not explain what is meant by the expression 'at or near his own place of work'. However, the *Code of Practice: Picketing (1992)* (see below) explains that lawful picketing normally involves attendance at an entrance to or exit from the premises (such as a factory, depot, shop or office block) at which the picket actually works. In other words, it is unlawful for a picket to attend at an entrance to, or exit from, any place of work which is not his own – even if those who work at that other place are employed by the same employer or covered by the same collective bargaining arrangements. Nor is it permissible in law for a person to picket in any part of premises which are private property. Pickets who trespass may be sued in the civil courts.

Note: Section 220(2) of the 1992 Act does, however, draw a distinction in the case of employees (eg mobile workers) who work at more than one place, and those for whom it is impracticable to picket at their own place of work because of the remoteness or location of the site. In those circumstances, it is lawful for such employees to picket those premises of their employer from which they work or from which their work is administered. Thus, it may be more appropriate for contract workers to register their protest at the entrance to their employer's administrative headquarters.

In the case of an employee who is no longer employed and whose previous employment was terminated in connection with a trade dispute, his 'place of work' for these purposes will be his former place of work (*ibid.* section 220(3)).

Secondary action and picketing

- As was indicated above, it is lawful for employees, who are in dispute with their employer, to picket peacefully at or near their own place of work – always assuming that the industrial action they have embarked upon is 'official'. In other words, it must have the support of a ballot conducted in accordance with the provisions of section 226 to 235 of the 1992 Act, must have been authorised or endorsed by the person specified on their ballot papers, and must have started within the period of four weeks beginning with the date of the ballot. Such pickets will be immune from any civil action for damages notwithstanding that they may have induced other employees to break their contracts of employment, or that they have disrupted the flow of goods and services to and from their employer's premises (*ibid.* sections 219 and 220).

- Cases may arise, however, where a trade union may induce its members employed by a supplier not to deliver goods to the premises of the employer in dispute with his workers. This is known as secondary industrial action (or 'sympathy' action). Such action is no longer lawful. In such cases, the supplier would be well within his (or her) rights to sue the trade union (and/or its representatives) for damages arising out of inducing his employees to break their contracts of employment and the interference with his contract to supply goods or services to the employer in dispute.

- In other words, secondary industrial action is lawful and immune from actions in tort if, but only if, it is done by employees in the course of peaceful picketing at or near their own place of work.

- Pickets who obstruct the highway, who damage property, or who use violent, intimidatory, threatening or abusive language or behaviour to 'persuade' workers, members of the public, van drivers, and the like, not to cross their picket lines are liable to arrest and could be prosecuted under the criminal law.

Code of practice on picketing

- The *Code of Practice: Picketing (1992)* referred to earlier was made by the Secretary of State for Employment and came into force on 1 May 1992 (replacing an earlier code made under section 3 of the Employment Act 1980). The code, which is available from The Stationery Office contains practical guidance for employers and trade unions on, amongst other things, picketing and the criminal law, the recommended number of pickets, the organisation of picketing, the role of the police, and so on, and should be studied with care. See also **Dismissal for taking industrial action, Strikes and strike ballots, Trade disputes and arbitration,** and **Trade union membership and activities,** elsewhere in this handbook.

POSTED WORKERS

Key points

- The term 'posted worker' is used to describe a worker who is sent from one EU Member State to another to carry out work (albeit for a limited period) in that other Member State. The relevance of the term is to be found in European Parliament and Council Directive 97/71/EC of 16 December 1996 'concerning the posting of workers in the framework of the provision of services'. The purpose of the Directive, which came into force in the UK on 16 December 1999, is to ensure that employers sending workers on temporary assignments to other EU countries, or tendering for contract work in another Member State, do not acquire a competitive edge by paying their workers less, or by offering terms and conditions below the legal minimum in that other Member State. A 'limited period', for these purposes, is a period of up to one year from the beginning of the posting (including any previous periods for which the post in question was filled by a posted worker).

- Implementation of the 'Posted Workers' Directive in the UK does not require specific legislation. However, the Directive has prompted minor amendments to the Sex Discrimination Act 1975, the Race Relations Act 1976, the Trade Union & Labour Relations (Consolidation) Act 1992, the Disability Discrimination Act 1995, and the Employment Rights Act 1996, each of which previously limited the application of certain employment rights to persons who ordinarily work in Great Britain. Those limitations have now been removed.

Note: The territorial limits in the enactments referred to above were repealed by section 32 of the Employment Relations Act (which came into force on 25 October 1999) and by the Equal Opportunities (Employment Legislation) (Territorial Limits) Regulations 1999 (which came into force on 16 December 1999).

Duties of employers

- UK employers sending one or more of their workers to carry out work for a limited period in another EU Member State must familiarise themselves with the laws, regulations and administrative provisions of that Member State, and/or (so far as building work is concerned) with any collective agreements or mandatory arbitration awards in that Member State which relate to:

  - maximum work periods and minimum rest periods;

  - minimum paid annual holidays;

  - minimum rates of pay (including overtime rates);

  - conditions for hiring out workers, notably workers supplied by temporary employment businesses (or 'employment agencies', as they are often, if incorrectly, referred to in the UK);

  - health, safety and hygiene at work;

  - protective measures with regard to the terms and conditions of employment of children, young persons and new or expectant mothers; and

  - equality of treatment between men and women, and other provisions prohibiting discriminatory treatment on specified grounds;

  and must guarantee that the workers posted to that Member State enjoy no less favourable terms and conditions during their periods of posting.

- It is, of course, open to employers to apply more favourable terms and conditions to those of their workers who are posted to other EU Member States for a limited period. If they are entitled (in any respect) to more favourable terms under their existing contracts of employment (whether imported by statute or otherwise), those more favourable terms must, of course, prevail.

- Article 4 of the Directive acknowledges that employers may have some difficulty 'tracking down' the employment laws and health and safety legislation of other Member States. To that end, Article 4 imposes a duty on each of the Member States to designate one or more liaison offices or one or more competent national bodies to provide that information. Furthermore, they must cooperate with each other to ensure that such information is disseminated and freely available. Until such time as the network, so to speak, is complete, interested readers should direct their enquiries to the labour attachés at the relevant embassies. See also *Further information* below.

- Employers in other EU Member States who post their workers to the UK for a limited period will, of course, need to familiarise themselves with (in chronological order):

    - the Employment of Women, Young Persons & Children Act 1920;

    - the Children & Young Persons Act 1933;

    - the Children & Young Persons (Scotland) Act 1937;

    - the Equal Pay Act 1970;

    - the Health & Safety at Work etc Act 1974;

    - the Sex Discrimination Act 1975;

    - the Race Relations Act 1976;

    - the Workplace (Health, Safety & Welfare) Regulations 1992;

    - the Disability Discrimination Act 1995;

    - the Employment Rights Act 1996;

    - the Working Time Regulations 1998;

    - the National Minimum Wage Regulations 1999;

    - the Maternity & Parental Leave etc Regulations 1999;

    - the Management of Health & Safety at Work Regulations 1999;

    - the Part-time Workers (Prevention of Less Favourable Treatment) Regulations 2000;

    - the Fixed-term Employees (Prevention of Less Favourable Treatment) Regulations 2002

    - legislation relating to adoption leave and pay, paternity leave, and flexible working (see Index);

and with health and safety legislation (such as the Diving at Work Regulations 1997, the Control of Lead at Work Regulations 2002, the Control of Substances Hazardous to Health Regulations 2002, etc) which contain measures for the protection of workers engaged in prescribed hazardous activities.

Categories of workers

- The Directive identifies three categories of workers. These are:

  (1) workers sent by their employers to another EU Member State to carry out work for customers or clients in that other Member State;

  (2) workers sent by their employer to work in a subsidiary or associated company established in that other Member State; and

  (3) temporary workers employed by an employment business (or placement agency) who are hired out on agreed terms to a client employer in another EU Member State.

Category (1) workers

- Typical of 'Category (1)' workers are people sent by their employers to carry out building work (see *Note* below) in another Member State (for a limited period) or to install plant and equipment (eg, a ventilation system or a refrigeration unit) purchased by a client or customer in that other Member State (where the installation of such equipment is an integral part of the contract for the supply of such equipment).

  Note: The expression 'building work' includes all work relating to the construction, repair, upkeep, alteration or demolition of buildings, and, in particular: excavation, earthmoving, actual building work, assembly and dismantling of prefabricated elements, fitting out or installation, alterations, renovations, repairs, dismantling, demolition, maintenance (including upkeep, painting and cleaning work) and improvements.

- However, the terms of the Directive do not apply to skilled or specialist workers sent by their employer (the supplier) to install plant and equipment in a customer or client's premises in another EU Member State (so long as the work in question does not amount to building work) if their posting to that other Member State does not last for more than eight days.

- Although it is uncommon nowadays for UK building workers to be sent by their employers to work on a construction site in another Member State, UK employers planning to do so should be alert to the existence (and complexity) of a variety of collective agreements and mandatory arbitration awards (peculiar to several EU Member States, notably Germany) which might well reduce the cost-effectiveness of such postings. It is more usual for UK workers to travel independently to other EU Member States looking for work on a building or construction site (as they have every right to do).

  Note: Article 3(3) of the Directive allows that a Member State may ('after consulting employers and labour') legislate for a derogation from the Directive's provisions relating to minimum rates of pay and overtime rates for workers in Categories (1) and (2) who are posted to another EU Member State for a period of one month or less. The UK government has decided (for the time being at least) not to exercise that option.

Category (2) workers

- The 'Category (2)' worker is a worker temporarily transferred by his (or her) UK employer to another branch of the organisation, or to a subsidiary or associated employer situated in another EU Member State, and who remains in the employ of his or her UK employer during the period of posting. Such workers must be treated no less favourably than resident workers during their stay in that Member State in terms of minimum pay rates, maximum working hours, minimum rest breaks and rest periods, annual holidays, equal treatment regardless of gender, race or disability, and health and safety protection.

Category (3) workers

- The third category of worker is the 'temp' or agency worker, who is employed under a contract of employment with an employment business (or placement agency) in one Member State, and who is hired out for a limited period to a 'user undertaking' in another EU Member State. So long as he or she remains in the employ of that business or agency throughout the period of posting, the hired-out worker must be paid no less than the minimum rates of pay and overtime rates applicable to comparable workers in the Member State in question and enjoy the same statutory protection (in terms of working hours, period of employment, rest breaks, holidays, health and safety measures, etc).

- Furthermore, Article 9 of the Directive provides that a Member State may take steps to ensure that employment businesses and placement agencies established in other Member States provide a guarantee that temporary workers posted to its territory are hired-out on terms and conditions no less favourable than those that apply to its own temporary workers.

Enforcement

- Any worker sent by his employer to work for a limited period in another EU Member State, whose wages or salary, working hours, holiday entitlement, etc are less favourable than those prescribed for workers normally resident in that Member State, may enforce his or her rights under the Posted Workers Directive by instituting proceedings before the appropriate tribunal or court in that Member State or in the Member State in which he normally works.

Likely implications for UK employers

- Nowadays, it is uncommon for relatively lowly paid workers in the UK or elsewhere to be sent by their employers to carry out short-term assignments in other EU Member States. Such postings are usually confined to businessmen and women, accountants, bankers, technicians, engineers, and the like (whose terms and conditions of employment are unlikely to fall below the minima prescribed for workers engaged in comparable activities in those other Member States). This will not necessarily be true of nurses, waiters, waitresses, secretaries, interpreters, bricklayers, carpenters, plumbers, etc employed by employment businesses (or placement agencies) who are hired out to clients in other Member States for limited periods. In the latter case, the Posted Workers Directive is applicable if, but only if, the workers in question remain in the employ of the relevant business or agency throughout the period of their postings.

Free movement of workers

- The nationals of one Member State who travel to another Member State in search of work (eg, as waiters, waitresses, builders, etc) usually do so independently – exercising their right under Article 39 (formerly Article 48) of the Treaty of Rome 'to move freely within the territory of Member States', 'to accept offers of employment actually made', 'to stay in a Member State for the purpose of employment', and 'to remain in the territory of a Member State after having been employed in that State'.

Further information

- Readers seeking further information about the Directive may telephone the DTI's Helpline on 0645 555105.

  The Directive itself may be viewed at:

  www.europa.eu.int/eur-lex/en/lif/dat/1996/en 396L0071.html

  See also **EEA nationals, employment of**, elsewhere in this handbook.

PREGNANT EMPLOYEES AND NURSING MOTHERS
(Rest facilities, risk assessment and suspension from work)

Key points

- Pregnant employees, breastfeeding mothers, and women who have given birth within the previous six months, enjoy a variety of rights under contemporary employment law and health and safety legislation. A pregnant employee has the right to be permitted a reasonable amount of paid time off work to attend at a clinic or similar place for ante-natal care. If her expected week of childbirth (EWC) begins on or after 6 April 2003, she has the right also to 26 weeks' ordinary maternity leave and, if she qualifies, a right to 26 weeks' additional maternity leave (beginning on the day immediately following the day on which her ordinary maternity leave period ends). If she has worked for her employer for at least 26 weeks by the end of the 15th week before her expected week of childbirth, and earns an average of £77 or more per week, she is entitled to up to 26 weeks' statutory maternity pay (SMP). Finally, she has the right to return to work with her employer after her baby is born and the right to take up to 13 weeks' unpaid parental leave (sections 47C and 99, Employment Rights Act 1996, supplemented by the Maternity & Parental Leave etc Regulations 1999). These issues are discussed at greater length elsewhere in this handbook in the sections titled **Maternity rights**, **Parental leave** and **Time off work: pregnant employees**. See also **Time off for dependants**.

Right not to be unfairly dismissed

- It is inadmissible and automatically unfair for an employer to dismiss a woman, select her for redundancy or subject her to any detriment because she is a woman; or because she is pregnant or has given birth to a child; or for having been suspended from work on maternity grounds (see below); or for exercising her statutory right to ordinary or additional maternity leave, parental leave or time off work for ante-natal care. The same rules apply if she is dismissed either for challenging her employer's refusal or failure to acknowledge her rights or, for bringing proceedings before a tribunal or court in order to enforce those rights (*ibid*. section 104) – as to which, please turn to the sections referred to at the end of the previous paragraph and the section titled **Dismissal for asserting a statutory right**.

Health and safety legislation

- There is also legislation which requires an employer to provide suitable rest facilities for pregnant employees and nursing mothers, to pay (or otherwise accommodate) women who have been suspended from work on maternity grounds, and to transfer a woman from night work to day work if her doctor or midwife certifies that this would be advisable.

Rest facilities

- Every employer (whether the proprietor of a fish and chip shop or the managing director of a multi-national corporation) is duty-bound to provide suitable rest facilities for those of his (or her) employees who are pregnant or nursing mothers, including (where necessary) the facility to lie down. Common sense will dictate what is suitable in relation to one workplace, and what is unsuitable in relation to another. In a large factory, office block, hotel or department store, an employer would be expected to set aside a small, well-ventilated room equipped with a toilet and washbasin and furnished with one or more beds or reclining chairs. In a small establishment, employing just a handful of employees, a small curtained-off area with a comfortable reclining chair would probably satisfy the requirement. However grand or modest, the room or facility must either be equipped with a toilet or washbasin or be conveniently situated in relation to the staff washrooms and toilets. A failure to provide such a facility is a criminal offence which could lead to prosecution and a heavy fine under the Health & Safety at Work etc Act 1974 (per regulation 25(4), Workplace (Health, Safety & Welfare) Regulations 1992).

Suspension from work on maternity grounds

- Under the Management of Health & Safety at Work Regulations 1999, the 'risk assessment' exercise necessarily carried out by *every* employer must include an assessment of the risk to the health and safety of *new or expectant mothers* (or to that of their babies) arising out of their working conditions, the type of work in which they are engaged (eg, manual handling of loads, noise, vibration, hot or humid conditions, etc), or their exposure to hazardous physical, biological or chemical agents. If there is a risk, the employer must either transfer a pregnant employee or new mother to suitable alternative employment or suspend her from work on full pay until that risk has passed (*ibid.* regulation 16).

Note: The expression 'new or expectant mother' means an employee who is pregnant; who has given birth within the previous six months; or who is breastfeeding (*ibid.* regulation 1(1)).

- The right of a new or expectant mother to be paid her normal wages or salary while suspended from work on maternity grounds is to be found in sections 66 to 68 of the Employment Rights Act 1996. Any woman denied her statutory rights in this respect may obtain redress by presenting a complaint to an employment tribunal. For further information, please turn to the section titled **Suspension from work on maternity grounds** elsewhere in this handbook.

- Similar provisions are to be found in the Control of Lead at Work Regulations 2002 and in the Ionising Radiations Regulations 1999, both of which require the suspension of a pregnant employee in specified circumstances. Indeed, both sets of Regulations caution that a 'woman of reproductive capacity' (that is to say, a woman who is capable of bearing a child, but who is not necessarily pregnant at the time) must be suspended from work involving exposure to lead or ionising radiation, on the advice of an employment medical adviser or HSE-appointed doctor, if her blood-lead or urinary-lead concentration or, as appropriate, the radiation dose limit for her abdomen is likely to be (or has been) exceeded.

Night work

- If a doctor or registered midwife certifies that a particular employee who is pregnant or breastfeeding (or has given birth to a child within the previous six months) should not work at night, her employer must either offer her suitable alternative work on the day shift or, if that is not reasonably practicable, suspend her from work on full pay until the danger has passed (regulation 17, Management of Health & Safety at Work Regulations 1999 (*qv*)).

- For further details, please turn to the sections in this handbook titled **Suspension from work on maternity grounds** and **Women and young persons, employment of**.

Further information

- The HSE publications listed below are available from HSE Books, PO Box 1999, Sudbury, Suffolk C010 6FS (Telephone: 01787 881165):

  New and Expectant Mothers at Work: A Guide for Employers (1994) ISBN 0 7176 0826 3

  Infections in the Workplace to New and Expectant Mothers (1997) ISBN 0 7176 1360 7

PUBLIC INTEREST DISCLOSURES

Key points

- Under the Public Interest Disclosure Act 1998, which came into force on 2 July 1999, any worker who makes a so-called protected disclosure has the right not to be dismissed, selected for redundancy or subjected to any other detriment (demotion, forfeiture of opportunities for promotion or training, etc) for having done so. Any term in a contract of employment or other document (such as a 'worker's contract') which purports to undermine or override a worker's right to make a protected disclosure is null and void.

Note:　The relevant provisions of the 1998 Act (commonly referred to as 'the Whistleblower's Act') have been inserted as Part IVA (sections 43A to 43L) of the Employment Rights Act 1996. Provisions in the 1998 Act relating to a worker's right not to be dismissed, selected for redundancy or subjected to any detriment for making a protected disclosure are to be found in sections 47B, 103A and 105 of the 1996 Act. The latter Act is hereinafter referred to as 'the 1996 Act').

Meaning of 'qualifying disclosure'

- Section 43A of the 1996 Act defines 'protected disclosure' as meaning a qualifying disclosure, that is to say, any disclosure of information which, in the reasonable belief of the worker making the disclosure, tends to show one or more of the following:

  (a) that a criminal offence has been, is being or is likely to be committed;

  (b) that a person has failed, is failing or is likely to fail to comply with a legal obligation to which he (or she) is subject;

  (c) that a miscarriage of justice has occurred, is occurring or is likely to occur;

  (d) that the health and safety of an individual has been, is being or is likely to be endangered;

  (e) that the environment has been, is being or is likely to be damaged; or

  (f) that information tending to show any matter falling within any one of the preceding paragraphs has been, or is likely to be deliberately concealed.

  It is important to note the use of the word 'worker', in this context. A worker is a person who is either an employee in the accepted sense (that is to say, a person employed under a contract of employment) or a person who undertakes to do or perform personally any work or service for an employer (perhaps as a freelance operator, a trainee, a casual labourer, or agency worker). The term does not however apply to any person who is genuinely self-employed.

- A worker prompted to make a disclosure about alleged wrongdoing by (or within) the organisation for which he (or she) works may do so:

  (a) to his employer (either directly or in accordance with established procedures for dealing with such allegations) or to another person whom the worker reasonably believes to be solely or mainly responsible for the alleged unlawful or criminal conduct;

  (b) to a legal adviser (if made in the course of obtaining legal advice);

  (c) to a Minister of the Crown (if the disclosure is made in good faith, and the worker in question is employed by a government-appointed person or public body);

  (d) to the appropriate enforcing authorities (such as the Health & Safety Executive, the Commissioners of the Inland Revenue, the Environment Agency, etc (see below));

  (e) (subject to certain conditions) to some other person or agency, if the disclosure relates to an exceptionally serious failure on the part of the worker's employer or some other person; or

  (f) (subject to certain conditions) to some other person or agency (eg, the media, or a professional body responsible for policing standards and conduct in a particular field).

Disclosure to employer or other responsible person

- A worker may make a qualifying disclosure directly to his (or her) employer, or to some other person whom he reasonably believes to be solely or mainly responsible for the alleged wrongdoing, and will enjoy the protection available to him under Part IVA of the 1996 Act, so long as he acts in good faith (*ibid.* section 43C).

- If an employer has developed or authorised a simple and readily accessible procedure to encourage workers to air their concerns about alleged wrongdoing within his organisation (eg, breaches of health and safety legislation), then those procedures should be exhausted before a worker takes it upon himself (or herself to air those concerns or allegations elsewhere (see *Disclosure in other cases* below). He may choose, on the other hand, to present his allegations of wrongdoing directly to the appropriate enforcing authorities (so long as he does so in good faith and reasonably believes those allegations to be substantially true).

- An employer's in-house procedures for dealing with allegations of wrongdoing are unlikely to inspire confidence unless they involve other members of the workforce or workforce representatives elected or appointed by their peers to deal with such issues and make representations to their employer. A reasonable employer will, of course, respond positively to qualifying disclosures about supposed criminal activities or other wrongdoing within his organisation. So long as those disclosures were made in good faith, it would be wholly irresponsible (not to mention costly) for an employer to react by disciplining the worker or workers concerned, or by dismissing them or subjecting them to some other detriment.

Disclosure to the 'appropriate authorities'

- A worker who makes a qualifying disclosure to a prescribed person or body – such as the Health & Safety Executive, the Inland Revenue, HM Customs & Excise, the Environment Agency, the Audit Commission, the Director General of Fair Trading, and the like (see *Note* below) – will enjoy the protection afforded by the 1996 Act, so long as he (or she) does so in good faith and reasonably believes that the allegations of wrongdoing he is making are substantially true (*ibid.* section 43F).

Note: A list of the persons and descriptions of persons prescribed for the purposes of section 43F of the 1996 Act is to be found in the Schedule to the Public Interest (Prescribed Persons) Order 1999 and is reproduced in DTI Booklet URN 99/511 (*Guide to the Public Interest Disclosure Act 1998*), copies of which are available free of charge from the DTI's Publications Orderline (Telephone: 0870 1502 500).

Disclosure in other cases

- A worker who makes a qualifying disclosure to some other person or body (other than his employer or the appropriate enforcing authority) will enjoy the protection of the law, if he (or she):

  (a) made the disclosure in good faith;

  (b) reasonably believed that the information disclosed, and any allegation contained in it, were substantially true;

  (c) did not make the disclosure for the purposes of personal gain;

  (d) reasonably believed (at the time he made the disclosure) that he would have been punished, dismissed, selected for redundancy or subjected to some other detriment had he made the disclosure to his employer or to the appropriate enforcing authority;

  (e) (in the absence of an appropriate enforcing authority) reasonably believed that his employer would have concealed or destroyed any incriminating evidence; or

(f) had previously made the same or a similar disclosure to his employer or the appropriate enforcing body without avail.

Whether or not it was reasonable for the worker to have made the qualifying disclosure to a person or body other than his (or her) immediate employer (or the appropriate enforcing authority) will depend in large part on the identity of the person or body to whom the disclosure was made. An employment tribunal will also consider the seriousness of the alleged wrongdoing (and the likelihood of its happening again), whether the disclosure in question contained information in breach of the employer's duty of confidentiality to another person (eg, a customer or client), the employer's or the prescribed enforcing authority's response (or failure to respond) to a previous disclosure of the same (or substantially similar) information, and whether, in making the same or similar allegations to his employer on a previous occasion, the worker had complied with any procedure whose use by him was authorised by his employer (*ibid.* section 43G).

- Challenging an employer's failure to pay the appropriate national minimum wage, or to comply with his (or her) duties under the Working Time Regulations 1998, or to provide personal protective equipment, or for discharging toxic chemicals into the environment, or for defrauding the Inland Revenue etc, may not achieve the desired result if made directly to the person allegedly responsible for such breaches of the law, or if doing so is likely to prompt the concealment of any damaging documents or other evidence before the relevant authorities have had an opportunity to make their own assessment of the situation.

- A worker might also be concerned about the risk to his livelihood, the more so if his previous allegations on the same or a similar theme have been dismissed out of hand or 'swept under the carpet', or he has been warned 'to keep his mouth shut'. Whether influenced by such considerations or otherwise, a worker has the right to make his disclosures about alleged wrongdoing to the body, person or authority responsible for investigating and enforcing the particular law which the worker reasonably believes has been, is being or is about to be broken.

Disclosures about exceptionally serious failures

A worker who has made a qualifying disclosure (eg, to a newspaper) about an *exceptionally serious failure* (either by his or her employer or by some other person) will enjoy the protection afforded by the 1996 Act if, but only if, he:

(a) made the disclosure in good faith;

(b) reasonably believed that the information disclosed, and any allegations contained in it were substantially true;

(c) did not make the disclosure for the purposes of personal gain; and

(d) in the circumstances, it was reasonable for him to have made the disclosure.

Whether or not the failure in question was exceptionally serious is a matter of fact, not of opinion. In other words, a worker's reasonable belief that a particular failure was exceptionally serious will not be enough. The failure must in fact have been exceptionally serious.

- In determining whether or not it was reasonable for the worker to have made the disclosure in question, an employment tribunal will have regard in particular to the identity of the person or organisation to whom the disclosure was made *(ibid.* section 43H). These requirements suggest that a worker would be well advised to obtain legal advice before making a qualifying disclosure which, if aired in the public domain, could not only undermine his right not to be dismissed or subjected to a detriment for doing so but could also lead to his being sued for defamation.

Other forms of protection

- It should be remembered that the 1996 Act offers considerable protection to employees who allege (in good faith) that their employer has infringed their statutory rights under that Act, the Trade Union & Labour Relations (Consolidation) Act 1992, or the Working Time Regulations 1998. Under the National Minimum Wage Act 1998, for example, Inland Revenue enforcement officers have the right to question workers and to act on any information supplied by those workers concerning their employer's alleged failure to pay the appropriate national minimum wage rate. There are any number of similar examples, all of which complement a worker's rights under the 'protected disclosures' provisions of the 1996 Act (eg, the right of employees under section 100 of the 1996 Act to bring to their employer's attention (by reasonable means) circumstances connected with their work which they reasonably believe to be harmful or potentially harmful to health or safety).

Complaint to an employment tribunal

- A worker may complain to an employment tribunal that he (or she) has been penalised, victimised or subjected to some other detriment for making a protected disclosure. Should the worker's complaint be upheld, his employer will be ordered to pay him such compensation as the tribunal considers appropriate in the circumstances (including compensation for the loss of any benefit that the worker might reasonably be expected to have enjoyed) but for his employer's conduct or failure to act.

- A worker (as 'employee') who has been dismissed (or selected for redundancy) for making a protected disclosure may complain to an employment tribunal and will be awarded a substantial amount of compensation if his (or her) complaint is upheld. A worker who is not an employee in the strict legal sense, but whose detrimental treatment amounted to a termination of his contract, may likewise complain to an employment tribunal, and will also be awarded compensation if his complaint is upheld. It is as well to point out that there is no upper limit on the amount of compensation that may be awarded in such cases.

- Complaints to an employment tribunal, in the circumstances described above, must be presented within three months of the effective date of termination of an employee's contract of employment, or within three months of the alleged detrimental treatment (including, in the case of a worker who is not an employee, detrimental treatment amounting to a termination of the worker's contract). Such complaints may be presented regardless of the worker's age or length of service at the material time.

See also **Dismissal** and **Victimisation** elsewhere in this handbook.

R

RACIAL DISCRIMINATION
(Employment and other fields)

Key points

- Under the provisions of the Race Relations Act 1976, it is unlawful for any person in Great Britain to discriminate against another person on grounds of colour, race, nationality or national or ethnic origins – whether in the field of employment or in the provision of goods, facilities or services.

- The 1976 Act, which repealed and replaced earlier Race Relations Acts, identifies three forms of racial discrimination, each of which is unlawful. These are:

  (a) **direct discrimination** (which occurs when a person is treated less favourably than other persons because of his or her colour, race, nationality, etc);

  (b) **indirect discrimination** (which occurs when a person is effectively denied access to employment opportunities, goods, facilities, services, etc by the imposition of an unjustifiable condition or requirement which places him or her at a disadvantage relative to persons of a different racial group); and

  (c) discrimination in the form of **victimisation or racial harassment** which can also occur when a person is treated less favourably by his (or her) employer, or some other person, for having brought proceedings for an alleged infringement of his rights under the 1976 Act.

Commission for Racial Equality

- The Commission for Racial Equality (CRE), which replaced the earlier Race Relations Board, has broad powers to undertake investigations for any purpose connected with the elimination of racial discrimination and the promotion of equality of opportunity and good relations between persons of different racial groups generally. Where the CRE uncovers evidence of racial discrimination, it may issue a non-discrimination notice requiring this to cease. It may bring proceedings against persistent offenders, and has similar powers to deal with unlawful discriminatory advertisements. It undertakes advisory and educational work, and may provide advice and assistance to persons or groups where there are special reasons for doing so. A *Code of Practice on Race Relations*, produced by the CRE, is available from The Stationery Office (see page 132).

Discrimination in the employment field

- It is unlawful for an employer in Great Britain to discriminate against an applicant or candidate for employment on racial grounds:

  (a) in the arrangements he (or she) makes for the purposes of determining who should or should not be offered that employment; or

  (b) by refusing or deliberately omitting to offer that person that employment,

  unless being of a particular racial group is a *genuine occupational qualification* for the job in question (see below) (*ibid.* sections 4(1) and 5(l)(A)).

- It is unlawful for an employer to discriminate on racial grounds:

  (a) by paying an employee less than his (or her) colleagues in the same employment or offering him less advantageous terms and conditions of employment;

  (b) by denying an employee equal access to opportunities for promotion, transfer or training, or to any other benefits, facilities or services, or by refusing or deliberately omitting to afford him access to them; or

  (c) by dismissing him or subjecting him to any other detriment (*ibid.* section 4(2)).

Note: Section 8 of the Asylum & Immigration Act 1996 cautions employers that they are liable to prosecution and a fine of up to £5,000 if they employ any person subject to immigration control who is aged 16 and who has not been granted leave to enter or remain in the UK or who does not have a valid and subsisting right to take up employment while in the UK. However, the mere act of screening job applicants (or a short-list of candidates for employment) in compliance with section 8 could unwittingly give rise to allegations of racial discrimination, an issue which is discussed elsewhere in this handbook in the section titled **Foreign nationals, employment of**. See also **Commonwealth citizens, employment of**.

Direct discrimination

- Direct discrimination occurs when a person is treated less favourably than other persons in the same employment because of his (or her) colour, race, nationality, or national or ethnic origins. An example is an employer's refusal to interview coloured applicants for vacancies, or a trade union's refusal to extend membership rights to coloured workers or foreign nationals. It can also manifest itself after employment has begun when an employer refuses (for no good reason) to promote coloured or foreign workers, or denies them access to training and facilities. Direct discrimination can be justified only if being of a particular racial group is a *genuine occupational qualification* for a particular vacancy (discussed below).

- An employer who openly or covertly instructs an employment agency not to submit coloured or foreign candidates for vacancies within his (or her) organisation, not only risks being served with a non-discrimination notice by the Commission for Racial Equality (with the attendant penalties if he does not mend his ways), but may also be ordered by an employment tribunal to pay compensation of such amount as the tribunal considers appropriate in the fight of a job applicant's loss of prospective earnings and injured feelings. The employment agency may likewise be served with a non-discrimination notice and, if it fails to comply with the terms of that notice, could be served with a county court injunction (or sheriff court order) restraining the agency from further unlawful acts (*ibid.* sections 14, 30, 56, 58 and 62). See also *Questions and replies* below.

Indirect discrimination

- An employer indirectly discriminates against an employee (or candidate for employment) on racial grounds by applying a condition or requirement which effectively excludes that person because of his (or her) race, colour, nationality, or national or ethnic origins. Thus, it is *prima facie* unlawful for an employer (employment agency or trade union) to require job applicants (or candidates for membership) to complete an unnecessarily complicated aptitude test, or to possess technical or professional qualifications which could only have been acquired in Great Britain either of which requirements might well deter otherwise suitable applicants from applying for work or membership, or taking their applications further, whether or not this effect was intended by the employer at the time.

- In *Hussein v Saints Complete House Furnishings* [1979] IRLR 337, an employer had stipulated that job applicants should reside outside Liverpool 7 and 8 postal districts. Persons recruited from those districts in the past had tended to bring with them their unemployed friends who were given to loitering outside the front entrance to his premises. An employment tribunal found that, although the employer had not intended to discriminate against coloured persons, his refusal to recruit persons from those two inner city postal districts had effectively eliminated some 50 per cent of the black community in Liverpool.

Note: In a not dissimilar case, a confectionery manufacturer in Edinburgh insisted that employees handling the company's products should be clean-shaven. A Mr Singh, a Sikh, applied for a job at the factory and was informed that he would not be accepted unless he agreed to shave off his beard. Mr Singh, whose religion forbade him to do so, refused. On a complaint of unlawful discrimination, the Employment Appeal Tribunal held that it was not unreasonable for a manufacturer of foodstuffs to insist on the highest standards of personal hygiene in order to avoid the possibility of food contamination. Mr Singh's appeal was dismissed (*Singh v Rowntree Mackintosh Ltd* [1979] IRLR 199).

Discrimination by way of victimisation

- An employer is guilty of racial discrimination by way of victimisation if he treats the employee victimised less favourably than he would other persons in similar circumstances, and does so because the employee in question:

  (a) has brought proceedings against him (or some other person) under the Race Relations Act 1976; or

  (b) has given evidence or information in connection with proceedings brought before a tribunal or court by any other person under the 1976 Act.

  The same rule applies if an employee is victimised or harassed for alleging that his employer's recruitment or employment policies amount to unlawful racial discrimination under the 1976 Act unless the evidence shows that the employee's allegations were false and not made in good faith (*ibid.* section 2).

Dismissal on racial grounds

- The dismissal of an employee on grounds of colour, race, nationality or national or ethnic origins is unlawful and automatically unfair and will nowadays attract a prohibitive award of compensation – including compensation for loss of earnings and damages for injured feelings (plus interest). See also **Dismissal** elsewhere in this handbook.

Instructions to discriminate

- It is unlawful for an employer to instruct any person over whom he (or she) has a measure of authority (eg personnel manager, head of department, foreman, supervisor, etc) to do any act which constitutes unlawful discrimination on racial grounds; or to induce, or attempt to induce, such a person to do any act which is unlawful (sections 30 and 31, Race Relations Act 1976).

  Note: In *Zarcynska v Levy* [1978] IRLR 532, a barmaid was dismissed when she disobeyed her employer's instructions not to serve black customers. The Employment Appeal Tribunal held that the employer's instructions constituted unlawful discrimination on racial grounds and that the barmaid (who was herself white and the innocent victim of that discrimination) had been unlawfully and unfairly dismissed.

Discriminatory advertisements

- It is unlawful for an employer to publish, or cause to be published, a job advertisement which indicates a clear or ill-concealed intention to discriminate against potential applicants on racial grounds, unless the advertisement indicates that persons of any class defined otherwise than by reference to colour, race, nationality or ethnic or national origins are required for employment outside Great Britain (*ibid.* section 29).

  Note: Proceedings in such cases may be brought only by the Commission for Racial Equality. Nowadays, of course, it is extremely unlikely that any newspaper proprietor or publisher will agree to publish an advertisement which is patently discriminatory (unless it was reasonable for the publisher to rely on a statement by the person wishing to publish that advertisement that it would not be unlawful under the 1976 Act) (*ibid.* section 29(4)). See also **Advertisements (discriminatory)** elsewhere in this handbook.

Genuine occupational qualification

- It is *not* unlawful for an employer to discriminate against job applicants on racial grounds if being of a particular racial group is *a genuine occupational qualification* for the vacancy, or vacancies, in question (*ibid.* section 5(1)). Being of a particular racial group is a genuine occupational qualification for a job if it involves working in a place where food or drink is (for payment or not) provided to and consumed by members of the public or a section of the public in a particular setting for which, in that job, a person of that racial group is required for reasons of authenticity (*ibid.* section 5(2)(c)).

  Note: It is therefore lawful for the proprietor of a Chinese restaurant to advertise for Chinese waiters and to turn away people who are not Chinese. The same is, of course, true of Indian restaurants, Pakistani restaurants, and so on. Whether an employment tribunal would take the same view in the case of advertisements for kitchen hands and 'bottle washers' in such establishments is another matter.

Questions and replies

- An employee (or candidate for employment), who believes that he or she may have been discriminated against on racial grounds (whether by his employer, or by a prospective employer), has the right under the 1976 Act to question the person concerned on the reasons for his apparently unlawful actions. If dissatisfied with that employer's answers (if answers were given), the employee or job applicant may admit them (or a refusal to answer) as evidence in proceedings before an employment tribunal (*ibid.* section 65). The purpose is to enable the person aggrieved to decide whether or not to bring legal proceedings against the employer concerned (the respondent).

- The procedure for submitting questions to an employer in such circumstances has been formalised by the Race Relations (Questions & Replies) Order 1977. The prescribed form is Form RR65 (available from any employment office, Job Centre or unemployment benefit office of the Department for Work & Pensioins; or from the Commission for Racial Equality).

  Note: Form RR65 is an eight-page document which not only provides space for preparing the questionnaire to be submitted, but also contains a deal of practical advice both to the person framing the questions and to the person to whom those questions are put. Although the document acknowledges that an employer is under no legal obligation to answer the questions put to him in Form RR65, it does caution that his failure or refusal to do so within a reasonable period could well put him in a difficult position should the questioner decide to refer the matter to an employment tribunal.

- To be admissible as evidence before an employment tribunal, the complainant's questionnaire (Form RR65) must be served on the respondent employer either:

  (a) before a complaint of unlawful racial discrimination is sent to the Regional Office of the Tribunals, but not more than three months after the date on which the alleged discrimination occurred; or

  (b) if the complaint has already been lodged, not later than 21 days after the date on which it was received by the Secretary to the Tribunals.

Complaint to an employment tribunal

- Any person who has been dismissed from his (or her) employment on racial grounds, or who considers that he has otherwise been discriminated against or subjected to any detriment (by his employer or by a prospective employer) in contravention of the Race Relations Act 1976, may present a complaint to an employment tribunal. An employee does not have to resign from his job in order to present a complaint of unlawful discrimination. Indeed, any employee victimised by his employer for complaining to an employment tribunal, or for alleging that his employer has committed an act of unlawful racial discrimination, can pursue a separate complaint on those grounds alone. An employee has the right to pursue a complaint of unlawful discrimination under the 1976 Act regardless of his (or her) age or length of service at the material time. However, he must present his complaint before the end of the period of three months beginning with the date on which the act complained of was done or, as appropriate, within three months of the effective date of termination of his contract of employment (*ibid.* section 68(1)).

Note: To pursue a complaint of unlawful racial discrimination (including a complaint of dismissal on racial grounds), the complainant should complete Form ET1, copies of which are available from employment offices, Job Centres and unemployment benefit offices of the Employment Department. See **Employment tribunals and procedure** elsewhere in this handbook. Once the complaint has been received and registered, the Secretary to the Tribunals will send a copy of Form IT1 to a conciliation officer of ACAS who will intervene to promote a settlement before the matter is put to an employment tribunal. Anything communicated to a conciliation officer (either by the complainant or by the respondent employer) is not admissible in evidence at any ensuing tribunal hearing, except with the express consent of the person concerned (*ibid.* section 55).

- If an employment tribunal decides that a complaint of unlawful discrimination is well-founded, it will make a declaration to that effect and will order the respondent employer to pay the employee or job applicant such compensation as it considers appropriate, including compensation for lost earnings or prospective lost earnings (if any) and injury to feelings. There is no upper limit on the amount of compensation which a tribunal can award in such cases (*per* the Race Relations (Remedies) Act 1994, which came into force on 3 July 1994). If the complainant is still employed, the tribunal will also recommend what the employer must do to avoid any further acts of discrimination against that employee (*ibid.* section 56). If the complainant has been unlawfully dismissed on racial grounds, the employer will be ordered to reinstate or re-engage that employee in the same or an equivalent job. If the employer refuses to comply (or the complainant indicates that he or she does not wish to be reinstated or re-engaged), the tribunal will take that factor (and the complainant's wishes) into account when calculating the amount of compensation to be awarded. For further particulars, see **Dismissal** elsewhere in this handbook.

Compromise and COT 3 agreements

- An employee considering bringing a complaint of unlawful racial discrimination against his (or her) employer may agree to settle 'out of court' by entering into a compromise agreement with his employer. Such an agreement is binding on both parties, so long as it is willingly entered into and is prepared in accordance with section 72(4A) of the 1976 Act, as to which see **Compromise agreements** elsewhere in this handbook.

- So-called COT 3 agreements are likewise binding on both parties; as to which, please turn to the section titled **Conciliation officers** (notably page 66).

  Note: Under section 212A of the Trade Union & Labour Relations (Consolidation) Act 1992 (as inserted by section 7 of the Employment Rights (Dispute Resolution) Act 1998), the Advisory, Conciliation & Arbitration Service (ACAS) is empowered to arbitrate in disputes involving proceedings or claims which could be the subject of unfair dismissal proceedings.

Assistance by Commission for Racial Equality

- A person contemplating bringing legal proceedings against his employer (or a particular employer) for alleged unlawful discrimination under the Race Relations Act 1976, may apply to the Commission for Racial Equality for help in preparing his (or her) case. If the Commission is agreeable (eg, on the ground that the case raises a question of principle), it may advise the complainant, attempt to procure an 'out of court' settlement (see previous paragraphs), arrange for the giving of advice or assistance by a solicitor or counsel, arrange for representation by any person (including all such assistance as is usually given by a solicitor or counsel in the steps preliminary or incidental to any proceedings, or in arriving at or giving effect to a compromise to avoid or bring to an end any proceedings), or give any other form of assistance which the Commission may consider appropriate (*ibid*. section 66(2)). See also **Disabled persons, Sex discrimination** and **Victimisation** elsewhere in this handbook.

REDUNDANCY
(*Rights of employees*)

Key points

- The Redundancy Payments Act 1965 (whose provisions have long since been repealed and largely re-enacted in the Employment Rights Act

1996) came into force on 6 December 1965. The two principal objectives of the Act were to require employers to compensate redundant employees for the loss of their livelihoods and to establish a Redundancy Fund from which employers would recoup a percentage (or rebate) of any statutory redundancy payment due and paid to a redundant employee. However, the already (by then) much-mutilated redundancy rebates scheme was abolished when the Employment Act 1989 came into force on 16 January 1990.

- It should be noted that the purpose of the redundancy payments scheme is to compensate a redundant employee for the loss of his (or her) investment in his job – not, as might be supposed, to provide him with sufficient funds to help him survive a period of unemployment. Accordingly, any employee who has lost his job because of redundancy may legitimately claim income support or the jobseeker's allowance, notwithstanding that he may already have received a substantial tax-free redundancy payment from his employer (see *Wynes v Southrepps Hall Broiler Farm* [1968] ITR 407).

Employer's liability to pay

- Subject to certain conditions (discussed in the following paragraphs), an employer is liable to pay statutory redundancy pay to any employee of his who has either been dismissed on grounds of redundancy or laid-off or kept on short-time working for a period of four consecutive weeks (or for an aggregate of six weeks in a period of 13 consecutive weeks) (sections 135 and 148, Employment Rights Act 1996).

- An employer cannot contract-out of his (or her) duty to pay a statutory redundancy payment to those of his employees who are entitled to receive such payments. Any provision in a contract of employment (or otherwise), which purports to exclude or limit that duty, or to deny an employee his right to bring proceedings before an employment tribunal, is null and void *(ibid.* section 203). However, there are two exceptions to this rule. A COT 3 agreement, concluded with the intervention of a conciliation officer of ACAS under section 18 of the Employment Tribunals Act 1996, is legally binding on both parties to the relevant dispute and serves to waive the right of the employee to bring proceedings in respect of that dispute before an employment tribunal. The same applies to a compromise agreement properly concluded between an employee and his or her employer. For further particulars, please turn to the sections titled **Conciliation officers** and **Compromise agreements** elsewhere in this handbook.

- There can also be an exemption in the case of a redundancy agreement concluded between an employer and one or more trade unions representing employees. If the employees covered by such an agreement have a right in certain circumstances to payments on the termination of their employment, and those payments are not less beneficial to those employees than the redundancy payments to which they would otherwise be entitled under the provisions of the 1996 Act, the Secretary of State for Education & Employment may (on the application of all parties to the agreement) make an order exempting that agreement from those provisions. However, the Secretary of State will *not* make such an order unless satisfied that the agreement allows questions to be put to an employment tribunal concerning the amount of (or the entitlement of an employee to) a payment under that agreement (*ibid.* section 157). To date, few redundancy agreements have been the subject of an exemption order by the Secretary of State.

Qualifying conditions

- As a general rule, a redundant employee will not qualify to be paid a statutory redundancy payment unless, at the *relevant date*, he or she:

  - was under age 65 or below the *normal retiring age* (whichever is the lower of those ages) for a person (male or female) holding the position which that employee held;

  - had been employed for a minimum period of two years calculated from the date on which his or her period of employment began or from his or her 18th birthday (whichever is the later) and ending with the *relevant date*; and

  - had not unreasonably refused an offer of *suitable alternative employment* (whether in writing or not) made by his or her present employer, an associated employer, or by the new owner if the employer's undertaking was sold or transferred to another employer.

Meaning of 'relevant date'

- The expression *relevant date* means the date on which the notice given to a redundant employee by his employer expired. However, if the employee was dismissed without notice or was given less than the minimum number of weeks' notice prescribed by section 86 of the 1996 Act (namely, one week's notice for each year of service up to a maximum of 12 years), the *relevant date* (for the purposes of calculating an employee's entitlement to a statutory redundancy payment) will be the date on which that statutory minimum period of notice would have expired had it been given on the date on which notice was actually given.

Excluded categories

- The following categories of employee are excluded from any entitlement to a statutory redundancy payment:

  (a) an employee who is dismissed on grounds of gross misconduct (whether with or without notice) while under notice of dismissal on grounds of redundancy (*ibid.* section 140(1)); and

  (b) an otherwise redundant employee who unreasonably refuses an offer of suitable alternative employment or who has agreed to 'try out' another job but unreasonably terminates his (or her) employment during the trial period (*ibid.* section 141(2) and (3)).

Note: Since 25 October 1999, when section 32 of the Employment Relations Act 1999 came into force, employees who are made redundant while outside Great Britain (including employees who ordinarily work outside Great Britain) no longer forfeit their right to a statutory redundancy payment on the termination of their employment. Furthermore, with the coming into force on 1 October 2002, of the Fixed-term Employees (Prevention of Less Favourable Treatment) Regulations 2002, waiver clauses, in a fixed-term contract lasting or expected to last for two years or more, are no longer permissible or enforceable – unless the contract in question (or its accompanying waiver clause) was agreed or inserted before 1 October 2002.

Meaning of redundancy

- A redundancy situation arises when an employee is dismissed from his (or her) employment, and the dismissal is wholly or mainly attributable to:

  – the fact that his employer has ceased, or intends to cease, to carry on the business for the purposes of which the employee was employed; or has ceased, or intends to cease, to carry on that business in the place where the employee was so employed; or

  – the fact that there is a reduced need for employees of the same category as that employee to carry out work of a particular kind in the place where that employee is employed (*ibid.* section 139(1) and (2)) – which underlines the rationale behind the inclusion of an employee's job title in the written statement of terms of employment prescribed by Part I of the 1996 Act.

In other words, an employer may decide for sound commercial reasons (1) to close down his (or her) business altogether; (2) to move his business to a different location; or (3) to reduce the number of people he employs in certain departments or sections within the business. For example, a sudden and apparently permanent decline in export orders may prompt a manufacturer to reduce the number of production workers in his factory. In an extreme situation, he may very well be forced to shut down completely. See also **Dismissal on grounds of redundancy** elsewhere in this handbook.

Lay-offs and short-time working

- A redundancy situation will also arise if an employee has been repeatedly laid off or kept on short-time working for four or more weeks. It must be emphasised at this point that an employer may not lay-off an employee or transfer him (or her) to short-time working – however serious the situation may be – unless the employee's contract of employment contains a clause which allows the employer to do so. An employee may, of course, agree to be laid off or placed on short-time working (as the more desirable alternative to redundancy); but that agreement (preferably in writing) must be sought and obtained by the employer before he puts any such arrangement into effect.

  Note: For the meaning of the expressions 'lay-off' and 'short-time working', please turn to the section titled **Lay-offs and short-time working** elsewhere in this handbook.

- Subject to the foregoing, any employee who has been laid-off or kept on short-time working for a period of four consecutive weeks (or for an aggregate of six weeks within a 13-week period), may serve written notice on his (or her) employer that he intends to claim a redundancy payment. However, the notice must be served not later than four weeks after the end of the last of the weeks in which the employee was laid-off or kept on short-time working. Furthermore, it must be accompanied by at least one week's notice of termination of employment (or such longer period as the employee is required to give under the terms of his contract of employment).

- If the employer does not dispute the employee's claim to a redundancy payment and/or cannot guarantee to provide the employee with a period of full employment lasting at least 13 weeks (to commence not later than four weeks after the date of service of the 'notice of intention to claim'), the employee is entitled to be paid a statutory redundancy payment (provided, of course, that he qualifies for such a payment in terms of his age and length of employment at the relevant date) (*ibid.* Part XI, Chapter III). For further particulars, please turn to the section titled **Lay-offs and short-time working** elsewhere in this handbook.

Employee anticipating expiry of employer's notice

- A redundant employee working out his (or her) employer's notice will still qualify for a redundancy payment even if he hands in his resignation to take effect on a date earlier than the date on which his employer's notice is due to expire (so long as he does so within the 'obligatory period of notice' (see next paragraph) and provided always that his employer does not object to his leaving prematurely). However, this rule does *not* apply if the employer writes to the employee instructing him to withdraw his letter of resignation and to continue working until the date originally specified in the employer's notice. An employee who unreasonably refuses to carry on working in such circumstances thereby forfeits his right to a redundancy payment, although the question as to whether the employee's refusal was 'unreasonable' will be a matter for an employment tribunal to decide (*ibid.* sections 136(3) and 142) (but see next paragraph).

  Note: Section 142 of the 1996 Act endorses the right of an employee under notice of redundancy to look for and, if need be, take up alternative employment before the expiry of his (or her) employer's notice. Provided that his employer does not insist on the employee working out his notice period, the employee will retain his right (if any) to a statutory redundancy payment on the termination of his employment. See also **Time off work and redundancy** elsewhere in this handbook.

- The 'obligatory period of notice' referred to in the previous paragraph is the period of notice to which an employee is entitled under his (or her) contract of employment, or the minimum notice required to be given by the employer in accordance with section 86(1) of the 1996 Act (that is say, a minimum of one week's notice for each of a maximum 12 years' continuous employment), whichever is the greater. Even though a redundancy situation exists, or is imminent, there can be no entitlement to a redundancy payment if an employee terminates his employment before the beginning of that obligatory notice period (*ibid.* section 136(4)).

- In *Pritchard-Rhodes Ltd v Boon and Milton* [1979] IRLR 19, two employees each received a letter from their employer informing them that they were to be made redundant at some future (unspecified) date. But the letter assured them that their jobs would last 'for at least seven months'. Taking the initiative (or, more appropriately, 'jumping the gun'), both men terminated their contracts some six weeks later and put in a claim for redundancy payments. The Employment Appeal Tribunal held that, as the employees had not tendered their notices within the obligatory period of notice required to be given by their employer under section 86(1) of the 1996 Act, they were not entitled to statutory redundancy pay.

Voluntary redundancies

- Voluntary redundancies occur when an employer and one or more of his employees agree to part company. This situation quite often arises when an employer invites employees to take part in a voluntary redundancy programme – the purpose often being to encourage older employees to accept dismissal in deference to younger workers. So long as there is a genuine redundancy situation, an employee's willingness to be made redundant will not deny him his (or her) statutory entitlement to a redundancy payment.

'Bumping'

- The question arises as to whether an employee is truly redundant (and therefore entitled to a redundancy payment) if he (or she) is 'bumped' out of his job in order to make way for a more senior or longer-serving employee whose own job has been made redundant. *In Gimber v Spurrett* (1967) 2 ITR 308 (followed by the EAT in *Elliott Turbomachinery Ltd v Bates* [1981] ICR 218), it was held that an employee dismissed in such circumstances had indeed been dismissed by reason of redundancy. But, in a more recent case, that *of Church v West Lancashire NHS Trust* [1998] ICR 423, the EAT ruled otherwise, declaring that, although 'bumping' was one way of managing a redundancy situation, the 'bumped' employee's dismissal was not of itself attributable to a diminution in the requirement for employees to do work of the kind done by that employee. Although the *Church* decision has been appealed to the Court of Appeal, the 'bumping' issue appears to have been resolved by the decision of the House of Lords in *Murray v Foyle Meats Limited* [1999] ICR 827; [1999] IRLR 562. There, the Law Lords held that an employee's dismissal could be due to redundancy even if the work on which he (or she) was engaged was unaffected by a fall in demand or a business set-back elsewhere within the employing organisation. There was no reason, they said, why the dismissal of such an employee should not be attributable to a diminution in the employer's need for employees to do work of a particular kind, although an employer in such a case would nonetheless need to explain the causal connection.

Offer of suitable alternative employment

- If an employer makes a written or verbal offer to an otherwise redundant employee, either to renew his (or her) existing contract of employment or to re-engage him under a new contract, the employee will *not* be entitled to a redundancy payment if he unreasonably refuses that offer. However, the employer's offer must be made to the employee *before* his previous contract comes to an end. Furthermore, the new job must not only be suitable in relation to the employee (see next paragraph) but must be available to the employee either immediately on the end of his former employment or within the next four weeks (*ibid.* sections 138(1) and 141 (1)).

- To be suitable, the terms and conditions under which the employee would be employed under the new or renewed contract (including the location and capacity in which he (or she) would be employed) must either be the same or similar to those enjoyed by the employee under his previous contract (*ibid.* section 141(1), (2) and (3)).

Trial period in new employment

- If, on the other hand, an otherwise redundant employee is offered re-employment in a job whose terms and conditions differ wholly or in part from the corresponding provisions of his (or her) previous contract, the employee has the right to try out that alternative job for a period of up to four weeks (or for an agreed longer period, if retraining **is** required) (*ibid.* sections 138(2) and 141(4)).

- If, during or at the end of the trial period, the employee decides that the new job is unsuitable, he (or she) will be treated in law as having been dismissed on the day his previous contract of employment came to an end, and will be entitled to be paid a redundancy payment calculated to that earlier date. If, however, the employee unreasonably terminates his new contract, for reasons which are not immediately apparent, his employer may dispute his obligation to pay a redundancy payment. As always, the matter may be referred to an employment tribunal for a determination (*ibid.*).

- The question whether an offer of alternative employment is 'suitable' in relation to an employee is one of fact to be decided by an employment tribunal (see *Hitchcock v St Ann's Hosiery Company Ltd* [1971] ITR 98, QBD). Having decided that an offer *is* suitable, an employment tribunal will then need to decide whether an employee had acted reasonably or unreasonably in refusing that offer. Factors to be taken into account may include matters such as distance, family commitments, the unemployment situation in the area, etc (see *John Laing & Son Ltd v Best* [1968] ITR 3).

Redundancy consultations

- An employer who has it in mind to make 20 or more employees redundant within a period of 90 days or less, is duty-bound to discuss his (or her) proposals with persons who are *appropriate representatives* of any of the employees who may be affected by the proposed dismissals or may be affected by measures taken in connection with those dismissals (per section 188, Trade Union & Labour Relations (Consolidation) Act 1992, as amended by the Collective Redundancies & Transfer of Undertakings (Protection of Employment) (Amendment) Regulations 1999).

For these purposes, the *appropriate representatives* of any affected employees are:

- representatives of an independent trade union (shop stewards or works convenors), if the employees in question are of a description in respect of which the trade union is recognised by their employer as having collective bargaining rights (*ibid.* section 188(1B)) or, if there is no trade union representation;

- existing employee representatives or representatives specifically elected by their colleagues or workmates to represent their interests, to be consulted about their employer's redundancy proposals, and to receive information from their employer concerning those proposals (*ibid.*).

- In short, if the would-be redundant employees are of a description in respect of which an independent trade union is recognised by their employer, their employer must consult representatives of that trade union. If there is no trade union representation, the employer must consult existing employee representatives. If there are no existing employee representatives, the employer must ensure that the would-be redundant employees are allowed sufficient time (and the facilities) to elect one or more of their number to represent their interests in consultations with their employer. It is up to the employer to decide how many employee representatives should be elected (*ibid.* sections 188 and 188A).

- If, in spite of having been invited to do so, the affected employees fail within a reasonable time to elect one or more of their colleagues to represent their interests, their employer must nonetheless ensure that each of those employees receives the written particulars referred to below.

When must the redundancy consultations begin?

- Consultations with appropriate representatives should begin at the earliest opportunity, and must in any event begin:

- at least 90 days before the first of the dismissals is to take effect, if 100 or more employees at one establishment are to be dismissed as redundant within a period of 90 days or less; or

- at least 30 days before the first dismissal takes effect, if 20 or more, but fewer than 100, employees at one establishment are to be dismissed as redundant within a period of 90 days or less.

An employer who refuses or fails to consult with the appropriate representatives is liable to be ordered to pay each affected employee an amount not exceeding the equivalent of 90 days' pay (as to which, please turn to the section titled **Disclosure of information** earlier in this handbook).

Scope of consultations

- Consultations with the appropriate representatives must include consultation about ways to:

    (a) avoid the dismissals;

    (b) reduce the number of employees to be dismissed; and

    (c) mitigate the consequences of the dismissals,

    and must be undertaken by the employer with a view to reaching agreement with those representatives (*ibid.* section 188(2)).

Written particulars

- For the purposes of the redundancy consultations, the employer must write to each of the relevant representatives:

    (a) explaining the reasons for the proposed redundancies;

    (b) listing the numbers and descriptions of employees whom it is proposed to make redundant;

    (c) specifying the total number of employees of any such description who are currently employed at the establishment in which the redundancies are to take place;

    (d) outlining the proposed method for selecting the employees who may be made redundant; and

    (e) explaining what severance payments (if any) are to be made to the redundant employees – in addition to their entitlement (if any) to statutory redundancy pay – and how those severance payments are to be calculated.

The letter or document containing the above particulars must either be delivered by hand to each representative or be posted to an address nominated by the representatives. In the case of trade union representatives, the letter should be sent by post to the union's head office (*ibid.* section 188(5)).

- Representatives involved in the consultation process must be allowed to talk to the employees who are on the list of likely candidates for redundancy and must be afforded access to an office and telephone ('such accommodation and facilities as may be appropriate') so as to enable them to conduct such meetings in private (*ibid.* section 188).

- It is neither acceptable nor lawful for an employer to refuse or fail to enter into consultations on the grounds that the decision to make 20 or more employees redundant was taken by a parent or holding company (perhaps located elsewhere in Great Britain, or overseas) and that he does not have the authority to explore ways and means of avoiding the redundancies or reducing the number of employees to be dismissed, or to take steps to mitigate the consequences of the dismissals. Nor can he use that same (or a similar) excuse to justify his refusal or failure to give the *written particulars* referred to earlier.

- For information about complaints to, and the penalties to be applied by, an employment tribunal, when an employer refuses or fails to comply with his obligation to enter into consultations with employee or trade union representatives (or with any associated duties), please turn to the section titled **Disclosure of information** earlier in this handbook.

Notifying the Secretary of State for Trade and Industry

- An employer proposing to make 20 or more employees redundant must not only consult with the appropriate employee representatives but must also notify the Secretary of State for Trade & Industry (in practice, the nearest Redundancy Payments Office of the Department of Trade & Industry (DTI)) *before* those proposals are put into effect (*ibid.* section 193).

- The notification must be given in writing (using form HR 1 supplied by the DTI):

  - at least 90 days before the first dismissal is to take effect, if 100 or more employees at the same establishment are to be dismissed as redundant within a period of 90 days or less; or

– at least 30 days before the first dismissal is to take effect, if 20 or more employees (but fewer than 100) at the same establishment are to be dismissed as redundant within a period of 30 days or less.

A copy of form HR 1 must also be sent to each of the employee and/or trade union representatives involved in the consultation process described earlier in this section (*ibid.* section 193).

- At any time after receiving formal notification of impending redundancies, the DTI may approach the employer in question for further information. Any employer who refuses or neglects to forewarn the DTI about his redundancy proposals, or who refuses to respond to a request for additional information, is guilty of an offence and liable, on summary conviction, to a fine of up to £5,000 (*ibid.* section 194).

Calculation of redundancy payments

- The method used for calculating redundancy payments is outlined in section 162 of the Employment Rights Act 1996. Just how much a redundant employee is entitled to be paid (assuming he (or she) satisfies the minimum qualifying conditions discussed earlier in this section) is determined by reference to his age, length of service (including any service with a previous employer which counts as part of his total period of continuous employment), and weekly pay at the effective date of termination of his contract of employment. Thus a redundant employee under normal retiring age at the time of his (or her) dismissal, who has worked for his employer for a minimum continuous period of two years (excluding any period of employment before his 18th birthday) must receive at least:

  – one-and-a-half weeks' pay for each year of employment in which he (or she) was not below the age of 41;

  – one week's pay for each year of employment in which he (or she) was below the age of 41 but not below the age of 22; and

  – a half week's pay for each year of employment in which the employee was below the age of 22 but not below the age of 18.

Calculations may lawfully exclude any period of service in excess of 20 years (counting backwards from the date on which the employment ends or is due to end) and may ignore weekly earnings (or average weekly earnings) in excess of £260 per week – which upper amount is reviewed in January of each year. Thus, the maximum *statutory* redundancy payment currently payable to an employee is £7,800 (ie, 20 × 1.5 × £260). Employers are, of course, free to 'top up' the statutory amount if they so wish.

Note: A Ready Reckoner for Redundancy Payments (Form RPL2) will be supplied on request by local employment offices of the Department for Work & Pensions. The Ready Reckoner is also reproduced in booklet PL 808 available from Job Centres, and *(Redundancy Payments)* available from Job Centres and local offices of the Employment Department.

- Furthermore, if a redundant employee (male or female) has already had his or her 64th birthday before the *relevant date* (see below), the amount of redundancy pay otherwise payable to that employee can legally be reduced by one-twelfth for each complete calendar month by which his or her age exceeds 64. Thus, a redundant employee aged 64 years and eight months when dismissed can expect to have his (or her) redundancy pay reduced by eight-twelfths (or two-thirds) (*ibid.,* section 162(4) and (5)).

- Reckonable employment, excluding periods which do not count but which do not break continuity, but including, where applicable, any relevant employment with a former employer (eg, the previous owner of the business – as to which, see **Continuous employment** elsewhere in this handbook) must be aggregated to make complete years. No payment is due for a fraction of a year. But excess reckonable employment in a higher age bracket will count towards employment in the age bracket immediately below. And, because of the upper service limit of 20 years referred to earlier, the number of complete years of continuous employment must be reckoned backwards from the date of expiry of notice (or, where no notice was given, the date of expiry of the statutory minimum period of notice which the employee would otherwise have been entitled to receive) (see **Notice of termination of employment** elsewhere in this handbook).

A week's pay

- A *week's pay* in the case of an employee paid monthly (whose salary is invariably expressed as an annual sum) is his (or her) annual income divided by 52. When an employee's pay varies with the amount of work done, as when pay is partly made up of bonuses or commission, the amount of a week's pay will be the average of that employee's weekly earnings over the 12-week period ending with the last complete week in which he or she actually worked. The same applies in the case of hourly-paid employees, when a week's pay will be the average of an employee's earnings over the same 12-week period. However, overtime premium payments will not feature in calculations – unless the employee's contract requires the employer to provide a specified number of overtime hours each week and requires the employee to work those extra hours. The fact that a redundant employee may have worked overtime, week in and week out, for many years will not entitle him to have his overtime income included in calculations for redundancy pay. If overtime working is in any sense voluntary, it (and the premium payments it generates) will be disregarded.

Note: If an employee's contract stipulates that he (or she) will be paid an annual bonus calculated as a fixed percentage of his salary or earnings during the previous period of 12 months, the relevant proportion of that bonus must be included in the amount of a week's pay. If, on the other hand, payment of a Christmas (or equivalent) bonus is at the absolute discretion of the employer, that bonus will *not* be included in calculations.

- For most employees, whose contracts of employment stipulate normal weekly working hours, it is relatively easy to calculate the amount of a week's pay. An Employment Department booklet titled *Rules Governing Continuous Employment and a Week's Pay* (Ref PL 711) explains the method for calculating a week's pay in the case of shift-workers and others whose working hours often vary from week to week. Copies of the booklet are available on request from any office of the Employment Service.

Note: In certain situations, an employer may choose to offset pensions (and lump sum payments) provided under an occupational pension scheme against statutory redundancy payments. Full details of the statutory provisions on account of pension, and examples showing the calculations are set out in Department for Work & Pensions leaflet PPL 1 (which should be readily available from Job Centres or unemployment benefit offices).

Calculations must be explained

- Every statutory redundancy payment must be accompanied by a written statement explaining precisely how that payment was calculated. Any employer who fails to comply with this requirement, without reasonable excuse, is guilty of an offence and liable on summary conviction to a fine of up to £200. An employer who fails to respond to a letter sent by a redundant employee demanding to be sent (or given) the explanatory statement within a specified period (not less than one week), is guilty of a further offence and liable on conviction to a fine of up to £1,000 (*ibid.* section 165).

References to an employment tribunal

- Any question as to the right of an employee to a redundancy payment, or as to the amount actually paid, must be referred to an employment tribunal within six months of the date of the employer's refusal or failure to pay (*ibid.* sections 163 and 164). If a tribunal upholds the employee's complaint, it will make a declaration to that effect and will order the employer to pay the amount of the redundancy payment due.

- If an employer is liable to pay a redundancy payment to an employee, but has either refused or is unable to do so because he (or she) is insolvent or in serious financial difficulties, the employee may apply to the Secretary of State for Education & Employment for a payment out of the National Insurance Fund. If the Department of Employment is satisfied that there is little chance of the employer being in a position to pay, it will pay the money directly to the claimant employee. The Department will then take the necessary steps to recover the money from the defaulting employer (or, as appropriate, from the relevant liquidator or trustee in bankruptcy) (*ibid.* sections 166 to 169).

Redundancy during maternity absence

- An employee absent from work on ordinary or additional maternity leave, who is not permitted to return to work because of redundancy, is entitled to be offered suitable alternative employment or (if there is nothing suitable for her to do) a redundancy payment. For further particulars, see **Maternity rights** elsewhere in this handbook.

Unlawful selection for redundancy

- Any employee dismissed or selected for redundancy for an inadmissible or unlawful reason, or for asserting one or other of his (or her) statutory employment rights will be treated in law as having been unfairly dismissed (*ibid.* sections 104 and 105); as to which, please turn to the sections titled **Dismissal** (notably the paragraphs headed *Inadmissible and unlawful reasons for dismissal*) and **Dismissal for asserting a statutory right**, elsewhere in this handbook.

  See also **Dismissal, Dismissal for refusing Sunday work, Dismissal in health and safety cases, Dismissal of an employee or workforce representative, Dismissal of a pension scheme trustee, Dismissal on grounds of redundancy, Dismissal on grounds of trade union membership, Insolvency of employer, Lay-offs and short-time working,** and **Time off work and redundancy.**

REFERENCES

Key points

- As the High Court remarked in *Lawton v BOC Transhield Ltd* [1987] IRLR 404, an employer is under no legal obligation to give a former employee a reference. But, if he (or she) does do so, he owes a duty to that employee to take reasonable care to ensure that the opinions he expresses in it are based on accurate facts and, in so far as the reference itself states facts, that those facts are themselves accurate. When an employer approaches another employer for information and opinions about one of the latter's employees (past or present), it should be self-evident, said the court, that the employee in question has proffered his (or her) former employer's name as referee, that he is being seriously considered for employment elsewhere, that he is relying on the former employer to get his facts right, and that an adverse report would almost certainly result in his being taken off the short list or remaining unemployed for an unspecified period. In other words, the employer's duty of care extends not only to the person seeking the relevant information but also to the employee in respect of whom that information is being sought.

Defamatory references

- There are a number of pitfalls facing employers who provide inaccurate, dishonest or malicious references. An employee may be prompted to bring an action for damages if a reference supplied by a former employer contains false or derogatory statements about him (or her) which result in the loss of his livelihood or affect his ability to find work or pursue his chosen trade or profession.

  Note: In *Spring v Guardian Assurance plc* [1993] IRLR 122, the High Court awarded damages and costs to an insurance salesman when it ruled that his former employer had been negligent in giving him a job reference that was the 'kiss of death' to his career. The reference, said Judge John Lever QC, was carelessly written, although not malicious. One of the main authors behind the reference, he said, had 'told a lie to bolster a conclusion he honestly believed to be true'. The other, while not malicious in intent, had failed to give 'a careful and accurate view' of the salesman's qualities. 'There should have been a careful and judicious review', added Judge-Lever, 'but his prejudice led him to play fast and loose with the facts.'

- If a defamatory reference is given in writing, it constitutes libel. If it is given orally (ie, over the telephone), it constitutes slander. For obvious reasons, slander is somewhat more difficult to prove than libel – which explains why many employers and personnel managers prefer to discuss a difficult employee's capabilities and recent conduct in person or over the telephone.

- An employer has three defences to an action for libel. He can plead, in the first instance, that the words used in the reference were incapable of having any defamatory meaning. He can also plead 'justification'. In other words, while admitting the truth of the employee's allegations, he can argue that the information given in the reference is true in substance and in fact (but see *Spent convictions* below). Finally, he can claim that the reference enjoyed 'qualified privilege', in the sense that the employer or person to whom it was given had an interest in learning of the employee's capabilities and shortcomings in order to assess his suitability for employment, and that no malice was intended. If either of the latter defences fails, the court will very likely order the employer who gave the reference to compensate the employee for the damage done to his reputation and employment prospects.

Note: It is because of the possible legal pitfalls that many employers nowadays refuse to supply more than a written statement of service – confirming a former employee's job title, length of employment, and his wage or salary at the time he or she left their employ.

Disclaimer of responsibility

- Giving an employee a wholly complimentary reference, which attributes to him (or her) skills, qualities and a level of competence which he does not possess, can be just as risky as giving him a reference which negligently misrepresents or downgrades his worth in the eyes of a prospective employer. Any employer who is deceived into hiring an employee on the strength of a commendatory or untrue reference may bring an action for damages against the employer who supplied the reference for the time, inconvenience and expense involved in taking-on an employee who is wholly unsuitable. To prevent this happening, an employer should always protect himself with a disclaimer of responsibility.

- As Mr Justice Tudor Evans remarked in the *Lawton* case referred to earlier, there is 'no reason why a disclaimer [in a reference] cannot be so framed as to exclude a liability not only to the recipient but also to the subject of the reference, and further to protect the actual servant who writes the reference. As to the subject of the reference, I cannot see,' he added, 'why an employer cannot effectively protect himself, either in the reference itself or by writing separately to the subject, indicating a willingness to give a reference but stating that it will be given without responsibility.

- Personnel managers and others charged with the responsibility for giving references (or 'vetting' them before they are issued) should ensure that every reference given to, or on behalf of, a former employee includes a statement to the effect that it is given 'without legal responsibility'. However, it is as well to sound a note of caution. While a disclaimer of responsibility couched in those terms will free an employer from liability when faced with an action for negligent misrepresentation, it unfortunately provides no defence against an action for libel. Indeed, it will be of little help if it can be shown that the employer (or person) who provided the reference deliberately and fraudulently misrepresented the employee's qualifications, skills, experience and capabilities.

The issue of confidentiality

- As a reference is usually given in confidence, an employer will not normally reveal its contents to the employee concerned without the express permission of the person or organisation who gave it. However, as the House of Lords remarked in the joined cases of *Nasse v Science Research Council and Vyas v Leyland Cars* [1979] IRLR 465, 'there is no principle in English law by which documents are protected from discovery by reason of confidentiality alone'. If a job applicant or employee believes that he (or she) has been the victim of unlawful discrimination or was denied employment (or dismissed) because of what was said about him in a reference, he has every right to apply to the tribunals or courts for a disclosure order.

- Under the Data Protection Act 1998, references issued by an employer (concerning an existing or former employer) are exempt from disclosure. But that exemption does *not* apply to references received by an employer from a former employer. For further information, please turn to the section titled **Data protection** elsewhere in this handbook.

Written reasons for dismissal

- A sympathetic employer might well be prompted to provide a 'charitable' or vaguely-worded reference to a dismissed employee (or to a prospective employer) rather than undermine his (or her) chances of finding work elsewhere. However, an employer should be alert to the possibility that that same employee might well decide to exercise his statutory right under section 92 of the Employment Rights Act 1996 to be given written reasons for his dismissal. If there is any contradiction between the opinions expressed in the one and the statements made in the other, an employment tribunal might well decide that the employee's dismissal was unfair. See **Written reasons for dismissal** elsewhere in this handbook.

Note: In *Castledine v Rothwell Engineering Ltd* [1973] IRLR 99, a dismissed employee produced a reference supplied by his former employer which stated that he 'had carried out his duties satisfactorily, often under difficult conditions'. The written statement of reasons for dismissal, also supplied by his employer, claimed that the employee had been dismissed on grounds of incompetence. When confronted with such conflicting evidence, an industrial tribunal had no difficulty concluding that the dismissal had been unfair.

Spent convictions

- Unless a former employee is known to be applying for a job in respect of which he (or she) is obliged to supply details of all **criminal** convictions – *spent* or otherwise – and the prospective new employer specifically asks for that information and gives reasons for doing so, an employer is under no legal obligation whatsoever to reveal particulars of *spent* convictions known to him when supplying a reference for that employee (section 4(2), Rehabilitation of Offenders Act 1974). For further details, see **Convicted persons, employment of** elsewhere in this handbook.

See also **Dismissal** and **Employment tribunals and procedure**.

REST BREAKS AND REST PERIODS
(*Statutory provisions*)

Key points

- Until the appearance of the Working Time Regulations 1998 – which came into force on 1 October 1998 – workers in Great Britain had no general statutory right to time off work for meals or rest; nor did they have the right to daily or weekly rest periods. Earlier factory legislation restricting the working hours and periods of employment of women and young persons (and, in some instances, men) was repealed some years ago by the Employment Act 1989. Before the appearance of the 1998 Regulations, the only other protection afforded to employees was (and is) to be found in the Road Traffic Act 1968 and, for drivers of vehicles of 3.5 tonnes and over, the relevant EC Regulations (as to which, please turn to the section titled **Working hours** elsewhere in this handbook.

Note: Legislation restricting the working hours and periods of employment of airline pilots, deep sea divers, and persons employed in specialist occupations will be familiar to employers in the industries in question and is beyond the scope of this handbook.

- The Working Time Regulations 1998, which extend to Great Britain only, implement Council Directive 93/104/EC (the 'Working Time Directive') of 23 November 1998 'concerning certain aspects of the organisation of working time'. They also incorporate Council Directive 94/33/EC of 22 June 1994 'on the protection of young people at work'.

- The reader will note that the 1998 Regulations give rights to 'workers' and not just to employees. In other words, they apply equally to casual, seasonal and temporary workers (including agency 'temps'), as well as to part-timers, trainees engaged on work experience, or training, and to freelances. They do *not*, however, apply to persons who are genuinely self-employed.

The Working Time Regulations 1998

The right to rest breaks and periods summarised

- Briefly, *adult* workers (other than those in *excluded sectors and occupations* and those to whom the term *other special cases apply* – see below) are entitled to a minimum in-work rest break of 20 minutes, if their working day or shift exceeds or is likely to exceed six hours; a minimum daily rest period of 11 hours between the end of one working day or shift and the beginning of the next; and a minimum weekly rest period of 24 hours (or 48 hours averaged over a fortnight).

- *Workers under the age of 18* are entitled to a minimum in-work rest break of 30 minutes during any working day or shift lasting or expected to last for more than four-and-a-half hours; a minimum daily rest period of 12 hours between the end of one working day or shift and the beginning of the next; and a minimum weekly rest period of 48 hours.

The 'ifs' and buts' attached to those rights are explained in more detail in the following pages.

Excluded sectors and occupations

- For the time being at least, the 1998 Regulations do not apply to *adult* workers who are sea fishermen, transport workers (ie, persons engaged in the air, rail, road, sea, inland waterway or lake transport industries, or in ancillary occupations), doctors in training, members of the police or armed forces, or civil protection workers. Nor do they apply to managing executives and other persons with autonomous decision-making powers (that is to say, people whose working time is not measured or predetermined by their employers or who determine their own patterns of work) (*ibid.* regulations 18 and 20). Young persons under 18 are, however, protected by the 1998 Regulations, regardless of whether they fall into one or other of the employment categories listed above.

- Even though *adult* workers in the sectors or occupations listed above do not enjoy specific protection under the 1998 Regulations, their employers should not lose sight of their overriding duty under the Health & Safety at Work etc Act 1974 to do all that they reasonably can to ensure the health, safety and welfare at work of each and every person in their employ. An employer's refusal or failure to provide suitable rest breaks and rest periods for workers (especially those engaged in heavy physical work, or work involving the operation of dangerous machines, or exposure to hazardous chemicals or substances) will not only undermine their health and general well-being, but could also expose them to the risk of physical injury directly attributable to fatigue, inattentiveness or carelessness. An employer successfully prosecuted under the 1974 Act could be ordered to pay a fine of up to £20,000.

Note: The DTI's *Guide to the Working Time Regulations* (see *Further information* below) cautions employers to consider granting regular rest breaks to production line workers and others engaged on uninterruptible or monotonous work in order to reduce any associated risks to their health and safety.

Other special cases

- The right to in-work rest breaks, and daily and weekly rest periods, *do not* apply to sales representatives and others whose duties keep them constantly 'on the move'. Nor do those rights apply to other workers who work away from home (occasionally working longer hours for short periods). Also excluded are workers who have no set pattern of work; journalists, television crews and broadcasters; security guards; doctors, nurses and hospital workers; workers in residential care homes; gas, electricity and water workers; postal and telecommunications workers; refuse collectors; farm workers; and so on.

- Workers whose working hours and periods of employment are affected by foreseeable surges in activity (eg, the summer tourist season, postal deliveries over Christmas and Easter, etc) will also forfeit their rights to rest breaks, etc at such times, as will workers affected by unforeseen circumstances (eg, an accident or dangerous occurrence at the workplace, or a last-minute rush order for goods or services).

- Once again, these exceptions described in the preceding two paragraphs apply only to *adult* workers – and are subject to the proviso that their employers must, wherever possible and within a reasonable time, allow those workers equivalent periods of compensatory rest. If, in exceptional circumstances, an employer finds it impossible to grant compensatory periods of rest, he (or she) must make other appropriate provisions to safeguard the health, safety and well-being of those employees (*ibid.* regulations 21 and 24).

In-work rest breaks

- Every *adult* worker whose working day or shift lasts or is expected to last for more than six hours, is entitled to take an uninterrupted rest break of at least 20 minutes in the course of that working day or shift. Workers under the age of 18, whose working day or shift lasts or is expected to last for more than four and a half hours, are each entitled to a minimum 30-minute rest break during those hours. Workers must be allowed to take their breaks away from their desks or workstations (*ibid.* regulation 12(1) and (2)).

- It is not acceptable for an employer to require his or her workers (adult or otherwise) to take their meal or rest breaks at the beginning or end of their working day or shift. Indeed, in the mainstream of industry and commerce, very few workers (let alone their representative trade unions) would be prepared to tolerate any such arrangement. Nor are they likely to accept meal and rest breaks lasting just 20 short minutes (whether in total or in the aggregate) in the course of a normal working day or shift. It has to be remembered that the 1998 Regulations lay down minimum (health and safety) requirements that (for most workplaces) bear little resemblance to contemporary employment practices.

- Arrangements for in-work meal and rest breaks (lunch breaks, coffee and tea breaks, etc will usually be incorporated into an employee's contract of employment or in either a *workforce agreement* (see *Note* below) or a collective agreement negotiated with a recognised independent trade union. Such agreements may modify or exclude the application of regulation 12(1) in relation to particular adult workers or groups of workers, so long as the workers covered by any such agreement are permitted to take equivalent periods of compensatory rest or receive other appropriate protection (ibid. regulations 23 and 24). See also *Other special cases* above.

Note: A 'workforce agreement' is a written agreement between an employer and his (or her) workers or a particular group of workers or their elected representatives, modifying or excluding one or more of the provisions of the 1998 Regulations, explained more fully in the DTI's *Guide to the Working Time Regulations* (see *Further information* below).

In-work rest breaks: paid or unpaid?

- The 1998 Regulations do not require employers to pay workers their normal wages or salaries during meal and rest breaks. It follows that contracts of employment and collective agreements should leave employees and workers in no doubt as to whether their in-work breaks are paid or unpaid.

Young persons and 'force majeure'

- Except in a case of *force majeure*, there is no exception to the rule prescribing minimum in-work rest breaks for workers under the age of 18. Young workers may be required to forego their right to such breaks if, but only if, there is some unusual or unforeseeable occurrence or problem (beyond their employer's control) that needs to be dealt with immediately, and for which there are no (or an insufficient number of) adult workers available to do the work. The same applies if there is an exceptional event that requires 'all hands to the pumps'. If a young person is required to forego an in-work rest break in such circumstances, the employer must see to it that he (or she) is allowed an equivalent period of compensatory rest *within the following three weeks* (*ibid.* regulation 27).

Daily rest periods

- In addition to the in-work rest breaks discussed in the preceding paragraphs, every *adult* worker is entitled to a rest period of not less than 11 consecutive hours in each 24-hour period during which he (or she) works for an employer. For workers *under the age of 18*, the minimum daily rest period is 12 consecutive hours in every such 24-hour period. For most workers, this means a minimum 11 or 12-hour work-free rest period between the end of one working day or shift and the beginning of the next (*ibid.* regulation 10).

No general exception for young workers

- Other than in a case of *force majeure* (discussed earlier), there is no general exception to the rule requiring young workers under 18 to be allowed a minimum 12-hour rest period in each 24-hour period. However, that rest period may be interrupted if a young person is engaged in activities involving periods of work that are split up over the day or are of short duration (*ibid.* regulations 10 and 27).

Exceptions for adult workers

- The right of *adult* workers to a minimum daily rest period of 11 consecutive hours in each 24-hour period may be modified or excluded by a workforce or collective agreement, so long as the workers covered by any such agreement are permitted to take equivalent periods of compensatory rest or receive other appropriate protection (ibid. regulations 23 and 24). See also *Other special cases* above (*ibid.* regulations 18, 20, 21 and 24).

Exceptions for adult shift workers, cleaning staff, etc

- There is an exception also in the case of *adult* shift workers. In brief, the right of adult workers to a minimum daily rest period of 11 consecutive hours does not apply when they change shifts and cannot take a daily rest period between the end of one shift and the start of the next. The same exception applies to adult cleaning staff and others engaged in activities involving periods of work split up over the day. In those circumstances, every affected worker must nonetheless be granted an equivalent period of compensatory rest within the next two or three weeks. If, in exceptional circumstances – which must, by definition, be rare – it is not possible to grant a compensatory rest period, the employer must nonetheless ensure that the worker is afforded 'appropriate protection' to safeguard his (or her) health and safety (*ibid.* regulations 22 and 24).

Patterns of work

- Under regulation 8 of the 1998 Regulations, employers are duty bound to ensure that every worker in their employ is given adequate rest breaks – the more so if the work on which the worker is engaged is monotonous or the work-rate is predetermined. A failure to comply with that duty could lead to prosecution by a health and safety inspector (or local authority environmental health officer). The penalty on summary conviction is a fine of up to £2,000 or, if the conviction is obtained on indictment, a fine of an unlimited amount.

Weekly rest periods

- In addition to their right to a minimum daily rest period of 11 consecutive hours, *adult* workers have the right to an uninterrupted weekly rest period of at least 24 hours in each seven-day period in addition to that 11-hour break. However, their employer may elect to adapt that right so that an adult worker is entitled either to two uninterrupted rest periods, each lasting not less than 24 hours, in each 14-day period, or one uninterrupted rest period lasting at least 48 hours in each 14-day period. A workforce or collective agreement may modify or exclude an adult employee's right to a minimum weekly rest break under the 1998 Regulations, so long as the employee is allowed to take an equivalent period of compensatory rest within the next week or two. If, in exceptional circumstances only, a substitute rest period is not possible, the employee is entitled to look to his (or her) employer for other 'appropriate protection'.

- This means, in brief, that adult workers are entitled to one day off work in every seven-day period (or week); or, if their employer so determines, either two separate days or two consecutive days off work in every fortnight. Unless a workforce or collective agreement (or a worker's contract) states otherwise, a 'week' for these purposes is the period of seven consecutive days from Monday to Sunday, inclusive.

- In some situations, it may not be possible for *adult* shift workers when they change shifts to take a weekly rest period between the end of one shift and the start of the next one. If this happens, their employer must nonetheless allow them to take equivalent periods of compensatory rest within a reasonable time afterwards (up to two months).

Young workers under 18

- Young workers under the age of 18 are entitled to a minimum two consecutive days off work (ie, 48 consecutive hours) in each seven-day period; in other words two days off work each week. Those minimum 48 hours may be interrupted if the worker's activities involve periods of work that are split up over the day or are of short duration. Furthermore, they may be reduced to *not less than 36 hours* if, but only if, justified by inherent technical or organisational reasons. Employers should be wary of creating such a reason (or abusing this facility) in order simply to deny a young worker his or her right to a minimum 48 consecutive hours off work each week (*ibid.* regulation 11(8)).

Complaints to an employment tribunal

- Complaints about an employer's refusal or failure to acknowledge an employee's rights to in-work rest breaks and/or daily and rest periods (including the right to take equivalent periods of compensatory rest) may be presented to an employment tribunal within three months of the alleged refusal or failure. Such complaints, may be presented regardless of the employee or worker's age or length of service at the material time. It is as well to add that a worker (as employee or otherwise) has no need to resign in order to present such a complaint.

- If the worker's complaint is upheld, the employer will be ordered to pay compensation to the worker of such amount as the tribunal considers just and equitable in all the circumstances. In determining the amount of compensation, the tribunal will have regard to the employer's default in refusing to permit the worker to exercise his (or her) statutory rights, and any resultant loss sustained by that worker.

- Any worker (as employee or otherwise) who is victimised (ie, punished, disciplined or subjected to any other detriment), dismissed or selected for redundancy for challenging his (or her) employer's refusal to allow the rest breaks and rest periods prescribed by the 1998 Regulations, may yet again register a complaint with an employment tribunal. Again, such a complaint may be presented regardless of the employee or worker's age or length of continuous service at the material time. If the complaint is upheld, the employer will be ordered to pay the complainant a quite substantial amount of compensation. A similar heavy penalty will apply if an employee or worker is dismissed or selected for redundancy for challenging his (or her) employer's intransigence or for asserting his statutory rights before a tribunal or court (*per* sections 45A, 101A, 104(4)(d) and 105(4A), Employment Rights Act 1996, as inserted by regulations 31 and 32 of the 1998 Regulations).

Written statement of employment particulars

- Employers have a duty under sections 1 to 7 of the Employment Rights Act 1996 to issue a written statement of terms of employment to *every* person in their employ. Strictly speaking, this right extends to employees only (although, this in no way undermines the rights of casual workers, freelances and others under the 1998 Regulations).

- The statement (commonly, although incorrectly, referred to as the 'contract of employment') must include particulars of any terms and conditions relating to hours of work (including any particulars relating to normal working hours, which, by definition, should include information about breaks for meals and rest and whether those breaks are paid or unpaid). If there are no particulars to be included under the heading of working hours, the statement must say as much. In the light of the changes introduced by the Working Time Regulations 1998, written statements issued before 1 October 1998 should by now have been amended and re-issued if an employee's contractual rights to rest breaks, etc fall short of his (or her) statutory rights under the 1998 Regulations.

- An employer's refusal or failure to provide each of his (or her) employees with a written statement, or to provide a statement that does not contain all of the particulars prescribed by the 1996 Act, may be referred to an employment tribunal by any disaffected employee. If the employee's complaint is upheld but the employer remains uncooperative, the tribunal may determine what particulars ought to be included in the written statement and will itself import those particulars into the employee's contract of employment, to be enforced, if need be, by another tribunal or (where appropriate) by a civil court. An employee has no need to resign in order to pursue his (or her) statutory rights before an employment tribunal. An employer who responds by dismissing such an employee will be ordered by a tribunal to pay that employee a substantial amount of compensation (*per* sections 11, 104 and 105, Employment Rights Act 1996).

Further information

- The Department of Trade & Industry (DTI) has published a comprehensive *Guide to the Working Time Regulations* (Ref URN 98/894), copies of which will be supplied (free of charge) by telephoning the DTI on 0845 6000 925.

  Further advice on the rights of employees to rest breaks and rest periods under the 1998 Regulations can be sought by contacting one or other of the following ACAS public enquiry points:

Birmingham	0121 456 5856
Bristol	0117 974 9500
Cardiff	029 2076 1126
Fleet	01252 811868
Glasgow	0141 204 2677
Leeds	0113 243 1371
Liverpool	0151 427 8881
London	020 7396 5100
Manchester	0161 833 8585
Newcastle	0191 261 2191
Nottingham	0115 969 3355

Health and safety legislation

- The notion that employees must be allowed meal and rest breaks in the interests of their health, safety and welfare is reinforced by regulation 25 of the Workplace (Health, Safety & Welfare) Regulations 1992, which imposes a duty on every employer to provide suitable and sufficient rest facilities for his employees, including suitable and sufficient facilities for eating meals, where meals are regularly eaten in the workplace.

- Indeed, there are safety regulations concerning work with prescribed dangerous or hazardous substances that forbid employees to eat or drink in workrooms or to wear work clothing during their meal breaks. In such circumstances, the employer is required to set aside a place where employees can take their meals in relative comfort. The Regulations in question are:

  - the Control of Asbestos at Work Regulations 2002 ;

  - the Control of Lead at Work Regulations 2002;

  - the Control of Substances Hazardous to Health Regulations 2002; and

  - the Ionising Radiations Regulations 1999 .

- For further particulars, please turn to the section titled **Canteens and rest rooms for employees** elsewhere in this handbook.

Pregnant employees and nursing mothers

- Regulation 25 of the Workplace (Health, Safety & Welfare) Regulations 1992 requires employers to provide suitable rest facilities for use by any employee who is pregnant or a nursing mother. Again, the implication is that an employer should think twice before denying a pregnant or breastfeeding mother (or any woman who has given birth within the previous six months) time off during the working day to make use of the rest facilities that he is duty-bound to provide for just such a contingency (as to which, see **Pregnant employees and nursing mothers** elsewhere in this handbook).

  A failure to provide suitable rest facilities for new or expectant mothers could lead to prosecution and a fine of up to £5,000.

S

SCHOOL LEAVING DATE

Key points

- In England and Wales the school leaving date for a child who turns 16 on or after the beginning of a school year is the last Friday in June. A child who turns 16 after that last Friday in June, but *before* the beginning of the next school year, may likewise lawfully leave school on that last Friday in June. In Scotland, a child who turns 16 during the period from 1 March to 30 September, inclusive, may leave school on 31 May of that same year. Children whose 16th birthdays occur outside that period must remain at school until the first day of the Christmas holidays.

- These provisions are currently to be found in section 8 of the Education Act 1996, supported by the Education (School Leaving Date) Order 1997, and (for Scotland) in section 31 of the Education (Scotland) Act 1980.

- Given the many restrictions on the employment of school-age children, employers (or would-be employers) who have doubts about the true age of young employees and job applicants would be wise to contact their local education authorities for further particulars. Alternatively, they should insist on the production of a birth certificate or (as is their right and on payment of a small fee) apply to the registrar or superintendent registrar of births, deaths and marriages for a certified copy of that birth certificate.

See also **Birth certificates, Children, employment of** and **Women and young persons, employment of** elsewhere in this handbook.

SEX DISCRIMINATION
(Employment and other fields)

Key points

- Under the provisions of the Sex Discrimination Act 1975 (as amended), it is unlawful for an employer in Great Britain to discriminate against an employee or job applicant (male or female) on grounds of sex or marital status or because the person in question intends to undergo, is undergoing, or has undergone 'gender reassignment' (as to which latter, see the *Note* below). The 1975 Act, which came into force on 29 December 1975, established the Equal opportunities Commission (EOC) with the function of working towards the elimination of sex discrimination and promoting equality of opportunity between men and women generally. With the coming into force, on 22 November 1993, of the Sex Discrimination & Equal Pay (Remedies) Regulations 1993, there is no longer an upper limit on the amount of compensation that can be awarded by the employment tribunals in sex discrimination cases.

Note: The Sex Discrimination (Gender Reassignment) Regulations 1999 came into force (in Great Britain) on 1 May 1999. The Regulations, which extend the Sex Discrimination Act 1975 to cover discrimination on grounds of gender reassignment in employment and vocational training, were prompted by the judgment of the European Court of Justice in *P v S and Cornwall County Council* (Case No C-13/94). The expression 'gender reassignment' means a process which is undertaken under medical supervision for the purpose of reassigning a person's sex by changing physiological or other characteristics of sex, and includes any part of such a process (*per* section 82 of the 1975 Act).

- It is important to bear in mind that the Sex Discrimination Act 1975 applies equally to the discriminatory treatment of men relative to women (*ibid.* section 2(1)). The same is true of the Equal Pay Act 1970 (*ibid.* section 13(1)). For convenience, the text below alludes primarily to discrimination against women (as most complaints of unlawful sex discrimination are brought by women).

- The 1975 Act identifies three forms of sex discrimination in the employment field, each of which is unlawful. These are:

  (a) **direct discrimination** (which occurs when a woman is treated less favourably than a man on the grounds of her sex, marital status or gender reassignment);

  Note: Sexual harassment at work, which may amount to unlawful direct discrimination, is discussed later in this section.

  (b) **indirect discrimination** (which occurs when a woman is effectively denied access to employment opportunities, promotion, etc by the imposition of a requirement or condition which places her and most other women at a disadvantage relative to men seeking the same opportunities); and

  (c) discrimination by way of **victimisation** (which may occur when a woman is treated less favourably by another person (usually her employer) for agitating for an improvement in her situation relative to men, or for having instituted proceedings against that person for an infringement of her rights under either or both of the Equal Pay Act 1970 or the Sex Discrimination Act 1975).

It is also unlawful for any person to discriminate against a woman (or man) because of her (or his) marital status by treating her less favourably than a man in the same circumstances (ibid. section 1(2)). Thus, it is *prima facie* unlawful for an employer to refuse to employ a woman with children on the grounds that he considers that, for that reason, she would probably be unreliable and a poor timekeeper (see *Hurley v Mustoe* [1981] IRLR 208).

Equal Opportunities Commission

- The Equal Opportunities Commission (EOC) is empowered to investigate any suspected contravention of the 1975 Act (whether by employers or by those responsible for the provision of goods, facilities or services). It may demand the production of documents and obtain written or oral evidence from involved parties. It may serve a Non-Discrimination Notice on an individual or company, and may institute proceedings against offenders (including persons who publish a discriminatory advertisement or cause any such advertisement to be published).

Code of practice

- Section 56A of the 1975 Act empowers the EOC to issue codes of practice containing practical guidance on steps to be taken by employers and others to eliminate sex discrimination and promote equality of opportunity between men and women in the field of employment. The current *Code of Practice for the Elimination of Discrimination on the Grounds of Sex and Marriage and the Promotion of Equality of Opportunity in Employment* is available from The Stationery Office. See also **Equal Opportunities Commission** elsewhere in this handbook.

Discrimination in the employment field

- It is unlawful for an employer in Great Britain to discriminate against an applicant or candidate for employment on grounds of sex, marital status or gender reassignment:

  (a) in the arrangements made for the purpose of determining who should be offered that employment;

(b) in the terms on which that employment is offered; or

(c) by refusing or deliberately omitting to offer her that employment,

unless being a man is a *genuine occupational qualification* for the job in question (*ibid.* sections 6(1) and 7(1)) (see below).

- It is unlawful for an employer to discriminate against a woman on grounds of her sex or marital status:

  - by denying her access to opportunities for promotion, transfer or training, or to any other benefits, facilities or services; or

  - by dismissing her, or subjecting her to any other detriment (*ibid.* section 6(2)).

An employee may complain to an employment tribunal that she (or he) has been unlawfully discriminated against on grounds of sex, marital status or gender reassignment. Please see *Complaint to an employment tribunal* below.

Absences from work associated with gender reassignment

- Any employee (male or female) who is absent from work (or from vocational training) while undergoing gender reassignment must not be treated less favourably than he (or she) otherwise would be if absent due to sickness or injury (*ibid.* section 2A(3)). What this means, in effect, is that an employee undergoing gender reassignment is entitled to the same access to an employer's occupational sick pay scheme (including SSP) as any other employee on sick leave – subject to the usual rules concerning notification and evidence of incapacity.

Direct discrimination

- Direct discrimination occurs when an employer gives less favourable treatment to a woman (or a man) on grounds of her sex or marital status, or because she intends to undergo, is undergoing, or has undergone gender reassignment. Direct discrimination can be inferred from an employer's recruitment policies. If, for instance, he consistently employs men and just as consistently turns women away, any of those women may refer the matter for investigation by the EOC and/or present a complaint of unlawful discrimination to an employment tribunal (*ibid.* section 63).

- In sex discrimination cases, the burden of proof ordinarily falls on the complainant. But, as the Court of Appeal for Northern Ireland pointed out in *Wallace v South Eastern Education & Library Board* [1980] IRLR 193, if the successful applicant for a job is a man and the unsuccessful, but better qualified applicant, is a woman, that of itself is evidence of discrimination on grounds of sex. The evidential burden of proof then falls on the employer who must satisfy the tribunal or court that there was no discrimination.

Discrimination in recruitment

* An intention to discriminate against a woman (or man) on grounds of sex, marital status or gender reassignment may be inferred from an employer's attitude at the employment interview. If an interviewer treats a female candidate in a peremptory fashion, or asks questions such as 'Are you on the pill?' (not uncommon) or 'Do you intend to have children?' or 'Do you really think you can look after your children as well as handle this job?', he (or she) could be said to be adopting a discriminatory attitude which could provide grounds for a complaint of unlawful discrimination under the 1975 Act. However, such questions do not of themselves contravene the Act. In the final analysis, it will be for the complainant to show that the interviewer's asking such questions, and his reactions to the answers, clearly indicated an intention to discriminate (see *Saunders v Richmond upon Thames Borough Council* [1977] IRLR 363).

* The tribunals have long since recognised the right of employers to manage their businesses to the best of their abilities. An employer may be able to justify his (or her) decision not to employ a pregnant woman on the ground that his is a relatively small business and that he does not have the resources to equip and train a woman who, in a few short weeks (or months), would be taking 26 weeks maternity leave. But this is not an entirely safe assumption to make. If a pregnant job applicant is clearly the best-qualified candidate for a particular job, the employer's refusal to hire her because she is pregnant or for a connected reason would ordinarily be held to constitute unlawful discrimination, regardless of the financial loss to the employer, because only women can be refused employment on the ground of pregnancy (per the European Court of Justice in *Dekker v Stichting Vormingscentrum Voor Jong Volwassenen (VJV-Centrum Plus)* [1991] IRLR 27).

* In *Webb v EMO Air Cargo (UK) Ltd* [1993] IRLR 27, HL, Lord Keith of Kinkel remarked that 'there can be no doubt that, in general, to dismiss a woman because she is pregnant or to refuse to employ a woman of child-bearing age because she may become pregnant is unlawful sex discrimination. Child-bearing and the capacity for child-bearing are

characteristics of the female sex. So to apply these characteristics as the criterion for dismissal or refusal to employ is to apply a gender-based criterion.'

- The 1975 Act also envisages situations which occur *after* employment has commenced, when a female employee is apparently denied opportunities for promotion, transfer or training on the grounds, perhaps, that she is married (or intends to marry) or is about to have a baby, and is, therefore, unlikely to pursue a long-term career with her employer. It is not open to an employer to make such presumptions. A disgruntled employee would be within her rights to serve notice on her employer that she intends to present a complaint of unlawful discrimination to an employment tribunal.

Discrimination on grounds of health and safety

- Section 51 of the 1975 Act states that an employer will not be guilty of unlawful sex discrimination if his refusal to appoint a woman to a particular job or occupation is justified by health and safety legislation which prohibits the employment of women or women of reproductive capacity in work involving exposure to specified hazardous substances or to a working environment which could put her own health and safety or that of a developing foetus or newborn child at risk (as to which, see **Women and young persons, Employment of** elsewhere in this handbook). However, an employer's reliance on health and safety legislation as justification for a refusal to employ a woman was challenged in *Mahlburg v Land Mecklenburg-Vorpommern* (2 February 2000). There, the ECJ ruled that it is not acceptable for an employer to refuse to employ a new or expectant mother in work otherwise prohibited to her on health and safety grounds *if the employment is intended to be permanent* and she is the best candidate for the job. In short, such a candidate must be appointed to the vacancy in question and either be offered suitable alternative employment until she begins her maternity leave period or be suspended from work on full pay until the risks associated with what is essentially a temporary indisposition have passed and she is in a position (legally) to take up her duties.

- In a not dissimilar case, that of *Habermann-Beltermann v Arbeiterwohlfahrt, Bezirksverband Ndb/Obf e V* (No. c-421/92), the ECJ ruled that termination of a pregnant employee's contract cannot be justified on the ground that a statutory prohibition, imposed because of pregnancy, temporarily prevents the employee from working at night. Since the prohibition takes effect only for a limited period in relation to the total length of what is intended to be a contract of employment for an indefinite period (as distinct from a fixed-term contract entered into for a specific purpose), a refusal to employ (or a termination) on such grounds, although in principle compatible with Article 2(3) of Council Directive 76/207/EEC (the 'Equal Treatment' Directive), would deprive the Directive of its effectiveness.

Genuine occupational qualification

- An employer can justify discrimination on grounds of sex if he can show that being of a particular sex is a *genuine occupational qualification* (GOQ) for the vacancy in question. For example, an employer is not obliged to employ a female attendant in a men's changing room or lavatory (however well-qualified she might be) or in any situation in which men might reasonably object to the presence of a woman because they are in a state of undress or using sanitary facilities. The reverse also applies. (See also *Gender reassignment as a supplementary GOQ* below).

- However, in *Etam plc v Rowan* [1989] IRLR 150, the EAT held that being a woman was *not* a GOQ for the job of sales assistant in a woman's clothing shop, given that a man could quite happily carry out the bulk of his duties without causing any inconvenience or difficulty for his employers. In delicate situations, said the EAT, he could always call upon one of the female assistants for help. In an earlier case, that of *Wylie v Dee & Co* [1978] IRLR 103, a woman was held to have been unlawfully discriminated against on grounds of sex when she was refused employment as a sales assistant in a menswear shop. In a decision which was applied in the *Etam* case, the tribunal pointed out that, if a customer objected to having his inside trouser leg measured by a woman, she could always call upon one of the male shop assistants for help.

- An employer is not obliged to offer a job to a woman if the nature or location of his establishment makes it impracticable for the jobholder to live elsewhere than in premises provided by the employer and 'the only such premises which *are* available are lived in, or normally lived in, by men and are not equipped with separate sleeping accommodation or sanitary facilities for women'. However, he would, in due course, be expected to provide such facilities in order to accommodate women in jobs traditionally (but not necessarily) occupied by men only. In other words, the 'no separate sleeping accommodation or loos' excuse will wear a little thin in time with the EOC if the employer has had ample time to put that situation to rights (*ibid.* section 7(2)).

- Being a man might also be a GOQ when an employer is contemplating the recruitment, transfer or promotion of persons to be sales representatives, consultants, engineers and the like, if such persons are likely to spend the greater part of their working time in certain countries (notably in the Middle East) whose laws, customs or cultural inclinations prohibit or preclude any business contacts or dealings with women *(ibid.* section 7(2)(g)). However, an employer would do well to check the facts before excluding an employee or job applicant on such grounds.

- More importantly, an employer need not (indeed, must not) employ a female if, by so doing, he would be in breach of health and safety legislation prohibiting or regulating the employment of women or girls in certain occupations *(ibid.* section 7(2)(t)). See **Women and young persons, employment of** elsewhere in this handbook.

- If an employer traditionally employs a married couple as caretaker and cook (or the vacancy is one of two to be held by a married couple), he is under no obligation to recruit two single people to fill those vacancies, the more so if the jobs are 'live-in' *(ibid.* section 7(2)(h)).

Gender reassignment as a supplementary GOQ

- The 1975 Act (as amended) allows that there will be circumstances in which it would be lawful to discriminate against an employee (or job applicant) on the grounds of gender reassignment if being a woman (or a man) is a supplementary GOQ for the employment in question.

- There is a supplementary GOQ for a job if the job holder is liable to be called upon to perform intimate physical searches pursuant to statutory powers (eg, immigration officers, customs officials, the police); or if the job involves living or working in a private home which necessarily involves close physical or social contact with the persons resident in that home or an intimate knowledge of those persons' lives. An employee (or job applicant) who intends to undergo or is undergoing gender reassignment might likewise be legitimately excluded from work which involves sharing communal accommodation with persons of the same or opposite sex where it would not be reasonably practicable for the employer to provide separate sleeping accommodation, toilets or washrooms. Such a person might also be legitimately denied access to work involving the provision of personal services to vulnerable individuals if, in the reasonable view of the employer (or would-be employer), such a person could not do so effectively. However, it would not be lawful to deny either of the latter jobs to a person who has already undergone gender reassignment, for that reason alone *(ibid.* section 7B).

Dress and appearance of employees

- An employer has the right (eg, in the interests of decency or propriety) to lay down certain ground rules concerning the conduct and appearance of his employees. Thus, in oft-quoted case of *Schmidt v Austicks Bookshops Ltd* [1977] IRLR 360, the Employment Appeal Tribunal (EAT) held that an employer was within his rights to introduce a rule forbidding female staff in his shop from wearing trousers. The fact that there was no comparable restriction on the appearance of male employees in the same shop was immaterial and, said the EAT, beyond the scope of the 1975 Act. In the light of recent developments, the *Schmidt* ruling would nowadays only be followed if male and female employees were required to wear uniforms at work. In *Burrett v West Birmingham Health Authority* [1994] IRLR 7, a staff nurse complained that she had been unlawfully discriminated against on the grounds of sex when she was disciplined and transferred to another department for refusing to wear her uniform cap. The EAT (quoting *Schmidt*) agreed with the tribunal that, as male nurses were also required to wear uniforms (albeit different uniforms), a female nurse could not claim to be treated less favourably than her male colleagues because she had to wear a cap which was part of her uniform – in spite of her honestly-held belief that the cap was ugly and demeaning to her sex.

- In a more recent case, that of *Fuller v Mastercare Service & Distribution* (EAT/0707/00), a male employee who had been dismissed for sporting long hair and a pony-tail, in open defiance of his employer's dress code, argued that he had been the victim of unlawful sex discrimination and that his employers had breached his right to freedom of expression under Article 10 of the European Convention on Human Rights. In evidence, the employee acknowledged that he had been informed during his pre-employment interview, and in writing, that he must at all times be well-groomed and presentable in appearance, the more so as his job involved face to face contact with customers. Indeed, that message was reinforced and amplified by posters in the workplace reminding male staff that their hair must be 'neatly groomed and conservatively cut (no long hair or ponytails)'. However, the only requirement for female staff was that their hair must be 'neatly groomed'. Although the complainant had initially complied with his employer's code on dress and appearance, he later chose to grow his hair long and wear it in a ponytail. His employers spoke to him about this on a number of occasions and repeatedly asked him to cut his hair. His refusal to do so eventually led to his dismissal. At the subsequent tribunal and appeal hearings, Mr Fuller argued that it was contradictory and patently discriminatory to allow a female employee to have long hair (so long as it was neatly groomed) while insisting that men should keep their hair short and conservatively cut. In dismissing the employee's complaint, the EAT, citing the judgment of the Court of Appeal in *Smith v Safeway plc* [1996] IRLR 456, held that (notwithstanding the effect on an employee's private life) employers have every right to lay down rules concerning their employee's dress and appearance at work. Such rules will not be discriminatory because their content is different for men and women if they enforce a common principle of smartness or conventionality and, taken as a whole (and not garment by garment or item by item), neither gender is treated less favourably in enforcing that principle. Whether or not having long hair or a pony-tail is unconventional for a male employee, said the EAT, is neither here nor there.

Dismissal

- The dismissal of an employee because she is a woman or pregnant (or for a connected reason), or because she is married, is *prima facie* inadmissible, unlawful and unfair. A complaint on such grounds may be presented to the Secretary of the Tribunals, regardless of the complainant's age, length of service or working hours at the material time.

Dismissing the pregnant employee

- In *Hayes v Malleable Working Men's Club & Institute* [1985] ICR 703, the Employment Appeal Tribunal held that it was unlawful under the Sex Discrimination Act 1975 for an employer to dismiss a pregnant employee simply because she was pregnant, or for a related reason, if he would not dismiss a sick man whose state of health rendered him temporarily incapable of carrying out the duties of his job. Nowadays, it is no longer necessary for employment tribunals to make such comparisons. Sections 99 and 105 of the Employment Rights Act 1996 caution that it is inadmissible and automatically unfair (regardless of her length of service) to dismiss a woman or select her for redundancy simply because she is pregnant, or because she has taken (or proposes to take) advantage of her right to maternity leave or her right to time off work for ante-natal care (or for any reason connected with pregnancy or childbirth).

Discrimination in retirement

- It is unlawful for an employer to specify different retirement ages for the men and women in his employ. If a man is permitted to continue working for his employer until age 65, a woman in the same employment must be afforded the same opportunity, and must *not* be denied opportunities for training, promotion or increases in pay because of the imminence of what was hitherto her normal retiring age. See also **Equal pay and conditions,** elsewhere in this handbook.

Indirect discrimination

- If an employer applies 'a requirement or condition which is such that the proportion of women who can comply with it is considerably smaller than the proportion of men', he is guilty of indirect discrimination – unless he can prove otherwise. For example, it is unlikely that as many women as men could comply with a requirement that they be at least 1.9 metres tall, or be able to lift and carry a sack weighing 50 kilograms or more. Similarly, an aptitude test (introduced by a Liverpool employer) requiring candidates for employment to name each of the players in the local football team, was held not to be a fair test of a woman's ability to memorise facts and figures or her suitability for employment as a tally clerk. Such tactics will almost certainly provide grounds for a complaint to an employment tribunal.

- On the other hand, an employer may be able to persuade an employment tribunal that he had good reasons for requiring employees doing certain jobs to be at least 5'9" tall (for example, safety or some peculiar operational factor related to the business in which he is engaged). The employer's hand would be strengthened if he could show that the rule applied equally to both male and female workers in his employ.

- An example of indirect discrimination on grounds of sex is illustrated by the oft-cited *Price v Civil Service Commission* [1977] IRLR 291 case. There, the Employment Appeal Tribunal (EAT) held that an advertisement requiring applicants for a civil service vacancy to be between the ages of 17 and 28 effectively prevented a great many women (many of whom had interrupted their careers to raise families) from re-entering the service. The advertisement was, therefore, an unlawful form of indirect discrimination. See **Advertisements (discriminatory)** elsewhere in this handbook.

Victimisation

- The 1975 Act specifically outlaws the victimisation or harassment of an employee who has brought, or is thinking about bringing, a complaint of unlawful discrimination against her employer. The reader should bear in mind that (as is the case with a great many statutory rights in employment) an employee has no need to leave her (or his) job in order to take her complaint before an employment tribunal. If the employer responds by 'sending her to Coventry' or by denying her a pay rise or an opportunity for promotion or further training, or by subjecting her to some other detriment, he is likely to pay dearly for his pains (*ibid.* section 4).

Sexual harassment

- In *Strathclyde Regional Council v Porcelli* [1986] IRLR 134, CS, Lord Emslie remarked that sexual harassment is 'a particularly degrading and unacceptable form of treatment which it must be taken to have been the intention of Parliament to restrain'. While it may well have been Parliament's intention to outlaw sexual harassment at work, the term does not appear in the 1975 Act. Indeed, the UK Government has so far resisted calls by the Equal Opportunities Commission and other organisations to amend the 1975 Act by including a definition of *sexual harassment* and by making unwelcome conduct of a sexual nature unlawful in its own right.

- As a result, the only way in which a victim of sexual harassment at work can obtain any form of legal redress is to persuade an employment tribunal that her treatment at the hands of her tormentors was tantamount to unlawful direct discrimination on the grounds of sex (contrary to section 1(l)(a) of the 1975 Act) and that she had been 'subjected to a detriment' as a result of that treatment (contrary to section 6(2)(b)). In short, she must show that she had received less favourable treatment than a man would have received in the same or comparable circumstances, and that the harassment had affected her health, general efficiency or peace of mind, had resulted in her being denied an expected pay rise, or had damaged her prospects for promotion, transfer or training – leaving her with no choice but to tender her resignation or apply for a transfer to another department or branch within the same organisation.

- In its Code of Practice on *Combating Sexual Harassment and Protecting the Dignity of Women and Men at Work* (COM (91) 1397 final, published on 7 November 1991), the European Commission defines sexual harassment as meaning unwanted conduct of a sexual nature, or other conduct based on sex, affecting the dignity of women and men at work, including any kind of unwanted physical, verbal or non-verbal behaviour which offends the dignity of the person, including:

    - physical contact (ranging from unnecessary touching, patting, pinching, and brushing against a person's body to molestation, assault, and coercing sexual intercourse), sexually-suggestive gestures, leering, whistling, or over-familiar comments about a person's appearance, physical attributes, or dress;

- insults or ridicule based on a person's sex or sexual orientation;

- displays of pornographic or sexually-suggestive pictures, objects or written material;

- suggestions that sexual favours may further a person's career (or that a refusal may damage it); and

- decisions affecting an employee's career based on her (or his) willingness or refusal to offer sexual favours.

Note: Although men are also vulnerable to sexual harassment (especially gay men and young men), the overwhelming majority of victims are women. The EU's Code of Practice (at paragraph 5) points to research in several Member States which suggests that those disproportionately at risk and especially vulnerable to sexual harassment are women who are divorced or separated, young women, new entrants to the labour market, women with irregular or precarious employment contracts, women in non-traditional jobs, women with disabilities, women from racial minorities, and lesbians.

Contributory fault?

- In *Snowball v Gardner Merchant Limited* [1987] IRLR 397, the EAT held that a complainant's attitude to matters of sexual behaviour was relevant and admissible for the purposes of determining the degree of injury to feelings she suffered (and hence the amount of compensation payable) as a result of sexual harassment. In *Wileman v Minilee Engineering Ltd* [1988] IRLR 144, the EAT held that, in determining whether sexual harassment constituted a job, health or career-threatening detriment, an employment tribunal were entitled to take into account the fact that, on occasion, the complainant wore scanty and provocative clothing to work. Upholding the tribunal's award of £50 in damages, Mr Justice Popplewell remarked (somewhat controversially) that 'if a girl on the shop floor goes around wearing provocative clothes and flaunting herself, it is not unlikely that other work people particularly the men – will make remarks about it. It is,' he concluded, 'an inevitable part of working life on the shop floor.'

Vicarious liability

- In *Bracebridge Engineering Limited v Darby* [1990] IRLR 3, an appellant employer claimed that he could not be held vicariously liable for a single act of sexual harassment perpetrated on a female employee by two male employees. They were not, he said, acting in the course of their employment at that time. In evidence, it was alleged that the works manager and a chargehand had accosted a female employee as she was preparing to leave work towards the end of her shift, picked her up by the arms and legs, carried her into the works manager's office, threatened her with a written warning for attempting to leave work early, placed her legs around the waist of one of them, and touched her private parts before releasing her. Early the next morning, feeling disgusted and degraded, the woman complained about the incident to the general manager. When challenged, the two men denied that anything untoward had taken place. In the light of their denials, the general manager decided that no further action was necessary. Upset that her complaint had not been properly investigated, the woman resigned a few days later and complained to an employment tribunal that she had been constructively dismissed and unlawfully discriminated against on grounds of sex. Both complaints were upheld and her employer was ordered to pay a total of £4,050 in compensation. The employer appealed.

- In dismissing the employer's appeal, the EAT upheld the employment tribunal's finding that, at the time of the incident, the works manager and chargehand *were* engaged in exercising (or in the course of exercising) a disciplinary and supervisory function and had, accordingly, been acting in the course of their employment. Their employer was therefore vicariously liable for their unlawful conduct.

Can a single act of harassment be a detriment?

- In the *Bracebridge* case referred to above, the appellants argued that an isolated incident could not properly be described as sexual harassment, and could not therefore have been a 'detriment' to the employee within the meaning of section 6(2)(b) of the 1975 Act. *The Shorter Oxford English Dictionary*, they said, defines 'harassment' as a continuing course of conduct. The EAT rejected that argument. ' "Sexual harassment",' they said, 'is a phrase which can embody a whole number of notions. Whether or not harassment is a continuing course of conduct is beside the point. What happened in this case,' said Mr justice Wood, 'was an act of unlawful discrimination against a woman because she was a woman. Furthermore, it was a most unpleasant act, and one which in our judgment clearly falls within the proper intention and meaning of the [1975] Act.'

Other legal consequences of sexual harassment

- Acts of sexual harassment may amount to unlawful assault, giving rise to civil or criminal liability. Indecent assault, in particular, is a serious criminal offence. Furthermore, where sexual harassment results in injury to an employee's health or places her (or him) under considerable stress, the employer might well be held to be in breach of his common law duty of care, let alone his general duty under section 2 of the Health & Safety at Work, etc. Act 1974 'to ensure, so far as is reasonably practicable, the health, safety and welfare at work of all his employees' – the more so if he was aware of the situation (or should have been) and took no steps to prevent it.

Protection from Harassment Act 1997

- Under the Protection from Harassment Act 1997, which came into force on 16 June 1997, it is a criminal offence for a person (whether in an in-work situation or otherwise) to pursue a course of conduct (that is to say, on at least two occasions) which amounts to the harassment of another person and which the harasser knows, or ought to know, amounts to such harassment. The term 'harassment' includes words or conduct calculated to alarm or distress the victim. A person guilty of such an offence is liable on summary conviction to a fine of up to £5,000 and/or imprisonment for a term not exceeding six months (*ibid.* sections 1 and 2).

- Furthermore, a person who is (or may be) the victim of harassment may bring a claim in civil proceedings against his or her tormentor. On such a claim, the perpetrator may be ordered to pay damages to the claimant for (among other things) any anxiety caused by the harassment and any resultant financial loss. The High Court or a county court may grant an order restraining the defendant from pursuing any conduct which amounts to harassment. A defendant who does anything prohibited by such an injunction is yet again guilty of an offence and liable, on conviction on indictment, to an unlimited fine and/or imprisonment for up to five years (*ibid.* section 3).

Public Order Act 1986

- Section 4A of the Public Order Act 1986 (inserted by section 154 of the Criminal Justice & Public Order Act 1994) cautions that a person is guilty of an offence and liable to a fine of up to £5,000 and/or imprisonment for up to six months 'if, with intent to cause a person harassment, alarm or distress, he (or she) uses threatening, abusive or insulting words or behaviour, or disorderly behaviour, or displays any writing, sign or other visible representation which is threatening, abusive or insulting, thereby causing that other person harassment, alarm or distress'.

- The offence may be committed in a public or private place, although there is no offence if the harassment occurs inside a private dwelling in which the perpetrator and the victim both reside.

Complaint to an employment tribunal

- A complaint of unlawful discrimination under the 1975 Act may be presented to the nearest Regional Office of the Employment Tribunals, regardless of the complainant's age or length of service at the material time. The complaint must be presented within three months of the alleged discriminatory act or, when dismissal has occurred, within three months of the effective date of termination of the employee's contract of employment. A tribunal may consider a complaint presented 'out of time' if, in all the circumstances of the case, it considers that it is just and equitable to do so (*ibid.* section 76(1) and (5)).

- If the employee's complaint is upheld, the tribunal will make a declaration to that effect and will order the employer to pay compensation to the complainant corresponding to any damages he (or she) could have been ordered to pay by a county or sheriff court, including damages for loss of earnings and for injured feelings. The tribunal may also make a recommendation directing the employer to take such steps as are necessary to reverse or modify his discriminatory activities and policies (*ibid.* section 65(l)(c)). If the employer declines to comply with such a recommendation, the EOC may apply to a county court for an injunction (or to the sheriff court for an order) restraining him from further unlawful discriminatory acts (*ibid.* section 71(1)).

Note: The reader is reminded that, since 22 November 1993, when the Sex Discrimination & Equal Pay (Remedies) Regulations 1993 came into force, there is no longer an upper limit on the amount of damages (or compensation) that can be awarded by an employment tribunal in sex discrimination cases. Indeed, such an award may now include a sum by way of interest on the amount awarded.

Burden of proof

- Under the Sex Discrimination (Indirect Discrimination & Burden of Proof) Regulations 2001, which came into force on 12 October 2001, once an employee (female or male) has established before an employment tribunal facts from which it may be presumed that she (or he) had been the victim of unlawful discrimination in the workplace, the burden of proving that no such discrimination occurred then devolves on the respondent employer. The *Questions & Replies* procedure explained in the next paragraph is designed to enable an employee who has been the victim of unlawful sex discrimination to formulate and present her (or his) case in the most effective manner.

Questions and replies

- Any employee (or job applicant), who believes that she (or he) has been discriminated against in contravention of the Sex Discrimination Act 1975 (whether by her employer, a particular employer, or whomever), may question the person concerned about the reasons for his apparently unlawful actions. If dissatisfied with that person's written explanation (if, indeed, an explanation is offered), the person aggrieved may admit that explanation (or failure to explain) as evidence in any ensuing proceedings before an employment tribunal (ibid. section 74).

  The procedure is explained in the Sex Discrimination (Questions & Replies) Order 1975. The Form prescribed is Form SD74 (obtainable from the Equal Opportunities Commission or from any Job Centre or unemployment benefit office of the Department for Education & Employment).

  Note: Form SD74 is an eight-page document which not only provides space for preparing the questionnaire to be submitted, but also gives a great deal of practical guidance both to the person aggrieved (the complainant) and to the person (the respondent) to whom the questions are directed. The document points out that the respondent cannot be compelled to reply to the complainant's questions or allegations. However, the respondent is cautioned that an employment tribunal (or court) may draw any such inference as is just and equitable from a failure, without reasonable excuse, to reply within a reasonable period, or from any evasive or equivocal reply, including an inference that the respondent (i.e. the person questioned) has discriminated unlawfully.

- To be admissible under the 'questions procedure' at any ensuing tribunal hearing, the complainant's questionnaire (Form SD74) must be served on the respondent either:

  (a) before a complaint about the treatment concerned is made to an employment tribunal, but not more than three months after the treatment in question; or

  (b) if a complaint has already been made to a tribunal, within the period of 21 days beginning with the date on which the complaint was received by the Secretary of the Tribunals.

  Note: To present a complaint of unlawful discrimination under the Sex Discrimination Act 1975, the complainant should complete Form IT1 (available from any employment office, Job Centre or unemployment benefit office of the Department of Employment) and submit it to the Secretary of the Employment Tribunals within the prescribed three-month period. See also **Employment tribunals and procedure** elsewhere in this handbook.

COT 3 and compromise agreements

- An employee who believes that she has been unlawfully discriminated against by her employer, and who is minded to pursue a complaint before an employment tribunal (or has already done so), may reach a legally-binding out-of-court settlement with her employer by means of a COT 3 or compromise agreement (*ibid*. sections 77(4)(a) and (aa)). A COT 3 agreement is concluded with the assistance of an ACAS conciliation officer. A compromise agreement (or contract), if properly concluded, will also serve to prevent the complainant from taking her case further. For further details, please turn to the sections titled **Compromise agreements** and **Conciliation officers** elsewhere in this handbook.

Discriminatory advertisements

- It is unlawful to publish (or cause to be published) an advertisement which indicates, or might reasonably be understood as indicating, an intention by a person to do an act which is or might be unlawful under the Sex Discrimination Act 1975. It is also a form of indirect discrimination to advertise job vacancies in a journal or magazine, the majority of whose readers are women (or men) (*ibid*. section 38(1)), unless being of a particular sex is a genuine occupational qualification for the vacancy in question.

- Use of a job title or job description with sexual connotations (such as 'waiter', 'barmaid', 'salesgirl', 'chambermaid', 'stewardess' etc) will be taken to indicate an intention to discriminate against men on grounds of sex unless the advertisement contains a clear indication to the contrary (*ibid*. section 38(3)). Any accompanying illustration should also reinforce that point. Showing a man carrying a briefcase would undoubtedly be interpreted as an intention to discriminate against female job applicants unless the advertisement shows a woman similarly equipped.

   Note: Given that the word 'manager' is not gender-specific (deriving, as it does, from the Italian *maneggiare* (to control) and, ultimately; from the Latin *manus* (hand)), there is no need to insert the (manufactured) word 'manageress' in the same job advertisement to avoid misplaced accusations of an intention to discriminate on grounds of sex. If the job title used in any advertisement is likely to be misunderstood, the accompanying text should clearly indicate that the vacancy is open to persons of either sex.

- The newspaper proprietor (or magazine owner) who publishes a job advertisement which appears to discriminate against women (or men) will not be liable under the 1975 Act if he (or she) can prove:

   (a) that he relied on a statement made to him by the person who paid for the advertisement to the effect that it would not be unlawful (eg, because being of a particular sex is a *genuine occupational qualification* for the vacancy in question); and

(b) that it was reasonable for him to rely on that statement (*ibid.* section 38(4)).

Any employer who knowingly or recklessly makes a false or misleading statement to a publisher is guilty of an offence under the 1975 Act and is liable, on summary conviction, to a fine not exceeding £5,000 (*ibid.* section 38(5)).

Note: The word *advertisement* includes every form of advertisement, whether to the public or not, and whether in a newspaper or other publication, by television or radio, by display of notices, signs, labels, show cards or goods (*ibid.* section 82(1)). The Equal Opportunities Commission alone is responsible for instituting proceedings against a person who publishes, or causes to be published, a discriminatory advertisement (*ibid.* section 72).

Employment agencies

● It is unlawful for an employment agency to discriminate against a woman (or a man):

(a) in the terms on which it offers to provide any of its services; or

(b) by refusing or deliberately omitting to provide such services; or

(c) in the way it provides any of its services,

unless it can prove that it acted in reliance on a statement made to it by an employer to the effect that the agency could lawfully refuse to offer a particular vacancy to a woman (or to a man), and that it was reasonable to rely on the statement (*ibid.* section 15).

Note: Any employer who quietly instructs an employment agency not to submit female (or male) candidates for vacancies within his organisation, not only risks being served with a non-discrimination notice by the EOC (reinforced by a court order) but could also be ordered to pay compensation (in the form of damages) to any person (woman or man) unlawfully discriminated against as a result of those instructions. The employment agency may also be served with a non-discrimination notice and/or a county court injunction (or sheriff court order). An employer who makes a false or misleading statement to an employment agency, is guilty of an offence and liable on summary conviction to a fine of up to £5,000 (section 15(6), Sex Discrimination Act 1975).

Instructions to discriminate

● It is unlawful for an employer to instruct any subordinate (eg, personnel officer, manager, supervisor, etc) to do any act which constitutes unlawful discrimination on grounds of sex or marital status; or to induce, or attempt to induce, a person to do any act which is unlawful under the 1975 Act (*ibid.* sections 39 and 40).

- Anything done by a person in the course of his (or her) employment will be treated for the purposes of the 1975 Act as having been done by the employer as well as by him, whether or not it was done with the employer's knowledge or approval. However, in proceedings before a court or tribunal, it will be a defence for the employer to prove that he took such steps as were reasonably practicable to prevent the employee from doing that act (*ibid.* section 41).

Assistance by Equal Opportunities Commission

- As was mentioned earlier in this section, persons who consider that they have been discriminated against in contravention of the Sex Discrimination Act 1975 have the right of direct access to the tribunals or courts for compensation or damages in respect of their complaints. However, the 1975 Act also gives the EOC discretion to assist an individual who has brought (or is considering bringing) proceedings against another person (whether employer or whoever). The Commission may assist if the case raises a question of principle; where it is unreasonable, having regard to the complexity of the case or the position of the individual relative to the other party to the proceedings (or intended proceedings) to expect the individual to deal with the case unaided; or where some other special consideration applies. In such cases, the Commission may give advice, seek a settlement between the parties and/or arrange for legal advice, assistance or representation (*ibid.* section 75).

  See also **Dismissal, Dismissal for asserting a statutory right, Equal pay and conditions, Employment tribunals and procedure, Pregnant employees and nursing mothers**, and **Maternity rights** elsewhere in this handbook.

SHOP ASSISTANTS
(*Conditions of employment*)

Key points

- Since 1 December 1994, when Part II of the Shops Act 1950 was revoked, there are no longer any *statutory* limits on the working hours and periods of employment of shop assistants. However, new limits have since been imposed by the Working Time Regulations 1998, which came into force on 1 October 1998. The new Regulations apply to all UK workers, regardless of the type of work in which they are engaged (although there are exceptions). In this context, the term 'shop assistants' encompasses persons employed in shops, department stores, supermarkets, restaurants, cafeterias, canteens, pubs, fast-food establishments, and in the public dining rooms and bars of hotels.

- Notwithstanding the repeal of the 1950 Act, shop assistants employed before 1 December 1994 remain entitled to those provisions of the 1950 Act necessarily imported into their contracts of employment, unless superseded by the 1998 Regulations discussed in the next paragraph.

Note: The Shops Act 1950 was repealed by sections 23 and 24 and Schedule 17 to the Deregulation & Contracting Out Act 1994 (by the Deregulation & Contracting Out Act 1994 (Commencement No 1) Order 1994, which came into force on 1 December 1994.

Working Time Regulations 1998

- Under the Working Time Regulations 1998, as amended by the Working Time (Amendment) Regulations 2002, adult workers (ie, workers aged 18 and over) in Great Britain and Northern Ireland cannot lawfully be required to work more than an average 48 hours in any week, calculated over a reference period of 17 consecutive weeks. Young workers under the age of 18, for their part, may not work or be required to work more than eight hours a day or more than 40 hours in any week – with no provision for averaging. The Regulations also include limits on night work and entitle workers to in-work rest breaks, daily and weekly rest periods and (from 23 November 1999) four weeks' paid annual holidays.

- The 1998 Regulations are, in large part, policed and enforced by health and safety inspectors. Prosecutions of recalcitrant employers for a breach of those Regulations could lead to heavy fines, akin to those imposed by the courts for a breach of an employer's duty under the Health & Safety at Work etc Act 1974. Workers who are denied their legal right to daily and weekly rest breaks (and rest periods), and to paid annual leave, may complain to an employment tribunal and are likely to be awarded compensation payable by their respective employers.

For further particulars, please turn to the sections titled **Holidays, annual, Overtime employment, Rest breaks and rest periods**, and **Working hours**, elsewhere in this handbook.

Sunday work

- The rights of shop workers, betting shop workers and others, in relation to Sunday work, are covered by the Sunday Trading Act 1994 (most of whose provisions have been imported into the Employment Rights Act 1996). Under that Act, a 'shop worker' is a person employed in a shop, supermarket, department store, or similar. The Act does *not*, however, apply to persons employed in premises such as restaurants, cafeterias, pubs, bars or the like, in which meals, refreshments or intoxicating liquor are sold for consumption on the premises. Nor does it apply to persons employed in 'take-away' establishments (or similar) in which meals or refreshments are prepared to order for immediate consumption off the premises. For further particulars, please turn to the section titled **Sunday work** elsewhere in this handbook.

Breakages and cash shortages

- Retail workers held responsible under their contracts of employment for breakages and cash shortages enjoy a degree of protection under Part II of the Employment Rights Act 1996. Deductions from pay and/or demands for payment in respect of such breakages or stock shortages are limited to 10 per cent of the gross pay due an employee on any one payday. For further particulars, please turn to the section titled **Deductions from pay** elsewhere in this handbook.

SICKNESS AND STATUTORY SICK PAY

Key points

- The Employer's Statutory Sick Pay (ESSP) Scheme was first introduced in the UK in April 1983. At that time, employers took over the administrative (if not the financial) burden of paying the equivalent of state sickness and injury benefits to employees incapacitated for work because of illness or injury. Initially, employers could reclaim 100 per cent of the SSP due and paid to their employees by deducting the amount in question from the National Insurance contributions routinely sent to the Inland Revenue Accounts Office at the end of each month. On 6 April 1994, the rebate scheme (already heavily eroded) was abolished altogether, although some relief was still available to small employers under the Small Employers' Relief Scheme. On 6 April 1995, the latter scheme was also abolished, to be replaced by a new scheme, known as the SSP Percentage Threshold Scheme. Under this scheme, employers can now reclaim in any one month that portion (if any) of their SSP costs which exceed 13 per cent of their gross (employer's and employees') National Insurance costs during that month. The procedure for reclaiming excessive SSP costs is explained in a booklet which is available from any local office of the Department of Social Security (DSS).

Note: The law relating to the payment of statutory sick pay is to be found in the Social Security Contributions & Benefits Act 1992 (as amended), and in the Statutory Sick Pay (General) Regulations 1982 (as amended).

An employee's right to SSP

- Provided he or she qualifies, an employee is entitled to be paid statutory sick pay (SSP) by his employer for up to 28 weeks in any period of incapacity for work (PIW), if, on the first day of that PIW, he (or she) was under the age of 65 and had average earnings equal to (or greater than) the current 'lower earnings limit' for SSP purposes.

- For the tax year 2003/04, the 'lower earnings limit' is £77 a week (which figure is reviewed annually). Employees who do not qualify for SSP, or who are excluded from SSP (see below), must apply to their local social security offices for the equivalent state benefits.

Note: An absentee employee must, of course, notify his (or her) employer that he is incapacitated for work because of illness or injury and must provide supporting evidence of incapacity for work, either in the form of a doctor's 'sick note' or (if the PIW lasts for fewer than seven days) a self-certificate (Form SC2 or the equivalent), both of which requirements are summarised later in this section.

- An employee who is entitled to be paid SSP by his employer is denied access to social security incapacity benefits until such time as he exhausts that entitlement or is otherwise disqualified from receiving (or continuing to receive) SSP.

SSP rate

- For the 2003/04 tax year, the weekly rate of SSP payable to an employee incapacitated for work on grounds of illness or injury is £64.35. The daily rate of SSP is the weekly rate divided by the number of *qualifying days* during the week in question. See also *Calculating average weekly earnings* below.

Note: The daily rate of SSP in a particular case may produce an odd fraction of a penny. However, rounding-up (not down) to the next whole penny must not occur until the total amount of SSP payable has been calculated.

SSP liable to deduction of PAYE and NI contributions

- SSP is *not* a tax-free benefit. In other words, it is liable to the deduction of income tax and National Insurance contributions (as well as any other sums ordinarily deducted from an employee's pay packet). In short, SSP must be treated in the same way as wages or salary.

Meaning of 'PIW'

- A PIW is a period of *four or more* consecutive whole days of incapacity for work (including Saturdays and Sundays, 'rest' days and bank and public holidays). A *whole* day in this context is a day on which an employee does no work at all for his employer. The PIW of an employee who is taken ill (or is injured) at work, even if he (or she) has only been at work for a minute or two, does not start until the beginning of the next day. It follows that a PIW ends on the day immediately preceding the day on which an employee returns to work.

- A 'day of incapacity for work', in relation to a particular contract of employment with a particular employer, is a day on which the employee in question 'is, or is deemed to be, incapable by reason of some specific disease or bodily or mental disablement of doing work which he can reasonably be expected to do under that contract'.

'Deemed' incapacity for work

- Regulation 2 of the Statutory Sick Pay (General) Regulations 1982 (*qv*) recognises that there will be occasions when an employee may not be physically incapable of carrying out his (or her) normal work, but has nonetheless been advised by his doctor 'to refrain from work' as a precautionary measure or for convalescent reasons following a recent or earlier period of illness or disability. Booklet M 270, produced by the DSS, cites the example also of the pregnant woman working with children at a place where there is an outbreak of rubella (German measles). Continuing to work at such a place would almost certainly place her unborn child at risk. The woman in question would be 'deemed' to be incapable of work within the meaning of section 1(3) of the 1982 Act, although not herself suffering from any specific disease or bodily or mental disablement.

- Employers in the catering industry will be familiar with the situation which arises when an employee (eg, a food handler) is issued with a certificate by the Medical Officer of Environmental Health (in Northern Ireland, the Chief Administrative Officer of the Health & Social

Services Board) directing him (or her) not to report for work by reason of his being a carrier, or having been in contact with a case, of infectious disease (*ibid.* regulation 2 (1)(b)). If a doctors' sick note or a certificate is issued to an employee in the circumstances described, the employee is 'deemed' to be incapable of work for SSP purposes and the employer should respond accordingly.

- Employees who are absent from work for the purposes of undergoing cosmetic surgery (eg, liposuction or the removal of a tattoo, etc) or, perhaps, for a vasectomy or vasectomy-reversal operation, are nonetheless deemed to be incapable of work and, subject to the usual conditions, would qualify for SSP in respect of such absences (including any attendant period of recuperation). This rule applies regardless of the voluntary nature of such operations. Whether or not such a person would also qualify for payment under his (or her) employer's occupational sick pay scheme is another matter.

- Under the Sex Discrimination Act 1975 (as amended by the Sex Discrimination (Gender Reassignment) Regulations 1999), an employee absent from work while undergoing gender reassignment must not be treated less favourably than any other person absent from work due to illness or injury (*ibid.* section 2A(3)). Such a person would be entitled to SSP and, subject to any procedural rules, equal access to his (or her) employer's occupational sick pay scheme.

The 'linking' rule

- One of the most important rules in the SSP scheme is the rule which states that a number of PIWs 'link' to form a single PIW if the gap between each PIW and its predecessor is 56 days or less. The link is broken and a new PIW is formed if, but only if, the gap between the last PIW and the next PIW is 57 days or more. A similar rule applies to new recruits. A PIW with a former employer links with a PIW with a new employer if the gap between those two periods is 56 days or less – but only if the employee had received SSP for one week or more in respect of the earlier PIW (See *Leaver's statements issued by former employers* below).

- The 'linking' rule is important for two reasons. First, a sick or injured employee is not entitled to SSP for more than a total (or aggregate of) 28 weeks in any single PIW. Secondly, only the first three qualifying days in a PIW are unpaid 'waiting days' – a condition which might well be misunderstood or misapplied when several PIWs 'link' to form a single PIW.

Meaning of a 'qualifying day'

- SSP can only be paid in respect of qualifying days occurring within a PIW. A *qualifying day* is a day agreed between an employer and an employee as being a day on which the employee is normally required to work under the terms of his contract of employment, or a day on which he is rostered or scheduled to work in a particular week. If an employee works a different pattern of days from week to week (eg, a system of rotating shifts), he (or she) will need to reach agreement with his employer as to which days of the week will be *qualifying days* for SSP purposes – given that, in some situations, employees may not be given more than a week or two's advance notice of the days of the week on which they have been rostered to work. One solution in such a situation would be for the employer to sit down with each of his employees and to examine the pattern of rostered working days, week by week, over a period of, say, three months – and then to select and agree upon those days of the week which most nearly reflect that pattern of working days (which days will be that employee's *qualifying days* for SSP purposes).

  Note: A special rule applies in the case of the nightshift worker whose normal working shift extends beyond midnight. For example, a factory worker might work a shift which extends from 10.00 pm in the evening to 6.00 am the following morning. If he (or she) starts work at 10.00 pm on Monday evening, goes on Tuesday morning, does not work the Tuesday night shift, but returns to work 10.00 pm on Wednesday evening, then Tuesday is deemed to be a day of incapacity for work, but Monday and Wednesday are not. The rule relating to nightshift workers (whose shifts span midnight) is laid down in regulation 2(2) of the Statutory Sick Pay (General) Regulations 1982 (*qv*) which states that an employee is deemed to be incapable of work throughout a day, if on that day, he (or she) does no work – except during a shift which ends on that day (having begun on the previous day) *and* does no work during a shift which begins on that day and ends on the next.

- It is *not* acceptable for an employer and employee simply to agree on a number of qualifying days in a week. Specific days of the week (eg, Monday, Tuesday, Wednesday, Thursday and Friday, or whatever) must be agreed and duly recorded on the employee's personal file (and kept available for inspection on demand by an inspector of the DSS), as to which see *Records of sickness absence* below. Nor is it acceptable for an employee to come to an understanding with his (or her) employer that qualifying days will be those days (if any) on which he is incapacitated for work by reason of illness or injury. Any such agreement (whether or not included as an express term in the employee's contract of employment) will be 'without effect'. There must be at least one qualifying day in every week. If an employer refuses to discuss or negotiate qualifying days with his workforce (in the misguided belief that he is thereby avoiding any liability to pay SSP), the DSS will assume the relevant qualifying day to be Wednesday.

Unpaid 'waiting days'

- The first three qualifying days in a PIW (linked or otherwise) are unpaid 'waiting days'. What this means is best illustrated by an example. Let us assume that an employee has three PIWs which 'link' to form a single PIW. In the first PIW there is just one qualifying day. In the second, there are two. In the third, there are four. As the first three qualifying days in a PIW are unpaid, the employee in question cannot be paid SSP during PIWs 1 and 2, but *is* entitled to SSP for *each* of the qualifying days in PIW 3.

Employees excluded from SSP

- Some employees are *excluded* from any entitlement to SSP because of the type of work they do; others (see below) are *disqualified* because of their particular circumstances on the first day of a PIW.

- The following are excluded from the SSP scheme:

    (a) temporary workers (or 'temps') hired-out by employment agencies – unless employed under a contract of employment by such agencies;

    (b) serving members of the armed forces (including the reserve forces); and

    (c) foreign-going mariners employed by a UK employer, while under a contract for which their employer pays a special rate of NI contributions.

Employees disqualified from receiving SSP

- An employee is disqualified (or excluded) from receiving SSP during a PIW if, on the *first day* of that PIW (or period of entitlement), he or she:

    (a) has done no work for his employer under his contract of employment; or

    (b) is over the age of 65; or

    (c) has average earnings below the 'lower earnings limit' for National Insurance contributions; or

    (d) is detained in legal custody or sentenced to a term of imprisonment (except where the sentence is suspended); or

    > Note: For the purposes of the SSP scheme, an employee is deemed to be in legal custody if he (or she) is in prison or has otherwise been detained in custody by the police. It is important to bear in mind that SSP in respect of a particular PIW does not resume when the employee is no longer in legal custody.

(e) has received (or been entitled to receive) a social security incapacity benefit or a maternity allowance or a severe disablement allowance within the period of eight weeks immediately preceding that day (in which event, the DSS will have issued him (or her) with one or other of forms BF 218, BF 220, BM 7 or BM 8); or

(f) is caught up in a stoppage of work due to a trade dispute unless he or she can prove that, at no time on or before the first day of that PIW did he (or she) have a direct interest in the trade dispute in question; or

(g) is or has been pregnant and the first day of that PIW falls within the 'disqualifying period' (which, in relation to a woman entitled to statutory maternity pay (SMP), is the maternity pay period; and, in relation to a woman entitled to the state maternity allowance, is the maternity allowance period);

Note: With the coming into force on 1 October 2002 of the Fixed-term Employees (Prevention of Less Favourable Treatment) Regulations 2002, employees on fixed-term contracts lasting or expected to last for three months or less are no longer excluded from entitlement to SSP.

Procedure when an employee is in an excluded or disqualified category

- If an employee is in an *excluded* category on the first day of a PIW, or is disqualified from any entitlement to SSP, his (or her) employer must complete and send to the employee a so-called 'change-over' form (Form SSP1), together with any current doctor's sick notes he is holding at the time. The form, which explains why the employee cannot be paid SSP, must be sent within seven days of the date on which the employee informed him (by whatever means) that he was incapacitated for work.

- On receipt of Form SSP1, the employee should complete and sign it where indicated and send it to (or hand it in at) his local social security office in support of his claim for social security benefits. He will also need to provide a sick note from his doctor.

Note: Stocks of Form SSP1 may be obtained from local Benefits Agency offices. However, supplies of that form will be issued in the ratio of one form for every 10 persons employed – presumably to limit any possibility of abuse or fraudulent misuse of the form. Supplies of other forms referred to in this section are available on request from the Employer's Orderline on 0845 7 646 646 or from website www.inlandrevenue.gov.uk/employers/emp-form.htm

Married women and widows paying a 'reduced stamp'

- Married women and widows, who have elected (and have retained the right) to pay reduced National Insurance contributions, are nonetheless entitled to be paid SSP by their employers when incapacitated for work due to illness or injury, provided they satisfy the usual rules and are not in one of the *excluded* categories described in the previous paragraph. However, they will still be denied access to social security benefits after exhaustion of their SSP entitlement, or if they later fall into an excluded or disqualified category.

When SSP must stop

- Payments of SSP to an employee must cease on the day *preceding* that on which he or she returns to work after an absence occasioned by illness or injury. SSP must also cease:

  (a) on the effective date of termination of employment if the employee in question resigns or is dismissed during a PIW, unless the employer's principal reason for dismissing the employee was to avoid having to pay any further SSP;

  (b) if a pregnant employee starts her 26-week maternity pay period during a PIW, in which situation SSP must cease on the Saturday of the week immediately preceding the week in which the maternity pay period begins;

  (c) if the PIW in question (consisting of a great number of 'shortish' linked PIWs with the same employer) runs on for longer than three years, in which (rare) event, the employer's liability to pay SSP stops at the end of the third year; or

  (d) if the employee is taken into legal custody or sentenced to a term of imprisonment (except where the sentence is suspended) during a PIW, in which event SSP must stop with the day on which the employee is taken into custody or sentenced.

  If any of the above situations occur, and the employee is still sick or otherwise incapable of work, the employer must complete and send the employee change-over form SSP1, plus any current sick notes he may be holding. If the employee resigns or is dismissed during a PIW, the employer may also need to provide a so-called leaver's statement (Form SSP1(L), referred to later in this section).

When an employer's SSP liability ends

- As an employer's liability to pay SSP to an employee is limited to a maximum 28 weeks in any single PIW (or series of *linked* PIWs), it is important that records are maintained showing the amount of SSP due and paid, and the remaining SSP liability in a PIW. The maintenance of these and other records is a legal requirement (*vide* regulation 13 of the Statutory Sick Pay (General) Regulations 1982). See also *Records of sickness absence below*.

- The method to be used to calculate an employee's residual entitlement to SSP in a particular PIW will depend on the number of agreed *qualifying days* in each week of that PIW. If, for example, there are five qualifying days in a week, each qualifying day in respect of which SSP is due and has been paid will reduce the residual SSP entitlement of the employee in question by one-fifth of a week. If there are four agreed qualifying days in a week, each day on which SSP is paid will reduce the entitlement by one-quarter of a week. This method is particularly useful in a situation where an employee with a varied or irregular pattern of working days, week by week, agrees that qualifying days in a particular week (eg, the first week of a PIW) will reflect his rostered working days in that week, and the same or different qualifying days for the following and any subsequent weeks of incapacity.

  For example: If, in a particular PIW, an employee has been paid SSP in respect of 11 qualifying days, in weeks of four qualifying days apiece (ie, 11×0.25 weeks, or 3.75 weeks), plus a further six qualifying days in weeks of five qualifying days apiece (ie, 6×0.20 weeks, or 1.20 weeks), he will have been paid 4.95 weeks' SSP in that PIW and will have a residual entitlement of 23.05 weeks' SSP during the remainder of that PIW. For further worked examples, the reader is referred to DSS booklet NI 270.

- If the indications are that an employee will very soon exhaust his (or her) entitlement to SSP, the employer should supply that employee with change-over form SSP1 at the beginning of the 23rd week of SSP. If the employee unexpectedly returns to work before he has exhausted his entitlement to SSP, his employer must issue him another SSP1 as soon as a further *linked* PIW begins. Issuing form SSP1 in advance, in these circumstances, will prepare the way for a smooth transition to social security benefits.

- If an employee seems certain to exhaust his (or her) 28-week entitlement to SSP, the employer should issue him with change-over form

SSP1 at the beginning of the 23rd week of SSP entitlement (that is to say, some five weeks before the employer's liability to pay SSP is due to end). Should the employee return to work before he (or she) has exhausted his maximum entitlement to SSP in that PIW, the form should be issued as soon as another *linked* PIW begins. If an employer's SSP liability is due to end before the 23rd week of SSP, the change-over form must be issued two weeks before the relevant date. If an employer's liability to pay SSP ends unexpectedly before the 23rd week of SSP (eg, sudden resignation), the change-over form must be issued as soon as possible.

When issuing an employee with form SSP1, an employer should also return any current sick notes, to enable the employee to submit his (or her) claim for state incapacity benefits.

Leaver's statements issued by former employers

- When an employee resigns or is dismissed (including a dismissal arising out of the non-renewal of his (or her) fixed-term contract), his employer must issue him with a leaver's statement (Form SSP1(L)) – but only if the employee has been paid (or was due) SSP for a week or more during a PIW ending within the last eight weeks of his employment. For this purpose, three or fewer SSP days must be rounded-down, and four or more SSP days rounded-up, to the nearest whole week.

  Form SSP1(L) must be sent (or handed) to the former employee not later than seven calendar days after the date on which his (or her) contract of employment ended. Supplies of the form may be obtained from the Employer's Orderline on 0845 7 646 646 or from website www.inlandrevenue.gov.uk/employers/emp-form.htm

Action on receipt of a leaver's statement

- An employee starting work with a new employer should hand over Form SSP1(L) (if any) supplied by his (or her) previous employer. Although a new recruit is under no legal obligation to hand over a leaver's statement, failing to do so could mean a long delay before he would be entitled to transfer to state incapacity benefit (payable at a higher base rate than SSP, with additions for dependants, etc). It is up to an employer to persuade a new recruit to hand over any leaver's statement he may be holding if he begins a PIW within the period of 56 days starting with the day on which his or her employment began.

Note: There is nothing to prevent an employer telephoning or writing to a previous employer to enquire whether a former employee (now in his employ) had been issued with Form SSP1 (L) when his employment ended.

- If a new recruit hands Form SSP1(L) to his (or her) new employer and begins a PIW within the first eight weeks of his employment, the new employer must first establish whether the interval between the last day for which SSP was due or paid by a previous employer and the first day of that PIW with him is eight weeks or less. If there is no *link*, the new employer's SSP liability in that PIW will be 28 weeks (in other words, his normal maximum SSP liability). But, if the two PIWs *do* link, the new employer's liability to pay SSP during that PIW will reduce by the number of weeks' SSP paid by the previous employer – as shown on the leaver's statement. In some instances, a leaver's statement will show that the employee in question had exhausted his 28 weeks' entitlement to SSP in that previous PIW – in which event, the employee is *excluded* from SSP in respect of the PIW in question and must be issued with a changeover form (Form SSP1, discussed below).

- A new recruit, who begins a PIW with his new employer within eight weeks of the commencement of his employment, should hand over Form SSP1(L) with seven days after the first *qualifying day* in that PIW. An employer may accept the late receipt of a leaver's statement if there is 'good cause' for the delay. Otherwise, he can disregard the amount of SSP shown on the leaver's statement. Indeed, he *must* do so if the employee fails to hand him Form SSP1(L) within 91 days after the first qualifying day in the relevant PIW.

Notification of sickness absence

- An employer has every right to insist that an employee notify him as soon as possible if he (or she) is unable to turn in for work on a particular day. Indeed, many employers have a rule which states that any employee who is unable to turn in for work must notify his manager or supervisor – by telephone or other means – within one hour of his normal starting time on that day. Such a requirement is understandable, given that the employer (or manager, as the case may be) has a business or department to run and may have to make other arrangements to cover the employee's job, particularly if that employee occupies a key position within the organisation. Indeed, any employee who repeatedly neglects to inform his (or her) employer that he will not be turning in for work (for whatever reason) is liable to disciplinary action, leading to dismissal if the situation does not improve.

- Under the SSP scheme, the rules for notifying sickness absence are somewhat less stringent. While those rules do not undermine an employer's right to discipline an employee who neglects to notify his (or her) superiors that he will not be attending for work, they *do* lay down less demanding conditions in relation to the payment of SSP. Thus, regulation 7 of the 1982 Regulations (*qv*) states:

  (a) that an employer must make it clear to his employees how he wants notification of sickness absence to be given (eg, whether by telephone, in writing, or both);

  (b) that an employer cannot insist on notification earlier than the end of the first *qualifying day* of a period of sickness absence;

  (c) that (for SSP purposes only) an employer cannot insist on notification by a specific time of day (in other words, notification given by an employee *at any time* during the first *qualifying day* of sickness absence will be in time for SSP purposes);

  (d) that, if an employer accepts written notification of sickness absence, he must treat that notification as having been given on the day on which the letter/postcard was posted, *not* on the day on which it is received;

  (e) that an employer cannot insist on the sick or injured employee giving notification in person (whether by telephone, letter, or otherwise);

  (f) that an employer cannot insist on notification in the form of a doctor's sick note (Form Med 3 or the equivalent), although a sick note will count as notification (see *Evidence of incapacity for work* below);

  (g) that (for SSP purposes only) an employer cannot insist on notification of continued absence more frequently than once every seven days;

  (h) that, if notification of absence is required in writing, an employer must be prepared (at least for SSP purposes) to accept any form of written notification so long as it contains sufficient details to show that the employee is ill or otherwise incapacitated for work (in other words, an employer cannot insist on the employee giving notification on a printed form designed and/or supplied by the employer);

  (i) that an employer must make his rules concerning notification of sickness absence readily available to his employees, eg, by means of a notice posted on a staff notice board or incorporated in an employee handbook.

Note: If an employer does not lay down 'house rules' for the notification of sickness absence, or such rules as he has prepared do not comply with the requirements laid down in (a) to (i) above, an employee will not forfeit any entitlement to SSP because of late notification, provided he (or she) gives written notification of sickness absence not later than seven calendar days from the beginning of the first qualifying day of that period of absence (*ibid.* regulation 7(l)(b)).

- Notwithstanding the above, an employer may withhold a day (or days) of SSP because of late notification if, but only if, he (or she) is *not* satisfied that the employee in question had a good reason for his or her tardiness. Nor is he under any obligation to withhold SSP – whether or not he is satisfied with the reasons for lateness put forward by the employee. Finally, days of SSP which are withheld because of late notification do not count towards the employer's 28 weeks of liability to pay SSP.

Evidence of incapacity for work

- Notification of sickness absence is one thing; *evidence* of incapacity is quite a different matter. Nowadays, doctors will not issue a sick note (Form Med 3 or the equivalent) unless the patient in question is likely to be incapacitated for work for seven or more days. It follows that employers cannot insist on the production of a sick note for a period of sickness absence lasting less than seven days (unless, of course, they are prepared to pay for such sick notes). However, once a PIW persists for seven days or longer, an employer can, of course, insist on the production of a sick note to cover the entire period of incapacity – and would be within his rights to withhold SSP if that evidence is not forthcoming.

- For shorter periods of incapacity for work (lasting less than seven calendar days), an employer may either require the employee to complete a form of self-certification for sickness absence (to be signed in the presence of his manager upon his return to work) or ask him to complete DSS Form SC2 – stocks of which are available from local Social Security offices. It is then up to the employer to decide whether a particular employee was genuinely incapable of work. If SSP is withheld because of suspected malingering (eg, a supposedly sick employee seen playing football), the employee in question is entitled to ask his employer for a written statement explaining his reasons for withholding SSP, and then apply to an adjudication officer of the DSS for a decision in the matter.

Note: Where an employee is frequently absent from work for periods of between four and seven days (for seemingly unrelated medical reasons) his (or her) employer may ask permission to approach the employee's GP for a medical report (see **Medical reports, access to** elsewhere in this handbook). If the employee refuses to cooperate, the employer may require him (or her) to attend for an independent medical examination by another doctor, at the employer's expense. If all else fails, the employer may write to his local office of the Inland Revenue offices asking Medical Services to intervene. The correct procedure is explained in the Inland Revenue's *Statutory Sick Pay Manual for Employers* (Ref. CA30).

- Whatever form of *evidence* of incapacity for work an employer requires, he should make his requirements known to his employees – so that they are left in no doubt as to what is expected of them should they be unable to attend for work because of illness or injury.

Calculating average weekly earnings

- In most SSP situations, an employer has no need to reach for his pocket calculator to determine whether or not an employee of his qualifies for the standard or lower rate of SSP. That will usually be self-evident. But, in borderline cases, the following procedures should be followed.

Employees paid weekly

- If an employee is paid once a week on the same day of the week, his (or her) average gross weekly earnings are calculated by totalling his gross earnings on the eight paydays ending with the last payday before the PIW (or series of *linked* PIWs) began. The result is divided by eight to produce the required weekly average. Any odd payments made to an employee in the eight calendar weeks ending with that last payday must also be included in calculations.

Note: The expression *earnings* in this context means an employee's gross earnings and includes any remuneration or profit derived from his (or her) employment. Overtime payments must be included, as must holiday pay, bonuses, tips and gratuities (if paid by the employer), maternity pay, and arrears of pay (including a protective award) ordered by an employment tribunal. Tips do not form part of an employee's earnings if received directly from customers, guests, etc – provided they are not indirect earnings – nor do payments in kind, such as the provision of board or lodging (or meals while at work) or of services or other facilities.

Employees paid monthly

- The average weekly earnings of a monthly-paid employee are calculated by adding together his (or her) gross wages or salary on each of the last two paydays before the relevant PIW (or series of *linked* PIWs) began. The total is then multiplied by six and divided by 52, in order to produce the required weekly average figure.

Employees paid at other intervals

- The average weekly earnings of an employee who is paid at other regular intervals (such as fortnightly or four-weekly), are calculated by taking the lowest number of *pay periods* which takes in at least eight calendar weeks before the PIW (or series of *linked PIWs*) began. The gross earnings paid on the number of normal paydays ending with the payday before the relevant PIW are then added together and divided by the number of weeks covered by the lowest number of pay periods referred to above.

New recruits who have worked for less than eight weeks

- The average weekly earnings of a new recruit, who has worked for his (or her) new employer for fewer than eight weeks before a PIW begins, are calculated by adding together any gross payments made to him since he first started work, and dividing the total by the number of weeks those payments represent. Odd days count as one-seventh of a week each.

New recruits who have not yet received any wages or salary

- If a new employee has not received any payment of wages or salary at the time a PIW (or series of *linked* PIWs) begins, his (or her) average gross earnings for SSP purposes will be the weekly (or equivalent weekly) remuneration to which he is entitled under the terms of his contract of employment.

Time and manner of payment of SSP

- SSP should ordinarily be paid on the first normal payday after a PIW begins. If that is impracticable (perhaps for administrative reasons, or because a PIW is formed just a day or two before the following relevant payday), payment may be deferred until the next payday – but *not* later than that payday.

- Regulation 8 of the 1982 Regulations (*qv*) states only that SSP may not be paid in kind or by way of the provision of board or lodging or of services or other facilities. DSS booklet NI 270 (at paragraph 99) says, quite simply, that an employer can use whatever means of payment he prefers, eg in cash, by cheque, credit transfer to an employee's bank account, etc. However, employers would be well-advised to consult with their employees before attempting to impose a method of payment of SSP which is unfamiliar to them and which could cause problems (eg, encashment of cheques).

SSP and occupational sick pay schemes

- Many employers run their own occupational sick pay schemes for the benefit of employees who are incapacitated for work because of sickness or injury. However, the benefits available under most occupational schemes are usually linked to an employee's status and/or length of service. Employers may opt-out of the Employers' SSP Scheme so long as the benefits 'enjoyed' by employees under their employer's occupational sick pay scheme are no less beneficial than those available to them under the Employers' SSP Scheme.

  Note: Employers with occupational sick pay schemes should long since have reviewed their occupational schemes in the light of their statutory duty to pay SSP to employees during periods of incapacity for work – bearing in mind that entitlement to SSP is not affected by considerations of status (ie whether an employee is full-time, part-time or, indeed, a seasonal worker) or length of service. Rules concerning notification and evidence of incapacity for work should also have been reviewed, bearing in mind that SSP rules on notification and the production of supporting medical are undoubtedly less stringent than those which usually apply under the provisions of an occupational scheme.

- Schedule 12 to the Social Security Contributions & Benefits Act 1992 states that any contractual remuneration paid to an employee by his (or her) employer in respect of a day of incapacity for work 'shall go towards discharging any liability of that employer to pay statutory sick pay to that employee in respect of that day'. Thus, if the amount paid to a sick employee under an occupational sick pay scheme – in respect of a particular day of sickness absence exceeds the amount of SSP due to that employee in respect of that *same* day, then the employer will have discharged his obligations under the SSP Scheme. If the amount in question is less than the daily rate of SSP due on that day, that amount will go towards discharging the employer's liability under the SSP Scheme. It must be stressed that any payment made under an occupational sick pay scheme may only be offset against SSP if the former is due and payable in respect of the same day (or days) on which the obligation to pay SSP arises. Thus, payment of occupational sick pay on the first three days (or *waiting days*) of a PIW (where liability to pay SSP does not arise) cannot be offset against SSP payable in respect of any subsequent *qualifying days* in that same PIW.

Records of sickness absence

- Employers have a legal obligation to maintain the following records for a minimum period of three years after the end of the tax year to which those records relate:

(a) dates of PIWs (ie, absences of four consecutive days or more, including Saturdays, Sundays, 'rest days' and public or bank holidays) formed by employees during the relevant tax year;

(b) particulars of any days within those PIWs for which SSP was not paid, and the reasons for non-payment; and

(c) details of the agreed *qualifying days* in each PIW.

These records must be kept accessible for examination on demand by Inland Revenue inspectors. See *Offences and penalties* below.

Note: Employers are also required to keep wage and other records showing particulars of SSP payments to individual employees for each payday in the relevant tax year, as well as details of pay, income tax (PAYE) and National Insurance contributions.

Disagreements about SSP

• An employee, who is unhappy about his (or her) employer's decision not to pay (or to cease paying) him the SSP to which he believes he is entitled, has the right to ask his employer for a written statement explaining the reasons for his decision – which statement must be handed or sent to the employee within a reasonable time. On receipt of the statement, the employee may refer the matter for determination by an officer of the Inland Revenue. An employer who refuses to provide the written statement, or who refuses to comply with a decision by the officer, is guilty of an offence under the 1992 Act and runs the risk of prosecution (per the Statutory Sick Pay & Statutory Maternity Pay (Decisions) Regulations 1999, which came into force on 1 April 1999). For further details, see next paragraph.

Offences and penalties

• An employer who fails to pay SSP within the time allowed (when an officer of the Inland Revenue has overturned his (or her) decision not to pay (or to cease paying) SSP to an employee), is guilty of an offence and liable, on summary conviction, to a fine of up to £1,000, plus a further fine of up to £40 per day for each day of continued non-compliance.

• An employer is also liable to a fine of up to £1,000 if he does not cooperate with the DSS when asked for written information about an employee, or if he fails to keep adequate SSP records, or if he refuses to issue either of Form SSP1 or a written statement explaining his reasons for not paying (or ceasing to pay) SSP.

- An employer who is entitled (or claims to be entitled) to 'Small Employer's Relief' is liable to a fine of up to £5,000 or imprisonment for up to three months if he produces, furnishes, or knowingly allows to be produced or furnished, any document or information which he knows to be false in a material particular, when purporting to recover amounts paid by way of SSP.

Miscellaneous

More about the three-year 'cut off' rule

- The effect of an employee's maximum entitlement of 28 weeks' SSP in a single (linked or unlinked) PIW, combined with the eight-week linking rule, could create a situation in which a single PIW (consisting of a large number of short-term linked PIWs) continues for more than eight years. To avoid this happening, the SSP Scheme introduces the notion of a three-year 'cut-off'. Thus, if a PIW with one employer (ignoring, in this instance, SSP paid by a previous employer) continues beyond three years, the employer's SSP liability in that PIW ceases at the end of the third year (in spite of the fact that the employee in question may not have exhausted his (or her) maximum SSP entitlement in that PIW). At the end of that third year, the employee must be issued with a 'change-over form' (Form SSP1) to enable him to transfer to the appropriate state benefit.

Dismissing an employee to avoid paying SSP

- An employer cannot avoid his liability to pay SSP to a sick or incapacitated employee by dismissing that employee. Regulation 4 of the Statutory Sick Pay (General) Regulations 1982 states that, if an employee is dismissed solely or mainly for the purpose of avoiding liability for SSP, the employer must nonetheless continue to pay SSP to that employee for so long as his (or her) illness or disability lasts (provided he does not exhaust his entitlement to SSP during the period of incapacity, or fall within one of the *excluded categories* described earlier).

Injury or ill-health caused by misconduct

- It is as well to point out that an employee is not to be denied access to SSP simply because his (or her) illness or disability has been caused by dangerous extra-curricular activities or wilful misconduct at the work-place. So long as the employee is genuinely incapable of carrying out his duties, his employer will have no option but to pay him SSP – provided, of course, that the employee is not in an excluded category, that he otherwise qualifies for SSP, and that he complies with his employer's rules concerning notification and evidence of incapacity.

Note: If an employee is injured while skylarking at work or indulging in 'horseplay' or a breach of his (or her) employer's health and safety rules etc, the employer has every right to discipline or dismiss him for conduct. If the employee is dismissed (as punishment for misconduct – not merely a ploy to evade liability for SSP), the employer's obligation to pay SSP ceases on the date of dismissal – at which time he must issue the employee with the 'change-over' form SSP1 discussed earlier in this section.

Employees with two jobs

- If an employee has two jobs, both employers are liable to pay SSP to that employee during a period of incapacity for work (assuming that the employee is not in an *excluded category*, because of low average earnings, or whatever). Each employer has a separate liability to pay that employee up to 28 weeks' SSP in any PIW.

Conclusion

- This section has been intended as a guide only (if a somewhat detailed guide) to the principal provisions of the statutory sick pay scheme. For a yet more comprehensive explanation of the intricacies of the scheme, the reader is referred to the current edition (with supplements) of the Inland Revenue's *Statutory Sick Pay Manual for Employers* (CA30) which is routinely supplied to all registered employers at the beginning of each tax year.

  See also **Dismissal on grounds of ill-health** and **Written particulars of terms of employment** elsewhere in this handbook.

STRIKES AND OTHER INDUSTRIAL ACTION

Key points

- Legislation relating to industrial action ballots (ie, ballots for strike action), and the rights and duties of trade unions and employers in relation to such action, is to be found in Part V of the Trade Union & Labour Relations (Consolidation) Act 1992.

- A trade union which organises a strike or some other form of industrial action against an employer (eg, an overtime ban or a work-to-rule), will enjoy a 'statutory immunity' against civil actions for damages arising out of any associated breaches of employment or commercial contracts:

  (a) if the industrial action is in contemplation or furtherance of a legitimate trade dispute (as defined below);

  (b) if the industrial action has the support of the members concerned through a properly conducted secret ballot;

  (c) if entitlement to vote in the ballot was accorded equally to all union members who it was reasonable at the time of the ballot for the union to believe would be induced to take part in the industrial action;

  Note: A trade union that unlawfully denies one or other of its members an opportunity to vote in a ballot for industrial action, and subsequently induces that member to take part (or to continue to take part) in that action, will lose its protection from liability in tort – unless the union had no reason to believe at the time of the ballot that the member in question would be induced to take part in that action.

  (d) if, following the ballot, the union gives the employer at least seven days' advance written notice of the date on which official industrial action is to begin; and

  (e) if the action does not involve unlawful picketing (as to which, see **Picketing** elsewhere in this handbook).

- If a strike or other form of industrial action fails to satisfy any of conditions (a) to (e), the union concerned (including the individuals responsible for organising what amounts to *unofficial* or unlawful action) has no statutory immunity and can be sued for damages by the employer himself, as well as by any other employer, supplier, customer, or member of the public whose business activities have been disrupted, whose commercial or employment contracts have been broken or interfered-with, or who have been deprived of (or denied access to) goods or services. Indeed, individuals engaged in unlawful secondary picketing (and the person or persons who organised that picketing) are themselves liable to be sued for interfering with (or inducing others to break or interfere with) contracts of employment or contracts for the supply of goods or services.

  Note: Although a trade union may be immune from certain legal proceedings for civil wrongs arising out of official 'industrial action, there is no protection against criminal prosecution for pickets and striking workers who commit acts of violence against persons or property, who engage in threatening or abusive behaviour, or who obstruct the public highway. See also *Criminal offences* below.

- Section 21 of the 1992 Act provides that a trade union will be taken to have endorsed or authorised unofficial industrial action, and will be liable in proceedings in tort for the actions of the officials, shop stewards or committees responsible for organising such action, unless the principal executive committee of the union, or its president or general secretary, acts speedily to repudiate and put an end to that action. In short, the executive committee, president or general secretary must:

  (a) write to the committee or official concerned telling them, him or her, in no uncertain terms, that the action they are contemplating or engaged in does *not* have the support of the union itself;

  (b) write to every member of the union, who the union has reason to believe is taking part (or might otherwise take part) in that unofficial action, in terms which must include the following statement:

  'Your union has repudiated the call (or calls) for industrial action to which this notice relates and will give no support to unofficial industrial action taken in response to it (or them). If you are dismissed while taking unofficial industrial action, you will have no right to complain of unfair dismissal.'

  (c) write to the employer in question informing him that the union unequivocally repudiates the industrial action (taken or proposed) by its local officials, shop stewards or other elected or appointed representatives.

  A trade union which take steps (a), (b) and (c) will not be treated in law as having repudiated the industrial action in question if, at any time after their purported repudiation of that action, the executive committee (or any of its members), president or general secretary:

  (d) behaves in a manner which is inconsistent with that repudiation; or

  (e) does not *immediately* confirm in writing, when asked to do so by a party to a commercial contract which has been (or may be) interfered with by the unofficial action, that the union has formally repudiated that action (although no such confirmation need be given if the request is made more than three months after the purported repudiation).

- Employees engaged in industrial action which has been repudiated by their trade union will forfeit any limited right they may have to complain of unfair dismissal unless they return to work by the end of the next working day after the day on which the repudiation took place. If, for example, an employee receives a letter from his (or her) union on Monday informing him that the industrial action in which he is engaged does not have the support of his union, he should return to work immediately or, at the very latest, before the end of his normal working day (or shift) on Tuesday. If he does not do so, he can be dismissed with impunity and will forfeit his right to complain to an employment tribunal that he was dismissed unfairly (*ibid.* section 237(4)). An employee in the same situation, who is dismissed before he has had an opportunity to return to work, will have the right to complain of unfair dismissal if, but only if, one or more of his striking colleagues were either not dismissed or were offered their jobs back within three months of his own dismissal. For further details, please turn to the section titled **Dismissal for taking industrial action** elsewhere in this handbook.

Remedies

- Any party whose contracts are broken or interfered with by unprotected industrial action (or by the threat of such action) may not only apply to the courts for an injunction restraining any further such acts but also may claim damages for the losses suffered.

- A trade union (or the officials or members concerned) will be in contempt of court and liable to heavy penalties (including, where appropriate, sequestration of the union's assets) if it or they do not obey an injunction to restrain from unofficial industrial action. At present (2003), the maximum damages which may be awarded in any proceedings against a trade union are as follows (depending on the size of the union):

No. of members	Max damages
Less than 5,000	£10,000
5,000–24,999	£50,000
25,000–99,999	£125,000
100,000 or more	£250,000

Meaning of a 'trade dispute'

- Section 244 of the 1992 Act defines *trade dispute* as meaning a dispute between workers and their employer which relates wholly or mainly to one or more of the following:

  (a) terms and conditions of employment or the physical conditions in which any workers are required to work;

  (b) engagement or non-engagement, or termination or suspension of employment or the duties of employment, of one or more workers;

(c) allocation of work or the duties of employment as between workers or groups of workers;

(d) matters of discipline;

(e) a worker's membership or non-membership of a trade union;

(f) facilities for officials of trade unions; and

(g) machinery for negotiation or consultation, and other procedures, relating to any of the foregoing matters, including the recognition by employers or employers' associations of the right of a trade union to represent workers in such negotiation or consultation or in the carrying out of such procedures (*ibid.* section 244).

Note: The expression 'worker', in relation to a trade dispute with an employer, means a worker still employed by that employer or a former employee, the termination of whose employment was either connected with the dispute or was one of the circumstances which gave rise to the dispute (*ibid.* section 244(5)).

- It follows that a legitimate trade dispute does not include:

  (a) unlawful secondary action (eg, a sympathy strike); or

  (b) action whose purpose it is to put pressure on an employer to accept a closed shop (or union membership agreement) or to deal only with contractors or suppliers who recognise, negotiate or consult with trade unions or trade union officials; or

  (c) action by way of protest against the dismissal of an employee sacked while taking part in unofficial industrial action.

  Nor does it include:

  (d) disputes between trade unions or groups of workers where no employer is involved in the dispute;

  (e) disputes between workers and an employer who is not *their* employer;

  (f) disputes between a trade union and an employer, when none of the latter's employees is in dispute with him;

  (g) disputes which are not wholly or mainly about employment-related matters (such as rates of pay and other terms and conditions of employment); or

  (h) disputes relating to events occurring overseas, unless the workers taking action in support of such a dispute are likely to be affected in a material way by its outcome.

Any form of industrial action, which is not in contemplation or further-ance of a legitimate trade dispute (as defined in the previous para-graph) is *unofficial* and, therefore, unprotected, whether or not it is authorised or endorsed by the trade union in question.

Requirement of a ballot before industrial action

- Section 226 of the 1992 Act cautions that any act done by a trade union to induce a person to take part (or to continue to take part) in industrial action will not be protected unless the industrial action in question has the support of a properly-conducted ballot. Nor is it protected in rela-tion to that person's employer (see *Note* below) unless the union writes to the employer, at least seven days beforehand, informing him of the date on which the ballot is to be held (when and where) giving details sufficient to enable the employer to make plans for dealing with the consequences of a possible strike or other form of industrial action, including (without identifying names) the number and categories of workers to be included in the ballot; and identifying those members of the workforce (by name, job title or description) who will be afforded an opportunity to vote in the ballot. Furthermore, not later than three days before the day on which the ballot is to take place, the union must send the employer a sample of the voting paper it intends to use in the ballot.

Note: If industrial action is 'unprotected' solely because of a trade union's failure to give an employer seven days' advance notice of its intention to conduct a ballot, or because of its failure to provide him with sample voting papers, it is only the employer concerned, or an individual deprived of goods or services by that action, who can sue the trade union for damages in such circumstances.

Entitlement to vote in a ballot

- Entitlement to vote in a ballot for industrial action must be accorded equally to all the members of the trade union who it is reasonable at the time of the ballot for the union to believe will be induced to take part or, as the case may be, to continue to take part in the industial action in question, and to no others. It is up to the trade union to decide whether any of its members who are outside Great Britain when the ballot is due to take place should be accorded entitlement to vote in a ballot. If those members *are* invited to vote, the information about the outcome of the ballot (which *must* be conveyed to those entitled to vote in the ballot after the votes have been counted) must distinguish between the votes cast by overseas members and other members, but need not be sent to those members who were overseas at the time. A member who is in Northern Ireland when votes are cast in the ballot should not be treated as an 'overseas member' (i) if the ballot is a *workplace ballot* and the member's place of work is in Great Britain, or (ii) if the ballot is a general ballot involving members both in Great Britain and Northern Ireland. See below for the meaning of the expressions *workplace ballot* and *general ballot*. See also *Reporting the results of a ballot* below.

- Section 232B of the 1992 Act allows that minor and accidental failures in determining who is (or is not) entitled to vote in a ballot for industrial action, and minor and genuine errors in the organisation or conduct of the ballot itself, will not invalidate the ballot, so long as they are on a scale that is unlikely to affect the outcome of the ballot.

Separate workplace ballots or a general ballot?

- Separate workplace ballots are not required when there is a company or industry-wide trade dispute involving members of the same trade union employed in the same or similar occupations, who share common terms and conditions of employment – so long as entitlement to vote in the ballot is accorded only to those members who share that common distinguishing factor. In short, an aggregate ballot (that is to say, across all or some of the affected workplaces) will be permissible if the dispute relates wholly or partly to a decision (or pending decision) by management concerning terms and conditions of employment, recruitment policy, suspensions, dismissals, redundancies, the allocation of work or the duties of employment, a worker's membership or non-membership of a trade union, or the provision of facilities for trade union officials – so long as that decision affects (or is likely to affect) one or more of the union's members at all (or some) of those workplaces.

- In other words, separate *workplace ballots* are necessary only if the trade union members entitled to vote in the ballot are employed at different locations, have a variety of occupations, enjoy different terms and conditions of employment, and have different branches or arrangements. In such circumstances, a majority vote in favour of industrial action at one location will lead to official industrial action; whereas industrial action taken at a second location (following a vote against industrial action) will be 'unofficial' and 'unprotected' (*ibid.* section 228).

Voting papers

- The following unqualified statement must (without being qualified or commented upon by anything else on the paper) appear on every voting paper:

'If you take part in a strike or other industrial action, you may be in breach of your contract of employment. However, if you are dismissed for taking part in strike or other industrial action which is called officially and is otherwise lawful, the dismissal will be unfair if it takes place fewer than eight weeks after you started taking part in the action, and, depending on the circumstances, may be unfair if it takes place later.'

- Furthermore, every voting paper must:

    (a) state the name of the independent scrutineer (unless the number of employees to be balloted does not exceed 50; in which case, there is no need for a scrutineer);

    (b) clearly specify the address to which, and the date by which, it is to be returned; and

    (c) be marked with a number which is one of a series of consecutive whole numbers used to give a different number to each voting paper.

The voting paper must also include at least one of the following questions which (however framed) requires the person answering it to say 'Yes' or 'No', namely:

    (d) whether he (or she) is prepared to take part or, as the case may be, to continue to take part in a strike;

    (e) whether he (or she) is prepared to take part or, as the case may be, to continue to take part in industrial action short of a strike (eg, an overtime or call-out ban).

Finally, the voting paper must:

    (f) name or describe (by title or function) the person or persons who, in the event of a majority vote in favour of industrial action, is (or are) authorised by the union to call upon the members concerned to take part (or continue to take part) in the industrial action.

The person or persons referred to in (f) may be the principal executive committee of the union (or any member of that committee), the president or general secretary, a regional, branch or local official, a works convenor, an elected or appointed shop steward, or any committee of the union constituted in accordance with the union's rules.

A ballot will be invalidated if the voting papers distributed to members do not comply with all of requirements (a) to (f) above (*ibid.* section 229).

Scrutiny of ballots

- When 50 or more of its members are entitled to vote in a ballot for industrial action, the trade union concerned must (before the ballot takes place) appoint a qualified and independent scrutineer whose job it is to ensure that the ballot is properly conducted. To be qualified, the scrutineer must be either a practising solicitor or qualified accountant, or a person nominated by one or other of the following three bodies, namely, the Electoral Reform Ballot Services Limited, the Industrial Society, or Unity Security Balloting Services Limited.

  Not later than four weeks after the ballot, the scrutineer must produce a report stating whether he (or she) is satisfied:

  (a) that the ballot was properly conducted;

  (b) that the security arrangements for producing, storing, distributing, returning and handling the voting papers, and for counting the votes cast in the ballot were sufficient to minimise the risk of unfairness or malpractice;

  (c) that there was no attempt by the trade union (or by any official, member or employee of that union) to interfere with or obstruct him in the conduct of his duties; and

  (d) that the union complied with his reasonable requests for information or assistance in the conduct of his duties.

  If the scrutineer is unhappy with the way in which the ballot was conducted, or with the way in which votes were collected or counted, he (or she) must say as much in his report.

- On receipt of the scrutineer's report, the trade union must send a copy on request (either for a modest fee or free of charge) to the relevant employer and to any member of the union who was entitled to vote in the ballot. However, the union need not respond to any requests for copies of the scrutineer's report if made more than six months after the date on which the ballot was conducted (*ibid.* sections 226B, 226C and 231B).

Conduct of ballot

- Trade union members exercising their right to vote in a ballot must, so far as is reasonably practicable, be allowed to do so in secret. The ballot itself must be properly conducted; and the votes given in it, counted fairly and accurately. Those voting must also be allowed to do so:

(a) without interference from, or constraint (eg, intimidation) imposed by, the union or any of its members, officials or employees; and

(b) without incurring any direct cost to themselves.

Furthermore, every person entitled to vote in the ballot must:

(c) have a voting paper sent to him (or her) by post at his home address or any other address which he has asked his trade union (in writing) to treat as his postal address; and

(d) be given a convenient opportunity to vote by post (again, at no cost to himself) (*ibid.* section 230).

Note: Merchant seamen who are likely to be at sea or outside Great Britain when a ballot for industrial action takes place must, so far as is reasonably practicable, be supplied with a voting paper and must be given an opportunity to vote while they are on board ship or in port (*ibid.* section 230(2A) and (2B)). This requirement will be amended when paragraph 7 of Schedule 3 to the Employment Relations Act 1999 comes into force (probably in mid-2000). Thereafter, a trade union must (if reasonably practicable) ballot a member on board ship, or at a port where the ship is, if the member will be at sea, or at a foreign port where the ship is, for all or part of the balloting period, so long as it is convenient for the member to receive the ballot paper and to vote in this way.

Reporting the results of a ballot

- Once the votes cast in a ballot have been counted, the trade union must, as soon as is reasonably practicable, inform every relevant employer and every person entitled to vote in the ballot of:

  (a) the number of votes cast in the ballot;

  (b) the number of individuals who answered 'Yes' to the question or, as the case may be, to each of the questions on the voting paper;

  (c) the number of individuals who answered 'No' to the question or, as the case may be, to each of the questions in the voting paper; and

  (d) the number of spoiled voting papers (if any) (*ibid.* sections 231 and 231B).

A trade union's failure to notify every relevant employer of the outcome of the ballot means that it may not lawfully call out those of its members whose employers were not correctly informed of the outcome of the ballot.

Majority vote in favour of industrial action

- If there has been a majority vote in favour of a strike and/or action short of industrial action, and the union decides to go ahead with that action, it must inform the affected employer (or employers), at least seven days beforehand (but not before it has informed the employer of the outcome of the ballot), of the date on which it intends to call its members out on strike or to instruct them to begin that other industrial action. The notice sent to the employer need not name names, but if the union possesses information as to the number, category or workplaces of the employees likely to be induced to take part in that action, the notice must contain that information. Furthermore, the notice must state whether the industrial action is to be 'continuous' or 'discontinuous' (eg, an uninterrupted strike or a series of one-day strikes). If it is to be 'discontinuous', the union must specify the dates or days on which that action is to take place. The notice must also state that it is given for the purposes of section 234A of the Trade Union & Labour Relations (Consolidation) Act 1992. The seven-day notice period referred to above may be suspended to enable the parties to a trade dispute to make last-minute attempts to negotiate a settlement. If such negotiations prove unsuccessful, it will not be necessary for the trade union to issue a fresh seven-day notice.

Note: Industrial action which has the support of a ballot will be 'unprotected' in relation to the employer if the trade union in question fails to give the employer seven days' advance notice of the date on which it intends to begin that industrial action. What this means is that, in those circumstances, only the employer or an individual deprived of goods or services by that action may pursue a civil action for damages (*ibid.* section 234A(l)).

- A trade union's call for industrial action, following a majority vote in favour of such action, must be made by the person or persons specified on the voting paper and must be made within four weeks of the date (or the last of the dates) on which the ballot took place. If it is not, the proposed industrial action will be 'unprotected' and 'unofficial' and (if proceeded with) will expose the trade union to the risk of civil actions for damages from all affected quarters. However, that four-week period may be extended by up to a further four weeks if, but only if, both the trade union and the employer in question agree to such an extension (eg, with a view to achieving a settlement of the dispute between them). Where there have been separate workplace ballots, an agreement to extend would apply to those workplaces only in which such an agreement has been reached.

- The industrial action must itself begin within those four weeks (or within the agreed extended period). However, the period must be deferred if, for one reason or another, there is a court order prohibiting the union from calling for industrial action during the whole or part of that period or the union has itself given an undertaking to the court not to proceed with such action. When the injunction or undertaking lapses or is set aside, the union may immediately apply to the court for an order extending that four-week or longer period. The court may refuse to do so if, following submissions by interested parties, it is persuaded that the result of the ballot no longer represents the views of the union members concerned, or something else has happened (or seems about to happen) which would prompt those members to vote against industrial action if offered another chance to vote in a ballot.

Criminal offences

- The statutory immunities (or protection) extended to trade unions engaged in official and lawful industrial action clearly do not extend to criminal offences. As is pointed out by section 240 of the 1992 Act, a person commits an offence who wilfully and maliciously breaks a contract of service or hiring, knowing or having reasonable cause to believe that the probable consequences of his so doing (either alone or in combination with others) will be to endanger human life or cause serious bodily injury, or to expose valuable property (whether real or personal) to destruction or serious injury. The penalty, on summary conviction, is imprisonment for a term not exceeding three months and/or a fine of up to £500 (level 2 on the standard scale).

- A person is liable to arrest without warrant if, with a view to compelling another person to do (or not to do) something which that other person has every legal right not to do (or to do), wilfully and without legal authority, he:

  (a) uses violence to or intimidates that person or his wife or children, or damages his property;

  (b) persistently follows that person about from place to place;

  (c) hides any tools, clothes or other property owned or used by that person, or deprives him of or hinders him in the use of such property;

  (d) watches or besets the house or other place where that person resides, works, carries on business or happens to be, or the approach to any such house or place; or

  (e) follows that person with two or more other persons in a disorderly manner in or through any street or road.

The penalty, on summary conviction, for any of the offences listed above, is imprisonment for a term of up to six months and/or a fine of up to £5,000 (level 5 on the standard scale).

See also **Codes of Practice**, **Dismissal for taking industrial action**, and **Trade union membership and activities**, elsewhere in this handbook.

SUNDAY WORK

Key points

- Although there is no general law in the UK which prohibits the employment of men, women or young persons on Sundays, there is legislation designed to protect the interests of shop workers and betting workers whose contracts of employment may or may not require them to work on Sundays. The statutes in question are the Sunday Trading Act 1994 and the Betting, Gaming & Lotteries Act 1963 (as amended) – the relevant provisions of which are now to be found in the Employment Rights Act 1996 (discussed below).

  Note: The reader is reminded that, under the provisions of the Working Time Regulations 1998, workers under the age of 18 cannot lawfully be required to work more than five days in any week (that is to say, in any period of seven consecutive days). In short, every adolescent worker must be allowed an uninterrupted 48-hour rest period each week, *in addition to* his or her minimum daily rest break of 12 hours. There are also restrictions on the employment of adult and young workers at night. For further details, please turn to the sections titled **Rest breaks and rest periods** and **Working hours**, elsewhere in this handbook. See also **Children, employment of**.

- Part II of the Shops Act 1950 (which contained provisions relating to the working hours and periods of employment of shop assistants) was repealed on 1 December 1994 by section 24 of the Deregulation & Contracting Out Act 1994 (*per* SI 1994/3037).

Shop workers

- With the repeal of the Shops Act 1950 came the Sunday Trading Act 1994. The relevant provisions of the latter enactment are now to be found in Part IV of the Employment Rights Act 1996. Since 26 August 1994, shop workers have had the right either to refuse to work on Sundays or to 'opt-out' of Sunday work. They also have the right not to be dismissed, selected for redundancy, or 'subjected to any detriment', for exercising (or proposing to exercise) that right.

Betting workers

- Under section 31A and Schedule 5A of the Betting, Gaming & Lotteries Act 1963, as inserted by section 20 and Schedule 8 to the Deregulation & Contracting Out Act 1994, betting workers likewise have the right to refuse to work on Sundays or, if employed before 3 January 1995 (under contracts of employment which require (or could require) them to work on Sundays), to opt-out of Sunday work. Those provisions have been consolidated and are now to be found in Part IV of the Employment Rights Act 1996.

Shop workers

Overview

- The Sunday Trading Act 1994 ('the 1994 Act') came into force on 26 August 1994. From that date, any shop in England or Wales may open all hours on a Sunday – unless it is a *large shop* (that is to say, a shop with a relevant floor area exceeding 280 square metres). Large shops may open for business for up to six hours on a Sunday subject to the proviso that they must not open before 10.00 am and must not remain open beyond 6.00 pm. The occupier of a large shop, who intends opening his (or her) premises on a Sunday must inform his local authority at least 14 days beforehand and must post conspicuous notices inside and outside his shop specifying the permitted Sunday opening hours for the shop. The owner or occupier of a large shop who ignores these rules is liable to a fine of up to £50,000.

    Note: The rules limiting the opening hours of *large shops* on Sundays do not apply to licensed pubs, registered pharmacies, shops in railway stations, shops in motorway service areas, petrol filling stations, shops selling motor vehicle and cycle parts and accessories, duty-free and other shops at airports (unless situated in a part of the airport which 'is not ordinarily used by people travelling by air'), and exhibition stands from which goods are sold to the public. A person of the Jewish religion, who is the occupier of a large shop may, if he intends not to open his shop on the Jewish Sabbath, serve notice to that effect on the local authority in the area in which his shop is situated.

Provisions for the protection of shop workers

- As well as lifting the previous restrictions on Sunday trading, the 1994 Act (at Schedule 4) also contained complicated provisions for the protection of shop workers whose contracts of employment may (or may not) have required them to work on Sundays. As was indicated earlier, Schedule 4 to the 1994 Act has since been repealed (with minor exceptions) and is now to be found in Part IV of the Employment Rights Act 1996 and in sections 45, 101, 105(4), 108(3)(d), 109(2)(d), 110(2)(c),

232 and 233 of that Act. Statutory references in the text which follows are references to the relevant provisions of the 1996 Act.

- A shop worker, for these purposes, is an employee who works in or about a shop on a day on which the shop is open for the serving of customers. The word *shop*, as used in the 1994 Act, refers to any premises in which a retail trade or business is carried on. For the purposes of the 1994 Act, the expression 'retail trade or business' does *not* apply to persons employed in restaurants, cafeterias, pubs, bars, or the like, in which meals, refreshments, or intoxicating liquor are sold for consumption on the premises. Nor does it apply to persons employed in 'take-away' establishments (or similar) in which meals or refreshments are prepared to order for immediate consumption off the premises (*ibid.* section 36(7)).

- There are four categories of shop worker to be considered in this context. These are:

  (a) the *protected shop* worker;

  (b) the *opted-out* shop worker;

  (c) the *opted-in* shop worker; and

  (d) the *'Sundays only'* shopworker.

  Shop workers in categories (a) and (b) have the right to refuse to do Sunday work, and the right also not to be dismissed or selected for redundancy, or otherwise victimised, for exercising that right or for challenging their employers' denial of that right (either before an employment tribunal or otherwise). Category (c) shop workers have renounced their *protected or opted-out* status and *can* be fairly dismissed for refusing to work on Sundays. For obvious reasons, the category (d) or 'Sundays only' shop worker is not protected in the same way as his or her colleagues in categories (a) and (b).

'Protected' shop workers

- The term *protected shop worker* describes a shop worker who was already a shop worker on 26 August 1994 (when the 1994 Act came into force) and is still employed as a shop worker (either by the same or an associated employer, or by a successor to that employer). The term also describes a shop worker recruited on or after 26 August 1994, whose contract of employment does *not* require him (or her) to do Sunday work.

- A *protected* shop worker has the right to refuse to work on Sundays, irrespective of any clause to the contrary in his (or her) contract of employment. He also has the right not to be dismissed, or selected for redundancy, or subjected to any detriment, for exercising (or proposing to exercise) that right (*ibid.* sections 45 and 101). See *Complaint to an employment tribunal* later in this section.

- It follows that any term in a *protected* shop worker's contract of employment which requires him (or her) to do Sunday work, or which requires his employer to provide him with Sunday work, is void and unenforceable. Although there is nothing to prevent a protected shop worker agreeing (or continuing) to work on Sundays, there is the risk that his employer may exercise *his* right to withdraw that facility at any time – given that he too can disregard any previous contractual obligation to provide that worker with Sunday work. If the employer exercises that right, there is very little that the protected shop worker can do about it. Indeed, if the shop worker's wages or salary are calculated by reference to his (former) contractual obligation to work on Sundays, he will very likely have to accept a cut in pay. The only way in which a *protected* shop worker can maintain the *status quo* (if that is what he wants) is to become an *opted-in* shop worker (see below).

'Opted-out' shop workers

- Employees recruited as shop workers on or after 26 August 1994, on terms which require them to work on Sundays, may (if they wish) opt-out of that contractual obligation. To do so, such a shop worker must give his (or her) employer three months' notice in writing (signed and dated), to the effect that he no longer wishes to work on Sundays. During that three-month notice period, the shop worker must continue to work on Sundays as required by his contract of employment. If he refuses, he is in breach of contract and can be fairly dismissed for that reason. But once those three months have elapsed, he becomes an *opted-out* shop worker and has the right to refuse to do any further Sunday work. At that point also, his contract of employment is treated in law as having been varied to accommodate that right. If an *opted-out* shop worker is dismissed or selected for redundancy, for refusing (or proposing to refuse) to work on Sundays, or on a particular Sunday, his dismissal will be held to have been unfair (*ibid.* section 101). If he is victimised or subjected to any detriment, he may complain to an employment tribunal and may be awarded compensation if his complaint is upheld (*ibid.* section 45).

Opted-out shop workers can opt back in to Sunday work if they wish. To do so they must follow the procedure described in the next paragraph.

'Opted-in' shop workers

- *Protected* shop workers can renounce their protected status if they are happy to work on Sundays (or if they are anxious to encourage an otherwise reluctant employer to continue to provide them with Sunday work). *Opted-out* shop workers who change their minds about working on Sundays may do the same.

- To forego his (or her) right to refuse to work on Sundays, a *protected or opted-out* shop worker must first:

   (a) give his employer an *opting-in notice* – that is to say, a notice in writing (signed and dated) in which he informs his employer that he wishes to work on Sundays or that he has no objection to doing so.

   Having done so, he must then:

   (b) enter into an agreement with his employer to do shop work on Sundays or on a particular Sunday. Once concluded, the agreement will be 'read into' his contract of employment and will be enforceable as such.

   An *opted-in* shop worker runs the risk of being dismissed (and fairly dismissed) if he (or she) breaks that agreement.

- An *opted-in* shop worker dismissed for refusing Sunday work will not normally qualify to present a complaint of unfair dismissal unless employed for a continuous period of two or more years and under normal retiring age at the effective date of termination of his (or her) contract of employment. But see **Dismissal for asserting a statutory right** elsewhere in this handbook.

   Note: A complaint by an *opted-in* shop worker that he (or she) has been unfairly dismissed for refusing to work on a particular Sunday might well be upheld by tribunal if, for example, there were circumstances beyond the worker's control (such as an urgent domestic crisis) which prevented him working on that Sunday. In other words, the employer would have to satisfy the tribunal that he had acted reasonably and fairly in treating the worker's non-attendance on that occasion as a sufficient reason for dismissing him.

   An *opted-in* shop worker, who no longer wishes to work on Sundays, may opt-out of Sunday work so long as he follows the correct procedure for doing so (explained earlier in this section).

'Sundays only' shop workers

- Shop workers, who have been recruited specifically to work on Sundays only, clearly do not enjoy the protection extended to their *protected* or *opted-out* colleagues. A 'Sundays only' shop worker cannot be unfairly dismissed for refusing to work on a Sunday (for that is what he or she has been employed to do); nor (short of resigning) can he or she opt-out of Sunday work.

Dismissal for refusing Sunday work

- As we have seen, every *protected* or *opted-out* shop worker has the right not to be dismissed or selected for redundancy for refusing (or proposing to refuse) to work on Sundays or on a particular Sunday. Any such worker who is dismissed or selected for redundancy for that reason may present a complaint to an employment tribunal, regardless of his or her age or length of service at the material time (*ibid.* sections 101, 108(3)(d) and 109(2)(d)). A worker who is dismissed, selected for redundancy, or subjected to any other detriment for asserting his or her statutory right not to work on Sundays is likewise entitled to complain to an employment tribunal and will be awarded a substantial amount of compensation (payable by the employer) if such a complaint is upheld. For further details, please turn to the sections titled **Dismissal for asserting a statutory right, Dismissal for refusing Sunday work**, and **Victimisation** elsewhere in this handbook.

- An *opted-in* shop worker, dismissed or selected for redundancy for refusing to work on a particular Sunday, may challenge the fairness of his (or her) dismissal before an employment tribunal. But, unlike his (or her) *protected* or *opted-out* colleagues, he will not qualify to do so unless continuously employed for a period of one year or more at the *effective date of termination* of his contract of employment. Furthermore, he must have been under *normal retiring* age at that time.

  Note: For the meaning of the expressions *effective date of termination* and *normal retiring age*, please turn to the section titled **Dismissal,** elsewhere in this handbook

Complaint to an employment tribunal

- A complaint of unfair dismissal (for whatever reason) must be presented to an employment tribunal within three months of the effective date of termination of the worker's contract of employment. A tribunal will not normally hear a complaint presented 'out of time' unless satisfied that it was not reasonably practicable for the complainant to have presented his complaint within the prescribed three-month period.

- If a tribunal finds that a shop worker has been unlawfully dismissed or selected for redundancy, it will order his (or her) employer either to pay compensation or to reinstate (or re-engage) the worker in his former job or in a job rated as equivalent. An employer who refuses to comply with a tribunal order to reinstate or re-engage a dismissed shop worker is liable to be ordered to pay that worker an increased amount of compensation. See **Dismissal** elsewhere in this handbook.

Victimisation for refusing Sunday work

- Apart from their right not to be dismissed for refusing Sunday work, *protected* and *opted-out* shop workers also have the right not to be victimised by their employer (or 'subjected to any detriment') for refusing (or proposing to refuse) to work on Sundays, or on a particular Sunday (*ibid.* section 45).

- A detriment might consist of a refusal to allow the worker to continue to work overtime on weekdays, or the withholding of an expected pay rise, or denying opportunities for promotion, transfer or training. However, there is nothing to prevent an employer adjusting a worker's pay to take account of the fact that he (or she) no longer works on a Sunday – so long as that adjustment does not amount to a cut in the worker's basic hourly rate of pay.

- A *protected* or *opted-out* shop worker, who believes that he (or she) has been unfairly disadvantaged or victimised in the circumstances described above, may complain to an employment tribunal. Unless the employer can justify his treatment of the complainant, the tribunal will not only caution him to 'set matters to rights' but may also order him to pay compensation in respect of any loss (including any loss of benefit) sustained by the worker as a result of his employer's actions. It is as well to point out that a shop worker has no need to resign in order to pursue a complaint in these circumstances. Indeed, as was indicated earlier, if he is dismissed for challenging his employer's actions, or for having referred the matter to an employment tribunal, his dismissal will be held to have been automatically unfair; as to which, see **Dismissal for asserting a statutory right** elsewhere in this handbook.

Employee's right to an explanatory statement

- When an employee is first recruited or employed as a shop worker, his (or her) employer must give him a written statement explaining his statutory rights in relation to Sunday work. This rule applies only to shop workers recruited *on or after* 26 August 1994, whose contracts of employment require them (or could require them) to work on Sundays. The requirement does *not* apply to shop workers who are employed to work only on Sundays (*ibid.* section 42).

- The written statement (in the form illustrated below) must be given to every relevant shop worker within two months of the date on which his (or her) employment began. An employer need not give the statement to a shop worker who has already exercised his right to opt-out of Sunday work. But if he otherwise fails to give the statement within the prescribed two-month period, the shop worker in question need only give one month's notice in writing of his intention to opt-out of Sunday working. In other words, an opting-out notice given in those circumstances will come into effect after one month instead of the usual three.

Employment Rights Act 1996 (Section 42(4))

STATUTORY RIGHTS IN RELATION TO SUNDAY SHOPWORK

(Form of statement to be issued to shop workers)

You have become employed as a shop worker and are or can be required under your contract of employment to do the Sunday work your contract provides for.

However, if you wish, you can give a notice, as described in the next paragraph, to your employer and you will then have the right not to work in or about a shop on any Sunday on which the shop is open once three months have passed from the date on which you gave the notice.

Your notice must:

be in writing;

be signed and dated by you;

say that you object to Sunday working.

For three months after you give the notice, your employer can still require you to do all the Sunday work your contract provides for. After the three-month period has ended, you have the right to complain to an employment tribunal if, because of your refusal to work on Sundays on which the shop is open, your employer:

dismisses you, or

does something else detrimental to you, for example,

failing to promote you.

Once you have the rights described, you can surrender them only by giving your employer a further notice, signed and dated by you, saying that you wish to work on Sunday or that you do not object to Sunday working and then agreeing with your employer to work on Sundays or on a particular Sunday.

Betting workers

- Schedule 5A to the Betting, Gaming & Lotteries Act 1963 (inserted by the Deregulation & Contracting Out Act 1994) came into force on 3 January 1995. As was indicated in the preamble to this section, Schedule 5A of the 1963 Act has since been repealed and reinstated in Part IV of the Employment Rights Act 1996.

- Betting workers (see *Definitions* below) enjoy the same statutory rights as shop workers. A betting worker employed *before* 3 January 1995 (other than as a *'Sundays only'* worker) has the right to refuse to work on Sundays or to 'opt-out' of Sunday work. He (or she) has the right also, as a *protected* or *opted-out* worker, not to be unfairly dismissed or victimised for refusing to work on a Sunday. If he is dismissed or victimised (ie, subjected to a detriment) for exercising his statutory rights under the 1996 Act, he may present a complaint to an employment tribunal regardless of his age or length of service at the material time. As the rights of betting workers *vis-à-vis* shop workers are essentially the same, interested employers should simply read the preceding pages – substituting 'betting worker' for 'shop worker' wherever the latter expression appears. There is, however, one minor difference. Betting workers have the right under the 1996 Act (as have shop workers) to be given an explanatory statement by their employers *within two months of the date on which their employment began.* As the wording differs slightly from that prescribed for the statement issued to shop workers, the full text of the 'betting worker' statement is reproduced below.

Definitions

- The term *betting worker* means an employee who, under his contract of employment, is either required to do betting work or may be required to do so. *Betting work* means work at a track in England or Wales for a bookmaker on a day on which the bookmaker acts as such at the track, being work which consists of or includes dealing with betting transactions, and work in a licensed betting office in England or Wales on a day on which the office is open for use for the effecting of betting transactions. Finally, the expression *betting transaction* includes the collection or payment of winnings on a bet and any transaction in which one or more of the parties is acting as a bookmaker (*ibid.* section 233).

Employment Rights Act 1996 (Section 42(5))

STATUTORY RIGHTS IN RELATION TO SUNDAY BETTING WORK

(Form of statement to be issued to betting workers)

You have become employed under a contract of employment under which you are or can be required to do Sunday betting work, that is to say, work –

at a track on a Sunday on which your employer is taking bets at the track, or

in a licensed betting office on a Sunday on which it is open for business.

However, if you wish, you can give a notice, as described in the next paragraph, to your employer and you will then have the right not to do Sunday betting once three months have passed from the date on which you gave the notice.

Your notice must –

be in writing;

be signed and dated by you;

say that you object to Sunday betting work.

For three months after you give the notice, your employer can still require you to do all the Sunday betting work your contract provides for. After the three-month period has ended, you have the right to complain to an employment tribunal if, because of your refusal to do Sunday betting work, your employer –

dismisses you, or

does something else detrimental to you, for example, failing to promote you.

Once you have the rights described, you can surrender them only by giving your employer a further notice, signed and dated by you, saying that you wish to do Sunday betting work or that you object to Sunday betting work and then agreeing with your employer to work on Sundays or on a particular Sunday.

SUSPENSION FROM WORK ON MATERNITY GROUNDS

Key points

- An employee who is suspended from work on maternity grounds is entitled to be paid her normal wages or salary during her enforced leave of absence – so long as she has not unreasonably refused an offer of suitable alternative work made to her by her employer before the suspension period began (per sections 66 to 68 of the Employment Rights Act 1996).

- Section 66 of the 1996 Act explains that an employee is to be treated as suspended from work on maternity grounds if, in consequence of any requirement imposed by health and safety legislation (or of any recommendation in a code of practice issued or approved under section 16 of the Health & Safety at Work etc Act 1974), she is suspended from work by her employer on the ground that she is pregnant or breastfeeding, or has given birth to a child within the previous six months.

Health and safety legislation

- Health and safety legislation in the UK has long restricted the employment (or continued employment) of pregnant women and women of 'reproductive capacity' in occupations that could expose them or their unborn children to risk. For example: the code of practice accompanying the Control of Lead at Work Regulations 2002 states that any woman of reproductive capacity, who is employed in work that exposes her to lead, must notify her employer if she becomes pregnant and must be suspended from such work if an employment medical adviser or appointed doctor certifies that it would be unsafe for her to continue doing that work – at least for the time being. There are similar provisions in the Ionising Radiations Regulations 1999 and in the all-embracing Management of Health & Safety at Work Regulations 1999. For further details, please turn to **Table 1** on pages 567 and 568 below.

- Any *new or expectant mother* doing a job that could expose her (or her baby) to risk – because of her condition – must either be transferred to more suitable work or be offered different working conditions and hours, or (if such measures are impracticable or unlikely to be effective) be suspended from work for so long as is necessary to avoid that risk. The risk may be related to her working conditions (eg, a hot or humid atmosphere), or to the type of work in which she is engaged (eg, lifting and carrying), or to the physical, biological or chemical agents (including those specified in Annexes I and II to Council Directive 92/85/EEC (the so-called 'pregnancy directive') 'on the introduction of measures to encourage improvements in the safety and health of pregnant workers and workers who have recently given birth or are breastfeeding' (as to which, see **Tables 2, 3 & 4** on pages 569 to 572 below).

Note: The term 'new or expectant mother' means an employee who is pregnant, or who has given birth within the previous six months, or who is breastfeeding. 'Given birth' means delivered of a living child or, after 24 weeks of pregnancy, a stillborn child. Regulation 3 of the Management of Health & Safety at Work Regulations 1999 (*qv*) imposes a duty on every employer to make a suitable and sufficient assessment of the risks to which his (or her) employees are (or may be) exposed while they are at work. Furthermore, if an employer's workforce includes women of child-bearing age, the assessment must include an assessment of the risks to the health and safety of a new or expectant mother (or to that of her baby) (*ibid*. regulation 16).

Prohibition on night work

- If a new or expectant mother works at night and produces a certificate signed by a doctor (or by a registered midwife) stating that night work could be detrimental to her health or safety, her employer must either transfer her to daytime work or, if this is impracticable, suspend her from work on full pay for the period specified in the certificate – unless she has unreasonably refused an offer of suitable alternative work. As is explained below, any dispute about an employee's right or otherwise to be paid during a period of maternity suspension may have to be resolved by an employment tribunal (*ibid*. regulation 17).

Employer's duty to offer suitable alternative work

- As was indicated earlier, an employee who would otherwise be suspended from work on maternity grounds has the right to be offered suitable alternative work by her employer if such work is available. Furthermore, the offer must be made *before* the suspension period is due to begin. If the employer fails to do so, or makes an offer of work that the employee considers unsuitable, she may complain to an employment tribunal. Her complaint must be presented within three months of the first day of the suspension period or within such further period as the tribunal considers reasonable in the circumstances. Unless satisfied that the employer had no suitable alternative work for the employee to do (or that the work that was offered *was* suitable), the tribunal will order him (or her) to pay the employee a 'just and equitable' amount of compensation – having regard to the infringement of the employee's right to be offered suitable alternative work and to any loss attributable to that infringement (section 67(1), Employment Rights Act 1996).

Meaning of 'suitable alternative work'

- 'Suitable alternative work' means work of a kind that is both suitable in relation to the employee and appropriate for her to do in the circumstances – bearing in mind the type of work she normally does and her status, qualifications, skills and experience. Furthermore, the terms and conditions applicable to that alternative work must not be substantially less favourable to her than the corresponding terms and conditions applicable to the work she normally performs under her contract of employment (*ibid.* section 67(2)).

Right to remuneration on suspension

- Section 68 of the 1996 Act states that an employee suspended from work on maternity grounds must be paid her normal wages or salary during the period of her suspension, unless (as was indicated earlier) she has unreasonably refused an offer of suitable alternative work. However, any payment made to her under her contract of employment in respect of that same period can be offset against that statutory entitlement, and *vice versa*.

- An employee can complain to an employment tribunal that her employer has failed to pay her her normal wages or salary while suspended on maternity grounds. She must do so within three months of the day on which payment was withheld, although a tribunal may consider a complaint presented 'out of time' if satisfied that it was not reasonably practicable for her to have acted sooner. If such a complaint is upheld, the tribunal will order the employer to pay the employee the amount of remuneration that it finds is due to her (*ibid.* section 70).

Dismissal for asserting a statutory right

- An employee who is dismissed (or selected for redundancy) for having been suspended on maternity grounds, or for asserting her statutory rights in relation to the suspension period, or for challenging her employer's refusal to acknowledge those rights (whether before an employment tribunal or otherwise), will be treated in law as having been unfairly dismissed (regardless of her length of service or working hours at the material time) and will be compensated accordingly (*ibid.* sections 104 and 105(7)).

  See also **Dismissal on grounds of pregnancy or childbirth** elsewhere in this handbook.

Table 1

UK health and safety provisions concerned with the protection of women who are pregnant or of 'reproductive capacity'

Regulations and Orders	Provision
Control of Lead at Work Regulations 2002 (regulation 10(8) and Schedule 1)	'Where the blood-level concentration or urinary lead concentration of an employee reaches the appropriate suspension level, the employer shall ensure that an entry is made in the health record of the employee by a relevant doctor certifying whether in the professional opinion of the doctor, the employee should be suspended from any work which is liable to expose that employee to lead…'
	The term 'suspension level' for a woman of reproductive capacity is a blood-level concentration of 20 µg/dl or a urinary lead concentration of 20 µg Pb/g creatinine.
Ionising Radiations Regulations 1999 (regulation 16(6) and Schedule 1, Parts IV and V)	'Where the employment medical adviser or appointed doctor has certified in the health record of an employee… that in his professional opinion that employee should not be engaged in work with ionising radiation or that he (or she) should only be so engaged under conditions he has specified in the health record, the employer shall not permit that employee to be engaged in work with ionising radiation except in accordance with the conditions, if any so specified.'
	The dose limit for the abdomen of a female employee of reproductive capacity, who is exposed to ionising radiation, is 13mSv in any consecutive three month interval. In the case of a pregnant employee, the dose limit averaged throughout the abdomen is 10mSv during the declared term of pregnancy.
Management of Health & Safety at Work Regulations 1999 (regulations 16 and 17)	'(1)(a) Where the persons working in an undertaking include women of child-bearing age; and (b) the work is of a kind which could involve risk, by reason of her condition, to the

health and safety of a new or expectant mother, or to that of her baby, from any processes or working conditions, or physical, biological or chemical agents, including those specified in Annexes I and II of Council Directive 92/85/EEC [*see Tables 2, 3 & 4 opposite and overleaf*] ... the assessment required by regulation 3(1) shall also include an assessment of such risk.

(2) Where, in the case of an individual employee, the taking of any other action the employer is required to take under the relevant statutory provisions would not avoid the risk referred to in paragraph (1)(a), the employer shall, if it is reasonable to do so, and would avoid such risks, alter her working conditions or hours of work.

(3) If it is not reasonable to alter the working conditions or hours of work or if it would not avoid such risk, the employer shall... suspend the employee from work for so long as is necessary to avoid such risk.'

Air Navigation Order 1985
(Article 20(8))

'A member of a flight crew who has reason to believe she is pregnant must notify her employers in writing without delay. Once her pregnancy is confirmed, she is deemed to be suspended from work and may only resume her duties during the initial stages of her pregnancy if it is considered safe for her to do so. But she will not be permitted to return to work as a member of a flight crew after her pregnancy has ended until she has been medically examined and pronounced fit to do so.'

Merchant Shipping Note M1331 (issued for the purposes of regulation 7 of the Merchant Shipping (Medical Examination) Regulations 1983

(a) Part X so far as relating to gynaecological conditions, and
(b) Part XI.

Table 2

Annex I (EC Directive 92/85/EEC)

Measures to encourage improvements in the safety and health at work of pregnant workers and workers who have recently given birth or are breastfeeding

NON-EXHAUSTIVE LIST OF AGENTS, PROCESSES AND WORKING CONDITIONS

A1. *Physical agents*

Where these are regarded as agents causing foetal lesions and/or likely to disrupt placental attachment, and in particular:

(a) shocks, vibration or movement;

(b) handling of loads entailing risks, particularly of a dorsolumbar nature;

(c) noise;

(d) ionising radiation;

(e) non-ionising radiation;

(f) extremes of cold or heat;

(g) movements and posture, travelling – either inside or outside the establishment – mental and physical fatigue and other physical burdens concerned with the activity of the worker within the meaning of Article 2 of the Directive.

A2. *Biological agents*

Biological agents of risk groups 2, 3 and 3* within the meaning of Article 2(d) numbers 2, 3 and 4 of Directive 90/679/EEC, in so far as it is known that these agents or the therapeutic measures necessitated by such agents endanger the health of pregnant women and the unborn child and in so far as they do not yet appear in Annex II. [* as per OJ text]

A3. *Chemical agents*

The following chemical agents in so far as it is known that they endanger the health of pregnant women and the unborn child and in so far as they do not yet appear in Annex II:

(f) substances labelled R40, R45, R46, and R47 under Directive 67/548/EEC in so far as they do not yet appear in Annex II;

(g) chemical agents in Annex I to Directive 90/394/EEC;

(h)   mercury and mercury derivatives;

(i)   antimitotic drugs;

(j)   carbon monoxide;

(k)   chemical agents of known and dangerous percutaneous absorption.

B. *Processes*

Industrial processes listed in Annex I to Directive 90/394/EEC (See Table 4 below).

C. *Working conditions*:

Underground mining work.

Table 3

Annex II (EC Directive 92/85/EEC)

Measures to encourage improvements in the safety and health at work of pregnant workers and workers who have recently given birth or are breast-feeding.

NON-EXHAUSTIVE LIST OF AGENTS, PROCESSES AND WORKING CONDITIONS

A. Pregnant workers within the meaning of Article 2(a)

1(a) Physical agents

Work in hyperbaric atmosphere, eg, pressurised enclosures and underwater diving.

1(b) Biological agents

The following biological agents

(a) toxiplasma,

(b) rubella virus,

unless the pregnant workers are proved to be adequately protected against such agents by immunisation.

1(c) Chemical agents

Lead and lead derivatives in so far as these agents are capable of being absorbed by the human organism.

2 Working conditions
Underground mining work.

B. Workers who are breastfeeding within the meaning of Article 2(c)

1(a) Chemical agents

Lead and lead derivatives in so far as these agents are capable of being absorbed by the human organism.

2 Working conditions

Underground mining work.

Table 4

**Annex I to Directive 90/394/EEC
on the protection of workers from the risks relating to
exposure to carcinogens at work**

**PROCESSES LIKELY TO POSE A RISK TO THE HEALTH
AND SAFETY OF NEW AND EXPECTANT MOTHERS**

1. Manufacture of auramine.

2. Work involving exposure to aromatic polycyclic hydrocarbons present in coal soots, tar, pitch, fumes or dust.

3. Work involving exposure to dusts, fumes and sprays produced during the roasting and electro-refining of cupro-nickel mattes.

4. Strong acid process in the manufacture of isopropyl alcohol.

| SUSPENSION FROM WORK ON MEDICAL GROUNDS |

Key points

- An employee suspended from work on medical grounds must be paid his (or her) normal wages or salary while he is so suspended for a period not exceeding 26 weeks (section 64, Employment Rights Act 1996) (but see *Qualifying conditions* below).

- There are currently three sets of health and safety regulations which provide for suspension from work on medical grounds (*ibid.* Schedule 1). Other regulations (and codes of practice) may follow. Under those regulations, an 'appointed' doctor or Employment Medical Adviser has the right to suspend an employee on medical grounds if there is evidence that the employee's continued exposure to certain hazardous substances or processes is likely to be detrimental to his (or her) health. The regulations in question are:

  (a) the **Control of Lead at Work Regulations 2002**, which contain provisions relating to exposure to lead (including lead alloys, any compounds of lead, and lead as a constituent of any substance or material) which is liable to be inhaled, ingested or otherwise absorbed by Persons, except where it is given off from the exhaust system of a vehicle on the road within the meaning of section 196(1) of the Road Traffic Act 1972;

  (b) the **Control of Substances Hazardous to Health Regulations 2002**, which deal (inter alia) with the health surveillance of employees engaged in specified processes which could give rise to exposure to one or other of the following substances listed in Schedule 6:

  vinyl chloride monomer (VCM);
  nitro or amino derivatives of phenol and of benzene or its
     homologues;
  potassium or sodium chlorate or dichromate;
  orthotolidine and its salts;
  dianasidine and its salts;
  dichlorobenzidine and its salts;
  auramine;
  magenta;
  carbon disulphide;
  disulphur dichloride;
  benzene, including benzol;
  carbon tetrachloride;
  trichloroethylene;
  pitch; and

(c) the **Ionising Radiations Regulations 1999**, which apply to exposure to electromagnetic or corpuscular radiation capable of producing ions and emitted from a radioactive substance or from a machine or apparatus that is intended to produce ionising radiation or in which charged particles are accelerated by a voltage of not less than five kilovolts.

Employers to whom the above regulations apply must develop and maintain suitable arrangements for the routine health surveillance of their employees and must keep comprehensive health records.

Note: Regulation 3 of the Management of Health & Safety at Work Regulations 1999 (*qv*) which apply to all employment situations (other than the ship-board activities of a ship's crew under the direction of the master) require every employer to assess the risks to which his employees are exposed while at work and to introduce health surveillance if that assessment shows that there is an identifiable disease or adverse health condition related to the work they do.

- An employee will usually be suspended from work because of the risks associated with his (or her) exposure to one or other of the hazardous substances listed above. He will not be ill or incapacitated for work in the accepted sense, but may well be showing signs of fatigue (headaches, etc) or have other potentially disabling symptoms. Indeed, a factory doctor or Employment Medical Advisor may decide to suspend an employee for a short or 'longish' period simply to enable further tests to be carried out. Until the employee receives the 'all clear', there can be no good reason why he should not be transferred to less hazardous work elsewhere in the same factory or workshop (discussed in the next paragraph).

Qualifying conditions

- To qualify to be paid his (or her) normal wages or salary during a period of suspension on medical grounds, the employee:

  (a) must have been continuously employed for a period of one month or more ending with the day before that on which the suspension begins;

  (b) must not otherwise be incapable of work by reason of disease or bodily or mental disablement (*ibid.* section 65(3)); and

  (c) must not have unreasonably refused an offer of suitable alternative work – whether or not work of a kind which he is employed under his contract to do; *or*, if his employer has nothing to offer immediately, must remain on standby (eg, at home or by a telephone) in case his employer *does* find something else for him to do (*ibid.* section 65(4)).

Medical suspension will not be appropriate if an employee is already incapacitated for work because of illness or injury (whether or not related to the hazardous nature of his or her work). Such an employee would either qualify for statutory sick pay (SSP) or be entitled to social security incapacity benefit. See **Sickness and statutory sick pay** elsewhere in this handbook.

Complaint to an employment tribunal

- An employee suspended from work on medical grounds (who satisfies the conditions explained earlier) may present a complaint to an employment tribunal that his (or her) employer has not paid him the whole or part of the wages or salary due to him during the suspension period. An employee need not resign in order to pursue his statutory rights, but must present his complaint (using Form ET1, available from local offices of the Employment Service) within three months of the day on which the expected payment was withheld. If the employee's complaint is upheld, the employment tribunal will order the employer to pay the disputed amount (*ibid.* section 70).

- An employee dismissed (or selected for redundancy) for having been suspended on medical grounds can present a complaint of unfair dismissal to an employment tribunal if he (or she) was under normal retiring age and had been continuously employed for a month or more ending with the effective date of termination of his contract of employment (*ibid.* section 108(2)).

- An employee who is dismissed (or selected for redundancy) for asserting his (or her) right to be paid his normal wages or salary during a period of suspension on medical grounds (or for questioning his employer's refusal to pay him) may complain to an employment tribunal regardless of his (or her) age or length of service at the material time (*ibid.* sections 104, 108(3)(g) and 109(2)(g)). If a complaint of unfair dismissal is upheld, the employer will be ordered either to reinstate or re-engage the complainant or pay compensation. For the meanings of the expressions *effective date of termination and normal retiring age* (and other details), please turn to the section titled **Dismissal** elsewhere in this handbook. See also **Dismissal for asserting a statutory right**.

SUSPENSION WITH/WITHOUT PAY

Key points

- An employer may not presume to suspend an employee *without* pay, whether as the more desirable alternative to dismissal or for some other reason, unless there is an express term in the employee's contract of employment which purportedly gives him the right to do so. The suspension of an employee without pay (in the absence of any such right) is technically a breach of contract which may lead to an action for damages before an employment tribunal or civil court (see below). Alternatively, the employee may choose to resign and pursue a complaint of unfair constructive dismissal; as to which, see **Constructive dismissal** elsewhere in this handbook.

- The written statement required to be given to an employee when he (or she) first starts work with an employer must include a note which either spells out any disciplinary rules applicable to the employee or refers him to a document which is reasonably accessible to the employee and contains the same information (section 3, Employment Rights Act 1996).

- ACAS Code of Practice 1 (*Disciplinary & Grievance Procedures*) adds that employees must be made aware of the likely consequences of breaking disciplinary rules. It is not open to the employer to impose whatever penalty he believes to be appropriate at the time. If the sanctions to be applied include suspension without pay, as well as dismissal, the employee must be made aware of the existence of such a penalty, the likely length of the suspension period and the circumstances in which it is to be applied. Notes to paragraph 15 of the Code caution that 'where a disciplinary suspension without pay is imposed, it should not exceed any period allowed by the contract of employment'.

Complaint to an employment tribunal

- The employment tribunals now have the jurisdiction to hear all breach of employment contract cases which arise or are outstanding on the termination of an employee's contract of employment. Any employee who has been suspended from work without pay (in breach of his contract of employment) may seek redress from an employment tribunal (or, if he chooses, from a civil court), but must present his claim to the Secretary of the Tribunals within three months of the effective date of termination of his contract of employment. See **Employment tribunals and procedure** elsewhere in this handbook.

Note: The relevant legislation is to be found in the Employment Tribunals Extension of Jurisdiction (England & Wales) Order 1994 and the Employment Tribunals Extension of Jurisdiction (Scotland) Order 1994.

Suspension with pay

- If an employee is guilty (or appears to be guilty) of gross misconduct sufficient to justify summary dismissal, his (or her) employer must nonetheless investigate the relevant circumstances and provide the employee with an opportunity to state his case before a final decision is made.

- If the employer's investigations are likely to take a little time, the employee may be suspended for a brief period on full pay. As was indicated earlier, suspension without pay on such occasions is generally unacceptable (see paragraph 15 of Code of Practice 1 (*qv*)). See also the sections in this handbook titled **Deductions from pay, Disciplinary rules and procedure, Dismissal, Lay-offs and short-time working, Suspension from work on maternity grounds, Suspension on medical grounds,** and **Written statement of employment particulars.**

T

TIME OFF FOR DEPENDANTS

Key points

- Every employee (regardless of his or her age, length of service or working hours) has the right to be permitted a reasonable amount of *unpaid* time off work to care for dependants (section 57A, Employment Rights Act 1996, as inserted by section 8, Schedule 4, Part 11, Employment Relations Act 1999).

- This statutory right, which came into effect on 15 December 1999, applies to a situation in which an employee needs time off work to take action which is necessary:

  (a) to provide assistance on an occasion when a dependant falls ill, gives birth, or is injured or assaulted;

  (b) to make arrangements for the provision of care for a dependant who is ill or injured;

  (c) in consequence of the death of a dependant;

  (d) because of the unexpected disruption (or termination) of existing arrangements for the care of a dependant; or

  (e) to deal with an incident at school involving one of the employee's children.

  For obvious reasons, an employee cannot be expected to give his (or her) employer advance warning of his need to take time off work in the circumstances described above. However, he must inform his employer of the situation as soon as is reasonably practicable (either by telephoning from home as soon as possible or, if suddenly called away from work, by notifying his supervisor or immediate manager of the situation before leaving the premises).

- It should be pointed out that, in the absence of any contractual arrangement to the contrary, an employee's right to take time off for dependants does not extend to dealing with other types of domestic emergency, such as a boiler explosion or gas leak, although employers should undoubtedly be prepared to be reasonable in such cases.

Meaning of 'dependant'

- For these purposes, a 'dependant' is an employee's wife, husband, partner, child, parent, or some other person living in the same household as the employee (other than as a tenant, lodger or boarder) who reasonably relies on the employee for assistance if he or she falls ill or is injured or assaulted, or to make arrangements for the provision of care in the event of illness or injury. The definition would also include a parent, grandparent, aged aunt or other close relative (whether or not living in the same household as the employee, but nearby) who is dependent on the employee for routine care and assistance.

- A live-in nanny or 'au pair' would also qualify (especially if living at a considerable distance from home), as would an elderly neighbour living alone who has no immediate family to call upon in an emergency. It is not yet clear whether a person sharing accommodation with an employee and one or two others (either as a live-in partner or friend) would fall within this category. In such circumstances, it is up to the employer to exercise a degree of judgement when asked to make a decision in the matter.

- It would be open to an employer to take disciplinary action against any employee who breaches his (or her) implied contractual duty of trust and confidence by abusing the right to time off in circumstances which do not warrant such time off.

How much time off is reasonable?

- Section 57A of the 1996 Act makes the point that an employee has the right to take a reasonable amount of unpaid time off work to *provide assistance* in a genuine emergency, *to make arrangements for* the care of a dependant, or *to collect a child from school* if he (or she) has had an accident or has been involved in some other incident. That right does not include taking extended leave of absence to care for an injured dependant or sick child or to wind-up a deceased relative's affairs. Should there be any dispute as to what and what does not constitute a reasonable amount of time off (given the circumstances), the matter should be dealt with through the usual 'grievance' channels (or, if need be, will be resolved by an employment tribunal). In some circumstances, it would not be unreasonable to require an employee to 'dip into' his or her annual holiday entitlement.

Complaint to an employment tribunal

- A complaint of an employer's refusal or failure to permit an employee to take time off for dependants must be lodged with an employment tribunal within three months of the date on which that refusal or failure occurred. Should the employee's complaint be upheld, the tribunal will make a declaration to that effect and will order the employer to pay the employee such compensation as it considers to be 'just and equitable' in the circumstances.

Protection from detriment

- Section 47C of the 1996 Act (supplemented by regulation 19 of the Maternity & Parental Leave etc Regulations 1999) cautions that an employee has the right not to be subjected to any detriment by any act, or by any deliberate failure to act, by his (or her) employer, done because the employee took or sought to take time off for dependants under section 57A of that Act. On a successful complaint to an employment tribunal, the employer would be ordered to pay the disadvantaged employee an appropriate amount of compensation, including compensation for the loss of any benefit which would otherwise have been available to the employee but for the employer's actions (or failure to act). See also **Victimisation** elsewhere in this handbook.

Unfair dismissal

- An employee who is dismissed or selected for redundancy will be held to have been unfairly dismissed if the reason (or, if more than one, the principal reason) for his (or her) dismissal or selection was that he had taken or sought to take time off for dependants under section 57A of the 1996 Act. A complaint of unfair dismissal in such circumstances (if upheld) would result in the employer being ordered to pay the employee a substantial amount of compensation (comprising a basic award of a maximum £7,800, a compensatory award of up to £53,500 and, where applicable, an additional award of between 26 and 52 weeks' pay). A complaint of unfair dismissal in such circumstances may be presented regardless of the employee's age or length of service at the material time. For further particulars, please turn to the sections titled **Dismissal** and **Dismissal for asserting a statutory right** elsewhere in this handbook.

Further information

- For further information, the reader is referred to DTI publication: *Time off for Dependants: A Guide for Employers and Employees* (Ref URN 99/1186), copies of which are available, free of charge, from:

  DTI Publications Orderline
  ADMAIL 528
  London
  SW1W 8YT
  Telephone: 0870 1502 600
  Fax: 0870 1502 333
  email: publications@dti.gsi.gov.uk

TIME OFF FOR STUDY OR TRAINING
(*Young persons*)

Key points

- Young employees aged 16 or 17, who have left full-time secondary or further education without having attained a prescribed 'standard of achievement', have the legal right to be permitted a reasonable amount of time off work, on full pay, to enable them to pursue studies or training leading to a 'relevant academic or vocational qualification', the attainment of which would be likely to enhance their employment prospects, either with their present employers or with any future employers. That same right extends to 18-year-old employees, who began their studies or training before their 18th birthday. Young persons employed by employment businesses (or 'employment agencies', as they are often referred to), who are hired out as 'temps' to client employers, also have the right to be permitted a reasonable amount of paid time off work for study or training. In the latter situation, the responsibility for providing a reasonable amount of paid time off work rests with the client employer.

- During a period of time off work for study or training, an employee must be paid his (or her) normal hourly rate of pay; or, if his working hours differ from week to week, his average hourly rate of pay calculated over a reference period of 12 weeks ending with the last complete week before the day on which the time off is taken. The hourly rate of pay for an employee who has worked for his employer for just a few weeks (or who has just started work) will be the rate which fairly represents his normal hourly rate of pay over a normal working week (*ibid.* section 63B).

- The time off may be taken either on the employer's (or client employer's) premises (eg, in facilities made available by the employer), or elsewhere (*ibid.* section 63A(7)). The word 'elsewhere' suggests occasional attendance at a college within easy distance of the employer's premises. When dealing with a request for time off for study or training, the sensible employer would ask for written confirmation that the employee in question is indeed pursuing a course of study or training leading to a relevant academic or vocational qualification (see below) and should take the opportunity to talk to the employee's tutors about the amount of time off work that the employee would sensibly need to enable him (or her) to 'keep up' with his studies or training.

- These provisions are to be found in section 63A of the Employment Rights Act 1996 (inserted by section 32 of the Teaching & Higher Education Act 1998, and supplemented by the Right to Time Off for Study or Training Regulations 1999), which came into force on 1 September 1999.

Standard of achievement

- The right to be permitted a reasonable amount of paid time off work for study or training extends only to those young employees who left school without achieving:

    (a) grades A* to C in five subjects in GCSE examinations; or

    (b) SQA Standard Grades at grades 1 to 3 in three subjects; or

    (c) one Intermediate level GNVQ or one GSVQ at level 2; or

    (d) one NVQ or SVQ at level 2; or

    (e) one BTEC First Certificate awarded by the Edexcel Foundation; or

    (f) one BTEC First Diploma awarded by the Edexcel Foundation; or

    (g) the City & Guilds of London Institute Diploma of Vocational Education at Intermediate level; or

    (h) 16 SQA unit assessment credits at least eight of which are at Intermediate 2 or above and the remainder at Intermediate 1, where unit credits are awarded on the basis of one per 40-hour SQA National Unit or National Certificate module or SQA Short

Course and *pro rata* for SQA National Units or National Certificate module of different duration,

and who are currently undertaking studies or training leading to:

grades A to E in one GCE 'A' level examination;

grades A to E in one GCE 'AS' level examination;

one Advanced Level GNVQ or one GSVQ at level 3;

one SQA Higher Grade at grades A to C;

one CSYS at grades A to C; or

one NVQ or SVQ at level 3,

awarded or authenticated by one or other of the 'awarding bodies' listed at the end of this section.

Note: 'BTEC' means Business & Technology Education Council; 'CSYS' means Certificate of Sixth Year Studies; 'GCE A level examination' and 'GCE AS examination' mean General Certificate of Education advanced level and advanced supplementary examinations, respectively; 'GCSE' means General Certificate of Secondary Examination; 'GNVQ' means a General National Vocational Qualification; 'GSVQ' means a General Scottish Vocational Qualification; 'NVQ' means a National Vocational Qualification; 'SQA' means the Scottish Qualifications Authority'; and SVQ, means a Scottish Vocational Qualification.

How much time off is reasonable?

- An employer who receives a request from a young employee for a period of paid time off work for study or training must respond reasonably to any such request. The amount of time off, and the number of occasions on which time off is to be permitted, will depend in large part on the demands placed on the employee by the course of study or training he (or she) is pursuing, the size of the employer's business and the effect of the employee's time off on the running of that business (ibid. section 63A(5)). These are the factors likely to be taken into account by an employment tribunal when dealing with a complaint of an employer's refusal or failure to accommodate an employee's legitimate request for paid time off work in these circumstances.

Complaint to an employment tribunal

- A complaint relating to an employer's refusal or failure to permit an employee to take time off for study or training, or to pay the employee for such time off, must be presented to an employment tribunal within three months of the date on which the alleged refusal or failure occurred. As always, an employee has no need to resign in order to do so. If the tribunal finds that the employee was not permitted to take time off, it will order the employer to pay the employee an amount equivalent to the remuneration he (or she) would have been paid had the time off been permitted. If the employee was not paid during permitted periods of time off, the employer will be ordered to pay the employee the amount that should have been paid in the first place (*ibid.* section 63C).

Detrimental treatment unlawful

- Section 47A of the 1996 Act cautions employers that it is unlawful to punish an employee or to subject him (or her) to any other detriment for exercising (or proposing to exercise) his statutory right to a reasonable amount of paid time off work for study or training. In such circumstances, an employee has no need to resign in order to seek redress before an employment tribunal. If the employee's complaint is upheld, the tribunal will make a declaration to that effect and will order the employer to pay the employee such compensation as is considered to be 'just and equitable' in all the circumstances. See also **Victimisation** elsewhere in this handbook.

Unlawful dismissal or selection for redundancy

- A young employee who is dismissed or selected for redundancy, principally for questioning or challenging his (or her) employer's refusal or failure to permit him a reasonable amount of paid time off work for study or training, or for bringing proceedings before an employment tribunal to enforce his statutory rights, may complain (yet again) to an employment tribunal regardless of his age or length of service at the material time. If the employee's complaint is upheld, the respondent employer will be ordered to pay the employee a substantial amount of compensation. See **Dismissal for asserting a statutory right** elsewhere in this handbook (*ibid.* sections 104 and 105).

Awarding bodies

A. GCSE and GNVQ Awarding Bodies

Assessment and Qualifications Alliance
Edexcel Foundation
Northern Ireland Council for the Curriculum, Examinations and Assessment
Oxford, Cambridge and RSA Examinations
Welsh Joint Education Committee

B. NVQ Awarding Bodies

Association of Accounting Technicians
Association of Industrial Truck Trainers
Automotive Management and Development Ltd
Awarding Body for the Built Environment
British Computer Society
British Horse Society
British Horseracing Training Board
British Polymar Training Association
CABWI Awarding Body
Central Council for Education and Training in Social Work
Chartered Institute of Bankers
City and Guilds of London Institute
Confederation of International Beauty Therapy and Cosmetology
Construction Industry Training Board
Construction Industry Training Board Northern Ireland
Council for Awards in Children's Care and Education
Distributive Occupational Standards Council
Edexcel Foundation
EMTA Awards Ltd
Engineering Construction Industry Training Board
Engineering Training Council (Northern Ireland)
EPIC
Fibreboard Awarding Body
Glass Qualifications Authority
Hospitality Awarding Body
Institute of Linguists Education Trust
Institute of Management Foundation
Institute of the Motor Industry
Institute of Personnel and Development
Institute for Supervision and Management
Joint Examining Board
Joint Industry Board for the Electrical Contracting Industry
Leather Producing Industry Vocational Qualifications Board
London Chamber of Commerce & Industry Examinations Board
Local Government Management Board
Management Verification Consortium Ltd
Meat Training Council
NCC Education Services Ltd
National Examining Board for Supervisory Management
National Fencing Training Authority
National Proficiency Tests Council
Oxford, Cambridge and RSA Examinations

Open University
Pitman Qualifications
Process Awards Authority
Qualifications for Industry Ltd
Royal College of Veterinary Surgeons
Security Industry Training Organisation/Parking Committee for London
Steel Industry Qualifications Board
Telecommunications Vocational Standards Council
Vocational Qualifications in Science, Engineering & Technology
Vocational Training Charitable Trust

C. National Entry Level Qualification Awarding Bodies

Assessment and Qualifications Alliance
Christian Theology Trust
Edexcel Foundation
Languages Development Centre (St Martin's College)
Oxford, Cambridge and RSA Examinations
Welsh Joint Education Committee

D. National Qualifications in Scotland Awarding Body

Scottish Qualifications Authority

E. SVQ Awarding Bodies

Association of Accounting Technicians
Association of Industrial Truck Trainers
Automotive Management and Development Ltd
British Horse Society
British Polymar Training Association
City and Guilds of London Institute
Confederation of International Beauty Therapy and Cosmetology
Electricity Training Association
EMTA Awards Ltd
Engineering Construction Industry Training Board
EPIC
Glass Qualifications Authority
Institute for Supervision and Management
Institute of the Motor Industry
Leather Producing Industry Vocational Qualifications Board
Local Government Management Board

Museum Training Institute
National Fencing Training Authority
National Proficiency Tests Council
NCC Education Services Ltd
Open University
Qualifications for Industry Ltd
Royal College of Veterinary Surgeons
Scottish Association of Master Bakers
Scottish Qualifications Authority
Travel Training Company Ltd
Vocational Qualifications in Science, Engineering and
    Technology
Vocational Training Charitable Trust

TIME OFF WORK: EMPLOYEE REPRESENTATIVES

Key points

- An *employee representative* has the legal right to be permitted a reasonable amount of paid time off work (during normal working hours) in order to perform his (or her) functions or to undergo training as such a representative. That same right extends to an employee who is a candidate for election to the post of employee representative (sections 61 and 62, Employment Rights Act 1996).

- Employee representatives, so-called, are persons elected by their fellow-employees to represent their interests in consultations with their employer concerning the latter's plans or proposals:

  (a) to make some or all of their number redundant; or

  (b) to sell or transfer part or all of his (or her) business as a 'going concern' (or to acquire another business)

- Before 26 October 1995, an employer had only to consult trade union representatives about his plans; and then only if the union they represented was a recognised independent trade union. That, said the European Court of Justice, was contrary to European Community Directive 75/129/EEC. This prompted the UK Government to introduce the Collective Redundancies & Transfer of Undertakings (Protection of Employment) (Amendment) Regulations 1995, since superseded by the eponymous 1999 Regulations, amending or inserting relevant provisions in the Trade Union & Labour Relations (Consolidation) Act 1992 and the Transfer of Undertakings (Protection of Employment) Regulations 1981.

- Under the Trade Union & Labour Relations (Consolidation) Act 1992 (as amended), employers proposing to dismiss 20 or more of their employees as redundant at one establishment must discuss their proposals with the *appropriate* representatives of those employees and listen to what they have to say. Under the Transfer of Undertakings (Protection of Employment) Regulations 1981 (as amended), the relevant employers must likewise consult *appropriate* representatives about their plans to sell or transfer the ownership of their business (or to acquire another business) and must inform them as to the likely effect on them of any such transfer or acquisition.

- *Appropriate* representatives are either *employee representatives* (elected by their peers) or *trade-union appointed representatives*. If an independent trade union is recognised by an employer as having bargaining rights in respect of the employees (or class of employees) affected by the employer's proposals, the employer is duty-bound to discuss his (or her) proposals or plans with representatives of that union. If there is no trade union representation, the employer must consult the relevant employee representatives. If there are no such representatives, the employer must ensure that the affected employees are afforded the time and facilities to nominate and elect one or more of their number to represent their interests. For further particulars, please turn to the section titled **Disclosure of information** elsewhere in this handbook.

Complaint to an employment tribunal

- An *employee representative* (or candidate for election as such a representative) who is denied his (or her) right to a reasonable amount of time off work, or who is not paid the whole of any wages or salary due to him in respect of that time off, or who is victimised, dismissed or selected for redundancy for carrying out (or proposing to carry out) his legitimate functions (or for challenging his employer's refusal to allow him to carry out those functions) may complain to an employment tribunal and will be awarded compensation if his complaint is upheld. Unless he has already resigned (or has been dismissed or made redundant) the employee representative has no need to resign from his employment in order to pursue his rights before an employment tribunal. Furthermore, a complaint may be brought regardless of the employee's length of service or age at the material time.

- Such a complaint must ordinarily be presented to an employment tribunal within three months of the employer's refusal or failure or unlawful action or (if the employee has resigned or been dismissed) within three months of the effective date of termination of the employee's contract of employment (*ibid.* section 63).

For further information, please turn to the sections titled **Disclosure of information, Dismissal, Dismissal for asserting a statutory right, Dismissal of an employee representative, Redundancy,** and **Victimisation** elsewhere in this handbook.

TIME OFF WORK: PENSION SCHEME TRUSTEES

Key points

- Any employee, who is a *pension scheme trustee* nominated and appointed (under section 16 of the Pensions Act 1995) to represent the interests of fellow-employees who are members of (or contribute to) a relevant occupational pension scheme (that is to say, a scheme established under a trust by their employer), has the legal right to be permitted a reasonable amount of paid time off work, during normal working hours, to enable him (or her):

(a) to perform any of his duties as such a trustee; or

(b) to undergo training relevant to the performance of those duties.

- Just how much time off is reasonable in such cases will depend in large part on the amount of time off work a pension scheme trustee needs to carry out his (or her) duties (or any particular duty) and how much time is needed to undergo relevant training. When considering a pension scheme trustee's request to be permitted time off, an employer is entitled to take into account the circumstances of his (or her) business and the effect the employee's absence will have on the naming of that business (sections 58 and 59, Employment Rights Act 1996).

Note: There must be at least two member-nominated pension scheme trustees (comprising at least one-third of the total number of trustees) – unless there are fewer than 100 members (employees) in the scheme, when one member-nominated trustee will suffice. Member-nominated trustees are appointed for a minimum period of three years and a maximum of six years (*ibid.*).

Complaint to an employment tribunal

- A pension scheme trustee who is denied his (or her) right to be permitted a reasonable amount of time off work to perform his duties (or undergo relevant training) as such a trustee, or who is not paid the whole of any wages or salary due to him in respect of that time off, or who is victimised, dismissed or selected for redundancy for carrying out (or proposing to carry out) those duties (or for challenging his employer's refusal to allow him to do so) may complain to an employment tribunal and will be awarded compensation if his complaint is upheld. Unless he has already resigned (or has been dismissed or made redundant) the employee representative does not have to resign from his employment in order to pursue his rights before an employment tribunal. Furthermore, a complaint may be brought regardless of the employee's length of service or age at the material time.

- Any such complaint must be presented to an employment tribunal within three months of the employer's refusal or failure or unlawful action, or (if the employee has resigned or been dismissed) within three months of the effective date of termination of the employee's contract of employment (*ibid.* section 60).

Please turn to the sections titled **Dismissal for asserting a statutory right, Dismissal of a pension scheme trustee, Redundancy,** and **Victimisation** elsewhere in this handbook.

TIME OFF WORK: PREGNANT EMPLOYEES
(Ante-natal care)

Key points

- 'An employee who is pregnant and who has, on the advice of a registered medical practitioner or registered midwife, made an appointment to attend at any place for the purpose of receiving ante-natal care… is entitled to be permitted by her employer to take time off during [her] working hours in order to enable her to keep the appointment.' Furthermore, a pregnant employee who is permitted to take time off during her working hours must be paid her normal wage or salary during her absence (sections 55 and 56, Employment Rights Act 1996).

- Section 55 imposes no limit on the number of occasions on which a pregnant employee may take paid time off work to attend at an ante-natal clinic. If an employer unreasonably intrudes upon that right, he may be called upon to justify his actions before an employment tribunal. However, the outcome is likely to depend on the tribunal's interpretation of the word 'unreasonable'. It might well decide that it is not unreasonable for an employer to urge an employee to make some of her ante-natal care appointments outside normal working hours – especially if his (or hers) is a small business which can ill afford having one of its employees off work two or three times a week. The same may apply if a pregnant employee occupies a key position within an organisation. Would it be unreasonable of her employer to suggest also that she arrange some of her appointments outside normal working hours or at the beginning or end of her working day? Each case will, of course, turn on its particular merits and there can be no hard and fast rule about what constitutes a reasonable or unreasonable denial of a pregnant employee's statutory rights in this respect.

Qualifying period of employment

- The right of a pregnant employee to be permitted paid time off work in these circumstances is available to all pregnant employees, regardless of their marital status or length of service. That right also extends to a pregnant employee who is married to her employer.

Production of medical certificate and appointment cards

- Before permitting a pregnant employee to take paid time off work for ante-natal care, an employer is entitled to demand to see:

  (a) a certificate from a doctor or registered midwife confirming that the employee in question is indeed pregnant (usually Form Mat B1);

  (b) an appointment card or equivalent document showing that she has made one or more appointments to attend at an ante-natal care clinic.

  For obvious reasons, an employer cannot demand to see an appointment card in respect of the first occasion on which a pregnant employee asks for paid time off work to attend an ante-natal clinic. This will ordinarily be provided during her first visit to the clinic and can only be presented for her employer's inspection after that first visit (*ibid.* section 55(2) and (3)).

Complaint to an employment tribunal

- An employee may present a complaint to an employment tribunal that her employer has unreasonably refused her time off work to attend for ante-natal care or that he (or she) has failed to pay her the whole or part of her normal earnings on any such occasion (*ibid.* section 57). Such a complaint must be presented within three months beginning with the day of the appointment concerned (or the day on which payment was withheld), or within such further period as the tribunal considers reasonable in a case where it is satisfied that it was not reasonably practicable for the complaint to have been presented within the prescribed three-month period.

- If an employment tribunal finds the employee's complaint to be well-founded, it will make a declaration to that effect; and

  (a) if the complaint is that the employer has unreasonably refused the employee time off work, the tribunal will order the employer to pay to the employee an amount equal to the remuneration to which she would have been entitled if that time off had not been refused; and

  (b) if the complaint is that the employer has failed to pay the employee the whole or part of the remuneration to which she was entitled, the tribunal will order the employer to pay to the employee the amount which it finds due to her (*ibid.* section 57(4) and (5)).

Unfair dismissal: assertion of statutory right

- Sections 104 and 105 of the 1996 Act provide that it is automatically unfair to dismiss any employee (or to select her for redundancy) if the reason or principal reason for the dismissal is that the employee has either brought proceedings to enforce a statutory right, including her right under sections 55 and 56 to be permitted to take paid time off work for ante-natal care, or that she has challenged her employer's authority by alleging that he (or she) has infringed that right.

- A complaint to an employment tribunal in these circumstances must be presented within three months of the effective date of termination of the employee's contract of employment. If the complaint is upheld, the employer will be ordered either to reinstate or re-engage the dismissed employee and/or pay compensation. An employer who refuses to comply with an order for reinstatement or re-engagement will be ordered to pay additional compensation of between 26 and 52 weeks' pay.

- See also **Dismissal on grounds of pregnancy or childbirth, Dismissal for asserting a statutory right, Employment tribunals and procedure,** and **Maternity rights** elsewhere in this handbook.

TIME OFF WORK: PUBLIC DUTIES

Key points

- Employees who perform specific official (or public) duties outside their regular employment have the legal right to be permitted a reasonable amount of time off work during their normal working hours to enable them to carry out some (if not all) of those public duties. This requirement is to be found in section 50 of the Employment Rights Act 1996.

- Section 50 states that an employer shall permit an employee of his (or hers) who is a justice of the peace to take time off during his (or her) working hours for the purposes of performing any of the duties of his office. That same obligation extends to any employee who is a member of:

    (a) a local authority;

    (b) a statutory tribunal (eg, an employment tribunal);

    (c) a police authority;

    (d) a board of prison visitors or a prison visiting committee;

    (e) a relevant health authority;

    (f) a relevant education body; or

    (g) the Environment Agency or the Scottish Environment Protection Agency.

Definitions

- *Local authority* means a local authority within the meaning of the Local Government Act 1972, or a council constituted under section 2 of the Local Government etc (Scotland) Act 1994, or the Common Council of the City of London, or a National Park authority, or the Broads Authority.

- *A member of a police authority* is a person appointed as such under Schedule 2 to the Police Act 1996.

- *A board of prison visitors* is a board of visitors appointed under section 6(2) of the Prisons Act 1952; and a *prison visiting committee* is a visiting committee appointed under section 19(3) of the Prisons (Scotland) Act 1989 or constituted by virtue of rules made under section 39 (as read with section 8(1)) of that Act.

- *Relevant health body* means a National Health Service trust established under Part I of the National Health Service & Community Care Act 1990 or the National Health Service (Scotland) Act 1978; or a health authority established under section 8 of the National Health Service Act 1977 or a special health authority established under section 11 of that Act; or a health board constituted under section 2 of the National Health Service (Scotland) Act 1978.

- The expression *relevant education body* means a managing or governing body of an educational establishment maintained by a local education authority; or a governing body of a grant-maintained school, further education corporation or higher education corporation; or a school council appointed under section 125(1) of the Local Government (Scotland) Act 1973; or a school board within the meaning of section 1(1) of the School Boards (Scotland) Act 1988; or a board of management of a self-governing school within the meaning of section 135(1) of the Education (Scotland) Act 1980; or a board of management of a college of further education within the meaning of section 36(1) of the Further & Higher Education (Scotland) Act 1992; or a governing body of a central institution within the meaning of section 135(1) of the Education (Scotland) Act 1980; or a governing body of a designated institution within the meaning of Part II of the Further & Higher Education (Scotland) Act 1992.

How much time off should be permitted?

- The 1996 Act does not provide any guidance on the amount of time off work an employee should be permitted to take in these circumstances, other than that the amount should be *reasonable* in all the circumstances. However, section 50 suggests that an employer should make it his (or her) business to find out precisely what duties are involved when an employee of his is a justice of the peace, or a public office-bearer, or a member of one or other of the authorities or bodies listed above.

- The Act also acknowledges that, when asked by one of his (or her) employees for yet more time off work, the employer is entitled to take account of the amount of time off the employee has already been permitted under section 50, as well as any time off he (or she) may have been granted under sections 168 and 170 of the Trade Union & Labour Relations (Consolidation) Act 1992 (time off for trade union duties and activities).

- The 1996 Act also recognises (by implication) that an employer has a business to run and that his (or her) principal concern must be the efficient running (and survival) of that business. When considering a request for time off work, the employer will quite properly consider what effect a particular employee's absence will have on his business (especially if he employs just a handful of people).

Note: It is as well to point out that an employer cannot compel an employee to work additional hours to make up for the time he (or she) has spent away from work while carrying out his functions as a justice of the peace or an official of a public body. Section 50(4) of the 1996 Act states that such an employee has a legal right to a *reasonable* amount of time off work. To require him to compensate his employer by working extra hours to make up for the lost time defeats that right (*vide Ratcliffe v Dorset County Council* [1979] IRLR 191). As to what constitutes an amount of time off, an employment tribunal held, in *Emmerson v Commissioners of Inland Revenue* [1977] IRLR 458 that it was unreasonable for the employer in that case to limit an employee to 18 days' leave of absence each year to attend to his official duties as a local authority councillor. A more appropriate period, said the tribunal, would have been 30 days a year.

Paid or unpaid?

- The 1996 Act is silent on the question of payment. It is generally assumed that an employee who is permitted time off work to attend to his (or her) public duties has no concomitant right to be paid his normal wages or salary during such absences. However, the Employment Appeal Tribunal has expressed the view that an employer's refusal to pay an employee who needs to take time off work to attend to his public duties *could* prove to be a deterrent sufficient to prevent that employee exercising that statutory right. In *Corner v Buckingham County Council* [1978] ICR 836, Slynn J remarked that 'in considering where there has been refusal to grant time off, the employment tribunal can look at the conditions subject to which an employer is prepared to grant time off (including conditions relating to pay) and could say that they really amounted to a refusal to allow time to be taken'.

Qualifying period of employment

- Employees who are office bearers or members of one or other of the public bodies described above can exercise their right to be permitted time off work to carry out their public duties, regardless of their length of service or the number of hours they work each week.

Complaints to an employment tribunal

- An employee who is a justice of the peace or member of a public body or authority may present a complaint to an employment tribunal that his (or her) employer has refused or failed to permit him to take time off work during his working hours so as to enable him to carry out his public duties (*ibid.* section 51). Such a complaint must be presented within three months of the date when the refusal or failure occurred. If the tribunal finds in favour of the complainant, it will make a declaration to that effect and may order the employer to pay compensation of such amount as the tribunal considers just and equitable in all the circumstances having regard to the employer's default in failing to permit the employee to take time off work and to any loss sustained by the employee attributable to that default (*ibid.* section 51(4)).

  See also **Dismissal for asserting a statutory right**, **Employment tribunals and procedure**, **Time off work: trade union members** and **Time off work: trade union officials**, elsewhere in this handbook.

TIME OFF WORK: REDUNDANCY

Key points

- 'An employee who is given notice of dismissal by reason of redundancy is entitled to be permitted by his (or her) employer to take reasonable time off during the employee's working hours, before the notice period expires, in order to look for new employment or make arrangements for training for future employment' (section 52, Employment Rights Act 1996).

- The period of notice referred to here is the notice required to be given by the employer under the terms of the employee's contract of employment, or the statutory minimum period of notice required under section 86 of the 1996 Act, whichever is the greater (see **Notice of termination of employment** elsewhere in this handbook).

- Thus, an employee under notice of redundancy can ask for and can expect to be allowed a reasonable amount of time off work during his (or her) notice period either to attend one or more employment interviews or to make arrangements for training for a new career or trade. Under such circumstances, an employer does *not* have the right to require an employee to produce evidence and particulars of job interviews he claims to have arranged with potential future employers (see *Dutton v Hawker Siddeley Aviation Limited* [1978] IRLR 390).

Paid or unpaid?

- An employee allowed time off work while working out his (or her) redundancy notice must be paid his or her normal salary or wages when attending employment interviews, looking for work or making arrangements for re-training (*ibid.* section 53).

Qualifying period of employment

- An employee under notice of redundancy will not be entitled to paid time off work to look for another job etc, unless, on the date on which his (or her) notice is due to expire, he will (or would) have been continuously employed for a period of two years or more (*ibid.* section 52(2)).

Reasonable time off

- Although section 52 of the 1996 Act does not specify just how much time off work would be considered *reasonable* in the circumstances described, it does offer a clue. Thus, section 54(4) states that an employment tribunal can award up to 40 per cent of a week's pay to any redundant employee who has been denied his (or her) statutory right to paid time off work while serving out his notice period. Assuming a normal working week of five days, this suggests that a redundant employee serving out his notice period should be allowed at least two days' paid time off work, in the aggregate (ie a half day here, an hour or two there), to attend employment interviews, visit the local Job Centre, etc – in short, to enable the employee to look for work elsewhere or to make arrangements for re-training.

  Note: An employee under notice of redundancy has the right to be allowed time off work with pay 'to make arrangements for training for future employment'. This means that such an employee has the right, for instance, to take time off work to visit his (or her) local polytechnic (or similar) and *sign-up* for a vocational training course to commence after his employment has come to an end. But, he does *not* have the right to take time off work to *attend* any such training course during his notice period.

Complaint to an employment tribunal

- A redundant employee may present a complaint to an employment tribunal that his (or her) employer has unreasonably refused to allow him time off work during his notice period or that he was not paid his normal wages or salary on those occasions on which he was permitted to take time off. Such a complaint must be presented within three months beginning with the day on which it is alleged that the time off should have been allowed or on which his wages or salary were docked (*ibid.* section 54(2)).

See also **Dismissal for asserting a statutory right, Dismissal on grounds of redundancy, Industrial tribunals and procedure**, and **Redundancy** elsewhere in this handbook.

TIME OFF WORK: SAFETY REPRESENTATIVES
(and representatives of employee safety)

Key points

- For these purposes, there are two types of safety representative. The first is the trade union-appointed safety representative operating in an establishment in which the employer recognises an independent trade union as having bargaining rights in respect of one or more groups of employees. The second is the *representative of employee safety* elected as such by his (or her) fellow employees (in a workplace in which there is either no trade union involvement at all, no recognition of a trade union (independent or otherwise), or in which trade union membership is fragmented or non-existent).

The employer's duty to consult and provide information

- An employer is duty-bound to consult either type of representative (or, if there is no elected or appointed safety representative, the employees themselves) on the introduction of any measure at the workplace which may substantially affect the health and safety of his (or her) employees; on his arrangements for appointing or nominating *competent persons* (as required by the Management of Health & Safety at Work Regulations 1999; on any information he is required to provide under existing health and safety legislation; on the planning and organisation of any health and safety training required by such legislation; and on the health and safety consequences attendant upon the introduction, or planned introduction, of new technologies into the workplace.

- The employer must also make available to those representatives such information as is necessary to enable them to participate fully and effectively in the consultation process. That information must include information contained in any record which the employer is required to keep under the provisions of the Reporting of Injuries, Diseases & Dangerous Occurrences Regulations 1995.

Time off for appointed safety representatives

- A safety representative appointed as such by a recognised independent trade union has the legal right to be granted such paid time off work during his (or her) normal working hours as may be necessary to enable him to perform his functions and to undergo relevant safety training (per regulation 4(2), Safety Representatives & Safety Committees Regulations 1977). The type of training envisaged by the 1977 Regulations includes training in the role of safety representative, as well as training in health and safety legislation, how to recognise and control workplace hazards, and so on.

   Note: Section 2(4) of the Health and Safety at Work etc Act 1974 gives a recognised independent trade union the right to appoint one or more safety representatives to represent the interests of employees in matters affecting their health and safety at work. The guidance notes accompanying the 1977 Relations (*qv*) (made under the 1974 Act) urge that any person appointed to the post of safety representative should normally have either worked for his (or her) employer throughout the preceding two years or have at least two years' experience in similar employment.

- Although a trade union-appointed safety representative has a right to investigate potential hazards and dangerous occurrences at the workplace, he (or she) cannot neglect his normal duties at a moment's notice to carry out an *ad hoc* inspection of his employer's premises. Under normal circumstances, he would be expected to liaise with his supervisor or other member of management to agree arrangements for workplace inspections, etc. If an appointed safety representative has it in mind to attend a safety training course, he should inform his employers several weeks in advance to enable them to make alternative arrangements to cover his absence.

- An appointed safety representative must be paid his (or her) normal wages or salary during any authorised period of time off work (*ibid.* regulation 4(2) and Schedule).

Code of practice

- A Code of Practice (COP 1) titled *Safety Representatives and Safety Committees* has been issued by the Health and Safety Commission and provides guidance for both employers and trade unions on the practical implications of a safety representative's legal right to paid time off work. Copies of the code (or *The Brown Book*, as it is known) (ISBN 0 11 883959 4) are available from:

HSE Books
PO Box 1999
Sudbury
Suffolk
CO10 6FS
Telephone: 01787 881165
Fax: 01787 313995

Time off work for 'representatives of employee safety'

- In a workplace in which there is no trade union recognition and no trade union-appointed safety representative, the employees themselves may, if they wish, elect one or more of their number to represent their interests in consultations with their employer on matters affecting their health and safety at work. Under the Health & Safety (Consultations with Employees) Regulations 1996, any person so elected is referred to, somewhat clumsily, as a *representative of employee safety*. As such, he (or she) has the right to be consulted by his employer on matters relating to health and safety in the workplace, and the right also:

    (a) to be permitted by his employer to take such time off work with pay (during normal working hours) as may be necessary to enable him to perform his functions under the 1996 Regulations; and

    (b) to be provided by his employer with such training (in respect of those functions) as may be reasonable in all the circumstances (the cost of which, including any associated travel and subsistence costs, must be met by the employer).

- Any employee who is standing as a candidate for election as a representative of employee safety, is entitled to be permitted a reasonable amount of paid time off work to perform his (or her) functions as such a candidate.

    Note: Although employees have the right to elect one of their number to represent their interests in consultations with their employer they are not bound to do so. If there is no elected representative, it nonetheless devolves on the employer to consult the employees themselves in good time on matters relating to their health and safety at work.

- As is the case with trade-union appointed safety representatives, *representatives of employee safety* should not simply abandon their work without notice (other than in an emergency) to conduct an *ad hoc* inspection of the workplace without coming to some prior arrange-ment with their immediate managers or supervisors. The same applies if an employee-elected representative wishes to attend an appropriate safety training course. This is a matter which needs to be discussed and agreed beforehand.

Complaint to employment tribunal

- A safety representative or *representative of employee safety* may complain to an employment tribunal that:

    (a) his (or her) employer has failed to permit him to take time off work for the purposes of performing his functions or undergoing train-ing in aspects of those functions; or

    (b) that his employer has failed to pay him his normal remuneration on such occasions.

    Such a complaint must be presented within three months of the date when the failure occurred. If the tribunal finds the complaint well-founded, it will make a declaration to that effect and may order the employer to pay compensation of such amount as the tribunal consid-ers just and equitable in all the circumstances. If a tribunal finds that the employer has failed to pay the employee the whole or part of the remu-neration due to him (or her), it will likewise order the employer to pay the employee the amount in question (*ibid.* regulation 11).

Right not to be victimised or dismissed

- Safety representatives (whether trade union-appointed or elected by their peers) have the right not to be victimised, penalised or 'subjected to any detriment' by their employer for carrying out their legitimate functions. They have the right also not to be dismissed for asserting their statutory rights or for challenging their employer's failure to allow them to carry out those functions.

    For further particulars, please turn to the sections titled **Dismissal in health and safety cases**, **Dismissal for asserting a statutory right**, and **Victimisation**, elsewhere in this handbook.

TIME OFF WORK: TRADE UNION MEMBERS

Key points

- 'An employer shall permit an employee of his (or hers) who is a member of an independent trade union recognised by the employer in respect of that description of employee to take time off during his (or her) working hours for the purposes of taking part in (a) any activities of the union, and (b) any activities in relation to which the employee is acting as a representative of the union' (section 170, Trade Union & Labour Relations (Consolidation) Act 1992).

Trade union activities

- The type of trade union activities envisaged by the 1992 Act include urgent shopfloor meetings of members, the voting-in of shop stewards, attendance at policy-making meetings of the trade union (a member attending as the elected representative of his colleagues on the shop floor), or representing the union on external bodies. But, activities which themselves consist of industrial action (whether or not in contemplation or furtherance of a trade dispute) do *not* qualify as trade union activities for this purpose.

- An employer is not obliged to pay trade union members whom he (or she) permits to take time off work in the circumstances described. Furthermore, every trade union member must give his (or her) immediate supervisor or manager advance notice of his intentions. He should not presume to abandon his desk or place of work without first obtaining the permission of his immediate supervisor or manager (which permission, however, should not be unreasonably withheld). Any dispute concerning the employee's rights in the matter will be determined by an employment tribunal (see below).

- Should several trade union members ask for time off work at the same time, their employer has the right to insist that one or more of their number remain at their workstations for safety or operational reasons – for example, to avoid disrupting the smooth flow of work, to keep the premises open to the public, or to maintain minimum manning levels.

- An employer has a business to run and has every right to insist that trade union members who are granted time off work are not absent from work for longer than is strictly necessary. Indeed, the employer can specify a time at which they must be back at work. The theme, as always, is that management and trade unions should 'get together' to discuss what is reasonable, and the need, wherever possible, for an early-warning system.

Note: ACAS Code of Practice 3, titled *Time off for Trade Union Duties and Activities* is available from ACAS Reader Limited on 01455 852225.

Qualifying period of employment

- So long as a trade union member is employed under a contract of employment, there is no qualifying period of continuous employment which restricts or limits his (or her) right to be permitted to take time off work in the circumstances described above.

Complaint to an employment tribunal

- An employee, who is a member of a recognised independent trade union, may complain to an employment tribunal that his (or her) employer has failed to permit him to take time off during his working hours to participate in the activities of his trade union (*ibid.* section 170(4)). The complaint must be presented within three months of the date when the failure occurred or, if 'satisfied that it was not reasonably practicable for the complaint to have been presented within that period, within such further period as the tribunal considers reasonable'. If the employee's complaint is upheld, the tribunal will make a declaration to that effect and will order the employer to pay compensation to the employee of such amount as the tribunal considers just and equitable in all the circumstances having regard to the employer's default and to any loss sustained by the employee in consequence of that default (*ibid.* section 172).

See also **Dismissal for asserting a statutory right, Employment tribunals and procedure, Time off work: trade union officials**, and **Trade union membership and activities**, elsewhere in this handbook.

TIME OFF WORK: TRADE UNION OFFICIALS

Key points

- 'An employer shall permit an employee of his (or hers) who is an official of an independent trade union recognised by the employer to take time off… during his working hours for the purposes of carrying out any duties of his, as such an official, concerned with:

(a) negotiations with the employer related to or connected with matters falling within section 178(2) (collective bargaining) in relation to which the trade union is recognised by the employer, or

(b) the performance on behalf of employees of the employer of functions related to or connected with matters falling within that provision which the employer has agreed may be so performed by the trade union'

(section 168, Trade Union & Labour Relations (Consolidation) Act 1992).

An employer must also permit a trade union official (shop steward, works convenor) to take a reasonable amount of paid time off during his (or her) working hours for the purposes of undergoing training in those aspects of industrial relations which are relevant to matters in respect of which his union has been afforded collective bargaining rights – so long as that training has been approved by the Trades Union Congress (TUC) or by the employee's own union (*ibid.* section 168(2)).

Note: Section 119 of the 1992 Act defines the 'official' (in relation to a trade union) as meaning an officer of the union or of a branch or section of the union, or a person elected or appointed in accordance with the rules of the union to be a representative of its members or of some of them, and includes a person so elected or appointed who is an employee of the same employer as the members or one or more of the members whom he (or she) is to represent.

- The amount of time off which an employee (in his or her capacity as a trade union official) is to be permitted to take, and the purposes for which, the occasions on which, and any conditions subject to which, time off may be taken are those that are reasonable in all the circumstances having regard to any relevant provisions of a code of practice issued by the Advisory, Conciliation and Arbitration Service (*ibid.* section 168(3)).

Note: Paragraph 12 of Code of Practice 3 (*Time Off for Trade Union Duties and Activities*) states that trade union officials should be allowed to take reasonable time off for duties concerned with negotiations or, with the employer's agreement, for duties concerned with related functions. Copies of the code (ISBN 0 11 701555 5) are available from ACAS Reader Limited on 01455 852225.

- An employee who is permitted by his (or her) employer to take time off work to carry out his duties as an official of a recognised independent trade union must be paid his normal wage or salary at such times. However, if he takes time off at a time when he would otherwise be working voluntary overtime (that is to say, overtime which he is not contractually obliged to work, nor his employer contractually bound to provide), he need only be paid his basic wage or salary (see *Davies & Alderton v Head Wrighton Teesdale Ltd* [1979] IRLR 170).

Note: Section 168 of the 1992 Act requires an employer to *permit* an employee of his, who is an official of a recognised independent trade union, to take time off work with pay in order to carry out his (or her) functions. Use of the word *permit* suggests that it is not open to a shop steward or works convenor simply to leave his (or her) department or place of work when and as he pleases. Indeed, paragraph 29 of the Code of Practice reminds union officials that management is responsible for maintaining production and service to customers, and for making arrangements for time off. If a shop steward needs time off, he must give as much advance notice to his supervisor or manager as is reasonable in the circumstances. He must say why he needs to take time off, where he will be, and how long he intends to be absent from his desk or workbench. Where necessary, managers and unions should develop contingency plans for other employees to cover the work of shop stewards who take time off to carry out their official duties or while absent on appropriate TUC or trade union-approved training courses.

How much time off is reasonable?

- Exactly what constitutes a *reasonable* amount of paid time off work is a matter for the tribunals to decide. At the workplace, much will depend on the attitudes of the parties concerned and the degree of cooperation between trade union officials (shop stewards, and the like) and their employers. If matters come to a head and there is no satisfactory conclusion, the trade union concerned may have no choice but to institute proceedings (see *Complaint to an employment tribunal* below).

Time off for training

- Paragraphs 15 to 19 of Code of Practice 3 (referred to earlier) state that trade union officials should be permitted a *reasonable* amount of paid leave of absence to attend TUC or trade union-approved training courses. But those courses must have a direct bearing on matters in respect of which the officials have been accorded negotiating rights with their respective employers, eg pay, working conditions, hours of work, health and safety, etc. Following amendments introduced by section 14 of the Employment Act 1989 (now incorporated in the 1992 Act), a shop steward no longer has the right to attend a training course in aspects of industrial relations which have no bearing on his (or her) day-to-day dealings with his employer.

Note: Here, too, a shop steward wishing to attend a training course is duty-bound to give as much advance warning to his (or her) employer as is possible (or reasonable) in the circumstances. Where there are a number of shop stewards (representing the same or different trade unions) on the same premises, it would be quite inappropriate to expect the employer to allow each to be absent from work at the same time. An employer has a business to run and cannot be expected to yield to every demand for paid time off work at short notice. He has a right to be consulted beforehand and, if need be, to refuse (or postpone) permission to take time off at certain times if the absence of one or more of his employees could present problems – particularly if his is a small operation or the trade union officials concerned occupy key positions within his organisation.

Qualifying period of employment

- A trade union official (shop steward or otherwise) has no need of a qualifying period of continuous employment to exercise his (or her) statutory right to be permitted a reasonable amount of paid time off work to carry out his duties or to attend an approved course of training. The only requirement is that he be employed under a contract of employment.

Complaint to an employment tribunal

- A shop steward or other official of a recognised independent trade union may complain to an employment tribunal that his (or her) employer has failed to permit him to take time off work to carry out his duties as such an official (or to attend an appropriate training course), or that he has refused to pay him the whole or part of his normal wages or salary at such times (*ibid.* section 168(4)).

  Note: A trade union is *recognised* if it is recognised by an employer to any extent for the purposes of collective bargaining (*ibid.* section 178(3)).

- Complaints to a tribunal in these circumstances must be presented within three months of the date when the employer's refusal or failure occurred. If any such complaint is upheld, the tribunal will make a declaration to that effect and will order the employer to pay compensation of such amount as it considers just and equitable in all the circumstances. If the employer has permitted time off work but has refused or failed to pay the official his (or her) normal wages or salary, the tribunal will order the employer to pay the employee the amount which it finds due to him (*ibid.* section 172).

  See also **Dismissal for asserting a statutory right, Employment tribunals and procedure**, and **Time off work: trade union members**, elsewhere in this handbook. See also **Trade union membership and activities**.

TRADE DISPUTES AND ARBITRATION

Key points

- If a trade dispute appears to be deadlocked, the parties to the dispute can ask the Advisory, Conciliation and Arbitration Service (ACAS) to intervene.

  With the consent of *both* parties, ACAS may refer all or any of the matters to which the dispute relates to the arbitration of:

  (a) one or more independent arbitrators appointed by ACAS for that purpose; or

  (b) the Central Arbitration Committee.

  Before referring a trade dispute to arbitration, ACAS will consider the likelihood of the dispute being settled by conciliation. Indeed, it will not consider arbitration unless satisfied that both sides to the dispute have exhausted all internal procedures for the settlement of disputes (section 212, Trade Union & Labour Relations (Consolidation) Act 1992).

  Note: Paragraph 129 of the ACAS *Code of Industrial Relations Practice* comments that when the parties to a trade dispute agree to go to arbitration, they should also agree to be bound by the decision of the arbitrators (or that of the Central Arbitration Committee). Without such an undertaking, says the Code, arbitration would succeed only in polarising the different positions of the parties.

Meaning of trade dispute

- Section 218 of the 1992 Act defines *trade dispute* as meaning a dispute between workers and their employer which relates wholly or mainly to one or more of the following:

  (a) terms and conditions of employment or the physical conditions in which any workers are required to work;

  (b) engagement or non-engagement, or termination or suspension of employment or the duties of employment, of one or more workers;

  (c) allocation of work or the duties of employment as between workers or groups of workers;

  (d) matters of discipline;

  (e) a worker's membership or non-membership of a trade union;

  (f) facilities for officials of trade unions; and

(g) machinery for negotiation or consultation, and other procedures, relating to any of the foregoing matters, including the recognition by employers or employers' associations of the right of a trade union to represent workers in any such negotiation or consultation or in the carrying out of such procedures.

Trades Union Congress (TUC) and inter-union disputes

- Disputes between TUC-affiliated unions are ordinarily referred to a TUC Disputes Committee for resolution.

  See also **Advisory, Conciliation & Arbitration Service** and **Central Arbitration Committee**, elsewhere in this handbook.

TRADE UNION MEMBERS
(*Rights of, as members and employees*)

Key points

- Members of trade unions have a number of legal rights, both in their dealings with the trade unions to which they belong and in their relationship with their employers (or prospective employers).

  Those rights (summarised below) are to be found in the Trade Union & Labour Relations (Consolidation) Act 1992 ('the 1992 Act'), as are the procedures to be followed when a trade union member wishes to seek legal redress for an infringement of those rights.

Rights as a member of a trade union

- In his (or her) dealings with the trade union to which he belongs, a member:

  (a) who claims that the union (i) has unlawfully used *trade union funds or property* to indemnify the unlawful conduct of any individual and (ii) has unreasonably failed to bring or continue proceedings in 'the court' (ie, the High Court or the Court of Session) to recover those funds (or the value of the property in question), has the right to apply to the court for permission to bring or continue proceedings to that end on the union's behalf (and at the union's expense) (section 15(3));

(b) who claims that the union's trustees have (or are proposing) to permit an *unlawful application of trade union property* at the direction of the union or otherwise), may apply to the court for an order requiring the trustees to recover (or protect) that property (section 16);

(c) may apply to the Certification Officer or the court for a declaration to the effect that the union has failed to compile and maintain a *register of the names and addresses of members*, or that the entries in the register are either inaccurate or not kept up-to-date (section 25);

(d) has a right (as has any member of the public) to be supplied on request (either free of charge or on payment of a reasonable fee) with a copy of the *rules of the union* (section 27);

(e) has a right to request access to any *accounting records* of the union which are available for inspection and relate to periods including a time when he (or she) was a member of the union. The union must make arrangements for him to inspect those records within 28 days, and allow him and any accountant accompanying him to inspect those records at an agreed time and place. The union may require the accountant to sign a confidentiality agreement, may impose a modest charge (not exceeding any reasonable expenses) for allowing the member and his accountant to inspect the records and take copies (so long as the member is forewarned that such a charge will be imposed and the basis on which that charge is calculated); and the right also to apply to the court for an order directing compliance (sections 30 and 31);

(f) has the right (as has any member of the public) to be supplied, either free of charge or on payment of a reasonable charge, with a copy of the union's *annual return to the Certification Officer*, revenue accounts, balance sheet, auditor's report, details of the salaries paid to and other benefits provided to the president, general secretary and members of the executive, etc) and a copy of the union's rules in force at the end of the period to which those accounts relate (section 32);

(g) has the right, within eight weeks of the day on which the annual return referred to in (f) was sent to the Certification Officer, either to receive or to read in the union's newspaper (or equivalent publication) a *'statement to members'* specifying the union's total income and expenditure for the period to which the return relates, and containing related information (including the auditor's report and details of the salaries and other benefits received by senior officers) required by section 32A which statement must also include the following statement:

STATEMENT TO MEMBERS

To be included in the statement relating to a trade union's financial affairs which the trade union must distribute to its members (or publish) within eight weeks of the date on which the union sent its annual return to the Certification Officer in accordance with section 32 of the Trade Union & Labour Relations (Consolidation) Act 1992) (ibid; section 32A(6)).

'A member who is concerned that some irregularity may be occurring, or have occurred, in the conduct of the financial affairs of the union may take steps with a view to investigating further, obtaining clarification and, if necessary, securing regularisation of that conduct.

The member may raise any such concern with such one or more of the following as it seems appropriate to raise it with: the officials of the union, the trustees of the property of the union, the auditor or auditors of the union, the Certification Officer (who is an independent officer appointed by the Secretary of State) and the police.

Where a member believes that the financial affairs of the union have been or are being conducted in breach of the law or in breach of rules of the union and contemplates bringing civil proceedings against the union or responsible officials or trustees, he should consider obtaining independent legal advice.'

(h) has the right to receive (free of charge) a copy of a qualified actuary's report on the trade union's proposals for a *members' superannuation scheme*, and a copy also of the actuary's subsequent periodic reports of the assets comprised in the fund and of the liabilities falling to be discharged out of it (sections 39 and 40);

(i) has the right not to be unreasonably excluded from standing as a candidate in union elections for the office of president, general secretary or member of the union's executive, and the right also to have his (or her) election address published and distributed, without being amended, altered or otherwise tampered with, and at no cost to himself (sections 47 and 48);

(j) (unless unemployed, or in arrears with his or her subscriptions or union dues, or an apprentice, trainee or new member, in accordance with the union's rules) the *right to vote* in any election referred to in (i) (section 50);

(k) the right not to be induced to take part (or continue to take part) in *industrial action* which does not have the support of a ballot, and to apply to the court for an order directing the trade union to take steps to ensure that no further such inducement takes place and that the unlawful industrial action is effectively called off (section 62);

(l)   the right not to be denied *access to the courts* in pursuance of his or her statutory rights, regardless of any stipulation to the contrary in the union's rulebook (section 63);

(m) the right (in accordance with sections 65 and 66) *not to be unjustifiably disciplined* by his or her union (ie, expelled, fined, deprived of benefits or facilities, or subjected to some other detriment, etc):

–   for refusing or failing, to participate in or support a strike, or for failing to break a term in his or her contract of employment (for a purpose connected with such a strike or other industrial action); or

–   for asserting (or for encouraging some other person to vindicate his or her assertion) that the union (or any official or representative of the union, or any trustee of its property) has contravened its own rules, or the terms of any agreement or any statutory duty (or is about to do so); or

–   for encouraging or assisting another person not to break his (or her) contract of employment in furtherance of a strike or other industrial action; or

–   for failing to agree (or withdrawing his agreement) to have monies representing his union dues deducted from his pay; or

–   for resigning (or proposing to resign) from the union or from another union, or for becoming, proposing to become, refusing to become, or for not being, a member of another union; or

–   for working with individuals who are not members of the union or of another union (or for proposing to do so); or

–   for working for an employer who employs individuals who are not members of the union or of another union (or for proposing to do so); or

–   for exercising his (or her) right either to require the union to comply with its statutory duties under the 1992 Act, or to apply to the court for an order directing the union to comply with those duties;

(n) has the *right to vote in a ballot on a political resolution* (which right must be accorded equally to all members of the union) (section 76);

(o) has the *right to apply to the Certification Officer* or court for a declaration to the effect that the union has held a ballot on a political resolution otherwise than in accordance with political ballot rules approved by the Certification Officer, or has failed in relation to any such proposed ballot to comply with the political ballot rules so approved (sections 79 and 81);

(p) has the *right not to be required to contribute to the union's political fund* as a condition for admission to the union; the right (after having served notice on the union to that effect) not to have to contribute to the union's political fund; and the right not to be denied access to any benefit or facility as a penalty for exercising those rights (sections 82 to 85);

(q) has the *right to complain to the Certification Officer* that the union has failed to comply with the rules and procedures in sections 97 to 108 of the 1992 Act relating to union amalgamations or those regulating the transfer of engagements to another trade union;

(r) has *the right not to be excluded or expelled from the trade union* other than for a reason permitted by section 174 (eg, because he no longer satisfies a legitimate and enforceable membership requirement, or because he no longer qualifies by reason of the union operating only in a particular part of Great Britain, or because membership is restricted to persons employed by a particular employer or by an employer within an association of employers) and he is no longer employed by any such employer, or because his exclusion or expulsion is entirely attributable to his conduct (section 174).

Note: A trade union which refuses or wilfully neglects to comply with its duties under paragraphs (d), (e), (f) or (h) above is guilty of an offence and liable, on conviction, to a fine of up to £5,000 (level 5 on the standard scale). If an offence is compounded by any union official or agent wilfully altering, destroying, mutilating or falsifying any document relating to the financial affairs of the union, or by fraudulently parting with, altering or deleting anything in any such document, or by making an explanation or providing a statement which he knows to be false in a material particular, the penalty rises to imprisonment for a term not exceeding six months and/or a fine of up to £5,000.

Relationship with employers

- In his (or her) dealings with his employer, a member of a trade union has the right (discussed elsewhere in this handbook):

  (a) (as a job applicant) *not to be denied access to employment* because of his trade union membership, or because of his unwillingness to accept a requirement to take steps to cease to be a member of that trade union or of any trade union (section 137);

(b) has the right (under section 146) *not to have action short of dismissal* taken against him with a view to:

- preventing or deterring him from being or seeking to become a member of an independent trade union, or penalising him for doing so,

- preventing or deterring him from taking part in the activities of an independent trade union at an appropriate time, or penalising him for doing so, or

- compelling him to be or become a member of any trade union or of a particular trade union or of one of a number of particular trade unions;

(c) has *the right not to be dismissed* (or selected for redundancy):

- for being or proposing to become a member of an independent trade union, or

- for taking part or proposing to take part in the activities of an independent trade union at an appropriate time (sections 152 and 153);

(d) has the right (as an official of a recognised independent trade union) to be permitted *to take paid time off work* for the purpose of carrying out such of his (or her) official duties as are concerned with matters in relation to which the trade union is recognised by his employer (and related functions) (section 168);

(e) has the right (as a member of a recognised independent trade union) to be permitted *to take time off work* in order to take part in the activities of that union and any activities in relation to which he (or she) is acting as a representative of that union (section 170);

(f) has the right to serve notice on his employer that he is exempt from any obligation *to contribute to his union's political fund, and* to insist that his employer make no further deductions from pay in respect of that fund (sections 86 to 88);

(g) has the right not to have *unauthorised or excessive trade union subscriptions* deducted from his (or her) pay (sections 68 and 68A).

- A trade union member may seek redress (ie, compensation) for an infringement of any of those rights by presenting a complaint to an employment tribunal (on Form IT1). Such a complaint must ordinarily be presented to the Secretary of the Tribunals within three months of the date on which the employer's failure or refusal occurred, although a complaint presented 'out of time' may be accepted in exceptional circumstances.

For further particulars, please turn to the sections titled **Access to employment, Deductions from pay, Dismissal for asserting a statutory right, Strikes and other industrial action, Time off: trade union members, Time off: trade union officials, Trade disputes and arbitration**, and **Trade union membership and activities** (next section).

TRADE UNION MEMBERSHIP AND ACTIVITIES

Key points

Access to employment

- Section 137(1) of the Trade Union & Labour Relations (Consolidation) Act 1992 cautions that it is unlawful for an employer to refuse to interview or employ a job applicant simply because the applicant is (or is not) a member of a trade union or because he (or she) is unwilling to accept a requirement to become (or cease to be, or to remain, or not to become) a member of a trade union. It is also unlawful for an employer to require a new employee to make one or more payments or to agree to have money deducted from his wages or salary as an alternative to trade union membership. The same rule applies to employment agencies, whether acting for themselves or on behalf of client employers.

- A job applicant may complain to an employment tribunal that he (or she) was refused employment (or a job interview) because of his trade union membership or non-membership. If the complaint is upheld, the tribunal will order the offending employer (or employment agency) to rectify the situation and/or pay damages for breach of statutory duty including compensation for injury to feelings. With the coming into force on 25 October 1999 of section 34(4) of the Employment Relations Act 1999, the maximum amount of compensation that can be awarded in such cases is now £50,000 (*ibid.* section 140(4)).

Trade union pressure

- If a trade union or other person (whether or not acting on behalf of a trade union) uses the threat of industrial action to *persuade* an employer not to recruit non-union employees, the employer or the complainant can ask the employment tribunal to direct that the person who exercised that pressure be joined or sisted as a party to the proceedings. Such a request must be made *before* the tribunal hearing begins or, in some cases, before the tribunal reaches its decision. But it will *not* be accepted if made afterwards. If the tribunal finds against the employer, it may order the responsible trade union (or other person) to pay the whole or part of any award of compensation payable to the complainant.

Victimisation and action short of dismissal

- 'Every employee shall have the right not to be subjected to any detriment as an individual by any act, or any deliberate failure to act, by his employer if the act or failure takes place for the purpose of:

    (a) preventing or deterring him from being or seeking to become a member of an independent trade union, or penalising him for doing so; or

    (b) preventing or deterring him from taking part in the activities of an independent trade union at any *appropriate time*, or penalising him for doing so; or

    (c) compelling him to be or become a member of any trade union or of a particular trade union or of one of a number of particular trade unions'

    (section 146(1), Trade Union & Labour Relations (Consolidation) Act 1992, as amended by section 2 and Schedule 2 to the Employment Relations Act 1999).

    Note: The expression 'appropriate time', in relation to an employee taking part in the activities of an independent trade union, means time which is either outside the employee's working hours, or is a time within his (or her) working hours during which, in accordance with arrangements agreed with, or consent given by, his employer, it is permissible for him to take part in those activities (*ibid.* section 146(2)).

- As was mentioned earlier, it is also unlawful for an employer to lay down a condition requiring an employee to make one or more payments, or to agree to have money deducted from his (or her) pay – payable to a trade union, charity or some other third party as a penalty for refusing to be or remain a member of a trade union, or as an alternative to the payment of trade union dues. Any such term in a contract of employment (or elsewhere in writing) is null and void (*ibid.* section 146(3) and (4)).

- Clearly, there are a number of ways (short of dismissal) in which an employer can make life difficult for employees who join trade unions or who encourage other employees to do the same. If an employer is opposed to any form of trade union activity on his (or her) premises, he may (unwisely) discriminate against those who refuse 'to toe the line' by giving them unpleasant jobs to do, by denying them pay rises or promotion or access to overtime, by criticising them in front of their workmates, and so on. An employee victimised or harassed in this way does *not* have to resign in order to present a complaint to an employment tribunal. Furthermore, he (or she) can do so regardless of his age or length of service at the material time. If the employee's complaint is upheld, the tribunal will order the employer to pay compensation to the employee of such amount as it considers 'just and equitable' in all the circumstances (*ibid.* section 146(5)) (see below).

- The same applies if an employer uses underhand tactics to compel one or other of his employees to join or remain a member of any trade union or of a particular trade union or of one of a number of particular trade unions. When determining the amount of compensation to be awarded in such circumstances, a tribunal will *not* be influenced by the employer's excuse that he acted in the way he did because of trade union pressure and the threat of industrial action (*ibid.*).

   Note: It is automatically unfair to dismiss an employee (or to select him (or her) for redundancy) either for alleging that his employer has infringed one or other of his statutory rights or for seeking to enforce that right by presenting a complaint to an employment tribunal (sections 104 and 105(7), Employment Rights Act 1996). See **Dismissal for asserting a statutory right** elsewhere in this handbook.

- Although an employee has the right to participate in the activities of an independent trade union at an *appropriate time* (see above), he (or she) does *not* have the right to disrupt the work of others or to make a nuisance of himself during working hours, eg by distributing leaflets or by taking time off to harangue other workers about the advantages of trade union membership. In the final analysis, the *reasonableness* of an employer's response to such misconduct will be determined by an employment tribunal – if, in the event, the employee believes he has been unfairly treated.

Complaint to an employment tribunal

- An employee may complain to an employment tribunal that his (or her) employer has harassed or victimised him in contravention of his legitimate right to be or not to be a member of a trade union or to participate (at an *appropriate time*) in the activities of an independent trade union (*ibid.* section 146(5)). Such a complaint must be presented to the Secretary to the Tribunals within the period of three months beginning with the date on which the incident complained of took place (or where that incident was one of a series of such incidents, the last of those incidents). If the tribunal finds the complaint well-founded, it will make a declaration to that effect and may make an award of compensation (to be paid by the employer to the employee) of such amount as the tribunal considers just and equitable in all the circumstances, having regard to the infringement of the employee's rights and any loss sustained by him as a consequence of his employer's actions (*ibid.* section 149).

Note: If the victimisation or harassment of an employee was prompted by a trade union or other person threatening a strike or other industrial action, the person exerting that pressure may be required (at the request of either the employer or the complainant) to be joined or sisted as a party to the tribunal proceedings, and may, in the event, be ordered to pay the whole or any part of any subsequent award of compensation (ibid. section 150).

See also **Closed shop**, **Dismissal on grounds of trade union membership**, and **Time off: trade union members**, elsewhere in this handbook.

TRADE UNION RECOGNITION
(*Schedule A1, Trade Union & Labour Relations (Consolidation) Act 1992*)

Key points

- Schedule A1 to the Trade Union & Labour Relations (Consolidation) Act 1992 (as inserted by section 1(1) and (3) and Schedule 1 to the Employment Relations Act 1999) lays down the (somewhat complicated) procedures attendant upon a request by a trade union for recognition and collective bargaining rights. It also contains no less complicated procedures for derecognition.

The new provisions summarised

- In brief, any employer with 21 or more workers 'on the payroll' may be presented with a valid request for trade union recognition. If the employer ignores or rejects such a request, or refuses to negotiate, the trade union may apply to the Central Arbitration Committee (CAC) for compulsory recognition. If the CAC is satisfied that the trade union's application is both valid and admissible, and accepts that more than 50 per cent of the workers in the proposed bargaining unit are members of that trade union, it will order the employer to recognise that trade union. If, on the other hand, the CAC is not entirely persuaded that a majority of the workers in the bargaining unit want the trade union to negotiate on their behalf, it will serve notice that it intends to arrange a secret ballot. If 40 per cent or more of the workers entitled to vote in the ballot, and a majority of those voting, vote in favour of recognition, the CAC will make a compulsory recognition order. A refusal to comply with such an order is a contempt of court, punishable by imprisonment or a fine.

Note: In the 1992 Act, the term 'worker' applies to any individual (other than a person who is genuinely self-employed) who works (or normally works) under a contract of employment or under any other contract whereby he (or she) undertakes to do or perform personally any work or services for another party to the contract. In other words, the term applies not only to employees in the accepted sense, but also to casual workers, seasonal workers, homeworkers and freelances engaged under some other contractual arrangement.

- The legislation also lay down procedures for derecognition (not discussed in any detail in this section). An application for derecognition may be made by either party to a recognition agreement, so long as the agreement in question was imposed by the CAC (in accordance with the procedures explained in this section). However, the CAC will not entertain an application for derecognition if made within three years of its original decision. If the number (or average number) employed in a particular organisation falls below 21, the employer may notify the union that his bargaining arrangements with the union are to end on a specified date (which must be not less than 35 working days after the date on which the employer notified the union of his decision). The union may challenge the validity of the employer's decision by making an application to the CAC. A voluntary recognition agreement may be terminated by either party at any time, without the need for the statutory procedure (so long as the CAC did not impose a method for collective bargaining in relation to that voluntary agreement).

Training

- A trade union that has been accorded recognition rights by the CAC in respect of a particular bargaining unit (and has adopted a method specified by the CAC for the conduct of collective bargaining) has the right to consult with their employer about his plans for training the workers within that bargaining unit (see page 626 below).

Earlier legislation

- Before Schedule A1 to the 1992 Act came into force, there were no statutory provisions for compulsory trade union recognition. Earlier statutory provisions in the Employment Protection Act 1975 were repealed by the Employment Act 1980 on 15 August 1980. Since then, collective bargaining agreements have been concluded on an entirely voluntary basis, with either party having the right to opt out on giving the appropriate or agreed period of notice.

- A number of statutory employment rights (eg, the right of trade union officials and members to a reasonable amount of paid or unpaid time off work, etc) hinges on their being officials or members of recognised independent trade unions. The same applies to a union's right to consult with employers concerning collective redundancies and 'relevant transfers' under the Transfer of Undertakings (Protection of Employment) Regulations 1981. Safety representatives, likewise, have no statutory right to perform their official functions unless the trade union that appointed them is a recognised independent trade union. An employer is not duty bound to disclose information to a trade union for the purposes of collective bargaining unless the union is a recognised independent trade union; and so on. Those rights (discussed elsewhere in this handbook) remain unaffected by the new statutory provisions.

The validity of a request for recognition

- Under the statutory recognition scheme, a trade union may submit a request for recognition to any employer in Great Britain who has 21 or more people on the payroll (including persons employed by an associated employer), or to any employer who has employed an average of 21 or more people over the previous 13 weeks. However, such a request will not be valid unless it:

  (a) is in writing (signed by one or more members (or an official) of the trade union in question);

      Note: Paragraph 9 of Schedule A1 to the 1992 Act permits the Secretary of State for Trade & Industry to make an order prescribing the form of requests for trade union recognition or the procedure for making them. Furthermore, the Schedule is silent as to whether a request for trade union recognition must be signed by a full-time trade union official or by the workers themselves. What is clear is that a request for recognition can only be made by workers who are themselves members of the union in question.

  (b) identifies the union making the request (which must be an 'independent' trade union);

      Note: A trade union is 'independent' if it has a certificate of independence issued by the Certification Officer in accordance with sections 2 to 9 of the 1992 Act, and that certificate has not been cancelled or withdrawn.

  (c) identifies the bargaining unit (or proposed bargaining unit), that is to say, the group or groups of workers the union wishes to represent in collective bargaining with the employer; and

(d) states that the request is made under Schedule A1 to the Trade Union & Labour Relations (Consolidation) Act 1992.

To determine whether an employer has 21 or more workers 'on the payroll', workers employed by any associated employer incorporated outside Great Britain must be ignored, unless they ordinarily work in Great Britain. A worker employed on board a ship registered under section 8 of the Merchant Shipping Act 1995 is to be treated as ordinarily working in Great Britain unless the ship is registered as belonging to a port outside Great Britain; or the employment is wholly outside Great Britain; or the worker is not ordinarily resident in Great Britain (*ibid.* paragraph 7(5)).

- A request for trade union recognition may be submitted by two or more trade unions acting in unison (or separately) in respect of two or more proposed bargaining units within the same organisation. For simplicity's sake, the legislation discussed in this section is in the context of one trade union applying for recognition in respect of one or more groups of employees (the 'bargaining unit').

Meaning of 'bargaining unit' and 'collective bargaining'

- Paragraphs 1 and 2 of Schedule A1 define the expression 'bargaining unit' (or 'proposed bargaining unit') as meaning the group or groups of workers on whose behalf a trade union is seeking recognition. 'Recognition' means recognition for the purposes of collective bargaining. In short, an independent trade union which is recognised by an employer (following a declaration to that effect by the CAC) has the statutory right to negotiate with that employer on matters relating to pay, working hours and holidays. It is, of course, open to the parties to agree to negotiate on other matters (eg, guarantee payments, sickness benefits, enhanced parental leave, etc) – whether the agreement is made before or after the Central Arbitration Committee (CAC) makes a declaration for trade union recognition (see below), or independently of any such declaration (*ibid.* paragraphs 1 and 2).

Note: For the purposes of Part I of Schedule A1 to the 1992 Act, the term 'collective bargaining' is restricted to negotiations in respect of pay, working hours and holidays. In short, the meaning of 'collective bargaining' given by section 178(1) of the 1992 Act does not apply to a declaration by the CAC that a trade union must be recognised by an employer for collective bargaining purposes. See also **Collective agreements** elsewhere in this handbook.

Voluntary or negotiated agreements

- Upon receiving a valid request for trade union recognition, an employer has 10 working days within which to accept it, ignore it or reject it. That period of 10 working days begins with the day following that on which the employer received that request.

- If the parties voluntarily agree a bargaining unit within those 10 working days and agree also that the union is to be recognised as entitled to conduct collective bargaining on behalf of that unit, the issue is settled. No further steps need be taken under Schedule Al to the 1992 Act. This rule also applies if a trade union has made an application to the CAC for compulsory recognition but withdraws that application before the CAC has declared automatic recognition or has notified the parties of its intention to arrange for a ballot (see below).

- If, on the other hand, the employer informs the union that he does not accept their request for recognition, but is willing to negotiate, the parties have a further 20 working days (30 in all) within which to reach agreement. However, there is nothing to prevent, the parties agreeing to conduct their negotiations over a longer period; the more so if the issues under discussion are likely to be complicated. If the parties reach agreement on recognition and on the composition of the bargaining unit within 20 working days (or within an agreed longer period), the trade union will be treated as recognised and no further steps are necessary under Schedule A1. It is then up to the parties to decide the scope and method of collective bargaining. During negotiations, both parties may invite the assistance of the Advisory, Conciliation & Arbitration Service (ACAS).

- If the negotiations fail, and there is no agreement before the end of the 20-day negotiating period (or within the longer agreed period), the union seeking recognition may apply to the Central Arbitration Committee (CAC) asking it to determine:

  (a) whether the proposed bargaining unit (or some other bargaining unit) is appropriate; and

  (b) whether the union has the support of a majority of the workers constituting the appropriate bargaining unit.

  If, on the other hand, the parties have agreed an appropriate bargaining unit, but have failed to reach agreement on the issue of recognition, the union may apply to the CAC to determine the question whether the union has the support of a majority of the workers constituting that bargaining unit.

- The CAC will decline to consider an application by a trade union in the circumstances described above if the evidence shows that the union had rejected (or failed to accept) a proposal by the employer that ACAS be invited to assist them with their negotiations – so long as the employer's proposal was made within the period of 10 working days beginning with the day following that on which the employer had indicated his willingness to negotiate.

Employer rejects request for trade union recognition

- If an employer ignores or rejects a valid request for trade union recognition (and has made it plain that he is unwilling to negotiate under any circumstances), the trade union may apply to the CAC to decide whether the proposed bargaining unit (or some other bargaining unit) is the appropriate bargaining unit; and whether the union in question has the support of a majority (more than 50 per cent) of the workers constituting the appropriate bargaining unit. The trade union must not submit its application to the CAC until 10 working days have elapsed (following the date on which the employer received their request for recognition).

'Preliminary tests' by the CAC

- Once the CAC has received and acknowledged a trade union's application for recognition (or for a decision concerning the appropriate bargaining unit) it must first decide (within the next 10 working days) whether the application is both valid and admissible. The 'validity test' was explained earlier in this section. To be admissible, the application must:

  (a) be made in such form as the CAC specifies; and

  (b) be supported by such documents as the CAC specifies.

  Furthermore, the trade union must have informed the employer of its decision to apply to the CAC and must have supplied the employer with a copy of its application and any supporting documents.

- Nor will the union's application be admissible unless the CAC is satisfied:

  (c) that at least 10 per cent of the workers constituting the proposed (or agreed) bargaining unit are members of the union in question;

  (d) that a majority of the workers constituting that proposed (or agreed) bargaining unit would be likely to favour recognition of the union as entitled to conduct collective bargaining on their behalf;

(e) that the application does not include any workers in the relevant bargaining unit in respect of whom the same union has already been recognised as being entitled to conduct collective bargaining (*unless* the matters in respect of which the union is entitled to conduct collective bargaining do not include pay, working hours or holidays);

(f) that the proposed bargaining unit does not overlap with another unit in respect of which the CAC has already accepted an application (ie, one or more workers apparently included in each of two or more bargaining units);

(g) that the application is not substantially the same as an application accepted by the CAC within the previous three years;

(h) that the application has not been made within three years of a previous declaration by the CAC that the union was *not* entitled to be recognised in respect of the same (or a substantially similar) bargaining unit;

(i) that the application has not been made within three years of the same union (or group of unions) having been derecognised in respect of the same (or substantially the same) bargaining unit; and

(j) (if the application has been made by two or more unions) that the unions will cooperate with each other in a manner likely to secure and maintain stable and effective collective bargaining arrangements, and show that they would be prepared also (if requested by the employer) to act together on behalf of the workers constituting the relevant bargaining unit (ie, to engage in single-table bargaining).

If the CAC accepts the union's application as being both valid and admissible, it must then proceed with that application.

- If the employer and the union have already agreed the bargaining unit, the CAC need do no more than determine the level of support for recognition. If the parties have not agreed a bargaining unit, the CAC must decide the appropriate bargaining unit before determining whether the majority of workers in that unit would be likely to favour recognition.

Acceptance of a trade union's application

- If the CAC proceeds with an application for trade union recognition, and is satisfied that a majority of the workers in the bargaining unit are members of the union in question, it must make a declaration that the union is recognised as entitled to conduct collective bargaining on behalf of the workers constituting the relevant bargaining unit, unless:

(a) satisfied that a secret ballot should nonetheless be held in the interests of good industrial relations; or

(b) a significant number of the union members within the bargaining unit inform the CAC that they do not want the union to conduct collective bargaining on their behalf; or

(c) evidence of trade union membership within the bargaining unit leads the CAC to conclude that there are doubts whether a significant number of the union members within that bargaining unit want the union to conduct collective bargaining on their behalf.

If none of conditions (a) to (c) in the preceding paragraph is met, the CAC must serve notice on the parties that it intends to hold a secret ballot of the workers in that bargaining unit. If, within the next 10 working days, the union asks the CAC not to conduct such a ballot (suspecting that it may not obtain a majority vote in favour of recognition) the CAC will take no further action and the union will *not* be recognised.

Conduct and outcome of a secret ballot for recognition

- If a secret ballot is to take place, the CAC must appoint a qualified independent person (a scrutineer) to conduct the ballot (eg, a person nominated by the Electoral Reform Society or a designated solicitor or accountant), and must inform the parties of the name of the person appointed, the period within which the ballot is to take place, and whether the ballot is to be a workplace or postal ballot (or a combination of both).

- The ballot must be conducted as quickly as possible, usually within 20 working days of the appointment of the independent scrutineer (or within such longer period as the CAC decides is appropriate, given the number and distribution of workers in the relevant bargaining unit). As indicated in the previous paragraph, the ballot may be held either at the workplace or by post (or by a combination of both methods (eg, if the workers are scattered throughout Great Britain or are 'on the road' or at sea at the time the ballot is to be held).

- Both the employer and the union (or unions) concerned must cooperate with the CAC in the conduct of the ballot and must share the costs.

The employer must (within 10 working days) supply the CAC with a list of the names and home addresses of the workers in the agreed or declared bargaining unit (but must not give that same information to the union). It must nonetheless allow the union reasonable access to all of those workers in that unit in order to solicit votes and ascertain their opinions. If asked to do so by the union, the independent scrutineer appointed by the CAC must send any pamphlets or other material to the home addresses of the workers entitled to vote in the ballot, provided the union bears all postage and other costs associated with sending that information to those workers.

- If the employer does not cooperate with the union(s) or with the independent scrutineer appointed to conduct the ballot, or denies the union reasonable access to the workers entitled to vote in the ballot, or is dilatory in supplying the CAC with the names and home addresses of the workers in the relevant bargaining unit, the CAC may order the employer to take the appropriate remedial steps with a specified period. Should the employer refuse or fail to comply with the order, the CAC may declare the union to be recognised; in which event it must take steps to cancel the ballot; or (if the ballot has already taken place) must ignore its outcome.

Ballot result

- Once the ballot has been held and the votes counted, the CAC must inform the employer and the union of the outcome. The CAC must declare the union to be recognised if, but only if, recognition was supported by a majority of those who voted in the ballot *and* by at least 40 per cent of those entitled to vote.

  For example, assume that the relevant bargaining unit comprises 100 workers, 60 of whom cast their votes in the ballot. If recognition is supported by 39 of those who voted, that would constitute a majority vote (65 per cent) in support of recognition but only by the workers who actually voted. But that does not amount to the required 40 per cent support amongst the 100 workers who were entitled to vote. In such a case, the CAC must declare that the trade union has not been recognised. If just one more worker had voted in favour of recognition, the outcome would have been different.

- If recognition is supported by a majority of those who voted in the ballot *and* by 40 per cent or more of those entitled to vote, the CAC must declare the trade union to be recognised as having collective bargaining rights in respect of the workers who comprise the relevant bargaining unit (limited to negotiations in relation to pay, working hours and holidays, although, as was indicated earlier in this section, there is nothing to prevent the parties agreeing to expand the scope of negotiations).

- If, within the next 30 working days, the parties are unable to agree on a method for conducting collective bargaining, they may ask the CAC to intervene. If there is no agreement within the next 20 working days, the CAC must specify the method for collective bargaining (unless the parties jointly and expressly ask it not to do so); but, again, that method will apply only to negotiations over pay, working hours and holidays, although the parties may agree to vary it to cover other matters as well.

- If the parties agree a method of collective bargaining (either with or without the assistance of the CAC), one of those parties may apply to CAC for help in brokering a second, more acceptable agreement. If the parties are still unable to agree, the CAC will impose a bargaining procedure.

- Any method of collective bargaining imposed by the CAC is legally binding on both the employer and the union, and may be enforced by a court order. A failure to comply with such an order (by either of the parties) will ordinarily constitute a contempt of court, with all that that entails.

No further application within three years

- Once an application for trade union recognition has been decided (eg, if there has been no CAC declaration for recognition), that decision may not be re-opened for another three years.

Training

- Once a trade union has been recognised by the CAC as having collective bargaining rights on behalf of a bargaining unit, and the CAC has specified a method for the conduct of such bargaining (unless the parties have varied or replaced that method or have agreed that the method is not to be legally enforceable), the employer must, from time to time, invite the trade union to send representatives to a meeting for the purpose of:

  (a) consulting about the employer's policy on training the workers within the bargaining unit;

  (b) consulting about his plans for training those workers within the period of six months following the date on which the meeting takes place; and

(c) reporting about the training provided for those workers since the previous meeting.

- Training meetings must be called at six-monthly intervals, starting with the date on which the CAC declaration for recognition was made. At least two weeks before each scheduled meeting, the employer must provide the trade union with any information it needs to enable it to participate fully in the meeting, save for:

  (a) information relating to a particular individual, unless the individual has consented to its being disclosed;

  (b) information communicated to the employer in confidence;

  (c) information whose disclosure would cause substantial injury to the employer's business interests (other than its effect on collective bargaining); or

  (d) information whose disclosure would be against the interests of national security or that the employer may not disclose without breaking the law or that has been obtained by the employer for the purposes of bringing, prosecuting or defending any legal proceedings.

  An employer must take account of any written representations about matters raised at a training meeting which he receives from the trade union within four weeks of the date on which the meeting took place (*ibid.* section 70B).

Complaint to an employment tribunal

- A trade union may present a complaint to an employment tribunal that an employer has failed to comply with his obligations (in relation to a bargaining unit) under section 70B of the 1992 Act. The complaint must be presented within three months of the employer's alleged failure.

- Should the trade union's complaint be upheld, the tribunal will make a declaration to that effect and may order the employer to pay up to two weeks' pay to each person who, at the time when the employer's failure occurred, was a member of the bargaining unit in question. For these purposes, the amount of a week's pay is subject to a maximum of £260 (2003/04) (*ibid.* section 70C).

Detrimental treatment of workers

- Part VIII of Schedule A1 to the 1992 Act cautions employers that a worker has the right not to be subjected to any detriment by any act (or by any deliberate failure to act) by his (or her) employer if the act or failure to act takes place because the worker:

(a) sought to prevent or secure trade union recognition; or

(b) supported or did not support his employer's proposal to recognise a trade union; or

(c) acted to prevent or secure the ending of collective bargaining arrangements, or indicated that he did or did not support the ending of those arrangements; or

(d) influenced or sought to influence the way in which fellow workers cast their votes in a CAC ballot relating to trade union recognition; or influenced or sought to influence other workers to vote or to abstain from voting in the ballot; or

(e) voted in such a ballot; or

(f) failed or declined (or proposed to fail or decline) to do any of the things referred to in paragraphs (a) to (e).

In other words, a worker must not be disciplined or otherwise victimised or punished (eg, forfeiture of an expected pay rise, or denial of opportunities for overtime, transfer, promotion, training, etc) for doing anything he (or she) is lawfully entitled to do in the context of a valid request (or an application to the CAC) for trade union recognition.

- On a successful complaint to an employment tribunal, the employer in question will be ordered to pay the worker such compensation as the tribunal considers 'just and equitable' in the circumstances, having regard to the infringement complained of and to any loss sustained by the complainant that is attributable to the employer's conduct or failure to act.

- A worker has no need to resign (or to terminate the contract under which he or she has been employed or engaged) in order to pursue a complaint of unlawful detrimental treatment. Nor are there any qualifying requirements in terms of age or length of service. However, the complaint must be presented within three months of the alleged detrimental treatment.

- A worker, who is not an employee, whose detrimental treatment effectively amounts to a dismissal, will be awarded compensation equivalent to the compensation he (or she) would have been awarded by an employment tribunal if, had he been an employee, he had successfully pursued a complaint of unfair dismissal against his former employer.

Dismissal of an employee

- A worker who is an employee, who has been dismissed (or selected for redundancy) for doing any of the things referred to in the previous paragraphs (relative to a request, or application to the CAC, for trade union recognition), may complain to an employment tribunal regardless of his (or her) age or length of service at the material tribunal. If such a complaint is upheld, the employer in question will be ordered to pay a substantial amount of compensation (as to which, please turn to the section titled **Dismissal** elsewhere in this handbook).

TRAINING OF EMPLOYEES

Key points

- Implicit in every contract of employment is the employer's duty to provide his employees with training sufficient to ensure that they carry out their duties safely and efficiently. Any employee injured in the course of his (or her) employment, as a direct consequence of his employer's negligence (including any failure to provide the proper degree of training necessary to minimise risks to health and safety), may sue the employer for damages in the ordinary courts.

  Note: It is for this reason that every employer carrying on any business in Great Britain has a duty, under the Employer's Liability (Compulsory Insurance) Act 1969, to insure against liability for bodily injury or disease sustained by his employees in the course of their employment. Furthermore, a copy of the certificate of insurance (or an extract from it) must be displayed at the employers place of business in a position where it can be easily seen and read by all his employees. If an employer does not insure his employees in accordance with the provisions of the 1969 Act, or does not display an up-to-date copy of the insurance certificate, he is guilty of an offence and is liable on conviction to a heavy fine. A leaflet (HSE 4), entitled *Short Guide to the Employer's Liability (Compulsory Insurance) Act* is available free of charge from HSE Books, PO Box 1999, Sudbury, Suffolk C010 6FS (Telephone: 01787 881165 or Fax: 01787 313995).

- Paragraphs 33 to 35 of the long-since-abandoned but nonetheless useful *Code of Industrial Relations Practice* cautioned that management should ensure that new employees are given induction training, including information about the main terms and conditions of their employment, disciplinary rules, etc as well as 'on the job' training designed to supplement previous education, training and experience. Young employees entering employment for the first time said the Code, must also receive broader initial training in the skills necessary to carry out their duties safely and without risks to health, plus training specific to the job that each has been employed to do. Any necessary further education and training should be provided where there is a significant change in job content; while employees should be encouraged to take advantage of relevant further education and training opportunities at all stages of their careers.

Health and Safety at Work etc Act 1974

- An employer who fails to discharge his duty under section 2(2)(c) of the Health and Safety at Work etc Act 1974, to provide such information, instruction, training and supervision as is necessary to ensure (so far as is reasonably practicable) the health and safety at work of his employees, is guilty of an offence and liable on summary conviction to a fine not exceeding £20,000; or, on conviction on indictment, to a fine of an unlimited amount (*ibid.* sections 2(2)(c) and 33(l)(a) and (1A)).

- It should be pointed out that an employer may be prosecuted under the 1974 Act whether or not an accident has occurred. A health and safety inspector may serve an improvement or (in extreme cases, a prohibition notice if he (or she) is less than happy with the standard of training provided by an employer or is worried about the ignorance displayed by employees whose work exposes them to hazardous substances. The penalty for failing to comply with the terms of an improvement or prohibition notice is a fine, on summary conviction, of up to £20,000; and, on conviction on indictment, in the case of a prohibition notice, a fine of an unlimited amount and/or imprisonment for a term not exceeding two years (*ibid.* section 33(l)(g) and (2A)).

Subordinate health and safety regulations

- Regulations made under (or saved by) the 1974 Act reinforce the general duty of employers to provide health and safety training. For example, regulation 13 of the Management of Health & Safety at Work Regulations 1999 – which apply to every workplace – warns that, when entrusting tasks to their employees, employers must take into account their capabilities as regards health and safety. Every employee, says regulation 13, must receive adequate health and safety training (a) when first recruited, (b) when exposed to new risks because of a promotion or transfer, and (c) when introduced to new working methods, equipment or technology. Furthermore, such training must take place during normal working hours, must be repeated as often as may be appropriate, and must be adapted to take account of any new or changed risks to the health and safety of the employees concerned. See also *Young persons* below.

- Similar provisions are to be found in hazard-specific regulations, including:

  - the Control of Asbestos at Work Regulations 2002;

  - the Electricity at Work Regulations 1989;

  - the Health & Safety (Display Screen Equipment) Regulations 1992;

  - the Control of Lead at Work Regulations 2002;

  - the Provision & Use of Work Equipment Regulations 1998;

  - the Control of Substances Hazardous to Health Regulations 2002; and

  - the Ionising Radiations Regulations 1999.

The penalty for a breach of these provisions is a fine, on summary conviction, of up to £5,000 or, on conviction on indictment, a fine of an unlimited amount (as laid down in section 33(l)(c) and (3) of the 1974 Act).

Young persons

- Regulation 19 of the Management of Health & Safety at Work Regulations 1999 (*qv*) states that any young person under 18 recruited by an employer to carry out work regarded as harmful, damaging or dangerous to young persons must be given 'comprehensible and relevant' information about any associated risks to their health and safety.

- That information (ideally complemented by training, whether formal or on-the-job) must include information about the steps taken by the employer to eliminate or minimise the risks to the young person's health and safety, the protective clothing and equipment which the young person must wear or use, the safety procedures and rules he or she must follow, the names of the competent persons appointed by the employer to implement and oversee emergency evacuation procedures, and the measures taken within the employer's premises to comply with the requirements and prohibitions imposed by the relevant health and safety legislation.

  Note: Under the Management of Health & Safety at Work Regulations 1999 (*qv*), an employer may not lawfully employ a young person under 18 in his (or her) premises unless and until he has made a suitable and sufficient assessment of risks confronting young persons while they are at work.

Safety representatives and representatives of employee safety

- Safety representatives (appointed by a recognised independent trade union) and *representatives of employee safety* (elected by their peers) have the right to be permitted reasonable paid time off work both to carry out their functions and to enable them to attend relevant safety training courses (at their employer's expense), as to which see **Time off work: safety representatives** elsewhere in this handbook.

Fire Precautions Act 1971

- A fire certificate issued under the aegis of the Fire Precautions Act 1971 ordinarily imposes a duty on the occupier or owner of the relevant premises to provide his employees with instruction and training appropriate to their responsibilities in the event of an emergency. Records of training provided and received (giving dates and names) must be maintained and kept available for inspection by an inspector of the fire authority.

- A person who contravenes any requirement of a fire certificate is guilty of an offence and liable on summary conviction to a fine not exceeding £2,000; or, on conviction on indictment, to a fine of an unlimited amount (section 7(4) and (5)).

- Regulation 4(2) of the Fire Precautions (Workplace) Regulations 1997 (as amended) cautions that an employer (or other person having control of an excepted workplace) must anticipate the possibility of a fire and consider how best to deal with it. He or she must develop and disseminate fire-fighting and evacuation procedures, inform and train employees, carry out regular fire drills, nominate and train a sufficient number of employees to oversee fire-fighting and evacuation procedures, and liaise with local emergency services, particularly as regards rescue work and firefighting (*ibid.* regulation 4(2)).

First aid

- Under the Health & Safety (First Aid) Regulations 1981, employers with 150 or more persons on the payroll must appoint one or more trained first-aiders (in the ratio of one first-aider to every 150 persons employed) to administer first aid when required and to take charge in an emergency. When deciding just how many trained first-aiders are needed in his establishment, an employer must ensure that there is adequate first aid coverage at all times when employees are at work. If there are two shifts (including night shifts), there must be two trained first-aiders on duty at the same (plus two persons nominated by the employer to take charge if one or other of those first-aiders is temporarily absent from work). An employer who refuses or neglects to comply with his duties under the 1981 Regulations is guilty of an offence under the 1974 Health & Safety at Work Act, and is liable to prosecution and a heavy fine if convicted.

Food Safety (General Food Hygiene) Regulations 1995

- The Food Safety (General Food Hygiene) Regulations 1995 impose a great many duties on food manufacturers, and on caterers, licensees, proprietors, supervisors and employees in restaurants, cafes, dining-rooms, staff and works canteens, pubs, bars, kitchens, stores, schools, hospitals, supermarkets, delicatessens, and the like, where food and/or drink intended for human consumption are manufactured, prepared, processed, handled, sold or supplied.

- Thus, food and drink must be protected from contamination. Food and drink handlers (such as factory operatives, counter attendants waiters and waitresses, chefs, cooks, kitchen porters, storemen, etc) must observe a high standard of personal cleanliness, must refrain from smoking while carrying out their duties, must cover or bandage open cuts and abrasions, must report to their supervisor or manager if they are suffering from (or are the carriers of) certain infections, must wash their hands after using the lavatory, and so on. All of which imposes a heavy responsibility, not only on the employees themselves, but more particularly on the management of the establishment in which they are working. It is, the manager's duty (under Chapter X of Schedule 1 to the 1995 Regulations) to ensure that food handlers receive adequate instruction and training, and that they are familiar with their obligations under those Regulations.

- Regulation 6 (*ibid.*) cautions that a person carrying on a 'food business' (which expression applies to premises in which food or drink is prepared, processed, manufactured, packaged, stored, transported, distributed, handled or offered for sale or supply) will be guilty of an offence if he fails to take all reasonable steps to secure the compliance by any person employed by him or under his control with his or her statutory duties. The penalty on summary conviction is a fine of up to £5,000 or, on conviction on indictment, a fine of an unlimited amount and/or imprisonment for a term not exceeding two years.

Training the allegedly incompetent employee

- If an employee is dismissed for alleged incompetence, the determination of the question whether the dismissal was fair or unfair will depend on whether, in the circumstances (including the size and administrative resources of the employer's undertaking), the employer had acted reasonably or unreasonably in treating lack of capability as a sufficient reason for dismissing the employee; and that question will be determined in accordance with equity and the substantial merits of the case (section 98, Employment Rights Act 1996).

- Case law has long since demonstrated that an employer's failure to train an allegedly incompetent employee, or to provide him (or her) with any advice or assistance before the decision was taken to dismiss him (the more so if he has a good service record and has but recently been transferred or promoted to an unfamiliar job, department or location), could lead to a finding of unfair dismissal. For further particulars, please turn to the section titled **Dismissal for incompetence** elsewhere in this handbook.

  See also **Induction training** and **Time off for study or training**.

TRANSFER OF UNDERTAKINGS

Key points

- Far and away the most controversial legislation to appear in the UK in the past 20 years has been the Transfer of Undertakings (Protection of Employment) Regulations 1981. The TUPE Regulations (so-called) – which came into force on 1 May 1982, implementing Council Directive 77/187/EEC of 14 February 1977 (the 'Acquired Rights' Directive) – protect the rights of employees when the undertaking (company, firm, trade or business) for which they work (or part of that undertaking) is sold or transferred as a 'going concern' to another employer. The 1981 Regulations have been amended on a number of occasions, while the parent directive was itself amended by a new Directive (98/50/EC) adopted on 29 June 1998. The provisions of both the original and amending Directives have since been consolidated in a further Directive (2001/23/EC) adopted on 12 March 2001. The UK (along with other EU Member States) had until 17 July 2001 in which to bring into force the regulations and administrative provisions necessary to comply with amending Directive 98/50/EC. But, while the Department of Trade & Industry published a consultation document in September 2001, outlining its proposals for reform of the TUPE Regulations, draft amending legislation has yet to appear (see *Future developments* at the end of this section).

- The TUPE Regulations apply to the transfer of a UK-based undertaking (or part of such an undertaking) from one person to another – whether effected by sale or by some other disposition (other than by the sale of shares), or by operation of law. Such a transfer (which may be effected by a series of two or more transactions, and may take place whether or not any property is transferred) is referred to in the Regulations as a 'relevant transfer'; and it is the meaning of that expression which has produced so many confusing and contradictory decisions in the courts (see *Meaning of 'relevant transfer'*, paras 17.30 to 17.41 below). The expression 'undertaking' includes any trade or business (Reg. 2).

- The person selling or disposing of his (or her) business (the seller) is referred to as the 'transferor'; while the person to whom the business is sold (the purchaser) is known as the 'transferee'.

Note: If the receiver, administrator or liquidator of a company which has gone into receivership or liquidation (or which is voluntarily wound-up by its creditors) transfers the company's undertaking, or part of the company's undertaking, to a wholly-owned subsidiary of the company, the 'relevant transfer' will be deemed not to have been effected until immediately before the transferee company ceases (otherwise than by reason of its being wound up) to be a wholly-owned subsidiary of the transferor company, or until immediately before the relevant undertaking is transferred by the transferee company to another person, whichever occurs first. For the purposes of the TUPE Regulations, the transfer of the relevant undertaking will be taken to have been effected immediately before that date by one transaction only (Reg. 4).

TUPE Regulations summarised

- When a TUPE transfer occurs, the transferee (the buyer) inherits the contracts of employment of the persons employed by the transferor (the seller) immediately before the transfer took place. In short, those contracts of employment do not come to an end (as they might other-wise have done under the common law) but are treated in law as if they had originally been made between the affected employees and the transferee. So, if food manufacturer A sells one of his (or her) factories to food manufacturer B, as a going concern, food manufacturer B inher-its the contracts of employment of every person employed in that factory (and their rights under those contracts) (*ibid.* regulation 5).

- A transferee who inherits the contracts of employment of persons employed in the undertaking immediately before the 'relevant transfer', (see paras 17.30 to 17.42 below) also inherits the transferor's rights, powers, duties and liabilities (including liability for redundancy payments, money in lieu of notice, compensation for unfair dismissal, subsisting allegations of sex discrimination, monies owed to employees, etc, but *not* any criminal liabilities) under, or in connection with, those contracts. Furthermore, anything done by the transferor *before* the transfer takes place, in or in relation to any such contract (or to a person employed in the undertaking in question), is deemed in law to have been done by the transferee.

- Once a 'relevant transfer' has taken place it is not open to the transferee to presume to vary the contracts of employment of the transferred employees with a view to harmonising their working hours, rates of pay, holiday entitlement, etc with those of his existing workforce. Nor may the transferee insert fresh terms, such as a restrictive covenant, in the transferred employees contracts (*Credit Suisse First Boston (Europe) Limited v Padiachy* [1998] IRLR 504, QBD; *Credit Suisse First Boston (Europe) Limited v Lister* [1998] IRLR 700, CA). This rule applies even if the employees in question are happy to accept any such variation in their terms and conditions of employment and are no worse off as a result of that variation (*Foreningen af Arbejdsledere i Danmark v Daddy's Dance Hall A/S* [1988] IRLR 315 and *Rask v ISS Kantineservice A/S* [1993] IRLR 133)). In the *Wilson/Bexendale* case (see next paragraph) Lord Slynn of Hadley opined (*obiter*) that any variation of the terms of an employee's contract, which is due to a TUPE transfer and for no other reason, is invalid. There can, however, be a valid variation, he said, for reasons that are not due to the transfer. 'It may be difficult' he concluded 'to decide whether the variation is due to the transfer or attributable to some separate cause, but there may come a time when the link with the transfer is broken or can be treated as no longer effective'.

- In *Wilson v St Helen's Borough Council/BFL v Baxendale & Meade* [1998] IRLR 706), the House of Lords held that a dismissal for a reason connected with a TUPE transfer (whether by the transferor or the transferee), while automatically unfair (unless for an ETO reason), is nonetheless legally effective and not a nullity – thereby overruling the Court of Appeal on that same point [1997] IRLR 505. An employee dismissed by a transferor cannot compel the transferee to employ him. Under English domestic law, said their Lordships, the dismissal of an employee by an employer brings to an end the working relationship between them. As a general rule, the English courts will not specifically enforce contracts of employment. If a dismissal is in breach of contract, the employee can claim damages for wrongful dismissal. If it is unfair, the employee may seek redress from an employment tribunal; in which event, the employer will be ordered either to reinstate or re-engage the dismissed employee and/or pay a substantial amount of compensation. But, save for the purpose of enforcing rights under it, the contract of employment is gone. As was indicated earlier, a transferee who does not take on the transferor's employees – because they have already been dismissed by the transferor or by the transferee himself – must, nonetheless, meet all the transferor's contractual and statutory obligations in relation to those employees, including a liability to pay damages for wrongful dismissal and/or compensation for unfair dismissal.

- All of which suggests that the only way a transferee can legitimately vary the terms of conditions of incoming TUPE-transferred employees is to dismiss them all (which dismissals will be automatically unfair if not for an ETO reason involving changes in the workforce) and then offer to re-engage some or all of them on a terms and conditions which they may or may not find acceptable. By any measure, this 'take it or leave it' option (and a willingness to pay compensation for unfair dismissal) cannot be in the interest of good industrial relations practice nor preferable to a negotiated and consensual variation in the terms and conditions of incoming employees.

- In the joined cases of *Bernadone v Pall Mall Services Group & Others* and *Martin v Lancashire County Council)* [2000] IRLR 487, the Court of Appeal held that the liabilities inherited by a transferee under TUPE include any and all liabilities of the transferor in tort. Although tortious liabilities do not arise 'under' the contract of employment, they do arise 'in connection with' the contract, given that the employer's common law duty of care arises out of the relationship of employer and employee. In short, an employee injured in the course of his (or her) employment with the transferor (his former employer) may nonetheless sue the transferee (his new employer) for damages in negligence. However, the former employer's right to an indemnity under his (or her) employer's liability insurance policy also transfers to the new employer. In other words, it is the transferor's insurers, not the transferee's, who must pay any damages awarded by the court in such circumstances.

- A transferee does *not*, however, inherit any term in an employee's contract of employment which relates to an occupational pension scheme as defined in section 1 of the Pension Schemes Act 1993 (but see *Future developments* at the end of this section).

- The phrase 'immediately before the transfer' is given a wide interpretation. It covers any person in the employ of the vendor who is dismissed in consequence of the proposed sale, whether or not negotiations for the sale had been completed or a buyer identified. It could apply where a liquidator trims the workforce before seeking purchasers to make a business more attractive, but not where he (or she) has run out of work and there is a true redundancy situation (*P Bork International A/S v Foreningen af Arbejdsledere i Danmark* [1989] IRLR 41, ECJ; *Litster v Forth Estuary Engineering Ltd* [1989] ICR 341, HL; and *Wendleboe v L J Music Aps* [1985] ECR 457, ECJ).

An employee's refusal to transfer

- There is no transfer of a contract of employment (or of the rights, powers, duties and liabilities under, or in connection with, that contract) if the employee in question informs the transferor (or the transferee) that he (or she) objects to becoming employed by the transferee (*ibid*. regulation 5(4A)).

- An employee who refuses to work for the new owner of his (or her) former employer's business, for whatever reason, effectively brings his contract of employment to an end. In short, the termination of his employment does not amount to a dismissal in law and the employee has no right to complain of unfair dismissal, regardless of his (or her) length of service at the material time (*ibid*. regulation 5(4B)) (*Katsikas v Konstantinidis* [1993] IRLR 179, ECJ).

- However, a substantial and detrimental change in the employee's working conditions immediately before the transfer might well amount to so serious a repudiation of his contract as to entitle him to resign (with or without notice) and pursue a complaint of unfair constructive dismissal (*ibid*. regulation 5(5)). That right would nonetheless be denied him if he had not been continuously employed for at least one year and was under normal retiring age at the effective date of termination of his contract of employment.

- In *Hay v George Hanson (Building Contractors) Ltd* [1996] IRLR 427, the Employment Appeal Tribunal said that an employee who had expressed unhappiness about the prospect of working for the transferee could not be said to have objected to (or refused) the transfer. Although the TUPE Regulations are not specific on this point, an employee who refuses outright to transfer should inform his (or her) employer in clear and unequivocal terms (whether by word or deed, or by a combination of the two) that he refuses to work for the transferor.

Effect of transfer on collective agreements

- If, at the time of the 'relevant transfer', the transferor has a collective agreement with a recognised trade union in respect of any employee whose contract is inherited by the transferee, the transferee inherits that collective agreement in respect of that same employee (and the rights and obligations that go with it) as if it had been made between himself (or herself) and the trade union in question (*ibid.* regulation 6).

  The transferee does *not*, however, inherit any term in a collective agreement as relates to an occupational pension scheme as defined in section 1 of the Pensions Act 1993.

Dismissal of employee because of relevant transfer

- If, either before or after the 'relevant transfer', the transferor (or the transferee) dismisses any employee of the transferor (or of the transferee) for a reason in any way linked to the transfer itself, the employee in question will be treated in law as having been unfairly dismissed. The only justification for such a dismissal would be an 'economic, technical or organisational reason entailing changes in the workforce' – often referred to as an 'ETO' reason – which, if genuine, will be treated by an employment tribunal as having been for 'some other substantial reason' of a kind such as to justify the dismissal of an employee holding the position which that employee held (*ibid.* regulation 8).

- In short, an employer (transferor or transferee) will need to justify his (or her) decision to dismiss one or more of the employees affected by the transfer on grounds which have nothing whatsoever to do with the transfer (eg misconduct) or for a genuine ETO reason involving changes in the workforce. For example, it is arguably absurd (in a situation in which an undertaking or part of an undertaking is absorbed within the transferee's organisation) for the transferee to be left with a duplicated management team (two marketing managers, two chief accountants, two personnel managers, etc), and (say) a hundred or more production workers (when he only needs 60) without being able to make the appropriate organisational changes. If he (or she) has a highly sophisticated production process requiring far fewer workers, logic dictates that a number of workers will have to be made redundant. If the transferee can justify those redundancies (and the redundancy selection process) on purely business grounds (ie an ETO reason), the dismissals are likely to be held fair.

- Curiously, an employee dismissed in consequence of a 'relevant transfer' does not qualify to present a complaint of unfair dismissal unless continuously employed for a minimum period of one or more years ending with the effective date of termination of his (or her) contract of employment and under 'normal retiring age' at that time (*ibid.* regulation 8(5)).

Effect of relevant transfer on trade union recognition

- If, after a 'relevant transfer' the undertaking (or part of the undertaking) transferred maintains an identity distinct from the remainder of the transferee's undertaking, any independent trade union recognised to any extent (or for any purpose) by the transferor shall be deemed to be recognised to that same extent (or purpose) by the transferee. If the transferred undertaking does *not* maintain an identity distinct from the remainder of the transferee's undertaking, but is simply absorbed within the latter undertaking, the recognition agreement no longer applies.

Duty to inform and consult representatives

- A 'relevant transfer' will inevitably impact on persons employed by both the transferor and transferee. Many will simply be concerned to know what effect the transfer is likely to have on their jobs, prospects or continued employment. To allay such concerns, the Regulations require both the transferor *and* the transferee, first, to inform the 'appropriate representatives' about the transfer and, second, consult them and listen to their representations.

- First, the representatives must be informed of:

    (a) the fact that the relevant transfer is to take place, when, approximately, it is to take place, and the reasons for it;

    (b) the legal, economic and social implications of the transfer for all affected employees;

    (c) the measures which the employer envisages will, in connection with the transfer, be taken in relation to those employees or, if it is envisaged that no measures will be so taken, that fact; and

    (d) if the employer is the transferor, the measures which the transferee envisages he (or she) will, in connection with the transfer, take in relation to such of those employees whose contracts of employment he will inherit after the transfer or, if he envisages that no measures will be taken, that fact.

The information in (a) to (d) must be conveyed to the 'appropriate representatives' long enough before the relevant transfer to enable them to take an active part in the subsequent consultations. To that same end, the transferee must likewise give the transferor advance information about his (or her) own intentions under (d) above.

- The term 'appropriate representatives' means employee representatives elected by the employees themselves or, if the employees are of a description in respect of which an independent trade union is recognised by the employer, representatives of that trade union (eg shop stewards). In an undertaking in which there are both employee-elected and trade-union appointed representatives, the employee must deal with those trade union representatives. If there is no trade union representing the interests of the affected employees (that is to say, the employees who may be affected by the transfer or may be affected by measures taken in connection with it) the employer must consult either with existing employee-elected representatives (who may have been elected for other purposes) or invite the affected employees to elect one or more of their number to represent their interests in consultations relating to the proposed transfer. If there are no elected employee representatives, the employers on both sides must invite the affected employees to elect one or more of their number to be representatives and give them sufficient time to carry out the election and to complete it *before* the information and consultation process takes place (*ibid*. regulation 10 & 10A).

  Note: When overseeing the election of employee representatives, the employer must do whatever is necessary to ensure that the election is fair. Although the employer has the right to decide on the appropriate number of representatives, he (or she) cannot presume to dictate which employees can put their names forward as candidates and which cannot. The employer must also allow the affected employees sufficient time to cast their votes *in secret*, and must see to it that the votes given at the election are accurately counted (*ibid*. regulation 10A)).

- Second, if either the transferor or transferees envisage taking (unspecified) measures in relation to any employees affected by the transfer, he (or she) must consult with the appropriate representatives with a view to seeking their agreement to those measures. During, the consultation process, the transferor or transferee must (a) consider any representations made by those representatives, (b) reply to those representations, and (c), if he rejects any of those representations, give his reasons for doing so. Before, during and after such consultations, the employer in question must allow those representatives access to the affected employees and provide whatever accommodation and facilities they may need in that respect (eg an office, tables and chairs and, perhaps, use of a telephone).

Penalties for failure to inform or consult

- An appropriate representative (or in the case of a trade union-appointed representative, the union in question) or one or more of the affected employees may complain to an employment tribunal that their employer had refused or failed to inform or consult them about the 'relevant transfer'. Such a complaint must be presented within the period of three months beginning with the date on which the relevant transfer took place. If the complaint is upheld, the tribunal will order the respondent employer to pay the complainant/s an appropriate amount of compensation; in short, such sum not exceeding 13 weeks' pay as the tribunal considers just and equitable having regard to the seriousness of the employer's failure to inform or consult. A complaint presented 'out of time' will not be entertained unless the tribunal is satisfied that it was not reasonably practicable for the applicant to have done so within that prescribed three-month period.

- A failure to pay the compensation referred to in the preceding paragraph will lead to a further complaint to a tribunal and to an order directing the employer to pay the relevant amount (*ibid.* regulation 11, as amended by the Collective Redundancies & Transfer of Undertakings (Protection of Employment) (Amendment) Regulations 1999 (SI 1999.1925)).

- An employer may defend his (or her) failure to comply with the duty to inform and consult if he can satisfy a tribunal that there were special circumstances which rendered it not reasonably practicable for him to do so, but that he took all such steps towards the performance of that duty as were reasonably practicable in those circumstances. However, it is no defence for the employer to argue (as transferor) that he (or she) was prevented from complying fully with his duty to inform the appropriate representatives because of the transferee's refusal or failure to provide the information referred to earlier in this section. If, on the other hand, the transferor has given notice to the transferee that he intends to show that fact, the giving of that notice will make the transferee a party to the proceedings (and liable in his turn to pay the whole or part of any award of compensation).

Restriction on contracting out

- Any provision of any agreement (whether a contract of employment or otherwise) will be void in so far as it purports to exclude or limit the operation of the TUPE Regulations or to preclude any person from presenting a complaint to an employment tribunal arising out of an employer's failure to inform or consult the appropriate representatives about the transfer (*ibid*. regulation 12).

* In *Thompson & Others v (1) Walon Car Delivery, (2) BRS Automotive Ltd*, EAT/256/96, the EAT held that a 'compromise agreement' concluded with the transferor several days after a 'relevant transfer', and purporting to exclude the right of an employee to bring proceedings under TUPE, could not be relied upon by the transferee.

Excluded classes

* Regulations 8, 10 & 11 of the TUPE Regulations do not apply to employees who, under their contracts of employment, ordinarily work outside the United Kingdom. A person employed to work on board a UK-registered ship is regarded as a person who ordinarily works in the UK unless the employment is wholly outside the UK or he (or she) is not ordinarily resident in the UK.

  Note: Regulation 8 relates to the dismissal of an employee because of a relevant transfer; regulation 10, to an employer's duty to inform and consult the appropriate representatives; and regulation 11, to the consequences of an employer's failure to inform and consult.

Meaning of 'relevant transfer'

* There has to be a 'transfer from one person to another'. The European Court of Justice (ECJ) has held that the Acquired Rights Directive provides protection where there is a change in the natural or legal person responsible for the running of an undertaking (*Landorganisationen i Danmark v Ny Molle Kro* [1989] ICR 330, ECJ), a view endorsed by the ECJ in (amongst others) *Dr Sophie Redmond Stichting v Bartol & Others* [1992] IRLR 366 and *Rask & Christensen v ISS Kantineservice A/S* [1993] IRLR 133.

* There has to be a transfer of a 'going concern' or an economic entity, so that the purchaser can carry on the business without interruption. It does not matter that there are modifications. Goodwill is often included but is not essential. Where there was a change of tenants at a public house owned by a brewery it was held that continuity was preserved for an employee who worked there. The new tenant had been put in possession of a going concern and was running the same business as that run by his predecessor (See *JMA Spijkers v Gebroers Benedik Abbatoir CV & Another* [1986] 2 CMLR 296 ECJ; *Kenny & Another v South Manchester College* [1993] IRLR 265, QBD; *McLellan v Cody & Cody*, 7 October 1986, EAT Oct. 7, 1986, EAT; and *Safebid Ltd v Ramiro & Others*, 3 May 1990, EAT).

- But where a firm holding a catering concession prematurely stopped running the business, which was then carried on temporarily with a different sort of catering facility by the company that had granted the concession, the EAT held that this was not a 'relevant transfer' within the meaning of the 1981 Regulations (*Caterleisure Ltd v TGWU & Others*, 14 October 1991, EAT).

- Where it is shown, on the other hand, that, shortly after the sale, the employees were re-engaged by the transferee, the Regulations would probably bite. A business was put out to tender. The company that previously ran it lost the contract to a competitor. That other company engaged nearly all the former employees who were previously engaged in the business. It was held that the 1981 Regulations applied (*Harrison Bowden Ltd v Bowden* [1994] ICR 186, EAT; and *Dines & Others v Initial Health Care Services Ltd & Another* [1994] IRLR 336, CA).

- The possible permutations are endless, but there have been several important rulings on what is meant by and what are the consequences of the TUPE Regulations. The tribunals and courts must apply a purposive construction to the relevant provisions so as to achieve what they are manifestly intended to achieve (*Marleasing SA v La Comercial Internacional de Alimentacion* [1990] ECR 4153, ECJ).

- It matters not how many transfers take place or between whom, provided that there is an economic entity in existence that the final employer carries on in some capacity, eg as purchaser of the business, or as franchisee or licensee (*Foreningen af Arbejdsledere i Danmark v Daddy's Dance Hall A/S* [1988] IRLR 315, ECJ; and *LMS Drains Ltd & Metro-Rod Services Ltd v Waugh*, 6 June 1991, EAT).

The 'Spijkers' test

- In *Spijkers v Gebroeders Benedik Abbatoir CV* [1986] 2 CMLR 486, the ECJ held that the decisive criterion for establishing the existence or otherwise of a TUPE transfer (or 'relevant transfer') is whether the undertaking (or part of the undertaking) transferred retains its identity after the change of ownership. In other words, are the activities or the nature of the trade or business carried on (or resumed) by the transferee essentially or identifiably the same as those carried on by the transferor before the transfer took place. The ECJ in *Spijkers* listed a number of factors to be taken into account in deciding whether these conditions are fulfilled:

  (a) the type of undertaking (trade or business) in question and the activities carried on by that business;

(b) whether or not tangible assets (including furniture and equipment, raw materials, stock in hand, finished products, and the like) were transferred to the new owner of the business;

(c) the value of intangible assets (such as 'goodwill') at the time of the alleged transfer;

(d) whether or not the majority of persons working in the business were taken over by the new employer;

(e) whether the new owner continued to do business with the same customers or clientele after the alleged transfer took place;

(f) the degree of similarity between the activities carried on before and after the transfer, and the period (if any) for which those activities are suspended.

Finally, it is for the national court to make the necessary factual appraisal, in order to establish where or not a TUPE transfer had occurred.

- The fact that an activity (i) was only ancillary, (ii) the business transferred only involved one person and (iii) there was no transfer of any tangible assets could not deprive an employee from the protection of the Regulations (*Christel Schmidt v Spar-undLeihkasse der früheren Amter Bordesholm, Kiel und Cronshagen, The Times*, 25 May 1994, ECJ).

The 'Süzen' and related cases

- In *Rygaard v Stro Molle Akustik* [1996] IRLR 151, the ECJ held that a transfer must involve the transfer of a 'stable economic entity'. But, the 'cat was set amongst the pigeons' (so to speak) in *Ayse Süzen v Zehnacker Gebïudereinguing GmbH Krankenhausservice & Lefarth GmbH* [1997] IRLR 255, when the ECJ ruled that, in the case of a 'second generation transfer', an activity does not of itself constitute such an entity. There would, they said, have to be a significant transfer of assets and a transfer of the majority of skilled workers from one contractor to the next before such a transfer could be held to be a 'relevant transfer' within the meaning of the 1981 Regulations. In the *Süzen* case, a cleaner who worked at a school in Germany, was dismissed (along with seven of her colleagues) by the cleaning company by whom she was employed when the latter lost its cleaning contract at the school. The contract was awarded to another cleaning company. The ECJ held (following the opinion of the Advocate-General) that a change of contractors does not qualify as a 'relevant transfer' unless significant tangible or intangible assets (or a majority of the workforce in terms of numbers and skills) also transfers to the second (or new) contractor. In labour-intensive undertakings (such as contract catering or cleaning), where there are no significant assets, there will not a transfer within the meaning of the TUPE Regulations unless a majority of the former contractor's workforce is taken on by the new contractor.

- Following swiftly on the heels of the *Süzen* decision came the decision on 26 March 1997 of the Court of Appeal in *Betts v Brintel Helicopters Limited and KLM Era Helicopters* [1997] IRLR 361. In the *Betts* case, Brintel Helicopters had a contract to 'ferry' men and equipment to and from a number of North Sea oil rigs owned by Shell. When Brintel's contract expired, the contract was awarded to KLM Era Helicopters who did not (nor needed to) take on any of Brintel's staff or equipment. The Court agreed with *Süzen* and held that the changeover of contractors did not constitute a 'relevant transfer'.

- *Süzen* was applied by the ECJ in *Francisco Hernández Vidal v Gomez Perez & Others* [1999] IRLR 132 and, again, in *Sanchez Hidalgo & Others v Asociación de Servicios Aser & Sociedad Cooperativa Minerva* [1999] IRLR 136. In the *Hernández Vidal* case, the ECJ held that a situation in which an organisation terminates its contract with a cleaning firm and decides to do its own cleaning would be covered by the 'Acquired Rights' Directive, so long as the operation is accompanied by the transfer of an economic entity between the last two undertakings. However, 'the mere fact that the maintenance work carried out, first, by the cleaning firm and then by the undertaking owning the premises, is similar, does not justify the conclusion that a transfer of such an entity has occurred'. And again: 'In certain sectors such as cleaning, the activity is essentially based on manpower. Thus, an organised grouping of wage earners, who are specifically and permanently assigned to a common task, may, in the absence of other factors of production, amount to an economic entity – a view repeated by the ECJ in the *Sanchez Hidalgo* case which was decided on a similar set of circumstances. In short, it is for the national court to determine whether the maintenance of the premises which awarded the contract was organised in the form of an economic activity within the outside cleaning firm before the firm awarding the contract decided to carry out the work itself.

- However, in *ECM (Vehicle Delivery Service) Limited v Cox* [1999] IRLR 416, the Court of Appeal (while distinguishing *Süzen* and cases like it, for reasons which are far from clear, given their similarity) held that an employer could not prevent the 1981 Regulations applying simply by refusing to take on the putative transferee's employees. Indeed, said the Court, an employment tribunal had every right to challenge those motives before deciding whether a TUPE transfer had in fact occurred.

Comment

- Over the years, the tribunals and courts have delivered a number of seemingly inconsistent (it not wholly contradictory) decisions on the interpretation of the 1981 Regulations. The old adage holds true: that each case must be decided on its particular merits – which is, of course, of little comfort to employers who (short of seeking an opinion from a tribunal or court) are left to decide for themselves whether their activities (notably the termination or non-renewal of cleaning, maintenance and related contracts, or the outsourcing of some of their operations, eg, payroll services) fall within the scope of the TUPE Regulations.

For further references in this handbook to the TUPE Regulations (and there are many) please consult the **Index**.

Future developments

- In September 2001, the Department of Trade & Industry (DTI) published a consultation document outlining the Government's proposals for reform of the TUPE Regulations in keeping with the provisions of the amending 'Acquired Rights Directive' (98/50/EC) adopted by the European Parliament and Commission on 29 June 1998. The proposals include the introduction of clearer rules on contracting-out and service provision transfers for public and private sectors alike; better protection for occupational schemes on transfer; more flexibility in applying existing insolvency rules to employers who might otherwise be prepared to acquire an insolvent employer's business; clarification of the rules concerning transfer-related dismissals and the circumstances in which a transferred employee's terms and conditions of employment may or may not be changed; and the imposition of a duty on transferors to give prospective purchasers advance written notification of all the rights and obligations in relation to employees who are likely to be transferred when the acquisition takes place, as well as a duty to write to the purchaser again giving details of any changes in those rights and obligations between the time of the earlier notification and the completion of the transfer. In an earlier consultation document, the DTI also proposed giving employers contemplating the sale or purchase of a business to obtain fast-track access to the employment tribunals for guidance on whether the intended purchase or sale is likely to constitute a 'relevant transfer' within the meaning of the TUPE Regulations. Although legislation implementing Council Directive 98/50/EC should have been introduced by mid-2001, no draft amending legislation has as yet been published. Copies of the consultation document (*Transfer of Undertakings (Protection of Employment)*

Regulations 1981 (TUPE): Government proposals for reform) can be obtained from the DTI's Publications Orderline on 0870 1502 500 (Fax: 0870 1502 333) or may be accessed and downloaded from website www.fti.gov.uk/er/tupe/longconsult.pdf.

V

VICTIMISATION

Key points

- Legislation nowadays protects employees who are victimised, harassed, penalised or subjected to any other detriment by any act (or any deliberate failure to act) by their employers for exercising (or proposing to exercise) certain of their statutory rights in employment.

- The relevant provisions are to be found in

  (a) the Sex Discrimination Act 1975;

  (b) the Race Relations Act 1976;

  (c) the Trade Union & Labour Relations (Consolidation) Act 1992;

  (d) the Disability Discrimination Act 1995;

  (e) the Employment Rights Act 1996 (as amended);

  (f) the Working Time Regulations 1998;

  (g) the National Minimum Wage Act 1998;

  (h) the Tax Credits Act 2002;

  (i) the Part-time Workers (Prevention of Less Favourable Treatment) Regulations 2000; and

  (j) the Fixed-term Employees (Prevention of Less Favourable Treatment) Regulations 2002.

- Employees (and, in some instances, workers) who have been victimised, penalised, harassed, discriminated against, or subjected to any detriment by any act (or any failure to act) by their employer, for choosing to exercise their statutory rights in employment (or simply for being who they are), may complain to an employment tribunal (regardless of their length of service or age at the material time) and will be awarded compensation (payable by their employer) if their complaints are upheld. It is important to bear in mind that an employee prompted to bring such a complaint has no need to terminate his (or her) employment in order to obtain a ruling from a tribunal. An employee who is dismissed or selected for redundancy either for challenging his employer's allegedly unlawful conduct, or for bringing proceedings before a tribunal or court, will be treated in law as having been dismissed unfairly and will be awarded a substantial amount of compensation.

Health and safety cases

- Section 44 of the Employment Rights Act 1996 Act states that an employee has the right not to be subjected to any detriment by any act, or by any deliberate failure to act, by his (or her) employer (eg, demotion, forfeiture of an expected pay rise, non-payment of an expected bonus, transfer to another department, etc) or to any other form of punishment or disciplinary action:

  (a) for carrying out (or proposing to carry out) his functions or duties as a trade union-appointed safety representative, a representative of employee safety, a member of a safety committee, or as a person designated by his employer to carry out activities in connection with preventing or reducing risks to health and safety;

  (b) in an establishment in which there is no safety representative (or representative of employee safety) or safety committee, for alerting his employer, by reasonable means, to circumstances connected with his work which he reasonably believed were harmful or potentially harmful to health or safety;

  (c) for leaving (or proposing to leave) his place of work in circumstances of danger which he reasonably believed to be serious and imminent and which he could not reasonably be expected to avert, or (while the danger persisted) for refusing to return to his place of work or any dangerous part of that place of work;

  (d) in circumstances of danger which the employee reasonably believed to be serious and imminent, for taking (or proposing to take) appropriate steps to protect himself or other persons from that danger (always provided that the steps the employee took or proposed to take in the particular circumstances *were* appropriate, in the light of his knowledge and the facilities and advice available to him at the time).

- An employee unlawfully victimised, harassed or subjected to any detriment, for acting (or proposing to act) in the manner described in paragraphs (a) to (d) above, has the right to complain to an employment tribunal, but must do so within three months of the relevant act, or failure to act. If the complaint is upheld, the tribunal will make a declaration to that effect and will order the employer to pay compensation. If the employee is dismissed or selected for redundancy for bringing proceedings against his (or her) employer, the dismissal will be held unfair and the employer will be ordered either to reinstate or re-engage the dismissed employee or pay a further substantial amount of compensation.

Employee representatives

- An employee representative, elected by his (or her) fellow-employees to represent their interests in consultations with the employer concerning his (or her) redundancy proposals or his plans to sell or transfer all or part of his business (or to acquire another business), has the legal right not to be subjected to any detriment by any act (or any deliberate failure to act) done, short of dismissal, for performing (or proposing to perform) his legitimate functions as such a representative (*ibid.* section 47).

- That right also extends to an employee who is a candidate for election to the role of employee representative and to any employee participating in such an election. The employer must permit the election to proceed unhindered and must not cajole the employee to withdraw his (or her) candidature by threatening or suggesting (for example) that his promotion prospects, pay, bonus, opportunities to work overtime etc, might be at risk if he proceeds. Other employees wishing to cast their votes in a ballot for the election of one or more employee representatives should likewise be permitted to do so unhindered (*ibid.*).

- Any employee representative (or candidate for that post), as well as any other employee who is victimised, harassed or disciplined by his (or her) employer, for the reasons given in the previous paragraph, may present a complaint to an employment tribunal and will be awarded compensation if his complaint is upheld. The employee need not resign in order to do so, but must present his complaint within three months of the alleged act (or failure to act) to which his complaint relates. If the complaint is upheld, the tribunal will order the employer to pay compensation.

- An employee representative, candidate or other employee who is dismissed or selected for redundancy for having challenged his employer's conduct or for having brought proceedings before a tribunal or court may complain yet again to an employment tribunal on grounds of unfair dismissal (*ibid.* sections 48 and 104). See **Dismissal for asserting a statutory right** elsewhere in this handbook.

Pension scheme trustees

- Any person who is a trustee of a relevant occupational pension scheme (that is to say, an occupational scheme established by his (or her) employer under a trust) has the right to perform his functions as such a trustee without being hindered, victimised or disciplined by his employer for doing so.

- An employer who victimises an employee of his, who is a pension scheme trustee, or subjects that person to any detriment for performing (or proposing to perform) his (or her) functions, will be ordered by an employment tribunal to pay compensation. If the employer responds by dismissing him or selecting him for redundancy, the employee has the right to pursue a further complaint (this time for unfair dismissal) and will again be awarded compensation if his complaint is upheld (*ibid.* sections 48 and 104). See **Dismissal of pension scheme trustees** elsewhere in this handbook.

Time off work for study or training

- With the coming into force on 1 September 1999 of the Right to Time Off for Study or Training Regulations 1999, young employees aged 16 or 17 who left full-time education without having attained the standard of achievement prescribed by those Regulations now have the statutory right to be permitted a reasonable amount of paid time off during normal working hours to undertake study or training leading to a 'relevant qualification'. The same rule applies to any 18-year-old employee already undertaking study or training leading to a relevant qualification – if he (or she) began such study or training before his 18th birthday. For further particulars, please turn to the section titled **Time off for study or training** elsewhere in this handbook.

- Section 47A of the Employment Rights Act 1996 cautions employers that they will be ordered to pay compensation to any employee of theirs who is victimised, disciplined or subjected to any other detriment for exercising (or proposing to exercise) his (or her) right to paid time off work for study or training. Likewise, a young employee who is dismissed (or selected for redundancy) for having questioned or challenged his employer's refusal or failure either to allow him a reasonable amount of paid time off work, or for having brought proceedings before a tribunal or court, may present a complaint of unfair dismissal to an employment tribunal; as to which, please turn to the section titled **Dismissal for asserting a statutory right** elsewhere in this handbook (*ibid.* sections 104 and 105(7)).

Trade union membership or non-membership

- 'Every employee shall have the right not to be subjected to any detriment as an individual by any act, or any deliberate failure to act, by his employer if the act or failure takes place for the purpose of:

  (a) preventing or deterring him from being or seeking to become a member of an independent trade union, or penalising him for doing so; or

  (b) preventing or deterring him from taking part in the activities of an independent trade union at any *appropriate time,* or penalising him for doing so; or

  (c) compelling him to be or become a member of any trade union or of a particular trade union or of one of a number of particular trade unions'

  (section 146(1), Trade Union & Labour Relations (Consolidation) Act 1992, as amended by section 2, Schedule 2 to the Employment Relations Act 1999).

  Note: The expression 'appropriate time', in relation to an employee taking part in the activities of an independent trade union, means time which is either outside the employee's working hours, or is a time within his (or her) working hours during which, in accordance with arrangements agreed with, or consent given by, his employer, it is permissible for him to take part in those activities (*ibid.* section 146(2)).

  For further particulars, please turn to the section titled **Trade union membership and activities.**

The closed shop

- Nowadays, the closed shop is a legal irrelevance. It can no longer be used as an excuse for denying a person a job or for dismissing (or disciplining) a person who refuses to be or remain a member of a trade union. Furthermore, an employer cannot lawfully demand a payment from a non-union employee (or presume to make a deduction from that employee's wages or salary) as an alternative to the payment of trade union dues. In short, an individual has the absolute right to decide whether or not he or she wishes to join (or remain a member of) a trade union. Any employer who undermines that right (or bows to trade union pressure to dismiss or victimise an employee who refuses to 'fall into line'), will be liable to pay very heavy compensation indeed. For further particulars, please turn to the sections titled **Dismissal** and **Dismissal on grounds of trade union membership** elsewhere in this handbook.

- It is also unlawful for an employer to refuse to interview or employ a job applicant who is not a member of a trade union (or of a particular trade union) or who has made it clear that he (or she) has no intention of joining a particular trade union or any trade union. A job applicant may complain to an employment tribunal if he (or she) suspects that he has been denied a job (or a job interview) for one or other of those reasons. The complaint must be presented within three months of the alleged unlawful act. If the complaint is upheld, the tribunal will order the employer to pay the complainant up to £50,000 by way of compensation (sections 137 and 140(4), Trade Union & Labour Relations (Consolidation) Act 1992).

- A person will be taken to have been refused employment because of his (or her) non-membership of a trade union (or because of his refusal to join a trade union) if an employer offers him a job on terms which no reasonable employer who wished to fill the post would offer.

Shop workers

- Apart from their right not to be dismissed for refusing Sunday *work*, *protected* and *opted-out* shop workers also have the right not to be subjected to any detriment by any act (or by any deliberate failure to act) by their employer for refusing (or proposing to refuse) to work on Sundays, or on a particular Sunday (*ibid.* section 45).

- A detriment might consist of a refusal to allow the worker to continue to work overtime on weekdays, the withholding of an expected pay rise, or the denial of opportunities for promotion, transfer or training. However, there is nothing to prevent an employer adjusting a worker's pay to take account of the fact that he (or she) no longer works on a Sunday – so long as that adjustment does not amount to a cut in the worker's basic hourly rate of pay.

- A *protected* or *opted-out* shop worker, who believes that he (or she) has been unfairly disadvantaged or victimised in the circumstances described above, may complain to an employment tribunal. Unless the employer can justify his treatment of the complainant, the tribunal will not only caution him to 'set matters to rights' but may also order him to pay compensation in respect of any loss (including any loss of benefit) sustained by the worker as a result of his employer's actions. It is as well to point out that a shop worker has no need to resign in order to pursue a complaint in these circumstances. Indeed, if he is dismissed or selected for redundancy for challenging his employer's actions or for having referred the matter to an employment tribunal, his dismissal will be held to have been automatically unfair; as to which, see **Dismissal for asserting a statutory right** elsewhere in this handbook.

Betting workers

- Betting workers enjoy the same statutory rights as shop workers. A betting worker employed *before* 3 January 1995 (other than as a 'Sundays only' worker) has the right to refuse to work on Sundays or to 'opt-out' of Sunday work. He (or she) has the right also, as a *protected* or *opted-out* worker, not to be victimised for refusing to work on a Sunday. If he is victimised (ie, subjected to a detriment) for exercising his statutory rights under the 1996 Act, he may present a complaint to an employment tribunal regardless of his age or length of service at the material time. The compensation payable in such circumstances is the same as for shop workers (described in the previous paragraph).

Victimisation by trade unions

- Under sections 65 and 66 of the Trade Union & Labour Relations (Consolidation) Act 1992, every member of a trade union has the right not to be *unjustifiably disciplined* by his or her union (ie, expelled, fined, deprived of benefits or facilities, or subjected to some other detriment, etc):

  - for refusing or failing to participate in or support a strike, or for failing to break a term in his or her contract of employment (for a purpose connected with such a strike or other industrial action); or

  - for asserting (or for encouraging some other person to vindicate his or her assertion) that the union (or any official or representative of the union, or any trustee of its property) has contravened its own rules, or the terms of any agreement or any statutory duty (or is about to do so); or

  - for encouraging or assisting another person not to break his (or her) contract of employment in furtherance of a strike or other industrial action; or

  - for failing to agree (or withdrawing his agreement) to have monies representing his union dues deducted from his pay; or

  - for resigning (or proposing to resign) from the union or from another union, or for becoming, proposing to become, refusing to become, or for not being, a member of another union; or

  - for working with individuals who are not members of the union or another union (or for proposing to do so); or

- for working for an employer who employs individuals who are not members of the union or of another union (or for proposing to do so); or

- for exercising his (or her) right either to require the union to comply with its statutory duties under the 1992 Act, or to apply to the court for an order directing the union to comply with those duties.

- An individual who claims that he has been unjustifiably disciplined by a trade union may present a complaint to an employment tribunal. The complaint must be presented within three months of the date on which the union's decision (or determination) was made. If it is upheld, the tribunal will make a declaration to that effect and will order the union to pay compensation (including repayment of any fine or similar penalty imposed on the individual by the union for the supposed breach of its rules). The amount of compensation will be such as the Employment Appeal Tribunal or employment tribunal considers just and equitable in all the circumstances (*ibid.* sections 66 and 67).

For further particulars, please turn to the section titled **Trade union members**.

Victimisation on grounds of race

- An employer is guilty of racial discrimination by way of victimisation if he treats an employee less favourably than he would other persons in similar circumstances, and does so because the employee in question:

  (a) has brought proceedings against him (or some other person) under the Race Relations Act 1976; or

  (b) has given evidence or information in connection with proceedings brought before a tribunal or court by any other person under the 1976 Act.

The same rule applies if an employee is victimised or harassed for alleging that his employer's recruitment or employment policies amount to unlawful racial discrimination under the 1976 Act unless the evidence shows that the employee's allegations were false and not made in good faith (*ibid.* section 2).

See **Racial discrimination** elsewhere in this handbook.

Victimisation on grounds of sex

- The Sex Discrimination Act 1975 specifically outlaws the victimisation or harassment of an employee who has brought, or is thinking about bringing, a complaint of unlawful discrimination against her employer. The reader should bear in mind that (as is the case with a great many statutory rights in employment) an employee has no need to leave her (or his) job in order to take her complaint before an employment tribunal. If the employer responds by 'sending her to Coventry' or by denying her a pay rise or an opportunity for promotion or further training, or by subjecting her to some other detriment, he (or she) is likely to pay dearly for his pains (*ibid.* section 4).

- It is also unlawful for any person to discriminate against a woman (or man) because of her (or his) marital status by treating her less favourably than a man in the same circumstances (*ibid.* section 1(2)). Thus, it is *prima facie* unlawful for an employer to refuse to employ a woman with children on the grounds that he considers that she would for that reason probably be unreliable and a poor timekeeper (see *Hurley v Mustoe* [1981] IRLR 208).

- Under the Sex Discrimination (Gender Reassignment) Regulations 1999, it is *prima facie* unlawful for an employer to treat an employee (or job applicant) less favourably on the ground that he (or she) intends to undergo, is undergoing or has undergone gender reassignment.

For further particulars, please turn to the section titled **Sex discrimination** elsewhere in this handbook.

Victimisation on grounds of disability

- It is unlawful for an employer to discriminate against a disabled job applicant (who is otherwise pre-eminently qualified to do the work in question) by refusing or omitting to interview that applicant, by refusing him (or her) employment, or by offering employment on terms less favourable than those that would have been offered to able-bodied candidates because of his disability (section 4(l)(2)(b), Disability Discrimination Act 1995).

- It is also unlawful for employers to discriminate against disabled persons in their employ by paying them lower wages or salaries (or associated payments) solely because they are disabled, or by offering other less favourable terms and conditions of employment. To refuse to promote or transfer a disabled employee, or to deny him (or her) opportunities for training for further advancement or to improve his skills, is likewise unlawful. An employee, who believes he has been discriminated against in this way, has every right to challenge his employer's actions before an employment tribunal, and is under no obligation to terminate his employment in order to do so. If his employer responds by victimising or disciplining the employee for having the effrontery to question his authority, that too is unlawful and will inevitably lead to a further hearing before a tribunal (*ibid.* sections 4(2) and 55).

For further particulars, please turn to the section titled **Disabled persons**. See also **Dismissal** and **Dismissal for asserting a statutory right**, elsewhere in this handbook.

Victimisation for exercising pregnancy, maternity and related rights

- New and expectant mothers, and the parents or adoptive parents of young children, have a number of statutory rights, including the right to maternity or adoption leave, the right to return to work after childbirth or adoption leave, the right to parental and paternity leave, and the right to time off for dependants. These rights are embodied in Part VIII of the Employment Rights Act 1996 (supported by the Maternity & Parental Leave etc Regulations 2002 and related legislation (discussed in more detail, under the appropriate subject heads, elsewhere in this handbook).

- Section 47C of the Employment Rights Act 1996 (as amended) cautions employers that they must not presume to penalise, victimise or otherwise 'punish' any employee of theirs who has exercised (or is proposing to exercise) one or other of those statutory rights. Any employer who contravenes section 47C will be ordered by an employment tribunal to pay that employee such compensation as the tribunal considers to be 'just and equitable' in all the circumstances having regard to the loss sustained by the employee as a result of her (or his) employer's intransigence. See also **Dismissal for asserting a statutory right, Maternity rights, Parental leave** and **Time off for dependants** elsewhere in this handbook.

'Tax credits' cases

- Under the Tax Credits Act 2002 (which repealed and replaced the Tax Credits Act 1999) and the Working Tax Credit (Payment by Employers) Regulations 2002, employers are duty-bound to pay tax credits (through the payroll) to those of their employees who have been awarded either or both of a child tax credit or a working tax credit by the Tax Credits Office (TCO).

- Section 70D of the Employment Rights Act 1996 (as inserted by Schedule 3 to the 2002 Act) cautions that employees have the right not to be victimised, disciplined or subjected to any other detriment by their employers for enforcing, or proposing to enforce their right to be paid tax credits on top of their normal wages or salaries, or for being entitled to tax credits. Should a complaint to an employment tribunal on those grounds be upheld the employer will be ordered to pay the employee such compensation as the tribunal considers to be 'just and equitable' in the circumstances, including compensation for any loss sustained by the employee as a direct consequence of his or her employer's action (or deliberate failure to act).

Part-time workers

- Under the Part-time Workers (Prevention of Less Favourable Treatment) Regulations 2000 (which came into force on 1 July 2000), a part-time employee has the right not to be treated less favourable than a comparable full-time employee:

  (a) as regards the terms of his contract of employment; or

  (b) by being subjected to any other detriment by any act, or by any deliberate failure to act, of his employer.

  The right not to be treated less favourably applies if the treatment is on the ground that the worker is a part-time worker, and that treatment is not otherwise justified on objective grounds.

- Should a worker's complaint of less favourable treatment be upheld by an employment tribunal, the offending employer will be ordered to pay the worker such compensation as it considers to be just and equitable in all the circumstances (including compensation for any loss of benefit sustained by the worker as a direct consequence of his (or her). employer's actions or deliberate failure to act. See also **Part-time workers** elsewhere in this handbook.

Fixed-term employees

- Under regulation 6 of the Fixed-term Employees (Prevention of Less Favourable Treatment) Regulations 2002, any employee who is dismissed or subjected to any detriment for challenging or questioning any alleged infringement of his (or her) rights under those Regulations (whether before an employment tribunal or otherwise) will be awarded such compensation as the tribunal considers just and equitable in all the circumstances, having regard to the infringement to which the complaint relates and any loss occurred by the complainant attributable to that infringement (including expenses reasonably incurred by the complainant in consequence of the infringement and the loss of any benefit which he or she might reasonably be expected to have had but for the infringement. See also **Fixed-term employees** elsewhere in this handbook.

W

WAGES, PAYMENT OF

Key points

- Employers nowadays have the right to decide what is the most cost-effective and secure way to pay an employee's wages. Before 1 January 1987, when section 11 and Schedule 1 to the Wages Act 1986 came into force (since repealed and replaced by sections 13 to 27 of the Employment Rights Act 1996), manual workers not only had the legal right to insist on being paid in cash but the right also to change their minds if they found payment by cheque or credit transfer not to their liking. The effect was to inhibit employers from promoting cashless wage payments.

- Nowadays, any employer wishing to abandon the payment of wages in cash may:

  (a) serve formal notice on his employees that he (or she) intends to adopt a cashless method of wage payments at a specified date in the future; and

  (b) insist that all new recruits be paid their wages or salary by cheque or by credit transfer to their bank accounts.

When negotiating or consulting with his (or her) employees (or their representatives) about his plans to introduce a system of cashless pay, an employer should not lose sight of the fact that employees currently paid in cash have the right to continue to be paid in that way if that is the method of payment specified in their contracts of employment or in a collective agreement concluded with a representative trade union. To repudiate that right is *prima facie* a breach of contract. An employer, on the other hand, has the acknowledged right to manage his business profitably and efficiently. At the end of the day, his decision to introduce a system of cashless pay is unlikely to be regarded as unreasonable by the tribunals or courts, so long as he has given reasonable advance warning of his intentions, perhaps equivalent to the amount of notice each employee is entitled to receive to terminate his contract of employment, and has consulted his workforce and considered their views.

- If a majority of the workforce is content to accept a system of cashless pay, the position of the minority will be considerably weakened, the more so if a tribunal is satisfied that the employer has done all that could be reasonably expected of him (or her) to ease the transition and any temporary hardship occasioned by the new method of payment. Once a system of cashless pay has been introduced, the employer should issue amended contracts of employment to all affected employees – as to which, please refer to the section titled **Written particulars of terms of employment** elsewhere in this handbook.

Payment of wages during illness

- Under the long since repealed Payment of Wages Act 1960, an employer, in the absence of any instructions to the contrary, could presume to pay an absentee worker's wages by postal order or money order sent by post to his (or her) home. Nowadays, any absentee employee normally paid by cheque or credit transfer can expect to receive his (or her) cheque in the post (unless he would prefer to have it collected on his behalf or held over until his return to work) or to have the amount due credited to his bank or building society account in the normal way. Again, if there is any term in a contract of employment or collective agreement specifying a different method for paying wages to absentee employees, that term will have to be renegotiated before any change is introduced.

  See also the sections titled **Deductions from pay** and **Dismissal for asserting a statutory right**, elsewhere in this handbook.

WOMEN AND YOUNG PERSONS, EMPLOYMENT OF

Key points

- Most of the legal restrictions on the working hours and periods of employment of women and young persons have long since been repealed or revoked, either by the Sex Discrimination Act 1986 or by the Employment Act 1989 – replaced, in the case of young persons under 18, by the Working Time Regulations 1998 (as amended on 6 April 2003 by the Working Time (Amendment) Regulations 2002). However, apart from restrictions on the working hours of young persons under 18, there remains a body of legislation that restricts or prohibits the employment of women and young persons in occupations that (for one reason or another) are viewed as potentially damaging to their health (but see the section on **Sex discrimination** elsewhere in this handbook).

- Restrictions on the employment of young persons under 18 are still to be found in the Licensing Act 1964 and in the Licensing (Scotland) Act 1976, both of which statutes prohibit the employment of young persons under 18 in the bar of licensed premises when that bar is open for the sale or consumption of intoxicating liquor. The prohibition on the employment of a young person under 18 'in the effecting of any betting transaction or in a licensed betting office' also remains (per section 21, Betting, Gaming & Lotteries Act 1963).

  Note: Section 170A of the Licensing Act 1964 (as inserted by the Deregulation (Employment in Bars) Order 1997) disapplies the prohibition on employing persons under 18 in bars (in England or Wales), so long as such persons are aged 16 or over and their employment is in accordance with a training scheme approved for the purpose by the Secretary of State.

The Management of Health and Safety at Work Regulations 1999

- Further restrictions on the employment of young persons under 18 are to be found in the Management of Health & Safety at Work Regulations 1999, regulation 19 of which imposes a duty on every employer to ensure that young persons under 18 employed by him (or her) are protected at work from any risks to their health and safety arising out of their lack of experience, their failure to appreciate potential risks, or the fact that, for the most part, they have not yet fully matured. Furthermore, the risk assessment necessarily carried out by employers in accordance with regulation 3 of those Regulations (and all subsequent reviews of that assessment) must include an assessment of the risks confronting young persons under the age of 18 because of those same considerations.

- Regulation 19 of the 1999 Regulations cautions that no employer may employ a young person under 18 for work which:

  (a) is beyond his (or her) physical or psychological capacity;

  (b) involves harmful exposure to agents that are toxic or carcinogenic, cause heritable genetic damage or harm to the unborn child, or that in any other way chronically affect human health;

  (c) involves harmful exposure to radiation;

  (d) involves the risk of accidents that it may reasonably be assumed cannot be recognised or avoided by young persons owing to their insufficient attention to safety or lack of experience or training; or

    (e) for work in which there is a risk to health from extreme cold or heat, noise, or vibration,

unless the work is necessary for the young person's training in circumstances in which he (or she) is supervised by a competent persons and the risks associated with that work are reduced to the lowest level that is reasonably practicable.

Table 1

RESTRICTIONS ON THE EMPLOYMENT OF WOMEN AND YOUNG PERSONS

Statutory provision	Prohibition/restriction
Working Time Regulations 1998 (as amended by the Working Time (Amendment) Regulations 2002 (Regulations 5A and 6A)	'A young worker's working time shall not exceed eight hours a day, or 40 hours a week.' 'An employer shall ensure that no young worker employed by him works during the restricted period'. The 'restricted period' is the period between 10:00 pm and 6:00 am or, where the worker's contract provides for him (or her) to work after 10:00 pm, the period between 11:00 pm and 7:00 am. *Note*: For details of the limited exceptions to these rules, please turn to the sections on **Overtime** and **Working Hours** elsewhere in this handbook.
Public Health Act 1936 (Section 205)	No woman or girl may be employed in a factory or workshop within four weeks after she has given birth to a child.
Control of Lead at Work Regulations 2002 (Regulation 4(2) and Schedule 1)	No employer shall employ a young person or a woman of reproductive capacity in lead smelting and refining processes involving the handling, treatment, sintering, smelting or refining of ores or materials containing not less than 5 per cent lead; or in the cleaning of any place where any of the above processes are carried out. Nor may an employer allow a young person or a woman of reproductive capacity in lead-acid battery manufacturing processes, ie the manipulation of lead oxides; mixing or pasting in connection with the manufacture or repair of lead-acid batteries; the melting or casting of lead; the trimming, abrading or cutting of pasted plates in connection with the manufacture or repair of lead-acid batteries; or in the cleaning of any place where any of the above processes are carried out.

	Note: The term 'lead oxides' means 'powdered lead oxides in the form of lead, lead monoxide, lead oxide, red lead or any combination of lead used in oxide manufacture or lead-acid battery pasting processes'.
Ionising Radiations Regulations 1999 (Regulations 11 and 22, and Schedule 4)	Dose limits for women of reproductive capacity.
	No person under the age of 18 may be designated as a 'classified person' (*ibid.* regulation 9(3)).
Employment Rights Act 1996 (Section 72)	'An employee entitled to ordinary maternity leave must not work, or be permitted by her employer to work, during the period of two weeks which commences with the day on which childbirth occurs.'
Air Navigation Order 1985 (Article 20(8))	A member of a flight crew who has reason to believe she is pregnant must notify her employers in writing without delay. Once her pregnancy is confirmed, she is deemed to be suspended from work and may only resume her duties during the initial stages of her pregnancy if it is considered safe for her to do so (see also **Table 1** on pages 567 to 568 of this handbook).
Merchant Shipping (Medical Examination) Regulations 1983 (Regulation 2)	Restrictions imposed on the employment (or continued employment) of women as laid down in Parts X (so far as relating to gynaecological conditions) and XI of the Merchant Shipping Notice No. M 1331. Please turn to the section titled **Suspension on maternity grounds** elsewhere in this handbook.

Note: The list above is not intended to be exhaustive, and does not include industry-specific legislation on activities or work situations beyond the scope of this handbook (mines and quarries, carriage of explosives, off-shore installations, etc), which will be well known to the employers concerned.

See also the sections titled **Children, employment of, Pregnant employees and nursing mothers**, and **Suspension on maternity grounds**, elsewhere in this handbook.

WORKING HOURS
(Restriction on, on health and safety grounds)

Key points

- Under the Working Time Regulations 1998 (as amended), workers in Great Britain and Northern Ireland (other than those in excluded categories) have the statutory right to four weeks' paid annual holidays, in-work rest breaks, and daily and weekly rest periods. There are also restrictions on night work and the length of the working week. The 1998 Regulations, implement Council Directive 93/104/EC (the 'Working Time Directive') of 23 November 1998 'concerning certain aspects of the organisation of working time'. They also incorporate Council Directive 94/33/EC of 22 June 1994 'on the protection of young people at work'. This section explains the legal limits on the working hours of adult workers and of young workers under the age of 18. *Those weekly working time limits are policed and enforced by the* Health & Safety enforcing authorities.

- Readers should note that, subject to exceptions (explained below), the 1998 Regulations apply not only to employees in the accepted sense of the word (that is to say, to individuals employed under contracts of employment) but also to every worker (full-time, part-time, temporary, permanent, seasonal or casual) who undertakes to do or perform personally any work or service for an employer. However, the Regulations do *not* apply to workers who are genuinely self-employed.

Adult workers

- Briefly, adult workers, that is to say, workers aged 18 and over, have the right:

  (a) not to be required to work more than an average 48 hours a week (including overtime hours) calculated over a reference period of 17 weeks (or, in appropriate circumstances, see below, a reference period of 26 or 52 weeks;

  (b) not to work at night for more than an average eight hours in any 24-hour period, calculated over a reference period of 17 weeks; and

  (c) to be offered free (and, where appropriate) repeat *health assessments* when assigned or transferred to night work.

The 48-hour week

- Adult workers in Great Britain (and Northern Ireland) cannot be required to work more than an average 48 hours a week (including overtime), calculated over a reference period of 17 weeks (but see *Extending the reference period* below). An adult worker may agree to work more than that average 48 hours, so long as he (or she) does so *individually, voluntarily* and *in writing*. A purported general opt-out for the workforce at large or for a particular group of workers under the terms of a workforce or collective agreement, is void and unenforceable. The same applies to any term in a contract that presumes to override a worker's rights under the 1998 Regulations. Furthermore, the opt-out agreement signed personally by an adult worker must remind that worker of his (or her) right to cancel the agreement on giving a specified period of notice (not exceeding three months). If the agreement makes no mention of the worker's right to change his mind, it may be cancelled by the worker giving his employer seven days' advance written notice of that decision (*ibid.* regulations 4 and 5).

  Note: In *Barber v RIB Mining (UK) Ltd* [1999] ICR 679; [1999] IRLR 308, the High Court held that (save for workers in excepted categories) there was an implied term in every contract of employment that an employee who has not signed an opting-out agreement could not be required to work more than an average 48 hours a week. In that case, six colliery workers had been working well in excess of 48 hours over a number of weeks to the extent that their average weekly hours would undoubtedly exceed that upper limit if they continued to work such long hours over the remainder of the reference period. What the High Court's declaration means, in effect, is that workers in such circumstances may either stop working for a time or insist on reducing their weekly hours until such time as their average weekly hours fell to the prescribed 48 hours a week.

- Any attempt on the part of an employer to pressurise an adult worker (or, for that matter, a young worker: see below) into opting out of the 48-hour week will not only invalidate the agreement but could also lead to criminal prosecution and a fine of up to £5,000; even higher, if a conviction is obtained on indictment. See also *Complaints to an employment tribunal* below.

Exceptions to the 48-hour rule

- The upper limit on working hours does not apply to managing executives and other persons with autonomous decision-making powers; nor does it apply to people whose working time is not measured or predetermined by their employers or who determine their own patterns of work (*ibid.* regulation 20(1)).

- Some workers (such as travelling salesmen, insurance brokers, etc) have contracts which, while stipulating that they must work a minimum number of hours each week, nonetheless give them the right (because of the specific characteristics of the work they do) to choose to work such additional hours as they themselves consider appropriate (visiting clients or would-be clients in their homes, and so on). In those circumstances, the Regulations allow that provisions relating to weekly working time and night work will only apply in relation to that part of the worker's work which is either measured or predetermined or cannot be determined by the worker himself (or herself) (*ibid.* regulation 20(2), inserted by regulation 4 of the Working Time Regulations 1999).

Extending the reference period

- The standard reference period of 17 weeks over which an adult worker's average weekly hours (including overtime) are calculated may be extended to up to 52 weeks under the terms of a collective or workforce agreement – if the extension is for objective or technical reasons or reasons concerning the organisation of work. The standard reference period may be a fixed period of 17 consecutive weeks (eg, January to April, inclusive) or a 'rolling' 17-week period (*ibid.* regulation 23).

- An employer may choose to increase the standard 17-week reference period to one of 26 weeks in the case of adult workers who routinely travel long distances and who work relatively long hours in order to complete a particular job or project on time. The same 26-week reference period may be used for workers engaged in security and surveillance work and for people working in hospitals, residential care homes, prisons, docks, and airports. Journalists, television and radio crews, farm workers, people employed by the water, gas and electricity 'utilities', refuse collectors, tour guides, postal workers, ambulance men/women and fire-fighters, and people operating continuous process machinery, would also fall within this category (*ibid.* regulation 4(5)).

Collective and workforce agreements

- A collective agreement is an agreement concluded with representatives of a recognised independent trade union on behalf of the whole workforce or one or more groups of workers. A workforce agreement is little different and is made in circumstances in which there is no union recognition or representation. With a workforce agreement, the employer must first allow time for workers to nominate and elect one or more of their number to represent their interests in negotiations with their employer. A workforce agreement (valid for up to five years, but no longer) must be in writing and cannot come into effect until it has been circulated in draft form to all affected workers (with accompanying guidance notes) and has been signed by each of the workforce representatives. If the employer has 20 or fewer workers, the agreement need only be signed by a majority of those workers. It is important to stress that a collective or workforce agreement does not (and cannot) impose an average working week in excess of 48 hours on the workers covered by such an agreement. As was pointed out earlier, a decision to opt-out can only be taken by individual adult workers.

Restrictions on night work: adult workers

- An adult night worker cannot lawfully be required to work more than an average eight hours in any 24-hour period, calculated over a reference period of 17 weeks. The term 'night worker' means a worker who either routinely, or for the majority of his (or her) working time, works at least three hours every night (that is to say, in the period of seven or more hours that encompasses the period between midnight and 5:00 am (but see next paragraph)). It is important to note that the 48-hour rule discussed earlier in this section applies equally to night workers as it does to day workers and to those who work shifts.

  Note: An employer's refusal or failure to comply with the requirements discussed here and in the following paragraphs could lead to prosecution and a fine of up to £5,000 (for each offence). See also *complaints to an employment tribunal* below.

- The standard 17-week reference period for adult night workers may be excluded or extended for particular workers or groups of workers by a collective or workforce agreement. However, in all such cases, the employer must nonetheless ensure that the workers in question take equivalent periods of compensatory rest; or, if that is not always possible, must ensure that they are afforded such protection as may be appropriate in order to safeguard their health and safety.

- An adult night worker whose work exposes him (or her) to *special* hazards or heavy physical or mental strain must not work for more than eight hours in any 24-hour period that includes a night shift involving exposure to such hazards. This is an *absolute* limit not an *average* limit. What constitutes a special hazard will be a matter for agreement between an employer and his (or her) workers in a collective or workforce agreement that recognises and takes account of the specific effects and hazards associated with night work. Otherwise, it is a hazard that poses a significant risk identified as such by the risk assessment exercise necessarily carried out by every employer under regulation 3 of the Management of Health & Safety at Work Regulations 1999. The absolute limit referred to here may, nonetheless, be modified or excluded by a collective or workforce agreement.

Exceptions to the night work rule

- The night work limit described in the previous paragraphs does not apply to managing executives and other persons with autonomous decision-making powers; nor does it apply to people whose working time is not measured or predetermined by their employers or who determine their own patterns of work. Also excepted are adult workers whose work activities take them to distant locations away from home and it is desirable for them to work relatively long hours over a short time span in order to complete a particular job or project.

- The exception applies also to adult workers engaged in security and surveillance work and to people working in hospitals, residential care homes, prisons, docks, and airports. Journalists, television and radio crews, farm workers, people employed by the water, gas and electricity 'utilities', refuse collectors, tour guides, postal workers, ambulance men/women and fire fighters, and people operating continuous process machinery, would also fall within that excepted category.

- However, in all such cases, their employers must ensure that the workers in question are allowed equivalent periods of compensatory rest; or, if that is not always possible, must ensure that they are afforded such protection as may be appropriate in order to safeguard their health and safety.

Health assessments for night workers

- The Regulations caution that adult workers should not be assigned or transferred to night work for the first time or on any subsequent occasion without first being offered the opportunity of a free health assessment. If a particular employee had a health assessment on a prior such occasion, the offer of yet another assessment will not be necessary if there is no reason to suppose that the previous assessment is no longer valid (*ibid*. regulation 7(1)).

- The result of any health assessment must not be disclosed to any person other than the worker to whom it relates, unless the worker has given his (or her) consent to the disclosure or the disclosure is confined to a statement that the worker in question is fit for night work.

- If an employer is informed by a doctor that a particular worker is suffering from health problems that are (or may be) connected with the fact that he or she works at night, the employer must, if possible, transfer that worker to suitable alternative work that does not involve work at night (either permanently or for so long as the doctor considers such a move to be necessary).

Young workers under 18

- Under regulation 5A of the 1998 Regulations, as inserted by the Working Time (Amendment) Regulations 2002, young workers under the age of 18 must not work or be required to work for more than 40 hours a week or for more than eight hours on any day. These limits are absolute. Although an adult worker's working hours may be averaged over a reference period of 17 weeks or longer, no such averaging is permitted in the case of young workers under the age of 18.

- However, Regulation 25 allows that the restrictions imposed by Regulation 5A do not apply in relation to a young worker: (a) if there is no adult worker available to perform the work; (b) if the work is necessary either to maintain continuity of service or production (or to respond to a surge in demand for a service or product; and (c) if performing the work would not adversely affect the young worker's education or training.

Night work by young workers

- There are also severe restrictions on the employment of young workers at night. Regulation 6A of the 1998 Regulations states that 'an employer shall ensure that no young worker employed by him, works during the restricted period'. For these purposes, the restricted period is the period between 10:00 pm and 6:00 am or, where the young worker's contract provides for him to work after 10:00 pm, the period between 11:00 pm and 7:00 am.

- However, the restriction on night does not apply to young workers employed in hospitals or similar establishments, or in connection with cultural, artistic, sporting or advertising activities, so long as they are supervised by adult workers (where such supervision is necessary for their protection) and are allowed a minimum half-hour rest break (or an equivalent period of compensatory rest) during any period of night work that lasts or is expected to last for more than than four-and-a-half hours.

- Regulation 25 of the 1998 Regulations also allows that the restrictions on night work imposed by regulation 6A need not apply to young workers employed in agriculture, retail trading, hotels, bakeries, catering establishments (including restaurants or bars), or in delivering newspapers or mail, if, but only if, (a) there is no adult worker available to perform the work; (b) if the work is necessary either to maintain continuity of service or production, or in response to a surge in demand for a service or product; and (c) if performing the work would not adversely affect the young worker's education or training. Furthermore, employers who take advantage of this permitted relaxation of the rules, must see to it that the young workers in question are supervised by one or more adult workers and are permitted to take the rest breaks and rest periods prescribed in the 1998 Regulations (see **Rest breaks and rest periods** elsewhere in this handbook). However, notwithstanding the permitted relaxation of the rules in relation to young workers employed in the establishments or sectors described above, there is an absolute prohibition on the employment of any such young person between midnight and 4:00 am, whatever the circumstances.

- Finally, employers must see to it that no young worker in their employment is assigned to work during the restricted period without first being offered the opportunity of a free health and capacities assessment – unless the worker in question had a health and capacities assessment before being assigned to work during the restricted period on an earlier occasion, and the employer has no reason to believe that the earlier assessment is no longer valid. The results of any health and capacities assessment must not be disclosed to any person other than the worker to whom it relates, unless the worker has given his (or her) consent to the disclosure or the disclosure is confined to a statement that the young worker in question is fit for night work.

Exceptions

- The restrictions on the working hours and employment at night of young persons, outlined in the preceding paragraphs, do not apply to young workers in domestic service or to those in the armed forces, or to young persons employed on ships whose employment is subject to regulation under section 52(2)(b) of the Merchant Shipping Act 1995. Nor do they yet apply to young workers employed in the excluded sectors and occupations listed in the next paragraph.

Excluded sectors and occupations

- It should be noted that the Working Time Regulations do not yet apply to workers enaged in sea fishing or other work at sea, or to mobile and non-mobile workers employed in the air, rail, road, sea, inland water-way or lake transport sectors; or to the activities of doctors in training, or to the police or members of the armed forces, or to certain activities in the civil protection services (*ibid.* regulation 18). But see *Drivers' hours* below.

- Even though workers in the sectors or occupations listed in the preceding paragraph do not enjoy specific protection under the 1998 Regulations, their employers should be conscious of their overriding duty under the Health & Safety at Work etc Act 1974 to do all that they reasonably can to ensure the health, safety and welfare at work of each and every person in their employ. An employer who pressurises any worker into working extremely long hours without a break is putting that workers' health and safety at risk and could be prosecuted (let alone sued for damages by an injured party) for any accident or dangerous occurrence directly attributable to fatigue, inattentiveness or carelessness.

Records of working hours

- Save for those adult workers who have agreed in writing to opt-out of the maximum 48-hour week, every employer is duty-bound to keep records sufficient to demonstrate compliance with the 'working time' provisions of the 1998 Regulations (but see next paragraph). For hourly-paid workers, time cards and pay records will probably suffice. There is no need to keep a separate running total of hours worked. For office workers, and others who do not routinely 'sign-in' or 'sign-out' at the beginning and end of a working day, management must develop a system designed to monitor the working hours of those workers who are in the habit of working more than 48 hours a week at busy times of the year or because of pressures of work. It will be for an employer to decide how best to reassure an inspector who suspects that the prescribed limits are being exceeded. Contracts of employment that prescribe working hours (including overtime) in excess of the 'working time' limits should by now have been amended to accommodate the 1998 Regulations (*ibid.* regulation 9).

- The working time records necessarily maintained by employers must be kept for a period of two years and must be made available for inspection on demand by the 'relevant enforcing authority' (ie, an HSE inspector or local authority environmental health officer). The penalty for failing to keep adequate records or for obstructing an inspector in the course of his duties is a fine similar to that likely to be imposed for a related offence under the Health & Safety at Work, etc Act 1974.

Inspectors have the right not only to examine workers' records but also to prohibit or restrict the working hours of any worker whose weekly working hours are likely to compromise his (or her) health and safety.

Maintenance of records

- Employers who employ people at night must maintain records sufficient to satisfy an HSE or local authority environmental health officer that they are complying with the night work limits imposed by the 1998 Regulations. The records must be kept for at least two years. A failure to do so is an offence that could lead to prosecution and a heavy fine.

Complaints to an employment tribunal

- A worker (including a worker elected by fellow workers to represent their interests in negotiations with their employer) may complain to an employment tribunal that he (or she) has been disciplined, dismissed, selected for redundancy, or subjected to some other detriment (including dismissal, in the case of a worker who is *not* an 'employee') either for challenging his employer's failure to acknowledge his rights under the 1998 Regulations (whether before an employment tribunal or otherwise) or for refusing to forego those rights, or for performing or proposing to perform his (or her) functions as an elected workforce representative. If such a complaint is upheld, the employer will be ordered to pay the worker a substantial (or further substantial) award of compensation.

- It is as well to point out that a worker has no need to resign in order to pursue his (or her) statutory rights before an employment tribunal, so long as the complaint is presented within three months of the employer's refusal or failure. If the worker has resigned or been dismissed, the complaint must be presented within three months of the effective date of termination of the worker's employment or within such further period as the tribunal considers reasonable in the circumstances (sections 45A and 101A, Employment Rights Act 1996).

Drivers' hours

- Although the Working Time Regulations 1998 do not yet apply to road transport workers and other transport sector workers (see *Future developments* below), the daily driving hours of drivers of goods and passenger vehicles operating within the UK are presently regulated by Part VI of the Road Transport Act 1968 (as amended) and by cognate legislation in Northern Ireland.

- The following is intended as a summary (no more) of the principal provisions of the 1968 Act. There are a great many subordinate regulations and orders, containing exemptions, modifications and dispensations, that are beyond the scope of this book. Part VI of the 1968 Act is intended to secure 'the observance of proper hours or periods of work by persons engaged in the carriage of passengers or goods by road and thereby protect the public in cases where the drivers of motor vehicles are suffering from fatigue' (*ibid.* section 95(1)).

- Section 96 of that Act restricts a driver's working day to 11 hours and the time he (or she) spends 'behind the wheel' to ten hours a day. A driver must not drive a goods vehicle (or any passenger transport vehicle) for more than five-and-a-half hours without a break of at least 30 minutes for rest and refreshment. In an 11-hour working day, this would entitle a driver to two half-hour meal and rest breaks.

- A driver of any vehicle to which the 1968 Act applies must be allowed an interval of at least 11 work-free hours between one working day and the next. He (or she) must not be on duty in any working week for more than 60 hours in the aggregate, and must be allowed an off-duty period of at least 24 uninterrupted hours in every period of seven consecutive days. The penalty for a contravention of the domestic drivers' hours code – whether by the driver or his employer, or both – is a fine not exceeding level 4 on the standard scale (currently £2,500).

- Section 97 of the 1968 Act (as substituted by the Passenger & Goods Vehicles (Recording Equipment) Regulations 1979) states that a tachograph must be installed in a goods vehicle in compliance with Council Regulation EEC/3821/85, as amended. A tachograph automatically records a driver's driving hours and rest periods, and must be installed in the cab of any goods vehicle with a gross plated weight of more than 3.5 tonnes. Any person who contravenes this requirement is liable on summary conviction to a fine not exceeding level 5 on the standard scale (currently £5,000).

EU Directives

- The daily and weekly driving hours (and daily and weekly rest periods) for drivers operating heavy goods vehicles to and from other EU member states, are regulated by provisions laid down in EC Regulations 3820/85 and 3821/85. As a rule, the driver of any such goods vehicle having a gross plated weight of more than 3.5 tonnes must not drive his vehicle for more than four-and-a-half hours without a break of at least 45 minutes (in total or in the aggregate) during the course of, or at the end of, that driving period. Two or more shorter breaks are permitted during those four-and-a-half hours so long as no single break lasts for less than 15 minutes and they add up to a total of 45 minutes or more. Any break lasting less than 15 minutes does not count as a rest period for these purposes.

- UK drivers operating in and out of the European Union must not drive for more than nine hours a day or for more than 56 hours in any week (subject to a fortnightly driving limit of 90 hours). Within those limits, a driver's daily hours can increase to ten hours on not more than two days a week. There must be an off-duty period of at least 11 consecutive hours in every 24-hour period, and a weekly rest period of 45 consecutive hours in every working week. The weekly rest period *can* reduce to 36 consecutive hours if taken at the driver's home base, or to 24 consecutive hours if taken elsewhere subject to the proviso that all rest hours lost in this way must be taken in a single rest period within the ensuing three weeks.

Future developments

- In a consultation document published on 31 October 2002, the Secretary of State for Trade & Industry outlined the Government's proposals for implementing a further 'working time' Directive (2000/34/EC), known as the Horizontal Amending Directive (HAD), adopted by the European Parliament and Council on 1 August 2002. UK legislation implementing the HAD Directive will come into force on 1 August 2003. From that date, the Working Time Regulations 1998 (as then amended) will encompass mobile and non-mobile workers in transport and related industries (as well as off-shore workers and junior doctors) hitherto excluded from those Regulations. Copies of the consultation document (URN 02/1424) 'on measures to implement Directive 2000/34/EC' can be obtained from the DTI's Publications Orderline on 0845 6000 925, or may be accessed and downloaded from website www.dti.gov.uk/er/work_time_regs/hadconsult.htm. The consultation period ended on 31 January 2003.

Further information

- *A Guide to the Working Time Regulations* (Ref URN 98/894) may be obtained from the Department of Trade & Undustry's (DTI's) Publications Orderline on 0870 1502 500 or from website www. dti.gov.uk/er. Employers needing further advice on working time limits, night work limits and health assessments may call the HSE Infoline on 0541 545550 or contact their local authority Environmental Health Department.

- See also the sections titled **Holidays, annual, Overtime employment**, and **Rest breaks and rest periods**, elsewhere in this handbook.

WRITTEN REASONS FOR DISMISSAL

Key points

- There are two situations in which the law requires an employer to provide a dismissed employee with a statement in writing explaining the reasons for his (or her) dismissal. In the first, the statement need only be provided if the employee requests it, always provided that he had worked for his employer for a continuous period of one year or more at the effective date of termination of his contract of employment. In the second, the statement must be provided automatically (that is to say, without any prompting by the employee) and regardless of the employee's length of service at the time of her dismissal (section 92, Employment Rights Act 1996).

Standard dismissal situation

- An employee who has been dismissed, with or without notice, for a reason other than pregnancy or childbirth (see below), and who had been *continuously employed* for one year or more at the effective date of termination of his (or her) contract of employment, may apply to his employer for a written statement, eg particulars of the reasons for his dismissal. The same rule applies if the employee in question was employed under a fixed-term contract lasting one year or more and the contract had expired without being renewed under the same contract.

- The employer must provide the written statement within 14 days of receiving the employee's request. If he refuses or neglects to do so (or provides a statement which is false or inadequate), he will be ordered by an employment tribunal to pay the employee the equivalent of two weeks' gross pay (*ibid.* section 93). It is as well to add that a written statement provided by an employer in accordance with section 92 is admissible in evidence in any proceedings before a tribunal or court.

Dismissal during pregnancy or maternity leave

- An employer who dismisses a pregnant employee (even if the dismissal has nothing to do with her being pregnant) or dismisses an employee after childbirth (in circumstances in which the dismissal cuts short her maternity leave period), must provide that employee with a written statement giving particulars of the reasons for her dismissal – whether or not she has asked for any such statement and regardless of her length of continuous service at the material time (*ibid.* section 92(4)).

Complaint to an employment tribunal

- An employee may complain to an employment tribunal (a) that his (or her) employer has unreasonably refused to provide him with a written statement of reasons for dismissal or (b) that the reasons given in the statement provided by the employer were inadequate or untrue. Either complaint must be presented to the Secretary of the Tribunals within three months of the *effective date of termination* of the employee's contract of employment (*ibid*. section 53(5)) or (in exceptional circumstances) within such further period as the tribunal considers reasonable.

  Note: For the meaning of the expression *effective date of termination*, please turn to the section titled **Dismissal** or to the appropriate entry in the **Index**.

- If an employment tribunal upholds the employee's complaint, it will make a declaration to that effect (including a declaration as to what it finds the employer's reasons were for dismissing the employee), and will (as indicated earlier) order the employer to pay compensation of an amount equal to the sum of two weeks' gross pay (*ibid*. section 93) – the amount being calculated by reference to the employee's *actual* weekly earnings at the time of his (or her) dismissal.

  Note: In *Castledine v Rothwell Engineering Ltd* [1973] IRLR 99, a dismissed employee produced a written statement of reasons for dismissal, supplied by his former employer, which claimed that he had been dismissed because he was incompetent. Admitted as evidence in the same proceedings was a reference supplied by the same employer which stated that the employee 'had carried out his duties satisfactorily, often under difficult conditions'. When confronted with documents which contradicted one another, the tribunal had little difficulty in concluding that the dismissal of the employee had been unfair. For a further discussion of the implications of providing an employee with a reference on the one hand, and a written statement of reasons for dismissal on the other, see the section titled **References**, elsewhere in this handbook.

  See also **Dismissal on grounds of pregnancy or childbirth** and **Maternity rights**.

WRITTEN STATEMENT OF EMPLOYMENT PARTICULARS

Key points

- Every person employed under a contract of employment (regardless of the number of hours he or she is required to work under that contract) has the legal right to receive a written statement from his (or her) employer containing specified particulars of the terms and conditions of his employment.

- The statement must be issued to a new recruit within two months of the date on which his (or her) employment began. If, within that same period of two months, the employee is sent to work overseas (ie, outside the UK) for one month or more, he must receive his written statement *before* he leaves the UK. A new employee still has the right to receive the written statement even if he resigns (or is dismissed) before the end of that two-month period, unless his employment continues for less than one month (sections 1, 2 and 198, Employment Rights Act 1996).

  Note: The written statement referred to in this section provides evidence of contractual terms but is not, as is often supposed, a contract of employment in the strict legal sense – the more so if it contains little more than the information required to be given by sections 1 to 4 of the 1996 Act. The employer who fails to provide an employee with a written statement is not thereby depriving that employee of his or her contractual rights (as some employers appear to believe). Nor has an employer anything to gain by withholding the written statement until an employee has completed two months' service. See also **Contract of employment** elsewhere in this handbook.

- As indicated earlier, an employee whose contract requires him (or her) to work outside the UK for a period of more than one month, must be given his written statement *before* he leaves the UK. Furthermore, the statement must contain the following information (in addition to the particulars described below):

  - the period for which the employee is required to work outside the UK;

  - the currency in which he (or she) is to be paid during that time;

  - any additional payment or benefits (such as an overseas allowance) to be provided by reason of his (or her) being required to work outside the UK; and

  - any terms and conditions relating to his (or her) return to the UK (*ibid.* section 1(4)(k)).

Particulars to be included in the statement

- The written statement must contain all of the particulars listed below. If there are no particulars to be entered in the statement under any of heads (a) to (n), the statement must say so. A 'Nil' return (or no mention at all of those missing particulars) is not acceptable and will entitle the employee to refer the matter to an employment tribunal. See *Reference to an employment tribunal* below.

- The written statement may be issued in instalments. However, one of those instalments (referred to in the 1996 Act as the 'principal statement') must contain the particulars listed in paragraphs (a), (b), (c), (g), (k) and (m) below. In the case of paragraphs (h) and (i), which deal with sick pay and pension rights, the statement may refer the employee to other documents which explain those particulars – so long as the employee has reasonable opportunities of reading those documents in the course of his (or her) employment. Alternatively, they must be made reasonably accessible to him in some other way. As to paragraph (j), the statement may either refer the employee to section 86 of the 1996 Act or (as appropriate) to the provisions of any collective agreement for particulars of the length of notice which he (or she) is required to give (or entitled to receive) to terminate his contract of employment. Here too, referring an employee to a collective agreement is acceptable only if the employee has reasonable opportunities of reading the agreement in the course of his employment or it is made reasonably accessible to him in some other way.

The written statement must contain the following particulars:

(a) the names of the employer and the employee;

(b) the date on which the employment began;

(c) the date on which the employee's period of continuous employment began, taking into account any employment with a previous employer which counts towards that period;

(d) the scale or rate of remuneration, or the method of calculating remuneration;

(e) the intervals at which wages or salary are to be paid (eg, weekly or monthly);

(f) any terms and conditions relating to hours of work (including any terms and conditions relating to normal working hours);

(g) any terms and conditions relating to the employee's entitlement to holidays, including public holidays and holiday pay (the particulars given being sufficient to enable the employee's entitlement, including any entitlement to accrued holiday pay on the termination of employment, to be precisely calculated);

(h) any terms and conditions relating to incapacity for work due to sickness or injury, including any provision for sick pay;

(i) any terms and conditions relating to pensions and pension schemes plus a note stating whether there is in force a contracting-out certificate (issued in accordance with Chapter I of Part III of the

Pension Schemes Act 1993) stating that the employment is contracted-out employment (for the purposes of that Part of that Act);

(j) the length of notice which the employee is obliged to give and entitled to receive to terminate his contract of employment;

(k) the title of the job which the employee is employed to do or a brief description of the work for which the employee is employed;

(l) where the employment is not intended to be permanent, the period for which it is expected to continue or, if it is for a fixed term, the date when it is to end;

(m) either the place of work or, where the employee is required or permitted to work at various places, an indication of that and of the address of the employer; and

(n) any collective agreements which directly affect the terms and conditions of the employment, including, where the employer is not a party, the persons by whom they were made.

Disciplinary rules and grievances

• The written statement must also include a note:

(o) specifying any disciplinary rules applicable to the employee or referring the employee to the provisions of a document which the employee has reasonable opportunities of reading in the course of his employment, or which is made reasonably accessible to him in some other way, and which specifies those rules, and specifying by description or otherwise a person to whom the employee can apply if he is dissatisfied with any disciplinary decision relating to him, and the manner in which any such application should be made; and, where there are any further steps consequent on any such application, explaining those steps or referring to the provisions of a document which the employee has reasonable opportunities of reading in the course of his employment, or is made reasonably accessible to him in some other way, and which explains them;

Note: This requirement does not apply if, on the date on which the employee's employment began, the relevant number of employees on the payroll was less than 20. That relevant number of employees includes persons employed by any associated employer (*ibid.* section 3(3)). However, once sections 35 to 38 of the Employment Act 2002 come into force (in the second half of 2003), all employers (large as well as small) will be required to develop statutory minimum disciplinary and dismissal procedures (DDPs) and statutory minimum grievance procedures (GPs). A refusal or failure to do so will result in awards of compensation for unfair dismissal being increased by up to 50 per cent.

(p) specifying, by description or otherwise, a person to whom the employee can apply for the purpose of seeking redress of any grievance relating to his employment, and the manner in which any such application should be made; and, where there are further steps consequent on any such application, explaining those steps or referring to the provisions of a document which the employee has reasonable opportunities of reading in the course of his employment, or is made reasonably accessible to him in some other way, and which explains them.

Note: Paragraphs (o) and (p) above do not apply to rules, disciplinary decisions, grievances or procedures relating to health or safety at work (*ibid.* section 3(2)), although an employer is perfectly within his rights to include such particulars in the written statement (in the light of their importance in the conduct of his business).

The written statement must be up to date

- The information contained in the written statement (including the information given in instalments and any associated documents, including collective agreements) must be correct at the time it is issued. Certainly, it must not be more than seven days out of date at that time (*ibid.* section 1(3)). Any change in the particulars to be included in the written statement must be notified to the employee in writing *not later than one month after that change* or, where the change results from the employee being required to work outside the UK for more than one month, before he (or she) leaves the UK (*ibid.* section 4).

- An employer may not vary any of the particulars given in the statement without the express permission of the employee himself (or herself). In practice, an alteration will not be challenged unless the change is to the employee's detriment, eg a unilateral reduction in wage or holiday benefits – in which event the employee might well be prompted to pursue a claim for damages for breach of contract or (if he has resigned in protest) to present a complaint of unfair constructive dismissal. If he is dismissed for bringing proceedings against his employer or for alleging that his employer had infringed one or other of his statutory rights (notably, in this instance, his right to be provided with an accurate and up-to-date 'written statement') his dismissal will be regarded as unfair; as to which, see **Dismissal for asserting a statutory right** elsewhere in this handbook. See also the sections titled **Contract of employment** and **Constructive dismissal.**

- There is nothing in the 1996 Act which requires an employee to sign the written statement. Indeed, many trade unions actively discourage their members from signing any document which purports to have legal force. A great deal will depend on the form of words used at the foot of the statement. A signature acknowledging receipt of the document should not present any difficulty.

Reference to an employment tribunal

- If an employer refuses to provide an employee with a written state-ment, or the statement he *does* provide does not comply fully with sections 1 to 6 of the 1996 Act, the affected employee may refer the matter to an employment tribunal. If there is no written statement, the tribunal will determine what particulars ought to have been included or referred to in it. If the statement issued to the employee is incom-plete or defective, the tribunal may amend the particulars given in the statement or substitute other particulars for them. In either case, the statement will be deemed to have been given by the employer in accor-dance with the decision of the tribunal, and will be enforceable as such (*ibid.* section 11). The reader should note that, once the *Dispute Resolution* provisions of the Employment Act 2002 come into force (in the second half of 2003), employers who fail to provide their employees with written statements will be ordered by the tribunals to pay compensation to those employees of an amount equivalent to up to four weeks' pay.

- An employee does not need to resign in order to challenge his (or her) employer's refusal or failure to provide a complete and up-to-date written statement. If he is no longer employed, he must make his complaint to an employment tribunal (on Form ET1) within three months of the date on which his employment ended (or within such further period as the tribunal considers reasonable in the circum-stances) (*ibid.* section 11(4)).

- If an employee is dismissed for challenging his employer's refusal or failure to provide him a written statement or for questioning the contents of that statement or for referring either matter to an employ-ment tribunal, his dismissal will be regarded as having been automati-cally unfair – whether or not the employee was entitled to the right in question and whether or not the employer had actually infringed that right (always provided that the employee had acted in good faith in making his allegations) (*ibid.* section 104). A complaint of unfair dismissal in such circumstances may be presented to an employment tribunal regardless of the employee's age or length of service at the time of his dismissal. For further particulars, please turn to the section titled **Dismissal for asserting a statutory right** elsewhere in this hand-book.

Please refer also to the sections titled **Bank and public holidays; Contract of employment; Disciplinary rules and procedure; Equal pay and conditions; Grievance procedure; Holidays, annual; Job title; Meal and rest breaks; Notice of termination of employment; Overtime employment; Pension schemes; Sickness and statutory sick pay;** and **Working hours,** elsewhere in this handbook.

WRONGFUL DISMISSAL

Key points

- An employee is treated in law as having been *wrongfully* dismissed by his (or her) employer if he has been dismissed without benefit of reasonable notice (or the notice to which he would otherwise have been entitled under the terms of his contract of employment), in circumstances which did not (or did not appear to) justify summary or instant dismissal.

- Since 12 July 1994, when the Industrial Tribunals (Extension of Jurisdiction) Orders 1994 came into force, employment tribunals have had jurisdiction to hear all breach of contract disputes which arise, or remain unresolved, on the termination of an employee's contract of employment – although there is an upper limit of £25,000 on the amount that a tribunal can award in respect of a successful claim for breach of contract. Employees (and, for that matter, employers) may, if they prefer, still pursue their claims through the civil courts.

  Note: Personal injury claims and claims relating to tied accommodation remain outside the remit of the employment tribunals, as do cases relating to intellectual property, obligations of confidence, and restrictive covenants.

Damages for wrongful dismissal

- An action for breach of contract to be heard by an employment tribunal must be brought within three months of the *effective date of termination* of an employee's contract of employment – although a tribunal may accept an 'out of time' complaint in exceptional circumstances. If an employer wishes to make a counter-claim, he must do so within six weeks of receiving a copy (from the tribunal) of the employee's originating application (Form ET1).

- An action before the civil courts can be brought at any time within the period of six years from the date of termination of an employee's contract of employment. At best, a county or sheriff court will award damages in respect of the actual loss sustained by the employee. Thus, if an employee had been dismissed without benefit of notice, the most that the courts can award is damages in respect of the relevant notice period (after consideration of the efforts made by the dismissed employee to mitigate his loss). It is for this reason that the bulk of wrongful dismissal claims before the civil courts are brought by persons (such as company directors) whose fixed-term contracts have been peremptorily ended by their employers before the expiry of the agreed term.

  See also the sections titled **Contract of employment, Fidelity and trust, employee's duty of** and **Notice of termination of employment** elsewhere in this handbook.

Appendix

Continuous Employment (Part XIV, Chapter I, Employment Right Act 1996)

Note: This Appendix should be read in conjunction with the section titled **Continuous employment** earlier in this handbook.

Introductory

210–(1) References in any provision of [the Employment Rights Act 1996] to a period of continuous employment are (unless provision is expressly made to the contrary) to a period computed in accordance with this Chapter.

(2) In any provision of this Act which refers to a period of continuous employment expressed in months or years–

> (a)   a month means a calendar month, and

> (b)   a year means a year of twelve calendar months.

(3) In computing an employee's period of continuous employment for the purposes of any provision of this Act, any question–

> (a)   whether the employee's employment is of a kind counting towards a period of continuous employment, or

> (b)   whether periods (consecutive or otherwise) are to be treated as forming a single period of continuous employment,

shall be determined week by week; but where it is necessary to compute the length of an employee's period of employment it shall be computed in months and years of twelve months in accordance with section 211.

(4) Subject to sections 215 to 217, a week which does not count in computing the length of a period of continuous employment breaks continuity of employment.

(5) A person's employment during any period shall, unless the contrary is shown, be presumed to have been continuous.

Period of continuous employment

211–(1) An employee's period of continuous employment for the purposes of any provisions of this Act–

(a)   subject to subsections (2) and (3) begins with the day on which the employee starts work, and

(b)   ends with the day by reference to which the length of the employee's period of continuous employment is to be ascertained for the purposes of the provision.

(2) For the purposes of sections 155 and 162(1), an employee's period of continuous employment shall be treated as beginning on the employee's eighteenth birthday if that day is later than the day on which the employee started work.

(3) If an employee's period of employment includes one or more periods which (by virtue of section 215, 216 or 217) while not counting in computing the length of the period do not break continuity of employment, the beginning of the period shall be treated as postponed by the number of days falling within that intervening period, or the aggregate number of days failing within those periods, calculated in accordance with the section in question.

Weeks counting in computing period

212–(1) Any week during the whole or part of which an employee's relations with his employer are governed by a contract of employment counts in computing the employee's period of employment.

(2) [*Revoked by Employment Relations Act 1999*]

(3) Subject to subsection (4), any week (not within subsection (1)) during the whole or part of which an employee is–

(a)   incapable of work in consequence of sickness or injury,

(b)   absent from work on account of a temporary cessation of work,

(c)   absent from work in circumstances such that, by arrangement or custom, he is regarded as continuing in the employment of his employer for any purpose, or

(d)   [*Revoked by Employment Relations Act 1999*]

counts in computing the employee's period of employment.

(4) Not more than twenty-six weeks count under subsection (3)(a) or (subject to subsection (2)) subsection (3)(d) between any periods falling under subsection (1).

Intervals in employment

213–(1) Where in the case of an employee a date later than the date which would be the effective date of termination by virtue of subsection (1) of section 97 is treated for certain purposes as the effective date of termination by virtue of subsection (2) or (4) of that section, the period of the interval between the two dates counts as a period of employment in ascertaining for the purposes of section 108(1) or 119(1) the period for which the employee has been continuously employed.

(2) Where an employee is by virtue of section 138(1) regarded for the purposes of Part XI as not having been dismissed by reason of a renewal or re-engagement taking effect after an interval, the period of the interval counts as a period of employment in ascertaining for the purposes of section 155 or 162(1) the period for which the employee has been continuously employed (except so far as it is to be disregarded under section 214 or 215).

(3) Where in the case of an employee a date later than the date which would be the relevant date by virtue of subsections (2) to (4) of section 145 is treated for certain purposes as the relevant date by virtue of subsection (5) of that section, the period of the interval between the two dates counts as a period of employment in ascertaining for the purposes of section 155 or 162(1) the period for which the employee has been continuously employed (except so far as it is to be disregarded under section 214 or 215).

Special provisions for redundancy payments

214–(1) This section applies where a period of continuous employment has to be determined in relation to an employee for the purposes of the application of section 155 or 162(1).

(2) The continuity of a period of employment is broken where–

    (a)   a redundancy payment has previously been paid to the employee (whether in respect of dismissal or in respect of lay-off or short-time), and

    (b)   the contract of employment under which the employee was employed was renewed (whether by the same or another employer) or the employee was re- engaged under a new contract of employment (whether by the same or another employer).

(3) The continuity of a period of employment is also broken where–

    (a)   a payment has been made to the employee (whether in respect of the termination of his employment or lay-off or short-time) in accordance with a scheme under section 1 of the Superannuation Act 1972 or arrangements falling within section 177(3), and

    (b)   he commenced new, or renewed, employment.

(4) The date on which the person's continuity of employment is broken by virtue of

this section–

    (a)   if the employment was under a contract of employment, is the date which was the relevant date in relation to the payment mentioned in subsection (2)(a) or (3)(a), and

    (b)   if the employment was otherwise than under a contract of employment, is the date which would have been the relevant date in relation to the payment mentioned in subsection (2)(a) or (3)(a) had the employment been under a contract of employment.

(5) For the purposes of this section a redundancy payment shall be treated as having been paid if–

    (a)   the whole of the payment has been paid to the employee by the employer,

    (b)   a tribunal has determined liability and found that the employer must pay part (but not all) of the redundancy payment and the employer has paid that part, or

    (c)   the Secretary of State has paid a sum to the employee in respect of the redundancy payment under section 167.

Employment abroad, etc

215–(1) This Chapter applies to a period of employment–

    (a)   (subject to the following provisions of this section) even where during the period the employee was engaged in work wholly or mainly outside Great Britain, and

    (b)   even where the employee was excluded by or under this Act from any right conferred by this Act.

(2) For the purposes of sections 155 and 162(1) a week of employment does not count in computing a period of employment if the employee–

    (a)   was employed outside Great Britain during the whole or part of the week, and

    (b)   was not during that week an employed earner for the purposes of the Social Security Contributions and Benefits Act 1992 in respect of whom a secondary Class 1 contribution was payable under that Act (whether or not contribution was in fact paid).

(3) Where by virtue of subsection (2) a week of employment does not count in

computing a period of employment, the continuity of the period is not broken by reason only that the week does not count in computing the period; and the number of days which, for the purposes of section 211(3), fall within the intervening period is seven for each week within this subsection.

(4) Any question arising under subsection (2) whether–

(a)   a person was an employed earner for the purposes of the Social Security Contributions and Benefits Act 1992, or

(b)   if so, whether a secondary Class 1 contribution was payable in respect of him under that Act,

shall be determined by the Secretary of State.

(5) Any legislation (including regulations) as to the determination of questions which under the Social Security Administration Act 1992 the Secretary of State is empowered to determine (including provisions as to the reference of questions for decision, or as to appeals, to the High Court or the Court of Sessions) apply to the determination of any question by the Secretary of State under subsection (4).

(6) Subsection (2) does not apply in relation to a person who is–

(a)   employed as a master or seaman in a British ship, and

(b)   ordinarily resident in Great Britain.

Industrial disputes

216–(1) A week does not count under section 212 if during the week, or any part of the week, the employee takes part in a strike.

(2) The continuity of an employee's period of employment is not broken by a week which does not count under this Chapter (whether or not by virtue only of subsection (1)) if during the week, or any part of the week, the employee takes part in a strike; and the number of days which, for the purposes of section 211(3), fall within the intervening period is the number of days between the last working day before the strike and the day on which work was resumed.

(3) The continuity of an employee's period of employment is not broken by a week if during the week, or any part of the week, the employee is absent from work because of a lock-out by the employer; and the number of days which, for the purposes of section 211(3), fall within the intervening period is the number of days between the last working day before the lock-out and the day on which work was resumed.

Reinstatement after military service

217–(1) If a person who is entitled to apply to his former employer under the Reserve Forces (Safeguard of Employment) Act 1985 enters the employment of the employer not later than the end of the six month period mentioned in section 1(4)(b) of that Act, his period of service in the armed forces of the Crown in the circumstances specified in section 1(1) of that Act does not break his continuity of employment.

(2) In the case of such a person the number of days which, for the purposes of section 211(3), fall within the intervening period is the number of days between the last day of his previous period of employment with the employer (or, if there was more than one such period, the last of them) and the first day of the period of employment beginning in the six month period.

Change of employer

218–(1) Subject to the provisions of this section, this Chapter relates only to employment by the one employer.

(2) If a trade or business, or an undertaking (whether or not established by or under an Act), is transferred from one person to another–

> (a)   the period of employment of an employee in the trade or business or undertaking at the time of the transfer counts as a period of employment with the transferee, and

> b)   the transfer does not break the continuity of the period of employment.

(3) If by or under an Act (whether public or local and whether passed before or after this Act) a contract of employment between any body corporate and an employee is modified and some other body corporate is substituted as the employer–

> (a)   the employee's period of employment at the time when the modification takes effect counts as a period of employment with the second body corporate, and

> (b)   the change of employer does not break the continuity of the period of employment.

(4) If on the death of an employer the employee is taken into the employment of the personal representatives or trustees of the deceased–

> (a)   the employee's period of employment at the time of the death counts as a period of employment with the employer's personal representatives or trustees, and

> (b)   the death does not break the continuity of the period of employment.

(5) If there is a change in the partners, personal representatives or trustees who

employ any person–

- (a) the employee's period of employment at the time of the change counts as a period of employment with the partners, personal representatives or trustees after the change, and

- (b) the change does not break the continuity of the period of employment.

(6) If an employee of an employer is taken into the employment of another employer who, at the time when the employee enters the second employer's employment, is an associated employer of the first employer–

- (a) the employee's period of employment at that time counts as a period of employment with the second employer, and

- (b) the change of employer does not break the continuity of the period of employment.

(7) If an employee of the governors of a school maintained by a local education authority is taken into the employment of the authority or an employee of a local education authority is taken into the employment of the governors of a school maintained by the authority–

- (a) his period of employment at the time of the change of employer counts as a period of employment with the second employer, and

- (b) the change does not break the continuity of the period of employment.

(8) If a person employed in relevant employment by a health service employer is taken into relevant employment by another such employer, his period of employment at the time of the change of employer counts as a period of employment with the second employer and the change does not break the continuity of the period of employment.

(9) For the purposes of subsection (8) employment is relevant employment if it is employment of a description–

- (a) in which persons are engaged while undergoing professional training which involves their being employed successively by a number of different health service employers, and

- (b) which is specified in an order made by the Secretary of State.

(10) The following are health service employers for the purposes of subsections (8) and (9)–

- (a) Health Authorities established under section 8 of the National Health Service Act 1977,

(b)   Special Health Authorities established under section 11 of that Act,

(c)   National Health Service trusts established under Part I of the National Health Service and Community Care Act 1990,

(d)   the Dental Practice Board, and

(e)   the Public Health Laboratory Service Board.

Reinstatement or re-engagement of dismissed employee

219–(1) Regulations made by the Secretary of State may make provision–

(a)   for preserving the continuity of a person's period of employment for the purposes of this Chapter or for the purposes of this Chapter as applied by or under any other enactment specified in the regulations, or

(b)   for modifying or excluding the operation of section 214 subject to the recovery of any such payment as is mentioned in that section,

in cases where a dismissed employee is reinstated, re-engaged or otherwise re-employed by his employer or by a successor or associated employer of that employer in any circumstances prescribed by the regulations.

Note: Section 219 above appears as amended by Schedule 1, paragraph 25, to the Employment Rights (Dispute Resolution) Act 1998.

Index

ACAS (see Advisory, Conciliation & Arbitration Service)
ACAS arbitration scheme   23, 59, 171
access to employment   4–11, 122, 468, 506
access to personal data   109
access to medical reports   405–09
accommodation, provision of   412, 414–15
accompanied, right to be, at disciplinary and grievance hearings   137, 331
accounting records of trade union, access to   609
accrued holiday pay   346
action short of dismissal see victimisation
addictions and disability   128
additional award of compensation (unfair dismissal)   189
additional maternity leave   375
additional adoption leave   12–15
adjustment to premises (disabled persons)   126
adoption leave   12–15
adoption pay see statutory adoption pay
advertisements (discriminatory)   15–20
  disability discrimination   16
  racial discrimination   19, 471
  sex discrimination   16, 279, 519
Advisory, Conciliation & Arbitration Service   21–24, 38, 48, 50
age, discrimination on grounds of   5, 15
age of majority   24, 33
agency 'temps'   255, 256, 411
alcohol addiction   128
annual holidays   32, 57, 338–50
ante-natal care, time off for   4, 590
appearance of employees   510
apprentices and the national minimum wage   412
aptitude tests, discriminatory   469
arbitration   22, 23, 59, 171
arbitration scheme (ACAS)   23, 59
armed forces, service with   691
asserting a statutory right, dismissal for   67, 176, 566, 592
assault (searching employees)   301
assault (sexual harassment)   515–17
attachment of earnings   25–28, 115

attendance record, poor   1–4, 135
average weekly earnings (SAP)   12–13
average weekly earnings (SMP)   392
average weekly earnings (SPP)   446
average weekly earnings (SSP)   524

bad workmanship, penalties for   29–30
ballot for industrial action   50, 542
  conduct of   549
  result of   551
  scrutiny of   549
  voting papers for   547
ballots for trade union elections   610
ballots, trade union recognition, for   50, 624
bank and public holidays   30–32, 681
bargaining unit, meaning of   620
basic award (unfair dismissal)   185–87, 357
betting workers   76, 216, 523, 554, 654
birth certificates   33
breach of contract   67, 69–76, 89, 90, 301
breastfeeding mothers   36, 459, 501
burden of proof   517
business reorganisations and dismissal   217

CAC see Central Arbitration Committee
capability, lack of, as reason for dismissal   232
canteens and rest rooms   34–37
care, employer's duty of   69
cash shortages, recovery of, from retail workers   117
cashless pay   661
Central Arbitration Committee   37–41, 617 et seq
Certification Officer   351, 609
change of employer   83, 692
'check-off' system (union dues)   119–20
chemical formulae (duty not to divulge)   297
cheque, payment of wages/salary by
child, meaning of   41

child tax credits   177–78
childbirth, meaning of   379
children, employment of   41–46
chronically sick and disabled persons   130
closed shop   47, 244, 653
codes of practice   48–52, 315
  ACAS, by   48
  ballots for industrial action, on   50
  collective bargaining, on   50
  Commission for Racial Equality, by   49
  disability discrimination, on   51, 129
  disciplinary and grievance procedures   50, 134, 209, 328, 330
  disclosure of information, on   49
  Equal Opportunities Commission, by   49, 51
  employment practices (data protection)   113
  equal pay, on   51
  failure to comply with   48
  health and safety, on   573
  legal status of   48, 140
  picketing, on   50
  racial discrimination, on   49, 57
  safety representatives and safety committees   52
  Secretary of State, by   49
  sex discrimination, on   49, 503
  sexual harassment, on   513
  smoking at work, on   37
  time off for trade union duties, etc   50
  trade unions and collective bargaining   50
  workplace health, safety and welfare   34
collective agreements   31, 86, 283, 336, 361, 669
  legal status of   53
  no strike' clauses in   53
  written statements, in   682
collective bargaining   38, 39, 50, 151, 191, 620
collective redundancies
  consultations concerning   153
  notification of, to DTI   159
Commission for Racial Equality   8, 49, 57–59, 467, 474
Commonwealth citizens, employment of   316
  working holidays by   323
'common travel area'   250

company property, employee's
  duty to return 362
compensation, invention by
  employee, for 360
compensation, unfair dismissal,
  for 184–89
compensatory award (unfair
  dismissal) 187–89
'competent persons' (safety) 164
compromise agreements 59–65,
  170, 473, 513
compulsory school age 41, 502
computerised personnel records
  106, 110
conciliation officers 21, 65–69
confidentiality, employee's duty of
  298
confinement, meaning of 379
constructive dismissal 69–76, 89,
  301
consultations *see also* disclosure of
  information
  appropriate representatives,
    with 481, 641
  collective redundancies,
    concerning 481
  employee representatives, with
    481, 640
  representatives of employee
    safety, with 599
  safety representatives, with
    598
  trade union representatives,
    with 481, 641
  transfer of undertakings,
    concerning 640
continuous employment 76–85,
contract of employment 31, 67,
  69, 70, 72, 85–92, 360
  breach of 90
  care, employer's implied duty
    of, under 69
  collective agreements,
    incorporation of, in 89
  confidentiality, employee's duty
    of 298
  cooperation, employee's duty of
    in 103–05
  duties of employee in 88
  duties of employer in 87
  equality clause in 89
  fidelity and trust, employee's
    implied duty of, in 168,
    297–303
  frustration of 238, 327–29
  illegal 91
  inventions by employee and
    359–62
  mobility clause in 71, 104, 682
  repudiation of, 69–76, 89, 301
  restrictive covenants in 88
  termination of 89
  transfer of undertakings and 6,
    35–638
  written statement of
    employment particulars,
    and 679–85

convicted persons, employment of
  92–103
  dismissal of 93, 124
cooperation, employee's duty of
  103–05
copyright, inventions and patents,
  ownership of 359–62
COT 3 agreements 59, 66, 170,
  473, 518
criminal conviction certificate
  (CCC) 99
criminal record certificate (CRC)
  100
  enhanced (ECRC) 100
criminal offences outside
  employment, relevance of
  211

daily rest periods 56, 496, 522
damaged goods, deductions in
  respect of 29–30
data protection 106–14, 491
data protection principles 108
deductions from pay 3, 9, 29, 47,
  114–21, 412
defamatory references 489
dependants, time off for 578–81
detrimental treatment, employees,
  of *see* victimisation
directors' reports 129
disability, meaning of 127
Disability Rights Commission 49
disabled persons, employment of
  121–31, 449
  discrimination against, unlawful
    5, 9
disciplinary hearing, right to be
  accompanied at 137, 331
disciplinary rules and procedures
  1, 50, 74, 133–49, 328, 330, 682
disclosure of information 149–68
discrimination on grounds of
  age 5, 15
  colour 467
  convictions, 'spent' 92–113
  disability 123
  ethnic origins 467
  gender reassignment 5, 503
  marital status 5, 503
  nationality 467
  political opinion 5
  race 467–74
  religion and beliefs 5, 9
  sex 502–21
  trade union membership or
    non-membership 614–17
disfigurements and disability 128
dishonesty and theft 70, 135,
  210
dismiss, pressure to, by trade
  union 614
dismissal (general) 168–98
  constructive 69–76
  convicted persons 93, 124
  fairness of 181
  inadmissible reasons for 76,
    173 *et seq*

meaning of 172
permitted reasons for 171
protected disclosures and 176,
  465–66
summary 421
trade union membership cases,
  in 54, 178, 243–45, 255
written reasons for 391, 491,
  678–79
wrongful 301, 423, 685
dismissal and 'TUPE' transfers
  198–200, 639
dismissal because of a statutory
  restriction 200–01
dismissal for asserting a statutory
  right 201–03
dismissal for incompetence
  204–06
dismissal for lack of qualifications
  206–08
dismissal for making a protected
  disclosure 176, 465–66
dismissal for misconduct 208–14,
  367
dismissal for refusing Sunday
  work 175, 214–17, 558
dismissal for 'some other
  substantial reason' 217–19
dismissal for taking industrial
  action 179, 219–24
dismissal in health and safety
  cases 174, 224–26
dismissal in 'tax credits' cases 177
dismissal in 'working time
  regulations' cases 175
dismissal of a pension scheme
  trustee 176
dismissal of an employee
  representative 228–30
dismissal on grounds of disability
  231–32, 254
dismissal on grounds of ill-health
  80, 232–40, 327
dismissal on grounds of
  pregnancy or childbirth 174,
  458, 511
dismissal on grounds of
  redundancy 241–42
dismissal on grounds of sex *see* sex
  discrimination
dismissal on grounds of trade
  union membership 54, 178,
  243–45, 255
dismissal on racial grounds *see*
  racial discrimination
dismissal procedures agreements
  54, 170, 357
disobedience 245–47
dress and appearance of
  employees 510
drivers' working hours 675
drug addiction 128
duty of fidelity, employee's
  implied 168, 297–303

EEA nationals, employment of
  248–50, 316

eating facilities for employees 34–37
effective date of termination 75, 77, 79, 168, 194–96, 233
elections, trade union 610
employee representatives 153
dismissal of 176, 228–30
election of 154
right of, to be consulted 481, 640
time off work for 587
employee safety, representatives of 225, 600
employees, appearance of 510
employees, duties of 88
employees, safety of 69
employment agencies 9, 250–58, 520
Employment Appeal Tribunal 258–60
employment particulars, written statement of 679–85
employment tribunals 260–78
awards of compensation by 184–89
award of costs or expenses by 276
constitution of 261
decision of 275
interim relief, order for *see* interim relief
jurisdiction of 261
originating application to 268
recoupment of State benefits, order for, by 276
restricted reporting order by 274
employment tribunals and procedure 260–78
documents, production of 271
notice of hearing 270
pre-hearing review 270
restricted reporting orders 274
rules of procedure 266, 273
vexatious proceedings 271
witnesses, attendance of 271–72
enhanced criminal record certificate (ECRC) 100
EOC *see* Equal Opportunities Commission
Equal Opportunities Commission 20, 49, 51, 279–80, 503, 521
equal pay and condition 87, 280–85
'equality clause' 89, 281, 284
equal treatment rule (occupational pension schemes) 449
ETO reasons for dismissal 199, 639
European works councils 40, 285–96
expectant mothers *see* new and expectant mothers
expenses, recovery of from wages, of 115

factory workers, eating facilities for 35
'fallback scheme' (parental leave) 435–37
fidelity and trust, employee's duty of 168, 297–303
fighting and physical assault 212
fire prevention and training 355, 632
first-aiders 632
fixed-term contracts 309
fixed-term employees 32, 57, 180, 303–09
flexible working 310–13
food safety and hygiene 633
foreign nationals, employment of 314–27
foul and abusive language by employer 73
full-tie workers, meaning of 439
frustration of contract 238, 327–29

gender reassignment 5, 503, 526
genuine occupational qualification (sex or race) 6, 7, 18, 19, 471, 507, 509
gratuities and tips (NMW) 413
grievance hearing, right to be accompanied at 331
grievances and procedure 50, 74, 330–34, 683
gross misconduct, dealing with 136, 209–10, 421, 577
guarantee payments 334–37, 373

HGV drivers 675
harassment 70, 467, 513–17
Health & Safety Commission 49
health and safety at work 87, 164, 353, 507, 564, 630
health and safety cases, dismissal in 174
health and capabilities assessments (young workers) 673
health assessments (night workers) 670
holidays, children, for 43
holidays and holiday pay 57, 338–50, 357, 522, 681
'holiday year', meaning of 339
hourly-paid workers 417
hours of work 667–77
adult workers 56, 522, 677
children 41–46
drivers 675
young workers 426, 522, 672

illegal contracts 91
illegal immigrants, penalties for employing 49
illegality of continued employment 200–01

ill-health, dismissal on grounds of 232–40, 327
statutory sick pay, and 238
implied contractual terms *see* contract of employment
inadmissible reasons for dismissal 76, 82, 457
incompetence, dismissal for 204–06, 634
independent trade unions 54, 151, 351–53
induction training 353–55
industrial action *see* strikes
industrial disputes 82, 337, 375, 691
industrial tribunals *see* employment tribunals
industrial undertakings, employment of children in 45
information, disclosure of *see* disclosure of information
insolvent and defaulting employers 61, 256–58
insubordination 245–47
interim relief 190, 264
health and safety cases, in 191, 226
pension scheme trustee, dismissal of, and 191, 227
employee representative, dismissal of, and 191
dismissal on grounds of trade union membership, and 191, 244
trade union recognition cases, in 191
workforce representative, dismissal of, and 191, 230
inventions, patents and copyright 359–62
in-work rest breaks 56, 495, 522
itemised pay statements 362–65
tax credits and 363

Jewish shops 555
job advertisements, discriminatory 15–20, 279, 471, 519
job applicants, discrimination against *see* access to employment
job descriptions 86, 272, 366
job title 366–67, 682
jurisdiction of employment tribunals *see* employment tribunals
jurors' allowances 369–71
jury service 368–71

late attendance and absenteeism 1–4
lay-offs and short-time working 334, 372–74, 478
leaver's statement (SSP) 532
legal custody, meaning of 528
legitimate or 'permitted' reasons for dismissal 171

libel   489
limited-term contracts   172   *see also* fixed-term employees
live-in accommodation (NMW)   412, 414–15
local authority byelaws, children and   44
local education authority   593
lock-outs   82, 375–76

maintenance orders *see* attachment of earnings
malingerers, dealing with   1
manual filing systems *see* data protection
married persons, discrimination against *see* sex discrimination
maternity allowance, State   404
Maternity Certificate (Form MAT B1)   381
maternity grounds, suspension on   564–72
maternity leave, compulsory   384, 665, 666
maternity leave   377–405
    additional   378, 386–92
    compulsory   384, 665, 666
    contractual rights during   382, 387
    contractual vis-à-vis statutory rights   379
    dismissal during   384, 388
    holidays during   343
    ordinary   380–86
    parental leave and   383, 389
    pregnancy-related illness and   382
    premature birth and   381
    redundancy during   384, 388, 488
    return to work after   383, 399
    return to work during   384, 390
maternity pay, statutory *see* statutory maternity pay
insolvent employer and   357
maternity rights   377–405
meal and rest breaks   56, 495, 522
meals, facilities for   34–37
medical grounds, suspension from work on   573–75
medical reports, access to   405–09
minimum wage, national (NMW)   410–20
misconduct, dismissal for   208–14, 367
misconduct, gross   136, 209–10, 421, 577
misconduct, injury cause by   541
military service, reinstatement after   692
mobility clauses   71, 104, 682
'moonlighting' by employees   302
mothers-to-be, rest facilities for   36, 459, 501
'mutuality of obligation'   85

national minimum wage (NMW)   59, 147, 167, 177, 255, 410–20
new and expectant mothers   36, 459, 501
nicotine addiction   128
night work   427, 670–73
    adult workers and   427, 670
    new mothers and   565
    pregnant employees and   565
    restrictions on, on health and safety grounds   565
    young persons and   427
    working time regulations and   670–73
NMW *see* national minimum wage
'no smoking' areas   36
'no strike' clauses   53
non-discrimination notices   20, 57, 58, 279
normal retiring age   75, 169, 233
notice of termination of employment   356, 420–24, 596, 682
notice period, rights of employee during   240, 422
notice, waiver of right to   421
nursing mothers, rest facilities for   36, 459, 501

occupational pension schemes   129
'equal treatment rule' in   284
occupational sick pay schemes   237, 538, 647
offenders, rehabilitation of   92–103
office workers, eating facilities for   35
ordinary adoption leave   12
ordinary maternity leave   378, 380–86
'out-of-court' settlements   23, 59–65, 66, 170, 473, 513, 518
overpaid wages or expenses, recovery of   115
overtime   104, 413, 425–30, 441

paper-based filing systems   106
parental leave   4, 383, 389, 431–38
part-time workers   32, 179, 345, 438–43
passive smoking   36
patents, ownership of   359–62
paternity leave   444–47
pay, deductions from   3, 9, 29, 47, 114–21, 412
    cash shortages, in respect of   117
    stock deficiencies, in respect of   117
    overpaid wages or salary, in respect of   115
pay statements, itemised   362–65
payments, demands for (by employers) *see* deductions from pay
pension scheme trustees   448
    dismissal of   176, 227–28

functions of   448
    time off work for   589–90
pension schemes (general)   358, 447–49, 681
period of incapacity for work (PIW)   525
permanent health insurance (PHI)   238
permitted reasons for dismissal   171
personal data   106, 107
personnel files/record, access to *see* data protection
PHI schemes *see* permanent health insurance
picketing   50, 450–52, 543
piece-workers and the NMW   417
PIW, meaning of *see* period of incapacity for work
political fund (trade union) contributions by employee to   120, 612
political opinion, discrimination on grounds of   5
pornographic displays   514
posted workers   452–57
pregnancy-related illness and maternity leave   382
pregnant employees and nursing mothers
    dismissal of, unlawful   76, 174, 238, 511
    night work and   459
    rest facilities for   36, 459, 501
    restrictions on employment of   565
    rights of *see* maternity rights
    suspension of, on maternity grounds   459, 564–72
    time off work by, ante-natal care   4, 590
    written statement of reasons for dismissal of   678
premature birth   381
pressure to dismiss (by trade union)   190
principal statement of terms of employment   31, 32, 681
protected disclosure   461–66
    dismissal for making   176, 465–66
'protected' industrial action   222–23
protective award (redundant employees)   157
public duties, time off for   593–96
public and bank holidays   30–32, 339, 681
public interest disclosures   151, 461–66
public performances, children, by

qualifications, dismissal for lack of   206–08
'qualifying' days (SSP)   527

qualifying disclosure *see* public interest disclosures
questions and replies
  disability discrimination 125
  equal pay, concerning 284
  racial discrimination 472
  sex discrimination 518

racial discrimination 7, 57, 59, 253, 467–74
  genuine occupational qualification justifying 471
  questions concerning alleged 472
racial harassment/abuse 70, 467
reasons for dismissal, written 391, 491, 678–79
recognition, trade union 39, 50, 331
records 418, 538, 674
recoupment notices 189
recruitment, discrimination in *see* access to employment
redundancy 474–88
  'bumping' and 480
  consultations concerning 153, 481
  information to DTI concerning 484
  lay-offs and short-time working and 372–74, 478
  maternity leave, during 384, 388, 488
  meaning of 477
  offer of alternative work, and 480
  selection for, unlawful 76, 241, 584, 613
  time off work during notice period 596
  trial periods and 158, 481
  unlawful selection for 488
  voluntary 480
redundancy pay
  calculation of 488
  employer's inability or refusal to pay 61
  excluded categories 477
redundancy payments, continuity of service and 81–82, 689
re-engagement, tribunal order for 82, 83, 182, 689
references 98, 489–92
registrar of births, deaths and marriages 33
rehabilitation of offenders 9, 92–103, 171
reinstatement, tribunal order for 82, 83, 182, 240, 694
'relevant filing system', meaning of 106
'relevant transfer' (TUPE), meaning of 643–46
religion, discrimination on grounds of 5, 9

replacement employee, dismissal of 218
representatives of employee safety 225, 600
repudiation of contract 67, 69–76, 89, 90, 301
rest areas for employees 34–37, 459, 501
rest breaks and rest periods 43, 56, 492–501
  adult workers 493
  children, for 43
  daily rest periods 56, 496, 522
  in-work rest breaks 56, 495, 522
  weekly rest periods 56, 497–98, 522
  young persons, for 493
restraint of trade 88, 301
restricted reporting orders 274
restrictive covenants 88, 301
retail workers, deductions from pay of 117
return to work after adoption leave 14
return to work after maternity leave 383, 399
return to work after parental leave 383, 399, 434–35

SAP *see* statutory adoption pay
SMP *see* statutory maternity pay
SPP *see* statutory paternity pay
SSP *see* statutory sick pay
safety at work 70, 72
safety policy, employer's 164
safety representatives 52, 166, 598–601
  dismissal of 224
  time off work 598
safety rules 211
salaried workers 415
salary or wages, overpaid, recovery of 115
sale or transfer of business or undertaking *see* transfer of undertakings
school holidays, employment during *see* children, employment of
school leaving age 502
searching employees 301
seasonal workers 338
secondary industrial action 451
self-employed person, meaning of 86
'sensitive personal data', meaning of 107
sex discrimination 5, 59, 253, 502–21
  direct 503, 505
  genuine occupational qualification justifying 508
  indirect 503, 512
  questions concerning alleged 518

sexual harassment 70, 513–17
  liability of employer for 514
shift allowances 413
shift workers 497
'shop', meaning of 215
shop assistants *see also* shop workers
  deductions from pay of 117
  dismissal of, for refusing Sunday work 214–17
  eating facilities for 35
  victimisation of 559, 654
shop workers 215, 553
  opted-in 557
  opted-out 76, 556, 654
  protected 76, 555, 556, 654
  'Sundays only' 555, 558
  victimisation of 559, 654
shortage occupations (work permits) 321
sick or injured employees, dismissal of 80, 232–40, 327
sick leave, holidays during 343
sick pay, occupational/contractual
sick pay schemes, employers' 681
sickness and statutory sick pay 523–41
slander 489
some other substantial reason for dismissal 217–19
special negotiating body 288
spent' convictions 9, 93, 171
stationery officer (HMSO) 132
statutory adoption pay (SAP) 13
statutory dismissal and dismissal procedures (DDPs) 140, 142, 143
statutory grievance procedures (GPs) 331–32
statutory maternity pay (SMP) 357, 378, 392–405
statutory paternity pay (SPP) 446
statutory right, assertion of 7, 176, 566, 592
statutory sick pay (SSP) 310, 523–41
stock deficiencies, deductions in respect of 117
strike ballots 541
strikes and other industrial action 88, 541–53, 613
  ballots for 541
  continuity of employment, effect of, on 82, 691
  dismissal for taking part in 219–24
  unofficial 220
striking workers, dismissal of, during 'protected period' 222–23
study or training, time off for 581–87
subscriptions to trade unions (union dues) 119
'suitable alternative employment' 205, 565

summary dismissal   421 *see also*
    gross misconduct
Sunday work   553–63
    dismissal for refusing   76, 17,
        85, 214–17
    betting workers and   523, 655
    shop workers and   523, 654
suspension on maternity grounds
        459, 564–72
    dismissal of replacement
        following   218
suspension on medical grounds
        264, 573–75
suspension with/without pay
        576–77
'sympathy' strikes   545

tachographs, use of   676
tax credits, duty to pay   177–78
temporary cessation of work and
        continuity   80
termination of employment *see*
        dismissal
terms and conditions of
        employment   2, 313, 348, 428,
        447, 499, 679–85
time off work
    ante-natal care   4, 590
    dependants, for   578–81
    employee representatives
        587–89
    parental leave   4,   383, 389,
        431–38
    paternity leave   444–47
    pension scheme trustees
        589–90
    pregnant employees   590–93
    public duties, for   593–96
    redundant employees   4,
        596–98
    representatives of employee
        safety   600
    safety representatives
        598–601
    study or training, for   581–87,
        605
    trade union members   3, 50, 602
    trade union officials   3, 50, 603
    young persons, study or
        training, for   581–87, 605
timekeeping   1–4
trade dispute, meaning of   545,
        607
trade disputes and arbitration   38,
        40, 607
trade secrets   297
trade union, expulsion from   612
    recognised, independent   54,
        151, 351–53

trade union duties and activities,
    time off for   3, 50, 602–03
trade union ballots on industrial
    action   50, 541
trade union dues   119–20
trade union members, rights of
        602, 608–14
trade union membership and
        activities   5, 9, 52, 241, 243,
        255, 614–17
trade union official   54
    dismissal of   214
    time off work   3, 50, 603
trade union recognition   39,
        617–29
    dismissal in connection with
        191
trade union representatives,
        consultations with   50, 149,
        641
trade union rules, access to   609
training and work experience
        322
training of employees   205, 353,
        399, 605, 618, 626, 629–34
training, time off for   581–87
transfers of undertakings   54, 84,
        161, 634–48
    dismissal in connection with
        198–200
trial period in new jobs
        (redundant employees)   158
tribunal proceedings *see*
        employment tribunals
TUPE transfers *see* transfers of
        undertakings

unfair, dismissal *see* dismissal
    compensation for   184–89
union dues   119–20
union membership agreements *see*
        closed shop
unlawful reasons for dismissal
        76, 82, 45
unofficial industrial action   543

vexatious and frivolous tribunal
        proceedings   271
vicarious liability of employer
        514
victimisation   649–60

wage, national minimum *see*
        national minimum wage
wages, overpaid, recovery of   115
wages, payment of   114, 661–62,
        682
    holiday, incorporation of, in
        344

'waiting days' (SSP)   528
'waiver clauses'   311
warnings of dismissal   138
week's pay, meaning of   486
weekly earnings, average *see*
        average weekly earnings
weekly rest period   497–98
'Whistleblowers' Act   461–66
witness statements   212
women and young persons,
        employment of   662–66
women's magazines, advertising
        in   16
work experience   46
work permits   316–27
'worker', meaning of   338, 411
workforce agreements   57,
        432–33, 668
workforce representatives   3,
        228–30, 669
working tax credits   177–78
working holidaymakers
        (Commonwealth citizens)
        323
working hours   70, 667–77
    adult workers   56, 522, 667
    children   41–46
    drivers   675 *et seq*
    young persons   522, 672
working time regulations   175,
        256, 522, 665
    annual holidays, minimum   57,
        338–50, 357, 522, 68
    rest breaks and rest periods   43,
        56, 492–501
    night work   427, 565, 670–73
    overtime   104, 413, 425–30, 441
    shift work   497
    working hours   70, 522, 667–77
written reasons for dismissal   391,
        491, 678–79
written statements
    fixed-term employees   310
    national minimum wage   411
    non-payment of SMP   399
    non-payment of SSP   529
    fixed-term employees   310
    part-time workers   441
written statement of initial
        employment particulars   2,
        213, 348, 428, 447, 499, 679–85
written warnings (dismissal)   138
wrongful dismissal   301, 423,
        685

young persons, employment of
        354, 427, 522, 631, 662–64, 672
young persons (time off for study
        or training)   581–87